John-Paul Himka

Ukrainian Nationalists and the Holocaust
OUN and UPA's Participation in the Destruction of Ukrainian Jewry, 1941–1944

No Longer Property of Washington University

Washington University Libraries

SAINT LOUIS, MISSOURI

UKRAINIAN VOICES

Collected by Andreas Umland

The book series "Ukrainian Voices" publishes English- and German-language monographs, edited volumes, document collections, and anthologies of articles authored and composed by Ukrainian politicians, intellectuals, activists, officials, researchers, and diplomats. The series' aim is to introduce Western and other audiences to Ukrainian explorations, deliberations and interpretations of historic and current, domestic, and international affairs. The purpose of these books is to make non-Ukrainian readers familiar with how some prominent Ukrainians approach, view and assess their country's development and position in the world. The series was founded and the volumes are collected by Andreas Umland, Dr. phil. (FU Berlin), Ph. D. (Cambridge), Associate Professor of Politics at the Kyiv-Mohyla Academy and Senior Expert at the Ukrainian Institute for the Future in Kyiv.

John-Paul Himka

UKRAINIAN NATIONALISTS AND THE HOLOCAUST

OUN and UPA's Participation in the Destruction of
Ukrainian Jewry, 1941–1944

ibidem
Verlag

Bibliografische Information der Deutschen Nationalbibliothek
Die Deutsche Nationalbibliothek verzeichnet diese Publikation in der Deutschen Nationalbibliografie; detaillierte bibliografische Daten sind im Internet über http://dnb.d-nb.de abrufbar.

Bibliographic information published by the Deutsche Nationalbibliothek
Die Deutsche Nationalbibliothek lists this publication in the Deutsche Nationalbibliografie; detailed bibliographic data are available in the Internet at http://dnb.d-nb.de.

Cover graphic: "The Pogromist Who Looks Like a Revolutionary" by Nikita Kadan.
In the collection of the Arsenał Gallery in Białystok.

ISBN-13: 978-3-8382-1548-8
© *ibidem*-Verlag, Stuttgart 2021
Alle Rechte vorbehalten

Das Werk einschließlich aller seiner Teile ist urheberrechtlich geschützt. Jede Verwertung außerhalb der engen Grenzen des Urheberrechtsgesetzes ist ohne Zustimmung des Verlages unzulässig und strafbar. Dies gilt insbesondere für Vervielfältigungen, Übersetzungen, Mikroverfilmungen und elektronische Speicherformen sowie die Einspeicherung und Verarbeitung in elektronischen Systemen.

All rights reserved. No part of this publication may be reproduced, stored in or introduced into a retrieval system, or transmitted, in any form, or by any means (electronical, mechanical, photocopying, recording or otherwise) without the prior written permission of the publisher. Any person who does any unauthorized act in relation to this publication may be liable to criminal prosecution and civil claims for damages.

Printed in the EU

For Chrystia
who stood beside me

Contents

Contents

Acknowledgments

I have received support for the research that went into this book from the Social Sciences and Humanities Research Council of Canada; Pinchas and Mark Wisen Fellowship at the Center for Advanced Holocaust Studies, United States Holocaust Memorial Museum; Killam Fund, University of Alberta; Support for the Advancement of Scholarship, Faculty of Arts, University of Alberta. I am very grateful for their generosity.

It has been a pleasure working with *ibidem*-Verlag, particularly with Jana Dävers, Valerie Lange, and Andreas Umland. I appreciate their guidance and respect for an author's vision of a book.

I have many people to thank. Although I am responsible for all the views put forward in this volume, I have had a great deal of help along the way. Persons who need to be singled out for their contribution to the appearance of this study are Vadim Altskan, Tarik Cyril Amar, Omer Bartov, Andriy Bolianovsky, Jeffrey Burds, Marco Carynnyk, Martin Dean, Sofia Dyak, Ernest Gyidel, Wendy Lower, Jared McBride, Oleksandr Melnyk, Ada Ogonowska, Dieter Pohl, Antony Polonsky, David Lee Preston, Per Anders Rudling, Roman Solchanyk, Wiesław Tokarczuk, and Larry Warwaruk. The following scholars worked at one point or another as research assistants for this book: Eduard Baidaus, Natalka Cmoc, Eva Himka, Rylan Kafara, Taras Kurylo, Mariya Melentyeva, Michal Mlynarz, Oksana Mykhed, Iaroslav Pankovskyi, and Grzegorz Rossoliński-Liebe. Those who read and helped me rework chapters were Raisa Ostapenko, Alan Rutkowski, the East Europeanist Circle at the University of Alberta led by Heather Coleman, and participants in the Danyliw Seminar in 2018. I wish I had the words I need to express the depth of my gratitude.

Abbreviations

AŻIH	Archiwum Żydowskiego Instytutu Historycznego
BA-MA	Bundesarchiv/Militärarchiv, Freiburg
CPSU	Communist Party of the Soviet Union
DALO	Derzhavnyi arkhiv L'vivs'koi oblasti
DAIFO	Derzhavnyi arkhiv Ivano-Frankivs'koi oblasti
DARO	Derzhavnyi arkhiv Rivnens'koi oblasti
DAZhO	Derzhavnyi arkhiv Zhytomyrs'koi oblasti
EM	*Ereignismeldungen UdSSR des Chefs der Sicherheits-polizei und SD* (title varies)
f.	folio
HDA SBU	Haluzevyi derzhavnyi arkhiv Sluzhby bezpeky Ukrainy
KGB	Komitet gosudarstvennoi bezopasnosti
KPZU	Komunistychna partiia Zakhidn'oi Ukrainy
NANU	Natsional'na Akademia nauk Ukrainy
NKGB	Narodnyi komissariat gosudarstvennoi bezopas-nosti
NKVD	Narodnyi komissariat vnutrennikh del
NTSh	Naukove tovarystvo im. Shevchenka
op.	opys
OUN	Organization of Ukrainian Nationalists
OUN-B	Organization of Ukrainian Nationalists (Bandera faction)
OUN-M	Organization of Ukrainian Nationalists (Melnyk faction)
P	Polish
PUN	Provid ukrains'kykh natsionalistiv
r.g.	record group
Ro	Romanian
RSHA	Reichssicherheitshauptamt
SB OUN	Sluzhba Bezpeky Orhanizatsii ukrains'kykh natsionalistiv
SBU	Sluzhba Bezpeky Ukrainy
SD	Sicherheitsdienst

spr.	sprava
TsDAHO	Tsentral'nyi derzhavnyi arkhiv hromads'kykh ob "iednan' Ukrainy
TsDAVO	Tsentral'nyi derzhavnyi arkhiv vyshchykh orhaniv vlady ta upravlinnia Ukrainy
TsDIAL	Tsentral'nyi derzhavnyi istorychnyi arkhiv Ukrainy, m. L'viv
TsGAOR	Tsentral'nyi gosudarstvennyi arkhiv Oktiabr'skoi revoliutsii, vysshikh organov gosudarstvennoi vlasti i organov gosudarstvennogo upravleniia SSSR
UCRDC	Ukrainian Canadian Research and Documentation Centre
UHVR	Ukrains'ka holovna vyzvol'na rada (Ukrainian Supreme Liberation Council)
UNDO	Ukrains'ke natsional'ne demokratychne ob"iednannia (Ukrainian National Democratic Union)
UPA	Ukrains'ka povstans'ka armiia (Ukrainian Insurgent Army)
USHMM	United States Holocaust Memorial Museum
UVO	Ukrains'ka viis'kova orhanizatsiia (Ukrainian Military Organization)
V	verso
YIUN	Yahad-in Unum Testimony
YVA	Yad Vashem Archives

Introduction

The Theme and Plan of the Book

This study concerns the participation of the Organization of Ukrainian Nationalists (OUN) and its armed force, the Ukrainian Insurgent Army (*Ukrains'ka povstans'ka armiia*, UPA), in the destruction of the Jewish population in Ukraine under German occupation, 1941-44. There were three major phases in which the nationalists contributed to the mass murder. (Since I do not use the definite article before OUN and UPA, readers would be advised to pronounce these terms as acronyms: o-OON, oo-PA.)

First, militias organized by OUN were key actors in the anti-Jewish violence of the summer of 1941, in the immediate aftermath of the German invasion of the Soviet Union. The militias arrested Jews in order to subject them to forced labor, humiliation, and murder; thousands of those arrested were executed by German units, mainly Einsatzgruppe C and Waffen-SS Division "Wiking." The Ukrainian nationalist militias assembled the Jews for the Germans' violence, since they could identify Jews more easily than the invaders and knew the localities, including Jewish neighborhoods in the cities. Sometimes the violence was accompanied by bloody public spectacles, as in the pogroms unleashed in Lviv and Zolochiv in early July 1941; sometimes the OUN militias murdered selected Jews and their families more discreetly, and sometimes they just murdered all the Jews in a village.

Second, OUN recruited for and infiltrated the Ukrainian Auxiliary Police in Galicia and the stationary Schutzmannschaften in Volhynia. These police units provided the indispensable manpower for the Holocaust. They rounded up Jews for deportation to the death camp at Bełżec or for execution by shooting; although most of the actual killing was done by the Germans, the Ukrainian policemen also killed in certain circumstances. These liquidation actions took place primarily from early 1942 through the middle of 1943.

Third, early in 1943 thousands of these Ukrainian policemen deserted from German service to join the OUN-led nationalist insurgency. Possessed of some military training and familiarity with both weapons and killing, they took leadership positions in UPA. As soon as the former policemen joined them, UPA launched a massive ethnic cleansing project, at first in Volhynia and later in Galicia. Although it was primarily directed against Poles, there were other non-Ukrainian victims, including Jews. In the winter of 1943-44, as the Red Army moved westward, UPA lured surviving Jews out of their hiding places in the forests, temporarily placed them in labor camps, and then murdered them.

In each of these three phases of anti-Jewish violence, the responsibility of OUN was different. In the first phase, the militias, and the OUN leadership which established them, were primarily responsible for rounding up Jews for the Germans, although the militias did some killing themselves. Altogether the militias were accomplices in the murder of thousands of Jews and shooters in the murder of many hundreds. In the second phase, OUN cannot be held responsible for all that Ukrainian policemen did in Galicia and Volhynia, since police structures were primarily under German control and by no means were all the policemen nationalists, at least initially. OUN's responsibility here lay in its strategy of deliberately infiltrating the police, which drew its members and sympathizers into the eye of the genocidal storm. For the most part, Ukrainian policemen rounded Jews up for others to kill, but sometimes they themselves killed Jews. Altogether the death toll from police round-ups was in the hundreds of thousands. In the third phase, OUN's responsibility was direct. Here, the organization was killing Jews primarily on its own initiative, as part of a far-reaching ethnic cleansing project; it was not only finding the Jews for murder, but its forces were perpetrating the killings themselves. The Jewish victims of OUN in this phase probably numbered in the thousands.

I have structured the book as follows. After this brief introduction, there are several chapters that provide context. The first is a rather extensive examination of the historiography. One factor contributing to the controversy surrounding the role of OUN and UPA in the murder of Jews stems from the peculiar way the historiography developed. For almost half a century after World War II, neither Holocaust scholars nor historians of the nationalists researched the topic. In this scholarly vacuum, accusations and denials were as if weightless, unanchored by evidence. Since about 1990, however, more and more information has come to light and many more scholars have examined the issues. But also since then, there has been a polarization of views over the issue of nationalist collaboration in the Holocaust, determined more by politics, specifically in the form of memory politics, than by contradictory evidence. The second chapter concerns sources. Here I outline the evidentiary record as we know it today and also discuss the particular problems the various kinds of source materials present.

After these two chapters, which present the epistemological context, I turn to the historical context for our problem. In the third chapter I look at OUN before Germany's invasion of the Soviet Union, with special attention to three issues: why it emerged and proved attractive to Ukrainian youth in Galicia, its relationship to fascism, and the place and nature of antisemitism in its ideology. In chapter four I turn to the first Soviet occupation of Western Ukraine (Galicia, Volhynia, Bukovina), in 1939-41. Some scholars argue that this historical interlude is crucial to understanding how the destruction of the Jews played out in these territories; I present my own understanding of how it affected perceptions and outcomes during the Holocaust.

The final three chapters are devoted to the phases of OUN's participation in the Holocaust: the anti-Jewish violence of the summer of 1941; the police's role in the systematic destruction of Jews in Galicia, Volhynia, and — to a lesser extent — elsewhere on Ukrainian lands in 1942-43, with special reference, of course, to the connections between the police and OUN; and, finally, UPA's murder of Jews in 1943 and 1944. The book ends with the presentation of the conclusions I have come to.

This book is not a study of how "Ukrainians" behaved during the Holocaust. It does not generalize about an entire national community but concentrates on a particular political movement. Although at the time this study is being written, powerful forces in Ukraine and in the Ukrainian diaspora aim to identify the entire

Ukrainian nation with the heritage of OUN and UPA, this is at the very least an intellectual error, especially in relation to the war period itself. Also, this is not a study of the whole range of collaboration of Ukrainians with the German wartime authorities. That is a much larger and much more complicated topic. Nor is this even a study of those Ukrainians who actively participated in the Holocaust. For example, the notorious "Ukrainian guards" of German camps, perhaps more properly known as Trawniki men after the camp at which they were trained, do not figure in this book. For the most part these were captured Red Army soldiers rather than ideological allies of the Nazis, and their work in German death and labor camps had no relation to OUN structures.

Geography

There is no consensus regarding the proper geographical nomenclature for borderland territories and localities, in which much of the events recounted in this study took place. For example, in this book I will frequently refer to "Galicia," a region that produced a very specific Ukrainian political and intellectual culture. Andrzej Zięba argues, however, that historians should abandon this term unless it is in relation to the Austrian crownland that existed from 1772 to 1918 or to the Distrikt Galizien established by the Germans that existed from August 1941 to July 1944. In his view, historians should use only the official state nomenclature of the Second Polish Republic; in the case of what I call Galicia, he would refer rather to the palatinates (*województwa*, voyvodships) of Lwów, Stanisławów, and Tarnopol. For certain studies, this is, I think, not only justified, but is a good practical choice.[1] But for this study, the regional specificity of what I call Galicia is important. It is the region where OUN emerged and achieved its greatest influence, and although UPA was active first in another region, Volhynia, its leadership was to a large degree of Galician origin. So by using this term, I mean to call attention to the regional specificity. Zięba also points out that

---

[1]   This procedure is used, for example, by Kopstein and Wittenberg, *Intimate Violence*.

Ukrainian historians, even when they use the term "Galicia," are really referring to Eastern Galicia, that is, the eastern part of the Austrian crownland, in which Ukrainians formed a majority of the population.[2] "Eastern Galicia" was also a geographical concept that demanded much attention from the diplomats who were working out the post-World-War-I settlements from 1918 through 1923. Martha Bohachevsky-Chomiak, who had used the term Eastern Galicia and Galicia in her earlier work, has lately been arguing that historians should designate what I call Galicia by its transliterated Ukrainian equivalent, Halychyna.[3] But as a linguistic conservative by inclination, I will retain the usage Galicia, which appears in my earlier publications and which is common practice in English-language studies of Ukraine. Today Galicia, as I am using it, comprises roughly the oblasts of Ivano-Frankivsk, Lviv, and Ternopil in Ukraine.

Just north of Galicia is a region I will refer to as Volhynia, although it does not encompass all of the territory to which that name has referred historically. Some scholars now employ the distinction Western Volhynia to refer to what I will be calling Volhynia. For this study, I mean the parts of historical Volhynia that were incorporated into Poland from 1921 to 1939. In 1941, under German occupation, Galicia became Distrikt Galizien within the General Government while Volhynia was incorporated into the Reichskommissariat Ukraine.[4] Volhynia had comprised the Volhynia palatinate in interwar Poland, which had its capital in Łuck, and comprises today Rivne oblast, a small part of Ternopil oblast, and Volhynia oblast (with its capital in Lutsk) in Ukraine. Galicia and Volhynia together comprised "Western Ukraine," a term used by the Soviet administration in 1939-41.

There are a few other territories I will refer to. When I write of Bukovina, I mean what is more accurately referred to as Northern Bukovina, that is, the territory which Soviet Ukraine annexed from

---

2   Zięba, "Ukraińcy, Polacy i niemiecka zagłada Żydów," xxvi-xxvii.

3   Bohachevsky-Chomiak, *Ukrainian Bishop, American Church*, xvi.

4   There is an excellent study of the Reichskommissariat Ukraine: Berkhoff, *Harvest of Despair*.

Romania in 1940 and which today comprises most of Chernivtsi oblast in independent Ukraine. By Transcarpathia, I mean the region which since 1945 has been Transcarpathia oblast, first in Soviet Ukraine and then in independent Ukraine.

It is always difficult to make choices about place names. In the period with which this book is concerned, borders and administrations shifted. What started out as the southeastern palatinates of the Second Polish Republic came under Soviet rule in September 1939, then passed to German rule from summer 1941 until summer 1944, and then returned under Soviet rule. Thus Lwów became Lviv, then Lemberg, and then Lviv again. Some scholars use the Polish names for all localities that existed in interwar Poland. I considered this same practice, but did not adopt it. My concern was that readers should be able to find the localities I mention on modern-day maps and geographic applications. Thus I use the Ukrainian name for all places within the boundaries of today's Ukraine. It would be cumbersome, even for a specialist, to find a present-day locality with only its Polish name. I had thought of using the names as they are found in Google Maps, but resigned from this idea after realizing that there were problems with consistency in that application. So I am rendering place names from Ukrainian, with modified Library of Congress transliteration (soft signs omitted; use of Y in place of I for the initial letter when followed by a vowel, so Yabloniv instead of Iabloniv). I think this method will most easily allow readers to search place names on the Internet and ascertain their location. Upon first mention in the text of localities that were in Poland between the wars, I will give the place name in Polish in parentheses. Localities that are in today's Poland rather than in Ukraine, such as Przemyśl, will only appear in their Polish forms. I will also provide the Romanian name for localities in Bukovina, which belonged to Romania between the wars. In some cases, the Polish or Romanian names are identical with the Ukrainian names. Cities and places that are well known in English by names that would violate the practices set out here, such as Warsaw (instead of Warszawa) and Babi Yar (instead of Babyn Yar), will be referred to by these common names. I think that the capital of Ukraine, Kyiv, is now becoming better known by its Ukrainian name, even though Kiev had once been more common. Many place names in Ukraine have changed since World War II. I will use both the modern and historical names as seems best for the context.

In sum, my choice of place name usage has not been guided by any considerations of historical correctness but rather by what I think will make geographic orientation easier for the reader.

Technical and Terminological Matters

In transliterating bibliographical data from the Cyrillic and Yiddish alphabets, I am using the Library of Congress systems without diacriticals. For Ukrainian and Russian names in the text, I am using the modified Library of Congress system devised by the Canadian Institute of Ukrainian studies; its main features are the elimination of soft and hard signs, the simplification of certain last-name endings to -sky, and the use of "Y" instead of "I" to transliterate the initial letters of certain names (e.g., Yuliian instead of Iuliian).

In this study I am using the term "nationalists" as shorthand for members and sympathizers of OUN and UPA. I do not mean to include all those who championed Ukrainian cultural and political independence. When I am using the word "nationalist" in a wider sense, I will signal that I am doing so.

I will be referring to folios of testimonies from the archive of the Jewish Historical Institute in Warsaw (AŻIH). Many individual testimonies are comprised of both a handwritten and typed copy, each with its separate pagination. I will be citing the folio numbers of the typed copies.

All translations are my own unless otherwise noted.

1. Historiography

It is a standard practice among historians to include in their monographs a survey of the existing historiography. Normally this does not constitute an entire chapter, but just a few pages. In this monograph, however, I consider it necessary to spend more time on the intellectual history of our problem, Ukrainian nationalist participation in the Holocaust. The topic has been a controversial one, and it needs to be placed in its complicated contexts. The historiography has emerged from different sources: Jewish survivors of the Holocaust, primarily in Israel; Ukrainian nationalist emigrés in North America and Western Europe; scholars in communist Poland; Soviet propagandists; scholars at universities in the West, primarily in Germany and North America; and scholars and activists in independent Ukraine. It has been impacted by major historical developments: the Holocaust itself, the establishment of communism in Eastern Europe, and the fall of that communism.

Pioneer Historiography of the Holocaust in Western Ukraine

A central figure in the early development of the historiography of the entire Jewish catastrophe survived the war in Western Ukraine, in Lviv (P Lwów). This was Philip Friedman, who had already made a name for himself in the interwar period as a historian of the Jewish population of Galicia. His doctoral dissertation from the University of Vienna, which was published in 1929, concerned the emancipation of Galicia's Jews in 1848-68.[5] He was an impeccably professional historian, who began to gather information on the Holocaust during the Holocaust itself. He survived the mass murder by hiding outside the ghetto, i.e., on the Aryan side, but his wife and daughter both perished. After the war, Friedman played a major role in collecting survivor testimony for the Central Jewish Historical Commission in Poland and was later active in many of the

---

5   Friedman, *Die galizischen Juden.*

early projects to gather sources for writing Holocaust history. He spent the last years of his life in the United States, mainly associated with Jewish scholarly institutions such as YIVO in New York and Yad Vashem in Israel, but he also lectured at Columbia University.[6]

Friedman wrote two short studies of particular relevance to this monograph. One was an account of the destruction of the Jews of his native Lviv; the first edition came out in 1945 and several expanded editions appeared later, the last in 1956.[7] He also wrote a survey, very careful and balanced, of Ukrainian-Jewish relations during the period of German rule, focusing almost exclusively on Galicia and Volhynia. Friedman was attuned to the problem of OUN-UPA participation in the mass murder of the Jews in the latter regions, but he was unable to arrive at the clarity made possible by later developments and later research. He usually did not make a distinction, which we shall see is important, between the Ukrainian National Militia and the Ukrainian Auxiliary Police.[8] He never realized the connection between the militia and the OUN, writing that the Ukrainian militia was "organized by the Germans in a hurry"[9] and consisted "of local volunteers."[10] He wrote about the UPA murder of Jews, but felt uncertain as to what had happened and wanted to learn more about it.[11] Like many historians of his era, he considered "authentic, official documents" to be the gold standard for Holocaust research;[12] yet so few of such documents had been

---

6   Aleksiun, "Invisible Web." Aleksiun, "Philip Friedman."

7   I have used the second, expanded edition of 1947 (Friedman, *Zagłada*) as well as the English translation of the 1956 Hebrew version (Friedman, "Destruction").

8   He noted correctly at one point that the Ukrainian militia was disbanded "and in its place was organized the Ukrainian auxiliary police under German direction," but otherwise used the terms militia and auxiliary police interchangeably. Quotation from Friedman, "Ukrainian-Jewish Relations," 181.

9   Friedman, *Zagłada*, 7.

10   Friedman, "Ukrainian-Jewish Relations," 181.

11   "In letters exchanged with fellow Jewish historians, Friedman expressed particular interest in exploring the attitudes of the Ukrainian leadership and military organisations, especially The Ukrainian Insurgent Army (Ukrayins'ka Povstans'ka Armiya, UPA) and their collaboration in the mass murder of the Jews." Aleksiun, "Invisible Web," 158. Aleksiun specifically cites a letter of Friedman to Szymon Datner, 30 April 1958.

12   Ibid., 152.

collected that he perforce relied heavily on testimonies and memoirs. Although Friedman was one of the first professional historians to engage with the Holocaust, his work was situated in the field of Jewish studies rather than within the scholarly discourse of modern European history.

The scholar who found study of the Holocaust at the margins of the historical discipline and, through the publication of his book *The Destruction of the European Jews*, pushed it almost to the center was Raul Hilberg. When Hilberg began to work on the murder of the Jews, he received some encouragement from his doctoral supervisor Franz Neumann, but there were also many nay-sayers. "During those days," he wrote a few decades later, "the academic world was oblivious to the subject, and publishers found it unwelcome. In fact, I was advised much more often not to pursue this topic than to persist in it."[13] His work had a tremendous impact on the way that scholars who came after him researched and wrote about the Holocaust. He is one of those rare figures of whom it is no cliché to say that he shaped a field. Some of his ideas were resisted almost immediately. He, like Hannah Arendt, whose essays in the *New Yorker* on the Eichmann trial appeared at the same time as Hilberg's *Destruction* (1961),[14] emphasized the passivity of the Jews during their slaughter and indicted the Jewish councils (*Judenräte*) for collaborationism. Their views provoked new research and publication on Jewish resistance[15] as well as a more nuanced investigation into the difficult situation of Jewish leaders in the *Judenräte*.[16]

Hilberg's great achievement was a cog-by-cog analysis of the machinery of destruction. While Friedman had lamented a lack of the official documentary sources he so highly prized, Hilberg had

---

13   Hilberg, *Destruction*, xiii (quotation from the preface to the revised edition, written in 1984). "Neumann said yes [to Hilberg's proposal to write a dissertation on "The Destruction of the European Jews"], but he knew that at this moment I was separating myself from the mainstream of academic research to tread in territory that had been avoided by the academic world and the public alike. What he said to me in three words was, 'It's your funeral.'" Hilberg, *Politics of Memory*, 66.

14   They formed the basis for her book *Eichmann in Jerusalem*.

15   For example, Ainsztein, *Jewish Resistance*, and Krakowski, *War of the Doomed*.

16   Trunk, *Judenrat*.

plenty of them, all emanating from the Germans themselves. The influential 1961 edition of his book could not yet make use of German sources in Soviet archives, but the third edition of 2003 was able to incorporate some of that source material. Hilberg's reliance almost exclusively on sources generated by the German perpetrators themselves established the methodology that dominated American and European scholarship on the Holocaust for decades thereafter. German sources became the main informants about what happened. The testimonies and memoirs of victims and eyewitnesses were relegated to the background if consulted at all. This produced a distorted picture. A one-sided source base was largely responsible for the exaggeration of Jewish passivity and for a one-sided emphasis on the complicity of the *Judenräte*. I believe it also resulted in an underestimation of help and rescue efforts on the part of non-Jews, to whom Hilberg also ascribed passivity.[17] The documents the Germans had produced tended to emphasize the successes of their extermination program and public cooperation with it. Also, the German documents noted instances of Jewish resistance and non-Jewish aid to Jews only when they were or threatened to be effective. But in the concrete circumstances of the Holocaust in Eastern Europe, neither resistance nor aid could be very effective, even if impulses and actions in these directions were more widespread than the German documents indicate. Both resistance and aid are much more evident in the documents and oral testimonies left by survivors.

Israeli scholars had objections to Hilberg's approach right from the start. Friedman, who had served on Hilberg's examining committee at Columbia, suggested to him that Yad Vashem in Jerusalem might co-publish his dissertation, but it refused: "Your book rests almost entirely on the authority of German sources and does not utilize primary sources in the languages of the occupied states,

---

17   "In fact the behavior of the population during the killing operations was characterized by a tendency toward passivity. This inertness was the product of conflicting emotions and opposing restraints. The Slavs had no particular liking for their Jewish neighbors, and they felt no overpowering urge to help the Jews in their hour of need. In so far as there were such inclinations, they were effectively curbed by fear of reprisals from the Germans." Hilberg, *Destruction*, 316.

or in Yiddish and Hebrew....The Jewish historians here make reservations...in respect of your appraisal of the Jewish resistance (active and passive during the Nazi occupation)."[18] Hilberg's work would always have a larger impact on scholarship in North America and in Western Europe than in Israel, except for provoking Israeli scholars to polemicize with his views on the lack of Jewish resistance and the complicity of the *Judenräte*.

Concentrated too narrowly on the narrative of Germans and Jews, Hilberg paid little attention to the "microbiota" of the Holocaust, the other, smaller actors, neither Jews nor Germans, who played significant roles. Unlike Friedman, Hilberg was not curious about OUN or UPA and their role in the Holocaust. In fact, he only once mentioned OUN, which he defined simply as "a pro-German organization of Ukrainians."[19] Evidently, he did not even care to inquire what the letters OUN stood for, since it appears in the index only as OUN, not as the Organization of Ukrainian Nationalists. So although Hilberg's *Destruction of the European Jews* remains an indispensable orientation text for studying the Holocaust, it has blind spots; and these blind spots have long dogged Western historiography on the topic. Jewish historiography in Israel continued along a different path, more like Friedman's.

A major contribution to the study of a territory where OUN and UPA were especially powerful was Shmuel Spector's history of the Holocaust in Volhynia, eleven editions of which were published in English and Hebrew between 1982 and 1990. Spector himself was born in Volhynia in 1922, in Kostopil (P Kostopol), Rivne oblast. When Germany attacked the Soviet Union, he fled to the Soviet interior. After the war he lived in Israel and worked at Yad Vashem. His book is interesting and very rich, with many details that make the wartime situation come alive. Spector possessed a deep knowledge of Volhynia's Jewish communities as well as its geography and terrain. Readers of his text can actually feel how highly motivated he was to figure out what had transpired in his home region during his absence. He made use of some German

---

18   Hilberg, *Politics of Memory*, 110.
19   Hilberg, *Destruction*, 312 n. 79.

documentation, particularly the Einsatzgruppen reports, but his main sources were Jewish survivor testimonies, primarily those collected by Yad Vashem and those published in memorial (yizkor) books. Since most of these testimonies were in Hebrew and Yiddish, his book is very useful to authors, such as me, who do not read Hebrew and have limited Yiddish. Spector's foremost interest was in the Jewish communities themselves, and his perspective is naturally somewhat Judeocentric. He was not as interested in the Germans as Hilberg was. But he *was* interested in the Polish and, especially, Ukrainian populations and their relation to the Holocaust. He lamented that there were not enough studies of the Ukrainian nationalist movement,[20] although he seems to have been unaware of John A. Armstrong's influential monograph on the subject (to be discussed below). Nonetheless, Spector managed to piece together a decent sketch of the history of OUN and UPA.[21] His book also frequently mentions UPA's murder of Volhynian Jews.

There is a short but (considering the paucity of available sources) well executed study of Ukrainian-Jewish relations in Galicia during the war written by the Israeli scholar Aharon Weiss.[22] Weiss had survived the war in Boryslav (P Borysław), where he was hidden by a Ukrainian woman whose son served in the Ukrainian Auxiliary Police.[23] Afterwards he emigrated to Israel and worked on Holocaust history at Yad Vashem. He understood in a general way that OUN was involved in the anti-Jewish violence of 1941 and mentioned explicitly the role of the "Ukrainian militia."[24] He was able to work with documents of the Ukrainian Auxiliary Police in Lviv but not able to connect OUN and the police.[25] He noted that

---

20   Spector, *Holocaust of Volhynian Jews*, 4-5.
21   Ibid., 233-38.
22   Weiss, "Jewish-Ukrainian Relations." I should disclose that in 1983 I thought quite differently and accused Weiss of a "nationalist view of history." "Roundtable," 493.
23   His very moving story is captured in an excellent documentary by Sarah Farhat and Olha Onyshko, *Three Stories of Galicia* (2010).
24   Weiss, "Jewish-Ukrainian Relations," 413.
25   Weiss presented his paper at the conference on Ukrainian-Jewish relations held at McMaster University in Hamilton, ON, from 17 to 20 October 1983. It is not recorded in the proceedings of that conference (Potichnyj and Aster, *Ukrainian-Jewish Relations*), but I recall a dramatic moment when Weiss was challenged by

few Jews who had been hiding in the Volhynian forests managed to survive and linked this fact to the control of the forests by UPA units, but he was unable to be more specific. He misidentified the Babii partisans who saved Jews as connected with the Ukrainian nationalists, although in fact they were a pro-Soviet formation.[26] The general thrust of his study is exemplified in its concluding sentence: "Full responsibility for these crimes falls on the Nazis, but if the attitude of the Ukrainian national movement and a great part of the Ukrainian population toward the Jews had been different, the number of survivors might well have been much larger."[27]

A book that is somewhat transitional in the historiography is Eliyahu Yones' study of "the Jews of Lviv in the years of the Second World War and the catastrophe of European Jewry, 1939-1944." It is transitional in the sense that it made limited use of newly opened Soviet archival materials that had been copied by Yad Vashem, but the text primarily relied on testimonies and memoirs, particularly Hebrew-language testimonies collected also by Yad Vashem. The text was originally presented as a doctoral dissertation at the Hebrew University of Jerusalem in 1993, at which time Yones was already advanced in years. He had been born in 1915 in Vilnius, but during the war he found himself in a labor camp in Lviv, hence his interest in the Holocaust in that city. His book was published in Hebrew as well as in German, English, Polish, and Russian translations. I primarily used the Russian-language version.[28] Although the primary focus of the book was Lviv, it also contained a great deal of material on the experience of Jews in other localities in Galicia. Yones devoted considerable attention to the persecution of Jews by the Bandera faction of OUN. His knowledge of OUN was

---

a man who claimed to have served in the Ukrainian Auxiliary Police and denied that the police had been involved in anti-Jewish actions during the war. Weiss countered by reading aloud from authentic police documents in the Ukrainian language that recorded how many Jews policemen had killed during an action.

26 See below, 431.
27 Weiss, "Jewish-Ukrainian Relations," 418.
28 Yones, *Evrei L'vova*. Other translations I consulted: Yones, *Smoke in the Sand*; Yones, *Die Strasse nach Lemberg*; Yones, *Die Juden in Lemberg*. In some earlier writings, I mistakenly stated that Yones first wrote and published his book in the 1950s.

incomplete; for example, he made the common error of conflating the militia and the police.[29] But the issue of Ukrainian nationalism and the Holocaust was very much on his mind, and his study provided much information on the topic.

Thus in this early stage of the historiography of Ukrainian nationalism and the Holocaust, the relevant studies were produced by Jewish scholars who were intimately familiar, from personal experience, with the terrain, languages, and societies of the regions where OUN and UPA had been active. They also relied extensively on the accounts of Jews who survived the mass murder. Where they all came up short, in terms of the project undertaken by this book, is that, although keenly interested in OUN and UPA, they did not have access to the kind of sources that would have given them more insight into the workings of the Ukrainian nationalist movement. They needed more definite and more extensive information, which would only become accessible after the collapse of communism. As to studies of the Holocaust in North American and European scholarship, the historiographical protocols established by Hilberg effectively prevented any focus on the role of OUN and UPA. If Western studies strayed into occupied Eastern Europe, they relied on German sources, neglected eyewitness testimony, and concentrated exclusively on the actions of Germans.

Histories of OUN and UPA Written prior to the Opening of Soviet Archives

The most detailed and solidly researched history of the pre-World-War-II OUN to appear in the period 1945-90 was written by Petro Mirchuk and published in 1968. Mirchuk had been a member of OUN since secondary school and was being entrusted with important assignments in the OUN propaganda apparatus by his early twenties (the mid-1930s). Like many in the nationalist underground, he was no stranger to Polish prisons. When war broke out in September 1939, he was in jail, but was released with all the other

---

29   He also mistakenly identified Taras Bulba-Borovets as an OUN leader. Yones, *Evrei L'vova*, 383 n. 6.

prisoners when the Polish forces in Lviv capitulated to the Germans. The insider knowledge he acquired in the movement contributed to a well-informed book. In addition, while writing his history, Mirchuk was able to consult a large number of original OUN documents as well as the interwar press, and his book reproduced many important texts of the era. He wrote from a thoroughly nationalist perspective.

Though rich in information, his book had its biases. One was that it sanitized OUN's record regarding its statements and actions against Jews in the 1930s as well as its relations with Nazi Germany. Mirchuk achieved this sanitization by avoiding these themes entirely. His omissions undoubtedly reflected OUN's postwar sensitivity about accusations of collaboration with the Nazis, especially with regard to participating in the Holocaust. But to be fair to Mirchuk, he had had a different experience with these issues than did most other OUN members. He only spent one month on Ukrainian ethnic territory during the entire war, namely mid-August to mid-September 1941. Then, at a low ebb of German-OUN relations, he was arrested by the Germans and spent the rest of the war in prisons and concentrations camps, mainly Auschwitz. He was only released when the Americans liberated the concentration camp at Ebensee on 6 May 1945.[30] Thus Mirchuk was not present to participate in the anti-Jewish violence of July 1941 and the ethnic cleansing campaign of 1943-44, and he had no love for the Germans. Another notable bias was that Mirchuk was a Bandera loyalist. When OUN split in 1940, he sided with Stepan Bandera against Andrii Melnyk; and when the Bandera faction split again after World War II, he remained with Bandera. His book, thus, presented the history of OUN from a partisan perspective. His depiction of the succession struggle after the assassination of OUN leader Yevhen Konovalets in 1938 was constructed so as to make the Bandera group's split from the emigré leadership seem reasonable and necessary. He also blamed Melnyk and his allies for turning OUN policy around and "betting on the German Hitlerite card." Until Melnyk assumed leadership, according to Mirchuk, there were "some contacts" with

---

30   Mirchuk, *In the German Mills of Death.*

Wehrmacht circles, who like OUN wanted a revision of the Versailles settlement, but OUN had had reservations about Hitlerite
ideology and politics, which viewed Eastern Europe as a territory
for colonization.[31]

Nowhere near as well researched, but even more partisan was
Polikarp Herasymenko's short book on "the Organization of
Ukrainian Nationalists during the Second World War." Herasymenko was neither a historian nor politically active for long;
instead he was a metallurgist who made a good career in the United
Kingdom and the United States after 1948. Born in Odessa, he fled
Soviet Ukraine to avoid arrest in 1921, living mainly in Prague until
the end of World War II. He was a member of the Melnyk faction
of OUN during the war years and for a short time thereafter.[32] Herasymenko's history was first published as a mimeographed text in
1947 and went through several editions over the following years.
The work made use of the interwar and wartime periodical press as
well as documents of both the united OUN and the Melnyk faction.
But overall, it was marred by one-sidedness. A major target of its
criticism was the Bandera faction. Herasymenko attributed its split
from the rest of OUN to foreign intrigue. Fearful of the power of
OUN, both the Germans and the Soviets had engineered the rift,
preying on the Bandera group's "political blindness, ambition,
primitiveness, moral indifference."[33] He condemned the rebellion
they led: "provoked by the enemy, they pushed the masses on the
path of a negative, in every respect unprepared, and therefore need-
lessly bloody 'insurgency.'"[34] Herasymenko quoted many OUN
documents critical of Nazi Germany and made no mention of pro-
German attitudes or cooperation with Nazi Germany on the part of
OUN. He made an exception, of course, for the Banderites, who, he
wrote, were both ignorant of Germany's plans for Ukraine and
ready to help the Germans by supplying them with hundreds of

---

31   Mirchuk, *Narys*, 582-83.
32   Kovaliv, "Herasymenko." I am grateful to Marco Carynnyk for first informing
      me that the pseudonymous H. Polikarpenko under whose name the history ap-
      peared was actually P. Herasymenko.
33   Herasymenko, *Orhanizatsiia Ukrains'kykh Natsionalistiv*, 43; see also 40-44, 50-51.
34   Ibid., 8.

interpreters. The many interpreters from the Melnyk faction working for the Germans were passed over in silence. There was also no
mention at all of the Melnykites' support for the Waffen-SS Division
Galizien. The Ukrainian police in German service, with whom both
factions of OUN were deeply involved, were almost completely absent from Herasymenko's account; there was a single passing mention in a wartime document calling upon Ukrainians in all stations
of life to remember that they were members of the "Ukrainian Nation, once free, glorious, and powerful, but today enslaved and
marked by blood and ruin."[35] Jews and the Holocaust were completely missing from Herasymenko's book.

Another veteran of the movement who wrote about OUN during World War II was Lev Shankovsky. Shankovsky had, as an ad-
olescent, served in the armed forces fighting for an independent
Ukraine during the revolutionary period that followed World War
I. His military experience later proved useful both for his activity in
OUN and UPA during World War II and for his postwar work as a
military historian of Ukraine. He was associated with the Bandera
wing of OUN during the war, but after the war he joined a faction
that broke with Bandera, the UHVR group[36] or so-called *dviikari*.
Led by Mykola Lebed and Lev Rebet, the *dviikari* adopted a more
democratic program than either the Banderites or Melnykites and
benefited from generous funding by the United States' Central Intelligence Agency.[37] Shankovsky's book on OUN-B's expeditionary
groups (*pokhidni hrupy*) in southern Ukraine[38] and Romanian-occu-
ped Transnistria created a picture of the past that fit well with the
postwar ideology of the UHVR. Shankovsky had fine narrative
skills and wrote with some verve, although his prose was not free
of jargon. I will spend more time analyzing this work, since it

---

35   Ibid., 131.
36   The UHVR or Ukrainian Supreme Liberation Council is discussed below, 375-
      76. Shankovsky was a founding member.
37   Yurkevich, "Ukrainian Nationalists and DP Politics." Rudling, "'Not Quite
      Klaus Barbie.'"
38   By southern Ukraine Shankovsky meant the Dnipropetrovsk, Kirovohrad, My-
      kolaiv, Odessa, Stalino (now Donetsk), Voroshylovhrad (now Luhansk), and
      Zaporizhzhia oblasts in their wartime boundaries as well as Crimea.
      Shankovs'kyi, *Pokhidni hrupy*, 27.

presented a narrative that has been very influential in the postwar Ukrainian diaspora, especially among historians and other intellectuals. It also offered a full enough account to serve here as a prominent example of a more general trend in OUN and UPA historiography.

The expeditionary groups were small OUN units that fanned out from Kraków and then across Ukraine, following the German advance. They were instrumental in establishing local civil administrations and militias wherever they went. In his account of them, Shankovsky emphasized that they fought against two enemies, both the Soviets and the Germans. He also described fierce persecution of members of OUN, especially OUN-B (the Bandera faction), by the Germans. While writing at length about the conflict between OUN and the Germans, Shankovsky completely omitted to mention moments of cooperation.

The main point of Shankovsky's book was to show that the more tolerant and democratic position adopted by the UHVR had its basis in the encounter between the Western Ukrainian nationalists and the population of Soviet Ukraine in its pre-1939 borders. His story is that the Western Ukrainian activists came into the rest of the Ukraine and discovered that the ideological baggage they had brought with them was unacceptable to the population there. The inhabitants of central, southern, and eastern Ukraine rejected the OUN's *Führerprinzip* and its intended single-party rule and wanted a democratic parliamentary system instead. They did not like OUN's voluntarism, amorality, exclusivity, and hunger for power, preferring ethical politics, toleration, and humaneness. They were not satisfied with the slogan of an independent Ukraine: they wanted to know the content of the envisaged state, its political structure and social policies. They were against imperialism and exploitation and wanted national minorities to have the rights of other citizens of the Ukrainian state. They did not accept OUN's slogan of "Ukraine above all." The Western Ukrainian activists, challenged by this encounter with the majority of Ukrainians, had to rethink their program, resulting in the more liberal OUN program of August 1943 and the establishment of the UHVR.[39] Here is how Shankovsky put it in his conclusions:

> ...I set myself a clearly defined goal that my work was supposed to achieve. I wanted—as extensively as possible—to present the ideological and political *evolution* that the pro-independence OUN underwent as a result of the direct encounter of the mass of its membership with the Ukrainian mainland and Ukrainian population in the Central Eastern Ukrainian Lands and Eastern Ukrainian Lands. The epic tale of the expeditionary groups in central and eastern Ukraine, the *discussion of ideas* conducted by the members of the expeditionary groups with the Ukrainian people of the Central Ukrainian Lands and Eastern Ukrainian Lands, and the integration (*usobornennia*) of the Organization of Ukrainian Nationalists through the mass entrance into it of Ukrainians from the Central Ukrainian Lands and the Eastern Ukrainian Lands were the reasons that much was thrown out from the political-programmatic decisions and directives of OUN, [the elimination of] which had been considered taboo in the conditions of Polish occupation. In particular, very decisively thrown out were all sorts of "isms" introduced onto Ukrainian soil from a foreign field: authoritarianism, elitism, totalitarianism, dogmatism, exclusivism, voluntaristic nationalism, and so on. Socioeconomic and political issues decisively took precedence over issues of worldview and philosophy; mysticism had to make way for a realistic strategy and tactics of liberation, and the despised leader system capitulated before democracy and parliamentarism, with its accompanying human freedoms.[40]

In addition to arguing for a fundamental shift in perspective within the OUN expeditionary groups as a result of the encounter with the east and south, Shankovsky also contended that under the impact of the encounter OUN began to shed its ethnocentrism and to develop a new openness to the national minority populations in Ukraine. He stated that the national minorities of southern Ukraine—"Russians, Greeks, Moldavians, and Tatars"[41]—warmed

---

39 This narrative permeates the book, but this particular summary is based on ibid., 21-22. On workers wanting free and fair elections and democracy and on their opposition to the leader principle, see 107. On the August 1943 program, see below, 368-70, 377.

40 Shankovs'kyi, *Pokhidni hrupy*, 317-18.

41 Ibid., 19.

to the idea of an independent Ukraine, with equal rights for the minorities.[42] "The broad masses of the Central and Eastern Ukrainian Lands most decisively rejected any possibility of an exterminatory or even discriminatory policy with regard to any national minority in Ukraine. Non-Ukrainians who live in Ukraine and are Ukrainian citizens should enjoy all the rights of Ukrainian citizens. It has to be recognized and emphasized that the leaders of the frontline expeditionary groups quickly oriented themselves in the situation and were able to conduct their propaganda in the direction of winning over non-Ukrainians for the Ukrainian liberation movement."[43] In Shankovsky's narrative, OUN in the Donbas reached out to Russians as full-fledged Ukrainian citizens.[44]

As to OUN's relations with the national minority with which this monograph is particularly concerned, i.e., the Jews, Shankovsky explained: "In this place we wish to underline that neither the Ukrainian population nor the members of the Ukrainian underground who came to the Central and Eastern Ukrainian Lands were in any way involved in anti-Jewish actions."[45] By contrast, Shankovsky wrote that the White Russian emigrés, who also came to Transnistria, were rabid antisemites who killed Jews on their own initiative, without prodding from the Romanian authorities.[46] Shankovsky also noted that the Jews in Transnistria were pro-Bolshevik.[47]

The heroic tale of OUN's transformation under the impact of this encounter could well contain some grains of truth, but to determine how many requires new and in-depth research. For the purposes of this monograph, though, it is necessary to point out some dubious claims, half-truths, and falsehoods in Shankovsky's narrative.

To begin with, I wonder how true is the claim that the young workers of the Donbas and indeed the general population of the

---

42   Ibid., 20, 56.
43   Ibid., 110.
44   Ibid., 163-64, 175.
45   Ibid., 66 n. 27.
46   Ibid., 237, 249.
47   Ibid., 249.

south were insisting on parliamentary democracy. Where would their knowledge of this political system have originated? Surely not from any personal experience, nor from anything they read in Soviet publications. And many years later, after parliamentary democracy was finally introduced in independent Ukraine, the Donbas stood out as the region of origin and the primary political base of the most authoritarian president and politicians in Ukraine's post-Soviet history (President Viktor Yanukovych and the Party of Regions). Thus I am skeptical of the assertion that a population molded by tsarism and Stalinism and later subject to Nazi occupation would have had a clear enough picture of representative democracy to summon it up as an ideal with which to challenge OUN. Much recent research in the history of Stalinism has shown that it was exceedingly difficult for Soviet citizens to think outside the communist box.[48] This is borne out by some of the original slogans the Donbas workers came up with during the German occupation, such as "Ukrainian Soviet power without the Bolsheviks" and "Soviet Ukraine without the Bolsheviks and without the dictatorship of the Communist party."[49]

And the picture of OUN being so open to non-Ukrainians, particularly Russians, is — at best — overdrawn. This is clear from a volume of documents published much later, in 2013, on OUN in the Donbas. The collection is decidedly pro-OUN; in fact, its editor conceived it as literature first and foremost for "radical youth and participants of Ukrainian paramilitary organizations."[50] The documents do show that some ethnic Russians participated in the nationalist movement, particularly a woman from Kramatorsk, Donetsk oblast, by the name of Serafima Petrovna Kutieva, who also figured in Shankovsky's book.[51] By Kutieva's own account to her NKGB interrogator in 1944, at first her Russian nationality did cause her OUN recruiter a moment's hesitation, but then she was accepted into the movement. It turned out that her Russian

---

48 A well known example of this subjectivist scholarship is Hellbeck, "Fashioning the Stalinist Soul."

49 Kuromiya, *Freedom and Terror in the Donbas*, 281.

50 Dobrovol's'kyi, *OUN na Donechchyni*, 3-4.

51 Shankovs'kyi, *Pokhidni hrupy*, 169, 172.

nationality worked out well for the OUN underground; her home could more effectively serve as a safe house for the movement. "...My apartment for them was above all suspicions since I am a Russian...."[52] In the course of her recruitment she discovered that not all OUN members were open to Russian ethnicity. One of her former husbands was her first recruiter, and he described the goal of the nationalist movement as the establishment of "an independent Ukrainian state which would be run exclusively by Ukrainians."[53] She described a fellow OUN activist from Vinnytsia as "stridently chauvinistically...inclined."[54] OUN members in the civil administration in Kostiantynivka, Donetsk oblast, advocated the replacement of ethnic Russians by ethnic Ukrainians.[55] OUN also promoted restrictions on the use of the Russian language in administration, the courts, signage, and education.[56]

The documentary collection also shows that OUN in the Donbas consistently propagated antisemitism while the Holocaust was proceeding. Several OUN proclamations are included as photoreproductions at the back of the book. The newspaper *Ukrains'kyi Donbas*, which was under OUN control, wrote in a front-page editorial on 18 December 1941:

> Under the powerful blows of the victorious German and Allied armies the bonds with which for twenty-three years day and night the Jewish-Bolshevik henchmen bound the freedom-loving Ukrainian people have burst asunder....[As the German and Italian forces approached,] for fifteen whole days Jewish commissars, Asiatic barbarians...destroyed the national property built by the sweat and blood of the Ukrainian people....We must accept the slogan "Ukraine for Ukrainians" as the fundamental principle in the work of a newly constructed state apparatus and take it as the starting point for

---

52   Dobrovol's'kyi, *OUN na Donechchyni*, 226. In addition, she continued, her husband enjoyed the trust of the German authorities.
53   Ibid., 218, 231.
54   Ibid., 221.
55   Ibid., 247.
56   Ibid., 265, 270-71, 273, 275-77, 291, 293.

orientation in solving all problems which every day of work on the construction of a new life brings.[57]

On the next page of the same issue appeared a proclamation to Ukrainian youth issued by OUN:

> The Jews forced us to call our dearest people enemies. They forced us to love alien Moscow and not our native Ukraine. In our country those who married Jewesses, and thereby contributed to the degeneration of the Ukrainian nation, were held in esteem. Jewboys were called Ukrainian musicians—all those Buses, Goldsteins, Davids, Oistrakhs. They gave them prizes, titled them Stalin laureates, but the truly talented Ukrainian youth was trampled and then withered on the vine. The institutes and schools swarmed with Jews because they had money....In the Komsomol and Pioneers the Jewish-Muscovite politicians tried to raise janissaries, champions of Red Moscow, haters of the Ukrainian people....Ukraine for Ukrainians![58]

And on the next page was yet another OUN proclamation, this one addressed to teachers:

> They forced us to poison the minds of children with Jewish internationalism....Jews wrote the grammar of the Ukrainian language....In the theaters and cinema they showed us performances and films directed by Jews, in which the best sons of the Ukrainian land were reviled and ridiculed....Schools for Ukrainians! Down with lying Jewish-communist education. In a Ukrainian school—Ukrainian children....Let us welcome the German army, the most cultured army in the world, which is driving from our lands the Jewish-communist scum. Let us help the Organization of Ukrainian Nationalists under the leadership of Stepan Bandera build a great Independent Ukrainian State. Ukraine for Ukrainians![59]

OUN members in the civil administration also promoted antisemitism. OUN member Anton Yastremsky was raion head in Olhynka, Donetsk oblast. On 17 September 1942 he issued an order to introduce the OUN greeting "Glory to Ukraine" in his raion. This

---

57 "Ukraintsi do pratsi!" Reproduced in Dobrovol's'kyi, *OUN na Donechchyni*, 342. *Ukrains'kyi Donbas* came out in Horlivka in Donetsk oblast.
58 "Ukrains'ka molod'!" Reproduced in Dobrovol's'kyi, *OUN na Donechchyni*, 343.
59 "Uchyteli ukraintsi!" Reproduced in Dobrovol's'kyi, *OUN na Donechchyni*, 344. A similar proclamation appeared in *Ukrains'kyi Donbas* on 18 January 1942: "Do napolehlyvoi pratsi!" Reproduced in Dobrovol's'kyi, *OUN na Donechchyni*, 346.

was intended to restore polite and respectful behavior after years of "hostile Jewish-Bolshevik" interpersonal relations, of "Bolshevik-Jewish barbarity."[60] The OUN-controlled city administration of Mariupol in Donetsk oblast ordered that civil servants take Ukrainian language courses since "as a consequence of Muscovite-Jewish rule in Ukraine our people lost their language, customs, and so on."[61]

The works on the history of OUN and UPA produced by veterans of the movement, such as those by Mirchuk, Herasymenko, and Shankovsky, but also by others (e.g., Mykola Lebed, Borys Lewytzkyj[62]), were marked by partisan perspectives. Their writings not only defended the positions of OUN but of their particular faction of OUN. They emphasized OUN's persecution at the hands of the German occupiers but downplayed the extent to which OUN collaborated with Germany. All of them avoided disclosure about the extent to which OUN and UPA were involved in ethnic cleansing, including participation in the Holocaust. Already in 1946, a prominent Ukrainian émigré from eastern Ukraine, Ivan Bahriany, accurately diagnosed the problem with the self-presentation of the emigrés associated with OUN: the nationalist camp, he wrote, was trying to repudiate its heritage of xenophobia, antisemitism, voluntarism, leaderism [vozhdyzm], and antidemocratism, but "not by overcoming these things, but by assuring us that they had not existed."[63]

In addition to the veterans' writings, a scholarly study of OUN and UPA appeared already in 1955 and went through three editions, the last appearing in 1990. John Armstrong's *Ukrainian Nationalism* relied primarily on three kinds of sources: German documentation, the wartime Ukrainian press, and interviews. The

---

60   Dobrovol's'kyi, *OUN na Donechchyni*, 273-74; photoreproduction of first page of the order, 339. Olhynka is no longer a raion capital.

61   Ibid., 268. For other indications of anti-Jewish sentiment among OUN members in the Donbas see 135, 215. On truth and legend about OUN in the Donbas, see also Radchenko, "'Two Policemen Came.'"

62   Lewytzkyj, "Natsional'nyi rukh pid chas Druhoi svitovoi viiny," is an interview, but to my knowledge it is the only attempt to sketch the history of the Mitrynga faction of OUN during World War II.

63   Bahrianyi, "Natsional'na ideia i 'natsionalizm,'" in Bahrianyi, *Publitsystyka*, 63.

interviews were conducted almost exclusively with prominent Ukrainian activists and politicians, and not just from the OUN camp. He had great sympathy for these men, although he was not uncritical in his admiration.[64] He did not interview Polish or Jewish survivors of OUN-UPA violence nor consult their testimonies and memoirs. The only book on the Holocaust listed in the bibliography of the 1990 edition is Hilberg's classic, in which, as we have seen, there was no room for a discussion of OUN. No works in Polish were cited. The result was a study that had very little to say about OUN operations against Poles and Jews.[65] The ethnic cleansing of the Poles was given cursory treatment, based entirely on German sources, on a few pages.[66] The question of OUN involvement in the pogroms of 1941 was discussed in one paragraph.[67] Like most scholars at that time, Armstrong did not understand the distinction between the militias organized by OUN and the later Ukrainian Auxiliary Police. He did, however, make mention of some anti-Jewish rhetoric employed by OUN.[68]

Armstrong wrote a rather sympathetic narrative of the nationalists, emphasizing their valor in fighting against two such powerful enemies as the Germans and the Soviets. He did not go far enough to please all the nationalist veterans, who felt, particularly, that he underestimated their success outside Western Ukrainian lands. Yevhen Stakhiv, a leading figure in the OUN-B expeditionary movement in the south and one of the major proponents of the

---

64   Armstrong, "Heroes and Human."
65   As I wrote in 2010: "In the mid-1980s the Solidarity underground in Poland wanted to publish texts about Ukrainian nationalism and requested through an intermediary, the late Janusz Radziejowski, that I convey to them copies of Armstrong's book as well as Alex Motyl's *Turn to the Right*. After reading them in Polish translation, Janusz wrote to me in 1988 that for all the scholarly value of these books, he was very disappointed that they took no cognizance of the tremendous tragedy of the Jews." Himka, "Organization of Ukrainian Nationalists," 87. Radziejowski's criticism was unfair in relation to Motyl's book, which only encompassed the period through 1929. For more on Armstrong's position, see Berkhoff and Carynnyk, "The Organization of Ukrainian Nationalists," 175 n. 22.
66   Armstrong, *Ukrainian Nationalism*, 110-12.
67   Ibid., 54, 56 (a map appears on p. 55). See below, 225-303.
68   Ibid., 79 n. 28, 118.

UHVR, made this objection,[69] as did Shankovsky in his history of the expeditionary groups. In fact, Shankovsky decided to write his history in the first place as a corrective to Armstrong's narrative.[70]

Another noteworthy study of Ukrainian nationalism from this period was Alexander J. Motyl's *The Turn to the Right*. It only covered the story up through the founding of OUN in 1929, so it was more of a prehistory than a history in relation to the theme of my own book. But it was important for its exploration of the ideological sources of Ukrainian nationalism and its interpretation of where Ukrainian nationalism stood in relation to the fascist movements emerging in Europe at that time. *Turn to the Right* was based on wide-ranging consultation of contemporary Ukrainian-language press and brochures as well as scholarly works on Ukrainian history and on right-wing and fascist ideology outside Ukraine. Its appearance in 1980, at a time when academic Ukrainian studies were just taking off in North America, meant that it gained considerable attention. Although later in life Motyl became an apologist for OUN, this first work was quite balanced.

Polish scholars contributed well informed works on OUN in wartime. In 1972 Ryszard Torzecki wrote a monograph on the Ukrainian policy of the Third Reich which, of course, devoted considerable attention to Ukrainian nationalism. Antoni Szcześniak and Wiesław Szota's *Droga do nikąd* (The Road to Nowhere) of 1973, which covered OUN and UPA from the 1920s into the postwar period, had an interesting, and rather sad, history. It was primarily based on Szcześniak's doctoral dissertation, but Szota wrote the introductory section on the interwar period. The text tried to work within the constraints of what could be said and what could not be said when Poland was a communist country within the Soviet orbit.[71] The reason this was tricky is that parts of what used to be Poland were now in the Ukrainian SSR, and the text had to avoid any

---

69   Dobrovol's'kyi, *OUN na Donechchyni*, 294 (reprint of excerpts from Stakhiv's memoir of 1956).
70   Shankovs'kyi, *Pokhidni hrupy*, 85-86, 94, 101-02, 147.
71   "...The authors have been guided, and this needs to be strongly emphasized, by Marxist-Leninist criteria in the national question and in the evaluation of social problems." Szcześniak and Szota. *Droga do nikąd*, 6.

suggestion that these territories were in some sense Polish. Thus, the events of 1939 were presented from a Soviet perspective: the alliance between Nazi Germany and the Soviet Union was glossed over and the population of western Ukraine was depicted as fervently desiring to be joined with Soviet Ukraine. But try as they did, the authors were unable to construct a narrative of OUN and UPA that the Soviets found acceptable. After the direct intervention of the Soviet embassy, the book was withdrawn from circulation as "harmful for current party propaganda"; the Soviets feared that "the book can be used propagandistically by the Ukrainian emigration in its fight against the Soviet system." The authors suffered for their mistakes, being pushed to the margins of the Polish scholarly establishment.[72] (Not many years later I heard that Szota committed suicide, but I cannot confirm this.) Aside from its ideological contortions, which of course included a less than even-handed and objective treatment of OUN and UPA, the work had value. It made use of abundant materials in Polish archives, materials that at that time Western scholars had no access to. The Ukrainian journalist and memoirist Ivan Kedryn Rudnytsky characterized the volume thus: "Although the tendency of this book is bad because — as the authors themselves declare in the introduction — they examined the problem 'through the prism of Marxism-Leninism,' nonetheless in it was gathered a mass of factual documentary-informational material — more than can be found in all the nationalist literature."[73] Kedryn did not explicitly mention it, but Szcześniak and Szota were very well aware of how Poles and Jews suffered at the hands of the Ukrainian nationalists and wrote about these matters in some detail.

As is clear from the case of *Droga do nikąd*, the Soviets had many sensitivities around the history of OUN and UPA, and it is not surprising that no real scholarship on the nationalists appeared in the Soviet Union. Aside from other considerations, the Soviets did not want to disturb the myth of a united Soviet people in struggle against the fascist occupiers by writing about collaboration with

---

72   Nowak, "'Droga do nikąd." This is a review of a reprint of *Droga do nikąd* in 2013.
73   Kedryn Rudnyts'kyi, *Zhytiia — podii — liudy*, 356.

the Germans and about a powerful anti-Soviet movement. The Soviets cloaked OUN and UPA under the term "Ukrainian-German
fascists" and were silent about their influence on the Ukrainian
population during the war. And in addition, the Soviet authorities
did not permit scholarship on the Holocaust. In fact, the subject of
the Holocaust made them uncomfortable.[74] It singled out the suffering of the Jews instead of the whole Soviet people, and this particular narrative of suffering could feed into Jewish nationalism,
i.e., Zionism. In the postwar period Soviet anti-Zionism could be
quite shrill and antisemitic.

But there was an exception to the Soviet reticence on our topic.
Beginning in the 1970s, the Soviets published tracts on Ukrainian
nationalist participation in the Holocaust and other war crimes.
Several were published under the name Valerii Styrkul in the 1980s,
after the airing of the influential television miniseries, *Holocaust*
(NBC, 1978), which heightened American interest in Nazi atrocities.[75] Styrkul concentrated on the Waffen-SS Division Galizien rather than on OUN. But the earliest and most influential of these
tracts was *Lest We Forget*, signed by the Ukrainian-American communist Michael Hanusiak (first edition 1973).[76] *Lest We Forget* did
publish documentary evidence of OUN antisemitism, notably extracts from the autobiography of OUN leader Yaroslav Stetsko from
July 1941, in which Stetsko endorsed German methods of annihilating Jews.[77] The book also contained documents and testimony on
crimes committed by both OUN and Ukrainian police units in German service with OUN connections. However, these documents
were unverifiable by scholars, since the archives they were housed
in were closed to researchers. And the presentation was so heavy-

---

74   Gitelman, "Politics and the Historiography of the Holocaust in the Soviet Un-
      ion." Amar, "Disturbed Silence."
75   On developments in America, see the classic study by Peter Novick, *The Holo-
      caust in American Life*.
76   There is an obituary of Hanusiak in the communist newspaper *People's World*:
      "Michael Hanusiak."
77   To be discussed below, 105-10.

handed and one-sided that scholars treated his revelations with scepticism or outright rejection.[78]

In fact, the brochure *Lest We Forget* was the product of a KGB operation. The head of the Ukrainian KGB, Vitalii Fedorchuk, wrote about it to the first secretary of the Ukrainian party, Volodymyr Shcherbytsky, in a memorandum dated 27 December 1973. It is worth quoting *in extenso*:

> Earlier the KGB of the Council of Ministers of the Ukrainian SSR reported that in order to incite enmity between Ukrainian nationalists and Zionists in the USA the brochure *Lest We Forget* was published in English; the publication exposes, on the basis of documents, the participation of OUNites during the Second World War in the mass destruction of the peaceful population, including in so-called "Jewish actions"....
>
> As "author" and publisher of the brochure figured one of the leaders of the progressive Ukrainian organizations, the League of American Ukrainians.[79] In recent years he has visited Ukraine and can thus explain how he obtained the materials utilized in the brochure.
>
> In order to popularize the brochure, the "author," at our recommendation, engaged one of the progressive Jewish activists of New York in the capacity of "copublisher."[80] The joint action of progressive

---

78   "Hanusiak's publication is utterly tendentious, and I refer to it with great caution." Weiss, "Jewish-Ukrainian Relations," 420 n. 36. Weiss's article cited here was originally delivered as a paper at a conference on Ukrainian-Jewish relations in 1983. At the same conference, during the roundtable discussion, I am recorded as having said: "...no matter how one claims that one is careful about this source, Hanushchak [sic] being a Ukrainian communist front, cannot be believed and one shouldn't even mention it in a text." "Round-Table Discussion [first edition]," 494. For the second edition of the conference proceedings I was permitted to clean up the language of my intervention and phrased the same thought somewhat differently, saying that Hanusiak was "a Ukrainian-American Communist with a political axe to grind; he is not a source to be cited in a scholarly text." "Round-Table Discussion [second edition]," 494. Somehow Taras Hunczak managed to misread this entirely: "I understand that when Aharon Weiss called Hanusiak's work 'utterly tendentious,' John-Paul Himka came to Hanusiak's defense." Hunczak, "Problems of Historiography," 136.

79   The organization was originally founded as the United Ukrainian Toilers Organization in 1924 and renamed the Union of Ukrainian Toilers in 1938 and the League of American Ukrainians in 1940. Kuropas, *The Ukrainian Americans*, 184, 196.

80   This was Sam Pevzner, a writer who contributed to such communist publications as *The Daily Worker* and *Jewish Life*. He had been subpoenaed by the House Committee on Un-American Activities as a communist propagandist in 1958.

Ukrainian and Jewish organizations in the USA against the OUNites as war criminals has had a certain political effect....

Since the demand for the brochure has exceeded the number printed, the Ukrainian and Jewish progressive organizations are preparing a second edition....

Given the interest in the brochure shown in the USA and Canada, measures are being taken by us to collect additional materials on the participation of nationalists in the eradication of the Jewish population for publication abroad.[81]

As the letter indicates, propaganda publications of this sort were intended for export and were published in the English language.

After surveying the state of the historiography before the 1990s, it should become apparent that it was very difficult at that time to arrive at a clear understanding of the behavior of OUN and UPA during the Holocaust. The Jewish scholars who came from the Western Ukrainian territories were aware of the nationalists' violence against the Jewish population, but they had too little knowledge of the nationalist movement to flesh out what had happened. They could not rely on the histories written by nationalist veterans, since the latter completely denied any responsibility for the persecution and murder of the Jewish population. Nor was Armstrong's scholarly study any help in this regard. Mainstream Holocaust history, as exemplified by Hilberg, did not have the conceptual framework and an inclusive enough source base to even consider investigating the role of OUN and UPA. Publications emanating from or inspired by the communist bloc were discounted by Western scholars; and in addition, the best informed of them, Szcześniak and Szota's *Droga do nikąd*, was very difficult to obtain.[82]

The Collapse of Communism in Europe

A decisive turn in the historiography resulted from the fall of communism in Eastern Europe and the dissolution of the Soviet Union

---

81   HDA SBU, fond 16, op. 4, spr. 2, tom 2, ff. 275-76.

82   Szcześniak and Szota's book came out while I was a graduate student at the University of Michigan. Our library had a publication exchange with Poland and received a copy of the book before it was removed from circulation.

in 1989-91. The opening of the Polish, Romanian, Slovak, and Soviet archives made available to scholars a vast amount of fresh material to understand the Holocaust in the east of Europe, including the activities of Ukrainian nationalists.[83] Moreover, the political restraints on research were removed. Scholars in the postcommunist sphere could now write whatever they wished, free from censorship and communist party control. Polish scholars no longer had to refrain from writing about the fate of Poles in territories that were once in the Soviet Union but now formed parts of independent Lithuania, Belarus, and Ukraine.[84] Even Ukrainian nationalists had been worried about writing their own history as long as Ukraine was communist, since revealing too much could lead to reprisals against nationalists and their families still residing in Soviet Ukraine.[85] Now those fears were gone. The result of these new sources and new freedoms was the blossoming of a diverse historiography on the question of the Ukrainian nationalists and the Jews during the Holocaust.

The first to professionally mine the new sources were two German scholars, Thomas Sandkühler and Dieter Pohl, who each produced a German-sized monograph on the Holocaust in Galicia, in 1996 and 1997 respectively. Both followed the practice of what was then mainstream Holocaust historiography: they paid relatively little attention to victims and their testimony and relied heavily on documents emanating from German structures. Pohl argued that the attitudes of the autochthonous, non-Jewish population were relatively unimportant in determining the general course and final outcome of the mass murder in Galicia: essentially the German occupation authorities made the decisions and executed them themselves. Whether resisting or aiding the Germans in the murder, the actions of what Pohl called "the Christian population" were of

---

83 The kinds of sources made available by the momentous changes of 1989-91 will be described in the next chapter.

84 The fact that "today" (the mid-1980s) Volhynia "lies outside the Polish territory poses delicate political problems for Polish authors." Spector, *Holocaust of Volhynian Jews*, 4.

85 Mirchuk, *Narys*, 9. Herasymenko, *Orhanizatsiia Ukrains'kykh Natsionalistiv*, 4. Shankovs'kyi, *Pokhidni hrupy*, 184, 198, 266, 291, 302 nn. 100-01, 329. Shtul', *V im"ia pravdy*, 7.

secondary importance in influencing events.[86] Pohl characterized the Bandera faction of OUN as antisemitic for much of the war, particularly in the spring and summer of 1941 and again in 1944, as the Soviets closed in, stating also that in 1942-43 OUN distanced itself from the Germans' murder of the Jews.[87] (During the latter period Ukrainian opinion in general had cooled towards the Germans and their "final solution.")[88] Pohl was not able to link OUN directly to any concrete war crimes. His treatment of the Ukrainian Insurgent Army in relation to the Holocaust reached no clear conclusion.[89] In my own review of Pohl's book, I characterized it as follows: "This is an ambitious and pioneering work. It is not a synthesis based on a corpus of pre-existing monographs; instead, it attempts a comprehensive portrayal of the Holocaust in Galicia largely on the basis of primary sources. It opens the field for further, in-depth monographic research of specific problems and incidents."[90]

It was in this period too that Jeffrey Burds began to lecture and write about OUN and UPA in an entirely new vein. Although the texts he published then did not directly concern the Holocaust but rather focused on the immediate postwar period,[91] they demonstrated that sources in the newly opened post-Soviet archives could provide a much deeper knowledge of the nationalists' actions than other historians had ever imagined. Also, his revelations about the ruthlessness of OUN and UPA helped break the spell of the nationalists' own historiography.

Directly related to wartime OUN's Jewish politics was a documentary publication by Karel C. Berkhoff and Marco Carynnyk: the full text, or rather texts, of the July 1941 autobiography of nationalist leader Yaroslav Stetsko, mentioned above in connection with Michael Hanusiak and to be discussed in some detail below.[92] In their introduction to the autobiography Berkhoff and Carynnyk

---

86   Pohl, *Nationalsozialistische Judenverfolgung*, 316.
87   Ibid., 40, 48-49, 375, 382.
88   Ibid., 316-17.
89   Ibid., 374-75.
90   Himka, Review of Pohl, *Nationalsozialistische Judenverfolgung*, 99.
91   Burds, "AGENTURA." Burds, *Early Cold War*. Burds, "Gender and Policing."
92   See 42, 105-10.

surveyed some of OUN's anti-Jewish pronouncements, which they found to be written in "vicious language" and to be encouraging "a deadly antisemitism."[93]

Martin Dean's *Collaboration in the Holocaust* investigated the actions of local police in certain regions of Belarus and Ukraine during the Nazi occupation. Although a very valuable study, it exemplified a trend that was still strong in the 1990s: Dean studied the Holocaust in Eastern Europe without knowledge of the relevant East European languages. Dean was trained in history (his first book was on Austrian policy during the late-eighteenth century wars with revolutionary France) and was then employed in the war crimes unit in Scotland Yard. He moved from there to the Center for Advanced Holocaust Studies at the United States Holocaust Memorial Museum (USHMM) in Washington, DC, where he has continued to write and compile impressive works on Holocaust history. *Collaboration in the Holocaust* was based on archival sources and eyewitness testimonies. It outlined the influence of OUN on the local Ukrainian police in German service and the role of those policemen later in UPA. But his work focused on areas outside the center of OUN and UPA activity, which was Galicia and Volhynia.

With the weakening and then total collapse of the Soviet system, OUN and UPA came under reexamination in Ukraine. After decades of condemnation of the nationalist organizations, calls for rehabilitation emerged in the public discourse, particularly in the Lviv newspaper *Za vil'nu Ukrainu*.[94] Already in March 1990, the foremost proponent of reform in Soviet Ukraine, Rukh (*Narodnyi Rukh Ukrainy*—People's Movement of Ukraine), raised the issue of the nationalists' political rehabilitation.[95] Before long, the government began to turn to Ukraine's scholarly establishment to advise on the issue. On 12 June 1991 the head of the commission on defense and state security of the Verkhovna Rada of the Ukrainian SSR, Vasyl Durdynets, wrote to the Ukrainian academy of sciences with

---

93 Berkhoff and Carynnyk, "The Organization of Ukrainian Nationalists," 152-56; quotations 156.

94 Marples, *Heroes and Villains*, 79-165.

95 Kul'chyts'kyi, *Orhanizatsiia ukrains'kykh natsionalistiv i Ukrains'ka povstans'ka armiia. Fakhovyi vysnovok*, 40.

the request to find someone to prepare a background paper on OUN, UPA, and the Waffen-SS Division Galizien. The task was entrusted to Viktor Koval, a historian in his mid-seventies specializing in the Second World War. Koval had studied in his native Kyiv and worked there in the academy's Institute of the History of Ukraine. The text he speedily produced, by 1 July, argued that "OUN and UPA conducted a national-liberation struggle for the construction of a sovereign and democratic Ukraine, in which people of all nationalities would enjoy the same political and social rights." Durdynets, who had long been an official in the Communist Party of Ukraine, repudiated the report and demanded that the academy withdraw it and replace it with another. The academy complied immediately, formally withdrawing Koval's report on 3 July.[96] But the OUN-UPA issue would not go away for the Ukrainian public, government, or academia. In particular, veterans' groups—Red Army veterans and UPA veterans—were confronting one another, especially on the occasion of the fiftieth anniversary of UPA celebrated in 1992. In 1993 the parliament (*Verkhovna Rada*) again decided that there was a need to investigate the legacy of OUN-UPA, but the efforts of a parliamentary committee proved insufficient to the task. Finally, in 1997 a working group of historians, under the leadership of Stanislav Kulchytsky, was charged with unearthing the true history of OUN-UPA and evaluating its heritage. The task proved more complicated than anyone expected, and the commission made no concrete progress until the early 2000s.

A few studies related to our topic did appear in Ukraine in the 1990s. Yakov Khonigsman's short book on the Catastrophe of Lviv Jewry, which came out in 1993, built on earlier studies, especially on the works of Philip Friedman and Tatiana Berenstein (the latter unavailable to me), as well as on a modest selection of documentation from Lviv archives. It made little use of memoirs and testimonies. In fact, in the foreword to the book, Bogdan Semenov stated

---

96   Koval', "Za shcho i z kym borolysia OUN-UPA." Quotation, 92. Koval's original report is reprinted in this article, 95-116. An entire section of Koval's report, "What Did UPA Fight for?" (112-14), is simply a long extract from the OUN program of August 1943.

that the volume "is not written from the words of eyewitnesses, where in the main the element of subjectivity or emotionality figures," but "according to the materials of archival documents."[97] Khonigsman avoided the topic of any OUN involvement in the events he described. Later, in 1998, Khonigsman published a book that looked at the Holocaust across Western Ukraine, encompassing the Ukrainian historical regions of Galicia, Volhynia, Bukovina, and Transcarpathia, but primarily concentrating on Galicia. This book made more use of survivor testimonies and was more deeply researched in archives, principally in the Lviv archives, but also in those of Kyiv and elsewhere. In this book Khonigsman pointed out how antisemitic OUN was.[98] Like many other historians before him, he did not differentiate the militia established by OUN from the Ukrainian auxiliary police established later by the Germans; hence he ascribed crimes of the militia to the auxiliary police.[99] Khonigsman had nothing to say about UPA and the Jews.

More interesting was a book on "the behavior of the local population of Eastern Galicia in the years of the 'final solution of the Jewish question'" — Zhanna Kovba's *Liudianist' u bezodni pekla* (Humaneness in the Abyss of Hell) published in 1998 by the Judaica Institute in Kyiv. Kovba conducted extensive archival research, consulting in particular the records of the Ukrainian Auxiliary Police in the State Archive of Lviv Oblast (DALO) and OUN documents in the Central State Archives of Supreme Bodies of Power and Government of Ukraine (TsDAVO). She consulted Jewish, Polish, and Ukrainian memoirs and also interviewed many people from throughout Galicia who had lived through the events of World War II. It was a book with an openly declared agenda: to destroy "the two fundamental deceitful myths which impede objective perception of the relations among peoples in these difficult times: that Ukrainians were almost the instigators of German crimes against the Jews...; that Jews were guilty of annihilating

---

97   Khonigsman, *Katastrofa l'vovskogo evreistva*, 2.
98   Khonigsman, *Katastrofa evreistva Zapadnoi Ukrainy*, 76, 122.
99   Ibid., 113, 125.

Ukrainians under Soviet rule."[100] And although Kovba had a tendency to make generalizations and prefer evidence that showed both Ukrainians and Jews in a favorable light,[101] she also included information that went against the grain of her overall interpretation. She was unwilling to hazard an evaluation of OUN's stance and actions during the Jewish tragedy because she found the evidence too contradictory; more research was required in order to make sense of things.[102] What comes through most clearly in Kovba's book is the mixed feelings of the 1990s: with the collapse of communism, both Jewish suffering and Ukrainian suffering were being articulated, and it was difficult to afford recognition to and reconcile them both.[103]

The emergence of a cult of OUN and UPA in Ukraine provoked a reaction from a maverick within the Ukrainian diaspora in North America, Viktor Polishchuk. Polishchuk had been born into an Orthodox family in Volhynia, but in 1940, during the first period of Soviet rule in the region, he and his mother and siblings were deported to Kazakhstan. (His father had been arrested by the Soviets in 1939 and was never seen again.) They were allowed to return to Ukraine after the Soviet reconquest in 1944, but to Dnipro oblast rather than Volhynia. In 1946 the family moved to Poland (Polishchuk's mother was Polish). Polishchuk studied law there and worked as a lawyer and a prosecutor; but after he openly declared his Ukrainian nationality in 1956 he was fired from the prosecutor's office and endured other instances of discrimination. In 1981 he emigrated to Canada, where, being very particular about proper Ukrainian usage, he worked as an editor in Ukrainian-

---

100 Kovba, *Liudianist' u bezodni pekla*, 203.

101 For example, Kovba sometimes suggested that the Poles, not the Ukrainians, were the real antisemites (e.g., 116). In her opinion, while the Polish and Jewish press printed tendentious accounts of the pogroms of 1917-20, Ukrainian publications offered "objective information" (29-30). She stated (29) that the "educated, tolerant Greek Catholic clergy was in its large majority free of antisemitic superstitions," but see the attempt in 1930 to prove the reality of the blood libel by the young Basilian monk Irynei Nazarko, "Piznaimo zhydiv!" (After World War II Nazarko became an influential church historian in the Ukrainian diaspora.)

102 Kovba, *Liudianist' u bezodni pekla*, 224, 228-29.

103 I have explored this theme also in "Debates in Ukraine," 354, 356.

language media. Based in Toronto and well informed through the circumstances of his employment about Ukrainian diaspora life, he came into contact with nationalist circles; he had not been acquainted with nationalists in Ukraine or Poland. Although he had no personal experience of what OUN-UPA had done in Volhynia during the war, he knew from friends and relatives that the nationalists had slaughtered many of its former Polish inhabitants, including members of his own extended family.[104]

A follower of the debates in Ukraine after the fall of communism, he was upset by prominent political and cultural figures calling for the rehabilitation of OUN and UPA and blamed the Ukrainian diaspora for reintroducing nationalism to Ukraine.[105] This is what provoked him to write *Hirka pravda* (Bitter Truth), published at his own cost in 1995. (The book appeared in Polish in the same year and later in an English translation.) The text was an indictment of OUN and UPA for the mass murder of the Polish inhabitants of Volhynia. At this time, by his own admission, Polishchuk did not have enough material to write about UPA's murder of Jews and others.[106] Later on he found plenty of relevant documentation,[107] but his documentary publications remained focused primarily on the murder of Poles.[108] His 1995 text did not yet use archival material, although he hoped that soon such material would become available.[109] Later Polishchuk did gain access to the relevant archival documents and cited and reproduced them in his publications. But the 1995 text was based entirely on published sources as well as some personal communications.

Polishchuk's book was not well received by Western, Ukrainian, or Polish historians, even though Polishchuk wrote from an anti-Soviet perspective and was careful to make a distinction

---

104 Polishchuk, *Hirka pravda*, 30-39, 215-16.
105 Ibid., 20-22, 25-26, 57, 245, 437-38.
106 Ibid., 10.
107 Kulińska, "Dowody zbrodni."
108 Polishchuk, *Integralny nacjonalizm ukraiński*, vols. 3-5 (these volumes bear an additional title: *Nacjonalizm ukraiński w dokumentach*).
109 Polishchuk, *Hirka pravda*, 12, 26.

between Ukrainians as such and OUN.[110] The prolific Canadian historian of modern Ukraine David Marples categorized the book as differing little from the Soviet perspective "in terms of the one-sidedness of the outline."[111] Volodymyr Serhiichuk, a pro-nationalist Ukrainian scholar best known for numerous documentary compilations on modern Ukrainian history, devoted a short book to a refutation of Polishchuk's *Hirka pravda*.[112] Polishchuk himself he called a "supposed Ukrainian" (*nibyto ukrainets'*). Yurii Shapoval, one of the first Ukrainian historians to work with NKVD documents, rejected Polishchuk's work as anti-Ukrainian.[113] The dean of Lviv's Ukrainian historians, the late Yaroslav Isaievych, labeled Polishchuk "a 'professional' of anti-Ukrainian hysteria."[114] Polish specialists in modern Ukrainian history were of a similar opinion. Ryszard Torzecki called him a former prosecutor for the NKVD (which he was not) and felt that he "was not worth talking about."[115] His views were also criticized by Rafał Wnuk, although not as vehemently: "W. Poliszczuk holds a special place among the non-scientists. As a Ukrainian political scientist who deals, so to speak, 'scientifically' with the problem of Ukrainian nationalism, he is sometimes seen as a credible person."[116] Both Shapoval and Torzecki equated Polishchuk with a much less credible writer, the propagandist Edward Prus.[117]

---

110 E.g., ibid., 22. His insistence on the innocence of the local Volhynian population and the guilt of the Galician nationalists led him to state categorically, and unfortunately incorrectly, that the local population of Volhynia took no part in the mass murder of the Jews, only the auxiliary police set up by OUN. Ibid., 342.

111 Marples, *Heroes and Villains*, 208. I also had been dismissive of Polishchuk's publications until I began my own research on the role of OUN and UPA in the Holocaust; before then I had absorbed the negative opinions of colleagues in Ukrainian studies and had only consulted his works superficially. I changed my thinking about Polishchuk when I read him carefully and with an open mind.

112 Serhiichuk, *Nasha krov — na svoii zemli*, 4.

113 Shapoval, "Chy podolano 'volyns'kyi syndrom'?"

114 Isaievych, "1943 rik."

115 Torzecki, "Mav ia do dila z endets'kym murom."

116 Wnuk, "Recent Polish Historiography," 10.

117 Polishchuk in fact criticized Prus more than once in his publications. For example, he wrote that Prus was wrong to seek the reasons for Ukrainian nationalist atrocities "in genetic or cultural factors of the Ukrainian people." Polishchuk, *Integralny nacjonalizm ukraiński*, 2:486.

In my opinion, this was not a fair equation. There are one-sided authors, and there are unbalanced authors. Prus, unfortunately, belonged to the latter category. In communist Poland he specialized in propaganda against the Ukrainian Greek Catholic church and Ukrainian nationalists and continued in the same vein after communism's collapse; in both eras he was closely associated with the Polish nationalist right. Prus had been born in and survived the war in Galicia. As a teenager he joined in the defence of Poles threatened by UPA and later fought UPA in the "destruction battalions" (*istrebitel'nye batal'ony*).[118] He later emigrated to Poland, earned a doctorate at the University of Warsaw, held various academic posts — none of any prominence, and wrote prolifically.

The book most relevant to the concerns of this monograph is Prus's *Holocaust po banderowsku* (Holocaust Banderite-Style), published in 1995. Among much else, the book included an account of a meeting Prus claimed he had in London with Karl Popper, whom he described as "undoubtedly one of the most outstanding Jewish thinkers of the twentieth century." According to Prus, Popper called him, i.e., Prus, "the most outstanding expert in this area [the history of UPA] in Poland, and not only in Poland." Also, Popper supposedly expressed amazement that the president of Ukraine at that time, Leonid Kravchuk, had not condemned the murders perpetrated by Ukrainian nationalists against Jews and Poles. "And he warned the Jews that they should stop playing together with Ukrainian nationalists at the expense of the Poles, because this fraternization with criminals under the flag of totalitarianism is a blind alley, a road to nowhere."[119] To me, this account sounds like a fantasy or at least a hearty embellishment. (Popper passed away shortly before *Holocaust po banderowsku* was published.)

---

118 The destruction battalions were militias that the Soviets organized to fight the nationalist insurgency after the reconquest of Western Ukraine. Many of the fighters were recruited from the Polish minority. On the battalions, see Statiev, *Soviet Counterinsurgency*, 209-29. Although these units are usually referred to as destruction battalions in the English-language literature, a more literal translation from the Russian would be exterminatory battalions.

119 Prus, *Holocaust po banderowsku*, 186-87.

I think there was also a strong dose of fantasy in the "evidence" he brought to bear. Much of what he had to say was based on personal communications in his possession and was therefore unverifiable. Sometimes he gave proper citations for material he quoted, but in other cases he offered no citations whatsoever. For example, *Holocaust po banderowsku* contained a long quotation very relevant to the theme of this study attributed to Mykhailo Stepaniak, a member of the central OUN leadership captured by the Soviets; the quotation concerned the Third Extraordinary Assembly of OUN (August 1943).[120] Prus offered no citation, although presumably the text would have been taken from the record of one of Stepaniak's interrogations. I have not, however, been able to find the passage Prus quoted in the archival record of Stepaniak's interrogation of 25 August 1944[121] nor in published versions of his interrogations.[122] Moreover, the quoted passage refers to the presence of Ivan Mitrynga at the congress, which seems highly unlikely, given that Mitrynga had broken with the Banderites in September 1941 and had joined forces with their rival Taras Bulba-Borovets. I suspect that the passage was the product of a vivid imagination rather than an excerpt from a genuinely existing document.

Moreover, he wrote in a style that had more in common with biblical prophecy than with historical scholarship. Referring to Stella Krenzbach, an alleged Jewish veteran of UPA to whom is attributed a memoir praising the Ukrainian nationalists,[123] Prus stated that she acted "undoubtedly from a whisper from Satan, because Satan directed the hand of the genocidaire of Polish and Jewish children," and that she was guilty of "blaspheming against Yahweh."[124] He also speculated that the apocalypse predicted by St. John the Revelator was not a once and final confrontation between good and evil but would be arriving in installments, one of which

---

120 Ibid., 156.

121 HDA SBU, fond 13, spr. 372, vol. 1, ff. 21-59.

122 "Vytiah z protokolu dopytu chlena tsentral'noho provodu OUN M. Stepaniaka," *Pol'shcha ta Ukraina u trydsiatykh-sorokovykh rokakh XX stolittlia*, 220-72, 442-44.

123 As we will see below, 112-15, Stella Krenzbach and her memoir were Ukrainian nationalist fabrications.

124 Prus, *Holocaust po banderowsku*, 164.

was the era of UPA. It was a time "of three clearly apocalyptic fig- ures, as Hitler, Stalin, and [UPA commander Roman] Shukhevych- 'Chuprynka,' and of three hells let loose in the cause of and with the active permission of those who supported them: Nazis, Bolshe- viks, and Ukrainian chauvinists."[125] In sum, Prus's texts are un- trustworthy and will not be cited in the narrative that follows. To equate Polishchuk with him is, I feel, a serious error.

A Conceptual Turn: Jan Gross's *Neighbors*

The publication of Jan Gross's short but explosive book *Neighbors* in 2000-01[126] transformed the historiography of the Holocaust as it transpired in Eastern Europe, including in Ukraine. The book de- scribed vividly, graphically how Poles in Jedwabne murdered the town's Jewish inhabitants in July 1941. It generated immense com- mentary and controversy, but the primary matters of contention (the number of victims and the presence or absence of Germans) have little bearing on how it affected historiography. There were three aspects of *Neighbors* that were revolutionary, even if they were not without some antecedents. The first was the focus on non-Ger- man participation in the extermination of the Jewish population. One might say that this turned the spotlight on the "microbiota" of the world war and the Holocaust, that is, on non-state actors fol- lowing their own agendas, which sometimes involved the murder of Jews. In particular, Gross directed attention to the anti-Jewish vi- olence of the summer of 1941, shortly after the German invasion of the Soviet Union but before the German leadership made the deci- sion to kill all of European Jewry. One result of Gross's work was that in the early twenty-first century a large literature on the pog- roms and related anti-Jewish violence in Western Ukraine ap- peared.[127] Particularly noteworthy was Kai Struve's detailed

---

125 Ibid., 189.
126 The Polish version appeared first, in 2000, the English version a year later.
127 Boll, "Złoczów" (2002); Bechtel, "De Jedwabne à Zolotchiv" (2005); Carynnyk, "Zolochiv movchyt'" (2005); Struve, "Ritual und Gewalt" (2005); Pohl, "Anti- Jewish Pogroms in Western Ukraine" (2007); Himka, "Dostovirnist' svidchen- nia" (2008); Kopstein and Wittenberg, "Deadly Communities" (2010); Kruglov "Pogromy v Vostochnoi Galitsii" (2010); Himka, "The Lviv Pogrom of 1941"

historical account of the violence across Galicia, which brought many new sources to bear and revealed the important role of German actors in the pogroms, especially the soldiers of Waffen-SS Wiking.[128] The interest in the pogroms also led to renewed research on one of their contextual factors, the mass murder of thousands of political prisoners by the NKVD, which occurred at different sites in western areas of Ukraine between the launch of the German invasion and the evacuation of Soviet forces.[129]

The second way in which Gross's little volume was revolutionary was that it placed the history of the Holocaust in Eastern Europe firmly within East European studies. Gross was an East Europeanist. Until *Neighbors* he was best known for two studies of Polish territories under German and Soviet occupation. He knew the languages, historical context, social relations, and culture of Poland before he embarked on his studies of the Holocaust and postwar antisemitism. He had earned his doctorate at Yale in 1975, and his book on Polish society under German occupation appeared four years later. He had behind him a quarter century of publications on Polish sociology and modern history before he published *Neighbors*. He had not dealt with the Holocaust in his earlier work, and when he finally came to that theme he brought a wealth of training and scholarly experience to it. Until *Neighbors*, East European studies and Holocaust studies had been on separate tracks. Friedman and Spector were Holocaust specialists; they came from Eastern Europe and so knew the languages and cultures, but their scholarly interests did not extend beyond Jewish history. Armstrong was an East Europeanist, but he avoided dealing with the Holocaust. Hilberg wrote his great work without much knowledge of Eastern Europe

---

(2011); Lower, "Pogroms" (2011); Struve, "Rites of Violence?" (2012); Prusin, "A 'Zone of Violence'" (2013); Rossoliński-Liebe, "Der Verlauf und die Täter" (2013); Struve, "Tremors in the Shatter-Zone of Empires" (2013); Kopstein and Wittenberg, *Intimate Violence* (2018).

128 Struve, *Deutsche Herrschaft* (2015).

129 Himka, "Ethnicity and the Reporting of Mass Murder" (2013); Kiebuzinski and Motyl, *The Great West Ukrainian Prison Massacre* (2017); Struve, "Masovi vbyvstva v"iazniv." Among earlier works on the same subject are Gross, *Revolution from Abroad* (1988), 144-86, and Romaniv and Fedushchak, *Zakhidnoukrains'ka trahediia* (2002).

and sometimes operated with stereotypes.[130] After *Neighbors* a number of persons trained in East European studies undertook work on the Holocaust. Aside from myself, examples include Kai Struve, who wrote an excellent study of peasant and nation in late nineteenth-century Galicia before he turned to an examination of the pogroms of 1941, and Per Anders Rudling, whose doctoral dissertation concerned the development of Belarusian nationalism but who has also worked on OUN-UPA and the Holocaust. What had occurred as a result of Gross's intervention was that the Holocaust in Eastern Europe had begun to be treated as a part of East European history. One could no longer just parachute intellectually into an East European locality and follow what the Germans did there — one had to have deeper contextual knowledge. In 1992 Christopher Browning published his pathbreaking study of Holocaust perpetrators, *Ordinary Men*. It followed a German reserve police battalion as it murdered its way through Poland but did not cite any sources in Polish. No scholar in the West in the 1990s thought this unusual. But when, at the end of the 1990s, Omer Bartov decided to write a history of interethnic relations and the Holocaust in the small Galician town of Buchach, the demands of scholarship were different. The immersion in the languages and cultures and physical space of Galicia required a large investment of time. In the end, it took this prolific author two decades to write his microhistory, *Anatomy of a Genocide*.

The third revolutionary feature of Gross's book was that it reintegrated victims' testimony into mainstream Holocaust scholarship, after decades of marginalization. His particular views on survivors' testimony will be discussed in the next chapter, on sources, but the overall point is that he demonstrated the crucial importance of moving beyond what perpetrators had to say and listening also

---

130   "The Ukrainians had never been considered pro-Jewish. Ukraine had been the scene of intermittent pogroms and oppression for 300 years. On the other hand, these people had no stamina for the long-range systematic German destruction process. Short violence followed by confession and absolution was one thing, organized killing was quite another." Hilberg, *Destruction*, 545. Aside from the essentialism here, Hilberg seemed unaware that some Ukrainians had proven quite capable of long-range systematic and organized killing—of the Polish population of Volhynia and Galicia.

to the victims. Christopher Browning exemplifies the change of attitude. When he wrote *Ordinary Men* back in the early 1990s, he did not use any testimonies or other first-person documents other than those of the perpetrators, except to establish chronology.[131] But in the twenty-first century he has become an advocate of reintegrating victim narratives into Holocaust studies. In a lecture he delivered at the USC Shoah Foundation in March 2018, he said:

> Using survivor testimony has difficulties....It is problematic evidence. But all historical evidence is problematic in one way or another. Anybody who relies on uncomplicated evidence isn't going to be able to write history. But the issue is not do we use it, but how do we use it. To not use survivor memories is to lose whole areas of the Holocaust that we have no other set of evidence for.[132]

The present monograph comes out of the post-*Neighbors* consensus: it examines non-German perpetrators, it proceeds from immersion in regional history and culture, and it makes copious use of testimonies and related ego documents. This is now becoming, at least in the West, the main stream of scholarship on the Holocaust in Ukraine and is represented by many, and diverse, practitioners, including Tarik Cyril Amar, Omer Bartov, Delphine Bechtel, Franziska Bruder, Jeffrey Burds, Marco Carynnyk, Simon Geissbühler, Taras Kurylo, Jared McBride, Grzegorz Rossoliński-Liebe,[133] Per Anders Rudling, and Kai Struve. Scholars sharing the same consensus have also been studying the Holocaust on territories adjacent to Ukraine, notably Diana Dumitru, Jan Grabowski, and Vladimir Solonari. A few other traits of this scholarly trend need to be mentioned. One is that it is in constant dialogue with Western scholarship on the Holocaust as well as with the historiography on twentieth-century Ukraine—in Western academia, the Ukrainian

---

131 Shortly after *Ordinary Men* was published, Browning visited Yad Vashem in Jerusalem, where Israeli scholars questioned his neglect of survivor testimony. Browning's arguments in defense of his approach are well laid out in Browning, *Collected Memories*, 40-42.
132 "Christopher Browning Talks."
133 Rossoliński-Liebe has also himself written several surveys of the historiography: "Debating, Obfuscating and Disciplining the Holocaust"; "Die antijüdische Massengewalt"; and "Survivor Testimonies."

diaspora, and in Ukraine itself. The main languages of its publications are English and German, but many of its texts have been translated into Ukrainian as well as Polish and Russian. The representatives of this historiographical tendency are critical of both the nationalists and their interpretation of the past.

Close to the group described above are other Western historians who have made important contributions to the history of the Holocaust in Ukraine. Wendy Lower has written on German perpetrators, co-edited a collective monograph on the Shoah in Ukraine as well as edited an English translation of one of the few diaries of a Jewish victim of the Holocaust in Galicia; she has also written on the bloody summer of 1941 in Ukraine. Vladimir Melamed, originally from Lviv and the author of a Russian-language history of Lviv's Jewish community, has written an original study of Ukrainian collaboration in the Holocaust based on the oral histories collected by the USC Shoah Foundation. Frank Golczewski has published a number of important studies that relate to OUN and to the Holocaust in Ukraine.

In the past few decades Polish historiography on OUN and UPA has been extensive and has been mainly concerned, of course, with the nationalists' slaughter of the Polish population in Volhynia and Galicia in 1943-44. One of the most important Polish historians working in this area is Grzegorz Motyka. His major study *Ukraińska partyzantka* (The Ukrainian Partisan Movement) contains a chapter on UPA and the Holocaust, but like Dieter Pohl a decade earlier he was unable to arrive at clear conclusions.

Contemporary Polish historiography remains divided over the scholarly contributions of Jan Gross. *Neighbors* has had, and continues to have, a controversial reception in Poland. Some prominent Polish historians and intellectuals reject Gross's work,[134] but mostly

---

134 See Polonsky and Michlic, *The Neighbors Respond*; Forum on Jan Gross's *Neighbors*; Michlic, "Coming to Terms with the 'Dark Past'"; Törnquist-Plewa, "The Jedwabne Killings." The government of the rightist, nationalist Law and Justice Party in Poland initiated libel proceedings against Gross in 2015 and attempted to strip him of his Order of Merit in 2016, but backed down in the face of protests. At issue was not *Neighbors* alone, but two other books by Gross, *Fear* and *Golden Harvest*.

in consideration of what it says or implies about Polish society. Worth singling out is Bogdan Musial's "*Konterrevolutionäre Elemente sind zu erschießen,*" an informative study of the violence—Soviet, Nazi, and Ukrainian nationalist—in the summer of 1941. It originally appeared in August 2000 and was less antagonistic to Gross's scholarship than Musial's later texts and those of other Polish historians in his camp (such as Marek Jan Chodakiewicz). But "*Konterrevolutionäre Elemente sind zu erschießen*" has been criticized by Western scholars for exaggerating the role of Jews in the Soviet apparatus in Eastern Poland/Western Ukraine in 1939-41 and thus implying a certain justification for the pogroms that broke out in the wake of the German invasion.[135]

The Rehabilitation of OUN and UPA in Ukraine

An even more important division has been created by the recrudescence of a pro-OUN historiography, this time in Ukraine rather than in the diaspora. It is a historiography that takes little notice of Western scholarship, except occasionally as an irritant. It also neglects or rejects the use of contemporary testimony by persons of non-Ukrainian ethnicity, particularly Poles and Jews. It does not conceal its political purpose, the exposition of a heroic national myth. Although it is not without genuine achievements, from the point of view of historical scholarship it is a historiographical silo.

As mentioned earlier, in the 1990s, as a response to calls to rehabilitate OUN-UPA as well as to protests of Red Army veterans and others against such rehabilitation, the Ukrainian parliament looked to Ukraine's historians to investigate the historical role of the nationalists and to provide information on which a decision could be based. In 1997 a working group was set up, headed by Stanislav Kulchytsky. In the mid-1980s Kulchytsky had been part of a Soviet Ukrainian commission to refute allegations that there had been a manmade famine in Ukraine in 1932-33. Later, when Ukraine became independent, and especially when President

---

135 Pohl, review of "*Konterrevolutionäre Elemente sind zu erschießen,*" and Rudling, "Bogdan Musial and the Question of Jewish Responsibility."

Viktor Yushchenko (2005-10) made the famine, the "Holodomor," a central component of his historical and identity politics, Kulchytsky changed his views and became the chief historian of the famine and a strong proponent of the idea that the Holodomor was a genocide.[136]

The working group produced two key texts in 2000-05 that were meant to clarify the history of OUN and UPA and provide expert guidance on the evaluation of the nationalists.[137] The first of these texts, *Problema OUN-UPA*, was produced in 2000 and intended as a preliminary outline of the issues.[138] A not unsimilar document was produced in 2005, which bore the subtitle "expert conclusion" (*fakhovyi vysnovok*) but actually made no overt recommendations.[139] In addition to these more programmatic documents, the working group published a collective monograph on the history of OUN and UPA.[140] Much of the text of the two shorter, programmatic publications was drawn word for word from the collective monograph. The collective monograph in turn was drawn from more extensive studies by working-group members that preceded the collective monograph. Particularly useful for this book were the substantive treatments of OUN and UPA by Anatolii Kentii and Ivan Patryliak. Although the oeuvre of members of the working group tended to have a generally positive attitude toward the nationalists and played down their dark sides, it harvested much rich material from post-Soviet Ukrainian archives.

The working group did not explicitly call for the rehabilitation of OUN and UPA, but that was clearly the direction in which their endeavors pointed. They were academics drafted to provide

---

136 There is a sympathetic account of Kulchytsky's career and the evolution of his views on the Holodomor which does not mention his contribution to the rehabilitation of OUN: Klid, "Stanislav Kulchytsky."

137 There is an excellent study of the working group within the context of a wider discussion of the effectiveness, or lack thereof, of historical commissions to resolve conflicts based on historical memory: Myshlovska, "Establishing the 'Irrefutable Facts.'"

138 Kul'chyts'kyi, *Problem OUN-UPA*.

139 Kul'chyts'kyi, *Orhanizatsiia ukrains'kykh natsionalistiv i Ukrains'ka povstans'ka armiia. Fakhovyi vysnovok*.

140 Kul'chyts'kyi, *Orhanizatsiia ukrains'kykh natsionalistiv i Ukrains'ka povstans'ka armiia. Istorychni narysy*.

historical answers to a political question that has divided Ukrainian public discourse ever since it became possible to freely discuss the nationalist heritage. Their work had nothing at all to say about antisemitism as a component of OUN ideology or about OUN-UPA participation in the Holocaust. In fact, the Holocaust itself is scarcely mentioned in their texts, although these texts all focus on World War II and on Ukraine, where a million and a half Jewish people were murdered. This omission can partly be explained by the working group's overall tendency to whitewash the nationalists' record. For example, it treated UPA's mass murder of the Polish population as a tragedy rather than a crime. It saw both Poles and Ukrainian nationalists as culpable in the violence, denying that the mass murder had anything to do with a nationalist ethnic cleansing project.[141]

But perhaps at least equally important was another factor, namely the terms of the political debate into which the historians were asked to intervene. The "expert conclusion" divided the parties privy to the dispute into "adherents to and opponents of the nationalists, veterans of OUN and the CPSU, of UPA and the Soviet army."[142] European norms, including European concerns about the Holocaust, were absent from the context. The working group was responding to the critique of the nationalists developed by the Soviets, who were not concerned with the Holocaust at all, nor with antisemitism, nor even — considering Stalinism's own record — with mass murder and ethnic cleansing. The working group was simply not thinking in a wider context. Most of the members of the working group were themselves products of the Soviet educational system and socialization. Kulchytsky and Kentii, perhaps the most influential individuals within the group, were both born in 1937. Four other historians who contributed to the collective monograph were

---

141   "Thus, the struggle of OUN-UPA was not about the destruction of the Poles as an ethnic minority on the territory of Ukraine, but about the removal of the 'Polish factor' as a weapon in the hands of the enemies of the Ukrainian liberation movement," i.e., the Germans and the Soviet partisans. Kentii in Kul'chyts'kyi, *Problem OUN-UPA*, 89-90.

142   Kul'chyts'kyi, *Orhanizatsiia ukrains'kykh natsionalistiv i Ukrains'ka povstans'ka armiia. Fakhovyi vysnovok*, 3.

born between 1955 and 1967, and thus were products of the Soviet higher educational system (Volodymyr Dziobak, Ihor Iliushyn, Heorhii Kasianov, Oleksandr Lysenko). The only member whose formative period was post-Soviet was Patryliak, who was born in 1976. Thus, the questions with which the working group wrestled were mainly those previosuly posed within Soviet discourse. As a result, issues of treason to the motherland and collaboration with the enemy were much more important for them at that time than whether OUN and UPA participated in the destruction of Ukraine's Jewish population.

Political developments in Ukraine affirmed the working group's attitude to OUN and UPA. The Orange Revolution of November 2004 brought Viktor Yushchenko to the presidency of Ukraine. He bestowed the honorific title "Heroes of Ukraine" upon both Roman Shukhevych, the commander of UPA, and Stepan Bandera, the leader of the most important faction of OUN. As he was leaving office in 2010, Yushchenko urged Ukrainians to name streets and public places after the heroes of OUN-UPA.[143] His successor as president, Viktor Yanukovych, rolled back the cult of OUN, but it returned with new energy after the Euromaidan in 2014.[144]

The working group was based in the Institute of the History of Ukraine in the National Academy of Sciences of Ukraine in Kyiv. Another, younger group of historians, based in the academy's Institute of Ukrainian Studies in Lviv, embraced OUN and UPA even more forthrightly. The leader of the Lviv group was Volodymyr Viatrovych, who was just twenty-five when he founded the Center for the Study of the Liberation Movement in 2002. Viatrovych remained director of the Center until 2008 when he was appointed head of the archive section of the Ukrainian Institute of National Memory, established by President Yushchenko. Shortly thereafter Viatrovych was also appointed head of the SBU archives. He became even more influential after the Euromaidan and headed the

143 Amar et al., Strasti za Banderoiu. Arel, Ukraine List, nos. 441 and 442.
144 On historical politics in independent Ukraine, see Kasianov, "History, Politics and Memory."

Ukrainian Institute of National Memory from 2014 to 2019. He consistently promoted the cult of OUN and UPA, downplaying their wartime crimes.[145] He and his associate Ruslan Zabily, who directs the pro-OUN Lontsky prison museum in Lviv,[146] have excellent connections with the Ukrainian diaspora in North America. They have spoken a number of times at the Harvard Ukrainian Research Institute and the Canadian Institute of Ukrainian Studies; both of these institutes have partnerships with the Center for the Study of the Liberation Movement.[147]

Of the publications of the Lviv group, the most relevant to our topic is Viatrovych's book on OUN's attitude toward Jews, which came out in 2006.[148] It sought to exonerate OUN and UPA from accusations of antisemitism and participation in the Holocaust, but it had serious flaws as a scholarly monograph. It handled sources in a one-sided manner, rejecting the authenticity or relevance of those that confirmed OUN's hostility to Jews while accepting as valid a fabricated memoir by an alleged Jewish member of UPA.[149] The latter was the only alleged Jewish survivor testimony that the book cited. It cited no sources or scholarly literature in German or English, nor did it take into account contextual or comparative factors that would have helped illuminate the issues. Also, it was apparent that Viatrovych could not recognize antisemitism when it appeared in OUN texts.[150] Viatrovych's book did, however, contribute to initiating a larger discussion about OUN and the Jews, and it published as an appendix two OUN texts on the subject.

Other historians working within a generally nationalist paradigm were more careful scholars than Viatrovych. In particular, Andrii Bolianovsky, also based in Lviv, published a number of useful, well researched articles on Galicia under German occupation

---

145 See McBride, "How Ukraine's New Memory Commissar Is Controlling the Nation's Past"; McBride, "Who's Afraid of Ukrainian Nationalism?" 657-62; Himka, "Legislating Historical Truth."
146 Himka, "The Lontsky Street Prison Memorial Museum."
147 The partnerships are featured on the Center's website, www.cdvr.org.ua (accessed 12 October 2018).
148 V"iatrovych, *Stavlennia OUN do ievreiv*.
149 This is discussed in the next chapter, 112-15.
150 Kurylo and Himka, "Iak OUN stavylasia do ievreiv?"

and — most important — two detailed monographs on Ukrainian military and police units in German service.[151] Moreover, other Lviv-based historians have written quite critically of OUN, including Marta Havryshko, who has published on the situation of women in UPA, and the prominent historians, essayists, and bloggers Yaroslav Hrytsak[152] and Vasyl Rasevych.[153] Oleksandr Zaitsev, at this writing head of the history department at the Ukrainian Catholic University in Lviv, has done particularly valuable work on OUN prior to 1941, including a detailed survey of integral nationalist ideology[154] and the publication of a text by a leading member of OUN advocating the ethnic cleansing of Ukraine.[155]

At present, some of the best researched and frankest discussion of OUN and Holocaust perpetration is being conducted in Ukraine by scholars younger than all the other Ukrainian scholars mentioned so far. An outstanding figure is Yuri Radchenko of Kharkiv, who knows *all* the languages necessary for Holocaust research, not only Slavic and Western languages but Hebrew and Yiddish as well. He has researched the Holocaust in Kharkiv and the Donbas and the memory politics surrounding the nationalists and their collaboration in the Holocaust, and he has broken new ground by working on the Melnyk wing of OUN in relation to the Holocaust.[156] Other younger, up-and-coming scholars are doing exciting work too, though much of what they have discovered has so far been presented only in unpublished papers. Andrii Usach started his scholarly career in the pro-OUN Center for the Study of the Liberation Movement in Lviv, but left that organization and now is assembling the most intimate portraits yet of Ukrainian Holocaust perpetrators.[157] Roman Shliakhtych of Kryvyi Rih has also been working on local perpetrators, particularly Ukrainian

151 Bolianovs'kyi, *Dyviziia "Halychyna"*; Bolianovs'kyi, *Ukrains'ki viis'kovi formuvannia*.
152 Hrytsak, *Strasti za natsionalizmom*.
153 E.g., Rasevych, "L'vivs'kyi pohrom"; Rasevych, "Vyverty propahandy."
154 Zaitsev, *Ukrains'kyi integral'nyi natsionalizm.*
155 Zaitsev, "Defiliada v Moskvi ta Varshavi"; Zaitsev, "Voienna doktryna."
156 He has also written his own account of the historiography. Radchenko, "Ukrainian Historiography."
157 Usach, "Chy mozhemo pochuty holos."

policemen in German service.[158] These excellent young historians —
and I am sure there are more of whom I am unaware — are certain
to redefine the contours of Ukrainian historiography on OUN and
UPA and their relation to the Holocaust. But it is not just young
historians who are making breakthroughs. Two older historians
from Ternopil, Oleh Klymenko and Serhii Tkachov, have done tremendous work in the archives of their city, producing two detailed
monographs on the Ukrainian police in the Ternopil and Kremenets
regions; both monographs treat both police involvement in the Holocaust and OUN involvement with the police in an open and balanced manner.

Finally, it is necessary to mention that the rehabilitation of
OUN and UPA attracted criticism from political circles in Ukraine
that took a more positive view of Russia and the Soviet past, notably the former Party of Regions. One of that party's deputies to the
Ukrainian parliament, Vadym Kolesnichenko, proposed a law in
May 2013 to ban the glorification and rehabilitation of the nationalists, whom he identified as fascists and Nazis.[159] Kolesnichenko and
his "International Antifascist Front" contributed nothing to the
scholarship on OUN and UPA, but in 2012 and 2013 they published
Russian and Ukrainian translations of articles written by Western
historians John-Paul Himka (i.e., this author), Grzegorz Rossoliński-Liebe, Per Anders Rudling, and Timothy Snyder. None of
these scholars had agreed to have their articles published by Kolesnichenko and had in fact specifically declined to be published by
him.[160] This was a clear case of the political instrumentalization of
critical scholarship on the Ukrainian nationalists.

Russian propaganda has also instrumentalized the scholarship of what I have termed the post-*Neighbors* consensus. Even before, but particularly since 2014, when Russia invaded Ukraine,
seized Crimea, and began a hybrid war in the eastern Donbas, the
Russian state under Putin has tried to link contemporary Ukrainian
aspirations for independence from Russian tutelage with fascism.

158 Shliakhtych, "Arkhivno-slidchi spravy politsaiv"; Shliakhtych, "Stvorennia ta
     funktsionuvannia"; Shliakhtych, "Uchast' mistsevoi dopomizhnoi politsii."
159 Kolesnichenko, "Reabilitatsiia ta heroizatsiia."
160 "Kolesnichenko vydav zbirnyk." Solod'ko, "Iak Kolesnichenko oskan-
     dalyvsia." "Kolesnichenko znovu potsupyv chuzhu pratsiu."

Yet serious scholarly monographs relevant to our theme have appeared in Russia within the framework of Russian historical politics, notably Aleksandr Diukov's study of OUN's attitude to Jews, its "second-rank enemy,"[161] and Aleksei Bakanov's more nuanced study of the national question in OUN ideology.[162]

161 Diukov, *Vtorostepennyi vrag* (two editions).
162 Bakanov, "*Ni katsapa.*"

2. Sources

The Increased Availability of Primary Sources

When I began my work as a historian in the early 1970s, conducting research was very different from what it is now. I wrote all my notes by hand on half-sheets of paper and all my bibliographic data on three-by-five index cards. I could photocopy texts and documents if I was working in the West, but photocopiers were not available in the communist bloc, where my most substantial research was undertaken. Microfilm and microfiche seemed to be the wave of the future, though now they seem mainly to take up valuable storage space in libraries and other repositories. I mention all this to underline just how different the world of research has become for scholars today. Had I been able to write this book, say, in the 1980s, my discussion of sources would have advanced from archive to archive, pointing out the relevant material that could be found in each.[163] But now the physical location of documents is not as determinative as it once was.

This is especially true for Holocaust studies. Much of the documentation most relevant to the history of the Holocaust in Ukraine was first microfilmed and later scanned by the United States Holocaust Memorial Museum (USHMM) in Washington, DC, and by Yad Vashem in Jerusalem. It is particularly easy to work with the materials at USHMM. On a trip there in spring 2018, it took me just a few hours to put thirteen thick volumes of Soviet Ukrainian war crimes trials on a USB drive.

Digitization has made a great difference to the work of a modern scholar. While tackling this project, I had vast source collections at my beck and call, including all the inestimably valuable survivor testimonies collected in Poland immediately after the war (the AŻIH collection) and the documentation on the wartime activities of OUN and UPA in Volhynia collected by Viktor Polishchuk. Both

---

163 There is actually a wonderful finding aid prepared along these lines: Berkhoff, "Ukraine under Nazi Rule."

fit easily on an external hard drive. Colleagues in the field have also usually been generous in sharing documents among themselves, giving us all the opportunity to develop rather large personal collections of documentary material. Furthermore, an abundance of sources is available on the Internet: vast electronic libraries of Ukrainian and Polish periodicals and books (such as a collection of publications from the Ukrainian diaspora, http://diasporiana. org.ua/) and specialized document collections (such as the electronic archive of the Ukrainian liberation movement, which comprised about 25,000 documents in autumn 2018, http://avr.org. ua/).

There are now also numerous printed collections of documents. In the mid-1950s Roman Ilnytzkyj, who was associated with the *dviikari*, published a collection of primarily German documents concerning relations between OUN and the Third Reich. While the title of his work promised that the compilation would encompass events from 1934 to 1945, the two volumes that appeared extended only into early 1942.[164] As John A. Armstrong noted, the collection was "highly partisan."[165] Philip Friedman pointed out a telling selective omission in Ilnytzkyj's collection. Ilnytzkyj cited a German police summary of a letter sent from the Bandera faction of OUN to the Gestapo in Lviv in October 1941. The part Ilnytzkyj cited indicated that the Banderites were breaking with the Germans, but omitted the phrase: "Long live greater independent Ukraine without Jews, Poles, and Germans. Poles behind the San, Germans to Berlin, Jews to the gallows."[166] This was typical of other source collections that emanated from the *dviikari*: they simply omitted or modified embarrassing passages and documents. For example, a collection of official OUN documents published in 1955[167] included portions of a text from May 1941, "Borot'ba i diial'nist' OUN pidchas viiny" (The Struggle and Activities of OUN during the War).

---

164 Ilnytzkyj, *Deutschland und die Ukraine 1934-1945*.
165 Armstrong, *Ukrainian Nationalism*, 39 n. 29.
166 Friedman, Philip. "Ukrainian-Jewish Relations," 181, 196 n. 15. EM, no. 126, 27 October 1941; translation from *Einsatzgruppen Reports*, 210.
167 *OUN v svitli postanov*.

As we will see below,[168] this document contained explicit instructions for OUN militants and security agents to "liquidate" and "neutralize" Jews in certain positions and to incite Red Army soldiers to murder Jews and Russians. But in the *dviikari* collection, "the passages about minorities were purged, without ellipses to mark the cuts."[169] Another example: in 1960 the *dviikari* published a small volume of documents about the NKVD murders of summer 1941.[170] Some of the documents were taken from the wartime newspaper *Krakivs'ki visti*. I carefully compared all the texts that were reprinted in the said volume with the originals published in the newspaper. Several of the original articles were vehemently antisemitic, but the offending passages were all eliminated or modified in the compilation of reprinted pieces.[171] Similar problems have dogged the documentary publications of OUN veteran Volodymyr Kosyk,[172] although the four volumes that came out in Lviv at the end of the 1990s and early 2000s do not omit or modify particular passages as they include photoreproductions of the German originals.

Another documentary and monographic series important for its sheer size is the *Litopys UPA*, which issued fifty volumes in its "main series" and another twenty-four (as of 2014) in its "new series." The volumes of the new series, which are academically

---

168 See below, 163, 165, 170-71, 225-26.
169 Berkhoff and Carynnyk, "The Organization of Ukrainian Nationalists," 177 n. 30.
170 *Zlochyny komunistychnoi Moskvy.*
171 Yevhen Stakhiv has related that in December 1941 he passed on a letter from the leader of one faction of OUN, Stepan Bandera, who was then imprisoned by the Gestapo in Berlin, to the underground head of OUN-B in the Homeland, Mykola Lebed, instructing OUN not to antagonize the Germans and to try to repair relations with Germany. About forty years later, Stakhiv reminded Lebed, who was then the leader of the *dviikari*, of Bandera's instructions, but Lebed claimed not to remember them. Again about five years later Stakhiv raised the subject with Lebed, and this time he allegedly answered: "Yes, I remember. But I didn't want you to tell people about it. It is not necessary for history to know the truth." Stakhiv, *Kriz' tiurmy*, 99-100. Although this story does seem to characterize the *dviikari*'s attitude to history, I lack faith in Stakhiv's reliability as a memoirist. The incident has been accepted as genuine, however, by Grzegorz Rossoliński-Liebe, "Ukrainian National Revolution," 106; *Stepan Bandera*, 41.
172 Kurylo and Himka, "Iak OUN stavylasia do ievreiv," 259.

superior to their predecessors, are all available online in the electronic library of the Institute of History of Ukraine of the National Academy of Sciences of Ukraine (NANU).[173] The series was initiated following a resolution of a congress of UPA veterans in 1973 to publish source materials on the nationalist army, and the first volume appeared in 1977 under the editorship of two UPA veterans, Peter J. Potichnyj and Yevhen Shtendera. Potichnyj had joined UPA as a fifteen-year-old child soldier; he cooperated with the *dviikari* in emigration and made an illustrious career in Ukrainian studies (he was a professor of political science at McMaster University in Canada). As one might expect of a veterans' publication, it tended to paint events with extra glory on its palette and was reticent or apologetic when it came to matters of ethnic cleansing and participation in the Holocaust. *Litopys UPA* has also been caught out omitting material that showed the nationalist army releasing German soldiers and murdering national minorities.[174]

On the whole, the best collections of OUN-UPA documents have been published in independent Ukraine since the mid-1990s, using material from archives that were not open under communism. Though they vary somewhat in quality, they are reliable on the whole. They might alter orthography or transcribe incorrectly, but they are freer of the ideological interference that sullied collections published by OUNites in the diaspora. Even collections put together by nationalists in Ukraine have not exhibited squeamishness about antisemitism, xenophobia, and ethnic cleansing. We saw an instance of this in the previous chapter, in the confrontation of Lev Shankovsky's idealized history of OUN-B in the Donbas with a post-Soviet documentary collection on the same topic.[175] Even Volodymyr Serhiichuk, whom we have already met as an UPA apologist polemicizing with Viktor Polishchuk,[176] included in

---

173 http://resource.history.org.ua/cgi-bin/eiu/history.exe?&I21DBN=ELIB&P21 DBN=ELIB&S21STN=1&S21REF=10&S21FMT=elib_all&C21COM=S&S21CN R=20&S21P01=0&S21P02=0&S21P03=ID=&S21STR=0013098, accessed 23 October 2018.

174 Berkhoff, *Harvest of Despair*, 287 and 428 n. 63.

175 See above, 31-38.

176 See above, 52.

his documentary collection on OUN-UPA a report from 1943 that frankly recounted that UPA had burned down a Polish village of eighty-six households, murdering all its inhabitants, and that it had completely cleansed another region in Volhynia of ethnic Germans (*Volksdeutsche*).[177] Among the best of the post-Soviet Ukrainian source collections are *Ukrains'ke derzhavotvorennia* edited by Orest Dziuban and a series on OUN during the years of World War II edited by Oleksandra Veselova and others. There is also a two-volume source collection published in Moscow on OUN and UPA during World War II containing documents from archives in the Russian Federation, Ukraine, and elsewhere.[178]

In summary, today documents relevant for research on OUN-UPA and the Holocaust are not as profoundly bound up with repositories in specific locations as they once were. A document that is in an archive in Ukraine might also be in Washington or Jerusalem, or in a scholar's personal collection of digitized literature and sources, or available on the Internet, or reprinted in a source publication. For this reason, this chapter on sources is not organized by particular repositories, as once was traditional in East European studies, but rather by types of sources. And for our study, in which cognizance of the individual perspectives of any given source is mandatory, this procedure makes the most sense.

Documents

German Documents

As already explained in the previous chapter, documents emanating from various offices and military units of the Third Reich have enjoyed primacy in Holocaust studies since the early 1960s. Though an undue reliance on them had a distorting influence on the field, they are nonetheless indispensable, since it was nationalist socialist Germany that initiated and bore most responsibility for the genocide of the Jewish people. Also, the Germans documented their murderous activities in great detail. They felt they were

---

177 Serhiichuk, *OUN-UPA v roky viiny*, 311-12.
178 Artizov, *Ukrainskie natsionalisticheskie organizatsii.*

undertaking, to use a Hegelian phrase, a deed of world-historical significance. They employed euphemisms, such as "Final Solution," "special handling," and "resettlement," but they wrote clearly enough about the plans and progress of their project to destroy what they considered to be "the Jewish race." They left a huge legacy of frank documentation, probably the most voluminous and transparent record of any genocidal operation in world history.

Particularly valuable for our purposes are reports from the Eastern front. Immediately after the invasion of the USSR, Nazi mobile killing units, the Einsatzgruppen, began to issue reports to the Reich Security Main Office (RSHA) on their activities.[179] The first report, which was dated 23 June 1941, bore the title *Sammelmeldung "UdSSR,"* no. 1; but no. 2, which had the same date, was renamed *Ereignismeldungen UdSSR* (EM). Altogether 195 EMs were prepared, the last of which was dated 27 February 1942. Another set of similar reports was also submitted to the RSHA by the Security Police (*Sicherheitspolizei*) and the Security Service (SD) in the occupied Soviet territories. These *Meldungen aus den besetzten Ostgebieten* began to appear on 5 January 1942; fifty-five were submitted, the last of which was dated 23 May 1943.[180] These reports, in addition to documenting the progress of the Holocaust across Ukraine, also provided copious information on the activities of the Bandera movement.

The records of the Ukrainian Auxiliary Police in Lviv have been especially useful, since they document the participation of the Ukrainian police in the major actions that destroyed the city's Jewish population. There is a related, but rather scanty set of records on the militia that existed prior to the formation of the auxiliary police force. Both sets of records are housed in the State Archives of Lviv Oblast in Lviv[181] but are difficult to access there; in spring 2011, a research assistant for this monograph was denied access to both sets of records.[182] Fortunately, the most important police

---

179 There is a very interesting book on the RHSA: Wildt, *An Uncompromising Generation.*
180 Headland, *Messages of Murder.*
181 DALO, fond R12, op. 1.
182 For more context on this, see Himka, "Legislating Historical Truth."

records, selected by Dieter Pohl, were microfilmed by USHMM,[183] and the militia records were microfilmed in their entirety by the United States Office of Special Investigations; thus, I have been able to study them.[184]

Kai Struve made excellent use of German military records to shed light on the anti-Jewish violence in Galicia in summer 1941. In this monograph I rely extensively on his research in these records, although I occasionally cite original documents. I also make occasional use of the records of German trials of Nazi war criminals, again relying more on Struve's research.

As was mentioned in the previous chapter, German documentation tended to emphasize the successes of the Reich's policies in the occupied Soviet Union and thus understated such irritating phenomena as Jewish resistance and non-Jewish aid to Jews, especially in survey reports like the EMs and *Meldungen*.

It is important to be aware that all the German documentation from the national socialist era reflects events through a highly racialized, ruthlessly imperialist prism. Many of the German documents incorporate the mindset of mass murderers and have to be used with care; the documents themselves exclude the perspectives of victims, but historians using them should keep those victims in mind.

Soviet Documents

The most important Soviet sources for this monograph are the interrogation and trials of members of OUN and UPA, housed in the archives of the Security Service of Ukraine (SBU) in Kyiv (HDA SBU).[185] These are problematic sources and require some care in interpretation. The minutes of the interrogations do not record the actual words used by the accused. Instead, they record summaries of each interrogation, translated into "Bolshevik speak," using

---

183 USHMM, Acc. 1995.A.1086, RG-31.001M.

184 I am grateful to David Alan Rich for sharing a copy of the militia files with me.

185 There are also regional SBU archives that I have not consulted, but the younger generation of Ukrainian historians (e.g., Marta Havryshko, Roman Shliakhtych, and Andrii Usach) has been making good use of them in their publications.

phrases the nationalists themselves would never employ.[186] These minutes, however, were signed by the accused, who thereby assented to the correctness of the information provided by the summary. More problematic, however, is that the Soviet interrogators often extracted information under duress, in particular through sleep deprivation and beatings, but also through even more vicious means. In his study of the Soviet counterinsurgency in Western Ukraine, Alexander Statiev wrote:

> A party inspector described how policemen connected electrical wires from a field telephone to the hands of an interrogated man and produced electric shocks by rotating the handle. Some interrogators burned suspects' skin with cigarettes. In March 1945, two police officers arrested without a warrant a Ukrainian woman they suspected of connection with the resistance and then interrogated her by placing her barefoot on a heated stove, severely burning her feet. When questioned by party inspectors, the policemen admitted that "grilling arrested persons on a stove...is a mediaeval method that should not be employed." The interrogators received 10-year jail terms, but torture remained among the major means of investigation until the end of Stalinism despite numerous directives ordering the police to observe the law.[187]

Thus these sources, i.e., the Soviet interrogation records — like the German documents discussed above and some of the films and photos to be discussed below — carry the moral taint of criminality, and in using them, I feel, we have to retain some cognizance of the circumstances surrounding their production.

But can they be relied upon at all? I think so. In the 1930s, as is well known, Stalinist interrogators extorted all manner of nonsense from their intimidated victims. In those days the secret police worked with the assumption that anyone who was arrested must be guilty and they felt it their duty to extract confessions by

---

186 This problem is fleshed out more fully in Solonari, "Patterns of Violence," 54-55.

187 Statiev, *The Soviet Counterinsurgency*, 247-48. We now have an excellent account of the methods used by the NKVD during the late 1930s in Soviet Ukraine based on NKVD interrogators' own admissions of "violations of socialist legality": Viola, *Stalinist Perpetrators on Trial*. See also a wrenching study of Stalinist interrogations in postwar Poland that was able to explore the issue more from prisoners' perspectives: Chodakiewicz, "The Dialectics of Pain."

whatever means necessary.[188] As a result, they forced people to confess to nonexistent conspiracies, to falsely admit to espionage for various foreign countries, and to name names of the confederates they worked with in these nefarious but fictitious antistate activities. How were the interrogations of the late-war and postwar period any different? As I read the situation, the fundamental difference between the 1930s and the period from 1943 into the 1950s is that in the former time truth did not matter at all, but in the latter time truth was of paramount importance.

The Soviets knew very little of what was going on in Western Ukraine during the German occupation. This became very clear to me when studying a volume on the Greek Catholic metropolitan Andrei Sheptytsky as he was reflected in the documents of Soviet security organs.[189] The volume contains detailed reports on the churchman from the period of the "first Soviets," i.e., the period from September 1939 until the end of June 1941, when Lviv was under Soviet rule. And again, there are many informative documents from the period after the Soviets regained Lviv in late July 1943 until Sheptytsky's death in early November 1944. But there is very little material on the period of the German occupation, i.e., the time period in between, and what there is from that period is full of inaccuracies. To me this signals a breakdown of the Soviet intelligence network in Western Ukraine. The Soviets were unable to follow events there. And no other documents I have encountered elsewhere indicate otherwise. Yet, as the Red partisans moved westward in spring 1943, they found themselves engaging in battle with Banderite forces (UPA), armed guerrillas who enjoyed more support than did the former from the local Ukrainian population. And once the Red Army reconquered Galicia and Volhynia, they faced the eruption of a dangerous insurgency led by UPA and the OUN underground. As a result, when SMERSH and other Soviet security and counterintelligence units were interrogating captured Ukrainian nationalists, they were not interested in fake conspiracies and false confederates: they wanted to understand exactly what they

---

188 This comes out very clearly in Viola, *Stalinist Perpetrators on Trial*.
189 Bohunov, *Mytropolyt Andrei Sheptyts'kyi*.

were coming up against. And overall, the interrogators had no incentive to fabricate information about the murder of Jews, since the particular suffering of the Jewish population was not of interest to their superiors.

Furthermore, I have sometimes been able to corroborate information from the Soviet interrogations by comparing them with other, non-Soviet sources. I have also not run across any patently evident falsehoods in the interrogations. Diana Dumitru too accepts the general reliability of Soviet Moldavian interrogations from the same period based on her own triangulation with other sources.[190] Vladimir Solonari, who worked with Soviet interrogations and trials from Moldavia and Bukovina, pointed to "plausible details of local life and death, such as the pillows that a killer brought from the killing site, a particular phrase that a Jew said before the execution of himself and his family, or what a perpetrator retorted to his neighbor when the latter rebuked him for his cruelty. It is highly unlikely that investigators would invent those details...."[191] Alexander Prusin, who examined interrogations and trials from Ukraine and the Baltic area, concurred: "While the testimonies...do not give exact dates or numbers of victims, they provide relatively accurate descriptions of the Holocaust in various localities. These descriptions are corroborated by archival documents and modern studies. Hence, there is no reason why the interrogation and trial records — if combined with other available materials — should not be used as historical sources relating to the sites and instances of genocide."[192] Another analyst of these same records, Tanja Penter, essentially agreed. In spite of problems which she carefully identified, "trial records represent an extremely valuable resource for the study of Nazi occupation and crimes in occupied Soviet territories. They contain detailed descriptions of the Holocaust in different local settings, towns and villages, and of life in ghettos and camps."[193]

---

190 Dumitru, "Analysis."
191 Solonari, "Patterns of Violence," 54-55.
192 Prusin, "'Fascist Criminals to the Gallows!'" 18.
193 Penter, "Local Collaborators on Trial," 21. See also Penter, "Collaboration on Trial."

The general validity of the information in Soviet interrogations was also accepted by the historical working group in Ukraine that provided the ammunition to rehabilitate OUN and UPA in the 1990s and early 2000s. Anatolii Kentii in particular used them for his work on OUN and UPA. Large extracts of these interrogations have also been published by the pro-UPA documentary series *Litopys UPA*.

Much of what has been said about interrogations also applies to Soviet trial records, but there are a few additional nuances. The records of trials, or simply of military tribunals, from the mid-1940s indicate to me that Soviet authorities in this era proceeded from some rough notions of justice—the courts and tribunals do not strike me as totally arbitrary. I was surprised, for instance, to discover in my research that accused war criminals, even members of OUN and UPA, were not convicted of murder on the basis of circumstantial evidence. There had to be eyewitness testimony or other evidence to convict. Thus, if an OUN militia executed a group of Jews in the summer of 1941, a participant in that execution could state that he was present at the execution but did not shoot; if none of his comrades betrayed him, he was likely to be convicted not of murder but of belonging to an anti-Soviet organization. A conviction of murder could result in execution, but participating in an anti-Soviet organization generally brought a sentence of ten years in a labor camp. Also, after the end of the Great Terror, i.e., from 1938 onwards, Soviet judicial proceedings became more professional and less arbitrary.[194]

The other point to make about trials is that the records of the 1940s tend to be fairly brief. But sometimes cases were reopened later with an eye towards a deeper investigation of instances of mass murder, and these reopened cases produced quite voluminous files. An example is the case of Yakiv Ostrovsky a former Ukrainian policeman (*Schutzmann*) in Volhynia who deserted German service to join UPA. In July 1944 he turned himself into the NKVD and was interrogated by a famous Soviet partisan leader, Aleksandr Saburov. Over the course of his interrogation, Ostrovsky

---

194 Comments of Tanja Penter in Coleman, "Roundtable," 235-37.

freely admitted to killing people as a policeman, but "not many — twenty-five to thirty people." Yet when sentenced to twenty years of hard labor in 1945, he was convicted not of murder, but of treason (as a policeman working for the Germans) and of membership in a counterrevolutionary organization (UPA). The case, however, was reopened in 1981. I suspect this happened in the context of growing global interest in the Holocaust and the Soviets' realization at that time of the propaganda value of linking Ukrainian nationalism to the murder of Jews.[195] In any case, new evidence came to light that allowed Ostrovsky's case to be reopened. It turned out that there had been an eyewitness after all to Ostrovsky killing Jews in an extermination action of 1942. The testimony had been recorded in July 1944, actually a day before Ostrovsky had turned himself in to the NKVD. But this testimony had been given not to the NKVD, but instead to the Extraordinary State Commission, the procedures and documents of which will be discussed immediately below. The lack of communication between the two Soviet investigative units meant that the relevant eyewitness testimony had not been considered at Ostrovsky's original trial. The eyewitness was a non-Jew who had been forced to bury the victims of the execution action, some of whom were still alive as he buried them. He had named Ostrovsky as one of the shooters. Ostrovsky was put on trial again in 1982, and much more evidence was brought to bear; this time Ostrovsky was convicted of murder and executed in the following year.[196]

Aside from investigation and trial records, another large collection of Soviet documentation relevant to our study are the documents of the Extraordinary State Commission for the Establishment and Investigation of the Crimes of the Fascist German Invaders and Their Accomplices, and of the Damage They Caused to Citizens, Collective Farms, Public Organizations, State Enterprises, and Institutions of the USSR. Established in 1942, its purpose was "to conduct investigations of Hitler's war crimes and to determine the

---

195 This is the same period in which the Soviets published the English-language tracts that appeared under the name Valerii Styrkul. See above, 42.

196 Himka, "'Skazhite, mnogo liudei vy rasstreliali?'"

material damage suffered by the USSR, to coordinate the activities of all Soviet organizations in this field, to reveal the names of war criminals, and to publish official reports on their findings."[197]

There were two tendencies in the work of the Extraordinary State Commission that affected how OUN and UPA were represented in its documentation. First, the Commission was interested in ascribing as much destruction and murder to the Germans as possible, with the aim of receiving large reparations. Second, the Commission avoided disturbing the image of a united Soviet people that resisted the fascist onslaught. Both of these factors led to downplaying the role of local, non-German accomplices. For example, the Commission compiled a list of persons responsible for war crimes committed in Lviv. Of the 69 persons on the list, only 3 were non-Germans,[198] although we know that the Ukrainian National Militia and later the Ukrainian Auxiliary Police were deeply involved in mass murder in the city. However, the Commission's investigations at the local, i.e., raion, levels were more open to information about local collaborators in Nazi crimes. But when summaries of these reports were drafted at the oblast level, the activities of non-German accomplices were often edited out. The higher the level of summary, the lower the profile of non-German perpetrators.

Moreover, the Commission's work was, as Solonari noted, "very uneven: in some districts it worked thoroughly, in others less so. Sometimes it could rely on relatively qualified personnel, but quite often barely literate party activists performed the entire task."[199] An example of the unreliability that Solonari describes appeared in the Commission's investigation of a horrendous pogrom in Hrymailiv (P Grzymałów), north of Husiatyn in Ternopil oblast, in which many young Ukrainian men of the town participated. Relying on local witnesses, the Commission stated that SS officer Daniel Nerling participated in the pogrom, which occurred on 5 July

---

197 Sorokina, "People and Procedures," 118, 121.
198 YVA, r.g. M.52, file 245.1 (6412889), frames 86-88; originally from DALO, 3/1/278. Extraordinary Commission documents.
199 Solonari, "Patterns of Violence," 55.

1941.[200] However, as we know from Nerling's trial in Lübeck in 1969, he did not arrive in Hrymailiv until late October 1941.[201]

On the more positive side, as Solonari also noted, the Commission would sometimes "collect handwritten accounts of the survivors or eyewitnesses and attach them to their minutes or would transcribe verbal testimony that contained vivid descriptions of the killing operations."[202] As we have seen, one of the eyewitness accounts in a Commission report led to the reopening of the trial of the policeman Ostrovsky in 1981.

One aspect of testimonies recorded by the Extraordinary Commission and similar bodies was always marred by outright falsification, namely testimony that concerned crimes against humanity committed by the Soviets themselves. A disturbing case of this involved the historian Friedman. In 1946 he testified to both the Extraordinary Commission and the Commission for the Study of the History of the Great Patriotic War that the Germans had rounded up Jews when they took Lviv on 30 June 1941, shot them in prisons, disguised their nationality, and blamed the episode on the NKVD. Here are his exact words: "The destruction of the Jews in the city of Lviv began from the first day of the arrival of the Germans, that is, on 30 June 1941. Moreover, at the very beginning the Germans conducted this destruction as a provocation. Taking advantage of the withdrawal of Soviet forces, the Germans led a portion of the Jewish population to the prisons and shot them there....At the same time they pursued a second aim: to present this as an example of the 'bestial crimes' of the NKVD, which before its departure from Lviv was allegedly shooting political prisoners."[203] In his

---

200 The Commission's investigation of Hrymailiv is found in GARF, fond 7021, opis 75, delo 94, ff. 1-4, 14-34v; USHMM RG-22.002M, reel 17.

201 *Justiz und NS-Verbrechen*, Lfd. Nr. 698, Lübeck 2 Ks 1/67 (vol. 31 of the printed edition), 483.

202 Solonari, "Patterns of Violence," 55.

203 Kovba, *Liudianist' u bezodni pekla*, 213. A photocopy of the complete testimony is online: https://training.ehri-project.eu/a10-1946-philip-friedman-recalls-po grom-lviv (accessed 15 January 2019). Kovba gives a different archival location and says the testimony was to the Extraordinary Commission. But the online testimony, which seems to be an identical text, was to the Commission for the Study of the History of the Great Patriotic War. I assume the same testimony was used for both commissions. I want to thank Alexander Melnyk for first

subsequent published scholarly work Friedman did not repeat the falsehood of a German provocation and correctly indicated that the corpses in the prisons were victims of the Soviets.[204] Similarly, the Soviets recorded testimony of a captured German Wehrmacht officer, Erwin Bingle, that blamed the Soviet mass murders at Vinnytsia from 1936-38 on the German SS and Ukrainian police.[205] Again, the murdered political prisoners were presented as murdered Jews. Bingle called the "frame-up" "baseless and utterly ridiculous."[206] Of course, the Soviets were unwilling to wash their bloody laundry in public but quite willing to add their own murders to the Germans' account, so they induced testimony that served their purposes. This was part of a general policy, the most notorious incident of which was blaming the Germans for the mass murder of Polish officers and intellectuals in 1940 at Katyń.

I found of particular value to my research a set of documents that were sent to the highest echelons of the Soviet Ukrainian communist party in the years 1943-44, as the Soviets entered and reconquered Western Ukrainian territory. These documents had various provenances, but what united them was that they contained information considered worthy of the notice of the top Soviet Ukrainian leadership. Many of these documents concerned OUN and UPA. Like the interrogation documents, these materials were also aimed at trying to understand what was happening. Of course, reports and analyses understood events through a Soviet ideological prism, but materials in this collection also included captured OUN and UPA documents, copies of the *Meldungen aus den besetzten*

turning my attention to this and providing me with information on the Commission for the Study of the History of the Great Patriotic War.

204 Philip Friedman, "The Destruction of the Jews of Lwów," 246. Friedman, "Ukrainian-Jewish Relations," 183, 198 n. 24.

205 On the Vinnytsia mass murders, see Paperno, "Exhuming the Bodies of Soviet Terror."

206 Korzen, "The Extermination of Two Ukrainian Jewish Communities," 311 (quote). *Yad Vashem Studies*, which published Bingle's testimony in 1959, apparently accepted this as good coin. Unfortunately, the publication of the testimony did not specify to which Soviet body the testimony was given.

Ostgebieten, and even the fascinating diary of a young man drafted into UPA.[207]

Information on UPA can also be found in the reports of the Soviet partisans who encountered them.

OUN Documents

There is a great variety of OUN and UPA documentation. Wartime OUN and UPA had well developed administrative structures that generated masses of documents. Some have been preserved by OUN members in the diaspora and have ended up in published collections as well as in archives, libraries, and museums across North America and Europe. But the richest trove is in archives in Ukraine, comprised primarily of documentation captured by the Soviets. Occasionally, too, OUN-UPA archives buried in containers for more than half a century have been unearthed.[208]

The most official of the OUN documents are the resolutions of the organization's congresses and conferences as well as various programmatic documents. But aside from these, there are many other kinds of documents, including:[209]

- drafts of programmatic documents;
- transcripts of meetings;
- orders and instructions to units of UPA and OUN's security service (SB OUN);
- field reports from units of UPA and SB OUN;
- SB OUN interrogation records;
- materials from OUN-UPA training courses;
- memoranda of both factions of OUN to various German offices;

---

207 The title of the collection is "Selected Records from Former Archives of the Communist Party of Ukraine, 1919-1937; 1941-1962; and 1965." USHMM RG-31.026 Acc. 2003.260; the documents are originally from TsDAHO. I would like to thank Vadim Altskan at USHMM for directing me to this collection.

208 For example, in 2017 an aluminum milk can full of well preserved OUN-UPA documents was found in the Yaniv woods near Lviv. The can had been buried in mid-1951. "Vidkopaly arkhiv UPA." Even more recently, in autumn 2019, OUN-UPA documents from 1945-46 were found in woods near Rohatyn in Ivano-Frankivsk oblast. Prystans'ka, "U lisakh Ivano-Frankivshchyny."

209 The OUN periodical press is discussed below, 101-02.

- proclamations and announcements to the population.

In using OUN-UPA documents, an important factor to consider is to whom a particular document is addressed. Leader Stepan Bandera himself stated: "One program should be addressed to the members and sympathizers of nationalism, and the second for external factors. The first should be the main credo for members and sympathizers. The second program should exist for external consumption. It can change according to the circumstances and external situation."[210] Particularly with regard to documents aimed for external audiences, it is necessary to consider the time and context in which documents emerged. There were moments when OUN was close to the Germans, other moments when they were enemies, yet other moments when OUN hoped to court the Western allies. In 1941 OUN was optimistic that the Germans would be victorious, but this ceased to be the case by 1943. Earlier, OUN competed ideologically with the Germans; later it did so with the Soviets. After it became clear that Germany would lose the war and that OUN's participation in the mass murder of Jews would blemish its reputation with the Western allies, OUN-B undertook to revise the historical record. On 27 October 1943, the OUN leadership in Ukraine issued an order to compile

> c. Lists that would confirm that the Germans carried out anti-Jewish pogroms and liquidations by themselves, without the participation or help of the Ukrainian police, and instead, before carrying out executions, urged the Jewish committee or the rogues themselves to confirm with their signatures the presence of the Ukrainian police and its involvement in the actions.
> d. Material that would clearly confirm that Poles had initiated and taken part in anti-Jewish pogroms....[211]

The order was sent "in strictest confidence" to "the oblast, circle, and county leaders" of OUN.

---

210 Cited in Patryliak, *Viis'kova diial'nist OUN (B)*, 322.
211 Translation by Marco Carynnyk. Carynnyk, "Foes of Our Rebirth," 345 (translation), 346 (photoreproduction of the original document).

Also, we know that not every order was written down, and sometimes we have to interpret the course and meanings of actions without documentation from OUN-UPA itself.

Yet in spite of efforts to dissemble and to doctor history, OUN produced written documents that testify to antisemitism, the pursuit of ethnic cleansing, and the murder of Jews.

Other Documentation

The USHMM has the stenographer's minutes of denaturalization hearings conducted by the United States Department of Justice, Office of Special Investigations in the 1980s of persons accused of having served as Ukrainian policemen under the Nazi occupation.[212] Useful in these documents is the witness testimony. Among those who testified are former Ukrainian policemen, their relatives, and Jewish survivors. They provide information that helps us better understand not only the Ukrainian Auxiliary Police in German service, but also the Ukrainian National Militia connected with OUN-B.

The Eastern Bureau of the Polish underground government reported on the situation in Galicia ("Eastern Little Poland" in its terminology) and Volhynia in 1943-44.[213]

Documentation of armed forces and governments other than those of the Germans and the Soviets who were active on Ukrainian territory during World War II has not been consulted for this study. But other scholars have made use of Hungarian, Romanian, and Slovak documentation; where relevant I cite it from their work.

Memoirs, Testimonies, Diaries

Jewish Testimony

Before his demise in Majdanek death camp, the Jewish historian Ignacy Schiper stated: "What we know about murdered peoples is only what their murderers vaingloriously cared to say about them.

---

212 USHMM RG-06.029.
213 Adamczyk, *Ziemie Wschodnie*.

Should our murderers be victorious, should *they* write the history of the war, our destruction will be presented as one of the most beautiful pages of world history, and future generations will pay tribute to them as dauntless crusaders."[214] The defeat of Nazi Germany prevented the scenario that Schiper feared, but the decades-long hegemony of Nazi documentaton in Holocaust research in the West has occluded for too long the input of the targeted victims. The memoirs, testimonies, and diaries of Jews who experienced the Holocaust comprise a huge and informative body of source material that needs to be taken into consideration by historians. As is the case for all the other sources discussed so far, the understanding and use of these particular sources require an awareness of their specific biases and limitations.

Jan Gross, as already explained, has been a champion of testimony, and his book *Neighbors* sparked a growing interest in the use of testimony in Holocaust studies in the West and in postcommunist Europe. In *Neighbors* he made a bold and controversial statement on the subject:

> ...I suggest that we should modify our approach to sources for this period. When considering survivors' testimonies, we would be well advised to change the starting premise in appraisal of their evidentiary contribution from a priori critical to in principle affirmative. By accepting what we read in a particular account as fact *until we find persuasive arguments to the contrary*, we would avoid more mistakes than we are likely to commit by adopting the opposite approach, which calls for cautious skepticism toward any testimony *until an independent confirmation of its content has been found*.[215] The greater the catastrophe, the fewer the survivors. We must be capable of listening to lonely voices reaching us from the abyss....[216]

Clearly this passage was carefully formulated, and so it has to be as carefully read. I am not sure that critics have been doing that. Gross was writing about historical likelihood, not proof. I therefore would disagree with the way Christopher R. Browning has criticized it. He wrote that in cases in which "there is only a handful of

---

214 Cited in Wieviorka, "The Witness in History," 386.
215 Emphases in original.
216 Gross, *Neighbors*, 92.

survivors, this [Gross's approach] is a tempting proposition. But however tempting, this default position still strikes me as too low an evidentiary threshold."[217] My own view is identical with that of Omer Bartov: "From the point of view of the historian, the single most important benefit of using testimonies is that they bring into history events that would otherwise remain completely unknown, since they are missing from more conventional documentation found in archives and mostly written by the perpetrators or organizers of genocide. Hence personal accounts can at times save events from oblivion."[218] In this book I will, as far as possible, triangulate sources, so that testimonies do not stand alone.

One persistent problem of victim narrative is how pervaded it is by trauma. Jewish testimony on the Holocaust expresses a traumatic subjectivity, reflecting deeply disturbing personal experience. The "subjectivity or emotionality" of eyewitness testimony has been one of the factors leading to the preference for putatively objective archival documents.[219] The main concern about horror and anger influencing survivor accounts seems to be the possibility that they might embellish or exaggerate. In my view, these same possibilities affect all sources, and I cannot agree with the proposition that what a murderer had to say is automatically more reliable than what a victim said. In this study I will frequently cite victim testimony and will leave it to the reader to judge whether it makes sense or not.

Another problem with victim accounts is that they express perspectives from a limited field of vision. Raul Hilberg and his successors in Holocaust studies preferred to work with German sources, among other reasons because the Germans had an overall, bird's-eye view of the operations that constituted their plan to kill all Jews. Such a viewpoint lent authority to the German documentation. Survivor testimony, by contrast, was fragmented into individual personal experiences in numerous localities. Moreover,

---

217 Browning, *Collected Memories*, 43.
218 Bartov, "Wartime Lies," 487; more generally on the importance of testimony as a source for the Holocaust, see 487-90 and 506-08.
219 See above, 49.

victims occupied a particular perspectival niche in the Holocaust. As Shmuel Spector put it: "...testimonies, their proximity to the events notwithstanding, are grounded in subjective perceptions; regardless of how much the witnesses strain to adhere to the truth, their field of vision remains, by necessity, narrow and restricted. Confined in the ghettoes and isolated from the society at large, Jews were in no position to obtain information about the outside world in general and the backrooms of the decision makers in particular."[220] In an earlier publication I analyzed a testimony taken shortly after the war by comparing what it said about events in the Lviv pogrom to photographic evidence of these same events. I did not find any contradiction between the testimony and the pictures and films. The testimony, I concluded, accurately described what the woman who wrote it experienced. I did note, however, that she was unable to learn much about the pogromists who attacked her.[221] Similarly, Alexander Prusin, writing of witnesses in Soviet war crimes trials, recorded that "only a few were able to identify the defendants or the units that carried out the murders."[222]

One result of this lack of knowledge about specific perpetrators was a tendency in testimony and memoirs to generalize. In the cases Prusin examined, a number of witnesses "identified the perpetrators merely as 'Germans,' or 'the Gestapo.'"[223] Many of the testimonies describing events in Ukrainian-inhabited territories refer to the perpetrators simply as "Ukrainians." Part of the task of this study is to sort out the actions of a particular group of perpetrators, OUN and its armed forces, from that of the general population of Ukrainians. Frank Golczewski, who wrote an important study of collaboration in the Holocaust on the territory of Ukraine, has emphasized the need for scholars to avoid generalization: "Who were these Ukrainians? If we here, as if it were something so apparently obvious, write about the behavior of an entire ethnic group, then it is from the outset problematic."[224] But for some survivors, such

---

220 Spector, *Holocaust of Volhynian Jews*, 1.
221 Himka, "Dostovirnist' svidchennia."
222 Prusin, "'Fascist Criminals to the Gallows!'" 20.
223 Ibid., 20.
224 Golczewski, "Die Kollaboration in der Ukraine," 156.

distinctions have been difficult to make, and there is concern on the part of some Holocaust scholars that testimony "may be affected by antipathy toward members of other groups."[225] As a result of traumatic experience, some survivors even have a physical aversion to the German, Lithuanian, or Ukrainian language. The cognitive psychologist Robert Kraft explained this phenomenon as follows:

> These responses are not the result of thoughtful resentment. They arise from implicit connections in core memory between the survivors' specific memories of trauma and the language of their tormentors. Prolonged trauma splits the self-concept, creating two separate selves, each supported by different memories that remain irreconcilable. When events in the world bring together these two sets of memories — Holocaust and post-Holocaust — this connection threatens the survivor's current self-concept, creating a powerful emotional response.[226]

There is also the issue of accuracy. In another publication I compared three testimonies about the same incident, the mass execution of Jews in Tovste (P Tłuste), north of Zalishchyky in Ternopil oblast. These were two testimonies from Jewish survivors a few years after the war and an interview I had taken myself in 2008 with a Ukrainian eyewitness. Numerous details were remembered differently — the number of Jews that were shot at one time, whether they stood on a plank or walked directly into the pit, the total number of victims, and so on. But all agreed on the main points: at least a thousand Jews were marched in groups through the town to the cemetery and shot there by the Germans.[227] I think that this is what we may expect of testimonies and memoirs — that they record the main points but cannot be relied upon for exact detail. Working with testimonies and memoirs, and not just Jewish ones or those related to the Holocaust, I have found that not infrequently specific dates and even years are incorrect.

---

225 Kopstein and Wittenberg, *Intimate Violence*, 44. I have explored the problem of antipathy and ethnic stereotypes in survivor memory in Himka, *Ukrainians, Jews and the Holocaust*, and Himka, "How to Think about Difficult Things."

226 Kraft, "Archival Memory," 321.

227 Himka, *Ukrainians, Jews and the Holocaust*, 12-21.

For this study, I have relied most of all on three sets of Jewish survivor testimonies, each with its own virtues: the Archive of the Jewish Historical Institute (AŻIH), videotaped testimonies collected by the USC Shoah Foundation, and published memoirs.

The Archive of the Jewish Historical Institute (AŻIH) has two fonds of relevance. Fond (*Zespół*) 301 has about seventy-two hundred testimonies in Polish, Yiddish, and other languages from Jews who survived the Holocaust on Polish or formerly Polish territory. Most of the testimonies I will be citing from this collection were taken within a few years of the end of the war, and this temporal proximity to the events described is one of the major strengths of this set of sources. The testimonies are short, averaging about ten pages.[228] A noteworthy feature of them is that most were recorded by staff from the Central Jewish Historical Commission,[229] who summarized what the survivors said and put their accounts into narrative form, sometimes endowing them with a genuine literary appeal. The Jewish Historical Institute in Warsaw has published a guide to these testimonies, with a most helpful geographical index.[230] There is also another fond, 302, which comprises just over three hundred and thirty longer, essentially book-length memoirs.

The testimonies collected by the USC Shoah Foundation Institute for Visual History and Education (abbreviated as Shoah Foundation in footnotes) are quite different. If there is a certain distance between the survivor and his or her testimony in the AŻIH collection, this disappears in the Shoah Foundations testimonies, which take the form of videos of the survivors themselves telling their stories in their own words. These personally narrated accounts often make a powerful impact on viewers. This is a vast collection of over fifty thousand survivor testimonies that are generously indexed: one can search by name and place, of course, but also by keywords (e.g., Ukrainians, UPA). The testimonies are in many languages and come from all over the globe. Each Shoah Foundation interview has been divided into numbered segments, which I refer to in the notes.

---

228 This estimate is taken from Kopstein and Wittenberg, *Intimate Violence*, 145 n. 2.
229 See Aleksiun, "The Central Jewish Historical Commission."
230 *Relacje z czasów Zagłady.*

Almost all these interviews were conducted between 1994 and 1999, which has its disadvantages but also a certain advantage.

The advantage is that the 1990s was when the former Soviet Union was just opening up, and many survivors were telling their stories for the first time. Recording their experiences would simply not have been possible earlier. The disadvantage, of course, is the distance in time from the Holocaust, a half century or more. As we know, these old memories could have been influenced by subsequent experience, books written by other survivors, and by films about the Holocaust. Certainly these kinds of problems plagued *German* memory in the same period.[231] Moreover, videotaping Holocaust testimony was intimately connected with television and film. Thus another major collection that began collecting earlier than the Shoah Foundation, namely the Fortunoff Video Archive for Holocaust Testimonies, was inspired by the television miniseries *The Holocaust*, which was aired in 1978, a year before the inception of what became the Fortunoff Archive. And the sponsor of the Shoah Foundation was Steven Spielberg, the director of the blockbuster film *Schindler's List*. Annette Wieviorka found this "troubling": "Two fictional films dealing with the genocide, viewed by dozens, even hundreds, of millions throughout the world, were also at the origin of the two most important testimony archives."[232]

My own experience has been that these later testimonies are generally as reliable as the early testimonies collected by the Central Jewish Historical Commission. When I have had the opportunity to compare testimony from the same person over several decades, I have found much more consistency than discrepancy.[233] Browning, when he began using testimonies for his project on the Starachowice slave labor camp, was surprised to discover that over time testimonies revealed "a firm core of shared memory" and that

---

231 Welzer, *"Opa war kein Nazi."*
232 Wieviorka, "The Witness in History," 392.
233 For example, these two texts, in spite of the name change, are by the same person: Lejb Wieliczker, AŻIH 302/26; Wells, *The Janowska Road*. They provide substantially the same information. The same is true of Kurt Lewin's memoir of 1946 and his testimony for the Shoah Foundation: Lewin, *Przeżyłem*; Shoah Foundation 25423 Kurt Lewin.

his expectations for greater change "were not realized."[234] Shmuel Spector has argued that later testimonies can be superior to their earlier versions: "A comparison of the different versions of the testimony given by the same witness, who related his or her story at different stages of evidence collection, reveals that the testimony given soon after the events it pertained to is not always the most reliable one. The main reason for this is that at that time some of the witnesses had not yet recovered from the horrors they had lived through; only later...they managed to leave them behind and their testimony became more objective and orderly."[235]

Kraft, the cognitive psychologist who studied the videotaped testimonies in the Fortunoff Archive, stated that "those survivors who returned to the [Fortunoff] archive a second time—in most cases, eight years after their first extended recall—gave testimony that was remarkably consistent in structure and content with the earlier testimony."[236] He explained this consistency from the perspective of his discipline:

> In the study of Holocaust testimony, the most pervasive finding about memory for atrocity is its extraordinary persistence. Specific memories can remain vivid and powerful for more than fifty years, causing people to cry suddenly, to break down uncontrollably, to become angry. Core memories can remain unchanged over very long periods of time, and memories can intrude forcefully into the consciousness of the individual....One consensus among cognitive theorists is that "memory is always dual." That is, the *present* self is aware of the *past* self experiencing the world....With survivors of atrocity, however, the subjective experience of memory is *not* always dual. Sometimes, when describing a scene, survivors may be drawn into core memory, losing contact with narrative memory and becoming immersed in visualizing the events of the past....When a person is *fully* visualizing, or 'back there,' as the survivors often say, the past self becomes the present self.

The third body of testimonies used in this study consists of Jewish memoirs produced independently of AŻIH and the Shoah

---

234 Browning, *Collected Memories*, 46-47.
235 Spector, *Holocaust of Volhynian Jews*, 2.
236 Kraft, "Archival Memory," 316 n. 3.

Foundation. I systematically examined the memoir collection in the library of the United States Holocaust Memorial Museum, which I was able to also supplement with additional items. I found that these memoirs, emanating from different people in different countries for over half a century, told the same basic story. There are also many testimonies contained in the memorial, yizkor books, many of which are also cited in the pages that follow.

Survivors' testimonies are somewhat unusual, since most Jews who remained on Ukrainian territory during World War II did not survive. We are fortunate that a few diaries of persons who perished in the Holocaust have been preserved and published.[237]

Ukrainian historians with a nationalist perspective discount or deny the evidential value of Jewish, and also Polish, testimonies about OUN and UPA. This is not surprising, but it is necessary to note that these same historians give great weight to Ukrainian testimonies about the manmade famine of 1932-33, the Holodomor, which took about four million lives in Ukraine. In fact, until the last days of communism and the opening of the archives, oral testimony was the only source that documented that terrible event. And even today, testimony remains a crucial source in understanding the famine. There exists then within Ukrainian studies a double standard with regard to testimony for which there is no intellectual justification.

Polish Accounts

Many Poles had been living in Galicia and Volhynia when war broke out in September 1939. The Soviets deported some of them, particularly persons associated with the former government and the economic elite, to the interior of the Soviet Union. Then, in 1943, UPA began to kill Polish civilians in mass operations, at first throughout Volhynia, then later in Galicia. Most of the Poles who survived in Ukraine after the war were resettled to Poland over the next few years by the Soviet authorities. During the ethnic cleansing campaign, Poles formed self-defense units that fought UPA,

---

237 Lower, *The Diary of Samuel Golfard*. I was not able to consult A. Klonicki-Klony-mus, *The Diary of Adam's Father* (Jerusalem, 1973).

sometimes independently, but sometimes in cooperation with the Germans and the Soviets. During the Soviet counterinsurgency in Western Ukraine, many ethnic Poles were recruited for the destruction battalions that were engaged against UPA. (As noted in the previous chapter, the propagandist Edward Prus had served in such a battalion.) Within the territory of People's Poland, campaigns against UPA were also conducted, and in 1947 the Ukrainian population of southeastern Poland was resettled to the west, to the former German territories annexed to the new Polish state (the Vistula Operation, *Akcja Wisła*). Thus many Poles were witnesses to what transpired in Galicia and Volhynia during the war, and they have preserved many written records and produced a large number of testimonies referring to the eastern borderlands (*Kresy Wschodnie*). As one would expect, these records and testimonies are hostile to OUN-UPA, but they are not particularly Judeophilic either. They constitute an additional body of sources relevant to Ukrainian nationalist participation in the Holocaust.

Unfortunately, I was not able personally to work in the largest repository of these Polish materials, namely the Eastern Archive (*Archiwum Wschodnie*) of the Karta Center in Warsaw, with branches in Poznań, Wrocław, and abroad. So I have had to confine myself to secondary literature which does make use of these materials (e.g., works by Bogdan Musiał and Timothy Snyder). But I have carefully gone through the two-volume collection of summarized testimonies compiled by Władysław Siemaszko and Ewa Siemaszko on "the genocide committed by Ukrainian nationalists on the Polish population of Volhynia 1939-45."[238] There are many references in it to the fate of the Jews. I also had the opportunity to read the wartime diary of Tadeusz Zaderecki, a Pole who had published a number of short, popular books on Judaism in the 1930s and who lived in Lviv during the war years.[239] Zaderecki's diary was edited by David Kahane and Aharon Weiss and published in a

---

238 Siemaszko and Siemaszko, *Ludobójstwo*. I would like to thank Michal Mlynarz for his invaluable help with this.

239 Andrzej, "Tadeusz Zaderecki." This article provides links to some of Zaderecki's publications of the 1930s.

Hebrew translation in 1982, but I have used the Polish original at Yad Vashem.[240] Yad Vashem also recently published an English translation.[241] The diary is permeated with an anti-Ukrainian animus, but it remains an important source on the Holocaust in Lviv.

Ukrainian Accounts

I have made every effort to consult as many relevant accounts by Ukrainians as I could, but for the most part, Ukrainian memoirs avoid the topic of the Holocaust. Shmuel Spector wrote of them: "...quite a few of the Ukrainians who after the war fled to the countries of Western Europe had collaborated with the Nazis, including active participation in the murder of Jews, either as policemen or as officials of the Nazi administration. Their memoirs and articles written after the war ignore completely the Jewish issue. There are even individuals seeking to present the authors of these memoirs as those who had saved Jews or helped them in their predicament."[242] This is too all-encompassing a generalization, but it does represent the bulk of what the historian finds in Ukrainian memoirs.

The Oseredok Ukrainian Cultural and Education Centre in Winnipeg held a memoir contest in 1947, which resulted in the submission of 64 memoirs. Not all are extant, but of those that are, 25 concerned the World-War-II period; of these, 14 mentioned, at least briefly, the Holocaust. As I wrote in the abstract to my published analysis of them:

> This body of memoirs is the earliest collection of Ukrainian memoirs of World War II that I am aware of, the closest in time to the events of the Holocaust. Already then, however, Ukrainians had become quite defensive about their behaviour towards the Jews; this perhaps explains why close to half the memoirs about the war omitted the fate of the Jews altogether and why the memoirs that do mention the Holocaust say almost nothing about Ukrainian involvement. The

---

240 Zaderecki, "Gdy swastyka Lwowem władała."

241 Tadeusz Zaderecki, *Lwów under the Swastika: The Destruction of the Jewish Community through the Eyes of a Polish Writer* (Jerusalem: Yad Vashem, 2018). I have been unable to consult this volume myself.

242 Spector, *Holocaust of Volhynian Jews*, 2-3.

memoirists did, however, reproduce the image of Jews as agents of communism, particularly active in the organs of repression. The majority of the 1947 memoirs nonetheless indicated horror at and disapproval of the murder of the Jews by the Germans. Perhaps characteristically, the account expressing the strongest such feelings was written by an older man from outside Western Ukraine. Conversely, the most outright expression of lack of sympathy with the Jews came from a man twelve years younger and from Galicia.[243]

I have examined carefully many of the memoirs of World War II collected by the Ukrainian Canadian Research and Documentation Centre (UCRDC) in Toronto.[244] This is an institution with a generally nationalist perspective, emphasizing Ukrainian victimhood and Ukrainian rescue efforts during the Holocaust and maintaining silence about Ukrainian perpetration.[245] Among items to be found here are the memoirs of a member of the Ukrainian Auxiliary Police; they are several hundred pages long and do not once mention the Holocaust.[246] Still, the memoirs provide information and context that have been useful for this study.

In May and June 2009 my daughter Eva Himka conducted interviews for me with twenty elderly nationalists in Lviv. They denied any Ukrainian involvement in the Holocaust at all, saying that Ukrainians uniformly sympathized with the Jews and only Germans and Poles killed Jews. The Ukrainian police were harmless and patriotic. UPA did not kill Jews and only fought a defensive war against the Poles. In their view, their own suffering, personal and national, at the hands of the Soviets was a more important story than what happened to the Jews. They still viewed Jews as

---

243 Himka, "Ukrainian Memories of the Holocaust," 427.

244 The memoir section is called "Spomyny."

245 See my analysis of a documentary put out by the Centre on Ukraine during World War II: Himka, "Victim Cinema."

246 UCRDC, "Spomyny," no. 33 (Ivan P"iatka). In 2014 the Lviv historian Andrii Bolianovsky brought to my attention that there is another memoir of a Ukrainian policeman in the UCRDC: B., "Ukrains'ka politsiia. Spomyn. Burlington, Ontario, 1988." When I made a request to see it in 2018, I was informed that access was "still restricted." Emails Andrii Bolianovsky to John-Paul Himka, 1 October 2014, UCRDC Office to John-Paul Himka, 28 May 2018. Subsequently Bolianovsky sent me photos of pages from the memoir, which he had clearly had access to.

communists and exploiters who inflicted the famine of 1932-33, the Holodomor, on the Ukrainian people.[247]

A major project of gathering Ukrainian testimonies has been undertaken by Father Patrick Desbois and his institution Yahad-In Unum founded in 2004. His team has been crisscrossing Ukraine to videotape eyewitnesses to the murder of the Jews. In Galicia the eyewitnesses they contacted were sometimes nationalists, e.g., one was a member of the Melnyk faction in Lviv,[248] another was a member of the Bandera group and had been his village's liaison with OUN,[249] and another was a member of the village administration set up by OUN (he ran the post office).[250] But there were also testimonies from Galicia and Volhynia that described events from a more neutral perspective and sometimes mentioned Ukrainian participation in killings. Testimonies from the territory of pre-1939 Soviet Ukraine are much more forthcoming about how the local population was drawn into the killing process. The USC Shoah Foundation also took some testimony from Ukrainian rescuers.[251]

Interesting texts that described the Holocaust in Lviv were written by Mariia Strutynska during and just after the war. One was the diary she began on 10 August 1941 and continued until 22 December 1949,[252] and another was a novel that she wrote in 1947 that was set during the first Soviet occupation of Galicia in 1939-41 and the first days of the German occupation.[253]

Unique among the Ukrainian ego-documents on the Holocaust is Yevhen Nakonechny's memoir of the "Shoah in Lviv."[254] Beautifully written, it described the destruction of Lviv's Jews from the point of view of a child, which Nakonechny had been at the

---

247 Himka and Himka, "Absence and Presence," 19-20.
248 Yahad-in Unum Testimony no. 737.
249 Ibid. no. 802.
250 Ibid. no. 827.
251 E.g., Shoah Foundation 36160 Dmitrii Omelianiuk; see also the film based on Ukrainian interviews for the Shoah Foundation: *Spell Your Name* (*Nazvy svoie im"ia*) (2006) directed by Sergei Bukovsky and presented by Steven Spielberg and Viktor Pinchuk.
252 Strutyns'ka, *Daleke zblyz'ka*, 145-246.
253 Strutyns'ka, *Buria nad L'vovom*.
254 Nakonechnyi, *"Shoa" u L'vovi*.

time. His childhood friends and neighbors, who were Jewish, perished in the Holocaust. He wrote with great sympathy for the victims. At the same time, he denied Ukrainian participation in these murders and excoriated "Ukrainophobes," such as the historian Eliyahu Yones, who thought otherwise. Nakonechny himself had been arrested as a member of an OUN youth group in 1949, at the age of seventeen, and he spent the next six years in the gulag. In his memoir he defended the innocence of OUN, even denying its antisemitism. It is a strange, but captivating book.[255]

Photographs and Films

Before the outbreak of the Second World War amateur photographers in Germany owned seven million cameras, and when the war broke out many German soldiers brought their cameras with them. It has been estimated that they took several million pictures in the occupied territories of the Soviet Union.[256] Like many soldiers, they were interested in atrocity photos; often, they made multiple copies to share, sell, or trade. In addition, official film crews, attached to particular military units or working for the propaganda ministry, made stills and movies of what they saw. One result of this is that historians have access to many photos and films that document the anti-Jewish violence of the summer of 1941, including on Ukrainian territories. Major repositories of photos and films related to the Holocaust are the Yad Vashem Archives (YVA) and the USHMM. A famous series of photos documenting the Lviv pogrom of 1 July 1941 is held by the Wiener Library in London. The prominent Philadelphia journalist David Lee Preston is a collector of materials, including photos, relating to Lviv during the Holocaust. Preston's mother survived the war in the sewers of Lviv;[257] and he has been very generous in allowing me to peruse and use his collection. A former master's student of mine, Arianna Selecky, discovered previously unknown footage of the Lviv pogrom in 2008 at the UCRDC

---

255 For a more extended analysis, see Himka, "Debates in Ukraine," 353-56.
256 Shepelev, "Fotografii," 431 n. 12.
257 See his beautiful and moving remembrance of her: Preston, "A Bird in the Wind."

in Toronto; it was taken by a photographer attached to the First Al-
pine Division (*1. Gebirgs-Division*). The original celluloid film has
disappeared, but a digital copy is available at USHMM.[258]

Although these films and photos are of historical importance,
they have to be used carefully and respectfully. As Georgii
Shepelev has noted: "Practically speaking, every photograph is not
only a document but the photographer's choice of subject, point of
view, and often—staging." And: "taking a photograph often turns
out to be an act of demonstrating domination."[259] This is very much
the case with pogrom photos. The prurient interests of some photographers come through clearly in images of sexual assault and
forced nakedness, especially during the Lviv pogrom. In the words
of Marianne Hirsch, "one might well argue that pedagogy demands
that the worst be shown, one might also worry about the violation
inherent in such displays: these women are doomed in perpetuity
to be displayed in the most humiliating, demeaning, dehumanizing
position."[260] In my opinion, the act of photographing sexual violence constituted participation in the violence. This view resonates
with the testimony of one of the victims of the violence, Róża Wagner: The Germans "walked around with the faces of rulers and photographed the tormented naked women: 'This will be in *Der
Stürmer*'; they were happy that their compatriots would have the
opportunity to look at the feats of their husbands and sons."[261] So
in using these photographs—and this applies to photographs also
of humiliation, physical assault, and murder—we must be cogni-
zant of the tainted circumstances of their production and of the perspective that they convey to the viewer.

The photographs discussed above are useful for establishing
and interpreting the role of OUN militiamen in the anti-Jewish violence of 1941. It is important to note that all these photographs were
taken by the Germans, not by members of OUN themselves; later,
when relations between OUN and the Germans became strained,

258 It is in the Steven Spielberg Film and Video Archive, acc. no. 2013.himka, RG-
     60.1414, film ID 2983. I also have a copy in my possession.
259 Shepelev, "Fotografii," 435, 441.
260 Hirsch, "Surviving Images," 37 n. 32.
261 AŻIH, 301/442, Róża Wagner, 3-4.

there were no German photographers to record atrocities committed by the nationalists. This may well be one of the reasons why I
have been unable to find photographs of OUN's activities in 1943-
44 of direct utility to this study. Hundreds of photos of UPA are
available for viewing online, but almost all of them are posed individual and mostly collective portraits, souvenirs for comrades-in-
arms. There are also photographs of Polish victims of UPA, but I
know of no photographic evidence of any Jewish actions undertaken by UPA.

Periodical Press

I have consulted many newspapers and periodicals of the 1930s and
1940s: OUN publications from the entire period, the legal Ukrainian
press under Nazi occupation, and postwar periodicals from displaced persons' camps in Germany and the POW camp in Rimini
(where soldiers of the Waffen-SS Division Galizien were interned).
Much of this research was conducted in the Stefanyk library in Lviv
and at Oseredok in Winnipeg. Many Ukrainian periodicals are
available online at *libraria.ua*.

Most useful for this study was the OUN press. The party organ
Rozbudova natsii came out legally in Prague in 1928-34 and was
smuggled into Ukrainian territories in Poland and Romania. It was
a venue for open debate and fresh ideas, within, of course, the limits
of nationalist discourse. Though it provides many insights into the
evolution of OUN thinking, it represented the émigré leadership
more than the activists and militants in Galicia and Volhynia. I
think one gets a better feel for the latter reading the OUN popular
press that came out of Galicia. *Nove Selo* was a weekly newspaper
that came out in Lviv in 1930-39; aimed at the peasantry, it contained much practical advice related to agriculture but also carried
articles of a more ideological nature. OUN also briefly managed to
publish a fortnightly newspaper aimed at workers. *Homin baseinu*,
intended for workers in the Boryslav oil basin, came out in
Drohobych (P Drohobycz) in 1937 and was renamed *Homin kraiu* in
December of that year; it lasted until the beginning of June 1938.
The workers' paper featured many articles aimed against

communism and the Soviet Union. Analysis of the Soviet Union was the specialty of the monthly *Het' z bol'shevyzmom* edited by Ivan Mitrynga. Only three issues of the journal came out, but it shows how seriously the Mitrynga group followed events in Soviet Ukraine and in the Soviet Union as a whole; *Het' z bol'shevyzmom* published academic Sovietology from a nationalist perspective. In 1942-46 OUN-B published an illegal, underground periodical, *Ideia i chyn*. It contained ideological articles, nationalist propaganda, and news.

The legal Ukrainian-language press that came out during the German occupation of Ukraine was often at least loosely affiliated with nationalist circles and sometimes, especially at the beginning of the occupation, served essentially as OUN organs. We have already seen an example of the latter from the Donbas in the previous chapter.[262] *Volyn'*, which came out in Rivne (P Równe) under the editorship of Ulas Samchuk, and *Ukrains'ke Slovo*, which came out in Kyiv under the editorship of Ivan Rohach, were both initially under the control of the Melnyk faction of OUN. But in February 1942 much stricter German censorship was introduced and leading nationalists in the press were repressed. Samchuk was arrested and Rohach executed; Olena Teliha, a major Ukrainian poet who contributed to both newspapers, was also executed.[263] *Krakivs'ki visti*, which appeared under the auspices of the Ukrainian Central Committee headed by Volodymyr Kubijovyč, was a cut above the other legal papers culturally and intellectually; it was loosely affiliated with the Melnyk faction as well and, like all the occupation papers, published antisemitic propaganda in abundance.[264] The Banderites initially controlled a weekly newspaper in Zboriv (P Zborów),

---

262 See above, 36-37.
263 On the successes and repression of the Melnykites in Kyiv, see Kurylo, "Syla ta slabkist'." On the antisemitism of the Melnykite milieus in light of contemporary Ukrainian historico-political controversies, see Radchenko, "'I todi braty.'" Myroslav Shkandrij wrote that after the repressions in *Ukrains'ke Slovo*, its replacement, *Nove ukrains'ke slovo*, was "anti-Ukrainian and antisemitic." Shkandrij, *Ukrainian Nationalism*, 176. This is true, but it implies that the Melnykite paper was not antisemitic beforehand, which was, as Radchenko shows, not the case.
264 Himka, "*Krakivski visti* and the Jews." Himka, "Ethnicity and the Reporting of Mass Murder."

Ternopil oblast, *Zborivs'ki visti*, which published for the first time the text of the declaration of 30 June 1941 proclaiming the renewal of Ukrainian statehood.

I examined numerous Ukrainian newspapers and periodicals published in displaced persons' camps and the POW camp in Rimini (1945-49). The general tone in this press was quite depressing. The Ukrainians who had followed the Germans out of Ukraine before the Red Army's advance saw their world collapsing. Not only had the Soviets returned to Ukraine and so many conscious Ukrainians become displaced to the West, but there was plenty of other bad news: communists coming to power throughout Eastern Europe, the suppression of the Greek Catholic church, the famine of 1946, the resettlement of the Ukrainian population in Poland, and the suppression of UPA in Poland and repression of its adherents. The Ukrainians in the camps were overwhelmed by their own memories of suffering and struggle and the bleak prospects for the future. The Ukrainians positioned themselves now as virulently anti-German, their initial flirtation with the Germans being presented as an honest error. And they remained anti-Soviet.

I was curious if the immediately postwar Ukrainian press continued to publish antisemitic articles and discovered that overt antisemitic statements had almost disappeared, even though many of the same journalists continued to work in the new environment. Although occasionally concerned with Polish-Ukrainian relations, Jewish-Ukrainian relations and the issue of the Holocaust and Ukrainian participation in it were hardly mentioned at all. What was developing, however, was a defense of Ukrainian behavior with regard to the Jews, although, as I've said, the issue was rarely treated at all.

There may well be more, but I found only two articles that confronted the stance of Ukrainians in the Holocaust. One was written in 1947 by Volodymyr Yaniv, an OUN activist who had been arrested several times by the Polish authorities. He published an article in defense of "the good name of the Ukrainian people," which was a response to generalizations about Ukrainians made by Eugen Kogon in his seminal work on the Nazi concentration camp system.[265] Yaniv did not deny that some Ukrainians took part in the Holocaust, but he said that certain things had to be taken into account: What was the extent of these Ukrainians' guilt? "Were they the initiators, or only the executors," and were they not acting under "bestial duress"? Kogon had also accused Latvians, Lithuanians, and Poles of antisemitism, "thus more or less all the nations on whose lands the mass liquidations of Jews occurred; this then is proof of an action coordinated from above rather than an expression of the genuine feelings of the above-mentioned nations. The 'antisemitism' of these nations was only a result of the pressure of the occupier." Yaniv considered participation in the Holocaust the responsibility of "criminal individuals" and omitted mention of any group that bore political responsibility. Yaniv blamed the robbery of Jews during their transit to the Lviv ghetto on "the Lviv rabble (motlokh)—in equal measure Ukrainian and Polish." One cannot, he admonished, generalize about the behavior of entire nations from such incidents. "It is well known: the rabble. The law of the mob."[266]

The other article, which also appeared in 1947 but in a different newspaper, was anonymous and simply entitled "Ukrainians and Jews." It reported that a Yiddish periodical, Ibergang, in discussing children rescued during the Holocaust had mentioned the efforts of the Greek Catholic metropolitan of Halych and archbishop of Lviv, Andrei Sheptytsky.[267] The article mentioned Sheptytsky's letter to Himmler condemning the murder of defenseless and innocent people. It concluded: "These facts most obviously contradict the malicious and baseless inventions of the enemies of Ukrainians about 'antisemitism' and 'pogromism' of the Ukrainian people."[268]

---

265 Kogon was a Christian who opposed the Nazis and paid for this with six years in Buchenwald. After the war he wrote the first major analysis of the concentration camp system, Der SS Staat (1946), published in English as The Theory and Practice of Hell.

266 Ianiv, "Za dobre im"ia ukrains'koho narodu."

267 The last major review of the metropolitan's thoughts and actions during the Holocaust was my own: Himka, "Metropolitan Andrei Sheptytsky and the Holocaust."

268 "Ukraintsi i zhydy."

Thus just a few years after the war we see expressions of the kind of argumentation that would be used in subsequent years to defend the record of OUN and UPA during the war. The Germans forced people to participate in anti-Jewish actions (which was indeed sometimes the case). The major offenders were not the Ukrainian educated elite but the lower classes, the rabble. Collaboration in the Holocaust was a matter of individual responsibility and guilt, and Ukrainians cannot be held collectively responsible for what happened. What is important about this formulation is that it excludes from consideration any intermediate actors between individuals and the national community as a whole, such as the occupation press, the local Ukrainian civil adminstration, OUN, UPA, and police and military units in German service. Also, Metropolitan Sheptytsky's condemnation of the Holocaust and rescue of Jewish children are understood to exonerate Ukrainians as a whole from charges of antisemitism and participation in the Holocaust.

Before leaving this general survey of the source base for understanding the connection between OUN-UPA and the Holocaust, I should explicitly state the obvious: I have not identified all the possible sources that a resourceful and imaginative historian can unearth. Some of the recent historiography has been quite impressive in bringing new and new types of documentation to light.[269]

Disputed Sources

Critics and defenders of OUN have argued over the authenticity and meaning of some sources, and in what follows I will look at three major controversies that have arisen.

Yaroslav Stetsko's Autobiography of July 1941

As we will describe in more detail later,[270] one of the most prominent leaders of OUN-B, Yaroslav Stetsko, declared the renewal of Ukrainian statehood in Lviv on 30 June 1941. OUN-B was hoping to present the Germans with a fait accompli, but they miscalculated,

---

and over the course of July a number of OUN-B leaders were arrested. Stetsko was arrested by the Security Police on 9 July and taken to Berlin; there on 12 July or within a day or two thereafter he wrote an autobiography in two languages, Ukrainian and German. A passage in the Ukrainian version reads:

> I consider Marxism to be a product of the Jewish mind, which, however, has been applied in practice in the Muscovite prison of peoples by the Muscovite-Asiatic people with the assistance of Jews. Moscow and Jewry are Ukraine's greatest enemies and bearers of corruptive Bolshevik international ideas.
>
> Although I consider Moscow, which in fact held Ukraine in captivity, and not Jewry, to be the main and decisive enemy, I nonetheless fully appreciate the undeniably harmful and hostile role of the Jews, who are helping Moscow to enslave Ukraine. I therefore support the destruction of the Jews and the expedience of bringing German methods of exterminating Jewry to Ukraine, barring their assimilation and the like.[271]

The corresponding passage in the German version is:

> Marxism is indeed to be considered as a creation of the Jewish brain, but its practical realization (also with Jewish help) was and is in the Muscovite prison of peoples, brought about by the Muscovite people. Moscow and Jewry are the greatest enemies of Ukraine and the carriers of disintegrative Bolshevik international Ideas.
>
> The main enemy of Ukraine is not Jewry, but Moscow, which has subjugated Ukraine; Muscovite imperialism is not to be confused with the disintegrative assistance of the Jews. Nevertheless the role of the Jews is not to be underestimated. I am of the opinion that in the struggle against Jewry in Ukraine German methods are to be employed.[272]

These passages were first published in the KGB-produced book *Lest We Forget* "authored" by Michael Hanusiak, and Western scholars were reluctant to rely on them.[273] But after the archives were opened in the 1990s, Karel C. Berkhoff and Marco Carynnyk

---

271 Translation taken from Berkhoff and Carynnyk, "The Organization of Ukrainian Nationalists," 170-71; Ukrainian text: 153, 162. Underlining in the original.

272 Author's translation. German text: Berkhoff and Carynnyk, "The Organization of Ukrainian Nationalists," 167. Underlining in the original.

273 See above, 42-44.

published the full texts of Stetsko's autobiography with extensive commentary in *Harvard Ukrainian Studies*. In a subsequent issue of that journal, Taras Hunczak cast doubt on the autobiography's authenticity.[274] Hunczak was a professor at Rutgers Newark who had made some solid contributions to the study of modern Ukrainian history, mainly of an editorial and compilatory nature. As a child during World War II, he had served as a courier for OUN, and later in the emigration he was associated with the Lebed group, the *dviikari*. He was also a passionate defender of Ukrainians against accusations of antisemitism; for example, he wrote an article exonerating Symon Petliura of responsibility for the pogroms that raged in Ukraine in 1919[275] and an account of Ukrainian-Jewish relations during World War II intended as a response to Judge Jules Deschênes' Commission of Inquiry on War Criminals in Canada.[276] So it is not unusual that he would take up the issue of the Stetsko memoirs and conclude that they were forgeries.

I will examine Hunczak's major arguments and then offer some additional considerations. First, he wondered why the memoirs were found in Ukraine rather than in Germany; he raised the question in order to buttress his final conclusion, which was that the autobiography "was written in the offices of KGB functionaries." At present, there is no precise answer to Hunczak's question. But there is a general answer: the Soviets took German records that interested them. Thus records of the RSHA are in Moscow and the records of the Einsatzstab Reichsleiter Rosenberg are in Kyiv; the Soviets also took records of the secret police and intelligence units. The best informed specialist on Soviet archives, Patricia Grimsted, explained:

> The seizure of Nazi records was specifically ordered by Allied Control Commission laws and paralleled similar seizures by the Western

---

274 Hunczak, "Problems of Historiography," 136-38.
275 Hunczak, "A Reappraisal." See also the response: Szajkowski, "'A Reappraisal.'"
276 Hunczak, "Ukrainian-Jewish Relations." The Deschênes Commission was active in 1985-86 investigating alleged war criminals among the Ukrainian and Baltic communities in Canada. Conflicts arose between these communities and some Jewish organizations over the use of Soviet evidence.

Allies. The only difference was that the Western Allies worked together with seized Nazi records, while Soviet authorities refused to
cooperate....[B]y the 1960s, the Western Allies had agreed to return to
West Germany almost all the Nazi records they had seized (with the
exception of some military and intelligence files), following analysis
and microfilming. Soviet authorities, by contrast, never even made
known which Nazi records they had retrieved.[277]

His second argument was that *Lest We Forget* was untrustworthy and outright deceitful. This was an accurate assessment, but it
does not follow logically that therefore everything in the book was
manufactured. Hunczak was able to show that "Hanusiak" deliberately distorted and misrepresented sources, but not that he used
fake evidence. For example, he analyzed a photograph of Metropolitan Andrei Sheptytsky that Hanusiak claimed was a picture of the
churchman receiving a swastika during a military exercise in 1939;
in fact, Hunczak had found the original of the photo in the Lviv
archives and determined that Sheptytsky was receiving a scout
(*Plast*) badge at a scouting camp in 1930. Thus the photo was real,
but the meaning the KGB wanted viewers to derive from it was not.
As the saying goes, even the devil can quote scripture.

The third argument he brought to bear was linguistic. He
maintained that the spelling of the adjective *pidpol'nyi* was "a transparent Russian variation of the Ukrainian *pidpillia*." But if he had
checked the spelling used by Lviv's major newspaper, *Dilo*, in the
1930s, he would have found the supposed "transparent Russian
variant" *pidpol'nyi* employed frequently.[278] Hunczak's major linguistic argument was that the spelling in the autobiography uses
an *h* (г) "where an individual from western Ukraine, particularly in
1941, would have used the letter *g*" (ґ). An example he cites is
"*propahanda* instead of *propaganda*." But the legal newspaper under
the German occupation, *L'vivs'ki visti*, used the spelling *propahanda*

---

277 Grimsted, "'Trophy' Archives," 6.
278 This is easily checkable in the searchable files of *Dilo* at libraria.ua.

in 1941, and Stetsko himself used the spelling *propahanda*.[279] The linguistic arguments, in sum, fail.[280]

In Hunczak's opinion, "the ultimate fraud" was a statement in the autobiography that Stetsko edited the journal *Ideia i chyn* in 1939-40. Again, Hunczak made an error, confusing the *Ideia i chyn* of 1942-46, in which Stetsko indeed had no role, with a periodical that bore the same title, but came out earlier and was in fact edited by Stetsko.[281] Thus none of Hunczak's proofs of fabrication hold up.

On the other hand, there are solid arguments in favor of the authenticity of the autobiography. For one thing, we know of no other example of the KGB seeding secret archives with false documents. We certainly know of Soviet falsifications, but not of falsifications that they secreted in archives that were basically closed to researchers. Moreover, the autobiography is an oddly preserved document. There is no full text of the German version; instead, there is a draft of the first page and then a fair copy of the rest of the pages, but some text missing in between. And there are also some discrepancies between the German and Ukrainian texts; for example, the German version notes that Stetsko was born in a priest's

---

279 There is a document from 1938 in which Stetsko added in his own hand the words "*Pryntsypy ukrains'koi propahandy.*" Reproduced in Carynnyk, "'A Knife in the Back,'" 7 (point 8a). This document has extensive additions in Stetsko's handwriting, and they can be compared to the handwritten additions in the small photoreproduction of a passage from the autobiography in Berkhoff and Carynnyk, "The Organization of Ukrainian Nationalists," 153. To me the handwriting and method of making insertions look the same, but I am not a specialist in analyzing handwriting and I have seen too little of the original of the Ukrainian autobiography. Stetsko's widow, Slava Stetsko, shown a copy of the autobiography by Zhanna Kovba, denied that it was her late husband's writing. Kovba, *Liudianist' u bezodni pekla*, 225.

280 On a more abstruse point, Hunczak was exercised about the typewriter, which at first he thought had no *g* (some Ukrainian keyboards lack them), but then he found examples of *g* in the autobiography. Thus, he argued, there was no reason for a Western Ukrainian not to be using a *g* where expected in the orthography and in the transcription of foreign words and place names. But I myself have used different Ukrainian keyboards, and more than once it has taken me a long time to discover whether the keyboard had a *g* as well as an *h*, since the placement of *g* on the keyboard was not and still has not been standardized. Stetsko was using an unfamiliar typewriter in Berlin and may not have found the *g* until near the end of his typescript, where the *g*'s in fact appear.

281 Herasymenko, *Orhanizatsiia Ukrains'kykh Natsionalistiv*, 28.

family, but the Ukrainian version omits that information. Would the KGB have put together such a sloppy document? These odd features smack of the irregularity of a genuine archival document.

Moreover, there was nothing unusual in the substance of the anti-Jewish passage of the document. As Berkhoff and Carynnyk pointed out when they published it,[282] and as we will see for ourselves in the next chapter, what Stetsko had to say in his autobiography of July 1941 was very similar to what other OUN leaders were saying at the same time and what Stetsko himself had been saying about Jews in previous years. In fact, the autobiography uses verbal formulations quite characteristic of Stetsko, as we can see by comparing it to an antisemitic article he published in 1939 in a Ukrainian nationalist newspaper in Canada, "Zhydivstvo i my" (Jewry and Us). The short article of 1939 uses the same vocabulary as the two paragraphs on Jews in the autobiography of 1941. (See Table 1.)

Table 1

"Жидівство і ми" 1939	Життєпис 1941
Москва є головним ворогом	головним ворогом — Москву
закріплювач (грали ролю закріплювача ворожого стану посідання)	закріповувати (помагають Москві закріпо[ву]вати Україну)
виключення всякої асиміляції	виключаючи її асиміляції
московський азіят	московсько-азіятський народ

In conclusion, there is no reason to doubt the authenticity of the 1941 Stetsko autobiography.[283]

---

282 Berkhoff and Carynnyk, "The Organization of Ukrainian Nationalists," 153-56.
283 The pro-OUN historian Volodymyr Kosyk also accepted the autobiography as genuine. See Berkhoff, "A Power Terrible for Its Opponents," 199 n. 10.

The Book of Facts

In 2008 the SBU released with great fanfare a document, *The Book of Facts*,[284] that it said exonerated OUN, and specifically its battalion Nachtigall, from participation in the anti-Jewish pogroms of the summer of 1941. As presented at that time, the *Book of Facts* was "essentially a chronicle of the activities of OUN during March-September 1941."[285] The relevant passage on the pogroms is interesting and short enough to present in full:

> 4-7 July 1941
> Representatives of Gestapo units, who came to Lviv in great number, by various paths approached Ukrainian circles that the Ukrainians should organize a three-day pogrom of the Jews. "Instead of organizing demonstrative funerals for political prisoners murdered by the Bolsheviks," they said, "it is better to execute a major revenge action against the Jews. Neither German police nor military authorities will interfere in this."
> The leading personnel of OUN, when they learned of this, informed all members that this was a German provocation in order to compromise the Ukrainians by pogroms, in order to provide a pretext for the German police to intervene and "restore order," and — most important — to divert the attention and energy of the Ukrainians in general from political problems and the struggle for independent statehood towards the slippery road of anarchy, crimes, and plunder.
> Already the Second Great Assembly of OUN expressed itself decisively against any Jewish pogroms,[286] condemning such tendencies as the attempts of occupiers to divert attention of the popular masses from the root problems of the liberation struggle. Now, in the first days of the German occupation, these decisions were realized in practice, prohibiting participation in the pogroms of Jews and counteracting German provocations. Only thanks to the decisive attitude of the OUN cadres there did not result in the first days after the retreat of the Bolsheviks a massive slaughter of Jews in Lviv and in other Ukrainian cities, in spite of the tremendous wave of indignation called forth by the Bolsheviks' murder of 80 thousand Ukrainian

284 Only three pages of *The Book of Facts* (*Knyha faktiv*) were made public at that time. But the whole 60-page text is available on line http://avr.org.ua/index.php/viewDoc/3188/ (accessed 10 December 2018).
285 "U Sluzhbi bezpeky Ukrainy vidbulys' Hromads'ki istorychni slukhannia." "Iak tvorylasia lehenda pro Nachtigall" (source of quotation). "Dokumenty SBU."
286 See below, 169-70.

political prisoners and in spite of the numerous provocations of the German Gestapo to incite Ukrainians to slaughter Jews.

After the publication of the text, both Marco Carynnyk and I raised questions about the status of the document. Both of us pointed out that it was no contemporary chronicle of 1941 but was in fact a chronological compilation put together some time after World War II was over.[287] We did not claim that *The Book of Facts* was a falsification, but rather that its presentation as a chronicle proving that OUN did not participate in the pogroms of July 1941 was a deception. Since our initial articles, the entire text of *The Book of Facts* has become available, and a well-researched study confirms that the book was compiled after the war, namely by OUN-UPA in Poland (*Zakerzonnia*) in 1946-47.[288]

Thus *The Book of Facts* was prepared after the Germans lost the war and after the crimes of the Holocaust had come to public attention throughout the world as a result of the Nuremberg trials. It belongs in the same category as the postwar OUN publications of the diaspora: it proves nothing about 1941, only about the postwar self-presentation of OUN. A good indication of how factual *The Book of Facts* is its assertion that "thanks to the decisive attitude of the OUN cadres there did not result in the first days after the retreat of the Bolsheviks a massive slaughter of Jews in Lviv and in other Ukrainian cities...."

Although patently unreliable, *The Book of Facts* served as a primary source for an exhibition on the Shoah in Lviv at the Lontsky Street Prison Memorial Museum in Lviv in 2013.[289]

The Stella Krenzbach Memoirs

In 1954 Ukrainian publications in Toronto and Buenos Aires published the memoirs of a Jewish woman, Stella Krenzbach (Krentsbakh), who had served as a nurse in UPA, both near the end of World War II and after the war, during the anti-Soviet

---

287 Rybakov, "Marko Tsarynnyk." Himka, "Be Wary."
288 Riabenko, "'Knyha faktiv,'" 103-08. Riabenko's study is well researched and at the same time a one-sided polemic.
289 Himka, "The Lontsky Street Prison Memorial Museum," 146-52.

insurgency. Her memoir said she was brought up in a small Galician town, in a family that spoke only perfect Hebrew among themselves, and her closest girlfriends were Ukrainian. She did not look like a typical Jewish girl of the region: in fact, she was a natural blond with cornflower blue eyes. Later she moved to Lviv to study. She hoped to go to medical school, but her application, along with the applications of thirty-eight Ukrainians, was rejected; she was the only Jewish girl not accepted. She studied philosophy instead, earning a doctorate. But that was in 1939, when war broke out.

Her experiences with the Bolsheviks were negative. She was arrested by the Soviet militia, who, she said, had orders to send all Jews to Siberia, but she managed to escape from them through a bathroom window. She claimed to be the only Jew who welcomed the Germans, since she thought they would build Ukraine. She was quickly disabused, obtained false papers with a Ukrainian last name, and worked in Ukrainian homes as a seamstress. She hated the passivity with which other Jews marched to their death. Having finished with the Jews, the Germans began to arrest the Ukrainians, shooting some, sending others to concentration camps. "But the Ukrainians were not meek, like the Jews: they repaid blood with blood, death with death." She heard rumors about UPA in Volhynia and suspected that one of her friends had connections with them. Her friend arranged for her to join the insurgent army. She said not to worry about her Jewishness, since the soldiers of UPA "do not divide people by races but by whether they are honest or not." She was given a six-month nursing course and served in an UPA hospital. Eventually the Bolsheviks decimated her unit, and the remainder fought their way into the American zone of Austria in the fall of 1946. From there she went to Israel.[290]

Only a few years passed before this beautiful tale was exposed as a fabrication. Friedman made an investigation into the memoir. When it was republished in Buenos Aires in 1957, a prominent Melnykite, Dmytro Andriievsky, filled in a bit more of Stella Krenzbach's life story. In Israel, he wrote, she went to work as a

---

290 Krentsbakh, "Zhyvu shche zavdiaky UPA."

secretary in the ministry of foreign affairs.[291] She first published her memoirs in the *Washington Post*, and a few weeks later she was murdered. Here is what Friedman discovered: "I checked the *Washington Post* of that period and did not find the memoirs. At my request, Dr. N.M. Gelber of Jerusalem made inquiry in the foreign ministry there; the reply was that the ministry had never had an employee by that name and that such a case of homicide was entirely unknown. Moreover, a careful analysis of the text of the 'memoirs' has led me to the conclusion that the entire story is a hoax."[292] One of the *dviikari*, Bohdan Kordiuk, also looked into the Stella Krenzbach question. His conclusion was very similar. He asked the UPA veterans he knew if they had known or heard of her; none had. In his opinion, "the tale of Dr. Stella Krenzbach has to be considered a mystification."[293]

But decades passed, Ukraine became independent, connections with the Ukrainian diaspora intensified, and some Western Ukrainians were calling for the rehabilitation of OUN and UPA. Not surprisingly, then, in 1993, a periodical connected with the Vasyl Stus Memorial Society in Lviv, *Poklyk sumlinnia*, reanimated Stella Krenzbach by republishing her memoir. The memoir fit perfectly with Zhanna Kovba's goal to give the lie to stereotypes of antisemitic Ukrainians and communist Jews, and she accepted it as good coin.[294] Volodymyr Viatrovych also cited her memoir in his 2006 book on OUN and the Jews to demonstrate the presence and acceptance of Jews in UPA.[295] Then as the controversies around OUN and UPA heated up near the end of Viktor Yushchenko's presidency, the Ukrainian-language Jewish poet Moishe Fishbein did a great deal to publicize the Krenzbach story. He gave a conference paper, frequently reprinted/reposted at the time, entitled "The Jewish Card in Russian Operations against Ukraine," which

---

291 This was also indicated in her published memoir: Ibid., 349.
292 Friedman, "Ukrainian-Jewish Relations," 203-04 n. 57.
293 Kordiuk, "Pro liudei." Kordiuk was one of the Banderites who was arrested and survived Auschwitz.
294 Kovba, *Liudianist' u bezodni pekla*, 113-14. She mistakenly wrote that the memoirs had been first published in Israel.
295 V"iatrovych, *Stavlennia OUN do ievreiv*, 79.

used the Krenzbach memoir to counter Russian claims that UPA was antisemitic. He also put the Krenzbach memoirs on his website in Ukrainian and in English translation.[296] Fishbein's efforts took in many people.[297]

* *

*

The controversies over the legitimacy of sources reaffirm the need to treat sources with care. In our survey, we saw the limitations and problems with every kind of source we looked at. The German documents do not constitute, as earlier Holocaust scholars believed, the touchstone of truth; instead they are marred by deep biases. Soviet documents are formulated using an ideological vocabulary and, more important, sometimes tailored information to serve the needs of the state. Internal OUN documents are much more reliable than documents produced for external consumption. Moreover, the researcher has to be careful about deliberate misrepresentation and even falsifications by OUN. Crucially, official documents of every provenance need to be triangulated, whenever possible, with other evidence, primarily eyewitness testimony, but also when relevant with photographs, films, and the periodical press. Jewish testimony is often marked by trauma and Ukrainian testimony by evasion. All sources need to be treated with care. Some sources, moreover, have imbedded problems as products of criminal practices: German documents and photographs are components of the atrocities they report on, and Soviet interrogations have their origins in torture. Questions around sources are not simple, but it is hoped that this survey has armed the reader with sufficient understanding to make reasonable judgments about the utility and reliability of the various sources and about the historical processes which they reflect.

---

296 http://mosesfishbein.blogspot.com/2009/10/memoirs-of-stella-krenzbach-i-am-alive.html (accessed 11 December 2018). The English translation was by Marta D. Olynyk. Apparently, Fishbein also had no luck in finding an original publication in the *Washington Post*.

297 Among those who fell for the Krenzbach fabrication was the well-known Sovietologist Paul Goble. Rudling, *The OUN, the UPA and the Holocaust*, 31-32.

3. The Organization of Ukrainian Nationalists

The intent of this chapter is to introduce the Organization of Ukrainian Nationalists as it existed before the German invasion of the USSR on 22 June 1941. The chapter looks at the historical circumstances attendant upon the birth and development of OUN, i.e., the local and international factors that led to the emergence of radical Ukrainian nationalism. It then sketches the history of the organization from its intellectual and organizational origins until the middle of 1941. Three sections then analyze particular aspects of OUN's thinking that appear relevant to understanding its subsequent participation in the Holocaust: its relationship to fascism, its ideas about creating a monoethnic Ukraine, and its antisemitism.

Contextual Origins of OUN

In this section I want to sketch the historical circumstances and political climate out of which OUN and its radical nationalist doctrines and practices emerged.

The formulation of a modern Ukrainian identity, one consciously separate from a Polish or Russian identity, occurred during the nineteenth century. A thin stratum of educated activists followed the typical program of that century's national revivals: the collection of folk songs, tales, and proverbs; the codification of the language; the invention of "national" instruments, costumes, and dances; the compilation of a history; the exaltation of a national poet; the delineation of national territory; and the imagination of an independent state.

The Ukrainian movement developed in two very different polities. Most people of Ukrainian nationality lived in the Russian empire, which produced the giants of the revival: the historians Mykola Kostomarov and Mykhailo Hrushevsky, the poet Taras Shevchenko, and the political thinker Mykhailo Drahomanov. But the movement here was top heavy, consisting of educated visionaries with little popular reach. Russian tsarism did all it could to stifle the nascent Ukrainian movement, including through a complete ban of education in Ukrainian and severe restrictions on publication in the Ukrainian language. Education in any language was also relatively neglected in Russia, which impeded the recruitment of peasants, who formed the vast majority of the ethnic Ukrainian population, into the national movement. Strict censorship of the press and autocratic government also stunted the propagation of the national revival among the mass of the population. The situation improved during the 1905 revolution, but the autocracy chipped away at the revolutionary gains in the years before World War I. Thus when tsarism collapsed in 1917, Ukrainian consciousness was weaker than demanded by the challenges of the time, and networks of pre-existing national organizations were absent. These structural flaws would make the Ukrainian revolution of 1917-20 chaotic and feeble in the former Russian empire.

The circumstances of national development were much more favorable in the Austrian crownland of Galicia, where Ukrainians also lived. From the very moment when this region was taken by the Habsburgs during the first partition of Poland in 1772, the absolutist emperors undertook a number of reforms that benefited the Ruthenians, as Ukrainians were then called, of Galicia. The most consequential of these reforms was the education of the Ruthenian clergy. Within a few decades, the clergy became an army of national awakeners, and later their children filled the ranks of a secular intelligentsia. When the Habsburg monarchy became a constitutional state in the 1860s, opportunities for the national movement expanded tremendously. Universal education was introduced, so that the vast majority of younger male peasants were literate by the outbreak of World War I. Moreover, in eastern Galicia Ukrainian was the language of instruction in most schools. The clergy and teachers founded numerous organizations in villages: reading clubs, which promoted both adult education and the national movement; cooperatives and credit unions; gymnastic societies, choirs, and fire brigades. In joining one of these organizations, peasants joined the nation that was under construction by the intelligentsia. Omer Bartov has reminded us that "before nationalism began to hate, it was also about education and enlightenment, material improvement, collective responsibility, and group identity. The path toward violence was neither foreseen nor inevitable."[298]

The peasants who benefited from the national movement were the children and grandchildren of serfs. Serfdom in Galicia and also in Right-Bank Ukraine was extremely oppressive. Serfs were forced to work without recompense on the landlord's land, at least several days a week, and resistance and shirking were punished corporally, generally by beating. They also paid rents in kind: eggs, cloth, honey, sheep, or whatever else the local peasant economy produced. The serfs fed and clothed themselves from their own small plots. The system of serfdom was abolished in the Habsburg monarchy in 1848, as a result of the revolution of that year, and in the Ukrainian-inhabited regions of the Russian empire between 1861 and 1864. Serfdom generated a long-lasting resentment among the peasant population.[299]

Before World War I, Ukrainian politics was generally on the left side of the political spectrum because the movement looked for its mass base in the peasantry. Drahomanov, the most important Ukrainian political thinker of the nineteenth century and a major influence on Galicia, defined himself as an anarchist and a socialist. The first Ukrainian political party in the Russian empire was the Revolutionary Ukrainian Party, which was generally socialist (and also a bit nationalist); activists from this party went on to found Ukrainian social democratic and social revolutionary parties. The latter were the major political parties during the Ukrainian revolution of 1917-20. In Galicia, the Ukrainian political party with the most influence was the national populist Ukrainian National

---

298 Bartov, *Anatomy of a Genocide*, 25.
299 I first learned of serfdom as a child from my grandmother, who was an illiterate peasant from Galicia. She learned of serfdom from *her* grandparents. My grandmother did not have an English word for serfdom, so I first learned of it as *panshchyna*. Grandma would always get upset when I volunteered for anything. She insisted that this was wrong, because *vzhe pomer davno toi, shcho robyv darmo* (long ago died the one who worked for free). In order to earn money to migrate to America, she worked as an agricultural laborer on her landlord's estate. Although a half century had passed since the abolition of serfdom, she was still regularly whipped to encourage her in her work. She told me she wished she could see her landlord suffering in hell. I do not know how exceptional she was in her rage.

Democratic Party, which had many socialists and former socialists in its leadership. There was also a smaller socialist peasant party, the Radical Party, and an even smaller Ukrainian Social Democratic party, since there were very few Ukrainian workers. The Ukrainian parties in Galicia organized and supported agricultural laborer strikes in the early twentieth century; they championed their nation and its peasant constituents.

As it did throughout Europe, the Great War that broke out in 1914, and even more the civil wars it unleashed, transformed the political constellation in Ukrainian lands. Ukraine experienced six years of uninterrupted warfare. Millions of young Ukrainian men underwent military training, learned to handle weapons, and participated in combat. They fought on both sides of World War I, in the Russian as well as the Austrian army. During the war the front crossed over Ukraine; the Russians were in Lviv for about ten months in 1914-15, and the Germans and Austrians were in Kyiv for about the same length of time in 1918.

A major result of the war was the collapse of empires. It started with Russia in February/March 1917. After Tsar Nicholas II abdicated, power was there for the taking. Leaders of the Ukrainian national movement initiated the Central Rada in Kyiv within days after the abdication. It was one of many local councils that emerged across Russia at that time (the Ukrainian word *rada* corresponded to the Russian *soviet*). The Rada was still very much in the tradition of prewar Ukrainian politics—democratic and headed by social revolutionaries and social democrats; the historian Hrushevsky presided over it. It called a number of congresses that were well attended by throngs of Ukrainians, but in essence it was a conglomeration of self-appointed leaders from the intelligentsia who were able to generate enthusiasm but unable to organize or retain the loyalty of the soldiers and peasants whom they saw as their base of support. By the end of 1917 they confronted an enemy that was better organized, better disciplined, and utterly ruthless in the pursuit of its aims—the Bolsheviks.

The events of 1918 came rapid-fire: the Rada declared the independence of the Ukrainian People's Republic; the Bolsheviks drove them out of Kyiv; then the Germans drove the Bolsheviks out and put the Rada back in charge; finding the Rada too difficult to work with, the Germans replaced it with the Hetmanate of Pavlo Skoropadsky; massive peasant insurrections exploded across the steppe led by charismatic warlords, mostly veterans of World War I; the Germans were defeated on the Western front; and forces of the Ukrainian People's Republic temporarily seized control of Kyiv. The next year, 1919, was even more chaotic. Vying for power in Ukraine were the Bolsheviks, the Russian Whites under General Anton Denikin, the Ukrainian forces under Supreme Otaman Symon Petliura, and various peasant warlords, including the famous anarchist Nestor Makhno. In 1920 the Poles under Commander-in-Chief Józef Piłsudski entered the fray. The low ebb of the Ukrainian national forces was the first half of 1919. They managed to hold Kyiv through the Christmas holidays, but the Bolsheviks drove them out by early February. They retreated to the southeast, to Podillia, where Petliura's undisciplined and poorly provisioned soldiers engaged in deadly pogroms against the Jewish population. In fact, during this period, forces allied with the Ukrainian movement were responsible for killing over fifty thousand Jews. Nearer the end of that year the forces of the Ukrainian People's Republic were ravaged by typhus and a freezing early winter. When major fighting came to an end in mid-1920, the Ukrainian revolution had been soundly defeated and its leaders went into exile, mainly to Warsaw and Prague, but also to Paris, Berlin, and Vienna.

There was a Ukrainian revolution in Galicia as well. While the Habsburg monarchy was collapsing under the impact of war, Ukrainian soldiers seized the city administration of Lviv and proclaimed the Western Ukrainian People's Republic on 1 November 1918. Ukrainians were a minority in the city, so Poles were able to seize control after a few weeks of fighting. But the Ukrainian republic continued to control most of the rest of eastern Galicia and was able to establish in the seven months of its existence a relatively viable governmental infrastructure. Had the Ukrainians been fighting only the local Poles, they would have won the Polish-Ukrainian war. In the end they were defeated largely thanks to the army of General Józef Haller, which had been trained and equipped by the French to fight against the Bolsheviks. The Ukrainian

Galician Army moved east in June 1919 and joined with Petliura's forces. Previously, in January 1919, the western Ukrainian republic had formally joined the Ukrainian People's Republic, which at that time was still in control of Kyiv. The Galicians were generally horrified by the chaotic condition of Petliura's army and government. The Ukrainian Galician Army effectively disintegrated in September 1919.

After the Polish-Soviet war of 1919-21, the territories inhabited by Ukrainians were divided among four countries: Poland (Galicia and Volhynia), Czechoslovakia (Transcarpathia and the Prešov region), Romania (Bukovina), and the Ukrainian SSR (all the rest). Thus at a time when hitherto unknown states were founded in east central Europe (Yugoslavia, Czechoslovakia, Finland, Latvia, Estonia) and long-dead states were revived (Lithuania, Poland), Ukrainians failed in their struggle to establish a state of their own. This was a source of great bitterness, and one of the factors that fueled radical Ukrainian nationalism. The "Decalogue" or "Ten Commandments of a Ukrainian Nationalist," composed by Stepan Lenkavsky for OUN in 1929, had as its first commandment: "You will attain a Ukrainian State or die in the struggle for it."[300] Numerous copies of the decalogue are among OUN and UPA documents captured by the Soviets in the latter part of World War II. A Ukrainian state was the nationalists' lodestar.

OUN was to envision and position itself as the direct continuation of the national-liberation struggle. Yevhen Konovalets was OUN's leader from its foundation in 1929 until his assassination in 1938. He was replaced by Andrii Melnyk, who led OUN until it split in 1940; he remained the head of his faction of OUN, OUN-M, until his death in 1964. These men were close friends and had been prominent in the struggle for Ukrainian statehood in 1917-19. Both were Galicians who had served in the Austrian army during World War I. Both had been captured by the Russians and escaped from their POW camps late in 1917. Instead of returning to their native region, however, they decided to aid the Ukrainian People's Republic in its struggle against the Bolsheviks and the Whites. In Kyiv they and

---

300 Mirchuk, *Narys*, 126.

other escaped Galician officers formed the Sich Riflemen[301] and served as colonels in that unit. After suffering defeat in the revolution and being released from Polish POW camps, both returned to Galicia and were among the founders of the Ukrainian Military Organization, perhaps better known by its Ukrainian initials, UVO. This organization waged an underground struggle against the Polish state. It was headed by Konovalets and was one of the predecessors of OUN. From the same milieu as Konovalets and Melnyk came others who were to be prominent in OUN, including Roman Sushko, who was also in the organization's leadership and formed nationalist military and police units in German service during World War II.

It is important to realize, however, that many prominent veterans of the Ukrainian struggle for independence later joined other political camps, ranging from communism to Catholic monarchism—OUN was not the only child of the failed revolution.

But feeding into the rise of nationalism was the conviction of some Ukrainians that the leaders of the Ukrainian movement had not been up to the task that history set for them. They were too democratic, too socialistic, too weak and accommodating. Certainly this criticism rings true with regard to the Central Rada, which misapprehended the moment entirely. Under the Rada's leadership, a number of Ukrainian military units were created. However, under pressure from the Russian Provisional Government of Aleksandr Kerensky, the Rada sent these units to the front to fight the Germans. At the very same time, Lenin and the Bolsheviks were urging soldiers to desert, bring their weapons home, and make a new revolution. While the Bolsheviks supported peasant seizures of landlords' land, the Rada insisted on waiting for a land reform to be worked out by a future Ukrainian constituent assembly, which, because of the defeat of the Ukrainian revolution, never convened. Instead of taking power on its own initiative and expropriating what it needed to function, the Rada constantly negotiated with the

---

301 Not to be confused with the Ukrainian Sich Riflemen, a unit in the Austrian army that evolved into the Ukrainian Galician Army. However, the Sich Riflemen of the Ukrainian People's Republic was named after the Galician unit.

Russian Provisional Government for recognition and funding. Even as the Bolshevik coup was proceeding successfully in Petrograd, a three-man delegation arrived there from the Rada to negotiate with the Provisional Government. Moreover, the Rada's commitment to independent statehood was minimal. When the Rada created the Ukrainian People's Republic in June 1917, it may have been in defiance of the Provisional Goverment, but it stopped short of creating an independent state — the republic was envisioned as an autonomous member of a democratic Russian federation. And the only reason that the Rada created an independent state in January 1918 was so that the Ukrainian People's Republic could sign a peace treaty with Germany; the Rada needed German military aid to repulse the Bolsheviks. The declaration of independence came at the last minute before the Rada was expelled from Kyiv — members of the Rada could hear Bolshevik artillery as they passed the Fourth Universal declaring Ukraine independent. And soon after the declaration, the president of the Rada, the historian Hrushevsky, published texts stating that the Rada preferred federation with a non-Bolshevik Russia to full independence.[302]

The nationalists had no intention of repeating these mistakes. As we will see, in 1941, as soon as it had the opportunity, OUN formed military and police units, set up a civil administration, and declared independent statehood. The nationalists' critique of the weakness of the democratic and socialist leadership of the Ukrainian movement in 1917-18 was somewhat analogous to the view of the German right, which considered that Germany had been betrayed by its politicians in 1918.

The conservative Ukrainian historian Ivan Lysiak-Rudnytsky summarized the situation well:

> In their search for causes of the failure of the Ukrainian revolution of 1917-21 nationalists became convinced that the masses had sought an independent state but had been frustrated and disillusioned by weak governmental leadership. Criticism of individual failings grew into a systematic rejection of the democratic and socialist principles that had been the hallmark of the Ukrainian movement in the late 19th

---

302 Hrushevs'kyi, *Vybrani pratsi*, 35, 37, 39.

and early 20th centuries. The humanist traditions of the prerevolutionary Ukrainian leadership were characterized as naive and lacking in national conviction. Nationalists believed that their era demanded new forms of revolutionary action that could match the ruthlessness and determination shown by Ukraine's enemies.[303]

The nationality policies of the interwar Polish state, which incorporated Galicia and Volhynia, also contributed to the national frustration that many Ukrainians felt. The state used the jobs and licenses it had at its disposal to favor Poles over national minorities. Opportunities for Ukrainians in education were also greatly reduced. Under Austria, Galician Ukrainians had enjoyed a flourishing Ukrainian-language school system. Much of this survived in Poland until 1924, at which time there existed 2151 Ukrainian-language schools. In that year the so-called "lex Grabski" rolled back minority-language education to the point where by 1929 only 716 Ukrainian-language schools remained in existence; the remainder were converted to bilingual schools. Though Poland had promised the Western powers it would open a Ukrainian university, it reneged; instead, it closed down the three existing chairs of Ukrainian studies at Jan Kazimierz University in Lviv and placed certain restrictions on Ukrainian admissions in the 1920s. An underground Ukrainian university flourished in the earlier 1920s but was repressed by the state. Ukrainians who managed to acquire a secondary or higher education faced discrimination in the workplace after graduation, resulting in a large body of unemployed or severely underemployed, yet well educated Ukrainian youth. This surplus intelligentsia was essentially limited to whatever livelihoods Ukrainian civic organizations could provide. The Ukrainian cooperative movement was the major source of funds for Ukrainian community life in Galicia.

In many other respects too, Ukrainians were second-class citizens in Poland. Land reform in Ukrainian-inhabited territories discriminated against them in favor of Polish large landowners and colonists from elsewhere in Poland. From 1920 onwards, the government pursued a policy of granting Polish veterans land holdings

---

303 *Encyclopedia of Ukraine*, s.v. "nationalism."

in the "eastern borderlands" (*kresy*). The idea was to reward the men who had fought for Poland, all the while establishing a forepost for the Polonization of territories largely inhabited by Ukrainians. The government's grandiose plans, however, required more resources than it had at its disposal. In the mid-1930s there were under six thousand of these colonists in the mainly Ukrainian palatinates of Volhynia and Polissia; altogether, colonists and their families made up only about 0.5 percent of the population of the *kresy*. But at the same time, rural overpopulation and land hunger were acute: in Galicia well over half of peasant holdings measured less than two hectares. A Polish expert on the colonization program, Janina Stobniak-Smogorzewska, wrote:

> The cardinal sin was the neglect of the interests of the local population in the division of the land....Giving the land to soldiers coming from other parts of Poland, without at the same time improving the economic situation of the local peasantry, provided trump cards to Ukrainian and Belarusian politicians in their anti-Polish endeavors throughout the existence of the Second Polish Republic. This situation contributed to the creation of the stereotype of the military colonization as aimed against the national aspirations of the non-Polish population there.[304]

Restrictions on Ukrainian church life were also galling, particularly the massive destruction and expropriation by Roman Catholics of hundreds of Ukrainian Orthodox churches in the Chełm region, Polissia, and Volhynia. The various assimilationist and repressive measures of the Polish state against its Ukrainian minority were not effective in reducing Ukrainian resistance to Polish rule; they simply increased Ukrainian contumacy and contributed to an atmosphere that fostered nationalist extremism. As Machiavelli pointed out: "Men must either be caressed or else annihilated; they will revenge themselves for small injuries, but cannot do so for great ones; the injury therefore that we do to a man must be such that we need not fear his vengeance."[305]

---

304 Stobniak-Smogorzewska, *Kresowe osadnictwo wojskowe*, 63, 103 (number of colonists).

305 This account of Poland's Ukrainian policy is based on Himka, "Western Ukraine between the Wars." For a more granular description of how this

If Poland did the Ukrainians small injuries, then great injuries were inflicted by the Soviet Union in the 1930s. But before then, in the 1920s *sovietofil'stvo* (Sovietophilism) was rampant among the disgruntled Ukrainian intelligentsia in Galicia. In the mid-late 1920s Soviet Ukraine was undergoing a state-sponsored Ukrainization. Cultural life was vibrant: Ukrainian literature, theater, and visual arts were exciting and innovative; many periodicals, books, and films were produced in the Ukrainian language; civil servants took courses in Ukrainian so that the administration could function in that language; ethnic Ukrainians played major roles in state and party leadership; a Ukrainian-language educational system, encompassing all levels, was built from scratch. Many Galician Ukrainian intellectuals looked at Soviet Ukraine as a land of opportunity, a place where they could find dignified employment and at the same time serve the development of the Ukrainian nation. Too many of them made the fatal mistake of emigrating to Soviet Ukraine.[306] In addition to cultural Sovietophilism, communism as such was also a force in political life. In Galicia, the Communist Party of Western Ukraine (KPZU), which could boast some brilliant and dedicated leaders in the 1920s, called for the union of Galicia and Volhynia with the Ukrainian Soviet Socialist Republic. Until the late 1920s, the party was very much a western Ukrainian variant of the national communism that existed in Soviet Ukraine. But by 1928 the policies of Ukrainization in the Ukrainian SSR began to be reversed, and in the following year the leaders of the KPZU were expelled from the Comintern. The KPZU continued to exist, but without Ukrainian leadership, until it was dissolved by Stalin, along with the entire Polish communist party, in 1938. The communists had a front organization, Sel-Rob, that retained adherents among the economically distressed Ukrainian peasantry, but by the 1930s it had grown very weak in Galicia, while remaining strong in Volhynia. An indication of the relative strength of communism as a mass movement in those two territories is given by an analysis of

---

discrimination looked at the local level (Buchach and environs), see Bartov, *Anatomy of a Genocide*, 117-20.
306 Gilley, "Reconciling the Irreconcilable," 348-51.

the last largely free Polish election, that of 1928: communist front parties received 13 percent of the vote in Galicia and 48 percent in Volhynia.[307] Many Western Ukrainian intellectuals who had been Sovietophiles or even communists later moved to the nationalist camp, including the writer and painter Sviatoslav Hordynsky; the writer Yurii Kosach, who continued to move back and forth later in life; the anthropologist and later racial theorist Rostyslav Yendyk; and the KPZU and Sel-Rob activist Mykhailo Stepaniak, who later advanced to the top leadership of OUN.

What happened in the 1930s in Soviet Ukraine was a bloodbath. Those Galicians who moved there to build a brighter future for themselves and for their nation were arrested and executed.[308] Major figures of the Soviet Ukrainian cultural renaissance, the party leader Mykola Skrypnyk and the celebrated writer Mykola Khvyliovy, committed suicide in 1933 in protest of Stalin's policies. Most of the rest of the Soviet Ukrainian cultural and political elite of the 1920s was exiled to the gulag, and many were shot during the great terror of 1937. A manmade famine, a direct result of central Soviet policy, killed four million people in Ukraine in 1932-33. Shortages of goods in 1930s Soviet Ukraine made impoverished Galicia and Volhynia look rich by comparison. Stalin had done great injuries to the Ukrainians who found themselves under his rule in the 1930s. One byproduct of this was an explosion of anticommunist sentiment among Ukrainians everywhere else, particularly in Galicia.

Stalinism essentially closed off the far-left option in Western Ukrainian politics. At the same time, the popularity of even liberalism and democracy was declining. The democratic countries of Europe and the United States were precisely the powers that had established the status quo that left Ukrainians stateless and at the mercy of the Polish authorities. (In 1923 the Conference of Ambassadors of the victorious powers awarded Eastern Galicia to Poland.) This undermined the Western Ukrainians' respect for democratic

---

307   Radziejowski, *The Communist Party of Western Ukraine*. Solchanyk, "The Communist Party of Western Ukraine."
308   Vividly described in Bertelsen and Shkandrij, "The Secret Police."

governance and liberal values. Moreover, there was a general trend towards authoritarianism in the 1930s across the continent, from Spain and Portugal, to Germany and Austria, to Italy, Stalinist Russia, and all East Central European states with the exception of Czechoslovakia.[309] Poland too participated in this authoritarian trend, which seemed to be the wave of the future. The great depression of the 1930s also made moderate progress within the limits of the law seem less attractive than radical political solutions. The loss of faith in communism and democracy worked in favor of nationalist recruitment in the dirty thirties.

In my own lifetime, I have lived through what I think of as political waves that engulf large populations, and especially youth. When I was a young man in the late 1960s and early 1970s, leftism was all the rage, and I was certainly affected. Then in the late 1980s and 1990s, as communism collapsed in Europe and apartheid disappeared in South Africa, faith in the unstoppable progress of democracy and human rights gripped much of Western society. Since the Iranian revolution of 1979 and the Soviet invasion of Afghanistan that same year, a wave of Islamism and jihadism has spread over the Middle East and other Muslim regions. At the time I am writing, a wave of right-wing populism has captured hearts and voters across the globe, from the United States to the United Kingdom to France to Brazil to the Philippines. I bring all this up because, given the outcome of the Second World War, it is often difficult for postwar generations to imagine how popular fascism actually was in Europe in the 1930s. Fascism was one of those political waves that washed over large territories and populations, just like leftism, unblinking faith in democratic progress, jihadism, and populism in more recent decades. The attractiveness of fascism and related ideologies in the 1930s is demonstrated by its widespread influence on European youth of the time, not just in Italy and Germany, but in Austria, Portugal, Spain, Romania, Czechoslovakia, and Yugoslavia. It would have been extraordinary had Ukrainian youth in Poland and Romania remained immune.

---

309 Czechoslovakia might perhaps be better classified as a partial exception since the two largest political parties were the communists and the Nazis.

The attraction of Ukrainian radicals to fascistic ideologies became more compelling when Hitler and the national socialists came to power in Germany in 1933. Ukrainian nationalists welcomed a leader who wanted to destroy the Versailles system and redivide Europe according to the ethnic principle: the annexation of Austria in 1938, i.e. the Anschluss, and of Czechoslovakia's Sudetenland later that year represented the unification of Germans in a single state. Moreover, Hitler was both anti-Soviet and anti-Polish; he was the enemy of the Ukrainian nationalists' enemies, and a powerful one. The orientation on Nazi Germany seemed to make geopolitical sense to radical Ukrainian nationalists, who preferred not to focus on Hitler's concept of *Lebensraum,* which had already been fully elaborated in his book *Mein Kampf* of 1925-26.

OUN: Historical Signposts

In this section my intention is to provide a chronological overview of the history of OUN before the German attack on the Soviet Union in June 1941, highlighting the major moments in its development, providing a temporal map for orientation.

A few words first about the movement's ideological origins. The first exponent of radical nationalism was the lawyer Mykola Mikhnovsky. An activist in student circles in Kyiv in the 1890s and then a lawyer in Kharkiv, he was one of the earliest explicit advocates of Ukrainian statehood. His brochure *Samostiina Ukraina* (Independent Ukraine) of 1900 was originally written as the program of the heterogeneous Revolutionary Ukrainian Party, but he went on to establish his own party, the Ukrainian People's Party (*Ukrains'ka narodnia partiia*) in 1902. Like other splinter groups from the Revolutionary Ukrainian Party, it positioned itself on the left as "a party of the working mass of the Ukrainian people, a party of the urban and rural proletariat." But unlike the other splinter groups, it held fast to the program of Ukrainian statehood and considered its task to include raising the national as well as the social consciousness of workers and peasants.[310] Perhaps the document of

---

310   Mirchuk, *Mykola Mikhnovs'kyi*, 33.

Mikhnovsky and his party that most influenced the nationalism of OUN was the 1903 "Ten Commandments" or "Code of Honor of a Conscious Ukrainian." As we have mentioned above,[311] the same ten-commandment structure was to be adopted just over a quarter of a century later by OUN ideologue Lenkavsky. Mikhnovsky's first commandment was: "One, Unified, Indivisible, Independent, Free, Democratic Ukraine, a Republic of working people—this is the ideal of the Ukrainian person, for the realization of which you must struggle, not sparing your own life." Other commandments concerned creating a Ukraine for Ukrainians, using the Ukrainian language at all times and places, honoring Ukrainian activists and despising renegades, supporting fellow Ukrainians, and eschewing non-Ukrainian wives (otherwise "your children will be your enemies") and anti-Ukrainian friends.[312] Mikhnovsky still used the language and phraseology of the socialistically inclined and democratic Ukrainian movement of the early twentieth century, but the content also contained a new message of national exclusivity and enmity.

A more proximate influence on the thinking of OUN was Dmytro Dontsov, an émigré from what was once Russian Ukraine who settled in Lviv in the early 1920s.[313] Before World War I Dontsov had been a Marxist, but after the war and revolutions he espoused an extreme form of nationalism. He published a book entitled *Natsionalizm* in 1926 which laid out many of his ideas. More important than his book was his work as an essayist and editor. In 1922 he assumed editorship of the most prestigious Galician cultural journal, *Literaturno-naukovyi vistnyk* (renamed *Vistnyk* in 1933). His numerous essays on literature and politics — flashy, emotional, provocative—attracted the youth, and a whole school of nationalist poets gathered around him. As Lev Shankovsky remarked, Dontsov "was the unofficial bible" of the 1930s.[314] In his articles, Dontsov demolished the enlightenment idols of reason,

---

311 See 122.
312 Mirchuk, *Mykola Mikhnovs'kyi*, 46.
313 On Dontsov, see Erlacher, "The Furies of Nationalism"; and Zaitsev, *Ukrains'kyi integral'nyi natsionalizm*, 157-237.
314 Shankovs'kyi, *Pokhidni hrupy*, 36.

brotherhood, and tolerance. He championed amorality, might, the aggressive warrior spirit. He reversed many of the old values, championing conflict over peace, hatred over love, hierarchy over equality, and will over logic. He despised weakness and passivity. He became a great admirer of Hitler and Mussolini and published both of their biographies. In his preface to the Hitler biography (written by Yendyk), Dontsov praised Hitlerism in the first place for its anticommunism and anti-Marxism but also for its antisemitism.[315] He believed in the regeneration or palingenesis of the Ukrainian nation in a new postliberal society based on the rule of strong races and nations.[316] Dontsov never himself became a member of OUN, but his thinking inspired many young people, particularly in Galicia.

We might think of three primary populations from which OUN was to be recruited. One was participants of the failed national revolution scattered across Europe: future leaders of OUN included Konovalets in Czechoslovakia, Italy, and Switzerland; Yevhen Onatsky in Rome; Mykola Stsiborsky in Prague and Paris; Dmytro Andriievsky in Belgium; Mykhailo Seleshko in Berlin. A second was Galician POWs interned in camps in Poland and Czechoslovakia after the defeat of Ukrainian forces. These camps became hothouses for the growth of radical nationalism, and after their release the internees brought their ideas back home with them to Galicia.

The third population was students. Because of restrictions, many young Ukrainians studied abroad, particularly in Czechoslovakia, but there was still a critical mass of higher-education students in Galicia. In the early 1930s, about 1500 Ukrainians were enrolled in higher education programs in Lviv (out of over 11,000 students in total).[317] The future leaders of OUN-B had been too young to participate in the struggle for national independence in 1917-20 but they shared an educational background at Jan Kazimierz

---

315 Zaitsev, *Ukrains'kyi integral'nyi natsionalizm*, 196. On Dontsov's antisemitism, see Kurylo, "The 'Jewish Question,'" 243-53.

316 Zaitsev, *Ukrains'kyi integral'nyi natsionalizm*, 206.

317 More detailed figures can be found in Zaitsev, *Natsionalizm i relihiia*, 112-13; this portion of the collective monograph was written by Oleh Behen.

University in Lviv or at other institutions of higher education in Galicia: Stepan Bandera, Yaroslav Stetsko, Roman Shukhevych, Stepan Lenkavsky, Ivan Klymiv, Yaroslav Starukh, Borys Lewytzkyj (Levytsky),[318] and Ivan Mitrynga (OUN-B historian Petro Mirchuk was also a student at the university in Lviv). In fact, one of the major organizational progenitors of OUN was the Union of Ukrainian Nationalist Youth, founded in 1926 and headquartered in the Ukrainian university student dormitory in Lviv.[319] Nationalists also recruited in the gymnasia and other institutions of secondary education in Galicia. Veterans returning from incarceration in POW camps sometimes enrolled in the gymnasia themselves to complete their interrupted education, inspiring in their younger classmates a passion to fight to the death for a Ukrainian state.[320] The younger students were organized in OUN's Youth (*Iunatstvo*), the organization for fifteen- to twenty-one-year olds. In 1929-30, this was the most developed membership structure in OUN, and by 1931, when OUN held it first homeland conference, there were only a few schools in Galicia with which the nationalists lacked contacts.[321]

The most direct forerunner of OUN was the Ukrainian Military Organization (UVO), founded by veterans in 1920 with the purpose of continuing the struggle for independence. There was a direct continuity between the leadership of UVO and of OUN. For most of its existence, UVO was headed by Konovalets, who was also to head OUN in 1929-38. His successor as leader of OUN was Melnyk, who had headed UVO in the homeland in 1922-24 (Konovalets was then in emigration). Subsequent homeland commanders of UVO were also to become prominent in the leadership of the united OUN and of the Melnyk faction: Sushko and Omelian

---

318 After the war Lewytzkyj moved to the left and became a prominent analyst of Soviet affairs in Germany; he used the transliteration Lewytzkyj for his writings in German and English.

319 Motyl, *Turn to the Right*, 140.

320 Golczewski, *Deutsche und Ukrainer*, 434 (point about veterans enrolling in gymnasia).

321 Skakun, *"Patsyfikatsiia,"* 24.

Senyk. Like OUN later on, UVO engaged in terrorist activities:[322] robbing post offices, burning Polish estates, and assassinating Polish civil servants and policemen as well as Ukrainians who co-operated with the Polish authorities. More notorious UVO actions included an attempt to kill Piłsudski in 1921; the successful murder in the following year of the Ukrainian editor and politician Sydir Tverdokhlib, who violated the UVO-enforced boycott of the 1922 Polish elections; the attempted execution of the Polish president Stanisław Wojciechowski in 1924; and the successful murder of the Lviv school inspector Jan Sobiński, in which future UPA commander Shukhevych, then nineteen years old, took part. UVO received support from Germany and Lithuania, both of which had territorial disputes with Poland. They supplied UVO with funding, some weapons, a place to print the organization's journal *Surma*, and military training. Among UVO members trained in Germany were Yevhen Vretsiona, who was to play a major role in the OUN militia in 1941, and Shukhevych.[323] UVO, as OUN later, also spied on behalf of its foreign benefactors.

OUN was founded at a congress held in Vienna over 28 January–3 February 1929 at which various nationalist groups as well as UVO were represented. Essentially, OUN was to adopt the practices of UVO and the doctrines of the nationalist organizations. Its first programmatic documents offered a vision of the future Ukrainian state that the nationalists wanted to achieve. Politically, the fledgling OUN envisioned the establishment of a dictatorship until the Ukrainian state got on its feet, and then some kind of representative government with a strong executive. Economically, the state would have a mixed economy, basically capitalism with some state monopolies. There would be a radical land reform, expropriating landlords without compensation. Landholding would be private, but commerce would exist in various forms: state, cooperative, and private. Socially, workers would have the right to strike

---

322   In using the term "terror" in reference to the activities of OUN and UPA I have in mind the technical meaning of violence and property destruction perpetrated by non-state actors.

323   Golczewski, *Deutsche und Ukrainer*, 450 (training of Vretsiona and Shukhevych).

and would enjoy an eight-hour day, with the perspective of further reduction. The state would provide unemployment insurance as well as social security for all citizens over sixty. In spite of relatively progressive social intentions, this could not be considered a liberal program, since it foresaw control of society in the hands of OUN and then of the new state it created. This early program never explicitly mentioned the place of national minorities in the envisioned state. There was no mention of Poles or Jews or of struggle against hostile nations, as opposed to hostile states. But the program was clearly written from the perspective of the dominance of the Ukrainian nation over all Ukrainian ethnic territory.[324]

The first major operation of OUN was the "sabotage action" of summer and early fall 1930. This was an initiative from the lower structures of OUN in Galicia, students on summer vacation, and it was not undertaken in understanding with the leadership of OUN, either in emigration or in the homeland. The leadership had been unsure whether OUN should maintain a legal presence, like the traditional Ukrainian political parties, or exist underground as a terrorist movement on the order of UVO. The youth's sabotage action decided the issue in favor of the latter. They burned down farm buildings and stacks of hay and grain belonging mainly to Polish manors; the government recorded 155 incidents of political arson in the three Galician palatinates of Lviv, Stanyslaviv (P Stanisławów; now Ivano-Frankivsk), and Ternopil (P Tarnopol).[325] The OUN youth also cut telegraph and telephone wires. There seems to have been a minimum of central planning, but the sabotage action spread through Galicia like wildfire. While the main thrust of these actions was anti-Polish, it is important to note for our study that the sabotage action was also directed against Jews. A circular found by the Polish authorities contained an order to the nationalist youth "to destroy the buildings of Jews, Poles, and Polish colonists."[326] In the

324 Mirchuk, *Narys*, 93-99.
325 Skakun, "*Patsyfikatsiia*," 39.
326 Ibid., 26.

period from August through October 1930, 131 Poles suffered from the sabotage action, but also 5 Ukrainians and 18 Jews.[327]

The Polish state responded with massive repression, known to historians as "the pacification of 1930." The government sent punitive expeditions into the Ukrainian countryside. Peasants were forced to quarter the troops sent to punish them. Polish soldiers beat and lashed Ukrainian activists, not just nationalists. They requisitioned property. In addition to hundreds of arrests on the local level, about twenty OUN and UVO leaders were arrested. Ukrainian community property, such as halls and libraries, were destroyed. The repressions did not selectively target nationalists but were aimed at the Ukrainian movement as a whole. While the beating and arrest of activists and the destruction of community infrastructure constituted a serious setback for the Ukrainian inhabitants of Galicia, the more important long-term result of the pacification was an even more profound alienation from the Polish state and all things Polish. This, of course, was to boost the attractiveness of the nationalists.

OUN engaged in terror throughout the 1930s. The nationalists undertook "expropriations," or *eksy* in the parlance of OUN militants, which frequently took the form of robbing post offices. They also attacked police stations. But their most effective propaganda of the deed was a series of sensational assassinations that brought OUN squarely into the public spotlight. In August 1931 they killed a prominent Polish politician, a member of the Sejm, Tadeusz Hołówko. Hołówko was a proponent of Ukrainian-Polish reconciliation and worked with members of the Ukrainian People's Republic in exile in Warsaw (the Promethean movement). OUN killed him because it felt that his influence could weaken the resolve of Ukrainians to overthrow Polish rule and establish their own state. In October 1933, Mykola Lemyk, a law student at Jan Kazimierz University who had joined the OUN Youth, murdered a Soviet consular official, Aleksei Mailov; he had intended to kill the consul himself, but mistook Mailov for the consul. The murder was in retaliation for the mass manmade famine of 1932-33 in Soviet

---

327 Ibid., 39.

Ukraine. This assassination and those subsequent were ordered and organized by the OUN homeland leadership, in which Bandera, Shukhevych, and Mykola Lebed played major roles. In June 1934 OUN killed the Polish minister of the interior, Bronisław Pieracki, and in the following month, the Ukrainian pedagogue Ivan Babii, the rector of the Lviv Academic Gymnasium who opposed OUN's influence among students.[328]

The assassination of Pieracki provoked Polish security organs to launch a major offensive against OUN. In June 1934 they arrested eight hundred suspected members of the organization.[329] The homeland leadership was devastated. Bandera and Lebed were condemned to death, a sentence commuted to life imprisonment; Shukhevych was sentenced to two years imprisonment. The repressions were a setback for OUN. Filling the vacuum in the leadership naturally produced tensions among the OUN activists at liberty. The new leadership steered OUN onto a somewhat different path. Spectacular assassinations gave way to a focus on organizational consolidation, the ideological formation and education of the membership, the expansion of underground periodicals, and the development of a legal press controlled by OUN.[330] OUN was able to restore its structures and to expand. The behavior of the defendants at their trials in Warsaw and Lviv in 1935 and 1936 elevated the OUN leaders, particularly Bandera, to the status of symbols of the national struggle and models for Ukrainian youth. The members of OUN in Western Ukraine developed "the typical elite consciousness of underground fighters."[331] Or, in the words of Kost Pankivsky, who knew the nationalists personally and well, "on the peaceful Galician soil was born in the ranks of OUN a new type of professional revolutionary, blindly obedient to the leadership, with dedication unto death, with a singular faith in the nation and the revolution, whose motto was: 'The nation above all!'"[332]

---

328 On the assassinations of Pieracki and Babii and the trials of the OUN perpetrators, see the well researched account in Rossoliński-Liebe, *Stepan Bandera*, 117-66.
329 Wysocki, *Organizacja*, 299.
330 Ibid., 308.
331 Plum, Report, 8.
332 Pan'kivs'kyi, *Roky nimets'koi okupatsii*, 138.

In the mid-1930s OUN also began to expand more beyond Ga-licia and into Volhynia. Volhynia had been a hotbed of communist activism in the 1920s, but the nationalists were winning more and more recruits among the youth. Altogether, according to a Polish scholar working with Polish military and security records, there were about 4500-5000 OUN members on the territory of Poland in 1935, about a fifth of them in Volhynia.[333] Ivan Patryliak, a specialist in the history of OUN, has estimated the strength of the organiza-tion to have been about eight or nine thousand members in 1939, up to twelve thousand if one were to include the most active sym-pathizers. But the total number of members and sympathizers, in his opinion, may have exceeded forty thousand.[334] OUN veteran Stefan Petelycky wrote about the strength of OUN in villages near Zolochiv in the late 1930s: "Most of the seventy Ukrainian families in the immediate area were sympathetic to the OUN.... Some Ukrainians did not want to get involved in our politics, of course, but I would estimate that no less than 75 per cent of the local com-munity supported us."[335]

The next major, and fateful, event in the history of the OUN was the assassination of its leader, Konovalets, in Rotterdam on 23 May 1938. This was to lead over the next two years to a battle for the overall OUN leadership between the homeland and the emigra-tion, between the youth and their elders. Tensions between the two centers of OUN and between generations had existed from the start, but Konovalets had the right skills and credentials to keep the or-ganization together. Whether he would have been able to maintain the unity of OUN in the longer term is uncertain, since the home-land leaders were developing their own charisma and authority. Konovalets's old comrade, Melnyk, stepped in as successor. For the while, his position was secure, since the most prestigious and expe-rienced homeland leaders were in prison and the new leadership was concentrating on infrastructural work that did not challenge the authority of the emigration.

---

333 Wysocki, *Organizacja*, 332-36.
334 Patryliak, *Viis'kova diial'nist OUN (B)*, 136 n.
335 Petelycky, *Into Auschwitz*, 4.

The year 1938 was also important in OUN history because of the emergence of Carpatho-Ukraine. This was the year that Hitler concentrated on the unification of ethnic Germans into a single Reich. In March 1938 he annexed Austria and in early autumn turned his attention to the Germans of Bohemia, the so-called Sudetenland Germans. Incorporating the latter into the Reich led to the restructuring of the Czechoslovak state. In October 1938, the western territories of Czechoslovakia, containing a large ethnic German population, were incorporated into Germany. At the same time, Czechoslovakia was reinvented as the hyphenated Czecho-Slovakia, composed of three territories: Bohemia and Moravia; autonomous Slovakia; and autonomous Subcarpathian Ruthenia, which was soon to call itself Carpatho-Ukraine. This territory in eastern Czecho-Slovakia was inhabited by Greek Catholics who spoke eastern Slavic dialects closely related to western Ukrainian dialects. However, they had adopted a Ukrainian identity only very late and never completely. Some of them regarded themselves as Rusyn-speaking Hungarians, others as a separate nationality of Rusyns, and still others as the westernmost branch of the Russian nation.[336] But the Ukrainophiles under the political leadership of the priest Avhustyn Voloshyn were able to assume power by the end of October.

The formation of Carpatho-Ukraine as a result of Hitler's revisionist policies electrified OUN. In November the Voloshyn government established the Carpathian Sich to defend its territory against Polish and Hungarian raids. At its height, the Carpathian Sich numbered about six thousand soldiers. About two thousand of these were Ukrainian volunteers from Galicia, mainly members of OUN. Leaders of OUN from Galicia also assumed leadership positions in the Sich: Mykhailo Kolodzinsky, who was to die in the struggle for an independent Carpatho-Ukraine, was chief of the general staff; Vretsiona was in charge of security; and Shukhevych was entrusted with important responsibilities in the general staff (recruitment, finances, and communications).

---

336 The best account of identity issues in this region is Magocsi, *With Their Backs to the Mountains*.

However, Carpatho-Ukraine did not last long. On 15 March 1939 Hitler invaded Bohemia and Moravia; on the previous day Slovakia had proclaimed its independence. The diet of Carpatho-Ukraine declared independence as well on 14 March and confirmed the declaration on the following day. But, with Hitler's permission, Hungary annexed Carpatho-Ukraine. Forty thousand Hungarian troops invaded on 15 March and subdued the vastly outnumbered Carpathian Sich. According to Mirchuk, five thousand members of Carpathian Sich, mostly locals from the region, perished in the struggle against the Hungarians.[337]

OUN's ideological fervor on the eve of the outbreak of World War II was palpable from the proceedings and resolutions of the Second Great Assembly of OUN, which was held on 27 August 1939 in Rome. The organization had been in existence for ten years, and this congress constituted the first major revision of its program. Unlike the initial congress at which OUN was founded, there was no discussion at the 1939 Assembly. The entire plenary session lasted only three hours. All it did was approve documents prepared in advance by an OUN committee consisting of Stsiborsky, who had become a leading ideologue of OUN, particularly after the publication of his treatise *Natsiokratiia* in 1935; Orest Chemerynsky; Senyk; and Stetsko. These documents were a "political program"[338] and an outline of the "structure" of OUN.[339] Striking elements of the program were a full-fledged corporatist view of society, which reflected Stsiborsky's influence, and the formulation of the leader principle.

The political program stated that the future Ukrainian state would be based on the principles of "natiocracy" (*natsiokratsiia*), which it defined as "the authority of the nation in the state, which is based on the organized and solidaristic cooperation of all socially

---

337 Mirchuk, *Narys*, 559.
338 "Politychna prohrama," in Provid ukrains'kykh natsionalistiv, *Politychna prohrama i ustrii*, 23-51; also in Hunczak and Solchanyk, *Ukrains'ka suspil'no-politychna dumka*, 2:399-410.
339 "Ustrii," in Provid ukrains'kykh natsionalistiv, *Politychna prohrama i ustrii*, 54-64; also in Hunczak and Solchanyk, *Ukrains'ka suspil'no-politychna dumka*, 411-16, and Mirchuk, *Narys*, 577-81.

useful strata, united — according to their social functions — in representative organs of state direction."[340] In line with this corporatist system, strikes and lockouts were to be prohibited in the future Ukraine, since they were "incompatible with the concept of a natiocratic state and contradictory to the principles of social solidarity."[341] In the name of the "solidaristic cooperation of all social-productive strata," the program explicitly rejected both capitalism and Marxism.[342]

The 1939 Assembly introduced a new term to OUN's political vocabulary: *vozhd'*, i.e. leader, by analogy to the Italian *duce*, German *Führer*, and Russian *Vozhd'*. During the war of liberation for a Ukrainian state, there was to be "a dictatorship of the Leader of the Nation." Then once the state was achieved, the Leader of the Nation would be head of state, "summoned [to this position] by the organized will of the nation."[343] The Leader of the Nation was also to be the commander-in-chief of Ukraine's armed forces.[344] "The head of the Leadership of the Ukrainian Nationalists (PUN) — as the helmsman and representative of the liberation efforts of the Ukrainian Nation — is its Leader."[345] The Rome Assembly confirmed that Melnyk was this Leader.

There were a number of other points in the new program that pointed to alignment with the rightward drift in Europe. "The existence of political parties will be prohibited by law. The only form of political organization for the population of the State will be OUN...."[346] Militarism was to be embraced.[347] There would be state control of cultural production. The state would plan the distribution of cultural goods; private production of the same would be controlled by the state. The state would control "all forms of publishing activity, especially the press...."[348] The program also

---

340 Provid ukrains'kykh natsionalistiv, *Politychna prohrama i ustrii*, 28.
341 Ibid., 38.
342 Ibid., 40.
343 Ibid., 29.
344 Ibid., 32.
345 Ibid., 55.
346 Ibid., 29.
347 Ibid., 31.
348 Ibid., 34-35.

contained a nod to the eugenic concerns so popular in that era: "The state will take measures to increase the population; it will prohibit matrimonial relations to those ill with certain diseases...."[349]

Of special relevance to the subject of our study is the position taken by the 1939 Assembly on the question of national minorities within the future Ukrainian state, an issue that the program of 1929 had omitted entirely. The 1939 program promised to take a differential approach to non-Ukrainians based on "their attitude towards the liberation efforts of Ukraine and its statehood."[350] Non-Ukrainians were to be prohibited from "material participation," i.e. ownership or investment, in publishing.[351] Commercial enterprises owned by "non-Ukrainians [chuzhyntsi] disloyal to the Ukrainian State will be confiscated without compensation." Non-Ukrainians would only be allowed to engage in commercial activities by special licenses issued by the government.[352] A similar spirit infused the nationalists' policy on minority religious groups. The 1939 program promised "freedom of conscience," but only "in so far as it does not go against the welfare and morality of the Ukrainian Nation." The state would favor the development of "both Ukrainian churches: Orthodox and Greek Catholic" and ban the propagation of atheism and "those religious cults that manifest antinational and immoral tendencies."[353]

Just a few days after the Rome Assembly, on 1 September 1939, Germany invaded Poland, thus launching World War II. On 17 September the USSR invaded eastern Poland (Western Ukraine and Western Belarus) and in June 1940 forced Romania to cede northern Bukovina. Thus Galicia, Volhynia, and Bukovina were to remain part of the Ukrainian Soviet Socialist Republic until the German and Romanian invasion of the USSR on 22 June 1941 began to push them out. With the destruction of Poland and incorporation of Western Ukraine into the Ukrainian SSR, OUN could concentrate

---

349 Ibid., 39.
350 Ibid., 30.
351 Ibid., 35.
352 Ibid., 49.
353 Ibid., 35.

its efforts on a single front, against what it considered its primary enemy, the Soviet Union.

Another consequence of the outbreak of war was the release of the OUN homeland leadership that had been arrested in 1934. Some of the leaders had already been at liberty, namely Stetsko and Shukhevych, but Bandera, Lebed, and others were released or allowed to escape as the Germans closed in.[354] The liberation of the young Galician leaders from Polish prisons was the "catalytic element"[355] that led to a split in OUN in early 1940 between the older, émigré and the younger, homeland nationalists.[356] The released leaders gathered in Kraków, in the German zone of occupied Poland, where several thousand other OUN members had transferred their activities after the Red Army occupied Galicia. In January the Galicians began to formally challenge Melnyk and the existing OUN leadership, and on 10 February 1940 they formed a new, "revolutionary" leadership headed by Bandera. Thereafter, OUN was divided into two factions: the Banderites or OUN-B and the Melnykites or OUN-M. The Ukrainian historian Ivan Patryliak has aptly encapsulated the "psychological" dimensions behind the split: "The majority of the people who for decades had lived in peaceful, secure, and comfortable conditions, 'overgrown' with families and material prosperity, did not understand the desperadoes who called to go under the bullets, who were not afraid to end up in prisons and camps."[357] The followers of Bandera and those of Melnyk did not much differ in ideology, but their primary bases of support were geographically distinct. The Bandera group was strongest in Galicia and Volhynia; the Melnyk group was strongest in emigation, particularly in the Reich and the Protectorate of Bohemia and Moravia, as well as in Bukovina. Here we will briefly look at the Bandera group's development in emigration, in Kraków. An

---

354 "The Polish police opened the doors of all prisons, concentration camps, with the result that dozens of leading activists of OUN were set free." Ishchuk and Ohorodnik, *Heneral Mykola Arsenych*, 52. This action stands in stark contrast to what the Soviets did when the Germans invaded in June 1941 — they murdered thousands of prisoners. See below, 194-97.

355 Armstrong, *Ukrainian Nationalism*, 36.

356 A classic account of the generational rift is Rud'ko, *Rozlam v OUN*.

357 Patryliak, *Viis'kova diial'nist OUN (B)*, 142.

account of OUN members who remained behind in Galicia and Volhynia under the Soviets will be offered in the next chapter.

The Banderites held their own Second Great Assembly of OUN in Kraków in early April 1941.[358] Its programmatic documents differed considerably from those produced at the Rome Assembly of 1939. They entirely repudiated the validity of the latter Assembly as well as Melnyk's leadership, whom they expelled from OUN altogether.[359] Corporatism was only briefly mentioned.[360] The resolutions referred to the late Konovalets as Leader (*Vozhd'*) but, unlike the 1939 program, did not have anything to say about the role of the Leader in OUN; however, supplementary documents of the 1941 Assembly did refer to a Leader, now called *Providnyk* in Ukrainian.[361] (The new Leader was, of course, Bandera.) The 1941 resolutions were less concerned with outlining the future state and more concerned with military issues and propaganda. Noteworthy in the 1941 resolutions was a declaration that was to guide the Banderites during and long after World War II: "OUN fights for the freedom of all nations enslaved by Moscow and for their right to their own state life."[362] Certain aspects of the 1941 resolutions will be discussed below, in the sections on OUN and fascism[363] and on OUN and Jews.[364] Soon after the Kraków Assembly of 1941, Bandera, Lenkavsky, Shukhevych, and Stetsko began to work on a detailed plan of action entitled "The Struggle and Activities of OUN in Wartime,"[365] which will also be discussed

---

358   The text of the resolutions of the 1941 Assembly has been bowdlerized in *OUN v svitli postanov*, 24-47, and in other source collections that derive from it, such as Hunczak and Solchanyk, *Ukrains'ka suspil'no-politychna dumka*, 3:7-22, and Veselova, *OUN v 1941 rotsi*, 35-50. I rely on a publication from 1941 that is available on line: *Postanovy II. Velykoho zboru*.

359   Ibid., 6, 24-26.

360   Ibid., 7.

361   Ibid., 27, 29.

362   Ibid., 9; see also 21.

363   See below, 145.

364   See below, 169-70.

365   Carynnyk, "Foes of Our Rebirth," 329. The text of this document, "Borot'ba i diial'nist' OUN pid chas viiny," has been repeatedly republished since the opening of the Soviet archives: Patryliak, *Viis'kova diial'nist OUN (B)*, 426-596; Dziuban, *Ukrains'ke derzhavotvorennia*, 15-56; Veselova, *OUN v 1941 rotsi*, 58-176

below in connection with OUN and antisemitism and in chapter 5 in connection with the formation of the Ukrainian National Militia.[366]

Were They Fascists?

The question of whether OUN was fascist has exercised a number of scholars, particularly since the rehabilitation of the nationalists in independent Ukraine.[367] OUN certainly looked fascist. At the trials of the OUN leaders in 1935-36, OUN defendants and witnesses shocked the courtroom by giving what a Polish newspaper called "the Hitlerite greeting."[368] This was a salute typical of the fascist movements of the time. Although widespread earlier in OUN, the form of the salute was defined for the first time in a programmatic document at the Banderite Assembly of 1941: "The organizational greeting has the form of raising the extended right arm to the right, higher than the crown of the head. The mandatory words of the full greeting: 'Glory to Ukraine!' with the answer 'Glory to the heroes.'"[369] The same document stipulated that the (Banderite) OUN was to have its own flag, in red and black,[370] which alluded to the German nationalist and national socialist concept of blood and soil

---

366 See below, 163, 165, 170, 219-21, 224-26.

367 Golczewski, *Deutsche und Ukrainer*, 571-92 ("Die Faschismus-Frage"). Gomza, "Elusive Proteus." Himka, "The Importance of the Situational Element." Kurylo, "Shche raz pro OUN ta faszyzm." Motyl, *Turn to the Right*, 163-69. Rossoliński-Liebe, *Fascist Kernel*. Rossoliński-Liebe, *Stepan Bandera*, passim. Statiev, "The Organization of Ukrainian Nationalists." Zaitsev, "Chy isnuvav ukrains'kyi natsional'no-vyzvol'nyi faszhyzm?" Zaitsev, "Fascism or Ustashism?" Zaitsev, "OUN i avtorytarno-natsionalistychni rukhy." Zaitsev, "OUN i fashyzm."

368 Rossoliński-Liebe, *Stepan Bandera*, 139-40, 152; for the term "Hitlerite greeting," see 152 nn. 189-90.

369 *Postanovy II. Velykoho zboru*, 23. This passage was expurgated from the resolutions as published in *OUN v svitli postanov*, 24-47, and in source collections derivative from it. The raising of the arm in the fascist style was prohibited after it became certain that Germany would lose the war. See, e.g., the order of the raion commandant of Kostopil raion of 1 September 1943; point 11 read: "To prohibit the outstretched arm when giving the salute, as was the case previously, but to give the salute to the cap as in the army, [if] without a cap, to stand at attention." DARO, fond R-30, op. 2, spr. 64, f. 40. I am grateful to Wiesław Tokarczuk for providing me with a photo of this document.

370 *Postanovy II. Velykoho zboru*, 23.

(*Blut und Boden*). Especially in the late 1930s, the vocabulary and ideology of the nationalists contained much that reflected the fascist zeitgeist, such as the authority of the Leader, the suppression of political parties, and the organization of society along corporatist lines.

OUN also aligned itself politically with the fascist great powers, Italy and Germany. For instance, OUN's legal newspaper for the peasantry, *Nove selo*, printed the following statement in April 1938: "Today we, the Ukrainians, **take pleasure in the victories of the nationalist states**, we take pleasure in the victories of Germany, Italy, and Japan. Every one of their successes we receive with great joy. But we are always aware...that **the total victory of nationalist states will only come about** *when the state ideal of the Ukrainian people is realized.*"[371] And on 2 May 1939 Melnyk, as Leader of OUN, assured German Foreign Minister Joachim von Ribbentrop that his organization was "related in world outlook to the same type of movements of Europe, in particular to National Socialism in Germany and fascism in Italy."[372] The fascist alignment was evident to Ukrainian observers outside OUN. In his memoirs of the German occupation, Kost Pankivsky, who himself collaborated with the Germans and took OUN to task for breaking with the Germans in the fall of 1941, identified the members of OUN as "people who for years had had contacts with the Germans, who were ideologically linked with fascism and Nazism, who in word and in print and in deed had for years been preaching totalitarianism and an orientation on Berlin and Rome."[373]

After World War II, OUN's own historians took pains to deny any connection with fascism. They doctored documents to eliminate overt expressions of that aspect of their past.[374] The Melnykite Polikarp Herasymenko devoted several pages of his short book on OUN in wartime to reproducing extracts critical of Italian fascism

---

371 "Povna peremoha natsionalistychnykh derzhav, ale koly?" *Nove selo* 9, no. 15 (416) (17 April 1938): 4. Bold and emphasis in the original.
372 Auswärtiges Amt, Politisches Archiv, AA, R 104430, Po. 26, No. 1m Pol. V. 4784, f. 2. This source was made available to me by Ray Brandon.
373 Pan'kivs'kyi, *Roky nimets'koi okupatsii*, 13.
374 See above, 70-71, 144.

and German national socialism from prewar OUN publications, omitting reference to the abundant OUN texts in praise of those political movements.[375] *Dviikar* Lev Shankovsky wrote: "Uncritical and politically illiterate people long considered, and perhaps someone even today considers, that Ukrainian nationalism is a movement identical with fascism or national socialism and that Ukrainian nationalists preached messianism, the superiority and chosenness of the Ukrainian people, the negation of all achievements of non-Ukrainian, especially Russian, culture, and a zoological intolerance toward national minorities. Of course, the absurdity of such ideas is not hard to prove. At the time Mikhnovsky created Ukrainian nationalism..., the creators of fascism and national socialism were still little children."[376] Of course, such distancing from past association with fascism was a result of the movement's defeat and disgrace in the world war.

Since the rehabilitation of OUN in Ukraine, pro-OUN forces in that country, in both politics and academia, have also endeavored to deny OUN's alignment with national socialism and fascism. As the Ukrainian political scientist Ivan Gomza has noted: "...fascist studies suffer from a memorial hindrance. Due to the trauma of World War II, fascism was branded as 'the Evil'; for this reason national communities (and, consequently, national scientific communities) aimed to prove that they had not been touched by the *mal du siècle*, or — in case of incriminating evidence — [that] there had been some extenuating circumstances."[377]

But what did the Ukrainian nationalists themselves think? Did they identify themselves as fascists? Some certainly did, but they were relatively marginal. There were two self-proclaimed fascists in the initial OUN leadership; they were gone by 1933 (although they had not been expelled for their fascist views).[378] For the most part, OUN thought of itself as a *sui generis* nationalist movement produced by the history and situation of the Ukrainian nation. It

---

375   Herasymenko, *Orhanizatsiia Ukrains'kykh Natsionalistiv*, 29-32.
376   Shankovs'kyi, *Pokhidni hrupy*, 20.
377   Gomza, "Elusive Proteus," 196.
378   Golczewski, *Deutsche und Ukrainer*, 571-73.

tended to think of Italian fascism and German national socialism not as sharing a common denominator as "fascist movements" but as individual manifestations of nationalism, produced by the specific circumstances and genii of the Italian and German nations.[379] Stsiborsky put it thus in his *Natsiokratiia* of 1935: "...Ukrainian nationalism, while recognizing the great historical service rendered by fascism and genuinely moving close to it in its ideological content, is at the same time a completely original movement and independent from anyone else. It orients itself only on the tasks of its own nation."[380] In his view, the future Ukrainian state would take into account the ideas and experience of fascism and national socialism, but it would be based on the aspirations of Ukrainian nationalism and would be, as he wrote, "neither fascist, nor national-socialist, nor 'primo-de-riverist.'"[381] The same idea was also expressed in an article in the OUN organ *Rozbudova natsii* in 1933: "...there is no universal doctrine of fascism, ...fascism is an exclusively Italian phenomenon, it is solely *a manifestation of Italian nationalism*, in Italian conditions, in conformity with the Italian national character and Italian historical tradition, it is the political movement of the Italian *state* nation (and not the *liberation* movement of an *enslaved* nation). Another manifestation of the active nationalism of a state people is the movement of the German 'Hakenkreuzlers,' which is absolutely distinct in its spirit from Italian fascism....One cannot equate both movements, and there is even less of a right and basis to call *every* active nationalism of various nations, and including even of *enslaved* nations, fascism." Our socialist opponents, he wrote, call us fascists, but we ourselves do not identify as such.[382]

---

379 E. Onats'kyi, "Ideol'ogichni i taktychni rozkhodzhennia mizh fashyzmom i natsional-sotsiializmom," *Rozbudova natsii* 7, no. 5-6 (76-77) (May-June 1934): 142-49. This article is also notable because of its criticism of national socialist racism, esp. 142-48.

380 Stsibors'kyi, *Natsiiokratiia*, 73.

381 Ibid., 65; by "primo-de-riverist" Stsiborsky was referring to the Falangist movement in Spain, founded by José Antonio Primo de Rivera.

382 "Ot khto ie ukrains'kymy fashystamy!" *Rozbudova natsii* 6, no. 1-2 (60-61) (January-February 1933): 53.

Based in Rome and greatly impressed with Mussolini and fascist theory and practice, Onatsky also considered fascism as something peculiarly Italian and distinct from Ukrainian nationalism. In an article that appeared in *Rozbudova natsii* a year before the founding of OUN, he made a point that was later to be picked up by some scholars (notably Alexander J. Motyl and Oleksandr Zaitsev): that the crucial differentiating point between fascism and Ukrainian nationalism was that Italian fascism was the movement of a nation with a state, while Ukrainian nationalism was the movement of a nation without one.

> Italian fascism always had its own state, which it was necessary only to support, renovate, lay new foundations, replace broken windows, paint the walls, and spruce up. Before young Ukrainian nationalism stands an entirely different task: it has to invent its state, facilitate its quickest and happiest possible birth, and support it with a firm hand when it begins to rise on its still feeble legs.
> The difference is one of tremendous, fundamental importance.
> Fascism is the nationalism of a state nation, which is inimical to any irredentas, which is ready to sacrifice absolutely anything for the cult of its already created state.
> Ukrainian nationalism is, on the contrary, the nationalism of a stateless nation, for which irredentism is its very life and which is ready to sacrifice absolutely anything in order to destroy the cult of those states which make its life impossible.[383]

To sum up the prevailing opinion among members of OUN in the 1930s: Ukrainian nationalism was not part of a larger collection of political entities called fascism, which included fascism in Italy and national socialism in Germany, but rather Italian fascism and German national socialism were part of a larger collection of entities called nationalism, which included Ukrainian nationalism.

Let us now look at the scholarship on the question of OUN's relationship to fascism. The first and very influential scholar of OUN, John A. Armstrong, classified the movement as "integral nationalist" rather than strictly fascist,[384] an idea that appealed to later

---

383 Evhen Onats'kyi, "Lysty z Italii, I. Deshcho pro fashyzm," *Rozbudova natsii* 1, no. 3 (March 1928): 93-96.
384 Armstrong, *Ukrainian Nationalism*, 12-15, 212.

defenders of OUN's legacy.[385] However, Armstrong also noted OUN's ideological proximity to fascism: "The theory and teachings of the Nationalists were very close to Fascism, and in some respects, such as the insistence on 'racial purity,' even went beyond the original Fascist doctrines."[386] And: "For many years the OUN had been closely tied to German policy. This alignment was furthered by the semi-Fascist nature of its ideology, and in turn the dependence on Germany tended to intensify Fascist trends in the organization."[387] Ukraine's working group in 2000-05 took a very similar position on the issue: it differentiated OUN's "integral nationalism" from both fascism and national socialism while admitting some ideological overlap.[388]

Much of contemporary scholarship now sees OUN as a typically fascist organization. This result derives mainly from the procedure of comparing OUN to some definition of fascism. For example, Per Anders Rudling wrote that "there are a number of definitions of fascism, and the OUN(b) fits rather neatly within most." He noted that OUN-B fulfilled "the six points of a 'fascist minimum' which Nolte regarded as the criteria for categorizing an organization as fascist: anti-Communism, anti-liberalism, anti-conservatism, the leadership principle, a party army, and the aim of totalitarianism."[389] Grzegorz Rossoliński-Liebe, who I think has made the most convincing case for OUN's fascism, relied primarily on the definition worked out by Roger Griffin which emphasizes ultranationalism and belief in palinogenesis (rebirth).[390] Gomza, inspired by the work of Roger Eatwell, used this three-point test for fascism: "(1) the rebirth of national community; (2) the search for some new form of political and economic organization, which transcends liberal democracy and collectivistic communism; (3) the use of threat

---

385 See for example, Zenon Kohut, "Ukrains'kyi natsionalizm. Lyst do redaktora Edmonton Journal, 10 liutoho 2010 r.," in Amar, *Strasti za Banderoiu*, 145-46.

386 Armstrong, *Ukrainian Nationalism*, 212.

387 Ibid., 28.

388 Kulchyts'kyi, *Problema*, 11.

389 Rudling, "Yushchenko's Fascist," 132.

390 Rossoliński-Liebe, *Fascist Kernel*. The same arguments also appear in a more dispersed form in his biography of Stepan Bandera.

and violence during its political struggle."[391] Gomza concluded, after exploring these factors, that OUN was indeed fascist and that only the "memorial hindrance" stood in the way of recognizing this fact.[392]

However, with a different definition of fascism, one can come to a different conclusion. Motyl took his cue from Onatsky's differentiation between state fascism and the nationalism of a nation still striving for statehood. For Motyl, fascism was only possible within an existing national state, and the state-nation relationship was at the core of what distinguished fascism from the nationalism of a stateless nation.[393] The most serious student of OUN's ideology, the Ukrainian historian Oleksandr Zaitsev, developed these ideas and proposed a new terminology. He named the nationalism of the stateless nations "Ustashism," after the Croatian movement, and classified it as something different from fascism.[394]

There is yet another way of proceeding. One can leave definitions aside and instead look for "family resemblances"[395] among various movements in a particular epoch. One can imagine 1930s Europe as a continent divided among three political camps: 1) communist, with its base in the Soviet Union, but uniting adherents in every country of Europe (and worldwide); 2) democratic, with Britain and France its most representative exponents; and 3) fascist, a congeries of movements and parties that extended across Europe, including the Falange in Spain, fascism in Italy, national socialism in Germany, the Legion of the Archangel Michael in Romania, the Arrow Cross in Hungary, the Ustaše in Croatia, and OUN in Galicia and Volhynia. Although this family resemblance makes a great deal of sense, it should not obscure the fact that there were substantial differences among the movements in the third camp.[396] Moreover, as Martin Broszat has pointed out, sorting out the movements in

---

391 Gomza, "Elusive Proteus," 197-98.
392 Ibid., 201.
393 Motyl, *Turn to the Right*, 163-69 (see esp. 164).
394 Zaitsev, "Chy isnuvav ukrains'kyi natsional'no-vyzvol'nyi faszhyzm?" Zaitsev, "Fascism or Ustashism?" Zaitsev, "OUN i avtorytarno-natsionalistychni rukhy." Zaitsev, "OUN i fashyzm."
395 See Gomza, "Elusive Proteus," 197.
396 See Himka, "The Importance of the Situational Element."

east central Europe is complicated by the need to distinguish "autochthonous fascism" from "the opportunistic adaptation of fascist models."[397]

My own position on this question is that it is not a mistake to label OUN as fascist, if one proceeds from an appropriate definition or from the family resemblance classification. But I have some caveats. "Fascism" is a constructed concept, and as we have seen, different constructions produce different results in regard to OUN (e.g., Rudling and Rossoliński-Liebe versus Motyl and Zaitsev). Also, "fascist" is not used solely as a scholarly term, but it also and perhaps more commonly figures as a pejorative term. As Gomza has written, there is a "memorial hindrance" to the investigation of OUN's relation to fascism, because since World War II fascism has been regarded as *the* evil; but in a highly polarized historiography there can also arise a desire to affix the label "fascist" on OUN precisely because it is so pejorative. I fear that labels can obscure substance: OUN needs to be judged in light of its own ideological visage and practices. Certainly OUN borrowed heavily from Italian fascism and, particularly in the second half of the 1930s, from German national socialism. It believed in dictatorship, an authoritarian leader, corporatism, censorship, and political violence against opponents. During World War II it engaged in the mass murder of non-Ukrainians. These beliefs and acts should serve as the basis of evaluation of the movement, not some classification or categorization. In general I am skeptical of definitions and constructions imposed on concrete historical phenomena,[398] and I am also a linguistic conservative. The members of OUN self-identified not as fascists, but as nationalists, so that is the term I am using in this study.

Visions of Monoethnicity:
Resettlement and Ethnic Cleansing

An impulse towards creating an essentially monoethnic Ukraine can first be discerned in Mikhnovsky's ten commandments of 1903,

---

397   Cited in Golczewski, *Deutsche und Ukrainer*, 579.
398   Himka, "Problems with the Category of Genocide."

although it was still formulated foggily. The second and third commandments read:

> 2. All people are your brothers. But the Muscovites, Poles, Hungarians, and Jews are the enemies of our nation, as long as they rule over us and exploit us.
> 3. Ukraine for Ukrainians! Therefore, drive out all her enemies-oppressors.[399]

Some ideologues of OUN expressed clearer visions of creating a Ukrainian state and removing non-Ukrainians by resettlement, expulsion, or murder. Some of this was linked with imperialist ambitions. There were prominent nationalists who envisioned a Ukrainian empire ruling over peoples to the east. Mykhailo Kolodzinsky, one of OUN's experts on military affairs, wrote a treatise in the late 1930s titled "the military doctrine of Ukrainian nationalists."[400] In it he wrote of a very large Ukrainian state that would include Moldavia, parts of Romania, Poland, Belarus, Russia, the northern Caucasus, and Baku and its nearby oil fields. Uzbeks, Tajiks, and Turkmens would be liberated from Russian dominance and come instead under Ukrainian influence. To the Kazakhs, however, he allotted another fate. They were "to perish or be reduced to the role that Indians play in America."[401] Ivan Mitrynga, often fantasized as a leftist within OUN, wrote a brochure sometime between mid-1940 and mid-1941 that saw Ukraine's geopolitical mission in expansion toward the Mediterranean Sea and Indian Ocean.[402]

A memorandum from the Leadership of the Ukrainian Nationalists (Melnyk group), dated 14 April 1941, was circulated to various German offices. It stated as a goal the creation of a large Ukrainian state extending into the north Caucasus, i.e., including the Kuban region and Kalmykia (both today in the Russian Federation). By the Melnykites' calculations, this Ukraine would have a population that would be over 70 percent ethnic Ukrainian. "But

---

399 Mirchuk, *Mykola Mikhnovs'kyi*, 46.
400 For background on this text, see Zaitsev, "Voienna doktryna Mykhaila Kolodzins'koho."
401 Zaitsev, *Ukrains'kyi integral'nyi natsionalizm*, 271.
402 Mitrynga, *Nash shliakh borot'by*, 1:42.

the Ukrainian nationalists' program intends to implement a very far-reaching population resettlement modelled on the Turkish-Greek population exchange or the recent repatriation of *Volks-deutsche* from which should emerge over the next few decades after liberation in place of a Ukrainian population majority in the future state a unitary Ukrainian-ethnic state (*eine ukrainische Volkseinheit*)." The memorandum specified how it would bring more ethnic Ukrainians into the large territory it claimed: they would be brought in from overpopulated rural districts of Galicia, from special settlements for exiles in northern Russia, and from Ukrainian-populated settlements in far eastern Siberia.[403]

The removal of non-Ukrainians from traditional Ukrainian ethnic territory was also something the ideologues thought about, and not as a peaceful process. Kolodzinsky, who was enamored with the idea of atrocity and violence, wrote: "Every insurrection is cruel and bloody, and even more so ours, a nationalist one....The idea, in whose name the uprising is made, justifies and sanctifies extreme vandalisms and the most ugly cruelties."[404] The struggle with hostile elements must be "merciless, cruel, and zoological."[405] Mitrynga, in a work written weeks or perhaps a few months before his brochure cited above, did not express himself so violently, but did note that "'ethical' prejudices" had no relevance for those who understood "the current wave."[406]

Kolodzinsky wrote: "Our insurrection does not just have the task of changing the political system. It must purge Ukraine from the alien, hostile element and from what is not good in our own people. Only during the insurrection will it be possible to sweep away literally to the last man the Polish element from the Western Ukrainian Lands and thus to end Polish pretensions with regard to the Polish character of these lands. The Polish element that actively resists must fall in battle, and the rest must be terrorized and forced to flee beyond the Vistula....The more of the hostile element that

---

403   Kosyk, *Ukraina v Druhii svitovii viini*, 1:24-25.
404   Kolodzins'kyi, "Natsionalistychne povstannia," 260-61.
405   Ibid., 266.
406   Mitrynga, *Borot'ba za novyi lad*, 15. This work shares the imperialist longings of *Nash shliakh borot'by* (see 14-15).

perishes during the insurrection, the easier it will be to rebuild the Ukrainian state, and the stronger it will be."[407] Mitrynga thought along the same lines: Certain nations have vitality, and they are the grave-diggers of parasite nations. They cleanse the earth of rotting nations.[408] "Our goal in Ukraine," he wrote, "which we will always be realizing, is to cleanse our nation of the non-Ukrainian element."[409] "The task of the Ukrainian revolution is to fundamentally pick the weeds from the Ukrainian national field, both the non-Ukrainian and Ukrainian degenerative element."[410] Stsiborsky wrote in 1938 that the post-revolutionary Ukrainian state would face "the burning issue of unloading alien national elements (almost all of them hostile to us) from the urban and industrial centers"; this would require being "as resolute as possible...because until our centers are thoroughly cleansed the internal order in the country will be constantly threatened." In the following year he wrote that the revolution itself would kill a "large part of the Russian, Polish, and other immigrants," while the rest would be removed administratively.[411]

In particular, OUN considered it necessary to expel Polish colonists, as the political program of the 1939 Rome Assembly made clear: "The lands and property of colonists, settled on our lands by the occupiers, will be confiscated, and the colonists themselves will be subject to forcible expulsion from the boundaries of the Ukrainian State." However, "an exception to this principle can be applied only to those colonists who have been settled in Ukraine for a very long time [z davnykh chasiv]." The language of this statement suggests that all Poles who lived on Ukrainian-inhabited territories were to be considered "colonists."[412] The actions of the local OUN

---

407 Kolodzins'kyi, "Natsionalistychne povstannia," 266-67.
408 Mitrynga, *Nash shliakh borot'by*, 1:9.
409 Ibid., 1:79.
410 Ibid., 1:84. "All visions of society-as-garden define parts of the social habitat as human weeds. Like all other weeds, they must be segregated, contained, prevented from spreading, removed and kept outside the society boundaries; if all these means prove insufficient, they must be killed." Bauman, *Modernity and the Holocaust*, 92.
411 Carynnyk, "Foes of Our Rebirth," 326. Carynnyk's translation.
412 Provid ukrains'kykh natsionalistiv, *Politychna prohrama i ustrii*, 43.

in the Radekhiv area in 1937 provided a foretaste of what was to come during the war. Hundreds of Ukrainian peasants surrounded a Polish colony, dragged the inhabitants from their houses, and burned the colony down.[413] One of the hot-headed youth who participated in this action, Bohdan Kazanivsky, recalled in his memoirs: "One of the fellows got a group of people together, and they made their way to the Polish colony near the village of Dmytriv. There they told all the colonists to pack their things onto wagons and leave for the west before sunrise, to go to their Polish land. If not, they will perish. It was a decree as harsh as the fate of an enslaved nation. The alien people felt the threat and loaded up their goods, and our boys helped them pack, to get them on the road faster....By sunrise there were no more colonists. Their houses were gone too, all dismantled. There was no nest left to which an alien bird could return."[414] This was an initiative of local OUN leaders rather than of the Homeland Executive. Kazanivsky identified Ivan Klymiv as the *spiritus movens* of the decolonizations in the Radekhiv region (Lviv oblast).[415] Klymiv, whom Armstrong characterized as "one of the most fanatical supporters which this fanatical movement of the younger generation could boast,"[416] was at that time head of OUN in the Sokal region. (Sokal was a somewhat larger town near Radekhiv.)

It is not clear to what extent these visions of monoethnicity were shared by the wider membership of OUN. In his airbrushed, but still informative memoirs, OUN activist Stefan Petelycky claimed to have opposed the enthusiasm for ethnic cleansing that was evident in the movement in the later 1930s: "Still, even at the time, I remember that I quarrelled with those nationalists (they were not a majority, but they were influential) who spoke of building a Ukraine that would be only for Ukrainians. I argued against that. If we ever tried to set up a state that excluded Poles, Jews, or the other minorities who lived among us, all of them would have

---

413 Mirchuk, *Narys*, 464.
414 Kazanivs'kyi, *Shliakhom Legendy*, 25.
415 Ibid., 23.
416 Armstrong, *Ukrainian Nationalism*, 48. For a portrait of Klymiv as a nasty xenophobe, see Carynnyk, "'Jews, Poles, and Other Scum.'"

no choice but to band together and try to liquidate us. And they might well succeed. We had to build a free Ukraine, I said, but a country that would be a home for everyone prepared to be a loyal citizen."[417]

Attitudes toward Jews

Earlier studies touching on OUN and its attitudes toward Jews generally did not consider OUN to be particularly antisemitic. Even historians not associated with or sympathetic to OUN thought this way. For example, Lysiak-Rudnytsky wrote in the 1980s: "Racist theory, in particular anti-Semitism, was not an intrinsic part of Ukrainian integral nationalism, although in the 1930s some publicists touched on anti-Semitic themes, and others began to examine the issue of the 'Ukrainian race.'"[418] And I myself wrote in the early 1990s: "Anti-Semitism in Ukraine is a poorly researched topic. It is clear, however, that anti-Semitism was never prominent in the platform of OUN or Ukrainian nationalism generally. In this respect right-wing Ukrainian nationalism differed profoundly from its Hungarian, Polish and Romanian counterparts."[419] Both of us were, it turned out, wrong. We were limited by the difficulty of gaining access to enough and sufficiently diverse sources and, to a lesser extent, by the modification of some sources by the OUN members who published them.

Now, there is a consensus among researchers that antisemitism was an important component of OUN ideology by the mid-1930s, particularly after Hitler came to power in Germany.[420] Perhaps it did not have to be that way.

---

417 Petelycky, *Into Auschwitz*, 4.
418 *Encyclopedia of Ukraine*, s.v. "nationalism."
419 Himka, "Western Ukraine between the Wars," 411 n. 50.
420 In Oleksandr Zaitsev's delicate phrasing, the orientation on national socialist Germany was primarily a "marriage of convenience" for OUN, "but it did not remain infertile in an ideological sense." Zaitsev, *Ukrains'kyi integral'nyi natsionalizm*, 319. The literature on OUN's antisemitism: Bakanov, "*Ni katsapa,*" 92-113. Carynnyk, "Foes of Our Rebirth." Diukov, *Vtorostepennyi vrag* (two editions). Himka, "What Were They Thinking?" Redlich, "Jewish-Ukrainian Relations." The outliers are: Motyl, "The Ukrainian Nationalist Movement and the Jews." V"iatrovych, *Stavlennia OUN do ievreiv*. Both of these publications provoked

There is a remarkable article written by Mykola Stsiborsky (in his characteristic ponderous style) and published in the party organ, *Rozbudova natsii*, in 1930 that outlined a different pattern of thought concerning the Jewish-Ukrainian relationship.[421] He believed that most Ukrainians had a negative attitude towards Jews and that this stemmed primarily from Jewish clannishness and materialism and from the socio-economic role that history had constructed for Jews. Also, during the Russian revolution, Jews favored Moscow over Ukrainian aspirations. Negative feelings were exacerbated by the assassination of Ukrainian revolutionary leader Symon Petliura in 1926 by a Jew who wanted to avenge the pogroms which Petliura's soldiers had perpetrated during the civil war. Registering all this, Stsiborsky went much further than was common in Ukrainian, let alone Ukrainian nationalist, reflections on their Jewish neighbors. He examined the historical factors that produced the traits that Ukrainians did not like and argued against essentializing them. A different historical turn would allow for the modification of those features of Jews that Ukrainians had objected to. The petty Jewish trader, so common and despised on Ukrainian territories, was the product of legal restrictions on Jewish participation in other economic spheres. Where these restrictions did not exist, as in France, the United States, or England, Jews entered other productive occupations. There was also a sound logic to Jews' preference for a centralized, democratic Russia over the young Ukrainian movement. Stsiborsky asked rhetorically: "And was there anything unusual in this indifference of the Jews to the Ukrainian movement when in the first period of the liberation struggle not only our masses, but also the Ukrainian leadership strata were unable to properly understand the spirit of the time and the genuine content of our national problem?!"

---

detailed responses backed by abundant evidence (respectively): Carynnyk, "'A Knife in the Back.'" Kurylo and Himka, "Iak OUN stavylasia do ievreiv?" In addition, see Kurylo, "The 'Jewish Question'," which focuses on Dontsov.

421   M. Stsibors'kyi, "Ukrains'kyi natsionalizm i zhydivstvo," *Rozbudova natsii* 3, no. 11-12 (November-December 1930): 266-73. It has been republished as an appendix to V"iatrovych, *Stavlennia OUN do ievreiv*, 115-29.

Of particular interest are Stsiborsky's views on the extent of Jewish support for Bolshevism:

> ...It would be a great mistake to accept without reservation the view of those who are inclined to see all of Jewry guilty of supporting the Bolsheviks. Actively joining the Bolshevik action were only a portion of the doctrinaire intelligentsia and the urban riff-raff (*shumovynnia*), some workers, artisanal apprentices, journeymen, etc. Most of the intelligentsia and the masses, in cities and on the periphery, took a stance of neutrality or opposition to communism. For Jewry as a whole the Bolshevik revolution, which brought the destruction of property, a change of the foundations of national-economic life and religious-customary ways, and so forth, was contradictory to its interests, tendencies, and psychology.[422]

This approach differed remarkably from what was soon to become the prevailing line in OUN. Its newspaper for the peasantry, *Nove selo*, reflected the kinds of ideas OUN members and sympathizers entertained about Jews in the countryside: that the struggle against Jews was identical with the struggle against communism,[423] that Jewish-socialist agitation had to be driven out from the villages,[424] and that Yids (*zhydky*) were luring susceptible young men into internationalism and communism.[425] An article in the paper stated that "Russian Jews killed many millions of Ukrainians in their own country through famine and forced labor."[426] The chorus to a popular OUN song called for "Death to the Muscovite-Jewish commune!"[427] Ideologue Yaroslav Stetsko wrote a text in 1938 identifying the Communist Party of Western Ukraine with Jews and identifying both Jews and Muscovites as secret police agents,

---

422 Stsibors'kyi, "Ukrains'kyi natsionalizm i zhydivstvo," 271.

423 "322 roky tiurmy za O.U.N.," *Nove selo* 8, no. 51 (402) (2 January 1938): 2-3.

424 Svidoma molod' Ilynets', "Het' zhydivs'kyi dukh z ukrains'kykh sil," *Nove selo* 9, no. 29 (430) (31 July 1938): 7.

425 Petro Sahaidak, "Zaiava," *Nove selo* 10, no. 25 (476) (25 June 1939): 7.

426 "Rumuniia prystala do fashystivs'koho taboru," *Nove selo* 9, no. 3 (404) (23 January 1938): 4.

427 "My zrodylys'...," *Homin voli*, unpaginated. A late in-law of mine, John (Ivan) Lahola, told me that this was a song he and his comrades sang in the summer of 1941 when they emerged from the underground. The text of the song is also in a handwritten UPA song collection from Volhynia. DARO, fond R30, op. spr. 108, f. 65v. OUN militiamen in Volhynia also sang the song in the summer of 1941. Siemaszko and Siemaszko, *Ludobójstwo*, 1:657, 1:720, 1:783, 2:1114, 2:1253.

informers, and political commissars who persecute Ukrainian activists in Soviet Ukraine.[428] Stetsko was probably also the person who drafted a resolution for the April 1941 Assembly in Kraków which stated that "the Jews in the USSR are the most devoted support of the ruling Bolshevik regime and the advance guard of Muscovite imperialism in Ukraine."[429]

Even when Judeocommunism became a commonplace in OUN thinking, there were those who did not share the view. OUN member Mykola Nitskevych sent a letter to Stetsko on 6 May 1938 that rejected Stetsko's identification of communism with Jews: "It is clear to everyone even a bit acquainted with Russian 'culture' that Bolshevism is by origin absolutely Muscovite.... Jews simply had nothing to do with it. They wheedled their way into the Bolshevik revolution just as they did into European capitalism."[430] Also, even though the Mitrynga group in OUN was by no means free of antisemitism, it seems to have felt that blaming the Jews had no explanatory value when it came to understanding Soviet communism.[431]

Stsiborsky's article of 1930 also took a different tack in its ideas about the Jewish economic role in the future Ukrainian state. While a few years later the OUN consensus was to be that Jews were exploiters and that their role in the economy needed to be severely restricted, Stsiborsky felt that Jews could make a major contribution to the revival of Ukrainian economic life after the overthrow of communism:

> ...Jews with their active character and entrepeneurship will be able both to find for themselves a favorable situation and to benefit the general process of state-building. In particular Jews can be very beneficial to themselves and to society in reviving free commodity-

---

428 The text was read over the OUN radio station "Radio Vienna" on New Year's eve 1938 and published in a Canadian Ukrainian-language newspaper in May 1939. Shkandrij, "Radio Vena," 211. Stets'ko, "Zhydivstvo i my."

429 Veselova, *OUN v 1941 rotsi*, 43.

430 The entire letter is reproduced as a photograph in Carynnyk, "Knife," 11-12.

431 Mitrynga put out three issues of a Sovietological journal, *Het' z bol'shevyzmom*, in 1937-38; it had nothing to say about Judeocommunism. Mitrynga's comrade Borys Lewytzkyj served for a short time in 1938 as the editor of *Nove selo*; although some antisemitic materials appeared in the paper under his editorship, these did not mention Jewish involvement in communism.

commercial circulation in Ukraine after Bolshevik rule, on condition of the regulation of their activities by a firm economic-state policy. The large stratum of Jewish artisans, whose social role is far from finished, can also provide much that is positive in the process of normalizing economic-productive relations in Ukraine, even considering the unfavorable conditions in which that stratum exists at present, especially in the Ukrainian SSR.[432]

Stsiborsky also argued that Jews could prove loyal to a future Ukrainian state and develop a conscious state patriotism. "Therefore, it will be the duty of the state authority to create for Jewry such conditions that they, preserving their organic racial, cultural, religious characteristics, would at the same time be drawn, as a factor with equal rights, into the circle of general social-state interests and positive creativity."[433]

Given the pressures of the historical environment, Stsiborsky was not able to hold these views over the long term. When he drafted a constitution for a future Ukrainian state, probably in 1940, he stipulated that "persons of Jewish nationality" were to be excluded from the provisions on citizenship and would be subject to "a special law."[434] As Kai Struve has noted, Stsiborsky's model here was likely the Nuremberg Laws.[435] A sentiment similar to Stsiborsky's was expressed by Mitrynga around the same time: "The Ukrainian revolution will not bring freedom to the non-Ukrainian individual in Ukraine. The freedom that the Ukrainian revolution will bring to the Ukrainian land is a gift exclusively reserved for the Ukrainian individual."[436] Already in the early 1930s OUN correspondents to the newspaper *Novyi shliakh* in Canada had proposed that in the future Ukrainian state, Jews should be denied citizenship rights.[437]

I have mentioned that the Stsiborsky of 1930, with his vision of the utility of Jewish economic activity for the future Ukrainian state, was an outlier. He was not just an outlier in OUN but within

---

432 Stsibors'kyi, "Ukrains'kyi natsionalizm i zhydivstvo," 272.
433 Ibid., 273.
434 Veselova, *OUN v 1941 rotsi*, 216. See also Carynnyk, "Foes of Our Rebirth," 324.
435 Struve, *Deutsche Herrschaft*, 86.
436 Mitrynga, *Nash shliakh borot'by*, 2:56.
437 Martynowych, "Sympathy for the Devil," 181.

the broader context of the Ukrainian national movement. Since the late nineteenth century, there had been two points of friction between Ukrainians and Jews in the economic sphere. One was the antagonism between Ukrainian peasants and Jewish tavernkeepers and merchants. It is difficult to sort out how much of this antagonism was due to actual economic relations and how much to an interpretation of these relations by the educated Ukrainians who led the national movement, but I am disposed to believe it was a bit of both.[438] There was a feeling widespread among Ukrainians that Jews exploited them, and this feeling was to play a part in the Holocaust: Ukrainian activists argued that the expropriation of Jews was justified in light of the ill-gotten nature of their property.[439]

OUN was an active purveyor of the stereotype of Jews as exploiters. In his 1938 text Stetsko wrote that Jews had taken over all trade in Ukrainian lands and lived "by deceit, exploitation, and serving the enemies of Ukraine."[440] Another 1938 text by another OUN ideologue, Volodymyr Martynets, said that parasitic Jews used taverns and usury to acquire peasant land.[441] In the same year OUN's Radio Vienna claimed that Jews had reduced the Ukrainian population of Carpatho-Ukraine to total economic dependence; they lent money at exorbitant interest and opposed Ukrainian private business in any way they could, including illegally.[442] The

---

438 Even an outline of this topic, which certainly requires revisiting by scholars, would take us too far afield. Works worth consulting include: Struve, *Bauern und Nation*. Himka, "Ukrainian-Jewish Antagonism." Tokarski, *Ethnic Conflict*. Although it has defects, I found fruitful for my own thinking Lehmann, *Symbiosis and Ambivalence*.

439 For example, the head of the Ukrainian Central Committee, Volodymyr Kubijovyč (Kubiiovych) wrote to Governor-General Hans Frank on 29 August 1941: "Considering that all Jewish property originally belonged for the most part to the Ukrainian people and only through ruthless law-breaking on the part of the Jews and through their exploitation of members of the Ukrainian people did it pass into Jewish possession, we deem it a requirement of justice, in order to make restitution to the Ukrainian people for moral and material damages, that a very considerable portion of confiscated Jewish property be returned to the Ukrainian people. In particular, all Jewish land holdings should be given to Ukrainian peasants." Veryha, *Correspondence of the Ukrainian Central Committee*, 1:342.

440 Stets'ko, "Zhydivstvo i my."

441 Martynets', *Zhydivs'ka probliema*, 4-6.

442 Shkandrij, "Radio Vena," 211. Shkandrij refers here to a broadcast dated 9 October 1938.

popular press of the nationalists disseminated the same message. In *Nove selo*, "a worker" informed the paper's peasant readers: "In our FOOTHILLS, live thousands of all kinds of alien freeloaders, and mostly Jewish ones, who exploit our peasants without mercy....Should we permit even now that with our money they built Palestine, organized the commune (*komuna*), while our children do not see a piece of bread?"[443] In the same issue, a peasant correspondent wrote: "The Poles have the government offices, the Jews everything else, and we nothing."[444] The workers' paper *Homin Kraiu* reported on a strike of brick workers in Jewish-owned brick factories in Przemyśl. "The Jews for this reason made a terrible cry....They are afraid that the 'goy' has at last seen clearly and does not want to be exploited any longer."[445] Economic distrust of Jews achieved an extreme formulation in "The Struggle and Activities of OUN in Wartime" of spring 1941, which stated: "If there should be an insurmountable need to leave a Jew in the economic administration [of postrevolutionary Ukraine], place one of our militiamen over him and liquidate him for the slightest offense."[446]

The second economic issue that separated Ukrainians and Jews was a conflict over commercial interests. In the disproportionate ethnic stratification of economic sectors in Galicia and Volhynia, Jews were overrepresented and Ukrainians underrepresented in commerce. Ukrainian activists promoted cooperative stores as well as stores privately owned by Ukrainians and urged the boycott of Jewish-owned stores. A popular Ukrainian byword of the time was *svii do svoho po svoie*, which meant: our own people should go to our own people for our own people's products. This was also a conflict that would play a role in the Holocaust. In 1939-41, the Soviets nationalized all stores and commercial enterprises in Western Ukraine, and these were mainly rather small and Jewish-owned. When the Germans came in, ownership was not, of course, restored to Jews, and many stores went into the hands of Ukrainians, as part

---

443 Robitnyk, "Do borot'by z vyzyskom," *Nove selo* 9, no. 2 (403) (9 January 1938): 15.
444 A. Voloshyn, "Po Boikivshchyni," *Nove selo* 9, no. 2 (403) (9 January 1938): 15.
445 "Proty zhydivs'koho vyzysku," *Homin Kraiu* 1, no. 11 (1 May 1938): 6.
446 Carynnyk, "Foes of Our Rebirth," 330. Carynnyk's translation.

of the network of Ukrainian cooperatives or else privately. An official of the civil administration in the Przemyśl region under the German occupation wrote in his memoirs in 1947: "In the cities, towns, and villages tens of thousands of Ukrainian stores appeared, cities took on a Ukrainian character."[447]

Martynets argued for the complete isolation of Ukraine's Jews. They could live among Ukrainians, but had to remain radically separate. "Do they want to engage in trade?" he asked. "Let them, but only among themselves."[448] The OUN newspaper for the peasantry published a call by the worker already cited for the total boycott of Jewish enterprises.[449] A peasant, also urging boycott, commented in the paper: "We have among us some people (*liudtsi*) who find it hard to live without the Jew." Some Ukrainian businesses even buy their hay from Jews. "When the peasants ask why these gentlemen do not buy their hay from them, the gentlemen answer that the merchandise is not good. I am curious to know where Jewry does its purchasing. Do they perhaps import the hay from Palestine?"[450] An OUN leaflet from a village in Volhynia from 1936 urged: "Let's not let the Jews rob us. Do not buy from a Jew. Do not sell to Jews. Drive Jews from the village. Let our watchword be: Away with the Jews."[451]

The nationalists accused Jews of supporting the dominant nations that oppressed Ukrainians, particularly the Russians and Poles but also the Czechs (in Carpatho-Ukraine),[452] and of being opposed to Ukrainian national aspirations. There was some truth to this claim (and a number of exceptions as well). As a vulnerable minority, Jews tended to assimilate culturally and politically to the stronger majorities; moreover, the largely peasant-based, stateless, and marginalized Ukrainian nation had little to attract outsiders. But the nationalists absolutized and essentialized the tendencies of Jews to ally with the powers-that-be rather than the Ukrainians. As

---

447 Dmytro Duchyns'kyi, "Moi spomyny," "Konkurs na spohady," Oseredok, 16-17.
448 Martynets', *Zhydivs'ka probliema*, 14.
449 Robitnyk, "Do borot'by z vyzyskom," *Nove Selo* 9, no. 2 (403) (9 January 1938): 15.
450 "Zhydivs'ki Ivany," *Nove Selo* 9, no. 14 (415) (10 April 1938): 9.
451 The leaflet is reproduced in Hon, *Iz kryvdoiu na samoti*, 76.
452 Shkandrij, "Radio Vena," 210.

early as 1929 Yurii Mylianych wrote an article in *Rozbudova natsii*, OUN's official organ, that stated: "In our struggle with Poland they reinforce the Polish front; in our struggle with Bolshevism, they support the Bolsheviks; in our battle with Russophilism (*rusotiapstvo*), they are the most consistent sowers of Muscovitism."[453] In his article, "Jewry and Us," Stetsko wrote that Jews helped enemies keep control of Ukraine "throughout all history." And of course now, he maintained, they served Bolshevism. Just as in the past Jewish leaseholders and taverners, who often held the keys to churches, exploited the Ukrainian people in their service to the alien lords, so now, according to Stetsko, they opposed the liberation movement of the Ukrainian people and helped Moscow and Bolshevism. Martynets put it thus: "For centuries [Jewry] has been the support of our national enemies, the bulwark of their regimes, a denationalizing factor and declared enemy of Ukrainian statehood, and moreover an enemy of Ukrainianism as a national phenomenon."[454]

At the same time the nationalists complained about the Jews' failure to support Ukrainian aspirations, they also closed the door on Jewish assimilation. Stetsko, who had responsibility for drafting policy in preparation for the 1939 Rome Assembly, wrote in his drafts: "All national minorities, except for the Jews, for whom there will be ghettos, will be denationalized and assimilated."[455] The spring 1941 "Struggle and Activities" stated: "Assimilation of Jews is excluded."[456] The ideologue Volodymyr Martynets, in a publication from 1938, agreed that Jews could not be assimilated: "from the racial point of view, this is an element unsuitable for mixture and assimilation."[457] He felt that attempting to assimilate the Jews would lead to a degeneration of the state-building instinct in

---

453 Iur Mylianych, "Zhydy, sionism i Ukraina," *Rozbudova natsii* 2, no. 8-9 (20-21) (August-September 1929): 271.
454 Martynets', *Zhydivs'ka probliema*, 6.
455 Zaitsev, *Ukrains'kyi integral'nyi natsionalizm*, 280.
456 Carynnyk, "Foes of Our Rebirth," 330. Carynnyk's translation.
457 Martynets', *Zhydivs'ka probliema*, 10. Kai Struve notes that Martynets took points made earlier in the OUN organ *Rozbudova natsiia* by Oleksandr Mytsiuk and radicalized them in a racist sense. On Mytsiuk's antisemitic publications, see Kurylo and Himka, "Iak OUN stavylasia do ievreiv?" 255-57.

Ukrainians; "the result would be not the liquidation of Jewry but the Jewification of our nation."[458] He was therefore against mixed marriages and for the total segregation of Jews. "Let the Jews live, but let them live *for themselves*, and — more importantly *from* themselves, and not off of us.... Do they want to live among us? Let them, but not in symbiosis with us."[459]

Not surprisingly, given this mental context, OUN's popular newspapers praised contemporary antisemitic movements and governments. *Nove selo* reported sympathetically on Nazi attacks on Jews in Germany in November 1938 (the November pogrom or *Kristallnacht*).[460] Both *Nove selo* and *Homin kraiu* also welcomed the antisemitic Goga-Cuza government, which came to power briefly in Romania at the end of 1937:

> Jewry screams that Hitler instigated Goga and the Romanians against the Jews. In reality the Jews themselves did the instigating with their arrogance. They're living like lords in Romania, so much so that they have taken into their hands all the industry and trade there. The Romanian peasant lives in great poverty in his own state, and the Jews are experiencing prosperity. But the Jews were not satisfied with this. They began to want to take power in the state. They began to organize socialist-communist organizations, purchased many periodicals, and began to spread communist propaganda....World Jewry has mobilized all the international powers [England, France, America] against the Romanian authorities.... And today, when the Romanian authorities have decided to take from the Jews only their right to exploit, i.e., tavernkeeping and commerce in the villages, then in their defense have stood all the "democratic" (read: Jewish) powers of the world.[461]

OUN did not limit itself to propagating anti-Jewish attitudes, but also engaged in the destruction of Jewish property. A leaflet

---

458 Martynets', *Zhydivs'ka probliema*, 11.
459 Ibid., 43.
460 "Pohrom zhydiv u Nimechchyni," *Nove Selo* 9, no. 45 (446) (20 November 1938): 6. "V kooperatyvi (Rozmovy na aktual'ni temy)," *Nove Selo* 9, no. 46 (447) (27 November 1938): 9.
461 "Rumuniia prystala do fashystivs'koho taboru," *Nove Selo* 9, no. 3 (404) (23 January 1938): 4. See also "Fashystivs'ka vlada Rumunii," *Nove Selo* 9, no 2 (403) (9 January 1938): 11. Protyzhydivs'ka aktsiia v sviti," *Homin Kraiu* 1, no. 5 (1 February 1938): 2.

from the Homeland Executive of OUN in 1931 incited its rural activists: "Let us break the windows of taverns, let us crush bottles of vodka, and we will chase the Jews from the village."[462] Indeed there was a major campaign of window breaking in Kalush, Stanyslaviv, Stryi, and Zhydachiv counties in Galicia in 1935.[463] OUN meetings in 1935 discussed ways to pressure Jews to leave Ukrainian villages, and among the proposals was setting fire to Jewish buildings.[464] OUN was responsible for a number of instances of arson against Jews in Kostopil county in Volhynia in 1936, including one which engendered such a fire that forty-one households were burned down, along with what they had harvested.[465] Although OUN destroyed the property of Jews, it rarely murdered them in the interwar era.[466]

A very interesting, and for this study particularly relevant, issue is OUN's attitude toward pogroms, which has not been examined in any depth in the existing literature. Particularly the older, émigré leadership of OUN strongly condemned pogroms. Konovalets had been horrified by what he witnessed in the aftermath of a murderous anti-Jewish pogrom committed by Petliura's troops in the town of Proskuriv (today the oblast capital Khmelnytskyi) in February 1919.[467] About 1500 Jews were killed on the pretext that they were behind a Bolshevik rebellion that broke out against the Ukrainian forces. Recalling this in his memoirs, Konovalets wrote: "In Proskuriv the Sich Sharpshooters encountered face to face the horrible phenomenon of the Jewish pogroms. We came to Proskuriv just about three days after the slaughter that

---

462 Posivnych, "Vydannia Kraiovoi Ekzekutyvy OUN 1931 r.," 14.

463 Hon, *Iz kryvdoiu na samoti*, 152.

464 Ibid., 149.

465 Police report from 16 September 1936, reproduced in Hon, *Iz kryvdoiu na samoti*, 153; and see also 79-80. The trial of the arsonists was covered in *Nove selo*: "322 roky tiurmy za O.U.N.," *Nove selo* 8, no. 51 (402) (2 January 1938): 2-3.

466 Maksym Hon identified three cases in which OUN murdered Jews. In none of these cases, however, were the victims killed because they were Jews, but for some other reason. Hon, *Iz kryvdoiu na samoti*, 154.

467 There is an account of the pogrom in Abramson, *A Prayer for the Government*, 122, 126-31. The pogrom was ordered by Otaman Ivan Semesenko, "commander of the Petliura brigade of the Zaporozhian Cossacks, 3rd Haidamak Regiment."

was executed there." He set up an investigative committee to determine "the causes of the pogrom, the main offenders and perpetrators, the actual course of the pogrom, and the losses borne by the
city and by the Jewish population."[468] On 13 January 1919, Melnyk,
who at the time held the rank of otaman in the armed forces of the
Ukrainian People's Republic, severely prohibited pogroms:

> The Ukrainian National Republic is engaged in a serious struggle for
> its independence and freedom, and therefore can deeply iden-
> tify...with the freedom of other peoples. Therefore I will prosecute
> decisively any provocateurs who argue that it is permissible to un-
> dertake Jewish pogroms and similar agitation. They will be given
> over to courts-martial, all criminals of the Ukrainian National Repub-
> lic....For pogrom-agitation [the following] were shot: Stanyslav Poli-
> anskyi and Nikanor Savel'ev.

And in April 1919 he issued another strong prohibition:

> Anarchy is more dangerous than the armed enemy who moves upon
> us from all sides. Remember, Cossacks, that through the pogroms
> may our power perish, for the death of innocent victims will provoke
> wrath against us and the numbers of our enemies will multiply. The
> Cossack's task is to conquer the enemy, whosoever he may be, not to
> fight women, children, old men, against whom you are being incited
> by our enemies, in order that our people and our sovereignty may be
> besmirched in the eyes of the world. Henceforth, I command you to
> arrest all persons who will be discovered conducting pogrom agita-
> tion among the Cossacks, and to bring them before the Extraordinary
> Tribunal. Suppress on the spot all attempts at pogrom agitation in the
> military detachments.[469]

In his 1930 article Stsiborsky, himself a veteran of the armed
forces of the Ukrainian People's Republic, also condemned "the
profoundly mistaken and thoughtless pogrom operation that took
place in Ukraine in the period 1919-20." The victims of the pogroms

---

468 Konovalets', *Prychynky do istorii ukrains'koi revoliutsii*, 28 n. I cite the 1928 edition, but it was republished in 1938 after Konovalets was assassinated. It would
be worthwhile to examine the materials of the investigative committee in
Proskuriv. I am grateful to Oleh Pavlyshyn for suggesting to me that they might
be preserved in the archives of the Shevchenko Scientific Society at the National
Library in Warsaw. See Svarnyk, *Arkhivni ta rukopysni zbirky*, 237-38.

469 Abramson, *A Prayer for the Government*, 145, 147-48.

were not actually pro-Bolshevik, since those Jews had retreated with the Red Army; the victims were the peaceful people left behind — storekeepers, tailors, shoemakers, and watchmakers. The pogroms "erected against us a whole wall of Jewish hostility, and that on a global scale." The pogroms also had a negative influence on the prospects of the Ukrainian cause in the international arena.[470]

The rejection of pogroms remained a part of mainstream OUN thinking even when antisemitism within the movement intensified in the late 1930s. Martynets' otherwise intensely antisemitic brochure of 1938 specified that to reduce the number of Jews on Ukrainian territory, "there is no need for pogroms nor forcible expulsion. It will be enough to separate completely from them."[471] This view was also reflected in an article published in *Nove selo* in 1939. Reporting on Czech fascists who stole bombs from a military arsenal and threw them into Jewish stores, the paper admonished: "But this kind of struggle, which the young Czech nationalists want to make use of, will lead to nothing. It is necessary to fight with the Jews by developing one's own industry and trade, propagating the slogan 'our people go to our people' and boycotting Jewish stores. Bombs are no help at all."[472] In his drafts for the 1939 Rome Assembly, Stetsko wrote: "The Jewish issue is important, but we have nothing cheerful to tell them (except perhaps that in the regulated Ukrainian State there will not be physical anti-Jewish pogroms)."[473] This position was codified in a resolution of the Banderite Assembly held in Kraków in April 1941 (partially cited earlier):

> The Jews in the USSR are the most devoted support of the ruling Bolshevik regime and the advance guard of Muscovite imperialism in Ukraine. The Muscovite-Bolshevik government exploits the anti-Jewish moods of the Ukrainian masses in order to divert their attention from the real source of evil and in order to direct them during the time of uprising into pogroms against Jews. The Organization of Ukrainian Nationalists struggles against the Jews as the support of

470 Stsibors'kyi, "Ukrains'kyi natsionalizm i zhydivstvo," 269, 271.
471 Martynets', *Zhydivs'ka probliema*, 22.
472 "Vzhe i chekhy napadaiut' na zhydivs'ki kramnytsi," *Nove Selo* 10, no 10 (461) (12 March 1939): 6.
473 Zaitsev, *Ukrains'kyi integral'nyi natsionalizm*, 280.

the Muscovite-Bolshevik regime, at the same time making the popular masses aware that Moscow is the main enemy.[474]

Nonetheless, the proponents of violent ethnic cleansing within OUN imagined the mass killing of Jews in the course of the national revolution. When Mitrynga wrote about the need to cleanse Ukraine of the non-Ukrainian element, he mentioned the Jews specifically. "The Jews, the Khazars, and all kinds of 'merchants' and 'wise men' from Asia Minor and the south have soiled our political thought, spoiled our will."[475] Jews were a dangerous internal enemy of the Ukrainian revolution and, he noted with consternation, there were almost four million of them in Ukraine.[476] Kolodzinsky did not mince words: "Without doubt, the anger of the Ukrainian people towards the Jews will be especially terrible. We have no need to restrain this anger, but on the contrary—increase it. The more Jews who die during the insurrection the better it will be for the Ukrainian state, because Jews will be the single minority which we do not dare include in our denationalization policy. All other minorities who come out alive from the insurrection we will denationalize." He considered his stance to be relatively moderate, since "some of the nationalists" preached the slaughter of all Ukraine's three and a half million Jews. He also thought that since every uprising inevitably involves cruelty, "then at least we have to be able to use it for the consolidation of our victory." Also, although he felt the insurrection would be marked by atrocities, with time fronts would stabilize, the insurgency would become a war, "and the cruelty will be alleviated."[477]

The spring 1941 "Struggle and Activities" also envisioned violence against Jews, calling for OUN security services to neutralize "Jews, both individually and as a national group."[478] All Jews were

---

474   Veselova, *OUN v 1941 rotsi*, 43.

475   Mitrynga, *Nash shliakh borot'by*, 1:79.

476   Ibid., 2:11. Perhaps there were close to four million Jews in the borders of the large Ukrainian state Mitrynga was imagining, but there were only two and a half million of them when World War II broke out within the borders of the independent Ukrainian state that was to emerge in 1991.

477   Kolodzins'kyi, "Natsionalistychne povstannia," 290. On the actual number of Jews in Ukraine, see the previous footnote.

478   Carynnyk, "Foes of Our Rebirth," 330. Carynnyk's translation.

obliged to report to a militia command post. In order to entice Red Army soldiers to the side of the Ukrainian revolution, OUN members were to encourage the soldiers to kill "Russians, Jews, NKVD agents, commissars, and everyone who wants war and death for us." In order to win over the workers, OUN was to issue them this instruction: "Don't allow the Red Army to destroy your factories while it is retreating. Kill the enemies among you—Jews and secret informers."[479]

Finally, though OUN had clearly become an antisemitic organization by the late 1930s, it would be a mistake to exaggerate this feature of its ideology before mid-1941 and the German attack on the USSR. The corpus of antisemitic writings published by OUN in this period would not fill a small book. OUN was not obsessed with Jews in the way the German national socialists or Romanian legionnaires were. Russians and Poles were considered the major national enemies in OUN's understanding. Jews were of secondary importance.

* *

*

OUN emerged as one of the responses to Ukrainians' failure to establish a state during the late phases and aftermath of World War I, a time when empires collapsed and new states emerged elsewhere in East Central Europe. OUN rejected the democratic and leftist politics of the leadership that proved inadequate to achieve Ukrainian statehood and embraced a more militant and aggressive platform. Veterans of the revolutionary era headed OUN and were actively involved in its founding. A transitional organization that bridged the revolutionary era and the appearance of OUN in 1929 was the underground terrorist formation UVO, whose head, veteran officer Yevhen Konovalets, would become the head of OUN. OUN also attracted many younger students in Galicia, who were imbued with nationalistic ideas and eager to revive the revolutionary struggle they had missed out on. The policies of the states in which most

---

479 Ibid., 332. Carynnyk's translation.

Ukrainians found themselves after 1920 nurtured nationalist resentment. Ukrainians in the Soviet Union in the 1930s suffered the loss of millions during the famine of 1932-33, and a great part of their intellectual elite was murdered by the regime. This made communism, which had enjoyed some serious support in Galicia in the 1920s, unacceptable to many politically conscious Ukrainians and pushed them to the right. Moreover, this occurred at a time when Europe was polarized between a fascist right and communist left. The Ukrainians in Poland, where OUN was primarily based, experienced discrimination in education and employment; this fanned discontent as early as the 1920s but became particularly exacerbated during the Great Depression.

OUN was heavily influenced by the fascist wave passing through Europe. At first OUN was enamored of fascist Italy, where Mussolini had been in power since 1922. The Italian influence was particularly evident in the writings of two prominent OUN thinkers, Yevhen Onatsky and Mykola Stsiborsky. But when Hitler came to power in 1933, OUN's attention was diverted to nationalist socialist Germany. Even before the Nazi seizure of power, OUN had developed close ties with Germany, and knowledge of the German language was widespread in Galicia. When Hitler began redrawing the boundaries of Europe in 1938, OUN became positively enthusiastic. One result of the adulation of national socialist Germany was an intensification of antisemitism in OUN.

4. The First Soviets, 1939–41

Several western Ukrainian territories came under Soviet rule as a result of the secret protocol of the German-Soviet Non-Aggression Pact of August 1939. The months spent under Soviet communism had consequences for further developments, including for the way the Holocaust was to play out in those territories. In this chapter I want to do four things: 1) survey in brief this first period of Soviet rule in Western Ukraine, often called "the first Soviets" by older Western Ukrainians; 2) examine the impact of Soviet rule on OUN; 3) look at how Jews responded to and were affected by Soviet rule; and 4) discuss the mass murder of political prisoners by the NKVD, the last act of the Soviets before retreating from the German advance.

The First Period of Soviet Rule in Western Ukraine

The German-Soviet Non-Aggression Pact, also commonly called the Molotov-Ribbentrop Pact, was signed on 23 August 1939. Though not explicitly stated in the pact, the point of this agreement was to facilitate a joint attack on Poland. The pact contained a secret protocol that divided Eastern Europe between Germany and the Soviet Union and foresaw the Soviets' incorporation of the eastern Polish territories largely inhabited by Ukrainians and Belarusians. The Germans attacked Poland on 1 September, quickly routing the Poles and reaching the outskirts of Lviv on 12 September. The Soviets launched their attack on 17 September, facing little resistance. According to figures released by Soviet foreign minister Viacheslav Molotov at the end of October of that year, the Red Army suffered fewer than three thousand casualties: 739 killed and 1862 wounded.[480] The Soviets took Rivne immediately, on 17 September; Lutsk (P Łuck) on the day after; and Lviv on 22 September. On 1 November Galicia and Volhynia were formally incorporated into

---

480 The figures were published in *Izvestiia* on 31 October 1939. Bilas, *Represyono-karal'na systema*, 1:112.

the Ukrainian SSR, remaining Soviet until the German invasion. Less than two years later, in 1941, Lutsk would fall to the Germans on 25 June, Rivne on 28 June, and Lviv on 30 June.

Though not actually envisioned in the initial agreement between Germany and the USSR, Northern Bukovina also became Soviet in this period. Molotov demanded Northern Bukovina and Bessarabia from Romania on 26 June 1940. Two days later the Red Army took Bukovina's capital, Chernivtsi. On 2 September 1940 Northern Bukovina was incorporated into Soviet Ukraine. Chernivtsi was to be retaken by the Romanians, with German support, on 6 July 1941.

As the Soviets presented their actions domestically and abroad, they were not so much attacking Poland in 1939 as liberating[481] Western Ukraine and Western Belarus. Therefore the brunt of Soviet repressions, especially at first, fell on the Polish political and economic elites. The primarily Polish landlords were all expropriated. The Soviets dismantled as much as they could of the former Polish state and gave Galicia and Volhynia a new, Soviet Ukrainian aspect. Jan Kazimierz University in Lviv was rechristened Ivan Franko University, after the most prominent Galician Ukrainian writer and scholar of the turn of the twentieth century. The language of instruction was officially changed from Polish to Ukrainian. Some local Ukrainians were recruited to the professoriate and Ukrainians imported from the older Soviet territories were given key posts in the university administration. The Polonization of the elementary school system was reversed. As early as in 1939 most schools in Galicia became Ukrainian; specifically, there were 5596 Ukrainian schools versus 922 Polish schools.[482] Many of the teachers were Ukrainians brought from the old Soviet territories to the east. It should be noted that local Ukrainians and Ukrainians from the east, "Easterners" (skhidniaky) as the Galicians called them, not only had very different political attitudes but also different cultural values.[483]

---

481 Older inhabitants of Lviv are fond of citing a witticism attributed to the composer Stanislav Liudkevych: *Nas vyzvolyly, i nema na to rady* (They liberated us, and there's nothing we can do about it).

482 Kovaliuk, "Kul'turolohichni ta dukhovni aspekty," 5.

483 Rich information on this theme can be found in Amar, *The Paradox of Ukrainian Lviv*.

Life, including everyday habits, changed radically under the new regime. Prior to 1939 the eastern regions of Poland were poor by European standards, but they seemed bountiful to the Red Army soldiers. There had been some malnutrition, but no famine in Galicia and Volhynia. Myriad household items, such as thimbles and soap, had been commonplace commodities in the former Poland, but were hard to obtain in the Soviet Union. Red Army soldiers were eager to obtain the riches they saw in stores. The Soviet authorities, perhaps fearing that otherwise undisciplined looting would erupt, prohibited the closure of shops and set the exchange rate between the Polish złoty and the Soviet ruble at a great advantage to the latter. As a result, soldiers bought up all they could and shipped many goods home.[484] The empty shops were soon to be nationalized in any case and then as scantily supplied with consumer goods as stores throughout the Soviet Union.

People also began to dress differently. While before September 1939, urbanites in eastern Poland/Western Ukraine took their fashion cues from the central European capitals, this could not be the case under Soviet rule. A Polish housewife from Baranavichy (now in Brest oblast, Belarus) wrote that "every passerby who was better dressed—and all of us Poles like to dress up—was taken in for interrogation."[485] Ivan Nimchuk, the last editor of the leading Ukrainian newspaper *Dilo*, recalled in his memoirs of 1950:

> It was interesting to observe at that time the conduct and attitude of Lviv's population, which from the moment of the arrival of the Bolsheviks in Lviv began to ratchet themselves not up, as had always been the case until then, but down. This became especially evident already before noon on the first Sunday: in the Ukrainian and Polish churches and on the streets you could rarely now see a woman in a hat—almost all Lviv ladies had ordinary babushkas on their heads; and many respectable citizens went about without ties and in old clothes.[486]

---

484 Gross, *Revolution from Abroad*, 46-48. Hrynevch, *Nepryborkane riznoholossia*, 213-14.

485 Cited in Gross, *Revolution from Abroad*, 147. Gross notes that the statement is somewhat exaggerated.

486 Nimchuk, *595 dniv soviets'kym viaznem*, 24-25. See also Hrynevch, *Nepryborkane riznoholossia*, 248.

The drabness of clothing was complemented by the drabness of the new Soviet newspapers. *Dilo* was replaced by *Vil'na Ukraina* (Free Ukraine), of which Nimchuk remarked: "...In Galicia no one up till then had ever read such a boring newspaper as *Vil'na Ukraina*."[487] With all the prewar press closed down, fifty-three newspapers came out in the western oblasts at the start of 1940. "And all these publications were, in terms of content, like twins, similar one to another and to their Kyivan and Muscovite 'sisters.' Not a trace was left of...the variegated information and polemics in the columns of the periodical publications of the previous period."[488] The closure of all previously existing sport, cultural, religious, and youth organizations also made life more monotonous.[489]

The face of the cities changed as Soviet monuments were erected and Soviet posters were pasted on walls and buildings.[490] Streets were renamed as well. In Lviv, the street that used to honor Haller's army, which defeated the Western Ukrainian People's Republic in 1919, was changed to honor the Budyonny cavalrymen, Bolshevik heroes who had helped defeat Petliura's forces. Piłsudski street became Red Army street; Sobieski street became Komsomol street; and Sapieha street was renamed Stalin street. All streets and squares with religious names were changed: St. Martin street became Decembrists street and Church street—Klara Zetkin street. The only partial exception was that St. George square became simply George square.[491]

Such transformations permeated life under the Soviets. Most disturbing to the populace, however, was the fury of repressions visited upon them. Altogether no less than 315,000 persons from eastern Poland, including Western Belarus as well as Western Ukraine, were deported to Kazakhstan, Siberia, and the far north. Of these, about 57.5 percent were Poles, 21.9 percent Jews, 10.4

---

487 Nimchuk, *595 dniv soviets'kym viaznem*, 31.
488 Kovaliuk, "Kul'turolohichni ta dukhovni aspekty," 9.
489 Hrynevch, *Nepryborkane riznoholossia*, 240.
490 Ibid., 248.
491 "Spisok ulits goroda L'vova, 1939," DALO, fond R-6, op. 1, spr. 48.

percent Ukrainians, and 7.6 percent Belarusians.[492] According to the Polish historian Grzegorz Hryciuk, from September 1939 until May 1941, 109,400 persons were arrested in the western oblasts of Ukraine and Belarus:

> Of the approximately 110,000 arrested persons, 9,465 persons were released in the course of investigations; 612 inmates died as a result of torture, harsh living conditions and illness; and 43 prisoners escaped. By May 1941, 1,208 death sentences had been issued. Part of these were carried out by 22 June 1941, another part immediately after the German invasion of the Soviet Union. To this number, it is necessary to add 7,305 persons murdered on the basis of a decision made by a special "troika" of the NKVD leadership in spring 1940.[493]

It was a brutal twenty-one months.

The OUN Underground

The repressions did not bypass OUN. While the first task of Soviet security was to neutralize the personnel of former Poland, the NKVD also turned its attention to Ukrainian nationalist counterrevolutionaries. On the night of 18-19 December 1939 OUN members in Zbarazh raion, Ternopil oblast, obviously hotheads, launched an armed insurrection, which, of course, failed; the NKVD arrested sixty-two persons.[494] In March-April 1940 the NKVD arrested 658 OUN members. They also arrested the entire homeland executive of OUN, but a new executive was reconstituted by early May. In September, however, this new executive was arrested as well, with the exception of its head, Dmytro Myron. In the September operation, the NKVD arrested 107 members.[495] And in another operation

---

492   Hryciuk, "Victims 1939-1941," 195. According to an NKVD document, there were a total of 210,271 persons from the western oblasts in the gulag as of August 1941: 117,800 Poles (including 8567 refugees from the German zone of occupation), 64,533 Jews (all refugees from the German zone), and 13,448 Ukrainians. Slyvka, *Deportatsii*, 1:154.
493   Hryciuk, "Victims 1939-1941," 182-83 (quotation from 183). On the abysmal conditions of detention in Soviet prisons and on torture of the prisoners, see Gross, *Revolution from Abroad*, 157-78. Severe beatings of prisoners are also mentioned in Nimchuk, *595 dniv soviets'kym viaznem*, 49-50, 57.
494   Danylenko and Kokin, *Radians'ki orhany*, 1:289-92.
495   Ibid., 1:314-15. Patryliak, *Viis'kova diial'nist OUN (B)*, 147-48.

in December 1940 and January 1941, the NKVD managed to arrest another 996 members.[496]

Several large trials of OUN members took place in 1941. In January fifty-nine OUN members were tried in Lviv, and all were found guilty of counterrevolutionary activities. Forty-two defendants were sentenced to death and the rest to ten years in distant labor camps; however, the women who were sentenced to death later had their punishment commuted to ten years in the camps.[497] Two trials of OUN members also took place in Drohobych in May, with a total of 101 defendants, about half of whom were also sentenced to death.[498] Altogether, 276 members of OUN were sentenced to death in Western Ukraine in January-May 1941.[499] The authorities also exiled the "bandits' accomplices," mainly the families of OUN members; in January-June 1941 over three thousand families (about 11,300 persons) were deported from the Western oblasts of Ukraine.[500]

In spite of these harsh repressions, the OUN underground survived Soviet rule and recruited new members, especially among youth. Ivan Patryliak, who estimated that on the eve of the Soviet invasion of Poland there were about eight or nine thousand members,[501] estimated that in the spring of 1941, on the eve of the German invasion of the Soviet Union, there were about twelve thousand members of OUN and seven thousand members of its Youth.[502] A more detailed recent study by Taras Hryvul estimated 7000-7500 members in the Soviet sector at the start of 1940 and about 20,000 members and an additional 30,000 sympathizers by June 1941.[503] Clearly, although its homeland leaders and many of

---

496 Patryliak, *Viis'kova diial'nist OUN (B)*, 151. Danylenko and Kokin, *Radians'ki orhany*, 1:329.

497 Baran and Tokars'kyi. "*Zachystka,*" 201-02. Patryliak, *Viis'kova diial'nist OUN (B)*, 152.

498 Baran and Tokars'kyi. "*Zachystka,*" 202. Patryliak, *Viis'kova diial'nist OUN (B)*, 152.

499 Baran and Tokars'kyi. "*Zachystka,*" 205.

500 Ibid., 205.

501 See above, 138.

502 Patryliak, *Viis'kova diial'nist OUN (B)*, 171.

503 Hryvul, "Chysel'nist'." The idea that OUN's numbers were "severely depleted by Soviet repression" is mistaken. Kopstein and Wittenberg, *Intimate Violence*, 97.

its militants were arrested and executed, OUN had grown. The blood of the martyrs was the seed of the nationalist church.

Although an OUN-B brochure from July-August 1941 boasted that the cadres in the underground just before the outbreak of the German-Soviet war were "an army of organized militants,"[504] it stands to reason that many of the new members of OUN were raw recruits and quite young.

OUN was able to survive because it drew on twenty years of experience in conspiracy. Some of its older members had belonged to the underground terrorist organization UVO, founded in 1920. When OUN emerged in 1929, it maintained an underground existence in Poland and, as we have seen, was capable of organizing many successful robberies and assassinations. OUN under the Poles, and even more so under the Soviets, could count on help from fellow Ukrainians. Underground OUN was able to "move amongst the people as a fish swims in the sea," as Mao was to put it. That OUN was so effective under the First Soviets becomes less surprising when one reflects on its resiliency under the Second Soviets, i.e., those who came in 1944. OUN was able to conduct guerilla warfare against the Soviet authorities for at least five years after the war was over, again recruiting effectively among the youth.

In addition to the underground in Galicia and Volhynia, several thousand leading cadres of OUN-B had gathered in Kraków, only three hundred kilometers to the west. There was, of course, a border between Kraków in the German zone and Lviv in the Soviet zone, but it was quite permeable at first. On 25 September 1939, the Germans closed the border to everyone but ethnic Germans (*Volksdeutsche*) and Ukrainian activists. Perhaps twenty to thirty thousand Ukrainian activists crossed the border into the German zone.[505] Later the border hardened, but OUN members continued crossing back and forth illegally, since they knew the terrain well and had sympathizers in the population. Crossing was risky, and sometimes the NKVD caught the activists and extracted information from them, sometimes even written information. OUN had

---

504 Hryvul, "Chysel'nist'," 267.
505 Hrynevch, *Nepryborkane riznoholossia*, 297.

a well-developed, if not one-hundred-percent effective system of couriers. This is clear from the results of the NKVD's anti-OUN operation of September 1940, when NKVD agents arrested eight couriers of the homeland executive, three oblast couriers, eleven circle and raion couriers, and nine persons who ran safe houses for OUN.[506] OUN used its communication across the border to pass on information to the Abwehr, i.e. German military intelligence,[507] but the border crossing mainly served OUN's own purposes of coordination and intelligence.

Of great importance for the near future was that, thanks to the Soviets, OUN became the only Ukrainian political organization to survive into 1941. Even before the invasion of Poland, in 1938, the Soviets strengthened the political right in Galicia and Volhynia by dissolving the Communist Party of Poland, including the Communist Party of Western Ukraine. Within days of taking Lviv, the Soviets began to look for and execute dissident communists, national communists and/or Trotskyists.[508] More important, all previously existing Ukrainian parties, including the centrist Ukrainian National Democratic Union (UNDO) and the leftist social democrats and socialist radicals, preemptively dissolved themselves before the end of September 1939.[509] Furthermore, they did not regroup in Kraków as did OUN-B. The result was that when the Germans invaded the Soviet Union on 22 June 1941, OUN was to face no rival Ukrainian political party: it had a clear field for action.

---

506 Danylenko and Kokin, *Radians'ki orhany*, 1:315.

507 Il'iushyn, *Ukrains'a povstans'ka armiia i Armiia kraiova*, 143.

508 Ivan Nimchuk, who was arrested within the first week of the Soviet occupation of Lviv, recalled in his memoirs that at his very first interrogation, he was asked about the whereabouts of Liudvyk "Chornyi" Rozenberg. Rozenberg and another prominent dissident communist, Stepan Rudyk, "disappeared without a trace in the Bolshevik thickets." Nimchuk, *595 dniv soviets'kym viaznem*, 35-36. Rozenberg and Rudyk, together with Roman Rosdolsky, had edited the journal *Zhyttia i slovo* in 1937-38, which, in addition to its criticism of fascism and Ukrainian nationalism, criticized Stalinism from Ukrainian national communist and Trotskyist positions. Rosdolsky managed to escape the Soviets by moving, like so many other Ukrainian activists, to Kraków; but here he was arrested for helping Jews who had escaped the ghetto and spent the rest of the war years in German camps, including Auschwitz.

509 Nimchuk, *595 dniv soviets'kym viaznem*, 25-26.

The situation favored OUN not only politically but militarily. OUN was able to collect weapons in September 1939 from Polish military units,[510] not only in Galicia and Volhynia, but also as they retreated from the Germans through Romanian Bukovina.[511] Stockpiling weapons was explicitly ordered by OUN-B in March 1940, along with setting up a "military section" in each OUN cell.[512] NKVD documents occasionally make reference to weapons confiscated from OUN; a document from December 1940 referred to 1 rifle, 4 revolvers, 4 grenades, and 94 rounds of ammunition (December 1940).[513] Another NKVD report mentioned that aside from having gathered weapons during the invasion of Poland, OUN used other methods to acquire weaponry, including the illegal importation of arms from Germany, the confiscation of weapons from the population (sometimes by posing as NKVD agents or militiamen), and the purchase of weapons.[514] According to an OUN document intercepted by the NKVD, the homeland executive had at its disposal in December 1940:

> 1859 rifles
> 147,797 rounds of rifle ammunition
> 897 pistols
> 14,026 rounds of pistol ammunition
> 21 machine guns
> 759 grenades
> 65 mines
> 211 kilograms of explosive materials
> 105 compasses
> 39 gas masks
> 53 pairs of binoculars
> 242 topographical maps[515]

OUN was, thus, modestly armed when it emerged from the underground in late June 1941.

---

510 Patryliak, *Viis'kova diial'nist OUN (B)*, 202. Moroz, *Zynovii Tershakovets'-"Fedir,"* 14.
511 Fostii, "Diial'nist' OUN na Bukovyni," 7.
512 Patryliak, *Viis'kova diial'nist OUN (B)*, 108-09.
513 Danylenko and Kokin, *Radians'ki orhany*, 1:329.
514 Dated 17 May 1940. Ibid., 1:116.
515 Ibid., 1:338.

It was also to emerge with some experience in insurrection, which helped inform "The Struggle and Activities of OUN in Wartime" of May 1941. As Poland was falling in September 1939, OUN considered whether to launch a full-scale insurrection or not. In the end, it decided that such a move was premature. Nevertheless, there were still many attacks on Poles and Polish property and institutions.[516] OUN undertook these armed forays both when the Germans initially encroached into parts of eastern Poland and after the Germans withdrew and left all of eastern Poland to the Soviets. OUN was able to operate in a context of lawlessness and violence as the Polish state collapsed and the Soviets encouraged class war in the countryside (Ukrainian peasants v. Polish landowners).[517]

The situation provided a favorable opportunity for OUN to infiltrate the Soviet militia. Jan Gross wrote that "whoever greeted the entering Soviets and cared to step forward in September 1939 was accepted and put in charge—as a militiaman or a committee member—in his village or town or gmina."[518] A former Polish policeman complained that "whoever took up weapons became a militiaman."[519] Nimchuk noted in his memoirs that at first almost all the Ukrainians who signed up for the Soviet militia were undercover OUN activists; later, he wrote, the Soviet authorities replaced them.[520] Other evidence shows that some of the militiamen from OUN survived in their posts.[521] While Bukovina was under Soviet rule in 1940-41, OUN ordered its members to infiltrate the Soviet militia.[522] Other sources confirm that OUN successfully infiltrated

---

516 There is a fairly large literature on OUN's activities in September 1939, including: Patryliak, "Zbroini vystupy," and Rukkas, "Zbroini zahony." Ewa Siemaszko counted at least 2242 Poles killed by OUN in Galicia and 1036 in Volhynia. Siemaszko, "Bilans zbrodni," 80-81.

517 See the description of the brutality of September 1939 in Gross, *Revolution from Abroad*, 35-45. Gross did not mention OUN.

518 Ibid., 52.

519 Ibid., 67.

520 Nimchuk, *595 dniv soviets'kym viaznem*, 21, 38.

521 See below, 220.

522 Fostii, "Diial'nist' OUN," 6.

local militias in Galicia.[523] The NKVD itself was concerned about the infiltration.[524]

The period of the first Soviet regime in Western Ukraine also brought OUN into direct contact with Soviet reality and Soviet Ukrainians, which would prove useful when they later followed the Germans into pre-1939 Soviet Ukraine. The nationalist military historian Lev Shankovsky stated that when the OUN expeditionary groups went into southern Ukraine in the summer and fall of 1941, they made use of contacts they had made previously to facilitate their work.[525] In September 1940 the head of the Ukrainian NKVD reported to the top leadership of the all-Union NKVD that OUN-B had plans underway to spread its influence to the eastern oblasts of Soviet Ukraine.[526]

In sum, the OUN underground survived severe repressions at the hands of the Soviet authorities in Western Ukraine, yet all the while growing in numbers and experience. It managed to accumulate a modest collection of weapons and military equipment and to make some contacts with Ukrainians from the oblasts that originally constituted Soviet Ukraine. A major gain for OUN from the first period of Soviet rule was the elimination of all its political rivals in Galicia and Volhynia.

Jews under the First Soviets

In his microhistory of the Holocaust in Buchach (P Buczcacz), Omer Bartov noted that "many Jews had an ambivalent response to Soviet rule" in 1939-41.[527] This is because the Stalinist system had aspects that hurt some Jews and other aspects that gave advantages to other Jews. Sometimes individual Jews or Jewish families experienced both benefits and harm, and much depended on particular

---

523 Struve, *Deutsche Herrschaft*, 144-45, 182 n. 164. Radchenko, "Stavlennia OUN do ievreiv....Chastyna persha" (information on Sloviatyn [P Słowiatyn], south of Berezhany in Ternopil oblast, September 1939).
524 Danylenko and Kokin, *Radians'ki orhany*, 1:114-15; report of 17 May 1940.
525 Shankovs'kyi, *Pokhidni hrupy*, 32.
526 Danylenko and Kokin, *Radians'ki orhany*, 1:317.
527 Bartov, *Anatomy of a Genocide*, 150; 150-54 discuss the situation of the Buchach Jews under the Soviets.

circumstances, such as an individual's occupation, age, political views, or place of residence. Before parsing these issues more sys-tematically, I would like to give voice to Jews from Lviv who sur-vived the Holocaust and looked back to the period of 1939-41 in recollections recorded by the USC Shoah Foundation. Their testi-monies reflect the complex human experience of Jews under the First Soviets.

Ana Merdinger, whose family was considered bourgeois, was hard hit by the Soviets' nationalization of property: her father's store in Lviv was expropriated and the family was left penniless; much the same happened to her husband's family in Zalishchyky (P Zaleszczyki), Ternopil oblast.[528] However, she appreciated that there was no killing under Soviet rule; "they were nice people," she said — "they would share their last crumbs with you." But towards the end of 1940, they began to send people away to camps.[529]

Edward Spicer's father owned a factory in Lviv. He gave it up immediately when the Soviets came in, but the workers themselves elected him to be the manager of the factory because he was the type of boss, his son said, who worked together with the people. For the young Spicer, Soviet rule brought the possibility of higher education. Under Poland there had been a quota for how many Jews could enroll in the polytechnicum; but when the Russians came in, he said, admissions were open, and before you knew it, about half the students were Jewish. They passed their exams, and the school was very good. He studied there in 1939-41, with aspira-tions to become an engineer. He was quite happy about his new situation. But then the Germans invaded.[530]

Bill Koenig said that he did not fare badly "under the Rus-sians." His father was angry at them because they took everything away from him. But his employees said he was a good man, so he was allowed to manage his foreign business. There were no pog-roms under the Russians, said Koenig. "I worked, minded my own

---

528 Shoah Foundation, 9640 Ana Merdinger, 14-16, 19. Soviet authorities, shortly after taking Lviv in 1939, compiled lists of store owners. The majority of names are recognizably Jewish. DALO, R-221/1/151.

529 Shoah Foundation, 9640 Ana Merdinger, 23-24.

530 Shoah Foundation, 12729 Edward Spicer, 16-18.

business; I made a good living during the Russians. I even had money enough to go to cabarets and enjoy life."[531]

Lidia Mayer was just in first grade when "the Russians came." They immediately took over part of her family's apartment and put another family in there. Under the Russians, in her opinion, it was not so bad for Jewish people, and later many of them fled with the Russians into Russia.[532]

Artur Weiser said that the Russians nationalized his father's store, but his father befriended a high-ranking officer who set him up with a good job in the main post office. But that did not prevent them from having to take a Russian officer and his wife into their home. The apartment became crowded, but the Russians who lived with them were cultured and polite, not a burden. They probably had instructions, he remarked. Life was much easier for Jews than it had been before the war. Antisemites did not want to reveal themselves: the Poles were afraid of repressions and the Ukrainians too kept quiet because they saw that many Jews occupied high positions in the Soviet apparatus, in the police, and in the NKVD. Life became more peaceful, and he was able to study at the Institute of Fine Arts in Lviv.[533]

Ann Speier, born in Lviv in 1922, said that the Soviets expropriated her father's business, thereby severing the family's means of support. It became very hard to buy anything and to make a living, "but at least they let us live," she said.[534] Rosa Sirota, born in Lviv in 1933, maintained that her life did not change much when the Soviets came; it changed after the Germans came.[535] Maria Gesiola put it thus: the Russians had taken our property, so we were initially hopeful about the Germans; but the Russians took property, while the Germans took lives.[536] Alexander Orlowski, who was a child of eleven when the Soviets entered his native Lviv, remembered that his family lived better under the Soviets than it did

---

531 Shoah Foundation, 12664 Bill Koenig, 37.
532 Shoah Foundation, 13265 Lidia Mayer, 16-17.
533 Shoah Foundation, 15611 Artur Weiser, 12-16.
534 Shoah Foundation, 14670 Ann Speier, 3-4.
535 Shoah Foundation, 12493 Rosa Sirota, 14.
536 Shoah Foundation, 29911 Maria Gesiola, 9.

in prewar Poland. (He also noted that after the Soviets retreated in 1941, his father would no longer sleep at home.)[537]

Matylda Wyszynska had nothing good to say about the Soviet regime: life was very hard, they requisitioned apartments, and they fired her father. The Soviets who requisitioned her family's apartment denounced them to the authorities.[538]

Anna Zaryn, a teenager in Lviv under the Soviets, also remembered that period as being very difficult. The Russians nationalized her father's factory, and he had to find other employment. The Soviets also appropriated two rooms in their flat. The Russians in the apartment were NKVD, so at least the family was protected from deportations. But when these Russians were sent back to Moscow, they took the furniture with them. When Matylda's mother asked them why they were taking the furniture, they responded: if you have any complaints, you will find yourselves where the polar bears live. Then another NKVD man moved in with his wife and mother. These Soviets took three rooms, including hers; she had to sleep in the dining room. But again the family was protected. This was important, because the Russians were making lists for deportation. Almost all the refugees from the west of Poland, i.e., from the German zone of occupation, were deported. At night the Russians used to come and take people away in large trucks. Medicine for her sick father had to be bought on the black market.[539]

After the Russians came to Lviv, recalled Zygfryd Atlas, everyone was trying to hide their wealth. Talking to people was risky because everybody was reporting everybody else. The Soviets were deporting people to Siberia; people were disappearing. Everyone had a twenty-kilogram bag packed for Siberia. The Soviets tried to force him to join the NKVD, to be a spy. A Georgian commissar took him aside and said he must report any anti-Soviet activities. His code name was "Football." "I nearly died," Atlas said: "I could never report a mouse." But this was in 1941, just a few months before the end of Russian rule. He was not willing to report on

---

537   Shoah Foundation, 43777 Alexander Orlowski, 36.
538   Shoah Foundation, 22876 Matylda Wyszynska, 29-32.
539   Shoah Foundation, 26130 Anna Zaryn, 25-36.

anyone, so he tried to join the Komsomol to show that he was a patriot. But the war broke out and nothing came of it.[540]

The wealthy Hornstein family had a difficult time under the Soviets. Lusia (Lisa) Hornstein, who was born in Lviv in 1925, recalled (the testimony here is somewhat abridged and edited):

> Our family owned the whole apartment building. My father had a wood business, selling wood for pencils (including to Faber in Germany), matches, etc. He exported specialized wood products all over Europe. He bought up forests and cut the wood to specifications. It was a very profitable business. The Soviets nationalized my father's business. They took it all. We had all the papers from my father's office. It was a cold winter, and we actually burned those papers to keep warm. About three weeks after the Russians came, NKVD officers searched our whole apartment and then told us to get out. It was early in the morning. My mother and I were still in nightgowns. They told us to get out and put a lock on the door. My father had connections, so he managed after about three weeks to get the apartment reopened. But the caretaker and his family moved up into one room of our apartment. And the same person who had locked our apartment moved into another room. At that point we still had four or five rooms, and we were quite happy....
>
> But we went to school, and my father went to work, so things settled down. But then the Russians started taking people away to Siberia. First they took the politically suspect, then the rich, then the refugees from the German zone. I knew many who were taken away to Siberia — they were in school with me. The Russians worked from a list and usually came at night. If you were not there, that was it, until the next time. We were hiding out every time there was a rumor that something was going to happen, hiding out in locked stores, basements, other peoples' houses. So it was tough. But between those times we lived relatively peaceful lives.
>
> In the second year of the Soviet occupation, the caretaker living with us denounced my father for hoarding silver and valuables. He was arrested and taken to Brygidky. He returned two days later with a large man, some kind of police officer. My father looked horrible. My father was showing this guy our rooms; then they left. He came back a few hours later. Then the officer and his wife and two children moved into two rooms of the apartment, so we were reduced to two rooms. My father was very intelligent and resourceful and in this way

---

540 Shoah Foundation, 20357 Zygfryd Atlas, 44-49.

bought his freedom. But that arrangement was fine by us. It was crowded. This woman was cooking in our kitchen. She would some-times whisper to us that she thought we better not sleep at home to-night. We became friendly with them. She and the other Russians did not cook kosher, and they would cook lobster. My grandmother al-most died....

As the Germans were approaching, the Soviet officer who lived with us offered to take us away in a taxi. To go to Russia was the last thing my father wanted. We stayed behind.[541]

In summary, the Jewish survivor testimonies collected by the Shoah Foundation reveal attitudes to the Soviet occupation that generally ranged from positive to mixed, though some were thor-oughly negative. The Soviets expropriated their businesses, but of-ten the Jewish owners could be hired back as the managers of their enterprises or be appointed to another good position.[542] Many Jew-ish families had to share their apartments with Soviet officials, sometimes as part of a quid pro quo. Some Jews were in danger of arrest and deportation, while others, particularly younger Jews, saw opportunities open up for them that were not available in in-terwar Poland. And a number of Jewish survivors stressed that Jews as Jews were safe under the Soviets, especially compared to the German regime that followed.

The testimonies cited above have already touched upon many of the issues that belong in a systematic presentation of those as-pects of Soviet rule in 1939-41 that affected the Jewish population. The expropriation of Jewish businesses affected all the territories that the Soviets acquired in 1939-40. Shmuel Spector has described the situation in Volhynia:

> Due to the nationalization of all commercial activities, store owners became the largest single group in the Jewish community which

---

541   Shoah Foundation, 14797 Lusia "Lisa" Hornstein, 1-2, 9-11, 13.

542   Among many such examples, Valerie Schatzker wrote to me about her hus-band's father, who lived in Liubyntsi (P Lubieńce), near Stryi (P Stryj) in Lviv oblast: "During the '39-'41 period, after the Soviets had confiscated their homes and businesses in Lubience, Henryk, who had graduated from the Polytechnic in L'viv as a forestry engineer, had a position running the state lumber enter-prise in Stryj, that probably included his former business." Email of Valerie Schatzker to the author, 7 April 2011.

suffered economically. Gradually, Jewish merchants in Volhynia (as we recall, they made up 44% of all Jewish breadwinners) were forced to abandon their trade....The end of 1939 was set as the deadline for retail merchants to liquidate their businesses. In the first days of the Soviet occupation they were ordered to open their businesses and sell merchandise at old prices in Polish currency, the zloty, for which a nominal rate of exchange was set: one zloty for one ruble. Army officers, soldiers and officials who arrived from the east were paid generous salaries in zlotys, thus creating a huge demand for goods. Unavoidably, stores were inundated with buyers. As there was no replenishing of stock, the locals joined the buying panic.[543]

As we have seen, Jewish businesspeople were sometimes able to regain control of their businesses as managers. Of course, there was a practical aspect to this — no one knew better than they how to run their businesses. Jews (and others, of course) could also bribe their way into lucrative positions.[544] While these circumstances mitigated Jewish economic losses, the Soviet nationalizations left the Jewish population economically weaker than they had been prior to 1939. This, combined with the destruction of Jewish political and public life, left the Jews in a weakened position — and this at a time, as Spector noted, that "they faced the prospect of physical extermination which was not late in coming."[545]

The Soviets persecuted and liquidated the preexisting Jewish political parties, arresting Zionists and Bundists in particular.[546] Zionists, especially members of Betar and Hashomer Hatzair,[547] went underground, but the NKVD succeeded in greatly diminishing their influence.[548] The Zionists were more vulnerable to Soviet persecution than was OUN, since OUN had had years of underground experience before the advent of Soviet rule; the Zionists, by contrast, had not only operated legally in Poland, but they were

543 Spector, *Holocaust of Volhynian Jews*, 30.
544 Hrynevch, *Nepryborkane riznoholossia*, 253.
545 Spector, *Holocaust of Volhynian Jews*, 42-43.
546 Hrynevch, *Nepryborkane riznoholossia*, 239. Spector, *Holocaust of Volhynian Jews*, 37. Yones, *Evrei L'vova*, 58.
547 Betar was the youth movement of the Revisionist Zionists founded by Vladimir Jabotinsky. Hashomer Hatzair, which was founded in Galicia, was the youth movement of the secular Socialist-Zionists.
548 Hrynevch, *Nepryborkane riznoholossia*, 293-97.

favored by the Polish authorities. The Soviets restricted Jewish religious life and closed Jewish civic organizations, such as sports clubs and cultural and youth organizations.[549] As the testimonies mention, many Jews fell victim to the massive Soviet deportations,[550] though those affected were mainly refugees from the German sector.[551]

The situation for Jews in Bukovina under Soviet rule was not much different. Activists in Jewish political parties such as the Zionists and social democrats of the Arbeiterbund were arrested and deported, along with prominent Jewish journalists. Some Jewish petty bourgeois ("craftsmen and merchants") were also deported. The shops and workshops of Jews were confiscated or nationalized, just as they were in Galicia. Jews who had been in the underground communist movement before 1940 were not generally given positions in the administration, since most positions went to personnel from Eastern Ukraine.[552]

Antisemitism was prohibited in the Soviet Union, which came as a relief to Jews who suffered from the frequent attacks of Polish and Ukrainian nationalists and antisemites. However, there is also evidence of increasing resentment towards Jews just under the surface of Soviet society,[553] especially in the Soviet military. In August 1939, for example, a drunken Soviet Red Army soldier was arrested for disturbing the peace. As he was being detained he shouted: "If Kolchak and Denikin didn't finish off the Jews, then the time is not far off when machine guns will mow the Jews down along with the commissars who are with them! Down with the revolution, with the blood-sucking commissars and *politruki* [political officers]; before long machine guns will mow down the Jews and commissars."[554] It seems likely that awareness of these moods influenced the authors of OUN's manual on "The Struggle and Activities of

---

549   Ibid., 240. Spector, *Holocaust of Volhynian Jews*, 33-43.
550   And see above, 176.
551   Struve, *Deutsche Herrschaft*, 155.
552   Solonari, "Stavlennia do ievreiv Bukovyny," 123.
553   Hrynevch, *Nepryborkane riznoholossia*, 228-30. Himka, "Ukrainian Memories of the Holocaust," 435-36. Barber, "Popular Reactions," 13-14.
554   Hrynevch, *Nepryborkane riznoholossia*, 203-05 (quotation 204).

OUN in Wartime" of May 1941; the manual instructed OUN activists to incite Red Army soldiers to murder "Russians, Jews, NKVD agents, commissars," since "Stalinist and Jewish commissars are the archenemies of the people."[555]

Because official Soviet policy did not discriminate against Jews, as had been the case in the former Poland, the First Soviets opened up hitherto impossible opportunities for some, especially for youth. Jewish quotas in higher education disappeared, and Jewish youth flocked to study medicine, engineering, and other subjects. Jews could also enter state service under the Soviets. As Spector has noted with regard to Volhynia: "The expansion of public services and state bureaucracy made possible the employment of many professional Jews....Jews found new prospects of employment which previously had been closed to them such as militia, rail service and others."[556] Jeffrey S. Kopstein and Jason Wittenberg pointed out with acuity that Jews were hired primarily at the lower levels of the administration, and precisely low-level state bureaucrats would have had "the most contact with the local non-Jewish populations."[557] Jewish entrance into the apparatus of repression, the militia and NKVD, further fed into the stereotype of Judeocommunism, which was to prove so deadly in the immediate aftermath of the first period of Soviet rule.

A very typical accusation, found in many Ukrainian and Polish memoirs, is that Jews denounced Ukrainians and Poles to the NKVD. A full and well-articulated example can be found in the memoirs of OUN member Stefan Petelycky:

> Many Jews, and not just poor ones, also welcomed the Soviets at first. They had seen the Poles as their oppressors, and more than a few of them were communist sympathizers. Lots of the poorer folk were given positions of authority in the new Soviet administration, as were many Jews. I also noticed that a lot of Jews served in the Red Army and as political propagandists. It must be said that some of the local

---

555 Carynnyk, "Foes of Our Rebirth," 332. Carynnyk's translation. For fuller context, see Patryliak, *Viis'kova diial'nist OUN (B)*, 566.
556 Spector, *Holocaust of Volhynian Jews*, 32.
557 Kopstein and Wittenberg, *Intimate Violence*, 4; see also the illuminating statistics cited on p. 6 for Białystok palatinate.

Jews, people who had lived beside us for years, who knew us and who could at least guess where our political sympathies lay, betrayed us to the Soviets. Whether they did so out of pro-communist convictions or in order to ingratiate themselves to their new masters I can't say. But that some Jews betrayed Ukrainian nationalists to the Soviet secret police is something I know happened, for I was there. And the Poles experienced the same thing. They remembered the names of those Jews and others who they felt, with some justification, had betrayed them and their state to the Soviets. Later they, too, would take their revenge.... Jews may not wish to remember this today, but in those days many of them were given preferential treatment by the Soviet regime. It wasn't just a question of being afforded equality with Poles or Ukrainians. Many Jews willingly took part in the Soviet administration of Western Ukraine. And, since the Soviet regime eventually began taking ever more active measures to root out Ukrainian and Polish nationalists, to do away with the priests and *intelligentsia*, and to liquidate the better-off classes, Jews were seen as the principal beneficiaries of the communist regime.... We all suffered. We also all remembered who had done what and to whom. Poles saw Ukrainians as insurgents and Jews as communists and traitors. Ukrainians felt little remorse at the collapse of interwar Poland and witnessed the greeting that many Jews gave to the Soviet forces. When, shortly thereafter, NKVD units began hunting down Ukrainian nationalists and Polish patriots, sometimes with Jewish collusion, the stage was set for future tragedies.[558]

The Jewish historian and memoirist Eliyahu Yones, who survived the Holocaust in Lviv and had been a Bundist activist, also recalled that young Jewish communists denounced leaders of other Jewish parties to the NKVD, with arrests in consequence.[559]

But even many Ukrainian memoirists remarked on the ambivalence of the Jewish response to the communist authorities. Immediately after the passages just quoted from his memoir, Petelycky added this sentence: "Some Jews certainly saw the Soviets as liberators and welcomed them, but others saw in them only new

---

558 Petelycky, *Into Auschwitz*, 7-9. Struve notes that the practice of denunciation afforded Jews "new power resources against those who had hitherto harassed them, namely Polish and Ukrainian nationalists, who under Soviet rule belonged to the most endangered groups." Struve, *Deutsche Herrschaft*, 161; for an excellent account of the situation and activities of Jews in 1939-41, see 145-61.

559 Yones, *Evrei L'vova*, 82.

oppressors."[560] A Galician teacher, Ivan Bodnaruk, stated in memoirs written only a few years after the war: "Justice requires me to state that many Galician Jewish intelligentsia, even those who once dreamed about the Bolshevik paradise, had a critical or even hostile attitude toward the Bolshevik regime....Perhaps it will not be an exaggeration to say that almost the entire Jewish intelligentsia in Galicia was hostile to bolshevism and communism."[561] Ivan Nimchuk also noted: "One can state with complete confidence that with the exception of those who benefited directly from the 'blessings' of the new regime (and these were only a few percent [of the population]), the overall population of Galicia – Ukrainians, Poles, and even Jews – adopted a clearly hostile stance to the Bolshevik regime and dreamed only about how to rid our land of this hated enemy."[562]

In sum, Jews in Soviet Western Ukraine on the immediate eve of the Holocaust found themselves, as did all inhabitants of the region, in a totally new situation. Many Jews were ambivalent about their experience of communist rule. They may have lost their business or part of their home or lost a friend or relative to the gulag, but they were no longer exposed to antisemitic attacks, whether physical or verbal, and perhaps they were able to pursue a new career or educational opportunity or otherwise climb the social hierarchy. Some lay as low as possible during this dangerous period; others cooperated with the Soviet authorities, to a greater or lesser extent, with more or less enthusiasm. Some denounced their neighbors to the NKVD or even joined its ranks. What happened was complicated, and different individual experiences and actions should not be reduced to generalizations or stereotypes, certainly not by scholars.[563] But in the actual historical situation of 1939-41,

---

560 Petelycky, *Into Auschwitz*, 9.

561 Himka, "Ukrainian Memories of the Holocaust," 436.

562 Nimchuk, *595 dniv soviets'kym viaznem*, 59.

563 The need to avoid collective stereotypes and to consider differentiating factors also applies to Ukrainians under the German occupation. Wendy Lower has made the point well in reference to the Zhytomyr region: "Ukrainians who were still haunted by the terrors of 1930s Stalinism did not uniformly embrace the Nazis as 'liberators.' While all Ukrainians viewed Germans as outsiders or foreigners, as individuals they experienced the occupation differently depending on where they lived, the character of the local German rulers, the type of work

generalizations and stereotypes arose and solidified in the public imagination, and the approaching period of Nazi rule was to exploit them to lethal effect.

The NKVD Murders

On 22 June 1941, Germany launched its surprise attack on the Soviet Union. At that moment, as was the case throughout the first period of Soviet rule in 1939-41, the NKVD prisons in Galicia and Volhynia were massively overcrowded. At first Poles constituted the majority of the inmates, since the Soviets began by arresting representatives of the previous regime and Polish political activists. But as Polish political prisoners were shipped east and NKVD attention shifted more to the Ukrainian nationalist underground, the demographics of the prison population changed. In June 1941, Ukrainians formed the largest proportion of political prisoners, though many Poles and Jews were still imprisoned alongside them, especially in larger cities like Lviv. Aware of OUN's orientation towards Germany, the NKVD rounded up many more suspected Ukrainian nationalists as soon as they learned of the German attack. In those same days, OUN launched armed attacks on the prisons to free their comrades. Moreover, the German advance was rapid, and initial plans to evacuate the prisoners to the east proved impossible to fulfill. Too many trains and other forms of transport were already being used for the Soviet retreat. In this tense situation, the NKVD chose to execute political prisoners throughout Galicia and Volhynia, perhaps at the direct orders of Lavrentii Beria.[564]

---

they obtained, whether they were male of female, old or young, and whether they could speak or read German." Lower, *Nazi Empire-Building*, 10.

564 Struve, *Deutsche Herrschaft*, 210-691, weaves a well researched account of these atrocities into his discussion of anti-Jewish violence in individual localities in the summer of 1941; see especially 212-21, 247-53, 271-88. A useful collection of excerpted sources and scholarly literature on the murders is Kiebuzinski and Motyl, *The Great West Ukrainian Prison Massacre*. The extraordinary microstudy of the Dubno prison executions by Marco Carynnyk deserves to be singled out. It is very deeply researched and reconstructs events with the literary flair of a Truman Capote: Carynnyk, "Palace on the Ikva."

Altogether, as per Kai Struve's careful estimate, between 7500 and 10,000 prisoners were murdered in Galicia alone.[565] Probably a somewhat smaller number were murdered in Volhynia, potentially bringing the total number of victims to about 15,000.[566] The deliberate massacre of so many civilians was still shocking in June and July 1941.

The murders were committed in the heat of summer, and the victims' bodies decomposed rapidly. Skin would fall off the corpses as they were exhumed from prisons and mass graves. Rumors began to spread that the prisoners had been cruelly tortured before death and even that a priest had been crucified. I agree with Kai Struve that it is unlikely that the NKVD executioners had the time to perform the refined tortures on the prisoners that rumor ascribed to them. Moreover, the rumors imagined practices that have not been documented elsewhere as part of the NKVD repertoire of torture and execution. Struve therefore ascribes the origin of the rumors about torture and mutilation to the advanced stage of decomposition of the victims.[567] But other scholars, including Ksenya Kiebuzinski and Alexander Motyl[568] as well as Jan T. Gross,[569] have accepted the rumors as accurate. A third camp, represented by Bogdan Musial[570] and Hannes Heer,[571] argued that OUN members deliberately mutilated the corpses of the victims before revealing them to the public in order to heighten hatred of the Bolsheviks.[572] Such and similar views circulated in Jewish and communist circles already at the time of the exhumations in summer 1941.[573]

---

565 Struve, *Deutsche Herrschaft*, 216.

566 There are, however, estimates as high as 40,000, a total that seems highly unlikely. Kiebuzinski and Motyl, *The Great West Ukrainian Prison Massacre*, 31.

567 Struve, *Deutsche Herrschaft*, 219-21, 278-88.

568 Kiebuzinski and Motyl, *The Great West Ukrainian Prison Massacre*, 31-33, 61-63. These are views expressed by Kiebuzinski and Motyl in their introduction, but material they include within their collection contradict their understanding of the issue; see 137, 139-40, 253, 287, 291, 323, 357, 368.

569 Gross, *Revolution from Abroad*, 181-82.

570 Musial, *"Konterrevolutionäre Elemente sind zu erschießen,"* 262-69.

571 Heer, "Lemberg 1941," 168-70.

572 This view was also shared by Prusin, "A 'Zone of Violence,'" 372.

573 A Jewish survivor, Roma Tcharnabroda, interviewed by David Broder in 1946, had been studying to be a nurse, and her husband was a military doctor. Both

Regardless of what actually occurred, the popular imagination at the time leaned towards the view that the NKVD had indeed orchestrated orgies of torture while killing the prisoners. Yevhen Nakonechny described what he heard from a family acquaintance, a Polish thief. The thief had been confined to Brygidky prison for six months when he became aware that Lviv was being bombed and that prisoners were being executed. He feared for his own life, but, as a mere criminal, he was eventually released instead of shot. He told the Nakonechny family that on his way out of the prison, NKVD men invited him to a little party they were having in the midst of the murders. They offered him vodka, sausage, bread, and pork fat (*salo*), an offer he simply pounced upon, having not eaten for a couple of days, as prison personnel were too busy with the killings to feed their charges. The NKVD men remarked on his appetite and wondered if abstention had also aroused his sexual appetite. One of them took him to a "room like a torture chamber. There on the tables lay absolutely naked young girls, with their hands tied to some hooks on the walls." The NKVD man urged him to take one of them, explaining that they were Polish girl scouts (*harcerki*), "crazy fascists" who were going to be killed soon in any case.[574] Such were the lurid tales circulating.

Press reports fanned the flames. The Nazi organ *Völkischer Beobachter* reported that "animals in human form," i.e. the NKVD operatives, ripped open the wombs of pregnant women and nailed the embryos to the wall. This article was translated into Ukrainian

she and her husband were in Lviv when the corpses were discovered in Brygidky prison. She said that the commission of doctors that performed a forensic examination noted that there was no blood around legs that had been chopped off. This indicated to her that the legs had been severed after the victims were already dead. In her opinion, the Germans themselves probably killed the prisoners. *Voices of the Holocaust,* http://voices.iit.edu/interview?doc=tcharnabrod aR&display=tcharnabrodaR_de (accessed 26 June 2019). Marian Tyrowicz was a teenager in Lviv in 1941 from a Jewish communist family. He recalled that there were various rumors about who had killed the prisoners— Ukrainians had killed Russians, Germans had killed the prisoners, and the guards had killed the prisoners. His family believed that either the Germans or the Ukrainians had been responsible. Shoah Foundation, 25867 Marian Tyrowicz, 67-68. See also AŻIH, 301/1096, Erna Klinger, 1; AŻIH, 302/201, Rachela Kleiner, 23.

574   Nakonechnyi, *"Shoa" u L'vovi,* 85.

and appeared in the daily *Krakivs'ki visti*. The same Ukrainian news-paper also reported on victims burned alive or subjected to the "red glove" torture, in which prisoners' arms and legs were plunged into boiling water and the skin flayed from the joints to the digits. The NKVD cut off noses and women's breasts, carved crosses on the chests of priests, and even crucified some of the priests. As is typical in such traumatic circumstances, the number of victims was greatly exaggerated.[575]

What happened in the NKVD prisons stoked a blind rage for revenge in some and also created a political opportunity for others, as we will see in the next chapter.

*   *

*

Overall, the first period of Soviet rule in Western Ukraine partially directed the course of the Holocaust there. The deportations and repressions solidified anti-Bolshevik sentiment among those — and they were the overwhelming majority — who did not directly bene-fit from the new regime. Moderate Ukrainian political parties were swept away, leaving the direction of Ukrainian politics to OUN. So-viet repressions hurt the OUN underground, but also seem to have spurred recruitment, so that OUN actually increased in size during the Soviet interlude. It also came out of this period with more weap-ons than it had acquired previously and with greater military expe-rience among its militants. Jews suffered economically, and their social institutions were destroyed or damaged under the Soviets; these circumstances undermined their chances of survival under German occupation. Many Ukrainians and Poles blamed Jews for denunciations to the NKVD and for collaboration with the Soviet state. As the Soviets retreated from Western Ukraine after the Ger-man attack, they murdered thousands of political prisoners. The decomposing and malodorous corpses were exhumed as soon as the Germans arrived, giving rise to nightmarish emotions.

---

575 Himka, "Ethnicity and Reporting," 381.

5. Anti-Jewish Violence in the Summer of 1941

The Wave of Pogroms

In the summer of 1941, beginning immediately after Germany's attack on the Soviet Union on 22 June, numerous incidents of anti-Jewish violence took place in a swath of territory roughly three hundred kilometers wide from west to east and stretching over a thousand kilometers from Riga in the north to Iași in the south. Almost all these incidents occurred on territory that had been acquired by the Soviets in 1939-40 as a result of their alliance with Nazi Germany but that had now come under occupation by the *Wehrmacht*.[576] Some of the incidents have become notorious, such as the murder of the Jews by their neighbors in Jedwabne and the horrific pogroms perpetrated in Kaunas (25-29 June) and Lviv (1 July). In Galicia and Volhynia alone, 153 pogroms have been counted for that summer.[577]

The number of victims across the Baltic states, eastern Poland, and Romania ran into the tens of thousands. This, however, was just a fraction of the million and a half Jews estimated to have been killed during the entire Holocaust, but primarily in 1942-43, across the territory of what is now Ukraine. But in the summer of 1941 in the westernmost fringes of the Soviet Union patterns were established that were soon refined into effective methods to murder almost all the Jews of Eastern Europe. The culmination of this wave of mass murder was the shooting of thirty-three thousand Jews at Babi Yar in Kyiv at the end of September 1941. Notably, these mass killings occurred before the Wannsee Conference (January 1942) and before the first death camp, Bełżec, became operational (March 1942).

Wherever the Nazis went, they orchestrated pogroms. When they took Vienna in March 1938, they forced Jews to clean the

---

576 There is a useful map: Gilbert, *Atlas of the Holocaust*, 67.
577 Kopstein and Wittenberg, *Intimate Violence*, 84.

sidewalks with toothbrushes or their bare hands and pulled the beards of older Jewish men. These and other humiliating rituals became stock features of pogroms over the next few years. Eight months after taking Vienna, the Nazis organized pogroms across Germany and the former Austria, known collectively as the November pogrom or *Kristallnacht*. Tomasz Szarota has written an excellent account of Nazi-sponsored pogroms in occupied Warsaw, Paris, Amsterdam, Antwerp, and Kaunas.[578] Kraków also experienced a pogrom in December 1939, as the Jewish population was moving from their former homes to the newly established ghetto. On the eve of the attack on the Soviet Union, Nazi leaders envisioned a wave of pogroms accompanying the German advance. The director of the Reich Security Main Office (RSHA), Reinhard Heydrich, invited dozens of SS and police personnel to Berlin on 17 June 1941 to a special meeting to receive instructions about encouraging "self-cleansing" actions in occupied Soviet territory.[579] The main points were summarized in a telegram he sent to Einsatzgruppe leaders on 29 June 1941, a week after the invason was launched:

> One should not put any obstacle in the way of efforts at self-cleansing arising in anticommunist and anti-Jewish circles on the territories to be newly occupied. On the contrary, one should provoke these, leaving no traces, intensify them if necessary, and direct them on the right track, but in such a way that local "self-defence groups" would not later be able to cite orders or political promises made.[580]

Holocaust historians have long been aware of a report to Heydrich submitted by the commander of Einsatzgruppe A, Franz Walther Stahlecker: "In the first hours after the entry of the forces [into Lithuania] we also persuaded, not without considerable difficulties, local antisemitic elements to start pogroms against the Jews....It was desirable, outwardly, to show that the first steps were made by the local population on its own initiative, as a natural reaction to the

---

578   Szarota, *U progu Zagłady*.
579   Ibid., 210-14.
580   Longereich and Pohl, *Die Ermordung der europäischen Juden*, 118-19.

subjugation at the hands of the Jews for decades, to the recent communist terror."[581]

The Germans created the context for the anti-Jewish violence and, in fact, they and their Romanian allies were directly responsible for most of the murders themselves, but, as Szarota has demonstrated, the Germans normally relied on local collaborators to instigate and orchestrate pogroms.[582] As we shall see in this chapter, the primary local accomplice of the Germans in such anti-Jewish violence in Galicia and Volhynia in the summer of 1941 was the Ukrainian National Militia established by OUN. Elsewhere in the former Poland the fascist Falanga served as the Nazis' instrument. In Lithuania the Germans worked with the Lithuanian Activist Front.

The utility of preexisting fascist movements was limited once the Germans crossed into the old, pre-1939 Soviet Union. Here, massive repressions, deportations, and executions had prevented the formation of any political entities outside the communist party, hence there were no local antisemitic organizations to rely upon. True, as we shall see in the next chapter, the Germans could draw on Russian and Ukrainian fascists and antisemites from elsewhere to staff the police forces they used to implement their murderous aims: both factions of OUN organized police in many localities in occupied Soviet Ukraine, and Russian fascists associated with the National Alliance of Russian Solidarists (perhaps better known by its Russian abbreviation NTS) were active in the police in eastern and southern Ukraine as well as in occupied Russia. But these imported fascists had little rooting in the local populace. As a result, on old Soviet territory, a wave of pogroms, such as affected the territories garnered by the Soviets in 1939-40, was absent.[583] There was

---

581   Cited in Bauer, *A History of the Holocaust*, 184 (Bauer's translation). Hilberg also cited the Stahlecker report (Hilberg, *Destruction of the European Jews*, 319; it appeared on p. 203 of the original 1961 edition). A pdf of the original report, which covered the activities of Einsatzgruppe A up to 15 October 1941, is available on the internet: https://alles-ueber-litauen.de/images/Litauen/Geschichte/Holocaust/Stahlecker_Report.pdf (accessed 26 August 2019).

582   Szarota, *U progu Zagłady*, passim.

583   For example, according to the research of Diana Dumitru and Carter Johnson, in Transnistria, the region around Odessa occupied by Romania, there is no

the occasional pogrom, to be sure,[584] but no cluster of such incidents. A report of Einsatzkommando 6 of Einsatzgruppe C from
pre-1939 Soviet Ukraine dated 12 September 1941 stated: "Almost
nowhere can the population be persuaded to take active steps
against the Jews. This may be explained by the fear of many people
that the Red Army may return."[585]

The concentration of the pogroms on the territories that had
been acquired by the Soviet Union in 1939-40 certainly had other
sources than the availability of local collaborationist groups.[586] Diana Dumitru and Carter Johnson have marshalled a compelling
case that the population of the old Soviet territories had been so-
cialized into a more open attitude to their Jewish compatriots, not
the more hostile them-and-us way of thinking prevalent in countries like Poland and Romania. They arrived at this conclusion
through a comparison of the behavior of local non-Jews in Bessarabia, which had been under Romanian rule since the end of World
War I until 1940, to the behavior in Transnistria, which had been
Soviet since the end of the Russian civil war and only came under
Romanian rule in 1941. They argued that three factors made the
pre-1939/40 territories less likely to produce pogroms: the Soviet
state granted full equality to Jews, suppressed antisemitism, and
integrated Jews into society.[587] I have myself observed in an investigation of memoirs of Ukrainian emigrants collected in 1947 that

---

evidence of any pogrom occurring in 1941. Dumitru and Johnson, "Constructing Interethnic Conflict and Cooperation," 24-25. They are not counting the
murder of several ten thousand Jews in Odessa in October 1941 carried out primarily by Romanian and German soldiery.

584 Mel'nyk, "Stalins'ka iustytsiia." Wendy Lower has observed: "But one cannot
state with certainty that 'no Jedwabnes occurred in central and eastern Ukraine;
this is because we have no sources for many smaller Jewish communities that
were destroyed, and because after the war Soviet investigations and war-crimes
trials played up the role of Ukrainian nationalists as collaborators but mini-
mized the popular antisemitism of ordinary 'peaceful Soviet citizens.'" Lower,
"Pogroms," 238.

585 Cited in Hilberg, *Destruction*, 317. A very similar report about eastern, formerly
Soviet Belarus is cited in Dumitru and Johnson, "Constructing Interethnic Conflict and Cooperation," 30.

586 For valuable reflections on the "historical and theoretical explanations of the
violence," see Lower, "Pogroms," 231-39.

587 Dumitru and Johnson, "Constructing Interethnic Conflict and Cooperation."

Ukrainians from the old Soviet territories were much more horrified by the mass killing of Jews and Roma than Galician Ukrainians, who often ignored the Holocaust altogether in memoirs of the Nazi occupation or even implied that the Jews deserved their treatment.[588] Nonetheless, the Germans were able to recruit and train professional killers from these same old-Soviet populations. They took ethnic Germans in Transnistria and formed them into "self-defense" units which killed about fifty thousand Jews in late December 1941 and for a few months in early 1942.[589] Beginning in September 1941 the German SS and police took Soviet POWs, trained them at a special camp, Trawniki, and used them as guards in labor, concentration, and death camps. So it was possible, in the right circumstances, to overcome the effects of Soviet socialization.

The territories acquired by the Soviets in 1939-40 were particularly fertile ground for the incitement of anti-Jewish violence. These were areas where anti-Soviet sentiment was extraordinarily high. Eastern Poland spent less than two years under the Soviets, the Baltic states and northern Bukovina just about one year. This was not long enough to create the mentality of homo sovieticus. But it was long enough for the population of these territories to experience mass deportations, mass arrests, and instant impoverishment. In particular, just on the eve of German occupation and the outbreak of the pogroms, the NKVD murdered tens of thousands of political prisoners from Estonia in the north to Galicia in the south. When the Germans entered, they ordered the corpses exhumed and laid out for the population to witness and identify. The stink of decomposing bodies polluted the air in cities such as Lviv. The perpetrators of these murders and of the earlier repressions had already retreated to the east. The anger of the population turned on "the Jews," who were widely, though inaccurately as we have seen, perceived to have been the main support of the Soviet regime. The German authorities and the German and collaborationist press repeatedly emphasized that "the Jews" should be held responsible.[590]

---

588 Himka, "Ukrainian Memories of the Holocaust."
589 Steinhart, *The Holocaust and the Germanization of Ukraine*.
590 Himka, "Ethnicity and the Reporting of Mass Murder." A Ukrainian eyewitness from Lviv remembered: "The press published reports and photographs. The cinemas showed newsreels with the horrific scenes [of the NKVD's victims].

We do not know why the Germans were interested in fostering popular violence against the Jews. Was this just an emanation of Nazi antisemitism or the inert continuation of practices that had been developing since the seizure of Vienna in March 1938? Raul Hilberg reflected on their motivations as follows:

> The reasons that prompted the killing units [Einsatzgruppen] to activate anti-Jewish outbursts were partly administrative, partly psychological. The administrative principle was very simple: every Jew killed in a pogrom was one less burden for the Einsatzgruppen. A pogrom brought them, as they expressed it, that much closer to the "cleanup goal" (*Säuberungsziel*). The psychological consideration was more weighty. The Einsatzgruppen wanted the population to take a part, and a major part at that, of the responsibility for the killing operations. "It was not less important, for future purposes," wrote Brigadeführer Dr. Stahlecker, "to establish as an unquestionable fact that the liberated population had resorted to the most severe measures against the Bolshevist and Jewish enemy, on its own initiative and without instructions from German authorities." In short, the pogroms were to become a defensive weapon with which to confront an accuser, or an element of blackmail that could be used against the local population.[591]

Szarota too thought that blackmail was an element in the Germans' intentions and considered that to be the reason they often photographed the pogroms.[592]

Szarota additionally suggested that the Germans provoked pogroms to facilitate ghettoization: after the pogroms, Jews would welcome separation from the neighbors who robbed and attacked them.[593] This hypothesis finds some reflection in the sources. According to the Stanyslaviv oblast branch of the Extraordinary State Commission, Hans Krüger, a captain in the Gestapo, held a speech

---

Placards and leaflets on the subject were issued. It was emphasized that precisely the Jews were guilty of the crimes." Nakonechnyi, "*Shoa*" *u L'vovi*, 100. Those who lived in North America during the terrorist attacks on 11 September 2001 might recall that the immediate reaction was an immense grief. The mood soon, however, turned to anger, and Americans began looking for someone to punish; the result was the invasions and wars in Afghanistan and Iraq.

591   Hilberg, *Destruction*, 318.
592   Szarota, *U progu Zagłady*, 32.
593   Ibid., 67, 272.

to the Jews of Stanyslaviv on 1 August 1941, in which he said: "Hitler...is a very good person, and during the war he is isolating the Jews from other nationalities so that they can live and work in peace."[594] Jewish survivor Rose Moskowitz recalled a relative calm descending upon the Jewish community in Lviv after the Germans put an end to the pogrom.[595] Historian Shmuel Spector also noted that "in this initial phase, the Jews [of Volhynia] regarded the German military administration as the power capable of defending them from the harassment of their neighbors."[596] After pogroms in Szczuczyn, northwest of Białystok, some Jews sought, and found, protection from German soldiers.[597] In the Baltic region (then "Ostland") the Germans began to issue instructions about ghettoization in mid-August, in the aftermath of the pogroms.[598] Of course, the Germans need not have had a plan to use the pogroms to lull and isolate the Jewish population; indeed, I think it more probable that they opportunistically made use of the pogroms when and where they could.

I also think it likely that the Germans had mixed motives in instigating pogroms in the western Soviet Union and above all that they were improvising, rather than following a particular strategy. Moreover, it seems to me that when they did begin to formulate the goal of killing all Jews, which occurred only after they entered old Soviet territory and could not rely on local organizations to spearhead pogroms, they realized that public participation in violence only slowed the killing process down. The latter notion is reflected in a report of Einsatzkommando 5 of Einsatzgruppe C of 21 July 1941: it stated that a pogrom perpetrated by Ukrainians and

---

594 YVA, r.g. M.52, file no. 558; microfilm no. 99.2698, frame 505; DAIFO. Two days later, according to the same source, Krüger began to extort, torture, and murder the leaders of the Jewish community. Krüger was the key figure in the "Bloody Sunday" massacre of about 10,000 Jews in Stanyslaviv on 12 October 1941. Pohl, *Nationalsozialistische Judenverfolgung*, 144-47.
595 Shoah Foundation, 9851 Rose Moskowitz, 20.
596 Spector, *Holocaust of Volhynian Jews*, 71.
597 Kopstein and Wittenberg, *Intimate Violence*, 76.
598 Matthäus, "Operation Barbarossa," 260.

German soldiers in Uman, in Cherkasy oblast on old Soviet territory, hampered them in the murder of the Jews of that city.[599]

Jeffrey S. Kopstein and Jason Wittenberg have advanced a novel explanation of the pogrom wave: "In occupied Poland pogroms were most likely to occur where there were lots of Jews, where those Jews sought national equality with Poles and Ukrainians, and where there was some non-Jewish support for parties advocating tolerance of minorities. In those areas local Poles and Ukrainians seized the opportunity provided by the German invasion to rid themselves once and for all of future political rivals."[600] They used a quantitative, statistical approach, comparing localities in which pogroms occurred (153 in Galicia and Volhynia) to localities in which Jews and non-Jews lived together but no pogrom occurred (1943 in the same regions). To test hypotheses, they used the Polish census of 1921 and results of the elections of 1928. They found a weak correlation between the strength of a communist movement in a locality and the outbreak of a pogrom. On the other hand, where the Zionists were strong, pogroms were more likely. Perhaps because Kopstein and Wittenberg come from a different discipline than I do, political science as opposed to history, I have my doubts. As a historian, I would have liked to have found some reflection in the sources of a resentment towards Zionist aspirations or to Jews as political rivals. Instead, I found the most popular justification of the pogromists to be that Jews had been instruments of the hated Soviet regime, and also that they were exploiters and (although this was expressed more rarely) Christ killers.

I am also not entirely sure about the suitability of using the 1928 election results as a proxy for the political configuration of individual localities in 1941. Much happened in the intervening years: the great depression; Stalinist repressions and famine in the USSR; Nazi rule in Germany; the descent of Poland into dictatorship; the emergence of OUN; the pacification of 1930 in Galicia and Volhynia; and the Soviet interlude of 1939/40-41. Kopstein and Wittenberg defended their use of the 1928 electoral data by citing

---

599   Snyder, *Bloodlands*, 198, citing "USHMM-SBU 4/1747/19-20."
600   Kopstein and Wittenberg, *Intimate Violence*, 129.

evidence that regional political attitudes persist over the long term.[601] I agree that there is often a historical basis for certain regional voting patterns. But I wonder if the Soviets' deportation of the Polish political and economic elite and suppression of the Zionists would not have changed precisely the political circumstances that Kopstein and Wittenberg were attempting to measure. Moreover, it is possible for historically based regional voting patterns to persist but for their content to change (e.g., formerly communist East Germany is, as I write, the stronghold of the right-wing, xenophobic Alternative für Deutschland).

Kopstein and Wittenberg's argument necessarily ascribes the initiative of the pogroms primarily to local civilians. But we have ample evidence that many of the incidents that they count as pogroms were the work of armed forces: the Wehrmacht, the Waffen-SS, the Einsatzgruppen, and OUN units such as the Ukrainian National Militia and Sich. Some incidents were hybrid, as we shall see clearly in the case of the Lviv pogrom, in which the Ukrainian National Militia rounded up the Jews, the urban crowd abused them, and a unit of Einsatzgruppe C shot hundreds of them during and shortly after the pogrom.[602] Kai Struve's careful study of anti-Jewish violence in the summer of 1941 in Galicia establishes that German soldiers or police played a significant role in the deadly pogroms in Berezhany (P Brzeżany) in Ternopil oblast), Boryslav in Lviv oblast, and Chortkiv (P Czortków) in Ternopil oblast, which also figure in Kopstein and Wittenberg's list of pogroms.[603] Struve also brought to attention the bloodthirsty rampages of Waffen-SS Wiking in Hrymailiv in Ternopil oblast, Skalat (P Skałat) in Ternopil oblast, Ternopil, Zboriv in Ternopil oblast, and Zolochiv (P Złoczów) in Lviv oblast, all of which localities also figure in the Kopstein-Wittenberg list.[604]

---

601 Ibid., 54-55.
602 Ibid., 104-08, deals with the Lviv pogrom. It places the major onus of responsibility for the pogrom on the crowd and does not discuss the mass shootings perpetrated by the Germans.
603 Struve, *Deutsche Herrschaft*, 668. Kopstein and Wittenberg, *Intimate Violence*, 137.
604 Struve, *Deutsche Herrschaft*, 561-630. Kopstein and Wittenberg, *Intimate Violence*, 138-42.

But it is not the task of this monograph to unearth and weigh the ultimate causes of the wave of anti-Jewish violence in the weeks after the Germans and Romanians occupied the Soviet western territories. Our goal instead is to ascertain the extent to which OUN participated in the violence, and this is the subject of the following sections.

Building the Nationalist Ukrainian State

The Germans arrived in Lviv on the morning of 30 June 1941. Along with them came the Nachtigall battalion, a unit in German service linked with OUN-B and led by Roman Shukhevych, the future commander of UPA. Stepan Bandera's chief lieutenant, Yaroslav Stetsko, also arrived in Lviv in the company of an OUN-B expeditionary group. That evening Stetsko held a meeting in the Prosvita building at which he proclaimed the renewal of Ukrainian statehood. The news spread quickly by radio, newspapers, posters, and word of mouth. OUN also organized public meetings in many localities to announce independence.[605]

The proclamation of statehood declared that "the renewed Ukrainian State will collaborate closely with National Socialist Greater Germany, which under the leadership of Adolf Hitler is creating a new order in Europe and the world and is helping the

---

605   Early in July OUN leaders and militiamen in Perevoloka (P Przewłoka), near Buchach in Ternopil oblast, rang the church bells at 6:00 or 7:00 in the morning, and about fifty people attended the meeting, according to an OUN militiaman later arrested by the Soviets. USHMM RG-31.018M, reel 60, frames 1062-63; GDA SBU Ternopil', spr. 4280, vol. 3. An OUN member and subsequently Ukrainian auxiliary policeman recalled at his deportation hearing in West Palm Beach, Florida a meeting in Halych (P Halicz) in Ivano-Frankivsk oblast: "Everybody, almost 95 percent of every village, the towns, all the people went there. That was the larger city and that took place of proclamation of our small region, so in my life, I had chance to see in one place tough fighters, crying in one place from happiness. I will always remember that....The church bells were ringing. It was very, very happy occasion." Testimony of Bohdan Koziy, USHMM RG-06.09.01*21, Box 21, case of Bohdan Koziy, 2 October 1981, 46. A Jewish survivor from Bolekhiv (P Bolechów) in Ivano-Frankivsk oblast also remembered that "a regional meeting was convened with the participation of representatives from nearby villages. They gathered at the 'Magistrate.' the town hall....There they proclaimed an autonomous Ukraine." Adler, "Chapters," 196. For more on such meetings, see Rossoliński-Liebe, "Ukrainian National Revolution."

Ukrainian people liberate themselves from Muscovite occupation...."[606] On 3 and 4 July Stetsko sent letters to the fascist leaders of Europe—Hitler, Mussolini, Franco, and Pavelić[607]—announcing the new state.[608] But neither Stetsko nor Bandera had cleared the establishment of a Ukrainian republic with the Germans, and the latter were not at all happy about the attempt at a *fait accompli*.[609] Not only did the Germans refuse to recognize the Ukrainian state, they arrested both Bandera, on 5 July, and Stetsko, on 9 July. Stetsko was released on 12 July and Bandera two days later, but neither was allowed to leave Berlin (at least officially)[610] and both had to report regularly to the police.[611] Other leaders of OUN-B were also detained, interrogated, and released at this time.

In July 1941 the Germans were finding certain services of OUN useful: in particular OUN was able to set up a relatively loyal local civil administration to replace what the Soviets had established, and the OUN militias helped them implement their anti-Jewish policies. The Germans were wary of OUN, particularly of OUN-B, because it had its own political agenda. But more substantive and harsher repressions were not visited on the nationalists until the second half of August and in September 1941. During the preceding, more tolerant period, OUN-B continued to hope for German

---

606 Dziuban, *Ukrains'ke derzhavotvorennia*, 123.

607 The letter to *Poglavnik* Ante Pavelić probably reflects the importance OUN-B attributed to Hitler and Mussolini's creation of an independent Croatia. Borys Lewytzkyj, who was a member of Ivan Mitrynga's faction in OUN, recalled the tremendous excitement that the announcement of the formation of an independent Croatia in April 1941 produced in the Banderite milieu in Kraków: "The Banderite leadership spontaneously decided to send a congratulatory telegram with a greeting, and the formation of this 'state' was treated as proof that there would be a similar 'independent Ukraine.' Mitrynga and comrades protested against such a telegram. Two of the main leaders at the time responded to our protest with a scene that cannot be forgotten: they marched around the room with their arms on each other's shoulders, shouting: 'We have never made a mistake, we will never make a mistake.'" Lewytzkyj, "Natsional'nyi rukh," 15.

608 The letters are published in Ukrainian translation in Dziuban, *Ukrains'ke derzhavotvorennia*, 137-39, 144-45.

609 EM 11, 3 July 1941.

610 Stetsko, however, managed to travel to Kraków, where he met with Mykola Lebed and turned over the Homeland command to him. Armstrong, *Ukrainian Nationalism*, 59-60.

611 Rossoliński-Liebe, *Stepan Bandera*, 247.

recognition of an independent Ukrainian state as a part of the New Europe. Even after the arrest of Bandera and Stetsko, OUN-B organized public meetings to proclaim the Ukrainian state and to appeal for German recognition.[612]

The state that the Banderites proclaimed was being built without delay. They set up a government, the Ukrainian State Administration (*Ukrains'ke Derzhavne Pravlinnia*), which was composed of leading OUN personnel as well as prominent Ukrainians from outside the organization. For example, from OUN they appointed, among others, Mykola Lebed, Lev Rebet, Roman Shukhevych, and Yaroslav Starukh—all of whom had played and would continue to play major roles in the nationalist project. They were given portfolios in the executive, security, the military, and propaganda. From outside were appointed: the physician Oleksandr Barvinsky; the agronomist Yevhen Khraplyvy; the historian Ivan Krypiakevych, who declined his post; and Kost Pankivsky, a lawyer who had defended OUN members on trial for assassinations and robberies. They were generally awarded posts in the areas of their expertise.[613] But all these appointments remained essentially on paper owing to the Germans' refusal to recognize the state and their arrest of the head of the government, Stetsko.

The Banderites had much more success in constructing the lower levels of their state. One of the consequences of the Soviet interlude of 1939-41 was a vacuum in local power. The Soviets dismissed and often deported Poles who had served in all levels of government of the Second Polish Republic, unless they were indispensable experts. They set up their own administration organized along the same lines as in the rest of the Soviet Union, with oblast, raion, municipal and village soviets. They imported cadres from eastern Ukraine to facilitate the sovietization of Western Ukraine. When the Germans invaded, many of the easterners and some locals who had cooperated closely with the communist regime fled to

---

612 Rossoliński-Liebe, "Ukrainian National Revolution," 106-13.
613 A full list of the composition of the Ukrainian State Administration can be found in Veselova, *OUN v 1941 rotsi*, 253-55.

the Soviet Union.[614] This was not a situation as in the rest of the General Government, where the Germans themselves replaced some mayors and village elders, often with local ethnic Germans, but left the majority of local officials in place, even forcing them to remain in place or face charges of sabotage.[615]

With the entrance of the Germans, it was not only OUN that was thinking about staffing the local administration. The head of the Greek Catholic church, Metropolitan Andrei Sheptytsky, issued a letter to his clergy on 10 July 1941, urging pastors and elders in the community to form local governments. "Where there is not yet an administration and local militia," he wrote, "it is necessary to organize the election of a community council, mayor, and chief of the militia." He instructed pastors to pick, on their own or after consulting with respected villagers, three farmers to serve as justices of the peace to settle disputes. His letter came a little late in the day, and his instructions were not backed by any effective measures of implementation. His purely moral admonition failed miserably.[616]

The Banderites were able to do much better. For one thing, they started much earlier. Ivan Klymiv reported to Bandera on 23 July 1941 that he had made appointments to local revolutionary committees and the civil administration already in early May; by the twentieth of that month he had appointed the commandants of militias in the villages and cities of the Western Ukrainian Lands.[617] Klymiv surely exaggerated his successes, but it is clear that the underground OUN-B had been preparing personnel in advance of the German invasion.

Once the invasion was underway, both factions of OUN dispatched expeditionary groups (*pokhidni hrupy*) from the German sector into the Homeland. When they arrived on the spot in

---

614 "...The evacuation of the Soviet administrative agencies created a power vacuum, mainly on the level of the local civilian and police administration. Local initiative quickly seized the opportunity to fill up the vacuum with Ukrainians, members or sympathizers of the Organization of Ukrainian Nationalists, whose various factions joined together for the purpose." Spector, *Holocaust of Volhynian Jews*, 62.

615 Grabowski, *Hunt for the Jews*, 64-65.

616 Himka, "Christianity and Radical Nationalism," 99-100.

617 Veselova, *OUN v 1941 rotsi*, 367.

Western Ukraine, these expeditionary groups set up local governments. An example of how this was done is contained in a fairly
detailed report of Starukh to Bandera of 29 June 1941. Starukh's expeditionary group, which included among its members Stetsko,
who was very soon to become head of state in Lviv, arrived in Yavoriv (P Jaworów) in Lviv oblast on 28 June. The first thing it did
was to hold a meeting of OUN members and sympathizers. Then it
appointed local government officials. It made Ivan Paslavsky head
of the county administration. Paslavsky, as a member of UVO, had
taken part in a robbery near Kalush (P Kałusz) in Ivano-Frankivsk
oblast in 1925, during the course of which he was wounded in a
shoot-out with the Polish police; he was sentenced to five years imprisonment in 1926.[618] At the head of the city administration the expeditionary group placed a certain Professor Kmetyk, who apparently taught in the Yavoriv gymnasium. As head of the militia it
appointed Yevhen Smuk, who joined OUN in 1935, was arrested
under the Poles and sent to the Bereza Kartuska concentration
camp in 1939, and was killed in 1948 as a local leader of UPA during
its anti-Soviet insurrection.[619] More appointments were made than
just to these three key positions, but who were chosen as deputies
and the like was not specified in Starukh's report.

The newly appointed leaders then swore an oath before
Stetsko, "according to the text of the instructions." Starukh here
was referring to the May 1941 text, which we have cited many times
before, "The Struggle and Activities of OUN in Wartime." The text
contained detailed instructions on how to set up the envisioned
Ukrainian state at all levels, including the local level. The oath read
as follows: "I swear to Ukraine that I will execute loyally [and] con-
scientiously all the obligations to the Ukrainian State entrusted to
me by the Organization of Ukrainian Nationalists under the

---

618 The footnote in ibid., 246, mistakenly identifies Paslavsky as one of the defendants at a Soviet trial of twelve OUN members held on 29 October 1940. The
source of the confusion is that Starukh referred to Paslavsky as "from the trial
of the twelve." But the number of UVO militants who were tried for the armed
robbery in Kalush was also twelve, and UVO even put out an effective propaganda brochure entitled "Twelve Ukrainians before the Court in Lviv." Mirchuk, *Istoriia OUN*, 31-32.

619 "Ievhen Smuk."

leadership of Stepan Bandera and that I will serve with all my strength and with my life the completely independent Ukrainian state and strive for its power and glory."[620] Although the oath referred to the "completely independent Ukrainian state" (*vid nikoho nezalezhnii Ukrains'kii derzhavi*), realities dictated that the next step was to send a small delegation, headed by Stetsko, to the German commandant of the city for approval of the appointments to the city administration. The commandant granted his approval without delay, but stipulated that a Pole be appointed as second deputy.

By evening a grandiose arc of triumph was erected in Yavoriv, decked out with the Ukrainian and German flags and with a sign saying "Glory to Ukraine—Glory to Bandera" in large letters. OUN called a meeting of the "entire community," but meaning only the Ukrainian community. "The beautifully decorated city hall was bathed in flowers. The hall was filled to overflowing, the mood upbeat, enthusiastic." Starukh called the new local leaders, Paslavsky and Kmetyk, to the podium and delivered a speech. The two leaders also briefly spoke. After shouts of glory to Ukraine and to the leader Bandera and the singing of the Ukrainian national anthem, the meeting concluded. "Then—meetings with the two leaders. Instructions on the organization of the militia. The entire machinery is in motion that should put the county on its feet."[621] Variations of this scenario were played out throughout Galicia and Volhynia in the first half of the summer of 1941. Although OUN-B did not control the entire civil administration in Galicia and Volhynia, it was the dominant force. Kai Struve has calculated that OUN controlled 187 of 200 raion administrations in Galicia.[622]

Both factions of OUN also sent their expeditionary forces to pre-1939 Soviet Ukraine and were able temporarily to control local administrations in a number of localities. OUN-M set up the governments in Kyiv,[623] Mykolaiv (the oblast capital), Poltava,

---

620 Patryliak, *Viis'kova diial'nist OUN (B)*, 490.
621 The report is printed in Veselova, *OUN v 1941 rotsi*, 245-47, and in Dziuban, *Ukrains'ke derzhavotvorennia*, 94-95.
622 Struve, *Deutsche Herrschaft*, 383.
623 Kurylo, "Syla ta slabkist'," 116-17.

Proskuriv (today Khmelnytskyi), and a number of smaller localities.[624] OUN-B had influence in Kherson[625] and in a number of localities in the Donbas.[626] Sometimes influence on local administration passed from OUN-B to OUN-M, as happened in Zhytomyr.[627] Members of OUN served as mayor of Krasnopillia raion, Sumy oblast, and deputy mayor of Sumy.[628] A comprehensive study of OUN influence on the civil administration, including in the old Soviet territories, is still lacking.[629]

The Germans were growing increasingly suspicious of the nationalists, who displayed a mind and goals of their own. Already in October 1941, an Einsatzgruppe report stated: "At the beginning of the campaign Bandera's adherents were assembled in small groups and received brief training. They were furthermore provided with money and propaganda material. Under the cover of carrying out tasks to establish order, such as appointing mayors, establishing a militia, and combatting Jews and communists, political work was being carried out."[630] The Germans began reining in and repressing OUN-B, primarily in Galicia and Volhynia, in mid-August and September 1941. The Banderite mayor of Kherson was apparently executed by the German Security Police before the end of 1941. The Germans tolerated OUN-M somewhat longer. The Melnykites were more active in the old Soviet territories, especially in Kyiv, rather than in Western Ukraine, but there they were exposed and easier to

---

624 Armstrong, *Ukrainian Nationalism*, 195-96, 200, 206.

625 Ibid., 206.

626 Dobrovol's'kyi, *OUN na Donechchyni*, 9-10.

627 Armstrong, *Ukrainian Nationalism*, 65-66.

628 Ivanushchenko, *OUN-UPA na Sumshchyni*, 9, 30.

629 In general, only the first steps are being taken in studying the civil administration of Ukraine under the German occupation. See Eikel and Sivaieva, "City Mayors," 407-08. A disappointing article from 2006 by an otherwise excellent historian demonstrates how little research has been conducted on the subject: Golczewski, "Local Government." The Ukrainian civil administration in the Kremenets region of Volhynia has been described in some detail in Klymenko and Tkachov, *Ukraintsi v politsii v reikhskomisariati "Ukraina,"* 17-33. The same authors have also treated the Ukrainian civil administration of the area around Ternopil in Galicia: Klymenko and Tkachov, *Ukraintsi v politsii v dystrykti "Halychyna,"* 30-52.

630 International Military Tribunal [Nuremburg trial]–102- R (Sechster Tätigkeitsund Lagebericht der Einsatzgruppen in der Sowjetunion vom 1.-31.10.1941). Ilnytzkyj, *Deutschland und die Ukraine*, 2:144.

purge: they stood out from the rest of the population by their language and attitudes, they did not possess the level of popular support that the Banderites enjoyed in Western Ukraine, and they had to compete with Russian émigrés for influence with the Germans. The Germans began murdering them in late November 1941 but intensified their repressions in January and February 1942.[631] They arrested the editors of the newspaper *Ukrains'ke slovo* in Kyiv on 12 December 1941 and later killed a number of prominent Melnykites associated with the paper, including the nationalist poet Olena Teliha (executed 21 February 1942). They also turned their attention to members of OUN in the civil administration; in December 1941 they arrested and in February 1942 executed the Melnykite mayor of Kyiv, Volodymyr Bahazii.[632] Also in 1942 German police shot the Melnykite mayor of Poltava.[633] In Vinnytsia, the Germans at first relied on emissaries from Western Ukraine, but "very few were able to conceal their nationalist sympathies and remain in the administration beyond the spring of 1942."[634]

Although OUN influence in the civil administration of the old Soviet territories was spotty and temporary, OUN-B was able to retain control of most of the local administration in Galicia and Volhynia. When OUN-B launched an anti-German insurrection and an anti-Polish ethnic cleansing project in spring 1943, parts of Volhynia were completely controlled by its armed force, UPA. As Timothy Snyder has noted: "Poles found little reason to distinguish UPA domination from German rule, since locally the same people with the same guns were in control."[635]

Whatever the motivation of locals entering the civil administration under the occupation, they were inevitably drawn into the machinery of the Holocaust. This was not just the case in Ukraine,

---

631 Armstrong, *Ukrainian Nationalism*, 77-78, 206.
632 Kurylo, "Syla ta slabkist',"119-21. Berkhoff, *Harvest of Despair*, 52. Eikel and Sivaieva, "City Mayors," 415. Shkandrij, *Ukrainian Nationalism*, 61-62. Kentii, *Narysy*, 106.
633 Armstrong, *Ukrainian Nationalism*, 200.
634 Lower, *Nazi Empire-Building*, 46.
635 Snyder, *Reconstruction of Nations*, 171.

but wherever the Nazis held power and influence in Europe.[636] The murder of millions of Jews required a huge bureaucratic apparatus, as Raul Hilberg's major work has demonstrated. The Germans depended on local administrations for the local knowledge necessary to implement their plans. These administrations were involved in the identification and registration of Jews, their economic exploitation,[637] and—particularly in the formerly Polish territories—their isolation from the non-Jewish population.

As the Germans were preparing to kill all the Jews in Galicia in 1942, mayors and community officials were ordered to submit Jewish birth records (so-called metrical books) and various genealogical information.[638] So, for example, the mayor of Rudky, just outside Lviv, Andrii Tershakovets, brother of prominent OUN-UPA leader Zynovii Tershakovets, provided the Germans with a list of 1349 Jews by name and year of birth.[639] Sometimes the local administration was charged with providing lists of Jews who had been activists under the Soviets;[640] the local officials of Otyniia (P

---

636 The role of the local government in the Holocaust in Dąbrowa Tarnowska county (about a third of the way from Kraków to Lviv) is well treated in Grabowski, *Hunt for the Jews*, 63-78.

637 In Radyvyliv in October 1941, "the Ukrainian committee issued a decree forbidding Jews to own any animals, horses, or sheep, under penalty of death; but they could sell their animals to the Ukrainians, although it was perfectly clear from the start that the exchange would be at half the price." Yitschak Vaynshteyn, "The Destruction of Radzivilov," https://www.jewishgen.org/yizkor/Radzivilov/rad199.html (accessed 30 March 2020).

638 A number of German documents ordering these materials are available on microfilm in Yad Vashem: YVA, r.g. M.52, file no. 261 (mf no. 99.2693, frames 942-1160; DALO, 24/1/252): "Perepiska s nachal'nikami sel'skikh i gorodskikh volosnykh sovetov o sostavlenii spiskov evreiskogo naseleniia prozhivaiushchego na territorii distrikta Galitsii"; file no. 262, frames 1165-98; DALO, 24/1/253. "Korespondentsiia nachal'nikov sel'sovetov...s otdelom naseleniia i...po voprosu personal'nykh knig" (the photo of the page did not encompass the right edge; the requests for documents came from the Lemberg-Land Amt für Innere Verwaltung, Bevölkerungswesen und Fürsorge); file no. 266; frames 1286-1382; DALO, 24/1/389. "Prikazy i perepiska po voprosu organi[zatsii]...prav evreiskogo naseleniia. Vedomosti o evreiskikh knigakh grazhdanskogo sostoianiia."

639 YVA, r.g. M.52, file no. 261 (mf no. 99.2693, frame 1010; DALO, 24/1/252). Andrii Tershakovets was an activist in the Ukrainian scouting organization Plast both in Ukraine and after the war in Canada. He died in Toronto in 1979. Kostiuk, "Pam"iati Andriia Tershakivtsia."

640 Spector, *Holocaust of Volhynian Jews*, 72.

Ottynia), northwest of Kolomyia in Ivano-Frankivsk oblast, for example, provided such a list to the OUN militia, who then murdered eighty-nine Jews in the summer of 1941.[641] The Germans asked the Ukrainian administration in Radyvyliv in Volhynia to compile a list of "dangerous Jews."[642] In Vinnytsia, one of the first tasks of the newly installed local administration was, according to Lower, "providing the locations of Jews, Roma, POWs, and other targeted groups."[643]

In August 1941 in Kamianets-Podilskyi in Khmelnytsky oblast, the SS killed 23,600 Jews — most of the town's Jewish inhabitants.

> On August 30, immediately after most Jews had been shot, the city administration asked all Jews still hiding in the Old Town to register with the local police. The city mayor distributed fifty copies of an announcement to the local police chief, specifying that all Jews in hiding had to register with the police office at the central square before 6 a.m. on August 31. The local administration and local police thereby helped the occupying authorities to complete the murder of the local Jewish population in as comprehensive a manner as possible.[644]

After the mass murder of Jewish communities, the local government was often tasked with processing and distributing the Jewish clothing and personal items left at the scenes of execution as well as belongings found in vacated Jewish homes.[645] Such was the

---

641 Struve, *Deutsche Herrschaft*, 641-42.

642 "The Ukrainians immediately drew up a list of a few Jews who fit that description and also provided an additional list of a few wealthy Jews. For some reason, they later reduced the first list to approximately 18 persons. These were the ones the Ukrainians wanted to destroy because of personal vendettas. These Jews hid money and various precious personal objects because they saw this as a pretext for confiscating and stealing their property." Yitschak Vaynshteyn, "The Destruction of Radzivilov," https://www.jewishgen.org/yizkor/Radzivilov/rad199.html (accessed 30 March 2020). See also "From the Memories of Jechiel Porochovnik," https://www.jewishgen.org/yizkor/Radzivilov/rad231.html (accessed 30 March 2020).

643 Lower, *Nazi Empire-Building*, 49.

644 Eikel and Sivaieva, "City Mayors," 421.

645 "On that day of liquidation Ukrainian police moved through the town and marked all the Jewish homes. Notices were put up in town warning that anyone found looting Jewish property — would be shot. For several weeks collections were carried out and all the belongings sorted out in special store-rooms. Part of the items were allotted to the Municipality, part to the Ukrainian institutions

case in Kamianets-Podilskyi, in Kyiv after the murder of over 33,000 Jews at Babi Yar, and in Bila Tserkva in Kyiv oblast.[646] Local governments also disposed of houses and apartments where Jews had lived before their murder.[647] In Volhynia, local officials "demanded that the Judenräte furnish the offices of the German and Ukrainian administration, as well as their living quarters, with the finest Jewish furniture and household utensils."[648] Civil administrations freely pressed Jews into forced labor on local projects.[649] In Lutsk, the capital of Volhynia oblast, the civil administration even succeeded in acquiring a forced labor camp in January 1942; previously it had been run by the SS "with particular severity and brutality," but conditions improved once the camp was transferred to the local administration.[650] In Kamianets-Podilskyi the Ukrainian mayor sought to protect some Jewish tailors and craftsmen because they were skilled and useful, and Ukrainians had not yet been sufficiently trained to replace them.[651]

Local administrations were active in establishing ghettos.[652] They had the knowledge of the local topography, and they also had an economic incentive to confiscate vacated Jewish housing for distribution. They determined the time line and rules for the transfer

---

or the needy families among the population who had applied for assistance and part, especially jewelry and expensive clothing, was sent by rail in special wagons to Germany (I witnessed with my own eyes these transports)." Ephrain Fishman, "As an Aryan in the Kovel Ghetto," *Kovel: Testimony and Memorial Book of Our Destroyed Community* https://www.jewishgen.org/yizkor/kovel1/kov442.html (accessed 21 March 2020).

646 Eikel and Sivaieva, "City Mayors," 415, 418, 420.

647 Ibid., "City Mayors," 419-20.

648 Spector, *Holocaust of Volhynian Jews*, 97.

649 Eikel and Sivaieva, "City Mayors," 421, 423-24. In Radyvyliv (P Radziwiłłów), the local administration impressed Jews to dig trenches to lay cable for the Lviv-Kyiv telephone line. Yitschak Vaynshteyn, "The Destruction of Radzivilov," https://www.jewishgen.org/yizkor/Radzivilov/rad199.html (accessed 30 March 2020).

650 Spector, *Holocaust of Volhynian Jews*, 125.

651 Eikel and Sivaieva, "City Mayors," 423.

652 A survivor from Kovel (P Kowel) recalled that about a year after the Germans occupied the city, "the Ukrainians" asked the Germans to establish a ghetto, since all other Volhynian towns already had ghettos. Ben-Zion Sher, "Thus the City Was Destroyed," Kovel: Testimony and Memorial Book of Our Destroyed Community https://www.jewishgen.org/yizkor/kovel1/kov407.html#Page411 (accessed 21 March 2020).

of Jews from their former homes into the ghetto.[653] They also had a major influence on the formation and composition of the Judenräte; again, they had local knowledge useful for this purpose.[654]

I repeat that OUN did not set up these civil administrations for the purpose of expediting the Germans' murder of the Jewish population; participation in the genocide was rather a result of the particular situation of local governments under Nazi occupation. The administration had many other matters to attend to in the wake of the Soviet retreat, which was often accompanied by the destruction of infrastructure. For example, in Vinnytsia, the new administration had to grapple with restoring electricity, running water, the post and telegraph, transport, and food supplies, all of which were urgent necessities.[655]

The Ukrainian National Militia

Instructions on the formation and duty of the National Militia, or Ukrainian National Militia, took up about a fifth of the planning document "The Struggle and Activities of OUN in Wartime," which, it may be recalled, was composed in May 1941 by the most authoritative figures in the Bandera faction of OUN: Bandera himself, Stepan Lenkavsky, Shukhevych, and Stetsko.[656] These were detailed instructions, specifying even the inscriptions on signs at militia posts and the size and design of the militia's rubber stamps.

The militiamen were to be identified primarily by their armbands: "All members of the Militia wear on their left arm yellow and blue armbands, and if these are unavailable then white armbands with the inscription 'National Militia.'"[657] If possible, the militia was to wear temporary uniforms, even Red Army or NKVD uniforms, but even so, militiamen had to wear the armband.[658] Even later, when the militia would be furnished with its own special

653 Spector, *Holocaust of Volhynian Jews*, 120-21.
654 Ibid., 151-53, 171. Eikel and Sivaieva, "City Mayors," 417, 421. AŻIH, 301/397, Mełamed and Zylberberg families, 4.
655 Lower, *Nazi Empire-Building*, 47.
656 Veselova, *OUN v 1941 rotsi*, 130-54
657 Ibid., 130.
658 Ibid., 135.

uniform (a point never actually reached), they were still to wear the armband "as the sign of belonging to the National Militia."[659] Many Jewish survivors were to remember these armbands as they recalled the violence of the summer of 1941, even when they did not understand their significance.[660]

Although a few passages in "Struggle and Activities" called for all male ethnic Ukrainians between the ages of eighteen and fifty to report for the militia,[661] this was an overly ambitious aspiration and it did not come to pass. The idea was that there would be permanent members of the militia, who were armed at all times, and a reserve force that was furnished with weapons only when required.[662] It seems that only permanent members of the militia were active in the summer of 1941. The instructions indicated who was to be recruited for regular service. Among the preferred recruits were ethnic Ukrainians who had served in the Soviet militia or even the NKVD, particularly officers, provided they were willing to support the nationalist revolution. OUN placed a high value on their professional training.[663] As indicated earlier, OUN had been infiltrating the militia during the Soviet occupation of 1939-40,[664] but almost none of these remained in service when the Germans invaded.[665] There were also a few cases in which militiamen changed allegiance from the Soviets to the nationalists.[666] In any case, the Holocaust survivor Leopold Iwanier remembered some militiamen in Lviv who served under both the Soviets and OUN: "These were the same Ukrainians who were in the Soviet militia.

---

659   Ibid., 140-41.
660   Himka, "Lviv Pogrom," 230.
661   Veselova, *OUN v 1941 rotsi*, 130, 148.
662   Ibid., 145.
663   Ibid., 130, 147, 150.
664   See above, 182.
665   Serhii Riabenko could only find once case in which a member of OUN served in the Soviet militia in Lviv and then entered the Ukrainian National Militia and, subsequently, the Ukrainian Auxiliary Police. Riabenko, "Ukrains'ka militsiia L'vova."
666   Apparently not many, however. Riabenko only found four Lviv militiamen born in Dnieper Ukraine and the Donbas and altogether just five former Soviet militiamen in the ranks of Lviv's militia. Riabenko, "Ukrains'ka militsiia L'vova."

They replaced the stars on their caps with tryzubs [stylized tridents—Ukrainian national symbols]. We knew them because we lived on their beat."[667] It was probably the former Soviet militiamen who were wearing uniforms during the Lviv pogrom of 1 July 1941. Uniforms were remembered by at least one pogrom survivor and appear in several photographs of the pogrom.[668]

In oblast centers and other large cities, where Ukrainians formed only a minority of the population, "Struggle and Activities" recommended recruiting for the militia among "workers, which is best, Red Army soldiers and Ukrainian militiamen, [and] persons brought in from the countryside."[669] About two-thirds of the militiamen in Lviv were born in villages.[670] The visibility of the young peasant men in the militia lowered its status in the eyes of their often more cosmopolitan victims. Jewish survivor Fanya Gottesfeld Heller, who spent her girlhood years in Skala-Podilska (P Skała), northeast of Borshchiv in Ternopil oblast, characterized them as follows: "The militiamen were all peasant boys who found it glamorous to carry a rifle, put on an armband, lord it over the Jews, and loot at will—and then get drunk and sleep it off."[671]

The leadership of the militia in Lviv was composed of OUN-B activists and sympathizers. Two of the leading figures in forming the militia there were survivors of the NKVD murders, Bohdan Kazanivsky and Omelian Matla. Also involved in the initial stage was Shukhevych himself.[672] OUN-B organized most of the militias in Galicia and Volhynia, but OUN-M controlled the militia in Rohatyn in Ivano-Frankivsk oblast.[673] The Ukrainian National Militia was organized by OUN, but not all militiamen were actual members of OUN. Serhii Riabenko, who studied the organization of the militia in Lviv in detail, has concluded that only a minority of the

---

667 Shoah Foundation, 48148, 45-47.
668 Himka, "Lviv Pogrom," 218, 229, 232.
669 Veselova, *OUN v 1941 rotsi*, 147-48.
670 Riabenko, "Ukrains'ka militsiia L'vova."
671 Heller, *Strange and Unexpected Love*, 54.
672 Himka, "Lviv Pogrom," 228.
673 Struve, *Deutsche Herrschaft*, 503.

militiamen in that city were OUN members.[674] This was certainly true of the militias elsewhere as well.

I will now present two cases of the formation of militias by OUN, one in Galicia and the other in Volhynia, to illustrate how militias were set up. The first case concerns the general area of Krakovets (P Krakowiec), west of Yavoriv in Lviv oblast, in the week after the German attack. Militias were established in a number of localities. In Kobylnica Ruska, a village near Krakovets but now in Poland, The expeditionary group under the command of Starukh, which we have already mentioned,[675] entrusted the Greek Catholic pastor, Father Lev Sohor to set up the militia, providing him with written authorization to do so. As Stetsko himself noted, "the village accepted it."[676] Another report from Kobylnica Ruska to the OUN leadership, dated 29 June, identified Father Sohor as "a very active priest and our sympathizer." The report stated that the militia in Kobylnica Ruska was sixteen men strong.[677] On 25 June Starukh's expeditionary group formed a militia in Mlyny (P Młyny), north of Nadvirna in Ivano-Frankivsk oblast. Twenty young men volunteered for the militia, all already wearing the required armbands. One had come from Kobylnica Ruska and two from the neighboring Kobylnica Wołoska. The entire afternoon was devoted to training the militia. They were given basic military training by Ivan Ravlyk, whom Stetsko was soon to entrust with the organization of the militia throughout Ukraine.[678] The recruits were then apprised of OUN's view of the situation and the tasks that lay ahead. The author of the report stated: "The guys were enthusiastic. [They constitute] very good material."[679] On 26 June, at a meeting chaired by Starukh, the head of the militia in Krakovets was

674 Riabenko, "Do pytannia stvorennia militsii," 57, 65. Riabenko, "Ukrains'ka militsiia L'vova."
675 See above, 212-31.
676 Report of Stetsko to Bandera, 25 June 1941 in Dziuban, *Ukrains'ke derzhavotvorennia*, 78.
677 Ibid., 93.
678 Stets'ko, *30 chervnia 1941*, 181-82.
679 The author of this report, dated 26 June, is unidentified. Dziuban, *Ukrains'ke derzhavotvorennia*, 82.

appointed.[680] On that same day, according to another report, from the village of Łazy, now in Poland in Gmina Radymno, "there came to us 6 people, who rode out to villages to create groups and create a militia under the leadership of Stepan Bandera." Through their efforts militias were established in Łazy and neighboring villages.[681]

The second case took place in the town of Rafalivka (P Rafałówka), southwest of Volodymyrets in Rivne oblast. We know about its formation from the testimony of a member of the militia, Volodymyr Panasiuk, who spoke about it at his first trial in 1944 and more extensively at his second in 1971. Two Galician nationalists came to Rafalivka in July 1941 to organize the Ukrainian National Militia. They said it was necessary to help the Germans in their battle with the Bolsheviks, Poles, and Jews, and urged all the Ukrainian men born in 1920-25 to join. Panasiuk, who had been born in 1921, did so. Two Galicians came and trained them in warfare and the use of firearms. The militiamen were told that Bandera had proclaimed an independent Ukraine, and they had to swear an oath to it. After swearing, they sang the Ukrainian national anthem "Shche ne vmerla." Then they celebrated with drinks. The militiamen wore the blue-and-yellow armbands.[682]

OUN expeditionary groups set up national militias in pre-1939 Soviet Ukraine as they followed the front eastward,[683] but these were short-lived, since in the autumn of 1941, the Germans were replacing the Ukrainian militias with a police force under their own control.

---

680 Report of Kosak, 26 June 1941 in ibid., 85.

681 Report of Kruk, 27 June 1941 in ibid., 85-86.

682 USHMM RG 31.018M, reel 20; HDA SBU, spr. 19090, vol. 1, ff. 9, 16, 16v, 17; vol. 3, ff. 3, 3v, 100, 101. When the militia was disbanded by the Germans, Panasiuk joined up in the stationary Schutzmannschaft, as the police in German service was called, and his duties included guarding the ghetto. He denied that he executed Jews, but admitted in 1971 that he escorted Jews to their execution. Later he was in a Sonderkommando under the command of the SS and SD. In an SS Sonderkommando he fought against Polish partisans in the Warsaw uprising. He wore a tryzub on his uniform.

683 Shankovs'kyi, Pokhidni hrupy, 45, 60, 160.

Nationalist politics aside, in the circumstance of the rapidity of the Soviet retreat, it was rational for communities to set up militias. Amateur historian George Moshinsky described the context for the formation of militias to the court at a deportation trial:

> As Soviets left and there was a vacuum of power, the population started immediately to organize a kind of self-defense group, which so often are being called by Germans as militia, militz....Those groups were organized solely by the population because the problem was very big. There were deserters from the army, Soviet deserters. There were people that couldn't retreat with their units, there were ordinary bandits, there were provocateurs, and in this case for the population it was very dangerous to live without any kind of power taking care. Usually in every country which it happens. So that Ukrainians, just like everywhere else, formed those militia units.[684]

Joseph Adler, a Jewish survivor from Bolekhiv recalled:

> A few days before the Soviet forces left Bolechow several Ukrainian activists approached the Soviet military command with the purpose of allowing them to organize a neutral militia force. This, they said, would ensure the safeguarding of the inhabitant's lives [sic] and property during the expected period of chaos resulting from the withdrawal of the Red Army. Permission was granted and soon one could see groups of 2-3 Ukrainian militiamen patrolling, bearing rifles, in plainclothes and wearing armbands.[685]

"Struggle and Activities" assigned a number of security tasks to the militia. They were to prevent looting and guard communication facilities (post and telegraph offices), train stations, bridges, industrial plant, and so forth.[686] They were to seek out NKVD records,[687] which they would use to identify collaborators with the Soviet organs of repression.[688] The raion commandant was responsible for drawing up lists of those who persecuted Ukrainians,

---

684 Testimony of George Moshinsky at deportation hearing, USHMM RG-06.09.01*43, Box 45, case of George Theodorovich, 11 March 1985, 837.
685 Adler, "Chapters," 196.
686 Veselova, *OUN v 1941 rotsi*, 132-33, 148.
687 Ibid., 131.
688 See, for example, Himka, "'Skazhite.'"

especially non-Ukrainians — Jews, Muscovites, and Poles.[689] The militia was to enforce curfews and issue passes to leave villages.[690]

In OUN's understanding, non-Ukrainians were security risks, and it was the militia's job to deal with them. This was clearly laid out in "Struggle and Activities." "We must remember," it said,

> that there exist factors, which as the main support of the power of the NKVD and Soviet authorities in Ukraine, must, in the creation of a new revolutionary order in Ukraine, be rendered harmless. These factors are:
>
> *Muscovites*, sent to Ukrainian lands to make Moscow's power in Ukraine secure.
>
> *Jews*, both individually, and as a national group.
>
> *Foreigners*, primarily various Asiatics, through whom Moscow colonizes Ukraine with the intention of creating in Ukraine a chessboard of nationalities.
>
> *Poles* in the western Ukrainian lands, who have not renounced their dreams of rebuilding a Greater Poland, precisely at the cost of Ukrainian lands, even if Poland had to be red [i.e., communist].[691]

The militia commandant of a particular locality, collective farm, or factory was to make sure that "all Jews" immediately report to the command post. Moreover, all inhabitants were obliged to report to the command post any "hidden Red Army personnel, NKVD operatives, Jews, informers...."[692]

The militia on collective farms was responsible for excluding from the farms the following categories of people: foreigners who enforced the exploitation of Ukrainian peasants; Jews employed on the collective farms as facilitators of Bolshevik power; and all representatives of Bolshevik power, including informers, persons associated with the NKVD, NKGB, and prosecutor's office, as well as correspondents of Bolshevik newspapers. "All non-members of the collective must be interned and locked under guard."[693] The commandant of the militia of industrial enterprises was to "arrange for the internment and the placement under guard of all elements

---

689 Veselova, *OUN v 1941 rotsi*, 145.
690 Ibid., 131, 136, 146, 150.
691 Ibid., 129.
692 Ibid., 131.
693 Ibid., 138.

hostile to the nationalist revolution and all uncertain elements. In particular, all Jews and collaborators with the NKVD and NKGB must be interned."[694] The raion militia was charged with responsibility for "the internment camp, designated for Jews, asocial elements, and prisoners of war."[695] In the actual course of events, the militia did not develop to the extent envisioned by "Struggles and Activities" and therefore never established internment camps. As we shall see, those who the instructions indicated should be interned were usually, in practice, shot or otherwise executed.

The xenophobia and antisemitism of "Struggles and Activities" marked the earliest actions of the militias. When the Starukh expeditionary group was setting up militias in Kobylnica Ruska and Mlyny, Stetsko reported directly to Bandera that the purpose of the militias was to "remove the Jews." He mentioned this twice in the same report, the whole of which was permeated with an antisemitic mindset.[696]

OUN never developed the centralized militia it had hoped for, but it did draw many men into the militia and thus into the movement and national revolution. German sources mention over thirty thousand militiamen by mid-August in 1941 in Galicia (at that time formally incorporated into the General Government as Distrikt Galizien).[697] Although I suspect that this number is inflated, the Germans in August 1941 were about to dissolve the militia and replace it with a police force under their direct control, and therefore they might well have tried to produce an accurate estimate.

"Struggle and Activities" had instructed the militia to be useful to the Germans: "The attitude and work of the National Militia must be such that the allied army and organs see also their own benefit in the existence of the National Militia."[698] However, given OUN's goal of establishing an independent state and the Nazis'

---

694   Ibid., 139.

695   Ibid., 143.

696   Stetsko's report of 25 June 1941 is in Dziuban, *Ukrains'ke derzhavotvorennia*, 77-78. And see the analysis of the antisemitism in the report in Struve, *Deutsche Herrschaft*, 266-68.

697   Pohl, *Nationalsozialistische Judenverfolgung*, 92. Plum, Report, 17.

698   Veselova, *OUN v 1941 rotsi*, 154.

goal of exploiting Ukrainian territory as a crucial part of Germany's *Lebensraum*, the working relationship between the Germans and OUN, especially OUN-B, was bound to be fragile and situational. OUN-B's disappointment with the Germans became greater after 1 August 1941 when Galicia was incorporated into the General Government, thus breaking up the unity of Ukrainian territories; Volhynia and much of the rest of Ukraine was about to become part of the Reichskommissariat Ukraine, officially created on 1 September 1941. For their part, the Germans were to arrest hundreds of adherents of the Bandera group in the latter part of August and in September 1941,[699] and dozens of them ended up in Auschwitz in 1942.[700] On 15 August, Stetsko and Bandera were imprisoned in Berlin and in the following year sent to Sachsenhausen concentration camp.[701]

The militias did prove useful to the Germans in the initial stage of anti-Jewish violence in Galicia and Volhynia, but almost from the outset the Germans were deeply suspicious of these armed formations in the service of a Ukrainian state they did not want to recognize. Already on 2 July 1941, Einsatzgruppe B reported: "Elements of the Bandera group under the leadership of Stetsko and Ravlyk have organized and brought to life a magistrate's office. The Einsatzgruppe has created a Ukrainian and political self-administration of the city [Lviv] as a counterweight to the Bandera group. Further measures against the Bandera-group, especially against Bandera himself, are in preparation. They will be carried out most expeditiously."[702] On that same day, according to Nazi Professor

---

699 German and OUN documents on these repressions can be found, respectively, in Kosyk, *Ukraina v Druhii svitovii viini*, 1:243-44, 279-82, 298-300, and Veselova, *OUN v 1941 rotsi*, 444-46, 504-05, 515. OUN-B blamed the arrests on the intrigues of OUN-M, and the intervention of the Melnykites was indeed a factor, but the contradictory visions of the Nazis and OUN about the future of Ukraine lay at the root of the repressions. For more on the context, see Armstrong, *Ukrainian Nationalism*, 69-70.

700 Bruder, "'Der Gerechtigkeit zu dienen.'" Among those who were imprisoned in Auschwitz were Bandera's two brothers, Oleksa and Vasyl, as well as Mykola Klymyshyn, Bohdan Kordiuk, and Petro Mirchuk. My in-law John Lahola, mentioned above (159), was also sent to Auschwitz. Lahola and Andrusiak, *Spohady*.

701 Kentii, *Narysy*, 74.

702 EM 10, 2 July 1941. Also in Kosyk, *Ukraina v Druhii svitovii viini*, 1:92-94.

Hans Joachim Beyer, who was serving then as a high SD official in Lviv, the city's militia was subordinated to the SS.[703]

By early August the Germans were expressing deep dissatisfaction with the Ukrainian National Militia. A report from the Security Police and SD in Kraków characterized it as undisciplined and unpopular: "In several places it was necessary to take action against the Ukrainian militia and its leaders, since plunderings and assaults were daily occurrences. In Ternopil and Rivne Polish families were murdered by them. In many places the local and field commandants had to disarm and dissolve the militias, arrest their leaders. The behavior of the militias is to some extent such that even the Ukrainian peasants call them 'Bolshevik hordes.'"[704] A few days later, a report from the same source stated that "Ukrainian militia commanders continue to shoot people they don't like."[705] In mid-August 1941 the Germans dissolved the Ukrainian militias and partially disarmed them. The militia was replaced by the Ukrainian Auxiliary Police in Galicia and by the stationary Schutzmannschaft in Volhynia, both of which were to be under direct German control. (These police formations will be the subject of the next chapter.)

The larger context of the replacement of the Ukrainian National Militia by police forces is that by late July Himmler was seeking to build up personnel for the systematic mass murder of East European Jews. On 1 August 1941 volunteer Lithuanian auxiliary police formations were subordinated to the German order police and renamed as Schutzmannschaften.[706]

Lviv in July 1941

The day after the proclamation of Stetsko's state, i.e. on 1 July 1941, OUN pasted posters around Lviv with Mykola Mikhnovsky's slogan "Ukraine for Ukrainians" printed in white letters against a red

---

703 Dziuban, *Ukrains'ke derzhavotvorennia*, 153; this document is a reprint of "Podii na zakhidn'o-ukrains'kykh zemliakh (Interviu z dots. d-rom H. I. Baierom)," *Krakivs'ki visti*, 6 July 1941. On Beyer, see Roth, "Heydrichs Professor."
704 EM 43, 5 August 1941. Similar accusations can be found in EM 54, 16 August 1941, and 56, 18 August 1941.
705 EM 47, 9 August 1941.
706 Breitman, "Himmler's Police Auxiliaries." Büchler, "Local Police Force."

background.[707] On the same day in Lviv and in many other localities of Galicia and Volhynia,[708] another poster appeared, authored by Klymiv sometime earlier; it instructed Ukrainians: "People! Know! Moscow, Poland, the Hungarians, the Jews are your enemies! Destroy them!"[709] And another placard was posted, in which Klymiv, styling himself as "the Chief Commandant of the Ukrainian National Revolutionary Army," told "the citizens of the Ukrainian State": "I am introducing collective responsibility (family and national) for all offences against the Ukrainian State, the Ukrainian Army, and OUN."[710] These posters issued a clear signal as to what non-Ukrainians in Lviv could expect. And in the conditions of Nazi occupation, the only non-Ukrainians that could be targeted with impunity were Jews.

But much more incendiary than any posters of the new nationalist state was the discovery of the hundreds of prisoners murdered in Lviv by the NKVD in the last days of Soviet rule.[711] Emotions ran high — rage, outrage, grief. Some people went inside the prisons to look for missing relatives. Famously, Roman Shukhevych discovered his brother Yurii's body in a mass grave in the NKVD prison on Lontsky Street.[712] When the corpses were exhumed and laid out in courtyards so that the public could search for relatives among the victims, a strong stench of rotting flesh permeated areas near the prisons. Photographs from the time show people with kerchiefs over their mouths and noses to blunt the stomach-churning

---

707 Nakonechnyi, "Shoa" u L'vovi, 118. There is a memoir of the printing operations conducted on 1 July 1941 by the man in charge of the printing press. Dmytro Honta, "Drukarstvo Zakhidnoi Ukrainy pidchas okupatsii," "Konkurs na spohady," Oseredok.
708 Struve, Deutsche Herrschaft, 295, 523, 653, 657. Shoah Foundation, 51758 Mark Tukan, 124-27. Siemaszko and Siemaszko, Ludobójstwo, 1:233, 1:526, 1:818, 1:976.
709 Carynnyk, "Foes of Our Rebirth," 332-33; this is Carynnyk's translation. Carynnyk published here a photocopy of the poster. It is also reprinted in Dziuban, Ukrains'ke derzhavotvorennia, 126-29.
710 My translation. Carynnyk, "Foes of Our Rebirth," 332, 334-35. Dziuban, Ukrains'ke derzhavotvorennia, 129-31.
711 On the course of the NKVD murders in Lviv, see Struve, Deutsche Herrschaft, 248-52.
712 Ibid., 181, 360. See also a contemporary newspaper report reprinted in Dziuban, Ukrains'ke derzhavotvorennia, 102-03; according to this report, Yurii Shukhevych was crucified, nailed to the prison wall while still alive.

smell.[713] Isolated incidents of anti-Jewish violence escalated into the Lviv pogrom of 1 July 1941.

The word "pogrom" has a number of meanings. The term originated with the incidents of anti-Jewish violence that erupted in cities on Ukrainian territories within the Russian empire in the early 1880s. These pogroms included much looting of Jewish businesses, beatings and rapes of Jews, and some murders. The pogroms of 1903-06 on the same territories were similar. But the pogroms in Ukraine of the civil war period, largely perpetrated by soldiers, were marked by great numbers of murders. Pogroms initiated by the Nazis, as when they seized Vienna in March 1938 and throughout the Reich in November 1938 (the November pogrom, often called *Kristallnacht*), primarily involved the destruction of Jewish property, the humiliation of Jews, and assaults, although there were also some murders. The Lviv pogrom of 1941 combined many features of the preceding pogroms: there were beatings, sexual assaults and humiliations, murders by the urban crowd, shooting by soldiers, and ritual humiliations; Jewish apartments were robbed,[714] but not their businesses, if we can speak of the businesses nationalized by the Soviets as in some sense still Jewish.[715]

The main stages of the pogrom were three prisons in Lviv where bodies of the NKVD victims were exhumed, although anti-Jewish violence and humiliations also occurred in other areas of the city, particularly in the central town square (*rynok*), but also near the opera house[716] and near the seat of the Greek Catholic metropolitan's residence, St. George's hill. Two of the prisons were close to largely Jewish neighborhoods: the Brygidky prison and the prison on Zamarstyniv street. As numerous Jewish survivors'

---

713 Such photographs are reproduced in Himka, "The Lviv Pogrom," 239, and Kiebuzinski and Motyl, *The Great West Ukrainian Prison Massacre*, 402.

714 Struve, *Deutsche Herrschaft*, 308-09. Nakonechnyi, *"Shoa" u L'vovi*, 115.

715 The best account of the Lviv pogrom is to be found in Struve, *Deutsche Herrschaft*, 304-79. In this monograph I have revised a number of the views advanced in Himka, "The Lviv Pogrom," but that article is still useful for the numerous quotations from Jewish survivors' testimonies and memoirs and for its photographs.

716 Jews were made to clean a street near the opera, much to the delight of onlookers. See the photograph in Himka, "The Lviv Pogrom," 212.

accounts make clear, members of the Ukrainian National Militia entered nearby apartment buildings and rounded up Jews, men and women, and took them to the prisons. The other prison, the NKVD prison on Lontsky Street (now a museum)[717] was closer to the center of the city, outside the Jewish neighborhood. For this prison Jews were rounded up off the street by militiamen and volunteers from the urban crowd. They were marched with their hands up, sometimes on all fours, to the prison.[718]

How did the pogrom start? It grew out of a general policy of the Wehrmacht to force Jews to do repairs and cleanup after war-related damage.[719] German troops made Jews repair streets in Lviv that had been damaged by bombardment.[720] Not infrequently, the impressment into labor was accompanied by physical harm or even death. On 30 June 1941 Czeslawa Budynska, her sister, and a neighbor girl were put to cleaning up battle sites in the city. The women were beaten and pushed as they carried out their tasks. Men were also drafted to the work, but according to Budynska, they were drowned later in the day.[721]

When the Germans entered Lviv, they discovered many hundreds of corpses in the prisons, heaped up or hastily buried in mass graves. Someone had to exhume the bodies, and it was not surprising that the Germans assigned Jews to this task, a nasty one, since the bodies fell apart as they were retrieved and the stench was unbearable. Outside Lviv too, Jews were routinely assigned to exhumation work in localities where NKVD victims were found.[722] Thus Jews, whom both the Nazis and Ukrainian nationalists identified as carriers and beneficiaries of Bolshevism, were placed at the forefront of the NKVD crime, in a position that appeared to be punishment for their own criminal responsibility. Moreover, this was in a context in which Ukrainian public opinion was being influenced to

---

717 Himka, "The Lontsky Street Prison."
718 See the photographs in Struve, *Deutsche Herrschaft*, 327-28, 331.
719 Ibid., 276-77. Drafting Jews for labor often accompanied pogroms in Nazi-occupied Europe. Szarota, *U progu Zagłady*, 21.
720 Pan'kivs'kyi, *Vid derzhavy do komitetu*, 35.
721 Shoah Foundation, 21303 Czeslawa Budynska, 31-42.
722 For example, in Ternopil. But in Berezhany, Ukrainians exhumed the bodies of NKVD victims. Struve, *Deutsche Herrschaft*, 609, 509-10.

regard the Jews as the main perpetrators of the refined tortures and mass killings that the numerous decomposing corpses indicated.[723]

Impressing Jews into work at the prisons posed a problem: finding and assembling Jews. As Dieter Pohl correctly noted:

> One should not underestimate the practical problems these SS men faced when they entered the Western Ukrainian towns. They did not know the population, the topography, and of course neither did they know the language. Thus, they were totally dependent on interpreters, local administrations or the militias that surfaced in June 1941.[724]

In Lviv, it was the Ukrainian National Militia that rounded up the Jews and participated in the violence against them. There is a photo from the time showing a uniformed militiaman pulling the hair of a half-undressed woman at the gate to the prison on Zamarstyniv St.[725] There is a film that shows a militiaman with his armband beating a Jew with a truncheon inside one of the Lviv prisons.[726] And numerous survivor testimonies and memoirs describe the arrests and brutality of the militiamen.[727] The militia rounded up many more Jews than could be put to use in the exhumation project. Jewish women were rounded up primarily for misogynist

---

723 See Himka, "Ethnicity and the Reporting of Mass Murder." The reports cited in this article were published after the Lviv pogrom but they indicate how perpetrators were ethnicized as Jews and Russians, and victims as Ukrainians. A notation in the war diary of the 49th German army corps in Lviv, dated 30 June 1941 at 3:00 pm stated: "Among the population a furious embitterment over the vile deeds of the Bolsheviks is being vented on the Jews who live in the city, who always collaborated with the Bolsheviks." Struve, *Deutsche Herrschaft*, 304-05.

724 Pohl, "Anti-Jewish Pogroms," 308.

725 Reproduced in Himka, "The Lviv Pogrom," 232; the same photo is in Struve, *Deutsche Herrschaft*, 342.

726 USHMM Film Archive, tape 202B, story RG-60.0328. The time code for the start of this film of the prison is 5:07:11; the beating by the militiaman occurs at 5:08:18–24.

727 Himka, "The Lviv Pogrom." Struve, *Deutsche Herrschaft*, 304-79. Melamed, "Organized and Unsolicited Collaboration."

sport.[728] The extra men just huddled in the courtyards of the prisons, trying to avoid additional assault (see figure 1).[729]

Figure 1: Wounded Jewish men in the courtyard of the NKVD prison on Lontsky St. On the other side of the photograph is written "Juden warten" (Jews are waiting). Collection of David Lee Preston, Philadelphia.

Although the militia played a major role in the pogrom of 1 July, it was not the only OUN contributor to the anti-Jewish violence on that day. Some part in the pogrom activities was also taken by a military unit in German service commanded by Shukhevych. This was the Nachtigall battalion, one of two battalions of what the nationalists called the Legion of Ukrainian Nationalists, although contemporaries also called it the Ukrainian Bandera legion.[730] The place of Nachtigall in the pogrom has been confused by a campaign

---

728 A German military photographer (or photographers) took a number of shots of women being physically and sexually assaulted during the Lviv pogrom. Some of these pictures have been reproduced in Himka, "Dostovirnist' svidchennia," 53-56, 58; the photographers are pictured on 60. See also Struve, *Deutsche Herrschaft*, 3, 343-44.

729 They can be seen in the background of figure 22 in Struve, *Deutsche Herrschaft*, 334.

730 That is how Jewish survivor Kurt Lewin referred to it in *Przeżyłem*, 61. On the formation and activities of Nachtigall, see Bolianovs'kyi, *Ukrains'ki viis'kovi formuvannia*, 41-74.

launched in 1959-60 by the German Democratic Republic and the Soviet Union aimed at taking down the government of Konrad Adenauer in the Federal Republic of Germany. Because Adenauer's Minister for Displaced Persons, Refugees, and Victims of War Theodor Oberländer had been a liaison with Nachtigall back in 1941, the East Germans and Soviets tried to blame the Lviv pogrom entirely on the nationalist unit. Many manufactured testimonies were collected to prove the case, and although the evidence was flimsy, Oberländer was forced to resign from Adenauer's cabinet. In February 2008 the Security Service of Ukraine (the SBU) released a number of documents that showed how the KGB had concocted the evidence against Oberländer, leaving no doubt about the falsity of their accusations against Nachtigall.[731]

However, there were a few survivor testimonies from the 1940s, thus written before the Oberländer campaign and its falsifications, that did point to the participation of some soldiers from Nachtigall in the violence at the prisons.[732] Struve, working with German records, established that at all three Lviv prisons where the major pogrom activities took place, detachments from Nachtigall were serving as guards until at least the evening of 1 July. He concluded that the soldiers of Nachtigall were one of several perpetrator groups at the prison and "were only responsible for a small part of the acts of violence."[733] However, we know a bit more about Nachtigall's participation in the killing of Jews from an autobiographical document prepared in 1946 for OUN's Security Service by a former soldier of Nachtigall who wrote under his nom de guerre Khmara. As historian Ivan Patryliak has noted, "the value of the document lies in that it was not intended for publication, and in it the author writes about the events of his life as they, of course,

---

731 Unfortunately, the SBU later removed the materials from their website. But the most relevant materials are contained in the SBU press release of from February 2008 on the website of Memorial: "SBU: Zvynuvachennia proty 'Nakhtihaliu.'" See also Himka, "The Lviv Pogrom," 225-26.

732 Lewin, *Przeżyłem*, 61 (Brygidky). AŻIH, 301/2242, Zygmunt Tune, 1 (Zamarstyniv St. prison).

733 Struve, *Deutsche Herrschaft*, 354-60 (quotation 360).

truly unfolded."[734] Khmara described Nachtigall's march from Lviv to Vinnytsia:

> At the time of our march we saw with our own eyes the victims of the Jewish-Bolshevik terror; this sight so intensified our hatred towards Jews that in two villages we shot all the Jews we encountered. I recall one fragment. During our march we saw many people wandering before one village. When questioned, they replied that the Jews are threatening them and they are afraid to sleep in their own houses. As a result of this we shot all the Jews we encountered.[735]

It is not possible to ascertain whom Khmara was referring to in speaking of Jews who threatened the villagers. Perhaps these were Jewish communists who frightened them with the return of the Red Army. But whoever did what, all the Jews whom Nachtigall laid hands on paid with their lives.

OUN may have been even more deeply involved in the Lviv pogrom. Jeffrey Burds identified a certain Ivan Kovalyshyn as a participant in the pogrom. Among the photographs of the pogrom taken by a German photo crew in the vicinity of the Zamarstyniv St. prison and held now by the Wiener Library in London, two show a man in a flat cap whose facial features seem to match the photograph in a militia ID card belonging to Kovalyshyn. Both photos show pogromists, among whom stands Kovalyshyn, mocking a naked Jewish woman, who also appears to have been physically assaulted.[736] Burds' discovery had indicated that some militiamen, without armbands or uniforms and dressed like the city's ruffians (*batiari*), took a leading role in guiding the pogrom. But Serhii Riabenko has argued against this view, on two grounds. He questioned whether the pogrom photos showed the same person as the militia ID card, remarking that the photo on the ID card was of poor quality. Also, he pointed out that, according to the ID card, Kovalyshyn only joined the militia on 21 July, almost three weeks after the

---

734   Patryliak, *Viis'kova diial'nist'*, 361-62.
735   Ibid., 362.
736   The photos of the pogrom scenes are WL 1645 and WL 1648. The ID card with photo are in DALO fond R12, op. 1, ff. 6-6v. A composite of the three photos has been published in Himka, "Dostovirnist' svidchennia," 61; Struve, *Deutsche Herrschaft*, 304; Riabenko, "Slidamy 'L'vivs'koho pohromu.'"

pogrom took place.[737] But Struve found that Kovalyshyn had actually joined the investigative unit of the militia, which seems to have been a branch of the OUN Security Service (SB), already on 3 July.[738] In my own view, the photo on the militia ID card and the two photos of the pogrom show the same individual, i.e. Ivan Kovalyshyn; perhaps at some point sophisticated facial recognition technology can help resolve the issue. Also, I continue to think that Kovalyshyn's presence in the thick of the violence was no accident but rather indicates that there were certain OUN operatives active in the pogrom in mufti. There are only ten militia ID cards with photographs that have been preserved to the present, and that one of the ten men pictured was where he was on 1 July seems to indicate the tip of an iceberg. There is also German evidence that plainsclothes OUN-B militants were active in the Zolochiv pogrom a few days later.[739] Moreover, from the very beginning of the formation of OUN SB, it was charged with "the organization of diversions (*dyversii*)."[740] In today's language, "diversions" might best be translated as "special ops." Perhaps future discoveries will throw more light on the issue.

The Lviv pogrom did great damage to the Jews of the city. Many men suffered wounds, especially head wounds, and many women suffered forms of sexual assault. All who were taken to the prisons suffered trauma, and the Jewish community of Lviv at large was put into a precarious position. It is hard to estimate the number of fatalities from the Lviv pogrom. For one thing, no one was keeping count. Also, many estimates of the number of victims of the pogrom are including in their tally the much more systematic violence that was to follow over the course of the rest of July. Struve, whose estimates of the number of victims tend to be conservative, argued that at most several hundred Jews perished during the pogrom.[741] A major portion of the murders were committed by members of Einsatzgruppe C, who shot about a hundred Jews at

---

737   Riabenko, "Slidamy 'L'vivs'koho pohromu.'"
738   Struve, *Deutsche Herrschaft*, 303-04.
739   Ibid., 583.
740   Ishchuk and Ohorodnik, *Heneral Mykola Arsenych*, 53.
741   Struve, *Deutsche Herrschaft*, 376-79.

Brygidky prison.[742] The rest were killed as a result of beatings with thick sticks, paving stones, shovels, and other objects by the remaining perpetrators: Nachtigall, German police battalions, the Ukrainian National Militia, the urban crowd, and the Wehrmacht.[743]

The lull in anti-Jewish violence in Lviv after the pogrom was very brief. Already on 3 July thousands of Jewish men were being detained and brought to a sports arena not far from the Citadel, where the NKVD had recently had its headquarters. The militia once again made most of the arrests, but they had some help from Einsatzgruppe C. Some of the men were picked up because they were on a list of Jews who had cooperated with the Soviet organs of repression; but many others were just grabbed at random because they were Jewish.[744] In the sports arena the Jews were tortured by the Germans; they were made to go up and down on the ground repeatedly and then to run around the arena while they were beaten with thick sticks. Most of them were taken by truck to woods outside the city and shot by the Einsatzgruppe. Altogether, about two thousand or more were executed in this way.[745] However, for reasons that are not certain, some of the assembled Jews were released. One of the killers active on 5 July, Felix Landau, ran across a group of these released Jews and described in his diary what they looked like after their experience in the arena:

> There were hundreds of Jews walking along the street with blood pouring down their faces, holes in their heads, their hands broken and their eyes hanging out of their sockets. They were covered in blood. Some of them were carrying others who had collapsed. We went to the citadel; there we saw things that few people have ever seen. At the entrance of the citadel there were soldiers standing guard. They were holding clubs as thick as a man's wrist and were lashing out and hitting anyone who crossed their path. The Jews were pouring out of the entrance. There were rows of Jews lying one on

---

742   Ibid., 360-66, 429.
743   Ibid., 353-76.
744   Ibid., 396.
745   Ibid., 402.

top of the other like pigs, whimpering horribly. The Jews kept streaming out of the citadel completely covered in blood.[746]

The role of the militia in this particular incident of torment and mass killing had been to arrest the Jews. Isolated recollections of the militia's presence within the arena or at the gate as the Jews were being released are most likely, as Struve suggests, failures of memory.[747]

Thus by the end of the first week of July, OUN was well aware of what its alliance with the Germans entailed with regard to the Jewish population: its militia was to help them by rounding up Jews for torment and mass murder. At this time the Germans had not yet determined to kill *all* Jews, but they were clearly aiming to kill a great many of them. How did the leadership of OUN-B react to the Germans' Jewish policy? We can answer that question with authoritative evidence.

First, we have the evidence from the head of the unrecognized Ukrainian state, one of the most influential figures in OUN, Yaroslav Stetsko. Arrested by the Germans on 9 July 1941 and taken from Lviv to Berlin, Stetsko composed an autobiography in both Ukrainian and German about a week later.[748] In it, he stated his position on the Jewish question in general and the Germans' Jewish policy in particular. He reiterated his long held view that Moscow, not the Jews, was the primary enemy of Ukraine, but that the Jews played an important role in helping Moscow to keep Ukraine enslaved. He therefore supported "the destruction of the Jews and the expedience of bringing German methods of exterminating Jewry to Ukraine, barring their assimilation and the like."[749] Thus he approved of the anti-Jewish violence in which his militia participated.

---

746   Klee et al., "*The Good Old Days,*" 91.

747   Himka, "Lviv Pogrom," 219-20. Struve, *Deutsche Herrschaft*, 398.

748   Berkhoff and Carynnyk, "The Organization of Ukrainian Nationalists," 150. See the discussion above, 150-10, on the genuineness of this document; along with the discussion on these pages are the full extracts in which Stetsko presented his views on Jews.

749   This sentence is from the Ukrainian version. The German version ended similarly: "I am of the opinion that in the struggle against the Jewry in Ukraine German methods are to be employed." Berkhoff and Carynnyk, "The Organization of Ukrainian Nationalists," 162-63, 167, 170-71. The translation from the

Only a few days later, on 18-19 July, OUN-B held a meeting of its propaganda sector in Lviv.[750] Among the topics discussed was national minorities, and in particular the Jewish minority. The first to raise the matter of Jews was Oles Hai-Holovko, a writer from pre-1939 Soviet Ukraine who had moved to Lviv during the first period of Soviet rule. Stetsko had named Hai-Holovko to head the propaganda section of his government.[751] In the course of delivering a report on Ukrainians in Kuban (then and now in the Russian republic), he noted: "There are a lot of Jews there who have trampled upon Ukrainian culture." The discussion continued about Ukrainians in areas outside Ukraine's territory, including Ukrainian settlements in Siberia. A certain Hupalo[752] said: "It would be good if they [the Germans] gave us the regions inhabited by Ukrainians. The main thing is that there are a lot of Jews everywhere. Especially in the centers. They shouldn't be allowed to live there. There should be a policy of expulsion. They will flee themselves. Or maybe we should assign them some cities, for example, Berdychiv [in Zhytomyr oblast]." Stepan Lenkavsky, then head of OUN-B's propaganda sector, addressed Hai-Holovko: "Characterize the Jews for me." The latter replied: "The Jews are very arrogant.

Ukrainian version is taken from Berkhoff and Carynnyk; the translation from German is the author's.

750 The beginning of the transcript of this meeting has been lost, so for several years after it began to be cited in the literature it was incorrectly thought that the meeting in question was a meeting of the Council of Seniors, an advisory body of Stetsko's government composed of such notables as Metropolitan Andrei Sheptytsky and the elder Galician statesman Kost Levytsky. See for example Pohl, *Nationalsozialistische Judenverfolgung*, 49, and Berkhoff and Carynnyk, "The Organization of Ukrainian Nationalists," 154, 178-79 n. 37. Berkhoff later acknowledged the error and accepted that the document in question was more likely an OUN meeting to plan propaganda. Berkhoff, "A Power Terrible for Its Opponents," 203, n. 14. The issue is treated in Struve, *Deutsche Herrschaft*, 414-15 n. 546. As we will see, the participants in the meeting included key figures involved in propaganda work and associated with OUN-B.

751 "Sklad Ukrains'koho derzhavnoho pravlinnia," in Veselova, *OUN v 1941 rotsi*, 253.

752 A Kostiantyn Hupalo was a writer active in OUN. He was murdered by the Germans with the rest of the editorial staff of Kyiv's *Ukrains'ke slovo* newspaper in February 1942. But he belonged to the Melnyk faction, at least at the time of his death.

One couldn't even use the word *zhyd*.[753] It is necessary to treat them very harshly. They cannot be kept in the center, absolutely. We must put an end to them." Then Borys Lewytzkyj, former editor of OUN's newspaper for the peasantry *Nove Slovo* and briefly of *Krakivs'ki visti*,[754] spoke:

> In Germany, the Jews have the Aryan paragraph.[755] More interesting for us is the issue of the General Government. There every Jew is marked (*naznacheno*). Every Jew had to be registered in a religious community. They were removed from some cities, for example from Kraków, and resettled to others, for example to Warsaw, with walled-off ghettos assigned to them. They have cinemas and theatres, but nothing to eat. The young who are fit for work go to work. A portion has to be destroyed. Although already some have been destroyed...[756] It is a fact that some have crept into Ukrainian blood; many married with Ukrainian women. In Germany there are various half-Jews, quarter-Jews, but this isn't possible for us. A German who marries a Jewish woman becomes a Jew.

Hai-Holovko added: "In Ukraine married couples with a Jewish woman are mainly in the cities. Jewish women married Ukrainians for a comfortable life; when Ukrainians went bankrupt, they divorced. Jews with Ukrainian women even lived well. I like the German attitude very much."

When Hupalo noted that "we have a lot of workers who are Jews, who are even respected, including some who converted to Christianity before the revolution," Lenkavsky conceded: "This has to be reviewed on an individual basis." Lewytzkyj added: "The Germans use specialists. In Kraków there are five Jews who do not

---

753 In Western Ukraine *zhyd* was the common word to use for "Jew;" Polish uses the same word (*Żyd*). In Russia and in Soviet and post-Soviet Ukraine, the word *zhid/zhyd* is considered derogatory and the politically correct term is *ievrei*.

754 *Krakivs'ki visti* was published by the Ukrainian Central Committee based in Kraków. The committee started out as a charity organization under the German occupation and evolved to become the chief liaison between the Germans and the Ukrainian population of the General Government. It was loosely affiliated with the Melnyk faction of OUN. On *Krakivs'ki visti*, see Gyidel, "The Ukrainian Legal Press"; Himka, "*Krakivs'ki visti* and the Jews"; Himka, "Ethnicity and the Reporting of Mass Murder."

755 A reference to the Nuremberg laws.

756 Ellipsis in original.

wear armbands because they are positive forces (*dobri syly*). In my opinion, the German approach to the Jewish issue does not work well for us. We have to examine individual cases on their own merits." Lenkavsky ended the discussion on Jews with the following pronouncement: "With regard to the Jews we will accept all methods that lead to their destruction."[757]

I have quoted the entire discussion of the propaganda sector on Jews, without interpretation. The conclusions that I see emerging from the discussion are: OUN's attitude remained anti-Jewish; OUN wanted to exempt some Jewish individuals from persecution; it also wanted to segregate Jews from the rest of the population and to kill many of them.

The Ukrainian National Militia in Lviv was to take part in one more major anti-Jewish action, the so-called Petliura days. This action clustered on the days 25-26 July, although some of the violence began a bit earlier and also continued for a few days after. It seems that it was the Germans, and specifically their security police, who named this action after Symon Petliura. Petliura, of course, was the leader of the Ukrainian People's Republic whose troops had unleashed numerous pogroms with tens of thousands of fatalities in 1919.[758] Kai Struve makes a convincing case that the security police were staging a "self-cleansing action" by Ukrainians such as Heydrich had called for about a month previously.[759] Struve links the action with a visit to Lviv by Himmler,[760] probably accompanied by the mass killer and SS commander Friedrich Jeckeln, on 21 July. The Petliura days differed from the Lviv pogrom that had occurred at the beginning of the month; there was very little public participation. The Ukrainians who took part were almost exclusively members of the militia.

757 The discussion on Jews is in Dziuban, *Ukrains'ke derzhavotvorennia*, 189-90.
758 See above, 121, 167-68.
759 Struve, *Deutsche Herrschaft*, 418-19, 426. On Heydrich and self-cleansing actions, see above, 200.
760 A visit by Himmler to Kryvyi Rih, in central Ukraine, seems also to have stimulated the largest massacre of Jews in that city in mid-October 1941. Twenty-five hundred Jews from Kryvyi Rih and eight hundred Jewish POWs were shot near one of the city's iron-ore mines. Shliakhtych, "Uchast' mistsevoi dopomizhnoi politsii," 82.

Let us first see how Jewish survivors remembered the event.

Janina Hescheles, who was at the time ten years old, remembered going out with her mother to visit her uncle. The streets seemed to be calm, but this was deceptive. At the entrance to their apartment building a man was lying on the ground, groaning and covered with blood. His shoes were missing. Suddenly "two boys with yellow-blue armbands" came up. They said, addressing first Janina's mother: "To work, please ma'am, and you, little one, go home." Janina went home, and her mother was taken to scrub floors in a school. Her mother returned home after an hour. The next day there was also unrest. That evening a neighbor appeared at the door with Janina's twelve-year old cousin Gustek, who was unconscious. His face was black and blue and swollen, his arm was bloody, his whole body bruised. When he came to, he said that he and others were taken by Ukrainians to the prison on Lontsky St. where they were beaten; he managed to escape. One of her uncles had also been seized from his apartment on ul. Staszica (today vul. Ye. Malaniuka), outside the Jewish quarter in the vicinity of the citadel, and did not return home for some days.[761]

Izak Weiser wrote that during the Petliura days he saw a group of men and women marched down ul. Pełczyńska (today vul. Dmytra Vyhovskoho) to the Lontsky St. prison. On Saturday, i.e. 26 July, a hundred seventy Gestapo men systematically beat the Jews at the prison all day long; no trace of these people was found later.[762] Henryk Baldinger was arrested on 25 July and taken to the Lontsky St. prison, where he and other Jewish men, women, and children over ten were systematically beaten by Germans and Ukrainians; when one group of beaters was tired, they were replaced by a fresh batch. Ukrainians armed with rifles maintained order. The Germans and Ukrainians confiscated all money, watches, pens, and other useful goods that their victims had on their persons. Physicians, including Baldinger, were released, but others were taken away in trucks. Baldinger said that later he found out from the Ukrainian who arrested him that the majority of the

---

761 Hescheles, *Oczyma dwunastoletniej dziewczyny*, 21-22.
762 AŻIH, 301/1584, Izak Weiser, 1.

victims were transported to "the Sands" outside Lviv and shot.[763] Salomon Goldman lost his brother to the violence of the Petliura days. He heard that people were being beaten in the Ukrainian police precincts, some to death, and others were taken out to "the Sands" and shot.[764] Lucyna Halbergsberg lost her husband. He was taken to Lontsky St. prison; she tried to get him released but failed. After three days the prisoners were taken to "the Sands" and, she heard, shot.[765]

Jan Badian was arrested on 25 July by "a Ukrainian from the civil militia" and taken, with the other Jewish men from his apartment building, to the nearest precinct station, that of the sixth commissariat on ul. Kurkowa (now vul. Lysenka). In a group of about a thousand Jews, he was marched to the prison on Lontsky St. As the Jews entered the prison courtyard, a broad-shouldered German beat each of them with a cudgel, bent as a saber from extensive use. He saw several other Germans and Ukrainians with such bent cudgels. There were women standing against a wall, but the men inside were in constant motion. The Germans and Ukrainians would drive them with beatings against one wall, then beat them again until they went to the other wall, back and forth. There were now, Badian estimated, about ten thousand people in the courtyard. There was a group of about sixty black-and-blue Jews who were made to hold their arms up and chant: "We Jews are to blame for the war." Trucks in the meantime were pulling up to the courtyard. Prisoners tried to escape from the beating and get on the trucks, which perhaps might be taking them to work. "It is unbelievable how many men can fit into a truck," wrote Badian later. The intensity of the torture in the courtyard did not let up. Zealous Ukrainians held wooden cudgels in one hand and iron bars in another. One of them told Badian that the Jews there were condemned to death. After 2:00 pm in the afternoon on 26 July, Badian and some

763 AŻIH, 301/1801, Henryk Baldinger, 1-4.Pet
764 AŻIH, 301/1864, Salomon Goldman, 5.
765 AŻIH, 301/2278, Lucyna Hallensberg, 1.

others were made to run the gauntlet between some Germans and then released into the street.[766]

Wolf Lichter did not use the term "Petliura days," but he recounted an incident that he said happened a few weeks after the German occupation began: Going with his mother to a non-Jewish neighborhood, where she thought he would be safer (he was then eleven years old), they saw a disheveled, screaming, pleading woman running and a band, mainly of men but including a few women, chasing after her. The "hoodlums" shouted: Kill the Jewess! Kill the Jewess! They caught up with her and beat and trampled her. She was pleading and begging until no more sounds came from her.[767]

Testimony given at the denaturalization proceedings of an alleged Ukrainian policeman also seems to refer to the so-called Petliura days, although the dating is off and the term was not used. A Jewish survivor, Joseph Romanski, described events that happened after Jews were forced to wear armbands with the Star of David, yet still in July 1941. This fits the chronology. He said that he was arrested by a Ukrainian militiaman and taken to the nearest precinct station. As he approached the station he saw a truck loaded with people leaving the building. In the lobby of the police station were seven or eight Jewish people. There were not enough of them to be loaded on the truck, and a heavy rain broke out which prevented militiamen from bringing in more Jews to fill a truck. While waiting there, he managed to bribe one of the militiamen with a Swiss watch and make his escape.[768]

When the various accounts are compared, the story that emerges is that the Ukrainian militia, together with members of Einsatzkommando Lemberg, first arrested a great number of Jews, mainly men but some women. They took the apprehended Jews to the closest militia station, and when enough were assembled, they marched them through the streets or drove them to the Lontsky St.

---

766   AŻIH, 301/4944, Jan Badian, 1-4.
767   Shoah Foundation, 29342 Wolf Lichter, 11.
768   USHMM RG-06.09.01*43, Box 45, case of George Theodorovich, 6 March 1985, 515-17.

prison. There the men were subjected to brutal beatings by both the militiamen and the Germans. As the beatings proceeded, trucks drove up; the Jewish men were crammed into the cargo beds and taken outside the city to be shot. The shooters were the Germans, not the militia.[769]

The involvement of the militia in the violence of the Petliura days is confirmed by a report from OUN's Main Propaganda Center in Lviv to the OUN Security Service, dated 28 July 1941:

> Protopriest Father [Petro] Tabinsky informs us of the following: Our militia is at present conducting, together with German organs, numerous arrests of Jews. The Jews defend themselves against liquidation in all kinds of ways, primarily with money. According to reports that Protopriest Father Tabinsky received, among our militiamen are supposedly people who for money or gold release Jews who are supposed to be arrested. We, unfortunately, have received no concrete facts regarding this matter, but nonetheless we provide you with this information to make use of.
> Glory to Ukraine![770]

Clearly the concern here was not that masses of Jews were being arrested by the militia and liquidated, but that some militiamen were accepting bribes to neglect their duty.

The number of victims during the Petliura days has been estimated at 1500,[771] 6000,[772] 10,000,[773] 15,000,[774] and 18,000-20,000.[775] Struve inclines toward the lowest of these figures as most probable.[776]

---

769   See the detailed treatment in Struve, *Deutsche Herrschaft*, 418-28.

770   Veselova, *OUN v 1941 rotsi*, 389. There are also a number of militia documents, including some signed by the head of the Lviv militia, Yevhen Vretsiona, that confirm the militia's participation in the Petliura Days. See Struve, *Deutsche Herrschaft*, 427.

771   Tadeusz Zaderecki, "Gdy swastyka Lwowem władała...(Wycinek z dziejów okupacji hitlerowskiej)," Yad Vashem Archives, 06/28, 63.

772   AŻIH, 301/1181, Lilith Stern, 3.

773   AŻIH, 301/4944, Jan Badian, 5.

774   AŻIH, 301/18, Ryszard Ryndner, 1. The same estimate is provided by the Soviet Extraordinary State Commission, "Akt, 1944 goda, noiabria, 1-6 dnia, gorod L'vov," Yad Vashem Archives, M 33/ 731, 5.

775   Gerstenfeld-Maltiel, *My Private War*, 61. The author worked for the Lviv Judenrat and uses their numbers.

776   Struve, *Deutsche Herrschaft*, 424-25.

Militia Violence Elsewhere in Galicia

Kai Struve has, in over two hundred dense pages, examined case by case almost every incident of anti-Jewish violence that took place in Galicia outside Lviv.[777] For a number of reasons, I am not going to go over these same incidents. I have no disagreements with Struve's narrative and interpretation, so to repeat what has already been done well does not make sense, especially given the length of such an exercise. Also, we will see plenty of concrete examples of what the Ukrainian National Militia did in the next sections of this chapter, dealing with Volhynia and Bukovina. In Volhynia, the same OUN-B structures were in place as in Galicia, so those who have not read Struve's study will gain a good idea of the kind of things that went on also in Galicia. In this section I just want to do two things: 1) to present a summary of Struve's findings, complemented by some material from my own research, and 2) to afford an insight into how OUN members understood their violence through a lengthy quotation from a former activist's memoir.

Essentially, there were two patterns of militia violence: 1) rounding up Jews for the Germans to execute and 2) killing communists and Jews on the militia's own initiative, usually just outside a town or village.

We saw in the case of Lviv that the militia was employed to round up Jews for Einsatzgruppe C to murder, and this was repeated in other localities in Galicia. As Struve has pointed out, the Ukrainian militia, unlike its counterparts that summer in the former Baltic states, was not usually involved in the actual shooting. Among the reasons Struve suggested might account for the different role of militiamen in Western Ukraine and the Baltics was that the Germans, and the Einsatzgruppen in particular, mistrusted the well organized OUN-B and its state-buiding agenda.[778]

One of Struve's most important discoveries was the role played by a single unit attached to the Wehrmacht, the Waffen-SS division Wiking. With its bloody work in just six localities, Wiking

---

777   Ibid., 432-667.
778   Ibid., 690. And see above, 227-28.

managed to be responsible for the majority of murders that occurred throughout Galicia, even including Lviv. In Ternopil, where
Wiking was able to incite a pogrom, this division and its accomplices killed between 2300 and 4000 Jews — more than anywhere
else in Galicia. In Zolochiv, Wiking killed between 600 and 1000.
Wiking accomplished what it did with the help of the Ukrainian
militia as well as civilians.

A horrific example is the town of Hrymailiv, where about 350-
500 of its approximately 2200 Jews were killed on 5 July 1941.[779] The
participation of OUN militia in the murders has been well documented. For example, Mykola Kubishyn had joined OUN in 1940
(although he told his Soviet interrogator in April 1944 that he had
only joined in 1943). At the time of the German invasion he held the
post of *stanychnyi* in Paivka (P Pajówka), a village not far from Hrymailiv.[780] Kubishyn appeared in Hrymailiv on the day of the murders, a sure sign that OUN was consciously prepared to take part
in the violence. On that day, a witness said, Kubishyn shot six Red
Army soldiers, although Kubishyn denied he did any killing at
all.[781] Also on that day, a Ukrainian communist in Hrymailiv told
his SMERSH interrogator, certain individuals who took part in the
mass killing wore the insignia "Ukrainian Army" on their cuffs. As
noted earlier, "Ukrainian Army" was a term employed by Ivan
Klymiv in one of his incendiary leaflets of 1 July.[782]

One of those wearing the insignia was Osyp Velychuk. A Jewish survivor, Markus Bliaikh [Bleich], told his SMERSH interrogator that he first encountered Velychuk on the day of the murders, 5
July. He was drafted to repair the highway under Velychuk's su-
pervision. He said that Velychyuk appeared in the town with a rifle

---

779 Struve, *Deutsche Herrschaft*, 626-28.
780 A *stanychnyi* was the head of a *stanytsia*. A *stanytsia* was defined in the May 1941
     instructions as "the lowest territorial-organizational unit. It encompasses in its
     activity a single village, usually, but in larger settlements it encompasses one
     large street, a neighborhood, a factory, or other not overly large concentration
     of people." Patryliak, *Viis'kova diial'nist OUN (B)*, 514.
781 References to the Soviet war crime trials come from: USHMM RG-31.018M, reel
     28; HDA SB, arkh. no. 4889, ugolovnoe delo no. 970, ff. 8-8v, 10-10v, 24-24v, 26-
     26v, 81-81v. Zaplitnyi, *Za tebe, kraiu mii*, 188-89.
782 See above, 229.

after the Germans arrived. Velychuk tormented Bliaikh and the seven other Jews who were impressed into highway work. He made them carry rocks from one place to another and also carry water from one well to another. He made them crawl on all fours. He would hit them with his rifle butt and make them kiss the ground. "Whose land is this?" Velychuk would ask. They were to answer that this is the land of free Ukraine. Similar mistreatment was reported elsewhere in Galicia during that violent summer.[783] Velychuk killed six of the Jews by beating them with his rifle butt. At one point Velychuk's attention was distracted, and Bliaikh made his escape. He returned home and was told that Velychuk had murdered seventy-two people. Velychuk eventually told his interrogators: "I beat Bliaikh with the butt of my rifle simply because he was a Jew." Another Jewish survivor from Hrymailiv, Volf Bernshtein, confirmed that when the Germans arrived, Velychuk began to walk around armed with insignia on his cuffs. He said he witnessed Velychuk murdering twenty-five to thirty Jews by the Hrymailiv bridge. Among his victims were a Jewish woman who had been in the Komsomol (communist youth league), as well as a mother and her child. On the next day he shot about twenty Red Army soldiers and took their boots; he also shot over thirty Jews that day. These shootings took place at the cemetery. Velychuk was also identified as one of the killers by witnesses to the Extraordinary State Commission.[784]

A Jewish survivor who was just passing through Hrymailiv told the Central Jewish Historical Commission that she was

---

783 Borys Arsen, of Jewish origin, had joined the Komsomol and worked as a teacher under the Soviets. After the Germans invaded, he was in his native village of Chesnyky (P Cześniki), east of Rohatyn in Ivano-Frankivsk oblast. Soon he was arrested by the OUN militia (identifiable by their blue-and-yellow armbands and weaponry) and beaten and interrogated. They beat him as he lay on the ground and repeated continually: "Tell us what this soil smells like, Jew." He was supposed to answer: "Ukraine." Arsen, *Moia hirka pravda*, 53-54. Arsen also provided his testimony to the Shoah Foundation. Melamed, "Organized and Unsolicited Collaboration," 222.

784 USHMM RG-22.002M, reel 17; GARF, fond 7021, op. 75, spr. 94, ff. 1-4, 14-34v

detained by "some Ukrainian boy with the armband of a militia-man."[785]

But the main motor behind the mass killings in Hrymailiv was Waffen-SS Wiking. And the men of Wiking were not content to simply work in a systematic fashion with the Ukrainian militia. They wanted to draw in as many perpetrators from the civilian population as they could. There is an illuminating interview about what happened that Fr. Patrick Desbois and his team captured on film in May 2009.[786] A haggard-faced old man named Stanyslav, born in 1913, delivered his shocking testimony in a dramatic manner. He told his interviewers that when the Germans, i.e. Wiking, came, they encouraged the "Catholics," i.e. the non-Jewish population, to shoot Jews. The Germans rounded up the Jews, gave rifles to local boys, and encouraged them to shoot. A German shot a Jew to get the massacre going, and then the Catholics began to shoot. Many people joined in, including boys in eighth and ninth grade. If someone refused to shoot, the German got angry. This happened right in the center of Hrymailiv. They rounded up Jews from their houses. "Hutsuls"[787] and others from villages outside the town had been warned in advance of the anti-Jewish action (actually they were OUN operatives). About forty of them came and, together with the inhabitants of Hrymailiv, killed the Jews. Jews were brought to the river and shot there. The shooters would execute one group, then make the next group stack their bodies on the shore. Soon the whole area began to stink from the corpses. (The old man wrinkled up his nose as he remembered the smell.)[788] Eventually the Jews were buried in the Jewish cemetery. Jews transported the bodies to the cemetery and dug the graves. Jews were also shot and thrown into a well. The shooting lasted a day, he said, and about two hundred Jews were killed.

---

785 AŻIH, 302/201, Rachaela Kleiner, 10-11.

786 USHMM RG-50.589*0246; Yahad-in Unum Testimony no. 796. Information on this interview is available online: https://www.yahadmap.org/#village/hrymailiv-grymailiv-ternopil-ukraine.85. (accessed 24 April 2020).

787 Hutsuls are a subethnic Ukrainian group of the Carpathian mountains with a distinct culture and dialect.

788 The horrible smell was also recorded in the diary of a Dutch perpetrator attached to Wiking. Struve, *Deutsche Herrschaft*, 627.

As pointed out earlier,[789] OUN did not approve of pogroms, understood as mob actions, with considerable elements of spontaneity and public involvement. The April 1941 resolution prohibiting participation in pogroms[790] had to be reconsidered in late June and early July, since the Germans wanted precisely such spectacles for their own purposes, which may not have been clearly defined; and OUN was hoping to please the Germans as they erected their own state. But the OUN antipathy to pogroms persisted. An article that appeared on 12 July 1941 in an OUN-controlled newspaper in Kolomyia (P Kołomyja), *Volia Pokuttia*, stressed that it was time to return to "normal life," to obey the laws of the Ukrainian state in an organized and disciplined fashion. The looting that had broken out in Kolomyia on 4 July, in which state and cooperative stores were robbed as well as Jewish stores, was caused by hostile elements who wanted to disrupt Ukrainian state building—members of the Komsomol who were taking orders from Moscow. They were interested in pogroms because they wanted people to think that it was the Jews, not the Muscovites, who were responsible for all the failures on the front and inside the USSR as well. They wanted to divert the struggle of the non-Muscovite nations against the Muscovite-Bolshevik empire into anti-Jewish pogroms.

> We declare that we do not want by this to defend the Jews, because we felt on our own skin the role that a part of this nation played, their heads turned by communist doctrines that were advantageous to them, standing in the advance guard of Muscovite Bolshevism, and also the role which almost the whole Jewish nation now plays in the camp of Anglo-American parasites-plutocrats. We simply want to point out to our citizenry the current goals of dying Moscow and to warn the Ukrainian population against provocations of this type, which have as their goal to discredit our Ukrainian state-building movement, displacing their criminal, anarchistic actions to the account of the Ukrainian citizenry.[791]

---

789 See above, 167-70.
790 See above, 169-70.
791 Dziuban, *Ukrains'ke derzhavotvorennia*, 262. The article also blamed Poles for the pogrom of 4 July.

There were a few other instances in which OUN-B scuttled pogroms. The Ukrainian militia in the small town of Obertyn prohibited excesses against the Jews as well as their execution.[792] There was also the ambiguous case of Bibrka (P̲ Bóbrka). According to Zhanna Kovba, in Bibrka, "the order of the circle (*okruzhnyi*) leader Yaroslav Diakun to maintain order in the locality was executed. The closed Jewish stores were protected (many of their owners had fled) as well as the property of those who had been evacuated. There were no actions of the local population against the Jews, neither as the Wehrmacht forces entered nor during the erection of the occupation administration."[793] Her source for this was Slava Stetsko, Yaroslav Stetsko's widow. But in his own investigation of Bibrka, Struve quoted a German report from the town, dated 3 July 1941, that said: "The rage of the Ukrainian population was directed against the local as well as the recently arrived Jews [i.e., those who fled from the former German sector of Poland into the Soviet sector before the German invasion]. These [expressions of rage] were by men armed with Russian infantry rifles and wearing blue and yellow armbands with the insignia "Ukrainian Army," who fetched [the Jews] from their houses and brought them to the prison," where the NKVD had massacred the inmates. Although the Jews were insulted and wounded, there is no evidence of fatalities at the prison site. However, a pogrom in the center of town resulted in 42-63 deaths. But there is no evidence that OUN took part in this.[794]

Kovba also identified, on the basis of private communications, two other localities in which OUN-B was said to have prevented pogroms: Krakovets and Hlyniany (P̲ Gliniany).[795] Neither of these two localities figure in the list of pogroms compiled by Aleksandr Kruglov.[796] But Hlyniany figures in both the list compiled by Jeffrey S. Kopstein and Jason Wittenberg for *Intimate Violence*[797] and in

---

792 Struve, *Deutsche Herrschaft*, 661.
793 Kovba, *Liudianist' u bezodni pekla*, 224.
794 Struve, *Deutsche Herrschaft*, 497-99 (quotation 497).
795 Kovba, *Liudianist' u bezodni pekla*, 224.
796 Kruglov, "Pogromy v Vostochnoi Galitsii."
797 Kopstein and Wittenberg, *Intimate Violence*, 138.

Struve's list of localities he did not study in detail.[798] Jewish survivor testimony confirms that Jews were murdered in Hlyniany by Ukrainians, and from the modus operandi it is clear that the shooters were militiamen. Janina Landau-Hescheles told the Central Jewish Historical Commission in April 1946 that after the Germans took Hlyniany on 1 July 1941, the Ukrainian authorities arrested ten Jews. The latter were taken out of town, allegedly for work, but in reality they were forced to dig their own graves and shot.[799] In a contribution to a Hlyniany yizkor book, Jonah Mehlman recalled: "In 1941 the local Ruthenians [Ukrainians] staged a mock trial and condemned 9 innocent Jews to be dragged to the forests and shot."[800] Salomon Speiser remembered something similar: "In the fall of 1941 the Ruthenians staged a people's court on the Gestapo style. The presiding judge was Fashkiewitz. They condemned 11 people to die, took them to the woods and shot them all."[801]

What seems to have happened in Hlyniany was fairly typical. Aside from killing Jews as accomplices of the Germans, the OUN militia executed dozens of Jews in dozens of localities, usually working from lists. We know that sometimes the militia was able to seize records of the former Soviet security organs to find out who had collaborated.[802] Otherwise, names were gathered on the basis of suspicion and denunciations from various individuals. In addition to Jews, Red Army soldiers and Ukrainians who held positions in the Soviet apparatus were also apprehended. The soldiers were usually killed, but local Ukrainians associated with the former

---

798   Struve, *Deutsche Herrschaft*, 670.

799   AŻIH, 302/1702, 1.

800   Jonah Mehlman, "Three Years of Nazi Rule in Gliniany," https://www.jewish gen.org/yizkor/Glinyany1/gli001.html#Page5 (accessed 27 April 2020).

801   "Letters from the Survivors of Gliniany and Vicinity," https://www.jewish gen.org/yizkor/Glinyany1/gli001.html#Page5 (accessed 27 April 2020).

802   For example, Yakiv Ostrovsky had informed on the nationalists in Vyshnivets (P Wiśniowiec), now in Ternopil oblast but formerly in Volhynia. When the Soviets retreated, this came to light, and he was advised to join the nationalist militia to expiate his guilt. Himka, "'Skazhite'" According to a Ukrainian Baptist memoirist from Volhynia, the militia seized NKVD records to find out who the informers were in order to arrest them. Podvorniak, *Viter z Volyni*, 126.

Soviet regime were sometimes tortured and released[803] or forced to serve the nationalists or simply released; many, of course, were murdered outright. The Jews on the list were not spared, and in many cases entire families were executed, this in keeping with Ivan Klymiv's instructions to impose "collective responsibility (family and national)."[804] In a minority of cases, the entire Jewish population of a particular locality was murdered by the militia. The murders were often committed at night, the victims taken from their homes to a place on the outskirts, often in or near a forest. The victims were usually forced to dig their own graves.

When estimating the number of Jewish victims in Galicia, Struve distinguished three zones: localities under the control of the Wehrmacht, localities visited by Waffen-SS Wiking, and localities under Hungarian occupation.[805] In the Wehrmacht zone, the militia worked with both the Wehrmacht and Einsatzgruppe C as well as undertook systematic executions. In this zone, only ten cases, generally but not exclusively in larger centers, resulted in or may have resulted in more than a hundred fatalities: Lviv (500-700), Skhidnytsia (P Schodnica) (200), Boryslav (160-350) Chortkiv (110-300), Berezhany (100-300), Yasenka Stetsiova (P Jasionka Steciowa) and nearby Isai (P Isaje) (100), Kosiv (P Kosów) (80-110), Sambir (P Sambor) (50-150), Drohobych (47-200), Stari Petlykivtsi (P Petlikowce Stare) and nearby Zaryvyntsi (P Żurawińce) (1-100). In the thirty-seven other localities that Struve investigated in this zone, there were 662-789 Jewish victims, so on average 18-21 victims per locality. Altogether in the Wehrmacht zone, there were from 2065 to 3354 victims.

In the second zone, i.e. in the six localities where Wiking was operating, there were from 4280 to 6950 Jewish victims, so from 713 to 1158 per locality.

---

803 Collective farm activists in Perevoloka were forced to hold burning Soviet propaganda material in their hands until the material was entirely consumed by fire. Although they suffered burns, they were allowed to live. Struve, *Deutsche Herrschaft*, 526-27.

804 See above, 229.

805 The estimates are presented in tabular form in Struve, *Deutsche Herrschaft*, 668-70.

In the third zone, occupied by the Hungarians, there were fewer Jewish fatalities than elsewhere in Galicia, since the Hungarians actively discouraged pogroms. Most of the murders here were the systematic executions from lists. Altogether, in the twelve localities where Jews were killed, there were 396-426 victims, i.e. 33-36 per locality.

In addition to these three zones, Struve made estimates for another twelve localities which he was unable to research in depth: altogether 554-579 victims.

When we add all these figures together, we get a total number of Jewish fatalities of 7295-11,309. Struve points out that as horrible as these atrocities were in specific localities, the anti-Jewish violence of the summer of 1941 claimed the lives of a relatively small proportion of Galicia's Jewish population, from 1.35 to 2.1 percent.[806] Another way to contextualize these murders is to consider in how many localities they occurred. In his study, Struve counted 77, obviously only a fraction of the localities in Galicia. In their monograph *Intimate Violence*, Kopstein and Wittenberg studied 1943 localities in Galicia and Volhynia inhabited by both Jews and non-Jews and determined that pogroms occurred in 153 of them.[807] Their larger number of pogroms not only reflects the inclusion of Volhynia but also their wider definition of a pogrom. Struve counted only localities where there were Jewish fatalities. Kruglov counted a total of 143 pogroms in Galicia, again including incidents without fatalities.[808]

OUN veterans have generally denied their involvement in anti-Jewish actions, so it is difficult to ascertain their view of what happened. But there is a memoir by a former OUN member, Stefan Petelycky, that gives us some insight into their attitudes. I need to state that there is no reason to believe that Petelycky himself was involved in the murders, but he was certainly a witness to one of the bloodiest moments in the bloody summer of 1941: the murder of hundreds of Jews by Wiking, the Ukrainian militia, and locals in

806 Ibid., 671.
807 Kopstein and Wittenberg, *Intimate Violence*, 84.
808 Kruglov, "Pogromy v Vostochnoi Galitsii," 335-40.

Zolochiv. For Petelycky, the murder by the NKVD of about 650 political prisoners was an extremely traumatic moment. There are certainly silences in his account,[809] but it is nonetheless as close as we
get to some kind of explanation:

> One of the local Jews, whom we called Shmulko and who had
> worked in the flour mill before the war, had joined the NKVD and
> worked at this prison [in Zolochiv]. He was captured near Sasiv and
> forced to show people the corpses of their family members, relatives,
> and friends. Then he was tied to a stake and stoned to death. He who
> lives by the sword dies by the sword. He was a strong man and so
> took a long time to die. I couldn't look at what was left of him. But I
> also couldn't feel sorry for him. Before he died, he confessed to a sec-
> ond burial pit that people had suspected but had not been able to
> find.
>
> The Germans forced many of the local Jews to dig up and clean the
> corpses and then place them outside for identification. After that SS
> troops executed these Jews. No Ukrainians participated in that mas-
> sacre, but when we saw what was happening to them we did noth-
> ing. We remembered all the Jews who had participated in the Soviet
> administration and had betrayed Ukrainian nationalists to the
> NKVD. We also held some of the Jews partly responsible for what
> had happened in that prison in the final weeks of the Soviet occupa-
> tion. Local Jewish collaborators had helped the Soviets.
>
> It was not fair to blame all the Jews for what had happened to our
> people. But you cannot imagine today what we saw in that prison
> yard.....
>
> We buried our victims together in a mass grave on the following Sun-
> day at the Ukrainian cemetery. We paid no heed to the deaths of their
> murderers or to the murder of the innocent Jews who were killed
> alongside the guilty ones. Some of them had been our neighbours,
> even friends. But now they were consigned to the ranks of our ene-
> mies. It was not entirely rational. It was not just or fair. But war was
> already hardening us, stripping away such basic human instincts as
> empathy, understanding, and forgiveness.[810]

---

809 See the brilliant essay by Marco Carynnyk, "Zolochiv movchyt'."
810 Petelycky, *Into Auschwitz*, 12–13.

Volhynia

Shmuel Spector listed 26 localities in Volhynia in which his research showed that pogroms had occurred in July 1941.[811] Kopstein and Wittenberg listed 28 pogrom localities in Volhynia palatinate in *Intimate Violence*.[812] For his 2014 dissertation on the violence in Nazi-occupied Volhynia, Jared McBride compiled a database of pogroms in the region. According to his data, there were 42 confirmed pogroms in Volhynia, but he estimated that there were at least twice as many, perhaps a hundred. In smaller localities there could well have been no survivors at all to bear witness after the retreat of the Germans. Also, the Extraordinary State Commission in Volhynia oblast, with its capital in Lutsk, was less interested in recording anti-Jewish violence than the commission that functioned in Rivne oblast, thus making it difficult to reconstruct what happened there.[813]

McBride, who has provided the most detailed account to date of the anti-Jewish violence in Volhynia in summer 1941,[814] pointed out that many local actors were involved in the violence in addition to the two factions of OUN: ordinary Ukrainians and Poles, criminal gangs, and smaller anti-Soviet and antisemitic forces that emerged that summer. He also explained that it is by no means easy to sort out who was responsible for what in this violence and especially the extent of OUN's culpability.[815] In his view, "participation of nationalist organizations can be confirmed in at least seven locations."[816]

In what follows I will look at a dozen localities where I believe the evidence points to OUN militia violence. Since in August and September the original militias were partly absorbed into and replaced by German-directed police units, to be discussed in the next chapter, I am confining my examples to a period when the militias

---

811 Spector, *Holocaust of Volhynian Jews*, 66-67.
812 Kopstein and Wittenberg, *Intimate Violence*, 137-42.
813 McBride, "'A Sea of Blood and Tears,'" 128.
814 Ibid., 87-149.
815 Ibid., 107-08, 130.
816 Ibid., 106.

definitely existed and remained ultimately under the command of OUN, i.e., late June, July, and the first few days of August 1941. There are a number of other localities in which I think OUN militias were likely to have been involved in this period, but I hesitate to confirm this view without more evidence.[817] As we will see in the next chapter, the dismantling of the Ukrainian National Militia and related OUN units actually continued into September. Thus, what I will be describing in relation to Volhynia considerably underreports instances of the militia's anti-Jewish violence. But even with this restriction, the nature of the violence in this region should emerge clearly.

Rivne and Lutsk

I will start with the two oblast capitals, Rivne and Lutsk. The Soviets carved Rivne and Volhynia oblasts out of the former Volhynia

---

817 These localities are: 1) Krymne (P Krymno), northwest of Kovel in Volhynia oblast. In July 1941 Ukrainian militiamen, who—at least later—had demonstrable connections with OUN, killed about ten Jews. Before killing them, they locked them in a small house for several days and deprived them of water. They also beat the Jews before shooting them near the village cemetery. Investigations of Volodymyr Kondrenko and Oleksii Hrysiuk, USHMM RG-31018M, reel 72, frames 346-53, 360-62, 382, 390-91, 408, 414, 429; HDA SBU, spr. 8650, vol. 1, ff. 36, 38-48, 75, 78-79, 111, 131. There is plenty of evidence that the militia on the raion level was controlled by OUN-B. USHMM RG-31018M, reel 32; HDA SBU, spr. 70, vols. 28-32. 2) Volodymyr-Volynskyi (P Włodzimierz Wołyński) in Volhynia oblast. See USHMM, *Encyclopedia of Camps and Ghettos*, s.v. "Włodzimerz Wołyński," by Ray Brandon; Katchanovski, "OUN(b) ta natsysts'ki masovi vbyvstva," 226; AŻIH, 301/2014, Józef Opatowski, 2-3; AŻIH, 301/1477, Ela Borenstein, 1. 3) Rozhyshche (P Rożyszcze) in Volhynia oblast. See USHMM, *Encyclopedia of Camps and Ghettos*, s.v. "Rożyszcze," by Alexander Kruglov and Martin Dean; Zvi Roiter, "A Child Watches the Germans Enter Rozhishch," https://www.jewishgen.org/yizkor/Rozyszcze/roz031.html (accessed 1 April 2020). 4) Radyvyliv. See USHMM, *Encyclopedia of Camps and Ghettos*, s.v. "Radziwiłłów," by Alexander Kruglov and Martin Dean; Yitschak Vaynshteyn, "Testimony," https://www.jewishgen.org/yizkor/Radzivilov/rad199.html (accessed 30 March 2020); Yitschak Vaynshteyn, "The Destruction of Radzivilov," https://www.jewishgen.org/yizkor/Radzivilov/rad199.html (accessed 30 March 2020); Jechiel Porochovnik," https://www.jewishgen.org/yizkor/Radzivilov/rad231.html (accessed 30 March 2020); Shifra Poltorak, "A Daughter of Radzilov on Her Town," https://www.jewishgen.org/yizkor/Radzivilov/rad251.html (accessed 30 March 2020). 5) Dubno in Rivne oblast. See USHMM, *Encyclopedia of Camps and Ghettos*, s.v. "Dubno," by Helen Segall; Klymyshyn, *V pokhodi do voli*, 319-21; AŻIH, 301/4918, Herman Guński, 1; AŻIH, 301/2168, Pinches Fingerhut, 1.

palatinate in 1939. OUN-B considered the two cities to be the capitals of their circle administration, with authority over their entire oblasts.[818]

Several high-powered expeditionary groups went through Rivne early on. The German Sixth Army took the city on 28 June 1941,[819] and OUN-B emissaries arrived less than a week later. According to Yuliia Lutska, the wife of a leading OUN-B activist, Oleksandr Lutsky, her expeditionary group left Chełm at the end of June and arrived in Rivne a few days later.[820] Mykola Klymyshyn arrived in Rivne in the first week of July 1941. There were already twenty members of his expeditionary group that had arrived on the previous day. "Rivne was very well organized." he wrote. "The OUN network there was very strong." As a result OUN-B was able to take over the city the day after the Bolsheviks retreated. "I found the city, raion, and oblast administration completely staffed and working intensely."[821] A militia was active no later than 8 July, since OUN-B activists on their way to Kyiv, including Starukh, were able to stay at the militia headquarters overnight on that date.[822] Starukh wrote in a report dated 15 July 1941 that in Rivne "the cause is positioned beautifully. Everything is going fine. The militia is functioning, the rest of the administration as well. There are three hundred underground members and a rather strong organizational network....We have a strong center here; no one even mentions Melnykism."[823] There is no room for doubt about who controlled the militia in Rivne.

---

818 Report of the deputy member of the Ukrainian State Administration Mykola Mostovych to the OUN leadership in Lviv on the activities of the local administration in Volhynia and Polissia, 31 August 1941, in Dziuban, *Ukrains'ke derzhavotvorennia*, 346.

819 USHMM, *Encyclopedia of Camps and Ghettos*, s.v. "Równe," by Alexander Kruglov. See also Burds, *Holocaust in Rovno*, 31.

820 Katchanovski, "OUN(b) ta natsysts'ki masovi vbyvstva," 227. (Her husband was at the time serving in Nachtigall.)

821 Klymyshyn, *V pokhodi do voli*, 321.

822 Katchanovski, "OUN(b) ta natsysts'ki masovi vbyvstva," 228. Testimony of Yurii Stelmashchuk in USHMM RG-31.026, reel 37, frames 180-84; TsDAHO, fond 1, op. 22, spr. 861, f. 22. Katchanovski cited the same testimony from a different repository. See also Dziuban, *Ukrains'ke derzhavotvorennia*, xvi.

823 Veselova, *OUN v 1941 rotsi*, 315.

Also in Rivne in July 1941 was Sonderkommando 4a of Einsatzgruppe C, commanded by Paul Blobel. This Sonderkommando was to be responsible for many murders in Volhynia. In two reports, Einsatzgruppe C informed Berlin that Sonderkommando 4a executed 240 Bolshevik and NKVD functionaries and agents, "primarily Jewish."[824] One report provided a laconic description of a mass execution that took place on 9 July, that is after the OUN-B militia was well in place: "So we were able in Rivne on 9 July 1941 at nightfall and with the aid of the militia to arrest 130 Bolsheviks, among them NKVD functionaries and informers, who in the meantime have been liquidated."[825] According to the Ukrainian Holocaust scholar Alexander Kruglov, Sonderkommando 4a and the Ukrainian militia "forced the victims to spend the night in the courtyard of the building of the State Bank." They were shot the next morning on the outskirts of the city.[826]

Rivne had a large Jewish population at the time, about 23,000 people, so a number of survivor accounts exist that give voice to their experience. Abraham Kirschner and his family fled to Rivne after surviving a massacre at Klevan (P Klewań), a village twenty kilometers north of Rivne.[827] As soon as Kirschner arrived in the oblast capital, he came upon a street roundup. Over 250 Jewish men were assembled, supposedly for work. Although at first no one knew what happened to these people, it was learned later from some people who lived at the edge of town that they could hear shooting the entire night. The sound was coming from the square at Biała St.[828] Another survivor's narrative was as follows: Many people fled as the Germans entered. When these returned, the

---

824 EM 19, 11 July 1941 and EM 28, 20 July 1941. Einsatzgruppe C reported that Einsatzkommando Brest was also stationed in Rivne in mid-July. EM 25, 17 July 1941.
825 EM 28, 20 July 1941.
826 USHMM, *Encyclopedia of Camps and Ghettos*, s.v. "Równe," by Alexander Kruglov.
827 On the killings in Klevan, aside from Kirschner's testimony, see USHMM, *Encyclopedia of Camps and Ghettos*, s.v. "Klewań," by Alexander Kruglov and Martin Dean; Burds, *Holocaust in Rovno*, 31-32 (includes a translation of much of Kirschner's wrenching testimony on Klevan); Al'tman, *Kholokost na territorii SSSR: entsyklopediia*, s.v. "Klevan'," by A.I. Kruglov.
828 AŻIH, 301/1190, Abraham Kirschner, 2-3.

Germans caught them, mainly Jewish men and former communists of different religions. They took them to Biała St. and shot them all there. The families of the murdered continued for some time to get news and greetings from them. "The Germans wanted in this perfidious manner to deceive the rest of the Jews."[829]

A fuller account was written by a Jewish woman who, like many other Jews in Rivne, was impressed into labor by the Ukrainian militia. The latter apprehended Jews on the streets and in their apartments. Tasks for Jewish laborers included digging ditches, carrying rocks and steel, and cleaning buildings after repair. Workdays lasted twelve hours, from 6:00 am to 6:00 pm, with a break for lunch between 12:00 and 1:00. Ukrainians supervised the work, though sometimes Germans did. During work they treated the workers inhumanely, beating and torturing them. Recounting the action of 8-9 July, she said that the Ukrainian militia and German gendarmerie rounded up Jewish men off the streets and from their homes, taking them also from the attics and cellars in which they hid. They loaded them all into cars and took them away in an unknown direction. They were told it was for work, but none of the arrested men returned. Such roundups of men occurred with some regularity. Each time they took several hundred persons.[830]

As to Lutsk, the Wehrmacht arrived there on 26 June 1941. As in some other localities in Western Ukraine, the Germans found in Lutsk a large number of corpses in the prison, victims of the NKVD. A study specifically devoted to the NKVD murders in Lutsk estimated that 1000-1400 prisoners were executed,[831] but Einsatz-

---

829 AŻIH, 301/2519, Lusia Jawec, 1.

830 AŻIH, 301/872, Adela and Inda Lieberman, 1. Kruglov confirms the recurrence of such actions: Einsatzgruppe C shot about 100 more Jews on the grounds of a brickyard about two kilometers from Rivne. "Several hundred more Jews were killed by a Sipo and SD squad of the Einsatzgruppe Special Duty (z.b.V.)." As noted above, Einsatzgruppe C reported that they had altogether performed 240 executions in Rivne by 11 July.

831 I was unable to consult the study: Mykola Kots and Volodymyr Zasiekin, *Rozstril v"iazniv luts'koi tiurmy 23 chervnia 1941 roku* (Lutsk: Volyns'ka oblasna drukarnia, 2010). But the estimate is cited in Katchanovski, "OUN(b) ta natsysts'ki masovi vbyvstva," 223; the estimate was based on memoirs of inmates who survived and Soviet documentation on the number of prisoners before the outbreak of war with Germany and on the execution itself.

gruppe C reported finding 2800 victims.[832] This enormous crime became a pretext for mass reprisals against the Jewish inhabitants of Lutsk. The Einsatzgruppe's report stated, citing the testimony of nineteen Ukrainians who had managed to survive the massacre, that "once again the Jews were prominent participants in the arrests and shootings."[833] An advance unit from Sonderkommando 4a arrived in Lutsk on 27 June[834] and the rest came in the first day or two of July.[835] Members of the Sonderkommando searched the Soviet offices and looked for "the Jews and communists" who were responsible for fires and pillage in the city. They were able to arrest three hundred Jews and twenty plunderers whom they executed on 30 June. Later on 2 July, the bodies of ten Wehrmacht soldiers were discovered. In reprisal for the murder of these German soldiers and of the Ukrainians, Sonderkommando 4a, aided by a unit of the order police and a Wehrmacht unit, shot 1160 Jews. On 6 July they executed fifty Polish "agents and spies."[836]

This Einsatzgruppe report did not mention any aid from Ukrainians and limited itself to listing those German units that participated in the actual shooting. However, the Germans would not have been able on their own to identify the hundreds of Jews they

---

832 A Banderite activist in his memoirs reported "over three thousand." Mechnyk, *Pid trioma okupantamy*, 106.

833 EM 24, 16 July 1941. The newspaper *Krakivs'ki visti* published an interview with a survivor of the prison murders in Lutsk. The article referred to "Muscovite-Jewish executioners." M.K., "Peklo bol'shevyts'kykh viaznyts'. Ochevydets' pro kryvavu masakru ukraintsiv u Luts'ku," *Krakivs'ki visti*, 15 July 1941. Even years after the war, Banderites continued to maintain Jewish culpability for participation in the murders. Someone who signed himself with the initials S.D. and who also survived the NKVD killings published a memoir in 1960 in the OUN-B newspaper *Shliakh peremohy*. He explained how, goaded on by machine-gun fire, prisoners broke through the barbed wire and jumped into the river Styr. "But no one managed to be saved, because the 'people's militia' (composed exclusively of Jews), which had been stationed in advance above the Styr, shot all the prisoners in the water. Although a few managed to break through this Jewish encirclement and swam on, [the Jews] caught up with them in boats and shot them too." Reprinted in Kiebuzinski and Motyl, *The Great West Ukrainian Prison Massacre*, 349.

834 EM 24, 16 July 1941.

835 EM 8, 30 June 1941; EM 9, 1 July 1941; 6 July 1941.

836 EM 24, 16 July 1941.

killed in an unfamiliar city—they needed local assistance.[837] As Jürgen Matthäus has observed: "Since the early stages of the war against the Soviet Union, non-Germans—in a kind of tacit division of labor—participated in anti-Jewish violence to a significant extent," including by identifying Jews.[838] A German soldier who was in Lutsk in the first week of the occupation, clearly recalled that Ukrainians helped round up the Jews.[839] And as we shall see, Jewish survivors also remembered Ukrainian participation in these early anti-Jewish actions. In Galicia, as Struve has demonstrated, the preferred partners for Germans in the roundup of Jews for execution were the OUN militias. And as we have seen in the case of Rivne and will see in a number of other localities, the Germans made use of OUN militias in Volhynia as well as in Galicia. Thus we have to look at how strong was the presence of OUN in Lutsk and whether and when it established militias.

Activists from the Melnyk faction of OUN followed the Germans from Chełm to Lutsk. And local OUN members, who would have aligned themselves with the Bandera faction, emerged from the underground.[840] According to the research of Ivan Katchanovski, the Volhynia oblast militia was headed by the local Banderite activist Oleksandr Kohut, who had been fortunate enough to survive the NKVD shootings in Lutsk. The city police were commanded by one of the leaders of the OUN-B in Volhynia oblast, Mykola Yakymchuk. In Katchanovski's view, there is sufficient evidence, from OUN, German, and Jewish survivor sources, to indicate that the OUN militia was formed before the mass execution of 30 June.[841] Stepan Mechnyk, an OUN-B activist who had served as a courier between Ivan Klymiv and Bandera, arrived in Lutsk at the end of June,[842] and, it seems, found that five squads

---

837 See above, 232.
838 Matthäus, "Operation Barbarossa," 268.
839 Struve, *Deutsche Herrschaft*, 244.
840 Klymenko and Tkachov, *Ukraintsi v politsii v reikhskomisariati "Ukraina,"* 56.
841 Katchanovski, "OUN(b) ta natsysts'ki masovi vbyvstva," 223-24.
842 In a documentary novel, Mechnyk stated that he heard the radio announcement of the proclamation of the Ukrainian state in Lviv on 30 June. Mechnyk, *Neskoreni*, 164. In a memoir, Mechnyk dated the radio announcement to 30 June, and he was already in Lutsk. Mechnyk, *Pid trioma okupantamy*, 108.

(*roi*) of OUN militants (about fifty men altogether) had preceded him there.[843] Even before he arrived, OUN-B activists had found the NKVD archive in Lutsk largely intact,[844] and Klymyshyn learned of this later (he arrived in Lutsk on 7 July).[845] Einsatzgruppe C also reported this discovery to their Berlin headquarters.[846] As Katchanovski noted, the circumstance that the OUN-B network in Lutsk and the Einsatzgruppe shared these records indicates that they were working together.[847]

The mass executions were described in the testimony of Jewish survivors. As Tatiana Kunica recalled the murder on 30 June, the Germans took several hundred Jewish men from their apartments on the pretext that they were being impressed for labor. But none of them returned from this work. A few days later, the Germans posted a notice that all Jewish men from 16 to 60 had to report to Lubart's Castle, originally built in the fourteenth century, with food for one day and with shovels to repair the sewage system. Four thousand men appeared. At 6:00 pm the whole city could hear rifle shots every 10-15 minutes. This lasted for several hours. Kunica at that time was working in the hospital as a doctor and had a boy in her section who recounted to her the whole course of the massacre. The Germans divided everyone into professionals and nonprofessionals. Then everyone had to turn over their cash, watches, and fountain pens. They had to dig their graves themselves. They shot them in groups. The boy fell after a salvo, but he was only wounded and was able to escape under cover of night. He was being treated for mental illness.[848]

Estera Bajdman-Ettinger remembered much the same. All of Lutsk was covered with announcements that the entire adult Jewish population was to report for work with shovels and pickaxes to Lubart's Castle. Those who did not show up were threatened with death. She herself and her family did not appear. After a few hours

843 Mechnyk, *Neskoreni*, 161.
844 Mechnyk, *Pid trioma okupantamy*, 106.
845 Klymyshyn, *V pokhodi do voli*, 322.
846 EM 24, 16 July 1941.
847 Katchanovski, "OUN(b) ta natsysts'ki masovi vbyvstva," 225.
848 AŻIH, 301/2565, Tatiana Kunica, 1-2.

on the empty Jewish streets, one could see silhouettes with a frightened aspect running in the direction of their homes. These were either elderly persons or persons who had documentation that they were professionals. These were released from the castle. The vast majority of people who went there never returned. They were all shot. "In the roundup of Jews the Ukrainians were most active; they had excellent circumstances for their activities and became the vampire of the Jewish population of Lutsk."[849] Yoysef Retseptor's narrative was similar. "...White posters announced that men aged 16 to 60 had to volunteer for work. They had to bring their own axes, shovels, pickaxes, hammers, crowbars, etc. They were to assemble at [Lubart's Castle]. About 3000 men presented themselves 'for work.' Alas, none of them was ever seen again. The Ukrainian and German murderers killed them with the very tools the victims had themselves brought."[850] Jankiel Baran also remembered that a week after the entrance of the Germans they took a number of Jews to the castle, with the very energetic help of the Ukrainians, and shot them there.[851]

Jewish survivors also remember Ukrainian attacks that took place outside the framework of helping the Germans in their executions. Retseptor recalled: "In the streets they chased Jews and beat them to death. Their dogs literally tore chunks of flesh from Jewish bodies. Jews were spit at and insulted. It became impossible to appear on the streets. Jews were forbidden to do business or to assemble; they were left to the mercy of murderous Germans and Ukrainians."[852]

Estera Bajdman-Ettinger remembered assaults on Jews by Ukrainian youth:

849   AŻIH, 301/5657, Estera Bajdman-Ettinger, 1.
850   Yoysef Retseptor, "Once There Was a Town Named Lutsk and It Was Destroyed," https://www.jewishgen.org/yizkor/lutsk/lutsk.html (accessed 28 March 2020).
851   AŻIH, 301/4941, Jankiel Baran, 1-2.
852   Yoysef Retseptor, "Once There Was a Town Named Lutsk and It Was Destroyed," https://www.jewishgen.org/yizkor/lutsk/lutsk.html (accessed 28 March 2020).

Our recent peers from the same school bench, from the same street, sometimes from the same apartment building became our most fervent enemies. A day did not pass without these Ukrainians storming into our homes, driving us onto the streets, beating and bullying old people and children. We had to stay in hiding all the time. One day at dawn, armed with revolvers and sticks, the gang of Ukrainian youth, headed by my good acquaintance from before the war, Drobitko (he lived on Shevchenko St.) closed off both sides of Ułańska St., positioning teenagers with sticks on both sides. Then with a loud shout of "Death to the Jews," they systematically broke into every apartment, driving all the Jewish youth out into the street and making them lie down in a giant puddle that covered the whole unpaved street, all to the accompaniment of the most horrible insults and beating with rifle butts. The [Jewish] boys started to flee. Shots were fired.

During this battle Bajdman-Ettinger was hiding in an attic and could see the street. She saw Jewish boys ripping up fencing and mounting a defense. Some were able to escape, but the Ukrainians pursued them. One Jewish boy was pushed into the machinery of a water pump and was crushed. This all happened in the last days of June 1941.[853] The presence of rifles and revolvers in this action suggest that these Ukrainian youth had some connection with the OUN militia.

Tuchyn, Horynhrad, and Kostopil

Next, I will look at a cluster of localities close to Rivne: Tuchyn (P Tuczyn); Horynhrad (P Horyńgród) I[854]; and Kostopil — all in Rivne oblast.

The German Sixth Army arrived in Tuchyn on 6 July. Alexander Kruglov and Martin Dean researched what happened in the town and summarized events as follows: "In the first days of the German occupation, antisemites from among the town's Ukrainian population organized a pogrom. In the course of the violence, about 60 or 70 Jews were killed and many homes looted. The next day, an Einsatzkommando of the Security Police (Sipo) and Security Service (SD), drawing on lists prepared by Ukrainians, arrested and

---

853 AŻIH, 301/5657, Estera Bajdman-Ettinger, 2-4.
854 There was also a Horynhrad II.

shot 20 Jews and 5 Ukrainians as Soviet activists and Communists."[855]

A great deal of documentation identifies the "antisemites from among the town's Ukrainian population" as the OUN militia. Early in 1942, Stepan Trofymchuk, an OUN-B activist who later became an UPA commander under the nom de guerre "Nedolia" (Misfortune), returned to Tuchyn, his home town, and met with his old comrades there from the organization. Tuchyn at that time had a large number of militants, who met regularly.[856] A Tatar woman who lived in Tuchyn during the war told the Extraordinary State Commission that when the Germans came to Tuchyn they formed a Ukrainian militia commanded by a Ukrainian nationalist. This militia began to maltreat the Jews and also shoot them.[857] Jewish survivors also explicitly identified Ukrainian nationalists and the Ukrainian national militia as perpetrators of anti-Jewish violence in Tuchyn in July 1941.[858]

A number of descriptions are extant of the first action against the Jews, which was perpetrated by the militia without German participation, about 6 or 7 July. Yosyf Zaltsman told the Extraordinary State Commission that Ukrainian nationalists prepared sticks with nails at their ends and went around the houses to kill the Jewish population. More than seventy persons were killed and tortured in this way. Those who were wounded but still alive went to the paramedic, a Ukrainian, who refused to help them. "Your authorities are finished," he said, and it's time for you to perish. But he

---

855 USHMM, *Encyclopedia of Camps and Ghettos*, s.v. "Tuczyn," by Alexander Kruglov and Martin Dean.

856 Marchuk and Perekhod'ko, *Kurinnyi UPA Stepan Trofymchuk*, 20.

857 Testimony of Halyna Tselminska to Extraordinary State Commission, 22 November 1944, USHMM RG-22.002M, reel 25; TsGAOR, fond 7021, op. 71, spr. 68, ff. 44-45v.

858 Yosyf Zaltsman testimony to the Extraordinary State Commission, USHMM RG-22.002M, reel 25; TsGAOR, fond 7021, op. 71, spr. 68, ff. 24-25. Testimony of Golda Rezelman to the Extraordinary State Commission, November 1944, USHMM RG-22.002M, reel 25; TsGAOR, fond 7021, op. 71, spr. 68, ff. 48-49. Testimony of Malka Elbert to the Extraordinary Commission, November 1944, USHMM RG-22.002M, reel 25; TsGAOR, fond 7021, op. 71, spr. 68, ff. 56-57. Testimony of Bella Shpilman to the Extraordinary Commision, 25 November 1944, USHMM RG-22.002M, reel 25; TsGAOR, fond 7021, op. 71, spr. 68, ff. 71-72.

treated the injuries of the Ukrainian nationalists, to whom he was quite respectful. The Jewish dead were buried in a mass grave in the Jewish cemetery. After the pogrom, the Ukrainian nationalists, headed by Prokop Polishchuk, imposed a contribution on the Jewish population, to deliver eight days' supply of food.[859] We know for certain that Polishchuk was a member of the local OUN-B network.[860]

Golda Rezelman told the Commission that the Ukrainian national militia proceeded from home to home among the Jewish population and killed families of Jews with axes, staves, shovels, and the like. She personally did not know how many people they killed, but heard from others of fifty murdered adults as well as many wounded. At this time there were no Germans present at all. It was the work of the Ukrainian administration that took over after the Red Army withdrew.[861]

Malka Elbert told the Extraordinary State Commission that the Ukrainians organized what they called a Ukrainian national militia and orchestrated a pogrom against the Jewish population. They killed up to 75 children and adults of the Jewish nation.[862]

The testimony of two Jewish families to the Central Jewish Historical Commission told a similar story. In the night, about 6 July, a group of Ukrainian policemen armed themselves with knives, axes, and boards with big nails and perpetrated a pogrom. They went from house to house, beating people's bodies with the nails, cutting out tongues, plucking out eyes, cutting bodies into pieces. The next morning they began to cart the corpses to the cemetery and the wounded to the hospital or to physicians. These same policemen who took part in the pogrom performed their service in the city in the morning, dispatched the wounded to their homes, and pretended to be amazed that so many corpses and wounded ended up in the city. In this pogrom sixty Jews were killed; ten died after longer or shorter sufferings, and a few dozen recovered. The

---

859 Yosyf Zaltsman testimony.
860 Marchuk and Perekhod'ko, *Kurinnyi UPA Stepan Trofymchuk*, 20.
861 Golda Rezelman testimony.
862 Malka Elbert testimony.

Ukrainian doctor (the same person as the "paramedic" of Yosyf Zaltsman's testimony) did not want to treat the wounded, saying that the Jews had lived long enough. A few days after the pogrom the Ukrainian police told the Jews to bring them bedclothes, bowls, cups, plates, and other household wares. Every house was allowed only one plate and a spoon.[863]

Ivan Stadnyk, one of those whom witnesses identified as a leading personage in the militia violence, denied to the Commission that he had taken part in these murders, although in the end, he was convicted of doing so.[864] He essentially confirmed the story of Jewish survivors: the Ukrainian national militia perpetrated the first pogrom against the Jewish population, using sticks with nails protruding; very many were killed.[865]

In the second major action, Germans played the leading role. Again, we have a number of eyewitness accounts. Yosyf Zaltsman recounted that after the first action, the Ukrainian nationalists ordered the Jewish population, under pain of death, to assemble at the raion administration building (Tuchyn was then a raion capital). About two thousand Jews gathered there. They took thirty Jews, including Zaltsman himself, whom they had put on a list as communists and forced them to sign the list. After they signed, the nationalists force-marched the Jews into the nearby village of Shubkiv (P Szubków) and added another ten persons. They locked them in a building there and tortured them, forcing them to beat each other. Whoever would not beat another Jew was beaten to death by the Ukrainian nationalists. But then the nationalists just dispersed the Jews. After a while "the Gestapo," as survivors' testimony often referred to units of the Einsatzgruppen, came from Rivne and under threat of death gathered twenty persons from the Jewish population. They shot the twenty Jews and buried them in the garden behind the leather-goods factory. (Leather had been produced in

---

863 AŻIH, 301/397, Mełamed and Zylberberg families, 2-3.
864 USHMM RG-22.002M, reel 25; TsGAOR, fond 7021, op. 71, spr. 68, ff. 73-73v.
865 Testimony of Ivan Stadnyk to the Extraordinary Committee, 24 November 1944, USHMM RG-22.002M, reel 25; TsGAOR, fond 7021, op. 71, spr. 68, ff. 58-60.

Tuchyn since tsarist times.) And they also shot and buried here five Ukrainians who had worked for the Soviets.[866]

Golda Rezelman also remembered the arrival of "the Gestapo." After inquiries, the Germans compiled a list of twenty, several Ukrainians and fifteen Jews. Ukrainian militiamen both provided the information and rounded up the listed persons by force of arms, delivering them to the Gestapo. The Gestapo shot them by the leather factory in Tuchyn and buried them. The victims dug their own grave.[867] Malka Elbert said much the same: the Gestapo came to Tuchyn, summoned twenty Jews and five Ukrainians who took leading roles in the work of the Soviet authorities, and shot them by the leather factory in Tuchyn.[868] And Bella Shpilman told the Extraordinary State Commission that the Gestapo from Rivne came, and the Germans turned to the Ukrainian nationalists to hand over the communists and Soviet workers. The Ukrainian nationalists gave them the names of the leading Soviet activists. Altogether they handed over eighteen people; all were shot by the leather factory.[869] Stadnyk, who may well have been involved in this action, told the Commission that he remembered the murder of the Soviet *aktiv* by the leather factory, but did not know the details.[870]

Horynhrad I is located just ten kilometers southwest of Tuchyn, and it seems that essentially the same militia that was active in Tuchyn arrested and killed Jews in Horynhrad. We have two testimonies about what happened here in early July. One was given to the Extraordinary State Commission by the former head of the village soviet, Mykola Pokhyliuk. He stated that shortly after the Germans arrived, about 5 July according to his recollection, "there appeared in [Tuchyn] raion 'the blue-and-yellow men,' the Ukrainian police." They called a meeting by the church in Horynhrad, sang

---

866 Yosyf Zaltsman testimony.
867 Golda Rezelman testimony.
868 Malka Elbert testimony.
869 Testimony of Bella Shpilman to the Extraordinary State Commission, 25 November 1944, USHMM RG-22.002M, reel 25; TsGAOR, fond 7021, op. 71, spr. 68, ff. 71-72.
870 Ivan Stadnyk testimony.

the anthem "Shche ne vmerla Ukraina," and demanded the population to turn over all Soviet functionaries. The militiamen said at the meeting that all Jews had to wear a white band with a six-pointed star on their left arm. About five or six days later, the Germans assembled the Jewish population and marched them northwest in the direction of Babyn (P̱ Babin), allegedly for work. They only took men, but no one ever saw them again. One of these, however, was only wounded and escaped. But the militiamen caught him, shot him, and threw him down the well in Jazłowce.[871] The Jews who were shot in Babyn were buried in a place called Lysa Hora (P̱ Łysa Góra), about four kilometers southwest of Horynhrad.[872]

The Mełamed family told the Jewish Historical Commission about their experience in Horynhrad, where they had lived when the war broke out. At that time, they said, there were about fifty Jewish families in the town. On 5 or 6 July, a taxi came to the town and five Ukrainians got out, peasants from the neighboring area. They were dressed as civilians but wore blue and yellow armbands. They said they had come for workers to help pull out a car that had gotten stuck by the river. They gathered twenty-five Jewish men, took them outside the city, told them to dig pits, and then shot them. These same Ukrainians on the next day put the corpses into the pits and covered them with earth. One of the Jews, badly wounded, managed to crawl home at night. After this incident, men began to flee from Horynhrad to other towns, such as Rivne, Tuchyn, and Hoshcha (P̱ Hoszcza). The Ukrainian police told the men to report for forced labor every day or their families would be shot. Then entire families began to leave Horynhrad. The Christian neighbors immediately robbed the abandoned Jewish homes. The police watched the roads and robbed and killed fleeing Jews. Only

---

871 Jazłowce (or Osada Jazłowiecka) was one of several Polish veterans' colonies established not far from Horynhrad in 1921 and no longer on the map; the inhabitants were sent to Siberia by the Soviets in 1941. "Osada wojskowa Krechowiecka," http://wolyn.freehost.pl/miejsca-k/krechowiecka-08.html (accessed 15 April 2020).

872 Testimony of Mykola Pokhyliuk to the Extraordinary State Commission, 20 November 1944, USHMM RG-22.002M, reel 25; TsGAOR, fond 7021, op. 71, spr. 68, ff. 28-29.

the old and infirm remained, about thirty persons. When the Melamed family left Horynhrad, there were still no German authorities there.[873]

Kostopil, a town about thirty kilometers northeast of Rivne, was occupied by the German Sixth Army in early July. Within the first days of the occupation, "local Ukrainians" organized a pogrom, during which Jewish property was plundered and Jews were beaten. In addition, six Jews suspected of being Soviet activists were executed.[874] The murder of pro-Soviet Jews indicates a militia action, and it is certain that OUN-B controlled the militia. An OUN-B press release informed readers that on 6 July the national militia was organized in Kostopil, which from the first day of its existence began to disarm Soviet forces. On 8 July the independence of the Ukrainian state was formally proclaimed in Kostopil; the Ukrainian national administration was established as well as the command structure of the Ukrainian national militia. "Twenty-seven villages belong to Kostopil raion. In these villages the Ukrainian national administration, the Ukrainian national militia, and commercial sectors have been established....With the help of the Ukrainian national militia a decisive battle is being waged with the vestiges of Soviet forces as well as with the element hostile to the Ukrainian state."[875]

Rafalivka, Volodymyrets, Olyka, Kremenets, and Vyshnivets

Between Lutsk and Rivne are four localities in which OUN perpetrated anti-Jewish violence. On the map, they form a fairly straight line running north-south. They are, from north to south: Rafalivka; Volodymyrets (P̱ Włodzimierzec) in Rivne oblast; Olyka (P̱ Ołyka) in Volhynia oblast; Kremenets (P̱ Krzemieniec), now in Ternopil oblast; and Vyshnivets.

---

873 AŻIH, 301/397, 1-2.
874 USHMM, Encyclopedia of Camps and Ghettos, s.v. "Kostopol," by Alexander Kruglov and Martin Dean. "Translation of 'Kostopol' Chapter from Pinkas Hakehillot Polin," https://www.jewishgen.org/yizkor/pinkas_poland/pol5_00168.html. (accessed 25 March 2020).
875 Press release on establishment of Ukrainian authorities in Kostopil raion, 8 July 1941, in Dziuban, *Ukrains'ke derzhavotvorennia*, 253. Delegations from the Kostopil region attended the celebration of Ukrainian statehood held at Lubart's Castle in Rivne on 27 July. Ibid., 301.

There were few fatalities in Rafalivka, but Jews were beaten and robbed. The Soviets began to withdraw from the town on 4 July, but the Germans, units of the Sixth Army, did not occupy it until mid-July. In the meantime, a Ukrainian administration and its militia took charge.[876] We have already seen that in July Banderites came up here from Galicia and organized a militia to help the Germans against Bolsheviks, Poles, and Jews.[877] The robbery of Jews by the Ukrainian nationalist militia is mentioned in the Soviet investigation of Oleksandr Sydorchuk, who deserted from the Red Army and joined the militia in Rafalivka in July 1941. Sydorchuk told his interrogator on 3 September 1948: "Yes, I am aware that Ukrainian nationalist bandits at that time robbed citizens of the Jewish nationality in the village of Stara Rafalivka. I did not take part in the robbery. This was in July 1941."[878]

The memoirs of Rafalivka Jews in the town's yizkor book depict the painful trauma they underwent during the Ukrainian nationalist interregnum. Fanya Bas recalled that after the Soviets left and before the Germans arrived, Ukrainians began robbing the Jewish population. "There were Ukrainians who hit Jews and tore babies out of their mothers' arms and threw them around. We waited for the Germans to come, thinking we would be better off, that there would be some order."[879] Leah Tziger recalled that "riots broke out when the Russians withdrew" from Rafalivka. "Murderers" broke into Jewish homes at night and stole and looted. She specifically recalled the Panasiuk brothers, one of whom we have met earlier, when he joined the militia.[880] They broke into some homes and killed a Jewish couple as well as a Jewish man. They also came for her uncle, but he ran away. They chased him but were unsuccessful in their pursuit. "It was a long difficult night. We sat in the dark in

---

876   USHMM, *Encyclopedia of Camps and Ghettos*, s.v. "Rafałówka," by Alexander Kruglov and Samuel Fishman.

877   See above, 223.

878   The investigation concluded that Sydorchuk, in spite of his denial, did take part. USHMM RG-31018M, reel 17; HDA SBU, [unfortunately, the title page with the number of the sprava was not microfilmed], 16a-v, 91.

879   Fanya Bas née Rosenfeld, "Grandma Fanya Tells Her Grandchildren," https://www.jewishgen.org/yizkor/rafalovka/raf139.html (accessed 31 March 2020).

880   See above, 223.

utter terror the entire night."[881] Another survivor, Meir Goldverin, wrote:

> During the interim, when the Russians left Rafalovka and the Germans had not yet arrived, the Ukrainians took the power in their hands. They started to rob the Jews of Rafalovka, took whatever came to their hands and slowly began to carry out a pogrom....A large mob of Ukrainians came to a Jew's house to steal. There was no passage to the house due to the large number of Ukrainians who crowded there. An oil lamp stood on the windowsill. The thug smashed the window panes from the outside and took the lamp. A Jew approached him and asked: "Mikita, what are you doing, are not you ashamed of your actions?" The Ukrainian replied—"Shut up dirty Jew."[882]

The pharmacist Yaakov Bas wrote a longer account. He explained that the Germans had already occupied the large cities in the area, but small towns like Rafalivka and Volodymyrets, about twenty-two kilometers to the northeast, were left without any authorities. The Ukrainians seized the opportunity to declare self-rule. Soon afterwards, Bas was visiting a teacher, a certain Mikolski, to express his misgivings about the new Ukrainian administration. While he was there he heard gunshots coming from town. He ran home to his family and found them huddled in a corner, paralyzed with fear. Shots as well as explosions continued to be heard, but they also heard someone banging on the door.

> The door was soon beaten down and a bunch of armed peasants walked in. They went into all the rooms and began searching. Some of them were acquaintances of mine who I had helped more than once. These men appeared uneasy about what they were doing, but one of them had no qualms at all. He came up to me and grabbed my hand. When he saw my wedding ring he started pulling at it forcefully and was about to break my finger. I started to scream from the pain. My wife handed them her wedding ring, pleading with them to take everything and spare our lives. And, indeed, they took whatever they pleased, threatening us and reminding us that our good years were over and that now we would be made to pay for all those years.

---

881 "Leah Tziger [née Pinchuk]," https://www.jewishgen.org/yizkor/rafalovka/raf139.html (accessed 31 March 2020).

882 Meir Goldverin, "We Didn't Find a Survivor," https://www.jewishgen.org/yizkor/rafalovka/raf093.html (accessed 31 March 2020).

The rest of our acquaintances, whom I had helped when they were sick or in need, took pity on us. The destruction and our helplessness no doubt made them feel contrite and they ordered the rioters to leave the house. They told us to shut the doors and not let anyone in the house. They crept away like thieves, but did not let go of their loot. We thanked God for this mercy they showed us. We closed the doors and the shutters and peeked out through the cracks. We heard the cries of women and children, gunshots, and the savage screams of the plunderers. We saw many peasant wagons full of Jewish property — bed linen and the like — leaving town. And in the streets, broken household utensils and feathers flying all around.

After the peasants quenched their first thirst for blood and left the town, it got quiet. I slowly opened the door and carefully went out to the street to see what they had done. I first went into the home of our neighbor, Mr. Rosenfeld. What I saw was a terrible sight. All the furniture was smashed and mixed in with the other household items. It was all in a pile — a heap of broken pieces. The Rosenfelds, pale and quietly weeping, were sitting among the wreckage. They were in shock, speechless, unable to utter a word.

The Jews of Rafalivka hoped that this would be the end of the persecutions, but on another day, Bas was conversing with Yona Rosenfeld when they heard "a horrifying cry of distress." Outside they saw a crowd of frightened Jews running. The fleeing Jews told Bas and Rosenfeld that a "large gang of thugs" was crossing the river Styr and heading towards town. The friends barely managed to get to their homes and families. But swept along by the rushing crowd, they were separated from most of their family members; Bas managed to hold on to his son and Rosenfeld his daughter. They could see, when they looked back, "many goyim, armed with all sorts of weapons." They were able to escape with the help of some local herdsmen. Hiding in a cowshed, they saw smoke and flames rising from Rafalivka. They feared for the other members of their families, but stayed in hiding until morning. Then they took a chance and, "hearts trembling," made their way back home. Fortunately, their families were intact. "We were extremely upset and swore to stay together in the future and never to leave each other again. We experienced days of terror and sleepless nights. We were always on guard, ready for trouble.... Rafalovka suffered the horrors of riots and bloodshed for three weeks. We were abandoned and humiliated."[883]

Olyka is about halfway between Rivne and Lutsk and seventy-five kilometers south of Rafalivka. The Sixth Army entered it on 27 or 28 June, but fighting continued here for several days.[884] A report from the head of the raion administration in the town of Olyka stated that the creation of the administration and militia was proclaimed at a meeting on 6 July 1941, but its leadership was formally approved "from above" ten days later. The militia was organized with the active participation of a representative from OUN "from the circle" (z okruhy). On 1 August it helped the Germans in Olyka shoot about 700 Jews, forced to the place of execution on the pretext of labor.[885]

About eight kilometers south of Olyka is Kremenets. Before the Germans succeeded in taking this city, the NKVD killed about a hundred fifty political prisoners.[886] As elsewhere in Western Ukraine, rumors immediately surfaced about the Soviets' extreme sadism.[887] Einsatzgruppe C reported to headquarters: "In part these Ukrainians were, it is said, thrown into a kettle of boiling water; the reason for this opinion is that during their exhumation the corpses were found without skin."[888] A Ukrainian newspaper reported that the victims included eight priests and a bishop. The Bolsheviks led

883 Yaakov Bas, "Bereavement and Wandering," https://www.jewishgen.org/yizkor/rafalovka/raf063.html (accessed 31 March 2020).

884 USHMM, *Encyclopedia of Camps and Ghettos*, s.v. "Ołyka," by Alexander Kruglov and Andrew Koss.

885 Katchanovski, "OUN(b) ta natsysts'ki masovi vbyvstva," 232. "682 Jewish men were caught and collected in the Radziwiłł Castle, where they were told they would perform forced labor. But instead they were escorted to the Jewish cemetery and shot." USHMM, Encyclopedia of Camps and Ghettos, s.v. "Ołyka," by Alexander Kruglov and Andrew Koss.

886 NKVD reports stated that there 350 prisoners in Kremenets at the time of the German attack on the USSR, but that 191 were able to escape. Kiebuzinski and Motyl, *The Great Ukrainian Prison Massacre*, 222, 231. Einsatzgruppe C reported that they found 100-150 victims in the prison. EM 28, 20 July 1941. The extract relating to Kremenets is reprinted in Kiebuzinski and Motyl, *The Great Ukrainian Prison Massacre*, 238. The Ukrainian newspaper *Krakivs'ki visti* reported 1500 murdered prisoners: "1500 ukraintsiv zamorduvaly bol'shevyky u Kremiantsi," *Krakivs'ki visti*, 6 August 1941.

887 See above, 195.

888 EM 28, 20 July 1941.

the latter, whose name was said to be Symon, naked through the streets to the prison. There they set fire to his beard, cut off his heels, nose, and tongue, and plucked out his eyes.[889] Although the story of the bishop has been repeated in Ukrainian and Ukrainian-diaspora publications,[890] it has no discernible basis in fact.[891] But of course, the ugly rumors fed an ugly and angry mood, and anti-Jewish violence exploded in Kremenets.

A large number of Jews were beaten to death. Einsatzgruppe C reported that "the Ukrainians took matters into their own hands and in retaliation clubbed 130 Jews to death."[892] Jewish survivors spoke of 300,[893] 400-500,[894] or 800[895] victims. The highest of these numbers has been accepted in the literature,[896] but this strikes me

---

889 "1500 ukraintsiv zamorduvaly bol'shevyky u Kremiantsi," *Krakivs'ki visti*, 6 August 1941.

890 *Zlochyny komunistychnoi Moskvy*, 42 (1960); Shevchuk et al., *Reabilitovani istoriieiu*, 44, 108 (2008).

891 Tymofii Minenko listed Volhynian clerics repressed by the Soviets in 1939-41; the list included no bishops, and no mention of anything like the scene described in *Krakiv'ski visti*. Minenko, *Pravoslavna tserkva*, 163-64. Nor is anything like this mentioned in the well informed book of Friedrich Heyer, who was in Ukraine during the Nazi occupation. He named Aleksii (Hromadsky) as bishop in Kremenets; the only Symon in the Volhynian episcopate under the Soviets was Symon (Ivanovsky), titular bishop of Ostroh. Both Aleksii and Symon survived the first Soviets. Heyer, *Kirchengeschichte*, 235-36. Aleksii went on to head up the Ukrainian Autonomous Orthodox Church during the Nazi occupation. This was a church oriented on the Moscow patriarchate, while its rival, the Ukrainian Autocephalous Orthodox Church, was associated with Ukrainian nationalists. In 1943, the nationalists, most likely members of the Melnyk faction, murdered Aleksii. Symon decided to remain in Ukraine after the Germans withdrew and served for short periods as a bishop under the Soviets, but he spent more time in the gulag than on an episcopal throne. He died in 1966.

892 EM 28, 20 July 1941.

893 Chayke Kiperman, "I Escaped the Germans and Bandera Gangs," https://www.jewishgen.org/yizkor/kremenets3/kre339.html#Page366 (accessed 27 March 2020).

894 Tova Teper-Kaplan, "The Story of the Extermination," https://www.jewishgen.org/yizkor/kremenets/kre251.html (accessed 26 March 2020).

895 "Translation of 'Krzeminiec' Chapter from *Pinkas Hakehillot Polin*," https://www.jewishgen.org/yizkor/pinkas_poland/pol5_00179e.html (accessed 25 March 2020). B. Shvarts, "Ghetto Martyrology and the Destruction of Kremenets," https://www.jewishgen.org/yizkor/kremenets/kre413.html (accessed 27 March 2020).

896 Spector, *Holocaust of Volhynian Jews*, 66. USHMM, *Encyclopedia of Camps and Ghettos*, s.v. "Krzemieniec," by Ester-Basya Vaisman. Vaisman's article also

as arbitrary. If the pogrom lasted for a few days, as survivors indicated, then it is likely that the Einsatzgruppe report referred to the victims of a single incident, but did not include the fatalities that occurred in the days that followed. Given too the propensity of survivors to increase the number of victims as an expression of the trauma of the experience, I think we are safest to think of hundreds of victims rather than of eight hundred.

It appears that here too, as in Rafalivka, Ukrainian nationalists were able to set up an administration and militias before the Germans arrived. Ester-Basya Vaisman, in the usually authoritative *Encyclopedia of Camps and Ghettos* published by the USHMM, states that the Germans arrived 3 July. However, Oleh Klymenko and Serhii Tkachov, working with detailed local records, concluded that Ukrainians took over the civil administration by 9 July 1941 and that this was days before the Germans arrived. The administration of the city, raion, and circle, they wrote, took orders from OUN.[897] Mykola Mostovych, deputy member of Stetsko's Ukrainian State Administration, reported to the OUN leadership in Lviv that OUN militias helped the Germans liquidate bands of diversionaries and, in localities with no German military, rounded up Bolshevik captives and turned them over to the Germans; he named Kremenets as one of those localities with no German military.[898] According to a Ukrainian Baptist memoirist, a Ukrainian militia was set up in Kremenets the day after the Soviets retreated,[899] and thus before the Germans installed themselves there. And although two Jewish survivor testimonies conflated the emergence of the Ukrainian administration and militia with the arrival of the Germans,[900] another

accepts the Einsatzgruppe's report that the NKVD apparently threw prisoners into cauldrons of boiling water. The article also errs in stating that the report dated the murder of 130 Jews to 3 July; no date was mentioned.

897 Klymenko and Tkachov, *Ukraintsi v politsii v reikhskomisariati "Ukraina,"* 18, 27.

898 Report on the activities of the local administration in Volhynia and Polissia, 31 August 1941, in Dziuban, *Ukrains'ke derzhavotvorennia*, 346.

899 Podvorniak, *Viter z Volyni*, 126.

900 Betsalel Shvarts, "The Holocaust," https://www.jewishgen.org/yizkor/kremenets/kre231.html (accessed 26 March 2020); Tova Teper-Kaplan, "The Story of the Extermination," https://www.jewishgen.org/yizkor/kremenets/kre251.html (accessed 26 March 2020).

stated that "before the Germans arrived, the Ukrainians were the police and the bosses of the city and attacked the retreating Russians from behind."[901] But the actual situation remains unclear. The head of Kremenets county, Mykhailo Redkyn, informed the population of Kremenets, city and county, that the "county Ukrainian government" had taken power as of 9 July; he said that its authority had been established by order of OUN-B and in understanding with the German military authorities.[902]

Both branches of OUN were involved in the Kremenets militias. An OUN-B press release stated that as of 9 July, "a section (*viddil*) of the Ukrainian army has been employed to cleanse the city of Bolsheviks, to find and gather weapons, and to cooperate with S. Bandera."[903] There were about eighty city militiamen in Kremenets in July. The city militia was headed by the Banderite Lev Yaskevych and came into frequent conflict with the circle militia headed by the Melnykite Mykola Niedzvedsky. Other members of the militia have also been identified as belonging to either OUN-M or OUN-B.[904]

Betsalel Shvarts, a survivor from Kremenets, recalled that the sudden outbreak of war left people unprepared and without provisions. Long bread lines formed at the bakeries. But Jews in the lines were unable to purchase loaves, because "the recently established Ukrainian militia attacked them and forced them out of the lines." Then, suddenly, the militia began to apprehend Jews, including women, children, and the elderly. "With cries of 'You have sucked our blood long enough!' the bandits began their killing spree. They caught everyone, old and young, arranged them in rows, and led them, beaten and bleeding," to the NKVD prison. There, as elsewhere in Western Ukraine, Jews had to "dig the corpses out with their bare hands and wash the bodies. They were beaten, and some died from the blows alone." Also, "bands of Ukrainian murderers

901 Chayke Kiperman, "I Escaped the Germans and Bandera Gangs," https://www.jewishgen.org/yizkor/kremenets3/kre339.html#Page366 (accessed 27 March 2020).
902 Dziuban, *Ukrains'ke derzhavotvorennia*, 255-56.
903 Press release, 14 July 1941, in ibid., 268.
904 Klymenko and Tkachov, *Ukraintsi v politsii v reikhskomisariati "Ukraina,"* 60, 91-93, 99, 102.

assembled from the surrounding villages, clubs in hands. They ganged up on the Jews, forced them from their homes, and beat and killed them."[905] As Struve has shown for Galicia, such bands of peasants convening on a scene of anti-Jewish violence turned out to be, upon closer inspection, "well organized groups of OUN-B militants."[906] This was also likely the case in Kremenets.

Shvarts's own wife was taken to the prison and barely survived: "My wife told me that she had been kidnapped from the bread line. She survived because the corpses covering her stopped the bullets fired toward her. She fainted, sleeping until nightfall, and at night crawled out of the pit, almost unconscious, and returned home via back roads." Other escapees went to surrounding settlements, where they took their chances, since some were caught, tortured, and "killed in all kinds of bizarre ways" by locals. "Women were raped." The violence continued for a few days until the German commander put a stop to it.[907]

Tova Teper-Kaplan recounted something similar, but noted the participation of German shooters: "A gathering of gentiles from the area's villages entered the town through the Dubna suburb,[908] armed with iron bars and assorted tools of destruction. They went from house to house, robbing and looting, and herded hundreds of people to the large jail, beating and wounding them without pity. Inside the jail, they were forced to wash the corpses of the murdered Ukrainians, then to dig pits near the jail and lie inside.

905 Betsalel Shvarts, "The Holocaust," https://www.jewishgen.org/yizkor/krem enets/kre231.html (accessed 26 March 2020); B. Shvarts, "Ghetto Martyrology and the Destruction of Kremenets," https://www.jewishgen.org/yizkor/krem enets/kre413.html (accessed 27 March 2020).

906 Struve, *Deutsche Herrschaft*, 678.

907 Betsalel Shvarts, "The Holocaust," https://www.jewishgen.org/yizkor/krem enets/kre231.html (accessed 26 March 2020); B. Shvarts, "Ghetto Martyrology and the Destruction of Kremenets," https://www.jewishgen.org/yizkor/krem enets/kre413.html (accessed 27 March 2020).

908 The Dubno suburb refers to an area on the north of the city, by the Dubno gate, where many Jews lived. According to Shvarts, "about 75 percent of residents of the Dubna suburb were killed and thrown into mass graves at that time." Betsalel Shvarts, "The Holocaust," https://www.jewishgen.org/yizkor/krem enets/kre231.html (accessed 26 March 2020).

German soldiers went from pit to pit and shot them to death."[909] Another Kremenets survivor, Chayke Kiperman, recalled that "the Ukrainians flew into a rage and began to 'seize Jews for labor.' At the same time, they beat up and murdered many Jews."[910]

Another well documented incident of OUN's anti-Jewish violence occurred in Vyshnivets, about 25 kilometers south of Kremenets. It is a town situated on the left bank of the Horyn River; across the river, on the right bank, is a village known as Staryi Vyshnivets (Old Vyshnivets, P Wiśniowiec Stary). The Germans arrived in Vyshnivets on 2 July.[911] Three larger anti-Jewish actions took place in that month. Around 10-12 July the Ukrainian militia murdered thirty-five to forty Jews in the former NKVD headquarters.[912] The second action was recorded by only a single survivor, who mentioned sixty-five Jews as victims and the date as 23 July. In the third action, perpetrated a week later, on 30 July, there were, according to different sources, 100,[913] 300,[914] or 400[915] victims. These murders occurred in Vyshnivets proper, but there was also a

---

909 Tova Teper-Kaplan, "The Story of the Extermination," https://www.jewish gen.org/yizkor/kremenets/kre251.html (accessed 26 March 2020).

910 Chayke Kiperman, "I Escaped the Germans and Bandera Gangs," https://www.jewishgen.org/yizkor/kremenets3/kre339.html#Page366 (accessed 27 March 2020).

911 USHMM, *Encyclopedia of Camps and Ghettos*, s.v. "Wiśniowiec," by Martin Dean and Andrew Koss.

912 A Survivor, "Nazi Atrocities in Vishnevets," https://www.jewishgen.org/yiz kor/Vishnevets/vis049.html (accessed 19 June 2020); Mendel Zinger, "The Destruction of Vishnevets, Volin (As Told by Shaul Shvarts)," https://www.jew ishgen.org/yizkor/Vishnevets/vis049.html (accessed 19 June 2020); Testimony of Mikhail Bulchak, of Jewish nationality, and a native of Vyshnivets, interrogated by SMERSH on 11 May 1944, USHMM, RG-31.018M, reel 60, frame 1690; HDA SBU Ternopil oblast, spr. 31882, f. 137v.

913 USHMM, RG-31.018M, reel 24; HDA SBU Ternopil oblast, spr. 33533, vol. 4, ff. 121-22, 126; vol. 7, f. 92. This is also the number accepted by Spector, *Holocaust of Volhynian Jews*, 67.

914 Mendel Zinger, "The Destruction of Vishnevets, Volin (As Told by Shaul Shvarts)," https://www.jewishgen.org/yizkor/Vishnevets/vis049.html (accessed 19 June 2020).

915 A Survivor, "Nazi Atrocities in Vishnevets," https://www.jewishgen.org/yizk or/Vishnevets/vis049.html (accessed 19 June 2020).

smaller action in July across the river in Staryi Vyshnivets, in which the militia brought eight to ten Jews for the Germans to shoot.[916]

The local militia called itself "Sich," as was often the case also in southern Galicia. It was commanded by a member of OUN-M, Anatolii Badasiuk.[917] A Soviet war crimes trial described the militiamen as armed with rifles, sporting blue and yellow armbands, and wearing caps with tridents on them.[918]

The first larger action has been described by several Jewish survivors. Mikhail Bulchak testified to SMERSH that "forty persons from the Jewish population were taken 'for labor'; they were taken into the basement of the NKVD building and shot there. Only the 'police' composed of Ukrainians of 'Independent Ukraine' took part in this."[919] An anonymous survivor who fled from the NKVD prison in Berdychiv as the Germans approached and returned to his residence in Vyshnivets, arrived in the town just as this action was underway. The victims, he said,

> weren't murdered with the usual tools of murder or in the usual way. It was strange, but the fact is that the way they [the thirty-five hostages] were murdered added more misery to the whole event. The Ukrainians received permission and orders from the Germans to kill them. They stormed the cellar, with the two Ostrovskis in the lead. Full of blood lust and the desire to kill, they tore down the entry door and threw heavy rocks and other heavy objects into the narrow room, pushing and shoving the prisoners into a corner and suffocating them little by little.
>
> The men died while watching death approaching them, step by step, centimeter by centimeter, with each stone thrown at them and with no means of escape.
>
> Alter, Makhtsi Ruach's son, was the only prisoner to survive. He was saved in a horrifying and amazing way. He was a small, skinny man. When the prisoners were pushed into the corner, he was covered up by a pile of human bodies twisting in the last moments of their lives

---

916 USHMM RG-31.018M, reel 61, frames 136-622; HDA SBU Ternopil oblast, 27414 (case of Oleksandr Khomytsky).

917 Klymenko and Tkachov, *Ukraintsi v politsii v reikhskomisariati "Ukraina,"* 165.

918 USHMM, RG-31.018M, reel 24; HDA SBU Ternopil oblast, spr. 33533, vol. 4, ff. 121-22, 126; vol. 7, f. 92.

919 USHMM, RG-31.018M, reel 60, frame 1690; HDA SBU Ternopil oblast, spr. 31882, f. 137v.

and slowly dying in agonizing spasms. Underneath the bodies, he succeeded in digging himself a hole, where he hid his head and survived.

In the evening, the Ukrainians left the murder site only after they had checked and found not a single sound of life coming from the bodies. Only then was Alter able to release himself from the pile of humans. He left his hiding place and found shelter in my house.[920]

Another survivor said that this first action was undertaken to avenge the murder of four men (three Ukrainians and a Jewish refugee from Germany) whom the Soviets executed before their retreat. For each NKVD victim they decided to kill ten Jews. "The Ukrainian police abducted the victims, and 40 Jews were murdered in a cellar in a town building."[921]

All the information about the second action is contained in the following passage from a survivor's account: "Early in the morning, we saw the Ukrainians running wildly. Suddenly, I saw them stop and pick up every person they came across in the Jewish streets. Shouting and laughing, they pulled them violently to one location. In all, they picked up 65 people. Later, they were all led to an unknown location. None of them came back. For many days, we tried to find out their fate and burial place, but all our inquiries came to nothing. Even now, nobody knows their fate."

The same survivor, in the lead-up to his account of the third action wrote: "A week passed without any special incidents. The Ukrainians and their German commanders were somewhat shaken by their own doings; they were frightened and tired." But on 30 July they returned to the work of killing the Jewish population. "The Ukrainians executed the same operation again, but on a larger scale. This time, they developed a new method for their killing. They collected almost 400 Jews, gathered them on the Boulevard in the center of town, and laid each one facing the ground. Then they walked over their backs with their spiky boots, holding heavy clubs in their

---

920   A Survivor, "Nazi Atrocities in Vishnevets," https://www.jewishgen.org/yiz kor/Vishnevets/vis049.html (accessed 19 June 2020).

921   Mendel Zinger, "The Destruction of Vishnevets, Volin (As Told by Shaul Shvarts)," https://www.jewishgen.org/yizkor/Vishnevets/vis049.html (accessed 19 June 2020).

hands. When a person raised his head to see what was happening or to see if it was over, a Ukrainian would jump on his back and beat him badly with the club he held. The Jews remained on the ground, wounded and bleeding, for a very long time, waiting for their fate or for the time when the Ukrainian animals would be satisfied with the groans and blood and let them go." Among the victims here were the author's oldest brother and the town rabbi. The militia accompanied them out of town and none of them were heard from again. The Ukrainians kept their secrets. "Even now [the account was published in 1970] there are no witnesses to or hints of where the 400 were murdered or how they disappeared. After each operation, the number of widows, orphans, and bereaved parents, whose world darkened, increased. Their lives entered a passage where everyone was thirsty to know the fate of their loved ones, who had been taken away from them to an unknown location."[922]

Another survivor, a teenager who told his story to an adult in Israel, recalled that one day hundreds of Jews, mostly women and teenagers, were rounded up and taken about five kilometers out of town to the estate of a Polish landowner named Rumel. Rumel had been exiled to Siberia by the Soviets. The abducted Jews were forced to dig a ditch 2 meters wide and 100 meters long and were told they would be buried in it. "The digging was done with heartbreaking wailing and crying. The Jews were kept under threat of execution by gunfire until late at night, and then they were allowed to go home....A few days later, Ukrainian policemen and the Gestapo conducted a house-to-house search and abducted around 300 Jewish men. The women were told they were taking the men to work." The men were all brought to the ravine near Rumel's estate, where they were shot and buried.[923]

A Soviet investigation of the incident said that the Ukrainian militia drove about one hundred persons of Jewish nationality into

---

922 A Survivor, "Nazi Atrocities in Vishnevets," https://www.jewishgen.org/yizk or/Vishnevets/vis049.html (accessed 19 June 2020).

923 Mendel Zinger, "The Destruction of Vishnevets, Volin (As Told by Shaul Shvarts)," https://www.jewishgen.org/yizkor/Vishnevets/vis049.html (accessed 19 June 2020).

the center of Vyshnivets. Among them were two former Soviet activists (such investigations were particularly concerned with the murder of Red Army soldiers and activists). All the Jews were made to kneel down while the militiamen beat them with sticks. Towards evening, they conveyed them to a ravine outside the town, Rumeliv Yar [Rumel's Ravine], and the Germans shot them. The militiamen surrounded the victims so that none of them escaped.[924]

Torchyn

The next locality we will look at is a large village about 25 kilometers west of Lutsk: Torchyn (P Torczyn) in Volhynia oblast. On 2 August 1941 German security forces arrested 284 people accused of collaborating with the Soviet authorities. These were mainly Jewish and Ukrainian directors of state enterprises and schools as well as local communists and members of the Komsomol. They were taken to woods near a small village, Buiany (P Bujanie), which was just a few kilometers east of Torchyn. Here they were shot, probably by the Security Police deployed at that time in Lutsk.[925] The German shooters were assisted by the raion militia, headed by the Banderite Panas Kovalchuk.[926] Mykola P. Kudelia, an OUN-M activist, was in Torchyn when the militia was being formed. He had a low opinion of Kovalchuk and the militia under his command. He saw how the militia "tortured (*molotyly*) the Jews so that they would admit where they hid gold and much else....I spat on all this."[927]

Jewish survivors depicted the action. On the Sabbath, the 9th day of Av, i.e., 2 August in 1941, the Torchyn Jews were told to

---

924 USHMM, RG-31.018M, reel 24; HDA SBU Ternopil oblast, spr. 33533, vol. 4, ff. 121-22, 126; vol. 7, f. 92.

925 USHMM, *Encyclopedia of Camps and Ghettos*, s.v. "Torczyn," by Alexander Kruglov and Martin Dean; Katchanovski, "OUN(b) ta natsysts'ki masovi vbyvstva," 227.

926 Katchanovski, "OUN(b) ta natsysts'ki masovi vbyvstva," 227; Antoniuk, *Dial'nist SB OUN na Volyni*, 160. Referring to this mass killing, a Jewish survivor wrote that "the Ukrainian police were assisting the Germans in all their bloody acts." Jack Kolnick and Aaron Katz, "The Extermination of Our People in Torchin," https://www.jewishgen.org/yizkor/Torchin/tor013.html#Page15 (accessed 20 June 2020).

927 Kudelia, *Kriz' buri lykholit'*, 26-28 (quotation 28).

assemble on the square near the Orthodox church. Forty able-bodied men were chosen and, with shovels on their shoulders, were marched to Buiany. "About two hours later, after checking names, 210 persons, among them six young women, all capable, young, the brains and brawn of the town, were forced into trucks that carried them into the woods" near Buiany." All of the 210 persons were shot and thrown into the pit previously dug by the former forty selectees who were killed in the same manner."[928]

Matsiiv

Finally, we will look at events in a locality in the northwest of Volhynia, not far from Kovel: Matsiiv (P Maciejów, later renamed Lukiv) northwest of Turiisk in Volhynia oblast.

The Wehrmacht took Matsiiv on 26 June. A few hours later OUN members arrived. They immediately set up a Ukrainian administration and militia. On 28 June the Germans gave the administration to the Poles, headed by the former mayor, but two days later OUN was able to restore these institutions into its own hands.[929]

On 18 July, the Ukrainian militia assisted a detachment of the Security Police and SD from Kovel, twenty-five kilometers to the east of Matsiiv, and the 1st and 4th Platoons of the 1st Company of Police Battalion 314. Together they rounded up about four hundred Jewish men on the pretext of registration and marched them to German headquarters, which was a Catholic nunnery beside the church. The Germans separated out Jews whose skills they considered useful, "while the larger group was attacked with dogs, beaten, and then shot...." The mass killing claimed 325 victims.[930]

---

928 Jack Kolnick and Aaron Katz, "The Extermination of Our People in Torchin," https://www.jewishgen.org/yizkor/Torchin/tor013.html#Page15 (accessed 20 June 2020).

929 Antoniuk, *Diial'nist SB OUN na Volyni*, 20.

930 USHMM, Encyclopedia of Camps and Ghettos, s.v. " Maciejów," by Alexander Kruglov and Martin Dean. See also Katchanovski, "OUN(b) ta natsysts'ki masovi vbyvstva," 226-27; "The Untold Stories...Maciejów," https://www.yadvashem.org/untoldstories/database/index.asp?cid=938 (accessed 22 June 2020).

Bukovina

As in Volhynia, a number of actors took part in the murder of Jews in Bukovina in July 1941: Romanian soldiers, Romanian anti-semites, criminals, ordinary villagers, and militiamen of both OUN-M and OUN-B.[931] Our focus, of course, remains only on the Ukrainian nationalists. OUN took off in Bukovina in 1934, when a number of independent nationalist organizations joined together as OUN of the Southwestern Ukrainian Lands. During the First Soviets, which in Bukovina lasted from June 1940 until early July 1941, the organization went underground. It suffered massive repressions—the NKVD arrested nearly 270 members and sympathizers[932]—but it was not crushed. A report, dated 23 July 1941, sent by Ivan Klymiv to Bandera claimed that there were eighty *stanytsi* in Chernivtsi oblast and up to five hundred OUN members.[933] In my opinion, Klymiv had a tendency to exaggerate, and even if he did not in this particular case, it is unlikely that the five hundred members were aligned with the faction of Klymiv and Bandera. The strength of the Bandera faction was on the territory of the former Poland, and the Melnykites were dominant in both the emigration and in Bukovina. Although most OUN members in Bukovina supported Melnyk, some went over to Bandera in 1941.

Some of the incidents of anti-Jewish violence in Bukovina have produced both rich documentary evidence and even some excellent scholarly literature, but for other incidents information is scant. Again, as in the case of Volhynia, I will proceed to examine a number of localities grouped into geographic clusters.

Borivtsi, Kyseliv, and Shyshkivtsi

I will start with two villages situated close to the Galician-Polish border. Borivtsi (<u>Ro</u> Borăuți) is only four kilometers west of that border. Closely neighboring it, to the southeast, is Kyseliv (<u>Ro</u> Chisălău). The case of Borivtsi is one of those that is exceptionally

---

931 See these valuable surveys: Geissbühler, *Blutiger Juli*, 61-71; Geissbühler, "'He Spoke Yiddish Like a Jew'"; Solonari, "Patterns of Violence."

932 Fostii, "Diial'nist' OUN," 1-9.

933 Veselova, *OUN v 1941 r.*, 365.

well documented. Most of what we know about it is based on what eyewitnesses recounted during Soviet investigations of war criminals, both the testimony of survivors and the confessions of perpetrators.[934] But one of the survivors who testified in 1944, Etti Preminger, recounted her experiences many times during subsequent decades, even as late as 2001.[935] The various accounts, from both perpetrator and victim perspectives, tell the same story with only minor variations. The most frequent variants arise from perpetrators trying to minimize their own personal guilt by shifting it to others among their comrades. For the Soviet investigators, the question of who did exactly what was of importance, but for our purposes it is the general picture of what the group of perpetrators did that is key. There is also some information about the events here in the records of the Extraordinary State Commission.[936]

Borivtsi was a major center of OUN activity. A native of the village, Vasyl Peleshaty, was arrested by the Romanian authorities in 1936 for participating in a demonstration in which the demonstrators employed Ukrainian national symbols. Peleshaty and his fellows spent four months in prison in Chernivtsi (Ro Cernăuți). After release, Peleshaty made contact with OUN and rose to be raion leader of OUN in the Zastavna region by the end of 1939. He spread OUN's message and recruited members in both Borivtsi and neighboring Kyseliv; he also had local members stockpile weapons. He was arrested by the Soviets in January 1941 and was one of the 222 prisoners shot by the NKVD in their prison in Chernivtsi after the German attack on the Soviet Union.[937]

---

934 USHMM RG-31018M, reel 85; HDA SBU, Chernivtsi.
935 Rodal, "A Village Massacre," 59-60.
936 USHMM RG-22.002M, reel 15; TsGAOR, fond 7021, op. 79, spr. 76.
937 Virna, "Do rokovyn." Fostii, "Diial'nist' OUN," 7, dates Peleshaty's arrest to 23 February 1941, which must be an error, since on the next page he discusses Peleshaty's interrogation already on 8 February. Reviewing the Borivtsi case in 1959, the deputy prosecutor of Chernivtsi oblast also highlighted Peleshaty's role in fostering OUN in the region, saying that in Borivtsi he organized the raion and nadraion (the level above raion) nationalist organization in three cells of the Melnyk faction. But the deputy prosecutor erroneously ascribed Peleshaty's activities to the spring of 1941, when, of course, he was in the NKVD prison in Chernivtsi. Decision of deputy prosecutor of Chernivtsi oblast, 13 January 1959, USHMM RG-31018M, reel 86; HDA SBU, Chernivtsi, spr. 5681, vol.

In the interregnum between the Soviet retreat and the arrival of Romanian troops, in early July, the local OUN took power in the village. As soon as it did so, it killed four or five Soviet functionaries of Ukrainian nationality. After an interval of a day or two, the leader of the group, Stepan Karbashevsky, ordered the annihilation of all the Jews in Borivtsi;[938] all the Jews in Kyseliv were also sentenced to death. In both places, OUN militias of about fifteen or more persons rounded up all the Jews in the two villages and marched them to a nearby lake. With rifles and sticks, the Jews were chased into the water, where, in the words of the Chernivtsi oblast deputy prosecutor, "it was proposed to them mockingly that they end their life by suicide."[939] The militiamen beat and drowned the Jews, and those whom they could not drown they shot. A few days later, the killers held in Borivtsi one of the celebrations of Ukrainian independent statehood that were widespread at that time also in Galicia and Volhynia; in fact, OUN activists came down from Stanyslaviv in Galicia to take part in the event.[940]

As usual, there are various estimates of the number of Jews murdered in this action. According to the Extraordinary State Commission, 41 Jews were killed in Borivtsi.[941] One of the perpetrators, Ivan Karbashevsky, spoke of 12-13 Jewish families.[942] Others mentioned 40 or 50-60.[943] In 1959, Soviet authorities worked with the figure of 44 for Borivtsi and 91 for Borivtsi and Kyseliv combined (thus 47 for Kyseliv).[944] Alti Rodal, citing handwritten lists in the

---

4, f. 365. See also the section on the OUN network in Borivtsi in Rodal, "A Village Massacre," 73-77.

938 A number of the perpetrators stated that they were following the orders of a Hungarian army commander, who also provided them with weapons. But Hungarian troops did not pass through Bukovina. I find Alti Rodal's suggestion quite plausible, that the Hungarian story was made up by Karbashevsky, who told it to his OUN comrades. Rodal, "A Village Massacre," 77.

939 Decision of deputy prosecutor of Chernivtsi oblast, 13 January 1959, USHMM RG-31018M, reel 86; HDA SBU, Chernivtsi, spr. 5681, vol. 4, f. 366.

940 Ibid., f. 369.

941 USHMM RG-22.002M, reel 15; TsGAOR, fond 7021, op. 79, spr. 76, ff. 39-45v.

942 Decision of prosecutor's office of Chernivtsi oblast, 12 May 1992. USHMM RG-31018M, reel 85; HDA SBU, Chernivtsi, spr. 9930, vol. 1, f. 140.

943 Ibid., ff. 97-99.

944 Decision of deputy prosecutor of Chernivtsi oblast, 13 January 1959, USHMM RG-31018M, reel 86; HDA SBU, Chernivtsi, spr. 5681, vol. 4, f. 368.

State Archive of the Russian Federation, wrote of "approximately 150 Jews" from Borivtsi and Kyseliv combined.[945]

There can be no doubt that the perpetrators were OUN men. A number of them are listed as OUN members in an annotated list of adherents of "the anti-Soviet resistance movement" in Chernivtsi oblast.[946] The connection with OUN is also confirmed in Soviet records.[947] Men from both factions of OUN worked together in the execution. By the time of the murders most had become associated with the Bandera faction instead of the Melnyk faction, which had firmer roots in Bukovina;[948] the proximity of Borivtsi and Kyseliv to Galicia probably accounts for this particular allegiance.

The killing operations of the OUN activists were events of extreme brutality. Because of the detailed investigation of what happened in Borivtsi, we are in a position to describe the kind of things that went on. Dmytro Skoreiko confessed that when he and Oleksandr Skoreiko[949] were arresting Jews, they picked up, among others, two small children and an eighty-year-old woman. The latter was unable to walk, so they dragged her out of her home and placed her and others on a cart.[950] Heorhii Voliansky, who was

---

945 Rodal, "A Village Massacre," 64.

946 Oleksandr Babiak (19), Petro Bakhur (21), Todor Fedoriak (143), Dmytro Skoreiko (217), Oleksandr Skoreiko (218), and Yurii Skoreiko (218). The figures in parentheses refer to page numbers in *Anotovanyi dovidnyk*.

947 See especially the decision of deputy prosecutor of Chernivtsi oblast, 13 January 1959, USHMM RG-31018M, reel 86; HDA SBU, Chernivtsi, spr. 5681, vol. 4, ff. 368-74.

948 Todor Bakhur joined OUN in 1939 and became a leader, at first of the Melnyk faction, but as of 1941 of the Bandera faction. Dmytro Hordei joined OUN in 1939 and switched from the Melnyk faction to OUN-B in 1941. Other killers joined OUN-B in early 1941: Stepan Farus, Mykola Fedoriak, Ivan Hrevul, and Vasyl Mykytiuk (Borivtsi). In Kyseliv the following members of OUN-B took part: Mykola Babiak, Oleksandr Babiak, Heorhii Voliansky, and Heorhii Yakivchuk. Decision of deputy prosecutor of Chernivtsi oblast, 13 January 1959, USHMM RG-31018M, reel 86; HDA SBU, Chernivtsi, spr. 5681, vol. 4, ff. 369-74. Fostii identifies Stepan Karbashevsky as the nadraion leader of the Melnykites at the time of the murders. Fostii, "Diial'nist' OUN," 13.

949 Rodal, "A Village Massacre," 76, mistakenly identifies them as brothers. But Dmytro was the son of Mykhailo Skoreiko and Oleksandr the son of Ivan Skoreiko.

950 Decision of prosecutor's office of Chernivtsi oblast, 12 May 1992. USHMM RG-31018M, reel 85; HDA SBU, Chernivtsi, spr. 9930, vol. 1, f. 142. Dmytro Skoreiko added, as was typical in such cases: "...I did not shoot them....I stood nearby and looked on."

active in Kyseliv, confessed that when he went to arrest the wife of Shulim Prostak, she grabbed the barrel of his rifle and began to yell. He ripped the rifle from her grasp and beat her with the butt. She fell on the ground and dropped her two-year-old child. Voliansky hit the baby once with his rifle butt. The toddler of course began to cry, and Mykola Kovalsky grabbed a stake and killed both the woman and her child.[951] Dmytro Kovalsky admitted that he drowned a half-dead child with his feet.[952]

As was the practice that summer in much of Eastern Europe, "the same people who had organized the pogrom afterward took charge of Jewish property as well."[953] Ivan Karbashevsky, who had been appointed elder of the village a few days before the violence, testified: "I did not take part in their execution but remained in the village, where I placed guards by the homes and property of the Jews who were shot....When the Ukrainian nationalists returned from the shooting, I began to distribute the property of the executed Jews....For myself I took two one-horse wagons."[954] Yurii Skoreiko got one of the victims' cows.[955] It seems that in spite of Ivan Karbashevsky's placement of guards at the Jewish homes, there was an outbreak of plundering. At least that is what the inhabitants of Borivtsi told Rodal when she visited it in 2001: "They were surprisingly open in sharing accounts of the horrors they witnessed and the disturbing scenes, such as villagers rushing into a Jewish home right after its occupants were taken away in order to take hold of what they could of the meager possessions inside."[956]

About five kilometers south of these two villages is Shyshkivtsi (Ro Şişcăuți). Fostii, working with local records, said that OUN murdered Jews here as well.[957] One of the perpetrators of Borivtsi,

---

951 Decision of deputy prosecutor of Chernivtsi oblast, 13 January 1959, USHMM RG-31018M, reel 86; HDA SBU, Chernivtsi, spr. 5681, vol. 4, f. 367.
952 Ibid., f. 375.
953 Gross, *Neighbors*, 67.
954 Decision of prosecutor's office of Chernivtsi oblast, 12 May 1992. USHMM RG-31018M, reel 85; HDA SBU, Chernivtsi, spr. 9930, vol. 1, ff. 140-41.
955 Decision of prosecutor's office of Chernivtsi oblast, 12 June 1992, USHMM RG-31018M, reel 86; HDA SBU, Chernivtsi, spr. 5648, vol. 1, f. 98.
956 Rodal, "A Village Massacre," 86.
957 Fostii, "Diial'nist' OUN u Bukovyni," 13.

Todor Bakhur, organized the OUN cell in Shyshkivtsi.[958] The Association of Jewish Organizations and Communities of Ukraine (VAAD) has included it on a list mass graves in Bukovina.[959]

Luzhany, Drachyntsi and Nepolokivtsi

Next I will look at three villages that are about 30 kilometers south of Borivtsi and Kyseliv and northwest of Chernivtsi: Luzhany (Ro Lujeni), Drachyntsi (Ro Dracinți), and Nepolokivtsi (Ro Nepolocăuți). These are localities where Fostii has also identified OUN violence against Jews.[960] The massacre at Luzhany is confirmed in a survivor testimony collected by Yad Vashem. Local Ukrainians robbed and killed Jews, shouting "Heil, Hitler! Now we will have a free Ukraine."[961] As to Drachyntsi, we know there were at least eleven fatalities.[962]

We have more information about the nature of the violence in Nepolokivtsi in the first days of July, but less clarity about OUN involvement. Vladimir Solonari, who studied the case, wrote that the Soviet investigators suspected that the group of perpetrators constituted "a nucleus of the Ukrainian nationalist organization. They pressed the issue with every eyewitness and defendant but invariably received a negative answer. The Chekists finally gave up their quest for the Ukrainian nationalist underground, though one may suspect that they were in fact misled by the villagers."[963] Aside from Fostii's attestation, the only link I have been able to discover between the perpetrators and OUN is that one of the perpetrators named by one of his comrades during interrogation was Vasyl Oliinyk, who was indeed a member of OUN.[964]

---

958 Decision of deputy prosecutor of Chernivtsi oblast, 13 January 1959, USHMM RG-31018M, reel 86; HDA SBU, Chernivtsi, spr. 5681, vol. 4, f. 368.
959 Geissbühler, *Blutiger Juli*, 68–69.
960 Fostii, "Diial'nist' OUN u Bukovyni," 13.
961 Geissbühler, "What We Now Know," 256.
962 Geissbühler, *Blutiger Juli*, 62.
963 Solonari, "Patterns of Violence," 64.
964 *Anotovanyi dovidnyk*, 176. He was named by Illia Oliinyk. Interrogation of Illia Oliinyk, date illegible, USHMM RG-31018M, reel 12; HDA SBU, spr. 7833, folio number illegible.

The course of the violence, however, which has been well documented, bears a marked similarity to other instances of OUN-led actions in Bukovina. Once again, this incident occurred after the Soviet retreat but before the arrival of the Romanians. Illia Oliinyk confessed that after the Soviets withdrew from Nepolokivtsi two members of an organized group came to his house at 10 in the evening and requested he join them in rounding up Jews and killing them. After all the Jews have done to us, they said, we have to destroy them. Oliinyk agreed. During his interrogation he named members of the band, eleven altogether. The men were armed primarily with stakes and pitchforks, but one of them had a rifle. They rounded up, according to Oliinyk, about 18-20 Jews, men, women, and children and took them to a bridge above the Prut River.[965] They beat all the Jews and pushed them from the bridge into the river.[966]

A Jewish woman managed to survive this action. She gave an identical account of the killing. After the Red Army left Kitsman raion and before the German-Romanian forces arrived, she and her family heard a clamor and crying on the streets. Together with her husband and daughter, she went out to see what the noise was about. They saw that Ukrainians were marching Jews towards the river Prut. Then Illia Oliinyk and another of the band ran up to them, armed with stakes and pitchforks. They took the family to the bridge above the Prut. They beat the Jews with stakes and killed some with pitchforks; they pushed them into the river.[967]

Nyzhni and Verkhni Stanivtsi

About fifteen kilometers south of Nepolokivtsi are two neighboring villages, Verkhni Stanivtsi (Ro Stănești de Sus) and Nyzhni Stanivtsi (Ro Stănești de Jos) (Upper and Lower Stanivtsi).[968] Before

---

965 Solonari, "Patterns of Violence," 64, and Geissbühler, "'He Spoke Yiddish Like a Jew,'" 435, mistakenly state that the bridge was above the Cheremosh River.

966 Interrogation of Illia Oliinyk, date illegible, USHMM RG-31018M, reel 12; HDA SBU, spr. 7833, folio number illegible.

967 Interrogation of a female Jewish survivor, name illegible, 1 November 1944, USHMM RG-31018M, reel 12; HDA SBU, spr. 7833, f. 105v.

968 The mass killing of Jews here has also been discussed by Solonari, "Patterns of Violence," 61-63, and Geissbühler, "'He Spoke Yiddish Like a Jew,'" 434.

examining what happened in these localities in early July 1941, I want to point out an appeal by one of the convicted perpetrators, Hryhorii Vyzyr, to the Supreme Court of the USSR in 1955, when many political prisoners were being amnestied. He still had about fifteen years to go in the gulag. Three points are of interest. First, the appeal confirmed what I noted earlier in the chapter on sources: that the NKVD often tortured suspects to elicit information.[969] Vyzyr protested that during his interrogation, he was beaten to the point of losing consciousness and was forced to sign the testimony which his interrogators composed. Second, as was common among almost all the accused, he denied that he personally was guilty. He said he was forced to accompany the group that killed Jews in Nyzhni Stanivtsi, but that he himself was innocent: he neither robbed nor killed Jews. He claimed that the witnesses who testified that they saw him beat a Jewish woman to death were not reliable because they bore a grudge against him. Third, he did not cast doubt on the general account of what happened. In fact, he wrote in his appeal that he saw a murdered Jewish woman and he saw others robbing Jews. Whether Vyzyr was innocent or not is not of concern for this study; it is not interested in personal responsibility, but only in group responsibility, OUN responsibility.

There can be no doubt of OUN responsibility in Nyzhni and Verkhni Stanivtsi. Jewish survivors understood it. One told the Shoah Foundation that "Ukrainian nationalists" killed Jews here in the interregnum after the Soviet withdrawal.[970] Two Jewish survivors told the Extraordinary State Commission in 1944 that the killers belonged to the "organization 'For an independent Ukraine.'"[971] At her interrogation as a witness by a representative of the Ukrainian Ministry of State Security (UMGB), a Ukrainian woman also blamed the murders on Ukrainian nationalists who took power in Nyzhni Stanivtsi in the name of an independent Ukraine.[972] The

---

969 See above, 76.

970 Shoah Foundation, 27158 Matias Tsvilling, 42-46.

971 Interrogations of Zhenia Rybker and Zhenia Rosenberg, 7 August 1944, to the Extraordinary State Commission, USHMM RG-22.002M, reel 15; TsGAOR, fond 7021, op. 79, spr. 70, ff. 40-41v.

972 Interrogation of Fevroniia Popadiuk, 26 August 1948, USHMM RG-31018M, reel 12; HDA SBU, spr. 1897, f. 171.

above-mentioned Hryhorii Vyzir stated that he was visited by the OUN leader, who asked him to participate in shooting Soviet citizens.[973] Two of the accused referred to the group that went to kill Jews as an "OUN band."[974] Finally, quite a few of the perpetrators named in the course of the investigation were members or sympathizers of OUN, as listed in the annotated handbook of the anti-Soviet resistance movement. These included Dmytro Hulia, startosta of Nyzhni Stanivtsi, who had been an OUN member since 1937 and a functionary in the nadraion leadership of OUN since 1939.[975]

Things proceeded in the usual way. The band leader gathered the others to kill the Jews. Vyzyr was approached and was asked to go "into the village to kill Jews, since the latter kill our Ukrainians." At first he didn't want to go, he testified, but they began to yell at him and he joined the group.[976] Stepan Oleniuk said that one of the band members recruited him, saying: "Let's arrest the Jews and kill them. We're done being subordinated to them."[977] Then they went to the homes of village Jews and rounded them up, armed with a few rifles, a sawed-off shotgun or two, thick sticks about a meter and a half in length,[978] and axes.[979] Roundups were always messy. The militia went to the home of a certain Zisman. The OUN band threw stones through the window to break it, and then threw stones at the family. The Zismans fled from the house and the OUN group chased after them, continuing to throw stones. The only one they could apprehend at first was Zisman's wife Ida. They beat her to

---

973 Vyzyr interrogation, 5 August 1948, USHMM RG-31018M, reel 12; HDA SBU, spr. 1897, f. 16v.

974 Interrogation of Mykola Kharena, 16 September 1948, and of Stepan Oleniuk, 29 August 1948USHMM RG-31018M, reel 12; HDA SBU, spr. 1897, f. 64v, 96.

975 *Anotovanyi dovidnyk*, 276. The other individuals are: Vasyl Floresku (member of OUN, ibid., 245), Heorhii Havdun (OUN sympathizer, ibid., 48), Stepan Kushnyriuk (OUN member, ibid., 137), Mykola Maksymiuk (OUN member, ibid., 152).

976 Vyzyr interrogation, 13 August 1948, USHMM RG-31018M, reel 12; HDA SBU, spr. 1897, f. 25.

977 Interrogation of Stepan Oleniuk, 8 September 1948, USHMM RG-31018M, reel 12; HDA SBU, spr. 1897, f. 97v.

978 USHMM RG-31018M, reel 12; HDA SBU, spr. 1897, ff. 25-25v, 98, 119v, 172.

979 Translation of the chapter "Unter Stanestie," *Geschichte der Juden in der Bukowina*, edited by Hugo Gold, https://www.jewishgen.org/yizkor/Bukowina-book/buk2_118b.html (accessed 4 July 2020).

death with staves. Eventually they caught Zisman's son and were about to kill him when a neighbor intervened and saved his life.[980]

The Jews rounded up were taken to the Nyzhni Stanivtsi courthouse and locked in for a day or so. They were taken out in small groups of four to six and killed at a location about a kilometer from the village.[981] According to the two Jewish women who offered their accounts to the Extraordinary State Commission, before killing some of them, the OUN band ripped out their arms and legs, cut off women's arms and breasts, and in general tortured them; but others were just shot.[982] However, this part of their testimony strikes me as questionable. Neither woman witnessed the actual murders. It is likely that they did not see the bodies until two weeks later and that they extrapolated their account of the torments on the basis of the condition of the corpses. One of the women noted that dogs had scattered the remains. It is also unlikely that all the victims were shot. It was normal practice to kill with staves and farm implements in order to save ammunition. Also, if the bodies were lying in the hot July sun for two weeks, decomposition could well have presented as traces of torture, as Struve argued was the case in Lviv.[983] One of the women, Zhenia Rybker, lost her father, an uncle, a grandmother, and a female cousin in this execution.[984]

---

980   Vyzyr interrogation 13 August 1948, Vyzyr interrogation, 13 August 1948, USHMM RG-31018M, reel 12; HDA SBU, spr. 1897, ff. 24v-25v. Interrogation of Mykola Kharena, 16 September 1948, USHMM RG-31018M, reel 12; HDA SBU, spr. 1897, ff. 62v-63v. Interrogation of Fevroniia Popadiuk, 26 August 1948, 172-73.

981   Interrogation of Zhenia Rybker, 7 August 1944, to the Extraordinary State Commission, USHMM RG-22.002M, reel 15; TsGAOR, fond 7021, op. 79, spr. 70, ff. 40-40v. Interrogation of Zhenia Rozenberg, 7 August 1944, to the Extraordinary State Commission, USHMM RG-22.002M, reel 15; TsGAOR, fond 7021, op. 79, spr. 70, ff. 41-41v. Apparently, this place of execution was "the hill overlooking the Fischer estate." Translation of the chapter "Unter Stanestie," *Geschichte der Juden in der Bukowina*, edited by Hugo Gold, https://www.jewishgen.org/yizkor/Bukowinabook/buk2_118b.html (accessed 4 July 2020).

982   Interrogation of Zhenia Rybker, 7 August 1944, to the Extraordinary State Commission, USHMM RG-22.002M, reel 15; TsGAOR, fond 7021, op. 79, ff. 40-40v. Interrogation of Zhenia Rozenberg, 7 August 1944, to the Extraordinary State Commission, USHMM RG-22.002M, reel 15; TsGAOR, fond 7021, op. 79, spr. 70, ff. 41-41v.

983   See above, 195.

984   Interrogation of Zhenia Rybker, 7 August 1944, to the Extraordinary State Commission, USHMM RG-22.002M, reel 15; TsGAOR, fond 7021, op. 79, spr. 70, ff. 40-40v.

Aside from the Jews killed at this location, others were killed at a sawmill in Nyzhni Stanivtsi.[985] While that was happening the Romanian military arrived and, according to the research of both Vladimir Solonari and Simon Geissbühler, the killings intensified.[986] At one point, a number of Jews were brought from Verkhni Stanivtsi to Nyzhni Stanivtsi to be murdered, but then they were marched back to Verkhni Stanivtsi and killed there.[987] One of the OUN band, Makovei Khodan, told his interrogator that he was ordered to convey nine arrested Jews from the hamlet of Vyviz, about ten kilometers south of Nyzhni Stanivtsi, to the latter village's startosta, Dmytro Hulia. Khodan said he brought the Jews into Nyzhni Stanivtsi, and let them go. Then he corrected himself and added, rather enigmatically, that he did not turn them over to the village administration as directed.[988]

And, as usual, the killers appropriated property of the dead Jewish families.[989] Stepan Oleniuk described how he had arrested an elderly Jewish man, by the name of Irsh, and Makovei Khodan

---

985 Interrogation of Mykola Kharena, 16 September 1948, USHMM RG-31018M, reel 12; HDA SBU, spr. 1897, f. 64v. Interrogation of Stepan Oleniuk, 8 September 1948, USHMM RG-31018M, reel 12; HDA SBU, spr. 1897, f. 97v. Interrogation of Khodan Makovei, 8 September 1948, USHMM RG-31018M, reel 12; HDA SBU, spr. 1897, f. 119v. Interrogation of Samson Huchok, 8 September 1948, USHMM RG-31018M, reel 12; HDA SBU, spr. 1897, f. 140v. Hugo Gold names the second site as "the saw mill on the Vivos." If this is meant to be a river, then there is no river in Chernivtsi oblast with a remotely similar name. I wonder if the reference is rather to the hamlet of Vyviz, which will be mentioned shortly.

986 Solonari, "Patterns of Violence," 62, and Geissbühler, "'He Spoke Yiddish Like a Jew,'" 434.

987 Interrogation of Zhenia Rybker, 7 August 1944, to the Extraordinary State Commission, USHMM RG-22.002M, reel 15; TsGAOR, fond 7021, op. 79, spr. 70, ff. 40–40v. Interrogation of Zhenia Rozenberg, 7 August 1944, to the Extraordinary State Commission, USHMM RG-22.002M, reel 15; TsGAOR, fond 7021, op. 79, spr. 70, ff. 41–41v.

988 Interrogation of Makovei Khodan, 8 September 1948, USHMM RG-31018M, reel 12; HDA SBU, spr. 1897, f. 119v. Vyviz is absent from most maps, but I visited it in June 2005 in connection with another project. I do not know what it was called in Romanian.

989 The killers "divided among themselves the property of the Jews they had shot." Interrogation of Zhenia Rozenberg, 7 August 1944, to the Extraordinary State Commission, USHMM RG-22.002M, reel 15; TsGAOR, fond 7021, op. 79, spr. 70, ff. 41–41v. In these days more than thirty Jewish homes were robbed, according to a Ukrainian witness. Interrogation of Fevroniia Popadiuk, 26 August 1948, USHMM RG-31018M, reel 12; HDA SBU, spr. 1897, f. 173.

took him to the sawmill for execution; Oleniuk said that he later heard from other villagers that Khodan himself had killed Irsh. Oleniuk went to the sawmill as well. As he was returning home from there, he passed Irsh's home and saw that people were taking things. He went into the house to take a look and saw Ivan Hulia with a bag of items he had taken. Hulia asked Oleniuk to help him carry the things across the river, which he did. They took the items to Khodan's home and then went back to Irsh's. There Oleniuk took a couple of packs of cigarettes and matches for himself. At that very time advance troops of the Romanian army arrived. When Hulia became aware of this, he gave Oleniuk his sawed-off shotgun and said to turn it over to the Romanian soldiers, because he himself did not want to be interrupted but wanted to continue to take things from Irsh's home. Oleniuk claimed he did as he was asked and then went home.[990]

The number of Jews killed in Nyzhni Stanivtsi has been variously given as over 30 or 35,[991] 54,[992] 65,[993] 80,[994] more than 80,[995] and 85.[996] The number of Jews killed in Verkhni Stanivtsi was said to be 50.[997]

990 Interrogation of Stepan Oleniuk, 8 September 1948, USHMM RG-31018M, reel 12; HDA SBU, spr. 1897, ff. 97v-98.
991 Interrogation of Fevroniia Popadiuk, 26 August 1948, USHMM RG-31018M, reel 12; HDA SBU, spr. 1897, f. 171, 173.
992 A "list of victims Soviet citizens shot and tortured by the German-Romanian invaders" in what was then Vashkivtsi raion names fifty-four victims from Nyzhni Stanivtsi, all Jews, men and women, born between 1871 and 1929. USHMM RG-22.002M, reel 15; TsGAOR, fond 7021, op. 79, spr. 70, ff. 68-69. Lists of victims tend to undercount, while numbers of victims as provided by survivors tend to overestimate.
993 Translation of the chapter "Unter Stanestie," *Geschichte der Juden in der Bukowina*, edited by Hugo Gold, https://www.jewishgen.org/yizkor/Bukowina book/buk2_118b.html (accessed 4 July 2020).
994 Interrogation of Zhenia Rybker, 7 August 1944, to the Extraordinary State Commission, USHMM RG-22.002M, reel 15; TsGAOR, fond 7021, op. 79, spr. 70, ff. 40-40v.
995 Recollection of a survivor interviewed for the Shoah Foundation cited in Geissbühler, "'He Spoke Yiddish Like a Jew,'" 434.
996 Interrogation of Zhenia Rozenberg, 7 August 1944, to the Extraordinary State Commission, USHMM RG-22.002M, reel 15; TsGAOR, fond 7021, op. 79, spr. 70, ff. 41-41v.
997 Interrogation of Zhenia Rybker, 7 August 1944, to the Extraordinary State Commission, USHMM RG-22.002M, reel 15; TsGAOR, fond 7021, op. 79, spr. 70, ff. 40-40v. Interrogation of Zhenia Rozenberg, 7 August 1944, to the Extraordinary

Banyliv and Miliieve

About twenty-five kilometers west of Nyzhni Stanivtsi are two villages, Banyliv (Ro Bănila pe Ceremuş), and about five kilometers to
the southeast, Miliieve (Ro Milie). Both localities have been identified by Fostii as sites of anti-Jewish violence organized by OUN.[998]

Aside from Fostii's indication that the murders in Banyliv
were committed by an OUN band, the only additional confirmation
I have found of OUN involvement was the testimony to the Extraordinary State Commission of a Jewish survivor who designated
the killers as "so-called OUNites." That survivor lost her husband,
her 10-year old son, and two of her brothers in the massacre. Some
of the victims, she said, were killed in their homes or in their yards
or in their farm buildings, but most were shot a kilometer away
from the village.[999]

A Ukrainian woman told the Commission that after the withdrawal of the Red Army, at the end of June or beginning of July, she
was an eyewitness to how a band shot her Jewish neighbors: three
families, including two women, a boy of thirteen, two elderly
women, one of whom was about eighty years old, and two old men
of about seventy. The murders took place near their houses in the
yard. She was lying behind potato plants in the garden and overheard the killers' conversations. They said: "Thank Hitler who
helped us kill the Jews, or else they would have killed us."[1000]

On 16 August 1944 a Soviet medical examiner inspected the
remains of the victims. They were in a state of advanced decomposition and, naturally enough, stank. There were marks of bullets on
various parts of the bodies, so it was clear they were shot. It was
also clear that the victims were killed at the same time, in the course
of two or three days, and that the victims had been lying in the

---

State Commission, USHMM RG-22.002M, reel 15; TsGAOR, fond 7021, op. 79,
spr. 70, ff. 41-41v.

998 Fostii, "Diial'nist' OUN u Bukovyni," 13.

999 Testimony of Iryna Hyrsh to the Extraordinary State Commission, 8 August 1944,
USHMM RG-22.002M, reel 15; TsGAOR, fond 7021, op. 79, spr. 70, ff. 58-59.

1000 Testimony of Anna Pasishnyk (b. 1914 in Banyliv) to the Extraordinary State
Commission, 8 August 1944, USHMM RG-22.002M, reel 15; TsGAOR, fond
7021, op. 79, spr. 70, ff. 60-60v.

grave for no more than three years.[1001] However, the examiner did not provide the number of bodies in the grave.

The Jewish witness to the Extraordinary State Commission spoke of 200 murders.[1002] A Jewish survivor, in testimony to Yad Vashem, spoke of more than 170.[1003] A "list of victims Soviet citizens shot and tortured by the German-Romanian invaders" in what was then Vashkivtsi raion named 64 from Banyliv, all of them Jews, men and women, born between 1861 and 1931.[1004]

Fostii himself described, on the basis of local records, what occurred in Miliieve. OUN-M leader Petro Voinovsky planned in advance a series of anti-Jewish actions to take place immediately after the withdrawal of Soviet troops. He also issued orders to execute all communists and active collaborators with the Soviet administration. He started in Milieive. On 5 July an OUN unit under his command, and an additional twenty or so volunteers, attacked the village with rifles, pistols, sawed-off shotguns, and agricultural implements. Dividing into groups of five to seven, they attacked the buildings in which Jewish families lived. Voinovsky personally took part and finished off wounded Jews with his revolver. Altogether, according to the testimony of the participants, they executed about 120 people that day.[1005] According to other sources, 175 people were murdered. A Jew who arrived immediately afterwards found no Jewish person alive in the village.[1006] Voinovsky formed a Bukovinian Battalion (*Bukovyns'kyi kurin'*) that marched on to Kyiv; some members of the Battalion are likely to have arrived in time for the mass murders at Babi Yar, but we do not know whether they took part in the killing.[1007]

1001 USHMM RG-22.002M, reel 15; TsGAOR, fond 7021, op. 79, spr. 70, ff. 62-62v.
1002 Testimony of Iryna Hyrsh to the Extraordinary State Commission, 8 August 1944, USHMM RG-22.002M, reel 15; TsGAOR, fond 7021, op. 79, spr. 70, ff. 58-59.
1003 Geissbühler, "'He Spoke Yiddish Like a Jew,'" 435.
1004 USHMM RG-22.002M, reel 15; TsGAOR, fond 7021, op. 79, spr. 70, ff. 69-70.
1005 Fostii, "Diial'nist' OUN u Bukovyni," 13. Voinovsky was in contact with the German SD in Chernivtsi and agreed to help the German army to seize hostile elements. Angrick, "Power Games," 117.
1006 Geissbühler, "'He Spoke Yiddish Like a Jew,'" 435.
1007 Nakhmanovych, "Bukovyns'kyi kurin'," argued that the Bukovinian Battalion had not yet entered Kyiv when the shooting occurred. Evidence subsequently provided by Karel Berkhoff undermines this case. Berkhoff, "Babi Yar." For the current state of the debate, see Radchenko, "Nashi 'sukyni deti.'"

Karapchiv

The final locality Fostii identified as a site of OUN violence against Jews was the village of Karapchiv (Ro Carapciu pe Ceremuş), located about halfway between Nyzhni Stanivtsi and Banyliv.[1008] I have an account by the political geographer Ladis K.D. Kristof, written in a letter to the historian Fred Stambrook. Kristof had read Stambrook's working paper on Bukovina's Jewish population in the Habsburg monarchy published by the Center for Austrian Studies in Minneapolis and was moved to share the history of his own village in Bukovina. The letter is worth quoting in full:

> I just read your paper "The Golden Age of the Jews of Bukowina, 1880-1914." Excellent historically and very interesting, especially for a person like me, born and raised in Bukowina. Of course, being born in 1918 my Bukowina was already different in various ways, that is, it was adapting to the fact that it was part of a national state where national interests, perspectives, policies, etc. were dominant or at least tried to be dominant. But the principle of "Leben und leben lassen" was in day-in-day-out respected until the nineteen-thirties when a hard core nationalism (fascism) began to seep in primarily from Iaşi and affecting mainly southern Bucovina but hardly the northern part where I was living in the village Carapciu pe Ceremuş, where half of the village declared themselves Romanians and the other half Ucrainians [sic] (or Ruthenians) but nobody spoke at home Romanian. There were also a few scattered families of Poles and at least two families of German origin who lost already their language.
>
> My family was of Armenian origin, an old immigration, who lost the language long time ago but kept the religion.
>
> Out of the population of 6000 a hundred families were Jewish, spread throughout the village. They had a synagogue, and until 1941 there were never any conflicts. In 1941 there was a pogrom (30 Jews killed) organized primarily by Ukrainians from the neighboring Galicja after the Soviets withdrew and before the Romanian authorities came back but then the Romanians evacuated and deported all Jews.
>
> Our families did not witness these turbulent events because we fled in June 1940 before the Soviets came in, and we came back only after the Romanian authorities were back. One Jew who was a very old employee of ours was killed by the Ukrainians in June 1941 before we came back.

1008 Fostii, "Diial'nist' OUN u Bukovyni," 13.

I visited my village in recent years. There are no Jews in the village or in the little town Vășcăuți (Waschkoutz) [Vaskhivtsi]. Only in Czernowitz [Chernivtsi] there are a few.

I thought you may be interested in the above reminiscences.[1009]

* *

*

For OUN's participation in the July bloodshed, I see two outstanding causes, though I recognize that no historical event has simple causalities.

First, one can easily see how OUN's intensified antisemitism in the late 1930s led to the May 1941 instructions to the militias to arrest and intern Jews. But during the German and Romanian attack on the USSR, the OUN leadership went further and ordered the murder of Jews, especially those who had been associated in some way with the Soviet authorities. Generally, in these executions, OUN militias killed a few dozen Jews, but sometimes they killed over a hundred. They often killed entire families, men and women, little children and elderly persons.

The second circumstance that facilitated the murders was the German and Romanian invasion. As we have seen, the militias often enough started killing the Jewish population in the interval between the withdrawal of the Soviets and the arrival of the invaders; but without the invasion, Soviet power would have remained in place. The Germans and Romanians, moreover, strongly encouraged the murder of Jews. When German units were rounding up Jews for execution, they frequently relied on the OUN militias. In these instances, in which the German military and mobile killing units were involved, the death toll tended to be much higher.

As Struve has pointed out, the July murders were responsible for only a small fraction of the victims of the Holocaust in

---

1009 Letter of Ladis K.D. Kristof to Fred Stambrook, 15 April 2007, in the author's possession. Underlining in the original. Professor Stambrook had already passed away when this letter was sent; however, his long-time companion, the historian Stella Hryniuk, sent me a copy of the letter because she knew I was working on the Holocaust in Ukraine.

Galicia.[1010] Adding up the estimates, low and high, of OUN murder victims in the nine localities in Bukovina for which I have numbers, I arrive at a minimum of 411 and a maximum of 566. But the total number of Jews murdered that summer, mostly by Romanian soldiers, came to 45,000-60,000 (figures for Bukovina and Bessarabia together). More than 90,000 surviving Bukovinian Jews were deported that fall to the Odessa region (Transnistria), where they were placed in camps and ghettos.[1011] Thus, the numerical contribution of the OUN militias' activities to the Holocaust was marginal. However, what the militias did, in the name of Ukraine, the Ukrainian state, and the Ukrainian nation, did its part to poison relations between Ukrainians and Jews for the rest of the period of occupation by Germany and its allies and for many years afterwards.

Zygmunt Bauman's brilliant essay on *Modernity and the Holocaust*, which emphasized bureaucratic, industrial killing, depicted a deathful but bloodless process. What we have seen in Galicia, Volhynia, and Bukovina was nothing like this. People were killed with stones, thick sticks, axes, and boards with protruding nails in addition to rifles and sawed-off shotguns. They were pushed off bridges, drowned. The perpetrators and the victims knew each other. This was intimate and therefore treacherous killing. I wish to make two points about the cruelty and brutality that I have described. First, there was nothing particularly "Ukrainian" about what happened in the summer of 1941. Nor was there, in spite of the notoriety of the events that summer in Jedwabne or Iași, anything particularly "Eastern European" about this. The Germans were certainly no better. Omer Bartov's study of Buchach in Galicia has a chapter on the capricious cruelty of the Germans in that occupied town. It is difficult to read. But even more difficult, more wrenching is Bartov's following chapter, which looks at how the German occupation was experienced by the living, breathing people who had happened to be born Jewish.[1012] My second point is

---

1010 See above, 254.
1011 Solonari, "Patterns of Violence," 56.
1012 Bartov, *Anatomy of a Genocide*, "Chapter 5: German Order," 158-231; "Chapter 6: The Daily Life of Genocide," 232-64.

that the kinds of scenes I have sketched above are common in genocidal situations. I am very much impressed by Jacques Semelin's astute observation:

> Even though the enemy is depicted by propaganda as having frightening, hideous features, he retains a dreadfully human face. This being the case, it could be why perpetrators of massacre feel a need to "disfigure" this fellow human as quickly as possible to prevent any risk of identification. To be able to kill him involves dehumanising him, not "just" in the imaginary constructs conveyed by propaganda, but now in one's acts....Cruelty is truly a mental operation on the body of the other, intended to destroy his humanity....Seen in this way, the perpetration of atrocities is the means by which perpetrators establish their own radical psychological distance from the victims, and convince themselves that these are in no way, and no longer, human beings.[1013]

I offer these perspectives not to mitigate the crimes of the militiamen of 1941 but to aid our understanding of how they happened. Ordinary men[1014] drawn into mass killing projects will do all the kinds of things that the OUN militias did.

1013 Semelin, *Purify and Destroy*, 296-97.
1014 According to "The Struggle and Activities of OUN in Wartime," the OUN militias were to be composed exclusively of men. However, one Jewish survivor mentioned a woman among the leadership of the perpetrators in Banyliv in Bukovina. Testimony of Iryna Hyrsh to the Extraordinary State Commission, 8 August 1944, USHMM RG-22.002M, reel 15; TsGAOR, fond 7021, op. 79, spr. 70, ff. 58-59. Women took an active part in looting the homes of murdered Jewish families. Survivors' testimonies contain information on the role of women in anti-Jewish violence and robbery, and this is a subject that should be looked into by future researchers. There is an excellent model in Wendy Lower's often hair-raising study of German women as perpetrators: Lower, *Hitler's Furies*.

6. The Organization of Ukrainian Nationalists and the Ukrainian Police in German Service

This chapter discusses the Ukrainian police in German service, their role in the Holocaust, and connections between the police and the Organization of Ukrainian Nationalists. The service of OUN members and sympathizers in the Ukrainian police was an important transitional stage in the nationalists' involvement in the Holocaust, bridging the anti-Jewish violence perpetrated by the Ukrainian National Militia in the summer of 1941 and the ethnic cleansing and murder of Jewish survivors by UPA from the spring of 1943 and into 1944. Although the auxiliary police were a different institution from the militia and were under the ultimate authority of Heinrich Himmler rather than Yaroslav Stetsko and Stepan Bandera, there were some notable continuities in personnel and tasks.

Ukrainian Police Structures in Distrikt Galizien and in Reichskommissariat Ukraine

In the late summer of 1941, the administrative structure of Western Ukraine changed fundamentally. Galicia and Volhynia—Western Ukraine—had shared the same governments since 1918, first under Poland, then under the Soviet Union. Much to the disappointment of most Ukrainians in these territories, the Germans decided to place Galicia and Volhynia in separate jurisdictions. On 1 August 1941, Galicia was incorporated, as Distrikt Galizien, into the General Government. To Ukrainians there it seemed that they were being reincorporated into Poland, even if under German rule. On 1 September the Reichskommissariat Ukraine was created, and Volhynia became part of it. Ukrainians in Distrikt Galizien were much better off than Ukrainians in the Reichskommissariat, even though the latter had the word "Ukraine" in its title. The nationalists perceived this division of jurisdictions as a hefty blow to their plans to create an integral (*soborna*) Ukrainian state, and the

Germans' decision further soured relations between OUN and the Germans.

The Ukrainian Auxiliary Police in Distrikt Galizien

The origin of the Ukrainian police in German service can be traced to 17 December 1939, when Hans Frank ordered the formation of police forces in the General Government recruited from the local population, namely the Polish ("Blue") police and the Ukrainian police. These forces were funded by local administrations and were subordinate to the German order police. The Ukrainian Central Committee in Kraków lobbied for the creation of a police school for Ukrainians, and in December 1939 the Germans created a police academy in the resort town of Zakopane, directed by Hans Krüger of the Gestapo. The school later moved to Rabka, a resort town located between Zakopane and Kraków. By mid-1940 similar academies were established in Kraków and Chełm. After the invasion of the USSR, many of the graduates of these police schools served as the basis for the formation of the Ukrainian Auxiliary Police.[1015] After the invasion of the USSR, police academies were also established in Lviv[1016] and Rivne.

But as we know, prior to the formation of the Ukrainian Auxiliary Police, OUN's Ukrainian National Militia provided local police services in Western Ukraine. The Germans decided to dissolve the latter in order to create the former. There were two main reasons motivating the Germans to replace the militia with the police. One we have already encountered: the Germans' growing distrust of OUN-B, and particularly the Einsatzgruppen's distrust of the Ukrainian militias.[1017] The second reason for the creation of local police forces was the Germans' intent to escalate the Holocaust. From late July 1941, Himmler urged the formation of local forces under firm German control to help with the expanded program of

---

1015 Martynenko, "Ukrains'ka Dopomizhna Politsiia," 154. Finder and Prusin, "Collaboration in Eastern Galicia," 103. Rudling, "'Not Quite Klaus Barbie.'" The Zakopane school achieved notoriety in the American left-liberal press. See Conason, "To Catch a Nazi."

1016 Pan'kivs'kyi, *Roky nimets'koi okupatsii*, 401.

1017 See above, 227-28.

mass killing. Such forces were created not only in Ukraine, but also in the Nazi-occupied Baltic states and Belarus.[1018] The Ukrainian police units in the General Government differed in some respects from the units in the Baltics and Belarus and in the Reichskommissariat Ukraine. One difference was that the Ukrainian police in Galicia and elsewhere in the General Government were almost exclusively Ukrainian by nationality, while the police units outside the General Government were purely territorial, and Russians and Poles could also enter them.[1019]

As of 2 August 1941, the day after Galicia was incorporated into the General Government, the OUN militias officially passed under German command. On 12 August the commandant of the German order police in Kraków ordered the dissolution of the Ukrainian National Militia, "and it was suggested to its members that they enter the units of the Ukrainian Auxiliary Police."[1020] But the transformation was not instant. Although as of mid-August the Germans began purging OUN members from the militia, the process took time. In Ternopil circle, for which we have more detailed information, the Germans ordered the dissolution of the Ukrainian National Militia in September, but disarming of the militias continued at least into early October.[1021]

During the course of the war the number of Ukrainian policemen grew, reaching its maximum during the period of the total liquidations of the Jewish population. In July 1943, just after the major killing operations concluded in Distrikt Galizien, there were 4047 Ukrainian policemen in the district.[1022] After that, numbers declined owing to desertions as the Soviets closed in. Thus in the Lviv Ukrainian Auxiliary Police there were 13 officers and 465 policemen in October 1942; in July 1943 there were 19 officers and 841 policemen. In the 5th commissariat on 17 May 1944, 9 of 59

1018 Büchler, "Local Police Force Participation," esp. 84-85. See also Breitman, "Himmler's Police Auxiliaries."
1019 Martynenko, "Ukrains'ka Dopomizhna Politsiia," 154.
1020 Ibid., 155-56.
1021 Klymenko and Tkachov, Ukraintsi v politsii v dystrykti "Halychyna," 266-67.
1022 Finder and Prusin, "Collaboration in Eastern Galicia," 106.

policemen deserted.[1023] An OUN-B report from 20 July 1944 described the panicked flight from Lviv as the Red Army approached the city. The report stated that the Ukrainian Auxiliary Police had been partially dissolved on 14 July and a few days later were evacuated in trucks to Sambir.[1024]

Policemen in Lviv were armed with wooden batons, pistols, or rifles.[1025]

The Schutzmannschaften in the Reichskommissariat Ukraine

The Germans began the dissolution of the Ukrainian National Militia in the Kremenets region of Volhynia at the end of August and beginning of September 1941. At first they subordinated some of the militias to the German gendarmerie and others to the German military command. Ukrainian officers were still in charge, but German officers were assigned to the former militias as well.[1026] By Himmler's order of 6 November 1941 the auxiliary police were created in the Reichskommissariat under the name Schutzmannschaft der Ordnungspolizei (Schuma for short).[1027] In December the police were put under direct German control—the Germans distrusted some of the local commanders and were trying to limit the influence of OUN.[1028] The replacement of the Ukrainian militias with Schutzmannschaften was completed in November and December 1941.[1029]

In addition to Schutzmannschaften that functioned as local police, there were also mobile Schutzmannschaft battalions that served the Germans. Some of these battalions were continuations of previous OUN military formations from outside the Reichskommissariat. The Nachtigall battalion commanded by Roman Shukhevych became Schutzmannschaft battalion 201 and put down partisan activity in Belarus.[1030] Petro Voinovsky's Bukovinian

---

1023 Martynenko, "Ukrains'ka Dopomizhna Politsiia," 157.
1024 Cited in Mick, *Kriegserfahrungen*, 539.
1025 Martynenko, "Ukrains'ka Dopomizhna Politsiia," 156.
1026 Klymenko and Tkachov, *Ukraintsi v politsii v reikhskomisariati "Ukraina,"* 65.
1027 Ibid., 65. Dereiko, *Mistsevi formuvannia*, 65.
1028 Klymenko and Tkachov, *Ukraintsi v politsii v reikhskomisariati "Ukraina,"* 65. Dereiko, *Mistsevi formuvannia*, 66.
1029 Klymenko and Tkachov, *Ukraintsi v politsii v reikhskomisariati "Ukraina,"* 66.
1030 Rudling, "Rehearsal for Volhynia."

Battalion became Schutzmannschaft battalion 118 and also engaged in antipartisan operations in Belarus.[1031] But Schutzmannschaft battalions were also recruited in the Reichskommissariat as territorial defensive units.[1032] Schutzbattalions 102 and 105 originated, for example, from the Kremenets region.[1033] In this monograph, these mobile Schutzmannschaften are not explored in any depth. This is mainly because there is no documentation available at present that shows that they took a significant part in the Holocaust, although the Germans' understanding of antipartisan warfare included the murder of Jews as a matter of course. In this study the focus is trained on local police Schutzmannschaften in Volhynia and elsewhere in the Reichskommissariat.

At least at first, there were about 40-50 policemen in a city,[1034] but the number grew in response to the massive killing operations of 1942 and early 1943. The Kremenets city police started with 50 policemen, but later grew to over 120.[1035] In villages there would be from 3 to 15 policemen. Each raion would have from 70 to 250.[1036] By the end of November 1942 there were about 8700 Ukrainian policemen in the cities of the Reichskommissariat and about 2800 German policemen; in the countryside the ratio of Ukrainian to German policemen was much higher: 42,600 Ukrainians to 3700 Germans.[1037] Earlier, in the spring of 1942, there had been only 14,452 policemen in rural localities.[1038] Again, this reflected the expansion of manpower for the Holocaust. In the General Circle Volhynia-Podillia[1039] in early 1943, there were 11,870 Ukrainian and 1407 German policemen, and 3500 Ukrainians and 1300 Germans in the mobile Schutzbattalions.[1040]

1031 Rudling, "Terror and Local Collaboration." Rudling, "Khatyn Massacre."

1032 Dereiko, *Mistsevi formuvannia*, 71-72.

1033 Klymenko and Tkachov, *Ukraintsi v politsii v reikhskomisariati "Ukraina,"* 171-235.

1034 Dereiko, *Mistsevi formuvannia*, 66.

1035 Klymenko and Tkachov, *Ukraintsi v politsii v reikhskomisariati "Ukraina,"* 65.

1036 Dereiko, *Mistsevi formuvannia*, 66.

1037 Berkhoff, *Harvest of Despair*, 42.

1038 Dereiko, *Mistsevi formuvannia*, 67.

1039 Generalbezirk Wolhynien-Podolien was larger than Volhynia proper, extending from Brest in the north to Kamianets-Podilskyi in the south.

1040 Spector, *Holocaust of Volhynian Jews*, 175 n. 145.

The primary arms of the Schutzmannschaften were the standard Soviet Mosin rifles. Ammunition was limited to five to ten rounds. As to uniforms, the first were makeshift—Soviet army uniforms with armbands. During the winter and spring of 1941-42 regular uniforms took their place, generally black uniforms modelled after or modified from those of the SS. The uniforms gave rise to some vernacular names for the police: the "black police," the "ravens," and "the storks."[1041] But in the Kremenets region, in addition to the black uniforms with yellow trimming, in common use was a uniform consisting of a grey greatcoat, a green shirt, a cap with a tryzub, and an armband with the word "Schutzpolizei." The police often just forced Jews to sew their uniforms, whether black or gray and green, with their own material. A frequent recompense for these Jewish tailors was a beating.[1042] A Jewish survivor from Rokytne, a raion capital in Rivne oblast, recalled: "In mid-September 1941, we were forced to make uniforms for the Ukrainian policemen. Their uniforms were made out of black gabardine and if there wasn't enough material provided we had to cut up our own holiday clothing."[1043]

Profile of the Ukrainian Police Personnel

In Distrikt Galizien aspiring Ukrainian policemen were obliged to meet the following requirements: Ukrainian nationality; good knowledge of the Ukrainian language, both oral and written; age 26-38; height over 165 cm; military training; doctor's certificate of health; and absence of a criminal record. No one who had belonged to communist organizations was to be allowed to join.[1044]

The average age of a Ukrainian policeman in Lviv in May 1943 was 27. Officers and NCOs were on average five years older, i.e., 33. Forty percent were in their early twenties (born 1919-23),[1045]

1041 Dereiko, *Mistsevi formuvannia*, 66.
1042 Klymenko and Tkachov, *Ukraintsi v politsii v reikhskomisariati "Ukraina,"* 67.
1043 Levin, *Under the Yellow & Red Stars*, 18.
1044 Pan'kivs'kyi, *Roky nimets'koi okupatsii*, 401.
1045 Calculated from the years of birth in lists of 336 policemen and 20 officers from May 1943 in USHMM RG Acc 1995 A 1086, reel 2; DALO, fond R12, op. 1, od. zb. 66a, ff. 1-22.

although originally, as already noted, the minimum age to become a policeman was set at 26. Obviously, the rules had to be adjusted to fit the circumstances. Policemen elsewhere tended to be even younger than those in Lviv. Martin Dean, using more fragmentary information than I had access to, worked out that in Mir, in Hrodna oblast, Belarus, about half the police force, including officers, were men under 25.[1046] In Volhynia, in the Kremenets circle and city police, the average age of rank-and-file policemen and officers in 1943 was only 20.[1047]

Most Lviv policemen had finished four to seven grades of elementary school, although some had gone to gymnasium and university. There were even individuals with specialized training, for example, in economics or theology. The men with higher education occupied positions of higher and middle rank. The autobiographies of 53 policemen of the third commissariat of the Lviv police in 1941-42 show that the great majority, 33, were of rural origin, 16 were craftsmen, and only 4 from the civil service. Most policemen, especially in 1943-44, came from poorer families and had worked in jobs with lower prestige, such as day laborers, janitors, building custodians, cloakroom attendants, and the like.[1048] The Lviv police were undoubtedly the best educated and socially most diverse force of the Ukrainian police in German service. In rural localities and in the towns of Volhynia the police would have been overwhelmingly peasant by social origin and less educated.

Motivations for Joining the Police under the Nazi Occupation

Police work attracted many men. There was, especially at first, no lack of volunteers for the Ukrainian Auxiliary Police. The Ukrainian Central Committee was inundated with requests to join, which it forwarded to the police command in Lviv.[1049] This was also true of

---

1046 Dean, *Collaboration during the Holocaust*, 73-74.

1047 Klymenko and Tkachov, *Ukraintsi v politsii v reikhskomisariati "Ukraina,"* 91-106, lists the personnel of the Kremenets police. Of 187 policemen listed, dates of birth are provided for 100 of them; their average year of birth was 1913.

1048 Martynenko, "Ukrains'ka Dopomizhna Politsiia," 159-60.

1049 "Sprava pryiniattia do Ukrains'koi Politsii v Halychyni," *Krakivs'ki visti*, 11 September 1941 (repeated 13 September). See also: "Zi L'vova i z kraiu. Ukrains'ka politsiia," *Krakivs'ki visti*, 28 August 1941.

the Jewish police (*Ordnungsdienst*) — it had more volunteers than places available.[1050]

Historian Taras Martynenko, referring to the Ukrainian police in Lviv specifically, although his observations have wider application, noted that some of the better educated men entered the police out of idealistic (or ideological) motives. They saw service in the Ukrainian police as an opportunity for military training and for strengthening Ukrainian influence in the city and region. Some of the rural cadres in the force had the same motivation. These were mainly individuals associated with Ukrainian organizations, such as Prosvita, Sich, Luh, Sokil, the radical nationalist Front of National Unity (*Front Natsional'noi Iednosti*), and OUN. (We will examine OUN's interest and influence in the police in the final section of this chapter.) These men joined not just because of their personal convictions but because their leaderships urged them to join in order to increase the influence of their members inside the police. The same tactic was used by Polish organizations with regard to the Blue police. There were also many cases of Revisionist Zionists joining the Jewish police in Lviv and elsewhere in the General Government.[1051] On the whole, those who served in the Ukrainian police

---

1050 Yones, *Evrei L'vova*, 135. At a time when only a remnant of Lviv's Jewish population was still alive, in the fall and winter of 1942, men who wanted to land a job with the Jewish police had to pay very large bribes to get on staff. Redner, *A Jewish Policeman in Lwów*, 238, 254.

1051 Ben Z. Redner, in his memoirs written in 1944, recalled "Szulim Goldberg, a young Revisonist from Stryj, shapely and agile, with his burning eyes under black eyebrows. In the early days of the police force, he represented Jewish-Revisionist idealism and honor. In general, the top positions in the force were staffed by Revisionists from Jabotinsky's Zionist paramilitary force, who nursed plans of armed resistance against the Germans." Redner, *A Jewish Policeman in Lwów*, 88. Yones, *Evrei L'vova*, 390 n. 59, cites a testimony in Hebrew — of Fishko Kravets (Tenenboim) — about Zionist youth serving in the Jewish police in Lviv; see also 145. Redner himself was a Revisionist Zionist, but he did not join the force out of ideological principles; he was simply looking for work. Redner, *A Jewish Policeman in Lwów*, 87, 137. Calel Perechodnik was a member of the Revisionist youth group Betar, but he too did not join the Jewish police in Otwock (near Warsaw) from ideological motivations. Perechodnik, *Czy ja jestem mordercą?* 6, 28. "Young Jewish men from Betar, who had been trained in the use of weapons by the Polish state, also showed a certain inclination to join the Jewish police." Snyder, *Black Earth*, 111; see also 266. In Żarki, about eighty kilometers northwest of Kraków, a Zionist served

out of idealistic motives occupied positions of higher and middle rank and did not constitute the majority of the rank-and-file policemen.[1052]

Sometimes these idealists were horrified by what they had to do in the force and found ways to quit. Oleh Klymenko and Serhii Tkachov, in their study of the police in the Kremenets region of Volhynia, wrote: "A certain part of the Ukrainian policemen, raised on solid national and moral principles, abandoned service in the police after a few weeks. This was the case with the former policeman from Pochaiv [P Poczajów] Vasyl Synkovsky. After what he saw, he expressed his opinion as: 'I thought the Germans were good people, that they are bringing us all better conditions of life, but they started to just laze about and do injury to the population; so I did not want to serve in the police any longer...to work in the German police you have to be a nonhuman, worse than any animal.'"[1053] The same phenomenon has been noted in reference to the Jewish police. At first the young intelligentsia went into the police, especially lawyers (who were now out of work because of Nazi laws); their commanders were former military men. But as the police increasingly became a German instrument, they left and were replaced by "representatives of the urban lower classes, criminals, hooligans, pathologically greedy persons." The *Ordnungsdienst* became "a criminal organization in service to a criminal regime."[1054]

Perhaps overlapping to some extent with the above category of the ideologically motivated were those who joined the police out of hatred towards the former Soviet regime. Ivan Dereiko collected information, not very systematically, however, about 119 members of the Schutzbattalions as well as 30 policemen, Ukrainian workers in the German Security Service (SD), and firemen in the

---

concurrently as chair of the Judenrat and commander of the Ordnungsdienst. A survivor remembered: "...His nationalist education and Zionist spirit stood him in good stead, and aided him in preserving a high moral level of behaviour at all times, and his actions revealed a great dedication to others, trying as he did in each instance to save Jewish lives." Weiss, "The Relations between the Judenrat and the Jewish Police," 5.

1052 Martynenko, "Ukrains'ka Dopomizhna Politsiia," 160.

1053 Klymenko and Tkachov, *Ukraintsi v politsii v reikhskomisariati "Ukraina,"* 70.

1054 Yones, *Evrei L'vova*, 135-36.

Reichskommissariat. Of the Schutzbattalion men, 13 had been repressed by the Soviet authorities and 15 had lost relatives in the regime-generated famine of 1932-33. Among the 30 policemen, 3 came from families repressed for participation in the Ukrainian national forces during the civil war of 1917-20, 2 lost members of their family during the famine, and 6 had been "dekulakized." Some of the men in both groups lost family members to attacks by Soviet partisans during the occupation.[1055] Eliyahu Yones observed the same about the Jewish police. Some of them were motivated by hatred of the Soviets, a hatred as strong as the Poles and Ukrainians felt to those who had imprisoned, exiled, and killed their relatives, friends, and neighbors; these Jewish policemen considered any instance of attempting to organize flight to the partisans to be aid to the Soviets.[1056]

In the ranks of the police throughout the Reichskommissariat were former NKVD militiamen, officers of the Red Army, and Soviet functionaries.[1057] The former head of the village soviet in Katerynivka (P Katerburg; now in Ternopil oblast, then in Volhynia) was forced to join the police in order to avoid persecution by the occupiers.[1058] Probably in the majority of cases, however, former party functionaries and members of the Soviet apparatus of repression entered the occupation police for other reasons; after all, they had formed a kind of management and security elite and may not have relished social demotion.[1059]

A reason frequently cited for joining the police was to avoid deportation for forced labor to Germany.[1060] This reason kicked in

---

1055 Dereiko, *Mistsevi formuvannia*, 85.

1056 Yones, *Evrei L'vova*, 143-44.

1057 Dereiko, *Mistsevi formuvannia*, 85.

1058 Klymenko and Tkachov, *Ukraintsi v politsii v reikhskomisariati "Ukraina,"* 68.

1059 Such behavior was known elsewhere in the Soviet Union during World War II: "The North Caucasian rebels had no common strategy. Many of their leaders were not ideological enemies of communism but opportunists who had attained lucrative positions in the Soviet administration, party, and police apparatus and strove to preserve power in the new conditions that emerged with the approach of the Germans." Statiev, "The Nature of Anti-Soviet Armed Resistance," 300.

1060 Martynenko, "Ukrains'ka Dopomizhna Politsiia," 161. Dereiko, *Mistsevi formuvannia*, 86. In 1965, Petro Chaika told his KGB interrogator that he joined the

about the middle of 1942. At first there were volunteers who went to Germany, but as word seeped back about the living conditions of the laborers (*Ostarbeiter*), volunteers dried up. At that point the Germans organized roundups of young Ukrainians and sent them to Germany whether they wanted to go or not. Policemen had to help with the roundups, but they themselves and their families were exempt. The loss of laboring hands in an agricultural environment, especially during the difficult wartime situation, was a disaster that families tried to avoid. Service in the police was some protection of policemen's families from other arbitrary injustices of the occupation authorities as well.[1061] One of the motivations young Jews had for joining the *Ordnungsdienst* was also to gain protection for their families.[1062] Of course, in their case, the catastrophe that otherwise would befall their families was much worse than forced labor, and the protection proved in the end to be flimsy.

There were also strong material incentives to enter the police. In Lviv the monthly salary of a rank-and-file Ukrainian policeman was about 230 złoty, of a decurion (*desiatnyk*) 300, of an officer 500. Although these salaries were half those of German policemen of equivalent rank, they were generous in comparison to civilian salaries. For example, an unskilled worker received 156-180 złoty, a skilled worker 264-300, and a professor 650. Policemen and their families were also eligible for social assistance. They enjoyed a discount on public transit, lower taxes, and, for a small monthly sum, meals in the police cafeteria. They also received a half liter of vodka and pack of cigarettes every month.[1063] A policeman in the Ternopil

---

Lviv police in February or March 1942 in order to avoid deportation to Germany. USHMM RG-31.018M, reel 99; HDA SBU, spr. 30853, vol. 2, ff. 6-7. Explaining to his NKGB interrogator on 13 November 1944 why he had joined the police in autumn 1941, Oleksii Slepchuk said that he did so because the village starosta was sending young people to Germany for work and he did not want to be sent. USHMM, RG-31.018M, reel 70, frame 2311; HDA SBU, spr. 21115, vol. 1, f. 13.

1061 Martynenko, "Ukrains'ka Dopomizhna Politsiia," 161.

1062 Yones, *Evrei L'vova*, 134. Redner, *A Jewish Policeman in Lwów*, 96, 176, 246-48. A famous Jewish boxer became a policeman in the Warsaw ghetto in 1941. One of his primary motivations was to protect his family. Finder, "Trial of Szepsl Rotholc," 66.

1063 Martynenko, "Ukrains'ka Dopomizhna Politsiia," 161.

region received the modest salary of 150 złoty a month, 100 cigarettes, a liter of 95 percent alcohol, 3 kilograms of groats, 3 kilograms of flour, butter, and eggs. This was certainly more than was
available to an ordinary peasant, and it drew young villagers into
the police force.[1064] Police in the Kremenets region in the
Reichskommissariat were paid 240 rubles a month if they were single and 540 if they had a family. They ate for free, received uniforms, footwear, underwear, fuel, and sometimes electricity.[1065] In
the words of Klymenko and Tkachov: "Under the influence of Hitlerite propaganda, the youth, especially rural youth who were sick
and tired of village life with its pitchforks, hoes, and shovels, ro-
manticized service in the police and SS units and regarded it
through rose-colored glasses. A handsome uniform, weapons,
power, money, food rations, a satisfied life, instead of hard work in
the field, became an irresistable stimulus drawing seekers after an
easy fortune which you just had to reach out and grasp."[1066] Jews
too were recruited to their police in German service on account of
extra rations and better accommodations as well as more freedom
of movement; they could eat better, dress better, and reduce exposure to illness and lice.[1067]

The Nazi occupation in the East was notoriously corrupt, and
the police forces in its service shared its reputation. For example,
one of the routine tasks of the police was to eliminate the production of moonshine. Usually the police confiscated the entire apparatus of production. But sometimes they just turned the equipment
over to other moonshiners, who made vodka specifically for the police.[1068] Work with the doomed Jews was often turned to profit by
policemen. Some of the latter sold food to the ghetto population at

---

1064 Klymenko and Tkachov, *Ukraintsi v politsii v dystrykti "Halychyna,"* 274.
1065 Klymenko and Tkachov, *Ukraintsi v politsii v reikhskomisariati "Ukraina,"* 74.
1066 Klymenko and Tkachov, *Ukraintsi v politsii v dystrykti "Halychyna,"* 274.
1067 Yones, *Evrei L'vova*, 134, 143. Thanks to his *Ordnungsdienst* cap and armband,
      a Jewish policeman was able to carry on a rather lively business of selling items
      on commission from Jews in the ghetto to non-Jews in the Aryan sections of
      the city. Among his customers was the prominent Ukrainian agronomist and
      appointee to Stetsko's Ukrainian State Administration Yevhen Khraplyvy.
      Redner, *A Jewish Policeman in Lwów*, 128-29, 149.
1068 Klymenko and Tkachov, *Ukraintsi v politsii v reikhskomisariati "Ukraina,"* 69.

astronomical prices. Some were able to enrich themselves considerably, acquiring gold coins and gold watches, jewelry and cash.[1069] The historian of the Holocaust in Volhynia, Shmuel Spector, remarked: "Various detachments of the Ukrainian police, as well as single policemen, engaged in blackmail, or simply robbed the Jews of money and property."[1070] Bribery was commonplace.[1071] It is important to realize that extorting bribes from the Jewish population amounted to stealing the wealth on which Jews often depended for survival. Stefan Petelycky, the OUN activist whose memoirs we have cited before to get an insight into the nationalists' thinking, had harsh words to say about corrupt police: "At this point I must say that among our people, as among the Jews, Poles, and *Volksdeutsche* (ethnic Germans), there were elements that I can only refer to as human garbage. These people were prepared to take advantage of the suffering and misery of others for their own gain."[1072] Jews also remembered some of their own *Ordnungsdienst* as "individuals from the underworld, criminals" and "the dregs of society."[1073] When the Gestapo wanted more contingents of Jews for forced labor, Jewish policemen also used the opportunity to collect bribes.[1074]

Some men were just drawn into the police by the nature of the work, by the exercise of power and violence, by the authority to choose who would live and who would die. This was true of individuals in both the Ukrainian and Jewish police forces.[1075]

1069 Ibid., 74-75.

1070 Spector, *Holocaust of Volhynian Jews*, 239. Police robbing the property of Jewish families in Volhynia is also recorded in Siemaszko and Siemaszko, *Ludobójstwo*, 1:218, 1:371.

1071 Prusin, "Ukrainskaia politsiia," 52. AŻIH, 301/305, Jakub Grinsberg, 2. AŻIH, 301/327, Izaak Szwarc, 1. AŻIH, 301/583, 1. AŻIH, 301/1181, Lilith Stern, 2. Sonia Orbuch's mother successfully bribed a policeman with her wedding ring to let her and her family escape. Shoah Foundation, 41647 Sonia Orbuch. Sometimes, of course, bribes were taken, but lives were not spared. Bartov, "Wartime Lies," 494. A Jewish policeman wrote that Ukrainian policemen were bribed by black marketeers. Redner, *A Jewish Policeman in Lwów*, 143.

1072 Petelycky, *Into Auschwitz*, 14.

1073 Spector, *Holocaust of Volhynian Jews*, 156.

1074 Yones, *Evrei L'vova*, 180. Redner, *A Jewish Policeman in Lwów*, 132-33.

1075 Martynenko, "Ukrains'ka Dopomizhna Politsiia," 161-62. Yones, *Evrei L'vova*, 143-44.

I have presented the motivations of both Ukrainian and Jewish men who joined the police during the occupation. I have done so for the purpose of comparison, a comparison which, I think, reveals a kind of template for the police forces in German service. I do not wish to suggest that Ukrainians and Jews were in a very similar situation, since the Jews, including Jews who were serving in the police, were earmarked for annihilation.

Evaluations of the Ukrainian Police

Ukrainian memory of the Ukrainian police is conflicted, which is not surprising considering the uneasy conjuncture of service to the Germans, simultaneous service to the Ukrainian movement, and notorious involvement in repressions and atrocities. Bohdan Koziy, who denied he was a Ukrainian policeman but faced deportation from the United States on the grounds that he was, told the court that the Ukrainian police were a normal force like any other:

> Q Do you know what the Ukrainian Police did in Stanislau?
> A What they did in Stanislau?
> Q What were their functions in Stanislau?
> A Just normal police in any country.
> Q What does that mean?
> A Keep the order, keep the hospitals, watch the banks, just like American police.[1076]

A bit later in the hearing he was asked directly about the police's involvement in the persecution of Galician Jews:

> Q Mr. Koziy, didn't the Ukrainian Police assist in leading Jews to the Ghetto in Stanislau and other big cities?
> A I don't know that. I never saw myself.
> Q You don't know anything about that?
> A No, sir.[1077]

The sister of another individual accused of being a Ukrainian policeman also told a deportation hearing in Baltimore that the Ukrainian police were just a normal force:

1076 Testimony of Bohdan Koziy at deportation hearing, USHMM RG-06.029.01*21, Box 21, case of Bohdan Koziy, 2 October 1981, 164.
1077 Ibid., 172.

Q At the time what was your understanding of what Ukrainian policemen had for duties?...
A I understood like in any other country police duties is to keep law
and order.[1078]

Similar benign presentations of the Ukrainian police as simply
a normal police force and even a rather pro-Ukrainian police force
can be found in the Galician testimonies collected by the Yahad-In
Unum project under the direction of Fr. Patrick Desbois[1079] as well
as in the interviews with elderly nationalists in Lviv conducted by
Eva Himka,[1080] although in both cases there were also dissenting
opinions. A former policeman who appeared at the Ukrainian-Jewish conference held in Canada in 1983 denied emphatically that the
Ukrainian police had anything to do with the Holocaust.[1081] On the
other hand, there have been nationalist memoirists who have written frankly about Ukrainian police atrocities against Jews, notably
Yevhen Nakonechny.[1082]

Kost Pankivsky, who worked in the Ukrainian civil administration, generally thought that the Ukrainian police were a positive factor. "From our point of view, it was a serious plus; it was
'our police'; the fact of its existence raised our prestige both in our
own community and among the other inhabitants of Galicia." He
dealt delicately with its involvement in the roundup of Jews for destruction: "...The German command used it to carry out certain orders which did not enter into the compass of its activities and which
the police were unable to decline."[1083] The Ukrainian writer Arkadii

---

1078 Testimony of Irene Rodd at deportation hearing, USHMM RG-06.029.01*43,
Box 45, case of George Theodorovich, 11 March 1985, 1190.
1079 YIUN, no. 764, Khlopivka [Khloptitsy in Yahad-in-Unum records], Ternopil
oblast, USHMM RG-50.589*0214. YIUN, no. 785, Skalat, USHMM RG-
50.589*0235. Ternopil oblast A member of OUN-M registered a negative opinion of the Ukrainian police, however, who, he said, behaved as badly as the
Germans. YIUN, no. 737, Lviv, USHMM RG-50.589*0187. Another man commented that the original militia was composed of patriots but the Ukrainian
police in German service was not. YIUN, no. 827, Ozerna, Zboriv raion, Ternopil oblast, USHMM RG-50.589*0276.
1080 Himka and Himka, "Absence and Presence."
1081 I was present.
1082 Nakonechnyi, "Shoa" u L'vovi, 244-46; see also 188 and 266.
1083 Pan'kivs'kyi, Roky nimets'koi okupatsii, 395.

Liubchenko was pleasantly surprised by the quality of the Ukrainian police (he was normally not well disposed to any kind of police). According to his diary entry of 7 April 1943 he had been drinking with a Ukrainian policeman and found him to be "a cultured man and a conscious Ukrainian." "It turns out that the bulk of the Ukrainian policemen in Galicia are people with secondary or higher education. Many engineers, teachers, scholars joined the police to keep it at the appropriate high level. Moreover, here people see in it the new seed of a Ukrainian army. The Poles hate it, and the yellow and blue police insignia with its trident is a knife in the heart of every Pole."[1084]

Jewish memory of the Ukrainian police was, of course, very different. Philip Friedman's opinion was: "The active pro-Nazi collaborationists included elements that would probably not have attained a position of power in Ukrainian society in normal times. The Ukrainian police was recruited mainly from among the rabble and criminals."[1085]

Sundry Duties of the Ukrainian Police in Relation to the Jewish Population

A principal task of the Ukrainian police (and of all other police forces in Eastern Europe at that time) was to enforce the Germans' Jewish policies. One of the first uses of police manpower in Galicia and Volhynia was to implement the transfer of the Jewish population from their homes into the newly created ghettos. During the hasty transfers in Volhynia, Ukrainian (and German) policemen helped themselves to Jewish goods.[1086] We can get an idea how these transfers were carried out from what we know about the transfer in Lviv. Jews were forced to move into the Lviv ghetto between 16 November and 15 December 1941. They had to pass an inspection station staffed by Ukrainian police, SS men, and Jewish

---

1084 Liubchenko, *Shchodennyk*, 140.
1085 Friedman, "Ukrainian-Jewish Relations," 187.
1086 Spector, *Holocaust of Volhynian Jews*, 121. Siemaszko and Siemaszko, *Ludobójstwo*, 1:771.

police — "a few Jewish outcasts," in the words of Philip Friedman. Friedman went on:

> The guards fastidiously inspected the never-ending stream of Jews carrying the pitiable remnants of their property....Whoever could not show a certificate of work, or seemed hungry, sick, or elderly, was immediately dragged over the fence to the old barracks. There they were slapped and beaten, often fatally, by the supervisors and gate keepers....Anyone who did not please the inspectors was arrested and was later transferred to the prison on Łąckiego [Lontsky] Street. The course from there was well known. Victims were thrown onto trucks which would take them to the forest for execution. The lives of thousands of Jews, many of them women, were lost in this "bridge of death" action [the inspection station was located under a railroad bridge]. This was the first major "action" in Lwów against Jewish women.[1087]

It has been estimated that there were five thousand victims of this "bridge action." Eliyahu Yones suggested that these murders were committed in order to reduce the number of Jews to be crowded into the small space allowed for the ghetto. A supplementary action was taken a short time later in which SS and Ukrainian police went house to house taking out the elderly, the infirm, and persons with disabilities. Ukrainian police then continued the action on their own initiative as a way to obtain bribes.[1088]

Once ghettos were established, Ukrainian police guarded its perimeter to make sure no one left without authorization. Inside the ghetto, the Jewish police were in charge. It was possible to bribe the Ukrainian police in order to leave the ghetto without arrest, but generally Jews were arrested if found outside the boundaries.[1089] A

1087 Friedman, "Destruction," 263.
1088 Yones, *Evrei L'vova*, 179-80, 206. See also Redner, *A Jewish Policeman in Lwów*, 103-06, 114.
1089 USHMM RG-31.018M, reel 60, fr. 1509; HDA SBU Ternopil, spr. 147. Testimony of former policeman Konstantyn Lubenetsky: "After the ghetto was organized [in Vyshnivets], we received an order to guard the ghetto. It was the duty of the police to guard the ghetto, not allowing anyone to leave. We did not have the right to enter the ghetto; it had its own Jewish police there." USHMM RG-31.018M, reel 60, frame 1509; HDA SBU, Ternopil oblast, spr. 18738, f. 312. Spector, *Holocaust of Volhynian Jews*, 122, 134 AŻIH, 301/3118, Juda Kneidel, 1.

survivor of the Stanyslaviv ghetto recalled that his father tried to leave, first dressing himself up in several suits so he would have something to sell. His attempt was unsuccessful, and he was beaten up by the Ukrainian police. They might have shot him, but instead they took his money and the suits and pushed him back into the ghetto.[1090] A child from Olyka who used to sneak into villages to barter for food wrote: "Many children like us were caught and killed by the Ukrainian police."[1091]

In general, the Ukrainian police were a terror to the Jews. In Volhynia there were restrictions on what Jews could buy in the markets, and if they purchased butter, eggs, ham, chicken, or sugar, the items were immediately confiscated by the police.[1092] Beatings were common currency. Yosef Laufer recalled that his maternal grandmother lost her only son after he was cruelly beaten by the Ukrainian police in Zhuravno (P Żurawno), southeast of Zhydachiv in Lviv oblast. He survived a few weeks after the beating and then died.[1093] Sexual violence was also not unknown. Pavlo Khvesiuk, of the Shumsk (P Szumsk) raion police, robbed the Jews in the ghetto mercilessly, and he also raped an underage Jewish girl.[1094] In Kamianka Strumylova (P Kamionka Strumiłowa, now Kamianka Buzka in Lviv oblast), Jews were held in a stable before execution in November 1941. According to one survivor from that town, Ukrainian policemen raped young girls there.[1095]

Among the common duties assigned to Ukrainian policemen was to guard Jewish forced laborers. They escorted laborers to and from their place of work; testimonies state that the Jews were brutally maltreated by the police.[1096] Policemen were also frequently

1090 USHMM, RG-50.030*0198, interview with Amalie Petranker Salsitz, 15 May 1990. Jews who broke the rules in the Vyshnivets ghetto were usually shot by the police. Klymenko and Tkachov, *Ukraintsi v politsii v reikhskomisariati "Ukraina,"* 72.

1091 Spector, *Holocaust of Volhynian Jews*, 103.

1092 Klymenko and Tkachov, *Ukraintsi v politsii v reikhskomisariati "Ukraina,"* 71.

1093 Tal, *The Fields of Ukraine*, 15.

1094 Klymenko and Tkachov, *Ukraintsi v politsii v reikhskomisariati "Ukraina,"* 74.

1095 AŽIH, 301/45, Alojzy Jazienicki. Members of the Belarusian police in Mir district Hrodna oblast, were said to have raped Jewish girls. Dean, *Collaboration during the Holocaust*, 70.

1096 Spector, *Holocaust of Volhynian Jews*, 102.

seconded to guard labor camps.[1097] Based on their study of the Ternopil area police, Klymenko and Tkachuk estimated that about 80 to 85 percent of the Ukrainian Auxiliary Police served at some point or other in forced labor camps.[1098] In Lviv's commissariat no. 2 in the second half of 1942, 5-6 policemen out of a total staff of 36 were seconded to guarding the ghetto and labor and concentration camps.[1099]

The guards at the Jewish labor camp in Lutsk were recruited from the Ukrainian police.[1100] A Ukrainian police contingent supervised the work at a labor camp set up in Sokilnyky (P Sokolniki), a suburban village south of Lviv. The laborers had to wade in swamps and perform exhausting work twelve hours a day. "From 70 to 80 percent of the workers were felled by illness, cold, lack of food, and inhuman housing conditions. Many died from wounds or from the blows that the Ukrainians inflicted on the 'lazy.'"[1101] Later in the war, Ukrainian police served as guards at the notorious Janowska camp, replacing SS personnel called to the front.[1102]

Some Ukrainian policemen became particularly notorious. The Jewish Historical Commission collected several testimonies about a Ukrainian policeman by the name of Skhab, perhaps as a prelude to a trial:

> Skhab killed on his own hundeds of Jews in Tovste and in the camps around Tovste, namely: Lysivtsi (P Lisowce), Holovchyntsi (P Hołowczyńce), Rozhanivka (P Rożanówka), Kozigóra, and Shershenivka (P Szerszeniowce).[1103]
>
> In the Lysivtsi camp I myself saw how Skhab shot a young Jew by the name of Ałter Grill. That same day he shot seven Jews in the camp in Lysivtsi. Among those he shot at the threshhold of the house was Grill's fiancée, named Małka Hertman, who was ill.

1097 As were Jewish police, who were paid extra for camp duty. Redner, *A Jewish Policeman in Lwów*, 177-78, 180, 183.

1098 Klymenko and Tkachov, *Ukraintsi v politsii v dystrykti "Halychyna,"* 283-84.

1099 Martynenko, "Ukrains'ka Dopomizhna Politsiia," 156, 163-64.

1100 Spector, *Holocaust of Volhynian Jews*, 125 n. 25.

1101 Friedman, "Destruction," 261-62.

1102 Ibid., 304. Friedman, *Zagłada*, 33.

1103 I have not been able to identify Kozigóra ("na Kozigórze" in the original). It is most likely a local toponym; the translation is Goat Hill.

Skhab shot at Grill and hit him in the hand. Grill fell and then got up. Skhab noticed this, went up to him, and shot him three times in the head so that he massacred him.

I was standing nearby on a hillock and saw it.

There was another time that Skhab came to the village and again shot a few people.

Skhab took part in roundups of Jews.

I was also taken with a group of twenty-some persons to Chortkiv, where they were supposed to kill us. But for some unknown reason they let us go. Those who were taken a day earlier to Chortkiv were also shot.

On the way to Chortkiv, Skhab beat and tortured us. He hit me with his truncheon on the thigh so hard that for several weeks I could neither lie nor sit on that side. On the way he shot a young Jewish boy. I saw it myself.

Skhab was the greatest criminal in Tovste during the German occupation.

...While in the Lysivtsi camp, Skhab hit me so hard with his rifle butt under the heart that I almost died.[1104]

Of course, as the German occupation continued and the project of the total annihilation of the Jewish population developed, the manifold of these anti-Jewish activities expanded and became more systematically lethal.

The Ukrainian Police and the Total Liquidations of 1942–43

Beginning in the fall of 1941, intensifying in 1942, and winding up in early summer 1943, the Einsatzgruppen and other German units engaged in a systematic campaign to completely eliminate the Jewish population in Distrikt Galizien and the Reichskommissariat Ukraine.[1105] Jews had already been concentrated in ghettos and

---

1104 AŻIH, 301/3882, Chana Fiderer, 1. See also AŻIH, 301/3883, Cyla Herman; 301/3384, Pepa Schwitzer; 301/3888, Maria Kenigsberg; 301/3889, Berł Glick; 301/3890, Hilary Kenigsberg; 301/3891, Mojżesz Szpigiel. An unnamed Ukrainian policeman in Tovste volunteered to shoot Jews after a roundup — could this have been the same individual? AŻIH, 301/327, Izaak Szwarc.

1105 For a concise and authoritative chronology of the mass liquidations in Ukraine, see Internet Encyclopedia of Ukraine, s.v. "Holocaust" by Dieter Pohl, http://

camps, and one by one these population clusters were either murdered on the spot (more frequently) or dispatched by train to a death camp (generally only in Galicia, usually to the death camp in Bełżec). In both Galicia[1106] and Volhynia[1107] Ukrainian police rounded up and conveyed Jews to their execution spots. This can be considered the most important function that the policemen performed in the implementation of the Final Solution.

Although in smaller localities, these liquidations involved a partnership of German punitive and police units with Ukrainian police, in Lviv the Jewish police also played a prominent role. Roundups during the March 1942 action in Lviv usually involved German, Ukrainian, and Jewish policemen, and this list is in the order of ascending magnitude of participation. The report of the sixth commissariat of the Lviv Ukrainian police, dated 25 March 1942, noted that the roundup of 160 Jews was conducted by 12 German policemen, 22 Ukrainian policemen, and 40 Jewish policemen.[1108] A report the same day from the first commissariat recorded 10 German, 20 Ukrainian, and 30 Jewish policemen who rounded up 512 Jews.[1109] On 27 March the sixth commissariat supplied 23 Ukrainian policemen, who worked with 12 German and 39 Jewish police.[1110] On 28 March, 16 German, 31 Ukrainian, and 38 Jewish policemen took part in the roundup in the fourth commissariat.[1111] The same

---

www.encyclopediaofukraine.com/display.asp?linkpath=pages%5CH%5CO%5CHolocaust.htm (accessed 26 August 2020).

1106 AŻIH, 301/3108, Edmund Mateusz Kessler. In his final report on "The Solution of the Jewish Question in Galicia," the head of the local SS and police, Fritz Katzmann, mentioned those who made it possible to create a *judenfrei* Galicia, namely "the Security and Order Police, the Gendarmerie, the *Sonderdienst*, and the Ukrainian Police." YVA, 06/28-1 — originally USA. Exhibit 277, L-18, dated 30 June 1943, International Military Tribunal in Nuremberg. "My cousin said that between January and April 1944, Ukrainian Militia working for the Germans rounded up the 15 Jewish families in Volkivtsi [Vovkivtsi, P̱ Wołkowce], and took them to Borschiv where they were shot and buried along with 2,000 other Jews from the surrounding villages. I saw the burial mound in the outskirts of Borschiv." Letter of Larry Warwaruk to the author, 5 February 2010.

1107 Podvorniak, *Viter z Volyni*, 152-53. YIUN, no. 570 & 571, Kalynivka, Sarny raion, Rivne oblast, USHMM RG-50.589*0168.

1108 USHMM RG Acc 1995 A 1086, reel 3; DALO, fond R12, op. 1, od. zb. 37, f. 3.

1109 Ibid., f. 8.

1110 Ibid., f. 34.

1111 Ibid., f. 42.

commissariat recorded 15 German *Schupo*, 31 Ukrainian policemen, and 38 Jewish *Ordnungsdienst* in the roundup on 30 March.[1112] No Jewish policemen worked on the roundup on 30 March in the sixth commissariat, just 14 German and 39 Ukrainian policemen.[1113] On 2 April 1942, 21 German, 30 Ukrainian, and 40 Jewish policemen rounded up 285 Jews in the first commissariat.[1114] Averaging these figures, we see that about 13 Germans worked with 26 Ukrainian and 37 Jewish policeman on each day in a single commissariat. The participation of Ukrainian together with Jewish policemen in the liquidation of the Lviv ghetto was noted by the Eastern Bureau of the Polish underground government[1115] and in the memoirs of a Jewish policeman as well.[1116]

On a roundup in the second commissariat on 24 June 1942, no Jewish policemen were employed. Instead, "the Ukrainian police assigned people to the action who were to undertake guard duties in the number of 11 people; the police school assigned 10 persons, the *Sonderdienst* 5 persons, and also the *Schutzpolizei* 5 persons."[1117] The roundup in the third commissariat on the same day also took place in the absence of Jewish policemen. Instead, the personnel involved were 23 Ukrainian policemen from the third commissariat, 20 policemen from the Ukrainian police academy, 10 members of the *Sonderdienst*, 3 *Schupo* men, and 1 Ukrainian and 1 German officer.[1118] In the fourth commissariat on that day, during which 52 Jews and 8 beggars were delivered to the assembly point, 36 men carried out the action: 17 Ukrainian policemen from the commissariat, 10 from the police school, 5 members of the *Sonderdienst*, 2 members of the Nationalist Socialist Motor Corps, and 2 members of the *Schupo*. Twelve others directed the action: 2 members of the

---

1112　Ibid., f. 76.
1113　Ibid., f. 57.
1114　USHMM RG Acc 1995 A 1086, reel 3; DALO, fond R12, op. 1, od. zb. 38, f. 9.
1115　E.g., Adamczyk, *Ziemie Wschodnie*, 32.
1116　Redner, *A Jewish Policeman in Lwów*, 160-61; an entire chapter of this memoir concerns the March action: 153-67.
1117　USHMM RG Acc 1995 A 1086, reel 3; DALO, fond R12, op. 1, od. zb. 38, f. 41.
1118　Ibid., f. 44.

German security police, 3 members of the Motor Corps, 1 *Schupo* officer, and 6 Ukrainian policemen.[1119]

Jewish policemen were not directly involved in the August action.[1120] An order to the Ukrainian police dated 9 August 1942 called for the commissariats to supply 82 Ukrainian policemen to help 88 Germans.[1121] In the fifth commissariat on 20 August, 24 Ukrainian policemen and 30 *Schupo* from Ternopil executed the roundup.[1122]

The preserved records of the Lviv Ukrainian police indicate that the March action took about five working days.[1123] On each of those days, on average, 26 Ukrainian policemen in each of six commissariats took part in the roundups, at a time when the total Ukrainian police force in Lviv was under five hundred.[1124] This suggests that the vast majority of Ukrainian policemen were involved at one point or another in the actions. In the course of the roundups, Ukrainian policemen sometimes shot Jews (they had to report the

---

1119 Ibid., f. 50.

1120 On the August action: "The Jewish police played an auxiliary role in transporting the victims to the Janowski camp, from where those condemned to the gas chambers at Bełżec were led in groups to the nearby Kleparów train station, where they were loaded onto freight cars. The Jewish police did not take part in the actual *Aktion* and the policemen and their families were spared." Redner, *A Jewish Policeman in Lwów*, 196. A survivor's testimony remembered the August action differently: "Three policemen—usually one German, one Ukrainian, and one from the Jewish police—came by to search all the houses for potential hiding places and then to inspect the occupants' cards." Rosenfeld, *From Lwów to Parma*, 32. From the records of the Ukrainian police and Redner's firsthand testimony, I am inclined to believe that this survivor conflated the August action with other, probably earlier, actions. Errors about time are fairly frequent in survivor testimonies.

1121 USHMM RG Acc 1995 A 1086, reel 3; DALO, fond R12, op. 1, od. zb. 40, f. 2. There were problems with absenteeism during this action. Report of the centurion (sotnyk) Liubomyr Ohonovsky to commander Volodymyr Pitulei, 10 August 1942. Ibid., f. 4.

1122 USHMM RG Acc 1995 A 1086, reel 3; DALO, fond R12, op. 1, od. zb. 39, f. 31.

1123 Perhaps only the records for five days have survived or were microfilmed. According to the memoir of a Jewish policeman, the action started on 13 March and ended on 3 April. Redner, *A Jewish Policeman in Lwów*, 153, 161.

1124 The largest manpower contingent in March 1942 was actually supplied by the Jewish police—37 per day per commissariat. There were 13 Germans per day as well. Information on the March actions comes from USHMM RG Acc 1995 A 1086, reel 3; DALO, fond R12, op. 1.

number of bullets they used to their superiors).[1125] A report from the fifth commissariat, dated 21 August 1942, stated that on the previous day's action Ukrainian police fired 49 bullets. Altogether 14 Jews who attempted to escape or offered resistance were shot to death and another 6 were wounded. It is likely that some of the shootings should be laid to the account of the *Schupo* men who accompanied the Ukrainian police on this action and made up a slight majority of the personnel involved.[1126] An acquaintance told Yosef Laufer that when the police were rounding up Jews in Zhuravno, one of them shot a Jewish woman known to the acquaintance who was not moving fast enough, who in fact was still lying in bed.[1127] In fact, as the roundups progressed over time, it became standard practice for German and Ukrainian policemen to shoot persons with disabilities and the elderly.[1128]

At the end of the roundups, at least before the final liquidation actions, the detained Jews were checked to make sure they were not protected from deportation. Laufer remembered that in Zhuravno detained members of the families of the Judenrat were allowed to return home.[1129] A report dated 25 March 1942 from Major Volodymyr Pitulei, commander of the Ukrainian police in Lviv, stated that 2254 Jews had been rounded up and held in the Sobieski school, but during the action about 1200 were released because they had appropriate documentation.[1130] On 30 March, the sixth commissariat of the Ukrainian police checked a total of 400 Jews, but only delivered 208 to the assembly point.[1131] The Ukrainian police of the second commissariat brought 127 Jews to the assembly point on 24 June 1942; after the *Schupo* vetted them, only 68 Jews remained in custody.[1132] In the third commissariat on that same day

1125 USHMM RG Acc 1995 A 1086, reel 3; DALO, fond R12, op. 1, od. zb. 39, f. 31. Tal, *The Fields of Ukraine*, 30.
1126 USHMM RG Acc 1995 A 1086, reel 3; DALO, fond R12, op. 1, od. zb. 39, f. 31.
1127 Tal, *The Fields of Ukraine*, 30.
1128 Redner, *A Jewish Policeman in Lwów*, 247-48. Spector, *Holocaust of Volhynian Jews*, 176.
1129 Tal, *The Fields of Ukraine*, 29.
1130 USHMM RG Acc 1995 A 1086, reel 3; DALO, fond R12, op. 1, od. zb. 37, f. 9.
1131 Ibid., f. 57.
1132 USHMM RG Acc 1995 A 1086, reel 3; DALO, fond R12, op. 1, od. zb. 38, f. 41.

300 Jews were rounded up, but only 171 were retained for deportation.[1133]

The Ukrainian police's participation in these actions deeply disturbed the head of the Greek Catholic church in Galicia, Metropolitan Andrei Sheptytsky. He protested directly to Himmler in February 1942 after Ukrainian policemen were used in the execution of the Jews of Rohatyn. From the March 1942 action in Lviv through the complete liquidation of Galicia's Jews in June 1943, Sheptytsky became almost obsessed with the role Ukrainian policemen played in the Holocaust. Numerous pastoral letters and other writings, including letters to the Vatican, testify to the great depth of his concern.[1134]

The Ukrainian police severely mishandled the Jews during the roundups. Survivor testimony frequently mentions beatings with whips, rifle butts, and iron bars.[1135] The Germans sometimes also noted that the Ukrainian police applied unnecessary brutality during the roundups. The *Schupo* commander in Lviv, Major Fritz Weise, wrote to the Ukrainian police commander that "during the roundup of Jews on 27 March 1942 there were violations that must under all circumstances be avoided....There are ever more frequent complaints that Jews are mistreated *without grounds*."[1136] At other times, Germans stood up for their Ukrainian colleagues. A Jewish woman complained that her leg was damaged from a beating by the Ukrainian police. The investigation of the matter was entrusted to representatives of the *Schupo* and SD, who determined that the woman had injured herself while escaping from a balcony.[1137]

Jewish survivor testimonies often mention that the Ukrainian policemen were quite susceptible to bribes.[1138] However, the archives of the Lviv police contain many slips of paper from

---

1133 Ibid., f. 44.

1134 Himka, "Metropolitan Andrei Sheptytsky and the Holocaust," 346-47.

1135 For example, AŻIH, 301/3109, Bronisław Teichholz, 1.

1136 USHMM RG Acc 1995 A 1086, reel 3; DALO, fond R12, op. 1, od. zb. 37, f. 43. Emphasis in the original.

1137 Report of sixth commissariat of the Ukrainian police, 30 March 1942, ibid., f. 57

1138 Jewish police also took bribes during roundups. Redner, *A Jewish Policeman in Lwów*, 33.

policemen that indicate that they handed in to their superiors cash or goods from attempted bribes during ghetto roundups. An example:

> To: the command of the Ukrainian Police in Lviv
> Re: Bribes during the Jewish action on 27 March 1942
> I attach 20 (twenty) zlotys with which the Jew Khama Shyfer, who resides at Ilkevych St. 22 wanted to bribe the policeman Roman Borukh.[1139]

The existence of such documentation would seem to contradict the image of the policemen portrayed in testimonies and memoirs, that is, as quite ready to take bribes. Is survivor testimony wrong on this point? It seems not. A monthly report from Ukrainian policeman Mykhailo Petruniak, dated 30 March 1942, stated: "During the Jewish action it is noteworthy that mainly poor Jews were rounded up."[1140] Moreover, since the slips of paper document massive attempts at bribing the Ukrainian policemen, what does it mean when a report from the sixth commissariat of the Lviv police (27 March 1942) states that "there were no attempts at bribery"? Most likely it means that the rule against bribery was not enforced at all in this particular action.[1141]

Ukrainian police were often assigned the job of stripping corpses of their valuables after a mass shooting. In Kryvyi Rih in the Reichskommissariat, 2500 Jews and 800 POWs, mainly of Jewish nationality, were shot at a mine pit on 14 October 1941. The police collected the valuables and turned them over to the German officers who commanded the operation.[1142] But some policemen also helped themselves to the loot. At least several policemen involved in the action managed to steal for themselves about 4000-5000 rubles each, a huge sum at the time. Earlier that morning,

---

1139 This and many other such documents can be found in USHMM RG Acc 1995 A 1086, reel 2; DALO, fond R12, op. 1, od. zb. 41. Unfortunately, it is not possible to identify the folio numbers for many documents on this reel. Such slips of paper can also be found in USHMM RG Acc 1995 A 1086, reel 3; DALO, fond R12, op. 1, od. zb. 37.
1140 USHMM RG Acc 1995 A 1086, reel 2; DALO, fond R12, op. 1, od. zb. 41.
1141 USHMM RG Acc 1995 A 1086, reel 3; DALO, fond R12, op. 1, od. zb. 37, f. 35.
1142 Shliakhtych, "Arkhivno-slidchi spravy politsaiv."

before the mass killing, policemen also collected watches, jewelry, and other personal items from the Jews who had been assembled in the synagogue. Some of what they took from them they delivered to their officers, and some items they were allowed to keep and sell.[1143] After the liquidation of ghettos in Volhynia, the Germans frequently gave Jewish property, especially furniture, to the Ukrainian policemen.[1144]

Oksana Surmach, author of a book on the Greek Catholic church under the Nazi occupation, said that for the Final Solution of the Jewish Question in Galicia, the Germans relied on the Jewish police, the kripo (criminal police), and Silesians (Polish-speaking Volks- and Reichsdeutsche). She then added: "Here and there they forced the local Ukrainian police subordinate to them to take part in their actions; the police were forced against their will to participate in Nazi roundups of the Jews and became a blind tool of the occupational regime."[1145] Bohdan Kazanivsky had stated something similar in his memoirs: "The Germans began to destroy in mass the Jewish population and frequently took Ukrainian policemen to guard a camp or ghetto. This was a function that the policemen did not at all want to perform, but they did so under explicit orders."[1146]

The notion that the Ukrainian police were reluctant to engage in anti-Jewish actions and did so only under duress is not supported by anything I have found in police records themselves — quite the contrary. The archival legacy of the Ukrainian Auxiliary Police in Lviv contains documents that comment on the Jewish police from the point of view of the Ukrainian police. Thus, a report from the March action (sixth commissariat, 25 March 1942), contained this passage: "The action was carried out listlessly on the part of the Jewish *Ordnungsdienst*. There was recorded an incident when a Jewish member of the *Ordnungsdienst*, no. 494, took

1143 Shliakhtych, "Uchast' mistsevoi dopomizhnoi politsii," 83-84.
1144 Klymenko and Tkachov, *Ukraintsi v politsii v reikhskomisariati "Ukraina,"* 74-75.
1145 Surmach, *Dni kryvavykh svastyk*, 100.
1146 Kazanivs'kyi, *Shliakhom Legendy*, 264. He also wrote here that Ivan Klymiv opposed having OUN members in the police take part in anti-Jewish actions. He is the only source for the latter contention.

correspondence from the escorted Jews and went away with the goal of delivering it."[1147] A report from the same commissariat of 27 March complained that "the action did not give the successful results that were expected" because the Jewish police warned people in advance and released "without grounds" certain Jews who had been rounded up.[1148] On 30 March, the sixth commissariat worked without the Jewish police, just with some Germans. It was pleased with the results obtained without the Jewish police placing obstacles in its way.[1149] According to the Polish underground government's Eastern Bureau, the Ukrainian police took part in the liquidation of Jewish policemen in Lviv: "On 13 February [1943] 170 Jewish policemen were taken away to the camp and their families were shot. Ukrainian militiamen executed this action, having first been made drunk on vodka by the Germans."[1150] However, I have found no other source confirming this allegation. After the final liquidation of the Lviv ghetto in June 1943, a report from the Polish Home Army said that the Ukrainian police helped in the murders "with zeal."[1151]

Sometimes Ukrainian police took part in mass executions, although my impression is that this was less common in Galicia than in Volhynia or elsewhere in the Reichskommissariat Ukraine.[1152] Sometimes the Germans took turns with the Ukrainians in murdering the Jews they had rounded up.[1153] Jeffrey Burds has found and published in English translation an account of a Polish man, Jurek

---

1147 USHMM RG Acc 1995 A 1086, reel 3; DALO, fond R12, op. 1, od. zb. 37, f. 3.
1148 Ibid., f. 35. The Jewish police did, in fact, sometimes attempt to sabotage or at least slow down actions. Redner, *A Jewish Policeman in Lwów*, 161.
1149 USHMM RG Acc 1995 A 1086, reel 3; DALO, fond R12, op. 1, od. zb. 37, f. 57.
1150 Adamczyk, *Ziemie Wschodnie*, 32.
1151 Cited in Mick, *Kriegserfahrungen*, 518.
1152 Livneh, *Pinkas hak'hilah Trisk*, 327. Martin Dean provided me with this source and an accompanying abridged translation into English. Zhulyns'kyi and Zhulyns'kyi, "*To tvii, synu, bat'ko,*" 107. YIUN, no. 841, Vyshnivets, Zbarazh raion, Ternopil oblast, USHMM RG-50.589*0290. Rothenberg, *List o zagładzie Żydów*, 12. USHMM RG-31.018M, reel 61, frames 57-135; HDA SBU Ternopil, spr. 7719/7788 (case of Kirill Filyk). Berkhoff, "'Total Annihilation,'" 87. Spector, *Holocaust of Volhynian Jews*, 183. Kovba, *Liudianist' u bezodni pekla*, 84. Siemaszko and Siemaszko, *Ludobójstwo*, 1:293-94, 1:402, 1:595.
1153 Kovba, *Liudianist' u bezodni pekla*, 84. Klymenko and Tkachov, *Ukraintsi v politsii v reikhskomisariati "Ukraina,"* 72-73.

Nowakowski, who was a friend of a Ukrainian policeman in Rivne, Heorhii Datsiuk. Datsiuk related to Nowakowski his experience of killing Jews:

> Datsiuk told me that at first it was "uncomfortable" for him to shoot defenseless people, moreover ones that were naked and lying on the ground face down. Among those whom he, Datsiuk, shot were several of his acquaintances, Jewish girls with whom he had met earlier on social occasions (*vecherinki*), some with whom he had even studied at school. But, Datsiuk said, he had to shoot even them. It was the norm, Datsiuk continued, to develop a taste for blood, for murder.[1154] An older policeman—I do not now recall his name—showed him by example how to do it, and then Datsiuk began to fire next: to shoot into the backs of their heads, and then to throw the bodies into the pit. They did not shoot the children—they didn't want to waste the bullets—and instead just hurled them live directly into the pit. I have survived [horrors], said Datsiuk, even Neron never faced.[1155]

After these systematic liquidations, total by intent, there were still some Jews hiding, with their Ukrainian or Polish neighbors, in sewers and hidey-holes, and in the forests. One of the jobs of Ukrainian police after the liquidations was to hunt these Jews down and either turn them over to the Germans or kill them themselves.[1156] For example, there are Ukrainian- and German-language reports from the Lviv Ukrainian police, dating from 4 February

---

1154 The Greek Catholic metropolitan of Galicia, Andrei Sheptytsky, observed in his pastoral letter "Thou Shalt Not Kill" of November 1942: "The sight of spilled blood calls forth in a person's soul a sensual desire, bound up with cruelty, which seeks satisfaction in dealing out suffering and death to its victims. The thirst for blood can become an uncontrollable passion, which finds the greatest delight in torturing and killing people....Crime becomes a necessary daily nourishment, without which [the killer] suffers torment, as though he suffered from some sickness of thirst and hunger which must be quenched." Sheptyts'kyi, *Pys'ma-poslannia*, 226. (I have read *prokliatoi* here as a typo for *proliatoi*.)

1155 Burds, *Holocaust in Rovno*, 61. The translation is Burds'. I believe that "Neron" is actually the Roman emperor Nero. *Neron* in Russian is Nero, just as *Platon* is Plato.

1156 Biber, *Survivors*, 128, 137. YIUN, no. 841, Vyshnivets, Zbarazh raion, Ternopil oblast, USHMM RG-50.589*0290. Klymenko and Tkachov, *Ukraintsi v politsii v dystrykti "Halychyna,"* 284-87. On the Polish Blue police's Jew hunts, see Grabowski, *Hunt*, esp. 101-20.

1943, of a house search in which they found two Jews hiding.[1157] Marian Bernacki, a Volhynian Pole and blacksmith, recalled: "Jews who escaped from the ghettos in various places, generally hid in the woods located near Polish villages, because Poles helped them. The Germans, and especially the nationalistic Ukrainian police, were well aware of this fact; [the Ukrainian police] would from time to time carry out roundups in these villages and would capture and shoot Jews who were hiding there." He went on to describe his personal encounter with a Jewish livestock dealer he knew who was being chased by the Ukrainian police.[1158] In 1942 Juda Kneidel and her family fled to the woods to escape the roundups in Khodoriv (P Chodorów), east of Zhydachiv in Lviv oblast. One night she went out looking for food. A Ukrainian policeman caught her and was taking her to the Gestapo, but she managed to break away. The policeman shot at her and missed, so she escaped.[1159] Ukrainian police in Sanok, which was outside Distrikt Galizien in the General Government's Krakau district, also took part in Jew hunts (*Judenjagden*). They rounded up hidden Jews and turned them over to the Germans to shoot. A Blue, i.e., Polish policeman who also participated in these hunts in Sanok testified that "every week there were very many such executions."[1160] When policemen found Jews in hiding places and discovered caches of money or valuables, they were rewarded with monetary bonuses.[1161]

A recurring scenario was when Jews were found hiding in a village and were brought to the mayor. The village authorities would be hesitant to report this to the Germans, lest there be negative repercussions for the locals who had hid them and indeed for the whole village. The prudent thing to do was to have a local Ukrainian policeman, who was in the employ of the local community, solve the problem.[1162] According to a Polish witness, this is

---

1157 The Jews managed in this case to escape. YVA, r.g. M.52, file no. 259, mf 99.2693, frames771-72; DALO, R-16/1/28, ff. 2-3.

1158 Wroński and Zwolakowa, *Polacy Żydzi*, 387.

1159 AŻIH, 301/3118, Juda Kneidel, 1.

1160 Grabowski, *Hunt*, 98.

1161 Martynenko, "Ukrains'ka Dopomizhna Politsiia," 163.

1162 This is well explained, but with reference to the Blue police, in Grabowski, *Hunt*, 106, 110.

what happened in the village of Kusnyshcha (P Kuśniszcze), north of Liuboml in Volhynia oblast. One day in early June 1942, a Ukrainian farmer armed with an axe brought three Jews into the village administration: a couple and their five-year-old daughter. The mayor was upset. He could neither release them nor hide them, so he called the local Ukrainian police. Two policemen came. One, a local boy, beat the husband unmercifully. The policemen ordered the mayor to find some men to dig a hole in a sandy area near the local cemetery. Later they took the Jews there and shot them.[1163]

Sometimes the executions were not so discreet and served as warnings to the local population not to hide Jews. In September 1943 survivor Henry Friedman, who was hiding with a Ukrainian family, the Symchuks, overheard a conversation between the man and wife:

> A [Jewish] couple with a child were caught hiding in an underground grotto in a forest. A Ukrainian family who had previously hidden them reported them to the Ukrainian police in [P] Suchowola [Sukhovolia near Brody in Lviv oblast]. The Jews had run out of ransom money and had fled to a hiding place in the woods. Their "friends" promised to supply them with food but instead betrayed them, never letting on that they had once hidden them. The villagers of Suchowola were called out to witness the Jews' execution.
> "Now watch this," one of the Ukrainian policemen said. "Any Jews, or anyone hiding a Jew, will meet with a similar fate."
> First they undressed the woman and asked if anyone wanted her. Mrs. Symchuck said she was very pretty. Since no one would lower himself to have sex in public with a Jew, not one person stepped forward. Her eight-year-old daughter stood by her mothers' side. "The child screamed hysterically," Mrs. Symchuck said. "Most of the people laughed. The police shot the husband first, then the wife, and, in the end, the poor child."

The violent spectacle had the desired effect on the Symchucks: "That same night, after witnessing the execution, Mr. Symchuck got very drunk. I heard the argument from above [in the attic]. 'Let's

---

1163 Łukasz Kuźmicz, "Oświadczenie świadka w sprawie zabójstwa Żydów przez ukraińską policję na Wołyniu"; I came into possession of a copy thanks to the generosity of Wiesław Tokarczuk.

get rid of them,' he yelled. 'I can't stand them and I am not going to have my family killed because of these damned Jews.'"[1164]

Mercy and Rescue

People who commit monstrous acts are not monsters. They remain people. SS men in Germany became respectable professors after the war. A Schutzmann who helped herd Belarusian villagers into a building and then manned a machine gun outside that building when it was set on fire could become a peaceful beekeeper in rural Quebec. A guard at a Nazi death camp could become a law-abiding auto worker in Cleveland. In other words, people who did horrible things at a certain time in their lives, in a certain place, and in a certain political conjuncture could be removed from that time, place, and conjuncture and function as ordinary citizens in a peace-time environment. They no longer robbed or killed. It turns out they were ordinary men after all.[1165]

Repentance for the kind of crimes the Ukrainian police committed has rarely been expressed publicly, but sometimes it has. Consider the case of the Volhynian policeman Mykola Dufanets. He was put on trial for a second time in 1980 after new evidence against him was discovered. In his opening statement he confessed to crimes he had committed. After a major shooting in Krymne in September 1942, he said, it was learned that there was still a Jewish physician alive in the village of Liubokhyny (P Lubochiny), about seven kilometers to the southeast. Dufanets went with a couple of other policeman to pick the doctor up, and Dufanets personally shot him. Soon afterwards Dufanets killed two or three families of "Gypsies." He testified that a fellow policeman "shot the Livak family; I only shot the two-year-old child." "Almost the entire

---

1164   Friedman, *I'm No Hero*, 31-32.

1165   In 2008 I had the pleasure of meeting Sima Samar, then the UN's special rap-porteur on the situation of human rights in Sudan, an Afghani by birth. When she arrived in Edmonton, she was horrified to recognize the taxi driver who picked her up at the airport: he had served in the Afghan Security Service dur-ing the communist period (1978-92) and had been responsible for the murder of over a dozen members of her extended family. He offered, as a kind of rec-ompense, to drive her around the city gratis.

police after such actions was drunk. I got drunk until I passed out and for me it meant nothing at that time to kill a person....I do not know where all this came from in me. I was a beast, that's all. I know that if I were to say that I repent, that I regret that I entered such a path, no one would believe me; and I myself would not believe it after all that happened." With regard to Jews, he said: "I did not have hostile feelings towards them; I felt sorry for the Jews, in my soul I felt sorry. I now feel that the highest court is the court of conscience. My conscience has gnawed at me my whole life; I knew I would have to answer for it. Do you think it is pleasant to fight with your conscience?"[1166]

One can feel the humanity behind this statement. I do not know if Dufanets ever spared anyone, but perpetrators were occasionally moved to mercy, although, of course, this had to be a marginal phenomenon given their duties and the historical circumstances. Actually, perpetrators, who had the power to do harm, could be among the most effective rescuers.[1167] An OUN militiaman during the Lviv pogrom saved the sister of one of his school friends.[1168] Jewish policeman Ben Z. Redner helped send many of the inhabitants of the Lviv ghetto to the gas chambers at Bełżec. But on one day during the March action he was sent to arrest "Rabbi Greenberg, father of the famous Hebrew-Revisionist poet Uri Zvi Greenberg." Redner was himself a Revisionist. The old rabbi had legs so swollen that he could not even put his shoes on. Moved by pity and a feeling of connection, Redner decided to do everything in his power to save the rabbi and his wife and daughter. His intention seemed thwarted when two German officers burst into the

---

1166 Minutes of the trial of Mykola Dufanets and others, 5-25 August 1980. USHMM RG-31018M, reel 32; HDA SBU, spr. 70, vol. 32, ff. 69, 71v, 72v, 74v, 75v. Dufanets was sentenced to execution by firing squad after the trial in 1980. A review of his case in 1997 concluded that his crimes were such that he could not be rehabilitated. USHMM RG-31018M, reel 33; HDA SBU, spr. 70, vol. 32, ff. 324-38.

1167 See the insightful dissertation of Nina Paulovicova, "Rescue of Jews in the Slovak State."

1168 Himka, "Lviv Pogrom," 219.

apartment. But Redner found a way to get the family to safety, not without serious risk to himself.[1169]

It should not, then, be surprising that Ukrainian policemen sometimes chose to rescue Jews. Jewish survivor Adam Landesberg, who was then twelve, was caught twice by the same Ukrainian policeman. Each time he cried and was released.[1170] A senior officer in the Ukrainian police helped a Jewish friend when his daughter was arrested by a young policeman; the daughter was released.[1171] A policeman in Vyshnivets told his Soviet interrogators that, although he had been involved in the murder of other Jews, he also let six Jews go free from the jail where they were being held for execution.[1172] In a diary entry of 11 August 1941, Mariia Strutynska, then in Lviv, said she saw a Gestapo patrol accompanied by an auxiliary Ukrainian policeman. She saw a Jew quickly disappear behind the corner and also saw the policeman urgently point the Germans in another direction. "I am almost certain that he saw the Jew and did this deliberately, though I cannot swear to it."[1173] There is evidence that some Ukrainian policemen made little effort to take aim and kill Jews escaping from *Aktionen*.[1174] Shmuel Spector noted that sometimes the Ukrainian police let Jews know in advance about an impending *Aktion*.[1175] This happened in Vyshnivets. The head of the town's police, Oleksii Voloshyn, in August 1942 warned the inhabitants of the ghetto about the preparation of an action; this led to the escape of over two hundred Jews.[1176] Spector wrote that bribed Ukrainian policemen facilitated a mass escape of hundreds of Dubrovytsia Jews from an *Aktion* in May 1942.[1177]

1169 Redner, *A Jewish Policeman in Lwów*, 157.

1170 AŻIH, 301/199, Adam Landesberg, 5.

1171 Rosenfeld *From Lwów to Parma*, 19-20.

1172 USHMM RG-31.018M, reel 60, fr. 1510; HDA SBU Ternopil, spr. 147, f. 313.

1173 Strutyns'ka, *Daleke zblyz'ka*, 173.

1174 Spector, *Holocaust of Volhynian Jews*, 193. Kovba, *Liudianist' u bezodni pekla*, 104.

1175 Spector, *Holocaust of Volhynian Jews*, 189.

1176 Klymenko and Tkachov, *Ukraintsi v politsii v reikhskomisariati "Ukraina,"* 70, citing HDA SBU, Ternopil, spr. 33526, vol. 2, f. 152.

1177 Spector, *Holocaust of Volhynian Jews*, 194.

OUN and the Ukrainian Police

From late 1941 through early 1943, the years in which the Ukrainian police played such a significant role in the Holocaust, OUN was in difficult straits. The Melnyk wing of the organization had virtually disappeared in Galicia and had never taken root in Volhynia,[1178] except in Kremenets. The Bandera movement, which was now effectively the sole representative of OUN on Western Ukrainian territory, was also at a loss. The German alliance had not worked out well, and the Bandera movement had made no plans on what to do if that happened. Originally, both factions of OUN had placed their hopes on the expeditionary groups that would follow the German invasion and transplant their nationalist movement into pre-1939 Soviet Ukraine. These efforts, however, failed to ignite the national revolution in that very different society.[1179] This failure was among the factors inclining OUN to put more emphasis on the police. Moreover, the one activity in which the expeditionary groups in Soviet Ukraine did enjoy relative success was setting up police units in German service.

Usefulness of Infiltrating the Police

In their joint article on the Ukrainian police in Galicia, Alexander Prusin and Gabriel Finder concentrated on the ideological underpinnings of Ukrainian police activity.[1180] They considered the Ukrainian police to be "the institutional epicentre of Ukrainian collusion with the Nazis in this region in the destruction of the Jews,"[1181] a finding that this monograph does not challenge. They also considered the Ukrainian police to be a cornerstone of Ukrainian nationalists' policy of creating a "Ukraine for Ukrainians." They killed "in the name of the reconstruction of society."[1182] This too is

---

1178 Adamczyk, *Ziemie Wschodnie*, 50.
1179 Kurylo, "Syla ta slabkist'." Armstrong, *Ukrainian Nationalism*, 84-86. Berkhoff, *Harvest of Despair*, 208-10, 218, 222, 226, 228-29. Weiner, *Making Sense of War*, 239-71, 314, 331-36.
1180 Finder and Prusin, "Collaboration in Eastern Galicia."
1181 Ibid., 96.
1182 Ibid., 97.

a finding that is not directly challenged here. But their view needs to be supplemented with more context. The relationship between the existence of certain ideas and the existence of certain practices is not often straightforward. There is usually a great deal of mediation. While not denying the role played by nationalist ideology, I consider it necessary to look also beyond OUN's strategies and aspirations for ethnic cleansing. The ideological underpinnings were only one factor explaining OUN's interest in the police; OUN also used the police to pursue various practical objectives. As Wendy Lower has perceptively noted, the "events that comprise 'the Holocaust' represent an intersection of German history and the varied local and regional histories of Europe."[1183]

OUN was not the only movement interested in infiltrating the police in German service. So too were the Polish Home Army and the Soviet partisans.[1184] Having one's own men in the police was very useful.

For OUN, the main point was that service in the police provided training and weapons for men who could later defect and serve the national revolution. According to Bohdan Kazanivsky, Ivan Klymiv early on was thinking that "the Ukrainian police will in future serve Ukraine."[1185] The Germans feared precisely such an outcome. An Einsatzgruppe report from 10 April 1942 said that OUN was trying to gain influence in the stationary Schutzmannschaften. It was trying to make the police units as strong as possible while German forces were overextended. "There is a telling saying: 'If one day fifty militiamen face five Germans, who will hold power then?'"[1186]

The police were able to issue false identity papers. OUN-B issued such papers to its own people and sometimes even to Jews.[1187] Arranging for false documentation was not simple, but it could be

---

1183 Lower, "Pogroms," 218.
1184 Dean, *Collaboration during the Holocaust*, 74-75. Hempel, *Pogrobowcy klęski, 211-62*. Dereiko, *Mistsevi formuvannia*, 100. Kentii, *Narysy*, 123.
1185 Kazanivs'kyi, *Shliakhom Legendy*, 266.
1186 EM 191, 10 April 1942.
1187 EM 187, 30 March 1942.

done. An OUN-B activist explained at his deportation hearing how it was accomplished:

> The Kennkartes — issue of the Kennkartes was performed by the German police with a Ukrainian assistance, Ukrainian policemen, so say, they come to Lisets [Staryi Lysets, a suburban village just southwest of Stanyslaviv, P Łysiec] once a month, or once in two months for issuing, for the population, the Kennkarte. So Marko, he was himself a member of our resistance movement. The only thing, he was policeman. So I deliver Marko only photography, ten, fifteen people, working with the German, exchanged. The main thing was the stamp. Kennkarte was easy to get for him than a stamp, so took me sometime long time, four, five, six weeks, but I always got it from him the Kennkartes....Each were very valuable to us.[1188]

Police also helped transport weapons and a radio transmitter for OUN.[1189] Some members of the police worked closely with intelligence and counterintelligence services of OUN and UPA, providing essential inside information.[1190] Police working in labor camps could also inform UPA of valuable skilled personnel, Jews, who might work for the insurgent army.[1191] The police were able to exempt certain Ukrainians from the roundups for forced labor to Germany and could even free people who were already in Germany and bring them back home;[1192] the utility of this power for an underground movement should be obvious. Police could also help OUN members evade arrest. A veteran of the Waffen-SS Division Galizien recalled: "There was a Ukrainian Police [in Galicia], but it was more subordinated to UPA than to the Germans. The police

---

1188 Testimony of Bohdan Koziy at deportation hearing, USHMM RG-06.029.01*21, Box 21, case of Bohdan Koziy, 2 October 1981, 56.

1189 Kazanivs'kyi, *Shliakhom Legendy*, 266-67.

1190 Klymenko and Tkachov, *Ukraintsi v politsii v reikhskomisariati "Ukraina,"* 77-78.

1191 Yones, *Evrei L'vova*, 298. Yones does not specifically mention the police as intermediaries, but that seems to be the most likely scenario.

1192 Vasyl' Onufryk, "Ukrains'ka politsiia. Spomyn," 54-57. This memoir was written in Burlington, ON in 1988. Andrii Bolianovskyi originally told me of its existence in an email of 1 October 2014, saying that he had consulted it at the UCRDC in Toronto. On 1 June 2018, he wrote that he had consulted the memoir about fifteen years earlier, and on 5 June 2018 he sent me photos of pp. 54-57 of the typescript. I corresponded with the UCRDC about the memoir. On 28 May 2018 the UCRDC Office informed me that the memoir "is still restricted." Another query to the UCRDC on 23 July 2020 resulted in the response that there was no record at all of the memoir.

would go out to arrest a member of OUN, but they almost never arrested him, because he would not be home when they came to arrest him. Someone had given him notice in advance. There were cases in which they transferred those arrested from Rohatyn to Berezhany, but on the way they were 'attacked' and freed. Someone just had to inform someone else in advance."[1193] OUN-M control of a police district in Kyiv allowed Oleh Kandyba (pseudonym Oleh Olzhych) to escape arrest in December 1941, when other OUN-M leaders were taken into custody by the Germans.[1194]

Grzegorz Motyka has reasonably suggested that some of the valuables and bribes that policemen collected from the Jews were deposited into OUN's war chest.[1195]

Militiamen in the Police

There was a certain continuity between the OUN militias and the police. Their tasks were essentially the same and some of the personnel of the Ukrainian National Militia also continued to serve in the Ukrainian Auxiliary Police and the Schutzmannschaften. As noted earlier, the order that was issued on 12 August 1941 to dissolve the Ukrainian militia also invited the militiamen to apply to the new police force.[1196]

Preserved in the Lviv oblast archives are 101 applications with autobiographies from men aspiring to join the newly formed Ukrainian Auxiliary Police. Fifty-eight of these applications came from former militiamen.[1197] David Alan Rich has written that at least a third of the Lviv militiamen (110 of 330) were incorporated into the auxiliary police, but over half of them (58) had left by autumn 1941.[1198] Prusin and Finder wrote that in March 1942, according to a contemporary estimate, there were still 122 former OUN

1193 Letter of P. Maslij to UCRDC, 29 January 1991. UCRDC, "Spomyny," no. 51.
1194 Armstrong, *Ukrainian Nationalism*, 80.
1195 Motyka, *Ukraińska partyzantka*, 289-90.
1196 See above, 307.
1197 Riabenko, "Ukrains'ka militsiia L'vova." Numerous such petitions, dated 13 August 1941, can be found in USHMM RG Acc 1995 A 1086, reel 1; DALO, fond R12, op. 1, od. zb. 4.
1198 Rich, "Armed Ukrainians in L'viv," 283.

militiamen in the Ukrainian police force in Lviv,[1199] of a total of under five hundred policemen. Bohdan Kazanivsky, who played an
important role in the formation of the militia in Lviv,[1200] saw a large
measure of continuity between the militia and police in the city:
"The Ukrainian militia was renamed as the police, over which the
German Schutzpolizei gradually took complete control."[1201] The
Ukrainian police force in Stanyslaviv is said to have been "seamlessly recruited" from the pre-existing force of three hundred OUN
militiamen.[1202] Militiamen also remained in the police in Sokal, in
the north of Lviv Oblast.[1203] After the dissolution of the militia in
Nove Selo (P Nowesioło), east of Zbarazh in Ternopil oblast, the
militia's commandant, who was also a *kushch* leader of OUN,[1204] ordered OUN members to go underground and infiltrate the new police force.[1205]

Only 31 militiamen from the Ternopil circle militia joined the
police, but most of them left in October and November 1941.[1206]
When I counted up all the militiamen listed by name in Klymenko
and Tkachov's study of the Ternopil region police, I came up with
a total of 815.[1207] Clearly, only a small fraction of the militiamen
found work in the new police force. But the small fraction may have
loomed larger within the smaller numbers of the Ukrainian Auxiliary Police. In September 1941, there were 110 policemen in the circle police, and in October — 122. Many of the Ternopil region militiamen went on to serve the Germans in other capacities. About
twenty militiamen from the Skalat region joined Schutzbattalion
109. Others joined the railroad police in Lviv, Ternopil, Chełm, and
Kraków. Still others joined various SS units.[1208]

1199 Finder and Prusin, "Collaboration in Eastern Galicia," 105.
1200 Kazanivs'kyi, *Shliakhom Legendy*, 212-14.
1201 Ibid., 263-65.
1202 Finder and Prusin, "Collaboration in Eastern Galicia," 105.
1203 Struve, *Deutsche Herrschaft*, 243.
1204 A *kushch* united five to seven villages or *stanytsi*.
1205 Klymenko and Tkachov, *Ukraintsi v politsii v dystrykti "Halychyna,"* 268.
1206 Ibid., 267.
1207 Ibid., 324-411.
1208 Ibid., 267.

In Volhynia, too, many of the original Ukrainian militiamen joined the Schutzmannschaft after the Ukrainian state was suppressed. A memoirist said that many militiamen simply returned home to their parents. But some "ignorant and [nationally] unconscious" elements entered the police from the militia in order to drink moonshine, rob the Jews, and run rampant in the villages. "Truth be told, there also remained in the police good lads as well, because the Germans punished those families whose sons returned. They were still in the police, but their souls were tortured and they awaited an opportunity to escape from there."[1209] Thus, a certain number of the militiamen – good and bad – remained subsequently in the police. A member of the propaganda apparatus of the OUN leadership told his Soviet captors during interrogation that the Banderites had set up the original Ukrainian police force in Volhynia, but that the Germans dissolved it in the fall of 1941. "Yet at the start of 1942 almost all the Ukrainian auxiliary units with the German police were once again filled with those same Banderites who had been expelled in the fall."[1210] When the militias were dissolved and the Schutzmannschaft formed in the Kremenets region, 35-37 percent of the new force was composed of former militiamen, and some former militias were incorporated into the mobile Schutzmannschaft battalions.[1211]

What the evidence points to is that about a third of the new police force in Galicia and Volhynia was, at least at first, composed of former militiamen. Some then left the service, others were purged by the Germans, but later other former militiamen joined or rejoined the police.

OUN in the Police

The first head of the Ukrainian Auxiliary Police in Lviv was longtime OUN activist Omelian Matla, until he was replaced by

---

1209 Podvorniak, *Viter z Volyni*, 138.
1210 Interrogation of Volodymyr Porendovsky, 15 February 1948. HDA SBU, fond 13, spr. 372, vol. 2, f. 197. Available online at http://avr.org.ua/viewDoc/21800/ (accessed 5 August 2020).
1211 Klymenko and Tkachov, *Ukraintsi v politsii v reikhskomisariati "Ukraina,"* 65-66.

Volodymyr Pitulei,[1212] an officer of the former Polish force. Pitulei personally knew some of the leading OUN figures in the police, such as Yevhen Kachmarsky, deputy commander of the fifth commissariat, but he never revealed them to the Germans in spite of their insistence that he do so. The OUN members served in the force on orders from the OUN leadership. As a result of the efforts of Ivan Klymiv, an OUN network was set up within the police in Lviv and environs, subordinate to its own leader, who held the rank of a raion leader.[1213] When an OUN-B member from Volhynia arrived in Lviv in the first half of August 1941 and had no place to sleep, he turned for help to the Lviv police, which he characterized as "at that time 'Banderite.'" They did indeed find a place for him to stay.[1214]

In Volhynia, the links between OUN-B and the police appear to have been quite strong. An Einsatzgruppe report stated that the police academy in Rivne had to be dissolved, because the police trained there were "considered to be a Banderite fighting organization." The Banderites also used their positions of authority in the academy to remove Melnykites from the teaching staff.[1215] A police school in Trostianets (P Trościaniec), northeast of Kivertsi in Volhynia oblast, was also under OUN-B control, as evidenced by its transformation into a center for training UPA officers in 1943.[1216]

Mykola Dufanets, whose penitent opening statement has been cited above, was appointed commandant of the raion police by the local OUN leadership.[1217] OUN-B controlled the police in the Sarny region.[1218] Oleksandr Danylevych, commandant of the Ratne (P Ratno) raion police in summer 1941 and until May 1942, had been

---

1212 Martynenko, "Ukrains'ka Dopomizhna Politsiia," 156.

1213 Kazanivsky, *Shliakhom Legendy*, 263-65.

1214 Petrenko, *Za Ukrainu*, 45.

1215 *Meldungen aus den besetzten Ostgebieten*, 22 May 1942, cited in Russian translation in Serhiichuk, *OUN-UPA v roky viiny*, 175-76.

1216 Siemaszko and Siemaszko, *Ludobójstwo*, 1:655.

1217 USHMM RG-31018M, reel 32; HDA SBU, spr. 70, vol. 29, f. 213. Indictment by Volhynia oblast prosecutor of Mykola Dufanets and others, 25 June 1980: USHMM RG-31018M, reel 32; HDA SBU, spr. 70, vol. 32, f. 4. Minutes of the trial of Mykola Dufanets and others, 5-25 August 1980: USHMM RG-31018M, reel 32; HDA SBU, spr. 70, vol. 32, ff. 68, 70-70v.

1218 Petrenko, *Za Ukrainu*, 35-36, 56, 115.

a member of OUN since 1931.[1219] A certain Chmyr, who recruited a Jewish doctor to serve as a physician for the insurgent army, was himself simultaneously both the commandant of the police in Koniukhy (P Koniuchy) northeast of Berezhany in Ternopil oblast and a member of UPA.[1220] According to Polish testimony, the deputy commandant of the police in Boremel, northwest of Demydivka in Rivne oblast, a certain Volochaiv, was a member of OUN.[1221]

The Germans were well aware of the Volhynian police's pro-OUN proclivities. After OUN-B launched an insurgency aimed against the German occupation, the Einsatzgruppen felt that the police were more loyal to OUN-UPA than to the Germans: "The Ukrainian Schutzmannschaften are in large part excluded from combating the Bandera group because they are in part strongly infiltrated by the Bandera people and at various times their members have gone over to the Bandera bandits. In the Ukrainian police school in Lviv the Ukrainian training officers engage in propaganda that is openly hostile to the Reich. The Ukrainian police sabotages the recruitment of labor [i.e., *Ostarbeiter*] in the most gross manner."[1222] In summer 1942, German security services, after studying captured OUN documents, summarized the nationalists' tactics with regard to Germany: "to infiltrate organs of authority, to wait, to preserve their forces, no unnecessary, thoughtless actions, but to conduct internal and organizational preparation, expand OUN's network, in order in the end to be able at the specified time to have 'the final say.'"[1223] The Eastern Bureau of the Polish underground government, describing the situation in Volhynia in early 1943, said that OUN was trying to base itself on the local government and on the police. It assessed its influence on the police as "rather significant," adding: "One gets the impression that the main organizational core in Volhynia are the c. 200 police stations which exist on

---

1219 Antoniuk, *Ukrains'kyi vyzvol'nyi rukh*, 238-39.

1220 Redlich, *Together and Apart*, 127.

1221 He was accused in the testimony of using living Jews as target practice for the men under his command. Siemaszko and Siemaszko, *Ludobójstwo*, 1:54.

1222 EM 46, 19 March 1943.

1223 *Meldungen aus den besetzten Ostgebieten*, 10 July 1942, cited in Ukrainian translation in Kentii, "Perekhid OUN(B)," 103.

that territory."[1224] Anecdotal confirmation of this assessment is the bizarre case in which a Jew using false identity papers was recruited into UPA as a result of taking his meals in the police cafeteria in Korets (P Korzec), east of Rivne.[1225] A young teacher from Pyriatyn (P Piratyn), sothwest of Dubno in Rivne oblast, wrote in his diary on 30 April 1943: "The police, whom the Germans kept as their dogs and fed, who shot parents, who drove out their brothers and sisters [to be forced laborers in Germany], have now become patriots of their nation (partisans, of whom many are in the forests)."[1226]

Aside from the mass transfer of Volhynian police to UPA, Ukrainian policemen from Galicia also joined UPA. Like many young nationalists from Galicia Ivan Stebelsky joined the Carpathian Sich to defend Carpatho-Ukraine in 1939. One of his friends there went by the pseudonym Mizerny. Mizerny, like Stebelsky, went on to join one of the nationalist legions in German service. He served as commandant of the Ukrainian police in Sanok (now in Poland) before losing his life as the commander of a company (sotnia) of UPA in 1947.[1227] Individuals in Galicia joined the police even without prior involvement in OUN and then went from the police into OUN and UPA; examples of this can be found in the records of Soviet prosecutions of policemen. According to an NKVD military tribunal, Yaroslav Melnychenko joined the Ukrainian police in the spring of 1943 and served in the town of Skala-Podilska. The NKVD accused him of involvement in the execution of Jews in the Skala woods. He denied it, admitting he was present, but stating that other policemen did the shooting. He did not seem to have any OUN background, at least none that the NKVD was able to uncover, but he joined UPA in December 1944 or earlier. Taking the pseudonym "Izhak," he served under "Kamin" in the Borshchiv region and was wounded in battle and captured in an NKVD

1224 Adamczyk, *Ziemie Wschodnie*, 22.
1225 See below, 430.
1226 Himka, "Refleksje żołnierza," 183. As we will see in the next chapter (377-78), this diarist changed his views after he was forcibly drafted into UPA later in the summer of 1943.
1227 Stebel's'kyi, *Shliakhamy molodosti i borot'by*, 47.

operation in April 1945.[1228] Petro Chaika really made the rounds. He started his career in the Soviet militia in 1939. Nineteen forty-one found him in the Red Army. He was wounded and captured by the Germans, but managed to escape. He joined the Ukrainian police in Lviv to avoid being sent to Germany as a forced laborer and also to avoid persecution for his past as a Soviet militiaman. As a Ukrainian policeman he took part in anti-Jewish actions, of course, and he confessed to his SMERSH interrogators that he had personally killed a Jewish woman and wounded a Jewish man and woman. He fell afoul of the Germans for not handing in keys from apartments in the ghetto. He escaped from a camp near Kraków in December 1943. He denied any OUN involvement, but it seems that in 1944 he joined an SB OUN unit headed by Dmytro Kupiak ("Klei"). Other members of the unit testified in 1965 that he had indeed been one of them.[1229] Other sources also confirm the importance of former policemen in Galicia. A Jewish survivor related that his Ukrainian wife's antisemitic uncle had helped the SS exterminate the Jews of Pinsk (P Pińsk). Although in 1945 he served briefly with the Red Army, he then led a Banderite underground unit near Sambir in Lviv oblast.[1230] Oleksandr Lutsky and Vasyl Sydor, who served as commanders of UPA-West, based mainly in Galicia, were both veterans of Schutzmannschaft Battalion 201.[1231]

Both factions of OUN deliberately infiltrated the police in the old Soviet territories, i.e., outside Western Ukraine. They were particularly interested in penetrating the police force in eastern Ukraine, where their movement was almost nonexistent. The OUN-B leadership issued instructions in March 1942 that said: "Ukrainian nationally conscious youth should volunteer in mass to join the Ukrainian Police" in the Eastern Ukrainian Lands. The instructions also called upon each *stanytsia* in Galicia to send ten men to join the

---

1228 USHMM RG-31.018M, reel 84; GDA SBU Ternopil', spr. 19710, vol. 1, Mel'nychenko Ia.V.
1229 USHMM RG-31.018M, reel 99; GDA SBU Lviv, spr. 30853, vols. 1-2, Chaika P.F.
1230 AŻIH, 301/2238, 6, 8.
1231 Katchanovski, "Terrorists or National Heroes," 14.

police in Ukraine's eastern territories.[1232] Although these instructions proved overly ambitious, they did bear some fruit. OUN had influence on the police in a number of eastern and southern localities.

OUN-M controlled police forces in cities just east of Western Ukraine, in Proskuriv (now Khmelnytskyi), Vinnytsia, and Zhytomyr. OUN-M also controlled "most of the Ukrainian police" in Kyiv.[1233] In fall 1941 there were significant numbers of members of both OUN factions in the police forces of Kyiv, Vasylkiv, Fastiv, Uman, and Bila Tserkva, but their numbers were later reduced by arrests.[1234] The chief of police in Fastiv was Ivan Lanovyi, who had arrived with an OUN-B expeditionary group in July 1941.[1235] According to the report of a Soviet partisan leader, nationalists from Galicia also staffed the police force in the Uman region.[1236] After organizing a series of pogroms in Bukovina, OUN-M leader Petro Voinovsky left twenty-five of his men to work as police in Kamianets Podilskyi.[1237] In Kharkiv, OUN-M emissaries headed by Bohdan Konyk organized the police force.[1238] Nationalists from Galicia organized meetings to elect the police in Kirovohrad oblast as well.[1239]

Kryvyi Rih, a center of the steel industry in south-central Ukraine, was occupied by the Germans in August 1941. OUN-B expeditionary groups controlled the local administration for the first four months of the occupation; the Banderite civil administration took part in the creation of the local police, and Banderites occupied

---

1232 "Instruktsii Providnomu aktyvovi OUN," 29 March 1942, TsDAVO, fond 3833, op. 1, spr. 46, f. 1. Patryliak, Viis'kova diial'nist OUN (B), 240. Kentii, Narysy, 95-96.

1233 Armstrong, *Ukrainian Nationalism*, 65, 67, 84, 195.

1234 OUN's control of the Kyiv police did not survive the Germans' purges during the winter of 1942. Hence when Alexander Prusin studied Soviet trials of 82 former Ukrainian policemen of the general district of Kyiv (Kyiv and Poltava oblasts), only 4 were members of OUN. Prusin, "Ukrainskaia politsiia," 43.

1235 Ibid., 44. Mondzelevs'kyi, "Pochatok viiny na Fastivshchyni."

1236 TsDAHO, fond 166, op. 2, spr. 58, f. 5. I am grateful to Oleksandr Melnyk for a transcript of this document.

1237 Fostii, *Pivnichna Bukovyna i Khotynshchyna*, 130-34.

1238 Radchenko, "'Ioho choboty ta esesivs'ka forma," 60. See also Skorobohatov, "OUN u Kharkovi," 83-87.

1239 TsDAHO, fond 166, op. 2, spr. 88, f. 5.

leading positions until purges in January 1942.[1240] OUN also had a significant influence on the Ukrainian police in the industrial Donbas. OUN-M organized the first police force in Stalino (now Donetsk, an oblast capital). OUN-B acquired leadership positions in the Ukrainian police of other centers in Donetsk oblast: Horlivka, Kostiantynivka, Mariupol, and Olhynka.[1241]

Yevhen Stakhiv, one of the most active and effective members of OUN-B sent from Galicia to work in the Donbas, also noted in his memoirs of 1956 that OUN-M had set up the police in Stalino. "Their work ended with forcing the policemen to wear tridents on their uniforms as well as blue and yellow....Under the brand of the Ukrainian national emblem they executed the most brutal orders of the German authorities."[1242] A Banderite report on the situation in July-August 1942 in the Southern Ukrainian Lands, which included the Donbas, offered a similar assessment of the police there: "The Germans have deprived the Ukrainian auxiliary police of their national visage and use the force in its predatory activity among the Ukrainian population, assigning it the most vexatious tasks, e.g., robbing bread, taking produce from the population, hunting in the bazaars and on the streets for workers for Germany, etc....Especially cruel are the so-called Ukrainian police in the Donbas, which still wear armbands of blue and yellow, even though they cannot explain [the meaning of] these colors."[1243]

A Banderite leaflet, probably also from the second half of 1942 or from early 1943, criticized both the stationary and mobile Schutzmannschaften in the Reichskommissariat. "Police and battalions — they were supposed to be the nucleus of a Ukrainian army, but [are instead] camps in which the Germans strive to produce the type of a pogromist. What's being made is a colonial army, which will have, and here and there already has had, the task of destroying

---

1240 Shliakhtych, "Stvorennia ta funktsionuvannia mistsevoi dopomizhnoi politsii na Kryvorizhzhi," 11-14.
1241 Dobrovol's'kyi, *OUN na Donechchyni*, 6, 10, 79-80, 115, 163, 169-70.
1242 Ibid., 291-92.
1243 Peter Potichnyj Collection on Insurgency and Counter-Insurgency in Ukraine, University of Toronto, box 76, file "Povstans'kyi rukh. Pivden' Ukrainy"; TsDAHO, fond 57, op. 4, spr. 348. I am grateful to Yuri Radchenko for providing me with a transcript of this document.

Ukrainian villages, shooting its own population, and also becoming a terror and dealer of death for other nations conquered by the Germans." The document also warned the Ukrainian police: "Do not take part in actions to hunt for Jews; leave this 'honorable work' to the Germans."[1244] The Banderite disenchantment with the police did not escape the attention of the occupiers. A German document from July 1942 affirmed: "...the Banderite organizations ordered their members no matter what not to join the police, and if a member of the Bandera movement joins the police, then he is automatically excluded from the Bandera movement...."[1245]

I doubt that OUN-B as a whole had completely given up on the police. As we will soon see, it was able to entice thousands of policemen to desert German service, with their weapons, and join its newly created armed force, the Ukrainian Insurgent Army (UPA). The disenchantment with the police seems to have been greatest among Banderite activists in pre-1939 Soviet Ukraine, perhaps partly because it lost ground there to the Melnykites. Also, the activists in the Donbas and elsewhere in southern Ukraine were moving toward the new ideological postures that resulted in what has often been considered a programmatic turn: the program adopted at the Third Extraordinary Congress of OUN-B in August 1943 and the "Universal" and "Platform" of the Ukrainian Supreme Liberation Council of July 1944 offered the population, including national minorities, basic civil rights.[1246] But we will examine this ideological turn more closely in the next chapter.

1244 Peter Potichnyj Collection on Insurgency and Counter-Insurgency in Ukraine, University of Toronto, box 76, file "Lystivky 1943"; TsDAHO, fond 57 op. 4, spr. 342. I am grateful to Yuri Radchenko for providing me with a transcript of this document. UPA in Galicia in February 1944 issued a similar admonition to Ukrainian police not to take part in "the German pogroms." Pohl, *Nationalsozialistische Judenverfolgung in Ostgalizien*, p. 375.

1245 *Meldungen aus den besetzten Ostgebieten*, 3 July 1942, cited in Russian translation in Serhiichuk, *OUN-UPA v roky viiny*, 182.

1246 Armstrong, *Ukrainian Nationalism*, 118-23. The documents referred to are reprinted in Hunczak and Solchanyk, *Ukrains'ka suspil'no-politychna dumka*, 3:65-73, 97-103.

Desertions from German Service

Grzegorz Motyka, one of the first scholars to study UPA in considerable detail, estimated that four or five thousand policemen in
Volhynia deserted German service to join OUN-B's insurgent
army.[1247] Some scholars have written that "virtually all"[1248] or "the
absolute majority"[1249] of the Volhynian Schutzmänner deserted to
UPA in spring 1943, but local studies indicate that this view requires modification.

A little context is in order. As we have seen, at least a faction
within OUN-B was dissatisfied with the Schutzmannschaften, since
they served the interests of the Germans against the interests of the
Ukrainian population. And indeed, Ukrainian policemen in
Volhynia, who might have considered the murder of the Jews justified, were increasingly disturbed with the tasks they were assigned in regard to their own, Ukrainian population. Volunteers for
labor in the Reich had virtually dried up, and the authorities in the
Reichskommissariat demanded from the police ever harsher methods to fill ever increasing quotas for forced labor. The police were
expected to round up young Ukrainians as if they were stray cattle
and to shoot them if they were noncompliant.[1250] And since the forests of Volhynia served as a good base for Soviet partisan activity,
police were expected to implement draconian antipartisan
measures, such as killing the families of suspected partisans and
burning down villages suspected of harboring partisans.[1251] During
the course of the occupation, ninety-seven localities in Volhynia oblast were set on fire and destroyed.[1252]

But also, as the war progressed, and particularly after the battles of Stalingrad (February 1943) and Kursk (July 1943), it became

---

1247 Motyka, *Ukraińska partyzantka*, 194-97. Jared McBride, in his dissertation on the
      violence in Volhynia, found that the number of deserters to UPA mentioned in
      the literature ranged from three to six thousand. McBride, "'A Sea of Blood and
      Tears,'" 292.
1248 Snyder, *Reconstruction of Nations*, 162.
1249 Dereiko, *Mistsevi formuvannia*, 99.
1250 Kentii, *Narysy*, 142.
1251 These activities are described with reference to southern Belarus in Dean, *Col-
      laboration in the Holocaust*, 127-34.
1252 Kentii, *Narysy*, 139n.

clear that the Germans were on the run in the face of the Soviet advance. For the policemen, the previous advantages of German service were about to turn into severe liabilities, so they looked for opportunities elsewhere. Some did indeed join UPA, but others joined Waffen-SS Division Galizien or the nationalist force commanded by Taras Bulba-Borovets or independent nationalist partisan formations or the Soviet partisans or the Red Army.

Thanks to the researches of Klymenko and Tkachov on the somewhat exceptional Kremenets region of Volhynia, we have a better idea about whom these policemen were deserting to. Few Kremenets-region policemen went over to the Soviet partisans — only 6. But 97 former policemen and Schutzbattalion men joined the Red Army. And over 20 served in the American army and French Foreign Legion.[1253] By late summer 1942, policemen were already considering participating in a Ukrainian national resistance to the German occupation. In August 1942, the leadership of the Dederkaly raion[1254] police established an OUN group of eighteen policemen. In September 1942 seven policemen of the Dederkaly raion police, to avoid repression by the Germans, fled to the forest, where insurgent groups were being formed by the Melnykites, but other policemen deserted to other Ukrainian partisan formations independent of OUN.

The largest mass desertion of Ukrainian police to Banderite and Melnykite armed units in the Kremenets region occurred in the second half of March 1943. At that time a Kremenets policeman intercepted a telephonogram from the German authorities ordering the arrest and disarming of "the untrustworthy element" in the police. The interceptor reported what he found to Mykhailo Danyliuk, responsible for military affairs in the Kremenets circle for OUN-M.

1253 Klymenko and Tkachov, *Ukraintsi v politsii v reikhskomisariati "Ukraina,"* 266. Lev Hloba, who served in the militia in Kremenets, then in the police, and then in Schutzbattalion 102, ended up deserting to the French Resistance. He was awarded the Croix de Guerre 1939-1945. "Hloba, Lev (Leon)," *Traces of War,* https://www.tracesofwar.com/persons/66692/Hloba-Lev-Leon.htm (accessed 3 October 2020). Zorian Stech delivered a talk about Hloba in the Toronto center of the Shevchenko Scientific Society of Canada on 18 September 2020 (I was able to attend the talk remotely).

1254 Velyki Dederkaly (P Dederkały Wielkie) is east of Kremenets.

Danyliuk and fellow Melnykite Mykola Niedzvedsky ("Khrin") organized the transfer of weapons and ammunition to the forest during the night of 22 March. Over a hundred policemen deserted,
forty-five of whom joined Niedzvedsky's insurgent unit. In that
same month UPA units attacked Shumsk, and the entire Shumsk
raion police deserted to the insurgents with their weapons. In early
1944 dozens of policemen from Sumy oblast, in the far northeast of
Ukraine, who had been evacuated to Kremenets, also joined
UPA.[1255]

As UPA gained in strength and the Germans grew ever more
distrustful of the Ukrainians in their police force, policemen were
put in a very difficult situation. On the one hand, UPA could kill
them for serving the Germans too slavishly, and on the other, the
Germans could arrest them on suspicion of contacts with UPA.[1256]
UPA killed five Kremenets-region policemen who preferred serving the Germans to cooperating with themselves.[1257]

Although the issue of desertions requires further research, the
massive presence of former policemen in UPA and other nationalist
formations is not in question. Numerous Soviet trials of former policemen record their defection to UPA.[1258] Dozens of Ukrainian

---

1255 Klymenko and Tkachov, *Ukraintsi v politsii v reikhskomisariati "Ukraina,"* 76-78, 265.

1256 Vasyl Yashan, who was deputy head of the civil administration of Stanyslaviv
oblast, tried to protect the police in his jurisdiction and to this end held a discussion with local UPA commander Vasyl Andrusiak ("Rizun") on 3 May 1944.
Iashan, *Pid brunatnym chobotom*, 145-46; see also 120, where he laments the "un-
enviable situation" of the police, caught between the Germans and UPA.

1257 Klymenko and Tkachov, *Ukraintsi v politsii v reikhskomisariati "Ukraina,"* 78, 265.

1258 Yakiv Ostrovsky, whom we met earlier as a militiaman and policeman (see
above, 79-80, 252), joined UPA in July 1943. USHMM, RG-31.018M, reel 29;
HDA SBU Ternopil oblast, spr. 33531, vol. 5, f. 35. From the Extraordinary State
Commission: USHMM RG-22.002M; TsGAOR (now GARF), fond 7021, op. 71,
spr. 52, "Zakliuchenie," 30 November 1944, f. 37. The document just cited lists
former policemen in Klesiv (P Klesów), east of Sarny in Rivne oblast, who were
now in "bands of 'UPA.'" Oleksii Senchyshyn served in the police in the area
of Vyshnivets and went for training at the police school in Kremenets. He
joined UPA May 1943, at first as a rank-and-file soldier, but was then promoted
to *chotovyi*, with thirty men under his command. Later, in 1944, he deserted to
the Soviet partisans, and UPA murdered his wife in retaliation. USHMM RG-
31.018M, reel 60, frames 2340-42, 2346, 2353-54; HDA SBU Ternopil, spr. 18474,
ff. 54-56, 59v-60, 84-85. Oleksandr Drobatiuk of Staryi Vyshnivets joined the
militia in July 1941, then served in the police, then deserted to UPA and was

members of Schutzmannschaft Battalion 118 joined UPA in Vo-
hynia,[1259] and the supreme commander of UPA, Roman Shukhevych, had been an officer in Schutzmannschaft Battalion 201.
Mykola Kovtoniuk (Yakymchuk), the commandant of the Lutsk
city police in 1941 and an OUN-B leader in Volhynia, became first
commander of the Turiv military district of UPA. Stepan Yanishev-
sky, deputy police commander in Vinnytsia in 1941-43, was acting
head of the Zahrava military district in 1944. Omelian Hrabets,
head of the regional police in Rivne in 1941 and OUN-B leader in
the Rivne region in 1941-42, was commander of UPA-South in 1943-
44.[1260]

The strong presence of police in nationalist guerrilla units is
reflected in Jewish survivor testimony. Aron Babouch, who was
hiding in the vicinity of Volodymyr-Volynskyi, thought that the
Germans had deliberately left the Banderite policemen behind to
fight the Soviets.[1261] Jacob Biber had been working as a tanner for a
Ukrainian in Siomaky (P Siomaki), not far from Lutsk, when a nationalist guerrilla unit was formed.[1262] He and his Ukrainian employer had rather different feelings about the significance of the
new armed force. His employer, Zachar, returned from town and
ran into the barn where Biber and his wife were staying. He excit-
edly told them: "The militz has split from the Germans....Our boys
have run off on orders from the nationalist underground. They
grabbed a lot of ammunition from the Germans and spread
throughout the village. They are preparing for a battle that will be

---

arrested by SMERSH in 1944. RG-31.018M, reel 61, frame 531; HDA SBU Ternopil oblast, spr. 27414, f. 169.

1259 Rudling, "Terror and Local Collaboration," 205.
1260 Katchanovski, "Terrorists or National Heroes," 11-12.
1261 Shoah Foundation, 26557 Aron Baboukh, 86.
1262 Biber, *Survivors*, 137-38. Biber referred to the forces of Taras Bulba-Borovets in
his memoirs. Bulba-Borovets commanded a conglomerate of different nationalist forces; among those under his command were insurgents associated with
OUN-M as well as the Mitrynga group of OUN-B. However, it is not certain
whether Biber was referring to the Bulba forces, as distinct from the Banderite
UPA, since these formations were often conflated in Jewish survivor testimony. See below, 363-64. Although Siomaky was located in territory that was
mainly controlled by OUN-B, scattered Melnykite formations were also active
in the vicinity. Armstrong, *Ukrainian Nationalism*, 108.

decisive in our struggle for independence....We are a force under the name of Taras Bulba." Biber said that he and his wife were not sure how good that news was, but they were glad that the Germans were losing ground. Zachar was sure that this was good news for the Bibers. That night as the nationalist unit marched through the village, Zachar told them: "From now on, you are free people." But Biber wrote in his memoirs: "We did not feel free. We had mixed emotions about the force going by. We knew how many killers there were in those lines of marching men to whom independence meant a chance to fill their own pockets." One of the "Bulbas" they encountered walking on the road one day was Ivan Riszhey [Ryzhy], whom they had known since childhood. Earlier he had volunteered for the militia under the Germans and once took a German soldier's place so that he could shoot Jews all day.[1263]

* *
*

Certain things are very clear about the police. They supplied manpower for the persecution and then systematic liquidation of the Jewish population throughout Distrikt Galizien and Reichskommissariat Ukraine; given the overextension of the German military and administration and the police's wealth of local knowledge, their aid in the Final Solution was indispensable. The Holocaust was a policy driven by the Germans, not by the Ukrainian nationalists, although the nationalists did not object to the murder of the Jews—it fit their vision of a monolithic Ukrainian nation state, a Ukraine for Ukrainians. We also know that, initially, both factions of OUN hoped to control the police force, seeing it as the nucleus of a Ukrainian army and as a vehicle for spreading their movement in pre-1939 Soviet Ukraine. The Germans did what they could to eliminate OUN influence, but OUN was always able to retain a foothold in the police. As German occupation policy became more desperate and ruthless, as manifested, for example, in the roundup of Ukrainian youth off the streets for forced labor in the Reich, the

---

1263 Biber, *Survivors*, 135-38.

population's disenchantment with the Germans and the nationalists' disappointment in the police increased. The policemen's own
situation grew more precarious as the German occupation faltered
and the prospect of a return to Soviet rule became imminent. Police
began to desert to nationalist formations already by late summer
1942, but after spring 1943 the desertions intensified. The Ukrainian
nationalist insurgency was not the beneficiary of all desertions, but
several thousand men — armed, trained in the use of their weapons,
and experienced in killing — rallied to the insurgency. Some of them
became commanders and officers in UPA. Thus OUN welcomed
into its army and placed in leadership positions many men who had
killed many innocent people.

7. The Fate of Jews in the Ukrainian Nationalist Insurgency

The Nationalist Insurgency

In 1942, at the same time that they were systematically murdering Jewish communities across Ukraine, the Germans ratcheted up the severity of their occupation policies, demanding ever more forced laborers for the Reich and repressing ever more ruthlessly any real or suspected activity by Soviet partisans. German policies in the Reichskommissariat Ukraine, including Volhynia, were excessively brutal and provoked acts of spontaneous resistance by ordinary Ukrainians. Soviet partisan activity was well underway by spring 1942, and the heavily forested region of Polissia, stretching across northern Ukraine from Volhynia to Chernihiv, furnished excellent terrain for partisan warfare.

The nationalists had originally hoped that the Germans would allow them to create their own Ukrainian state, allied to the New Order in Europe. That hope was slow to die, even after the Germans arrested the Banderite leadership in July 1941 and repressed the Melnykites in Kyiv in the winter of 1941-42. There was always hope that the Germans would come to their senses and harness the nationalism of the non-Russian peoples of the USSR. Partially generating that hope was the relatively pro-Ukrainian stance of Alfred Rosenberg, Reich Minister for the Occupied Eastern Territories. But Rosenberg did not actually exercise much influence, and men full of contempt for the Slavic populations, notably Himmler and Reichskommissar Erich Koch, determined policy in the occupied territories. Now Ukrainian nationalists faced a situation in which their association with the Germans was compromising them in the eyes of the population of Volhynia and the only organized resistance to the Germans came from Soviet partisans. Moreover, communism had enjoyed considerable popularity in Volhynia in the interwar era,[1264] before the policies of the First Soviets

---

1264 Himka, "Western Ukraine between the Wars," 407.

discredited it and before the nationalist militias killed pro-Soviet elements in the summer of 1941; but by the next summer communism, or at least the pro-Soviet resistance movement, could tap into the sentiments and personnel of the interwar movement. Could the nationalists afford to just step aside and watch the Volhynian population's loyalties shift from themselves to the Soviets?

The situation in Galicia was quite different. Ukrainian national consciousness had always been strongest here, and anti-Soviet attitudes remained intense. There was no Soviet partisan activity in Galicia until Sydir Kovpak made a raid across Polissia and then entered Galicia south of Ternopil in early July 1943. These Soviet guerillas could survive in Galicia only for a matter of weeks. According to John A. Armstrong, "it appears that a decisive factor in the rapid destruction of the band was the hostile attitude of the Galician population."[1265] Ukrainians in Distrikt Galizien had less reason to be dissatisfied with the German occupation than Ukrainians in the Reichskommissariat. Although Galician Ukrainians also experienced the roundups of youth for labor, the regime here was generally less repressive, and Ukrainians were favored over their archrivals, the Poles. The differences in attitude between Galicia and Volhynia are illustrated by developments in the spring and summer of 1943. At that time, the Ukrainian Insurgent Army (UPA) was at its military height in Volhynia, while in Galicia tens of thousands of young men volunteered to serve in a German unit, the Waffen-SS Division Galizien. UPA largely dissolved in Volhynia after the Soviets drove out the Germans. It moved its main base of operations to Galicia, where the Carpathian mountains provided suitable terrain for guerilla forces. UPA flourished in Galicia for several years and received considerable support from the Ukrainian population, but it was not fighting the Germans, who were already defeated, but the Soviets.

The anti-German resistance of Ukrainian nationalist forces in Volhynia was constrained by several factors. Obviously, this was a classic case of asymmetrical warfare: the Wehrmacht was a mighty,

---

1265 Armstrong, *Ukrainian Nationalism*, 110.

modern army with tanks, planes, and artillery, while the nationalist forces consisted of scattered bands in the woods, armed mainly with rifles and cold weapons. Like all guerillas, the nationalist insurgents avoided pitched battles and instead organized smaller operations, such as ambushing a German patrol, interrupting the deportation of Ukrainian youth for forced labor in Germany, assassinating representatives of German authority, and freeing prisoners. Unlike the Soviet partisans, however, the nationalists had no interest in sabotage operations that would have undermined the German war effort against the Soviets, such as derailing supply trains destined for the Eastern front.[1266] They were quite happy to have the Germans and the Soviets destroy each other. Also constraining the anti-German resistance was that the nationalists had more than the Germans to reckon with. They fought Soviet partisans, sometimes in small pitched battles. UPA, moreover, started killing the Polish population of Volhynia. The ethnic cleansing resulted in clashes with the underground Polish Home Army (AK), spontaneously formed Polish self-defense units, and largely Polish detachments serving either with the Soviet partisans or in the Schutzmannschaften (replacing Ukrainian policemen who had been deserting in mass). In addition to fighting against several enemies, the Ukrainian nationalist insurgents had a pragmatic reason why they could not concentrate on anti-German resistance: it did not make sense to squander military resources on an enemy that was already being pummeled by another of its enemies, the Soviets. Thus the anti-German resistance was calibrated to do two things: to demonstrate that the nationalists had turned against the hated occupiers to defend the local Ukrainian population and to draw the discontented to their own forces rather than to the Soviet partisans. A sign that OUN-B had turned against the Germans was a change in vocabulary. Instead of calling the Germans *nimtsi*, the normal

---

1266 A Jew who ended up in an UPA unit wrote in his memoir: "Our policy was not to blow up trains or sabotage German supply lines. This would have helped the Red Army on the Eastern Front, and why should we aid our mortal enemies?" Heiman, "We Fought for Ukraine," 42. Heiman was not the author of the memoir. See below, 429.

Ukrainian word, the Banderites began calling them *nimaky*, intended to be as derogatory as *moskali* for Russians and *liakhy* for Poles.

The first to offer resistance to the Germans, albeit in a very limited way, was Taras Bulba-Borovets. In 1941 he had commanded a fairly large militia force in Polissia called Polis'ka Sich. Based in Volhynia and eventually establishing headquarters in Olevsk, in northern Zhytomyr oblast, Polis'ka Sich engaged in the same kind of activities as the OUN militias, that is, cooperating with the Germans, disarming or executing Red Army stragglers, and killing communists and Jews.[1267] As in the case of the OUN militias, the Germans dissolved Polis'ka Sich in November 1941 in favor of the Schutzmannschaften under direct German control. But Bulba-Borovets reactivated his forces in the spring of 1942, now with an anti-German orientation and with a new name: the Ukrainian Insurgent Army (UPA). The Bulbaite forces were not under the control of OUN. Instead, Bulba-Borovets oriented himself on the leadership of the Ukrainian People's Republic in exile, headed by Andrii Livytsky in Warsaw. Soon, though, Bulba-Borovets was able to attract volunteers from OUN, both from the Melnyk faction and from the dissident Mitrynga faction that had formerly been aligned with OUN-B. His movement grew over the course of 1942 and early 1943 and so did its resistance to the Germans.

Meanwhile, OUN-B gathered its forces but was hesitant to engage in anti-German activities. In May 1943 OUN-B undertook negotiations with Bulba-Borovets and the Melnykites to form a united movement, but the negotiations failed because OUN-B was unwilling to subordinate itself to any leadership it did not itself control. After the failure of the talks, the leader of OUN-B in Volhynia, Dmytro Kliachkivsky, appropriated the name UPA for his own

---

1267 The best work on the Bulba forces is that of Jared McBride. Aside from his dissertation ("'A Sea of Blood and Tears'"), see McBride, "'To Be Stored Forever,'" which discusses some of the recent Ukrainian historiography on Borovets, and USHMM, *Encyclopedia of Camps and Ghettos*, s.v. "Olevsk," by Jared McBride and Alexander Kruglov. Although silent on many of the issues that relate to the present monograph, Borovets' autobiography is quite interesting: Bul'ba-Borovets', *Armiia bez derzhavy*.

Banderite forces, and in July and August the Banderites in Volhynia successfully attacked both the various Melnykite units and then those of Bulba-Borovets. After these encounters, the Banderites were able to incorporate many of the fighters from the units they defeated;[1268] they also thus became the primary force for nationalistically inclined policemen to desert to. They even became powerful enough to institute a draft, and many young Volhynian Ukrainians were forced to enter their ranks. Before long the Banderite UPA had a force of perhaps forty thousand men.

In discussing these events, Armstrong remarked that Kliachkivsky had adopted the name UPA "to secure the prestige attached to it by 'Bul'ba's' earlier start."[1269] One of the consequences of this decision was to create confusion in the Volhynian population about terminology. This confusion has affected Jewish survivor testimony, as we have already briefly noted in the previous chapter,[1270] and as we shall see again as we proceed in this chapter. A Jewish survivor blamed Bulbaites for killing three Jews in the woods near Krutyliv (P Kręciłów), north of Husiatyn in Ternopil oblast.[1271] However, the Bulba forces had never entered that region, which was quite far south of their base of operations. On the other hand, an eyewitness of a pogrom organized by the genuine Bulbaites, interviewed in Olevsk in 2011 or 2012 by Jared McBride, referred to the Bulbaites as "*banderovtsy.*"[1272] A report of Rivne oblast partisan commander Vasyl Behma, dated 11 April 1943, stated: "The nationalists are conducting mass terror against the Polish population. In villages in the raion centers of Stepan [P Stepań], Derazhne [P Derażne], Rafalivka, and Klevan the Bulbaites do not kill, but butcher each and every one, old and small, and completely burn down Polish settlements."[1273] Yet this was surely the Banderite UPA,

---

1268 Bulba and OUN-M forces were severely weakened in Volhynia as of mid-August 1943 and for the most part vacated the region in November 1943. Armstrong, *Ukrainian Nationalism*, 113.
1269 Ibid., 112.
1270 See above, 355.
1271 Weissbrod, *Death of a Shtetl*, 65.
1272 McBride, "Ukrainian Holocaust Perpetrators."
1273 Cited, almost surely in Ukrainian translation from Russian, in Il'iushyn, "Boiovi dii," 250.

which was then several weeks into its massacre of Volhynian Poles, a project that Bulba-Borovets roundly condemned.[1274] Jewish survivor Moshe Vaysberg tried to explain the taxonomy of the murderous nationalist bands in Volhynia. He identified them as "1) the UNRA (*Ukrain'ska Narodova Revoliutsiina Armiia*), headed by Bandera..., and 2) UPA (*Ukrains'ka Povstancha Armiia*), headed by Bulba."[1275] In fact, though, Vaysberg had matters backward: the UNRA was what Bulba renamed his forces after the Banderites had appropriated the name UPA. In these cases just cited, it has been possible to spot the confusion and clarify the situation. But in a number of other accounts it is not clear, in spite of the terminology employed, whether the Banderites or Bulbaites were responsible for the murders ascribed to them. For that reason, I will also reference testimonies that refer to the Bulbaites, even though this was not an OUN formation. Local studies should eventually be able to sort things out.

Before proceeding to the fate of the Jews in the insurgency, I have to sketch some context that helps clarify why they became particularly endangered as the Red Army closed in. That is when the Banderite UPA launched a paranoid cleansing of its own ranks and of various elements in the general population. In the words of Anatol Kentii:

> An intensification of the struggle between Ukrainian insurgents and Red partisans at the end of 1943 was objectively inevitable. Because the front line was rapidly approaching Western Ukrainian lands, which constituted the rear of the liberation movement, the attempts of the partisans to consolidate themselves in the western region mortally endangered UPA. After the partisans came the Red Army, and after it Soviet power with its punitive-repressive apparatus. In order to properly oppose this threat, the Ukrainian nationalists had to

---

1274 In an open letter to the OUN-B leadership, Bulba-Borovets deplored the opening of a "Polish front": "The axe and the flail have gone into motion. Whole families are butchered and hanged, and Polish settlements are set on fire. The 'hatchet men,' to their shame, butcher and hang defenseless women and children....By such work Ukrainians not only do a favor for the [German] SD, but also present themselves in the eyes of the world as barbarians." Polishchuk, *Rik 1943*, 14.

1275 YVA, RG 104, folder 441, Moshe Vaysberg.

dismantle the anti-German front and, even before the arrival of Soviet forces, cleanse their territories of Red partisans and those elements who were considered to be "agents of Moscow."[1276]

In the course of its growth, UPA had drawn Eastern Ukrainians and even Russians into its ranks, mainly deserters from German service. OUN-B marked them for liquidation as the Soviets approached. Yurii Stelmashchuk, an UPA officer under the command of Dmytro Kliachkivsky, testified during interrogation that Kliachkivsky had orally ordered the "physical liquidation of all members of UPA of Russian nationality. The directive suggested to carry out the eradication [*istreblenie*] under the pretext of members of UPA being transferred to special 'Russian legions.'" Still another secret order "suggested to physically destroy all family members of persons suspected of anti-OUN attitudes, not excluding breast-feeding children nor women nor old people." All these secret orders, according to Stelmashchuk, emanated from "the central leadership of OUN."[1277]

Danylo Shumuk, a native Volhynian serving as a political instructor in UPA, was shocked by the murder of sixteen Ukrainian families, including children, by SB OUN in January 1944. In his memoirs he recalled conversations he had had about this incident with representatives of the middle OUN leadership, specifically with Oleksandr Prysiazhniuk ("Mitla"), SB *referent* for the land leadership of the Northwest Ukrainian Lands, and Panas Matviichuk ("Krylach"), commander of the rear (*komendant zapillia)* in the Turiv region of UPA's Army North—Shumuk designated him as "oblast leader." The OUN-UPA leadership justified the atrocities that disturbed Shumuk as the preemptive murder of potential Soviet agents:

> "Soon the Soviet forces will occupy all Volhynia. Do you want us to leave a network of Soviet agents behind to await their arrival?" Krylach asked.

1276 Kentii, "'Dvofrontova' borot'ba," 205.
1277 USHMM RG-31.026, reel 37, frames 204-05; TsDAHO, fond 1, op. 22, spr. 861, ff. 47-48.

"We should root out everyone the Soviet authorities can rely on while we still can," added Mitla....

"Do you know what the Bolsheviks did in prisons when they retreated before the German advance?" Krylach asked. "Were you in Lutsk, and did you see how many young people were shot there without any investigation or trial?"[1278]

Krylach, of course, was reminding Shumuk that preemptive murder had become the norm from the moment the German-Soviet war broke out.

Stelmashchuk also testified during interrogation that Kliachkivsky had given him an oral order to physically liquidate "all Soviet POWs located on the territory of the western oblasts of Ukraine as facilitating the spread of Bolshevism."[1279] Ukrainian memoirs bear this out. A Melnykite remembered that "there came an order to destroy the undependable element." The most tragic result of this, he felt, was the Banderites' murder of Ukrainian POWs who had been released from the camps and were living in the villages of Volhynia.[1280] A Ukrainian Baptist remembered the same: UPA murdered Soviet POWs working for farmers out of fear they would join the Soviet partisans.[1281]

Such a paranoid mood would not bode well for Jewish survivors hiding in the forests of Volhynia.

UPA Attitudes towards the Jewish Minority

In the year preceding the formation of the Banderite UPA, OUN-B realized that its association with the Germans' mass murder of the Jews was becoming a liability in the international arena. Having at least tentatively broken with the Germans by the beginning of 1942, it now had to work on presenting itself as a movement more appealing to the Western Allies. In April 1942, the second conference of OUN resolved: "Notwithstanding the negative attitude to Jews

---

1278 Shumuk, *Life Sentence*, 116-17.
1279 USHMM RG-31.026, reel 37, frames 204-05; TsDAHO, fond 1, op. 22, spr. 861, ff. 47-48.
1280 Shtul', *V im"ia pravdy*, 30.
1281 Podvorniak, *Viter z Volyni*, 143, 186. See also Polishchuk, *Rik 1943*, 28, and Biber, *Survivors*, 146.

as an instrument of Muscovite-Bolshevik imperialism, we consider it inexpedient at the present moment in the international situation to take part in anti-Jewish activity, in order not to become a blind tool in foreign hands and to not turn the attention of the masses away from the main enemies."[1282] Nonetheless, on the first anniversary of the proclamation of the renewal of Ukrainian statehood, in the summer of 1942, OUN-B distributed a leaflet throughout Western Ukraine that took pride in the "partisan actions" the organization had engaged in during the previous summer and its participation in the physical liquidation of "the Muscovite-Jewish occupier."[1283]

In October 1942 in Lviv, OUN-B held its first military conference. No documents emanating directly from that conference have survived, but an account of its decisions was passed on to Soviet security organs by a member of OUN who was an informant. The conference decided that all Poles should be resettled from Ukrainian territory, with the right to take some of their property. Those who refused to leave should be destroyed. This was the prelude to a major ethnic cleansing action against the Poles, which was to claim tens of thousands of victims. The conference also made a decision with regard to the Jewish population: "The Jews should not be destroyed, but resettled from Ukraine, after having granted them the possibility to take out some of their property. It is necessary to be careful with them in as much as they have great influence in England and America."[1284] OUN had long believed that Jews had disproportionate control over the foreign policies of the democratic

---

1282 Polishchuk, *Integralny nacjonalizm ukraiński*, 3:220, citing DARO, fond R-30, opys 1, spr. 10; opys 2, spr. 1. Polishchuk wrote that Hunczak and Solchanyk, *Ukrains'ka suspil'no-politychna dumka*, omits this passage; however, the documentation of this particular conference is not included in the collection, so the passage could not have been omitted. The passage can also be found in the Banderite organ *Ideia i chyn* 1, no. 1 (1 November 1942): 14; however, the periodical did not register the date of the conference.

1283 Kentii, *Narysy*, 135.

1284 Shapoval, "Pro vyznannia I znannia," 18, citing HDA SBU, Kyiv, fond 13, spr. 372, vol. 5, ff. 37-38. See also Carynnyk, "Knife in the Back," 25-26.

countries,[1285] and this conviction was to persist for a long time after the war.[1286]

It is in this context of looking to America and Britain that we should understand the programmatic changes that OUN-B adopted at its Third Extraordinary Great Assembly of OUN, held in Zolota Sloboda (P Słoboda Złota), a village southwest of Ternopil in Galicia, on 21-25 August 1943. By this time the Germans had been defeated at Stalingrad as well as at Kursk, the latter city not even 150 kilometers from the border of the Ukrainian SSR. The Western Allies were the nationalists' only hope, and to actualize the possibility of American and British aid for their cause required some programmatic window dressing. The materials and decisions of the Third Extraordinary Great Assembly broke from OUN's past positions by espousing equal rights for national minorities in the Ukrainian State, although it also included a contemptuous reference to Jewish passivity in the Holocaust:

> The Ukrainian nation, which does not want to allow itself to be slaughtered without defending themselves in the manner of the Jews, must oppose in an organized way and with arms the pretensions of the Bolshevik imperialists....
> I. Programmatic decisions....In the ranks of OUN, Ukrainian peasants, workers, and intelligentsia struggle....for a new state order and a new social structure....
> 11. For the full right of national minorities to develop their own national culture, individual in form and content.
> 12. For the equality of all citizens of Ukraine, regardless of their nationality, in state and civic rights and responsibilities, for the equal right to work, wages, and rest.
> Political decisions....

1285 See above, 166. For further exploration of this topic, see Himka, "What Were They Thinking," esp. the section on "Other Stereotypes."

1286 The Melnykite Mykola P. Kudelia wrote in his memoirs in 1997 that the nationalists hoped, especially after Churchill's "Iron Curtain" speech in Fulton, MO, that the democratic Allies would soon begin a war against Bolshevism, "but world Jewry, headed by the American President Roosevelt, and the Jewish directors of the Muscovite Kremlin did not allow this to happen." Kudelia, *Kriz' buri lykholit'*, 72.

14. The national minorities of Ukraine, conscious of their common fate with the Ukrainian nation, fight together with it for the Ukrainian State.[1287]

Declarations and deeds did not match. At the same time as OUN-B was proclaiming equal rights for national minorities, it was also killing Polish civilians en masse in Volhynia. UPA officer Yurii Stelmashchuk confessed to the following during his interrogation by the Rivne NKVD on 20 February 1945:

> On 29 and 30 August 1943 [not even a week after the Third Great Assembly] I with my unit, which numbered seven hundred armed bandits, at the order of the Commander of the Military Circle "Oleh,"[1288] slaughtered, with no exceptions, the entire Polish population on the territory of Holoby (P Hołoby), Kovel, Sedlyshche (P Siedliszcze), Matsiiv, and Liuboml (P Luboml) raions, robbing all their movable property and burning all their real estate.
> Altogether in those raions on 29 and 30 August 1943, I slaughtered and shot over fifteen thousand civilians, among them old people, women, and children.
> We did this as follows:
> After we drove the entire Polish population, each and every one of them, into one place, we would surround them and start the slaughter. When there was no longer a single one of them left alive, we dug large pits, threw the corpses into them, covered them with earth to hide traces of the horrific mass grave, started huge fires on top of it, and went further on our way.
> In this way we travelled from village to village until we had destroyed the entire population, over fifteen thousand people.
> We took all the livestock, valuables, property, and food, but set fire to the buildings and the rest of the property.[1289]

1287 Hunczak and Solchanyk, *Ukrains'ka suspil'no-politychna dumka*, 3:64-71. The materials of the Third Extraordinary Great Assembly have been published in English translation in Potichnyj and Shtendera, *Political Thought*, 333-53.

1288 "Oleh" was the pseudonym of Mykola Yakymchuk, who was commander of UPA's Turiv Military Circle.

1289 USHMM RG-31.026, reel 37, frames 199-200; TsDAHO, fond 1, op. 22, spr. 861, ff. 42-43. The same is in Polishchuk, *Integralny nacjonalizm ukraiński*, 4:457, citing acts of spr. 1647 of the NKVD of Rivne oblast, from a microfilm in DARO. Stelmashchuk later, at his trial, stated that his unit killed only five thousand, not fifteen thousand Poles. Ibid., 4:464. Later in the trial he said that "Savur" (Dmytro Kliachkivsky) and "Oleh" (Mykola Yakymchuk) had summoned him and demanded that he destroy the Poles. The murders were supposed to take place 25-

July and August 1943 were, in fact, the months of the most intense ethnic cleansing of the Poles in Volhynia, probably accounting for well over half of the mass killings in that year.[1290] OUN-UPA's treatment of the Poles is indicative of how little the August 1943 statements on the rights of national minorities were implemented in practice.

Before turning to UPA's expressed attitudes to the Jewish minority, two absences should be noted. The first absence was delineated by the most conceptually-oriented historian of Ukraine, Ivan Lysiak-Rudnytsky. He was responding to statements by OUN veteran Myroslav Prokop that in 1943 and later OUN-B was not xenophobic and chauvinistic. Rudnytsky countered:

> As we all know, there occurred in Ukraine during the Nazi occupation an unprecedented tragedy: the total genocide of the Jewish population. Responsibility for this terrible crime falls upon the German Nazi regime, although one cannot deny that some Ukrainians (the organs of the local administration, the "Ukrainian" police) also played an auxiliary role. Who was called upon to protest in the name of the Ukrainian people against Hitlerite criminality? Given the situation at that time, only the nationalist underground operated independently of the occupying authorities. After all, OUN, especially the Banderite OUN, held illegal conferences, promulgated various declarations, published an uncensored press, and so forth. Therefore, there was no objective obstacle to OUN-R [OUN-B] condemning the genocide of the Jews and warning Ukrainians not to take part in Nazi bestialities. There are situations when it is impermissible to remain silent, because whoever has the ability to protest and does not do so shows by this that they are in agreement. The silence of the OUN

---

30 August and to be conducted by both UPA and SB OUN units. Ibid., 4:467. And again in October, Kliachkivsky ordered him to murder the Poles who could not be killed in August because of well armed resistance. Ibid., 4:468.

1290 Władysław Siemaszko and Ewa Siemaszko put the total number of Poles murdered in Volhynia in 1943 at 33,347-33,454 (of whom 18,186-18,208 were known by name); July accounted for 10,473-10,527 (5595-5597 known by name) and August for 8280-8298 (5441-5447 known by name). These numbers refer to Poles murdered in 1943 "by OUN-UPA and Ukrainian policemen." Siemaszko and Siemaszko, *Ludobójstwo*, 2:1045. By July and August so many Ukrainian policemen had deserted German service that the Germans recruited Poles to replace them.

camp in the face of the tragedy of Ukrainian Jewry is very elo-quent.[1291]

The second absence to note is that OUN-UPA never estab-lished an organization like Żegota, which the Polish underground set up to aid the Jewish population.

Antisemitic statements continued to appear in various texts associated with OUN-B. In August 1943 the Banderites issued a leaflet to Ukrainians of the Chełm region and Podlachia that stated: "...The eternal enemy of Ukraine, Moscow, sends bands of Gypsies, Muscovites, Jews, and other rabble, the so-called 'red partisans' for the destruction of the Ukrainian nation."[1292] A one-page, typewrit-ten leaflet dated 31 December 1943 appealed to the youth of Volhynia not to treat Eastern Ukrainians with suspicion any more, because they too are taking part in the national struggle. One of the reasons that the East possesses less national consciousness, the leaf-let said, is that it has spent a quarter of a century "in Jewish-Bolshe-vik slavery." The leaflet does not seem to have been official, but ra-ther to have been authored by an Eastern Ukrainian serving in UPA.[1293] (At this time OUN-B, and especially its Youth organiza-tion, were killing many Eastern Ukrainian POWs.) Antisemitic songs continued to be created. The following song, sung to the tune of the popular folk song *I shumyt', i hude*, was entered into a note-book of songs and verses on 20 May 1944:

> І шумить і гуде ось повстанець іде
> Тікай, тікай вражий жиду [sic], бо загинеш як найде.
> Озирається жидяк і не знає що то є,
> А повстанець український вже по спині його б'є.
> Україна не для вас утікайте жидяки
> В Україні нашій славній запанують козаки.
> Чи то лях, чи москаль, чи румун, чи німак
> Всі покинуть Україну, як скоштують наш кулак.[1294]

1291 Rudnytsky, "Natsionalizm i totalitaryzm," 85.
1292 Serhiichuk, *OUN-UPA v roky viiny*, 366.
1293 Voron, "Druzi ukraintsi." USHMM RG-31.017M, reel 1; DARO, fond 30, op. 1, spr. 16, f. 52.
1294 There's a murmur and a buzz, see the insurgent on the move. / Flee, flee evil Jew, because you will perish if he finds you. / The kike looks around and

UPA kept count of the Jews surviving on territory it controlled. Reports from the commandant of the Iskra region noted "about one hundred" Jews in mid-September 1943 and "about two hundred" at the end of the month. A report from the Zahrava military district from mid-October noted: "A band of locals and Jews numbering about sixty persons, mainly poorly armed, are circulating in the regions of Ozersk [P Jeziersk] and Svarytsevychi [P Swarycewicze]" (north of Sarny, up against the Belarusian border).[1295]

A number of sources, of varied provenance, attest to an oral order for SB OUN and UPA to kill Jews they found. In early August 1943 all members of the SB OUN were summoned to a conference in the village of Diadkovychi (P Diatkowicze), about fifteen kilometers west of Rivne. According to Mykola Slobodiuk, testifying to the Soviet authorities on 13 April 1944, the security personnel were told "to annihilate all 'enemies of UPA,' which was to be understood as all Poles, Czechs, Jews, Komsomol members, Red Army officers, workers of the militia, and all Ukrainians who have even the slightest sympathy for Soviet power."[1296] Another UPA member told his NKVD interrogator that in the spring of 1943 his unit was instructed "to kill and rob all Poles and Jews on the territory of Dederkaly raion."[1297] A Polish testimony also spoke about an order to kill all the Poles, Jews, and communists in the region of Kysylyn (P Kisielin), east of Volodymyr-Volynskyi, and throughout Ukraine.

---

doesn't know what's happening, / And the Ukrainian insurgent is beating him on the back. / Ukraine is not for you; run away, you kikes. / In our glorious Ukraine the Cossacks are in charge. / Whether a Pole or a Russian or a Romanian or a German, / all of them will leave Ukraine when they get a taste of our fist. DARO, fond R30, opys 2, spr. 108, f. 57.

1295 "Zvit komandanta voiennoho terenu 'Iskra' Nevmyrushchoho za chas vid 12.08. po 12.09.1943," DARO, fond R30, opys 2, spr. 34, f. 94. "Zvit komandanta terenu 'Iskra' Nevmyrushchoho, 30.09.1943," DARO, fond R30, opys 2, spr. 34, f. 99. "Zvit ch. 1 hrupy UPA 'Zahrava' z nadraionu Stolyn, 17.10.1943," DARO, fond R30, opys 2, spr. 35, f. 100. Also published in Polishchuk, *Integralny nacjonalizm ukraiński*, 4:355.

1296 Rosov, "Chem zanimalas' SB OUN." See also McBride, *Contesting the Malyn Massacre*, 18.

1297 "Protokol doprosa Vozniuka Fedora Iradionovicha," https://szturman.live journal.com/270073.html (accessed 14 November 2020), citing HDA SBU, fond 13, spr. 1020, ff. 221-29.

The author of the testimony heard about this from a Ukrainian friend who fed them while he and his family hid in the forest.[1298] Some documentation emanating from OUN-UPA itself told the same story. An entry in an SB OUN operative's notebook dated 12 July 1943 read: "We liquidate all units which are not subordinated to UPA as opportunists. All national minorities."[1299] The notes appear to be from a training session for new recruits to OUN's security service. An order from the OUN leadership to the SB OUN, undated, but probably from the end of 1943, told security personnel to get rid of their uniforms, tridents, "all their bright ornaments. The SB is now underground....8. Return to conspiracy. 9. Persons against whom there are [compromising] materials, cannot be shot without informing the acting superior, except for Jews, Poles, and Germans."[1300] A report of Timofei Strokach, chief of staff of the Ukrainian partisan movement, dated 21 January 1944, stated that the partisans had captured a report from an SB UPA agent with the code name Zhburt (no date given). Zhburt's report said: "Earlier the SB issued an order to annihilate all Jews who are not specialists, this to be done conspiratorially, so that Jews and even our own people would not know; and that they put out propaganda that he went [sic] to the Bolsheviks."[1301] On 11 March 1944, by which time both Lutsk and Rivne, but not all of Volhynia, had been taken by Soviet forces, the OUN SB in Volhynia issued an order "to liquidate without delay communists and Jews."[1302] Yet another order said "to destroy NKVD personnel, informers, Jews, and Poles."[1303]

There was also an order to kill anyone who hid Jews. In the notebook of the SB OUN operative we have already cited, another entry read: "For hiding Jews or Poles, everyone will be shot."[1304] A

1298 Siemaszko and Siemaszko, *Ludobójstwo*, 1:150.

1299 DARO, fond R30, opys 2, spr. 15, f. 127.

1300 Polishchuk, *Integralny nacjonalizm ukraiński*, 4:420, citing DARO, fond R30, opys 2, spr. 15, ff. 53-54.

1301 Kentii, *Borot'ba proty UPA i natsionalistychnoho pidpillia*, book 1, 126. Zhburt's original report has not surfaced.

1302 Motyka, *Ukraińska partyzantka*, 293-94, citing TsDAVO, fond 3838, op. 1, spr. 57, f. 6. The order was signed by "Berkut."

1303 Motyka, *Ukraińska partyzantka*, 294, citing TsDAHO, fond 1, op. 23, spr. 928, f. 190.

1304 DARO, fond R30, opys 2, spr. 15, f. 126.

Jewish survivor recalled what happened in the village of Staryky (P Staryki) southeast of Radyvyliv in Rivne oblast:

> The Banderovtzis threatened the villagers that they would kill them if they helped Jews. Landau and I stayed with a kind-hearted peasant. We sewed hats and earned our keep.... At Easter 1943 there was a big conference of Banderovtzis in the village of Tinna [Tynne, southeast of Sarny in Rivne oblast]. Our host also attended the conference even though he was not one of the Banderovtzis. Yakov and I went to the village to watch the Easter festivities. We felt that many of the young people were lying in wait for us. We took a roundabout route back to our shelter. Late in the evening our host returned full of fear. He told us that at the conference an officer of the Banderovtzis gave a speech warning everyone that anyone who hid Jews would suffer the consequences.[1305]

Two Jewish survivor memoirs mention that the Banderites in the Kremenets region killed Ukrainians, including a priest, who gave shelter to Jews.[1306]

There are a few, but very few, indications of countervailing tendencies, which may have been connected more with the political leadership of OUN-B in Galicia (Mykola Lebed and others) than with the military and security leadership in Volhynia (Dmytro Kliachkivsky and others). I mentioned in the previous chapter that some Banderites had called for the Ukrainian police to refrain from participation in anti-Jewish actions.[1307] An order from the Supreme Leadership of UPA on 1 November 1943 told its propagandists to spread the word that in the future Ukrainian state Jews will be treated as citizens with full rights. It recommended that discussions on this topic be initiated with Jews who worked with UPA as physicians or in other professional capacities. Grzegorz Motyka saw this as the beginning of a change in attitude towards Jews, but I suspect the change in this case was limited to the sphere of

---

1305 Aharon Lifshitz, "The Struggle for Life," https://www.jewishgen.org/yizk or/rokitnoye/rok317.html (accessed 1 April 2020).

1306 Betsalel Shvarts, "The Holocaust," https://www.jewishgen.org/yizkor/krem enets/kre231.html (accessed 26 March 2020). Chayke Kiperman, "I Escaped the Germans and Bandera Gangs," https://www.jewishgen.org/yizkor/krem enets3/kre339.html#Page366 (accessed 27 March 2020).

1307 See above, 351.

propaganda.[1308] We have the notebook of a course conspectus written by a certain Mykhailo Smenchak, who was undergoing political training with OUN or UPA in 1943 in Volhynia. Lesson twelve concerned "our relations towards national minorities." About Jews he wrote down: "We consider them agents of Muscovite imperialism, formerly tsarist but now proletarian. Still, we have to first beat the Muscovites and then the surviving Jews (*zhydiv nedobytkiv*)."[1309] A letter of instruction the OUN-B leadership addressed to political referents of larger districts [*nadraiony*], dated 8 January 1944, said simply: "We do not attack [*ne vystupaiemo proty*] the Jews."[1310] This was a document addressed internally.

In early July 1944, just a few weeks before Galicia was reconquered by the Soviets, OUN-B held a conference establishing the Ukrainian Supreme Liberation Council (UHVR). Armstrong called the program of the UHVR a "mixture of social egalitarianism and romantic authoritarianism which characterized the new OUN-B ideology."[1311] The new organization's "Universal" stated: "We call upon all national minorities that live on Ukrainian lands to join in the Ukrainian liberation struggle. We guarantee them full civil rights in the Ukrainian state." Its "Platform" also promised "the guarantee of all civil rights to all national minorities in Ukraine."[1312] Yurii Stelmashchuk, a high-ranking officer in UPA and simultaneously deputy of the Land Leader of OUN in Volhynia, told his Soviet captors that UHVR was simply invented to deceive public opinion in the democratic countries. "...No such organization as the UHVR exists....UHVR exists only on paper, in OUN's printed

1308 Motyka, *Ukraińska partyzantka*, 295-96. When interrogated by the Soviets, UPA homeland leader (*kraiovyi providnyk*) Fedir Vorobets claimed to have recruited a Jew from Korosten, Zhytomyr oblast, to spread rumors that the Ukrainian nationalists considered Jews to be an "equal nation." "Vytiah z protokolu dopytu F. Vorobtsia," 691.

1309 USHMM RG-31.017M, reel 1; DARO, f. 30, op. 2, spr. 82, ff. 36v-37. There is a handwritten transcript of the same text in DARO, fond R30, op. 1, spr. 9, f. 3; I am grateful to Wiesław Tokarczuk for a photocopy.

1310 Serhiichuk, *OUN-UPA v roky viiny*, 379.

1311 Armstrong, *Ukrainian Nationalism*, 119.

1312 Hunczak and Solchanyk, *Ukrains'ka suspil'no-politychna dumka*, 3:99, 102. An English translation of the materials of the UHVR are in Potichnyj and Shtendera, *Political Thought*, 355-76.

propaganda."[1313] As noted earlier in this book, some of the figures associated with UHVR broke with the Bandera faction in emigration and were able to use their democratic program to find favor with the American CIA, which supported their publications.[1314] There were also some OUN-UPA propagandists in the underground in Ukraine who, after the Soviet reconquest, publicized the more democratic and socially conscious line of the UHVR.[1315]

A unique source that sheds light on the attitude towards national minorities is the diary of an UPA soldier by the name of Oleksandr Povshuk.[1316] He started his diary on 17 September 1939, when the Soviets took Volhynia, and he continued it until 3 August 1944, which must have been shortly before his death. He was seventeen when he started the diary. Under the Soviets he acquired a secondary education, and under the Nazis he became a teacher in Pyriatyn. When UPA first appeared on his horizon, he was not at all impressed. He wrote in his diary on 30 April 1943:

> I sit and my heart aches when it looks at our people....Instead of fighting with its open and dangerous enemy, they fight the Poles. At first in 1941 they worked for the Germans—they made trouble for the Bolsheviks, went with the Germans against the world, e.g., America, where there are Ukrainian millionaires who could have helped. Now the world press has covered the Ukrainians in shame, and the German is suffocating [us].[1317]

Two weeks later, on 15 May, he wrote:

> All the Poles are leaving their homes for the cities and are enrolling in the police; the German takes the rest to his own country. At present you do not see a single Pole who's living in the village. Our partisan movement hunts and destroys them....There are cases when the partisans pass through and the Germans don't touch them. These politics amaze me, and I am against this tactic of struggle. You will not win your independence by [taking] the life of the peaceful Polish

---

1313 USHMM RG-31.026, reel 37, frame 205; TsDAHO, fond 1, op. 22, spr. 861, f. 48.
1314 See above, 31.
1315 Their writings were the ones selected for inclusion in Potichnyj and Shtendera, *Political Thought.*
1316 USHMM RG-31.026, reel 1; TsDAHO, fond 7, op. 4, spr. 344. I have published a large selection of the diary entries in Himka, "Refleksje."
1317 Himka, "Refleksje," 183. And see above, 347.

population, when the enemy stands untouched; instead, two enslaved nations perish. If they want to destroy [the Poles], then at least
not now. People in the villages do not sleep and fear one another.[1318]

And again on 20 June, he wrote: "In the evening outside the
village they set Polish houses on fire. Everywhere they burn them.
In the village you do not see a single Pole."[1319]

But later that summer, like many other young Volhynians, he
was drafted into UPA. He felt that the rich peasants in his village
drafted him to get rid of him, because he thought too independently. Once drafted, Povshuk began to exhibit different attitudes. His vocabulary changed: he no longer wrote about "the German" as a *nimets'* but, using the recently adopted OUN-B term, *ni-
mak*. In August 1944, by which time the Germans had gone and the
Soviets had arrived in Volhynia, he read the text of the program
adopted at the Third Extraordinary Great Assembly of OUN-B a
year earlier. Evidently, it took time for such official programmatic
documents to reach the rank-and-file soldiers of UPA. Povshuk was
in ecstasy. He wrote in his diary on 5 August 1944: "Generally I will
say that after all my spiritual dissatisfactions and spontaneous reactions against injustice, the wonderful program of OUN, worked
out through life, relieves me. Here there is no chauvinism, as the
Bolsheviks call it. All minorities have equal rights in the Ukrainian
state." Then he listed all the social benefits for women, workers, and
peasants promised by the program. "I only realized that to fight
and die for such aims is a holy thing....[The local nationalists]
thought that Ukraine was for Ukrainians, which I opposed....And
the program written at the third congress of OUN I consider sacred,
something worth dying for."[1320]

In this same entry, however, he wrote that, while there should
be no discrimination by nation, it was something altogether different "when a nation tries to rule us and enslave us, e.g., the Poles
live on our land and create organizations and at their assemblies
demean us and trade us like cattle, like livestock to pull the yoke."

1318 Himka, "Refleksje," 184.
1319 Ibid.
1320 Ibid., 186-87.

Not only had his attitude towards the local Polish population turned 180 degrees, but he also began writing about Jews, something he had not done previously in his diary. On 1 August 1944 he wrote about how workers and collective farm workers in the USSR were starving. "These are the results of Jewish politics." Terrified into silence and passivity, Ukrainian peasants can offer no resistance to state grain requisitions. "...And Moishe will take as much as he can, leaving only as much to prevent the collective farm worker from dying." It was Jews who found suckers to participate in the Stakhanovite movement. A Jew thought up the idea of infantrymen attacking German Tiger tanks. Formerly a Darwinist and atheist, battle taught Povshuk to rethink his attitude towards religion. But "I do not believe and will not believe in the Old Testament, since it is a Jewish lie." The God of the Old Testament sent Joshua into battle to kill two thousand non-Jews. "But this is not evidence that there is no God. The Jews did not necessarily know or not know whether there was a God. And if they knew, then they were unable to understand it like we do, but imagined and adjusted [the deity] as they needed him and for what they needed him."[1321] Clearly, a year in UPA had wrought a profound change of perspective in the young teacher-soldier.

Murders

Numerous testimonies from Jewish and Polish survivors of OUN-UPA violence, from Soviet investigations, and from reports generated by UPA and SB OUN themselves confirm that OUN-UPA was killing Jews in the period between the liquidations of the ghettos, primarily in 1942 and early 1943, and the reconquest of Ukraine by the Soviets in the summer and fall of 1944. I will present a number of such cases, but hardly an exhaustive account. I remind the reader that until August 1943, when the Bulbaites for the most part exited the scene, it is possible that some of the violence attributed to the Banderites in Volhynia was actually perpetrated by the Bulbaites, and vice versa. This is the first set of murders that I will recount.

1321 Ibid.

Shalom Segal lost his wife Idis to a Banderite band, who discovered her hiding with a Ukrainian. Her host was forced to ask her to leave the house. "These Ukrainian murderers found her in a field, on her way back to Lanowitz [Lanivtsi, P Łanowce]. They buried her alive together with Shmuel and Aaron Mehlman, Misha Grisham, and the daughter of Sarah Weissman, the daughter of Shalom Weissman."[1322] Lea Rog was in Rafalivka when, after the German defeat at Stalingrad, some of the Ukrainian police escaped to the forest and joined the Banderites who fought for an independent Ukraine. "They murdered every Jew who crossed their path or had found a hiding place from the threat of death at the farms of friendly people who believed in righteousness, the Righteous Gentiles of the Nations."[1323] Also in the vicinity of Rafalivka at the time, Meir Goldverin remembered that "there was danger to the Jews from the '*Bandérivtis,*' Ukrainian Nationalists who murdered Jews."[1324]

Max Grosblat was hiding with a group of about a hundred Jewish, but not Soviet, partisans somewhere in the woods of Volhynia. He remembered that both the Banderites and the Bulbaites attacked them continually, wanting to clear the woods of Jews.[1325] Another Jewish survivor, Laizer Blitt wrote, in his memoir:

> Conditions for the Jewish community of Kortiless [Kortelisy, about twenty-five kilometers south of Ratne] went from bad to worse. They began to suffer casualties, not so much at the hands of Germans in the forced labor details, but mainly at the hands of various armed marauding Ukrainian groups. Some of these called themselves Partisans, who favored Russia; others went by the name of Bulbovtsi, who were Ukrainian nationalists; and there were those who were plain criminals. These groups fought among themselves, and the only

---

1322 Shalom Segal, "How My Daughter Was Saved," https://www.jewishgen. org/yizkor/Lanovtsy/lan076.html (accessed 28 March 2020).
1323 Lea Rog, "In the Footsteps of the Ukrainian Murderers," https://www.jewish gen.org/yizkor/Melnitsa/mele047.html (accessed 28 March 2020).
1324 Meir Goldverin, "We Didn't Find a Survivor," https://www.jewishgen.org/ yizkor/rafalovka/raf093.html (accessed 31 March 2020).
1325 Shoah Foundation, 11957 Max Grosblat, 40-41.

thing they had in common was that they robbed from farmers and killed Jews.[1326]

Survivor Baruch Goldman wrote in the Rokytne yizkor book:

We were in the marshland between the villages of Chabel [P Czabel, southeast of Sarny, Rivne oblast] and Lenchin [Linchyn, P Łęczyn, southwest of Rokytne, Rivne oblast] when two Baptists, acquaintances of my father, passed by. One of them, Afanas, told us he was returning from a large gathering of Banderovtzis in the village of Tinna [Tynne]. It had been decided there that night they would go to Berdocha [U Berdukha, P Berducha], an agricultural farm near Tinna, to kill 21 Polish families. The following night they would go to kill the Jews hiding in the forests in the area. The Banderovtzis even knew the names of those Jews....When my father and Aharon Lifshitz heard about the fate awaiting these Jews, they decided not to waste a minute and to save them immediately. They hurried to the site and told them they must escape or else they would not remain alive. At first, they refused to leave. Firstly, they did not believe the situation was so drastic and secondly, they did not want to abandon their belongings. However, the pleas of Lifshitz and my father finally opened their eyes and they joined us. We went together to the village of Bober [U Rudnia Bobrovska, P Rudnia Bobrowska][1327] where [Soviet partisan leader Dmitrii] Medvedev's regiment was camped.
On the way my father and Lifshitz wanted to save two young women hidden by a peasant, but they were too late. The Banderovtzis had, in the meantime, killed Batya Grinshpan. Rachel Hammer managed to run out of the house. She hid in a barrel in the yard and was spared. Our acquaintances, area peasants, reported that the Banderovtzis did come at night to kill all the Jews. When they did not find them, they became angry and burned all the shelters where they had hidden.[1328]

A Jewish partisan in Volhynia recalled: "A large group of Jews, over thirty persons, were hiding in a bunker in the woods of Count Plater. These were refugees from Dubrovytsia [P Dąbrowica], Berezhnytsia [P Bereżnica], and Vysotsk [P Wysock]. The Banderites found their hiding place and 'liquidated' the whole

---

1326 Blitt, *No Strength to Forget*, 45.
1327 The village no longer exists.
1328 Baruch Goldman, "The Great Rescue," https://www.jewishgen.org/yizkor/ rokitnoye/rok317.html (accessed 1 April 2020).

group, applying torture and torment. Only a few of the Jews managed to escape to us in the Svarytsevychi forest."[1329]

Another Jewish partisan recalled:

> ...the Ukrainians and the Poles had started to fight. At first, the Ukrainians had helped the Germans, so the Germans kept them as "favorites" for a year or a year and a half. While the Ukrainian were with the Germans, they had hit the Poles. Then the Ukrainians saw that the Germans were exploiting them, so they started to take to the woods and form assassin bands, nationalist terrorist bands. These were not decent, partisan groups; these Ukrainian nationalist bands were out to make the area clean of Jews, clean of everybody except themselves.[1330]

The Jewish partisan Yitzhak Geller wrote: "The Ukrainian peasants admired the ["Bulbaite"] gang members and saw them as national heroes. Church pastors would bless their weapons, machine guns, and even their throats. Eighty-five percent of Jewish refugees in the forests were killed by Ukrainian nationalists who abused the Jews. They cut their limbs off and pierced their eyes. They would torture a captive Jew while he was alive and continue abusing his corpse after he died."[1331]

Shmuel Spector has also recorded several cases of UPA's murder of Jews. Young Jews Dubina and Levkovich of [P] Ludwipol (Liudvypil, since 1946 Sosnove) were being marched to the Gestapo offices in Kostopil when they turned on their escorts and seized their weapons. They fled to the forest. "Unfortunately, they came upon Ukrainian partisans, who murdered them."[1332] Five brothers by the last name of Spasov "ran into a UPA unit by mistake" and were murdered.[1333]

According to Polish testimonies, in the second half of June 1943, UPA shot a Jew hiding in the colony Jeziorany Czeskie (near today's Ozeriany, south of Lutsk). Nine other Jews hiding there

---

1329 Bakal'chuk-Felyn, *Vospominaniia*, 95.
1330 Kohn and Roiter, *Voice from the Forest*, 93.
1331 *Sefer ha-partizanim ha-Yehudim*, 1:681. Translation by Alan Rutkowski.
1332 Spector, *Holocaust of Volhynian Jews*, 209, citing Ludwipol memorial book.
1333 Spector, *Holocaust of Volhynian Jews*, 271.

managed to escape.[1334] A Jewish survivor remembered that Jews hiding in the woods near Osova (P Osowa, between Rivne and Rafalivka) in 1943 were systematically hunted and murdered by UPA.[1335]

Policeman Ivan Fedoruk, who was tried by the Soviets, had participated in the murder of Jews in Ostrozhets (P Ostrożec), north of Dubno in Rivne oblast, in spring 1942. In spring 1943 he joined UPA and was assigned to the SB OUN under the pseudonym "Chornyi." He and three other Banderites took two Jewish adolescents who had been in hiding at the edge of the village, near the forest, and executed them.[1336] Yosyf Zaltsman testified before the Extraordinary Commission. During the murder of two thousand Jews in Tuchyn, some managed to escape into the forest, including Zaltsman. "They began to catch us and shoot us in the forest. All this was done by Ukrainian nationalists."[1337]

We now turn to Volhynia in the fall of 1943 and winter 1944. By this time the Bulbaites were out of the picture, and UPA was the primary nationalist force in the region. It was in this period too that the Soviets reconquered much of Volhynia. As the Red Army closed in, the murder of Jews accelerated.

Jakub Grinsburg, a boy of fifteen who was hiding in and around Radyvyliv, in the second half of 1943 and early 1944, had known two Jews whom the Banderites killed in the nearby village of Sytne (P Sitno). He himself was caught by a "Ukrainian-Banderite." The Banderite was taking him to a field in order to kill him, but Grinsburg managed to escape.[1338] Osada Osowa, Kostopil county, was a Jewish settlement with a prewar population of about nine hundred. By 1943 Jewish survivors of Osowa were hiding in the nearby woods, which were systematically searched by UPA. When UPA found these survivors, they murdered them.[1339] In the Czech

---

1334 Siemaszko and Siemaszko, *Ludobójstwo*, 1:597.
1335 Cited in ibid., 1:313.
1336 HDA SBU, spr. 7843, ff. 252, 258.
1337 USHMM RG-22.002M, reel 25; TsGAOR, fond 7021, op. 71, spr. 68, ff. 25v.
1338 AŻIH, 301/305, 2.
1339 Siemaszko and Siemaszko, *Ludobójstwo*, 1:313, citing memoirs of Daniel Kac. does not seem to have survived the war.

village of Novyny (P̲ Nowiny Czeskie), northeast of Mlyniv in Rivne oblast, about twenty Jews were still alive at some point in 1943 when an UPA soldier pretending to be a Soviet partisan lured them to the forest, supposedly to the partisans. Instead, they were murdered there.[1340]

Jewish survivor Emil Goldbarten related that there were many Jews hiding in woods in the vicinity of Mizoch (P̲ Mizocz), southwest of Zdolbuniv in Rivne oblast. The Germans were afraid to go into the woods because of UPA activity there. (UPA had its headquarters not far away in Derman monastery.) Although UPA kept the Germans out, they killed the Jews in the woods themselves. In January 1944 Goldbarten was captured by three Ukrainian partisans, who took him to a house and gave him a bed. They said, You are an intelligent man, you are going to work for us. But this was a lie, Goldbarten said in his testimony: they killed all the Jews whom they caught. In the house where he was supposed to stay was a young girl who used to work for Goldbarten before the war. She asked one of the UPA partisans what they were going to do with him. He answered, What are we going to do? We're going to kill him. And she said, He was such a nice man, I used to work for him, he was so nice to me. Goldbarten overheard this conversation and managed to escape. He was hiding in a barn in the straw and heard the partisans searching for him, asking, Did you see a Jew here? The housewife said, No. They took a pitchfork and stuck it in the straw. Goldbarten had not had time to dig a proper cavity in the straw and was all cramped up. The partisan stood above him, sticking and sticking his pitchfork into the straw, but never striking his hidden target. What the hell, he said. Where did he disappear to? Two or three weeks later Goldbarten was liberated.[1341]

Aron Baboukh was surviving in villages in the vicinity of Volodymyr-Volynskyi and was kept alive primarily through the

1340 Siemaszko and Siemaszko, *Ludobójstwo*, 1:91-92. Spector, *Holocaust of Volhynian Jews*, 271. A Jewish woman who joined the Soviet partisans also noted a case in which nationalist partisans successfully posed as Red Army men and inflicted many casualties. USC Shoah Foundation Institute for Visual History and Education, 41647 Sonia Orbuch.

1341 Shoah Foundation, 7722 Emil Goldbarten, 62-69.

efforts of Ukrainian rescuers who hid him from the Banderites. In February 1944 many Banderites suddenly appeared in the village where he and his friend were hiding in a bunker, and the village became dangerous for them. One day, searching for fuel, he and his friend stumbled upon some Banderites who tried to capture them and shot at them. The Banderites found the bunker with more Jewish refugees and shot every one of them. Baboukh claimed that the Banderites killed hundreds of Jews, and that he was an eyewitness to their atrocities.[1342]

Near the end of the German occupation, Sonyah Sherer was hiding in in Khorokhoryn (P Chorochoryń), west of Lutsk, with a man, Lionyk Pavlovsky, whose father was Polish and mother Ukrainian. Pavlovsky had Banderite connections. Since Pavlovsky's home was a bit distant from the front at the time, Banderites, including Pavlovsky's uncle, visited the home. Pavlovsky's uncle "had killed my uncle, and I had to sit next to him at the table. Banderites came and related how they killed Jews, and I had to listen to all this."[1343]

According to a Polish testimony, in the fall of 1943 UPA killed a Jew named Moszek in the village of Bubniv (P Bubnów), west of Lutsk.[1344]

In confirmation of the eyewitness testimonies regarding UPA's murders of the Jewish population in Volhynia in 1943 we can adduce evidence from the Book of Reports (*Knyha zvitiv*) of the Mykhailo Kolodzinsky division (*zahin*) of UPA. The division operated in the forests of Volhynia; it routinely killed any surviving Jews it encountered and reported on this to its superiors. "On 14 November [1943] the platoon..., following up a denunciation, attacked Jews who had settled in the forest near Ostrivtsi. Having shot four Jews, two escaped, and they caught two alive." Ostrivtsi (P Ostrowce) is a village about half way between Rafalivka and Volodymyrets in Rivne oblast. "On 15 December [1943] the [unit's]

1342 Shoah Foundation, 26557 Aron Baboukh, 114-25.
1343 Shoah Foundation, 17221 Sonyah Sherer. This testimony was in Hebrew; I am grateful to Mykhailo Tiahlyi for providing me with a Ukrainian translation.
1344 Siemaszko and Siemaszko, *Ludobójstwo*, 1:189.

cavalry in the village of Selets caught ten Hungarian Jews who had left a work battalion. That very day they were dispatched to 'the bosom of Abraham.'" Selets (P Sielec) is immediately north of Dubrovytsia, Rivne oblast.[1345] The Kolodzinsky division was part of UPA Army-North. Based near Dubrovytsia, it reported to the commander of the Zahrava military district.[1346]

Historian Franziska Bruder also found an OUN-UPA report from 20 September 1943 that said: "[The Jews,] almost completely liquidated, in small groups or as individuals hide in the woods and wait for a change in the political situation. We ourselves liquidated in the Horyn [River] region seven Jewish men and a Jewish woman."[1347] A report from Stolin nadraion of UPA (Stolin is now in Brest oblast, Belarus) noted that in the first half of December 1943 "a local unit captured four Jews, whom they killed."[1348]

As the Red Army was about to take over Volhynia, many UPA units crossed into Galicia, spreading the murder of Poles and Jews to this region as well.

Murray Burgman was in a forced labor camp in a Carpathian village which he referred to as Limanova.[1349] Jews from the labor camp worked in the mountain forests and used the opportunity to

---

1345 USHMM RG-31.017M, reel 1; DARO, fond 30, op. 2, spr. 89, 7v, 11v. The microfilm copy at USHMM is hard to read. I thank Wiesław Tokarczuk for providing me with a more legible scan from the DARO original. Germans also liked the "bosom of Abraham" witticism. A soldier in a Schutzkommando in Poland wrote to his wife on 12 November 1942: "For a couple of weeks we have been sending the Jews to the bosom of Abraham." Grabowski, *Hunt*, 40-41.

1346 Petro Sodol', "Orhanizatsiina struktura UPA," http://forum.ottawa-litopys. org/documents/dos0301_u.htm (accessed 26 October 2009).

1347 Bruder, *"Den ukrainischen Staat erkämpfen oder sterben!"* 219. Bruder thought there was a typographical error in the report because it said "na tereni Horyni." She thought it must have been referring to the locality Horynka. The Horyn River, however, runs through territory that figures in Jewish testimonies as the home of hiding survivors and the site of UPA massacres.

1348 DARO, fond R30, op. 1, spr. 21, f. 29. I am grateful to Wiesław Tokarczuk for a photocopy of this document.

1349 The Limanova referred to here is not the Limanowa which is today in southeastern Poland. Rather, it was a labor camp near Boryslav in Distrikt Galizien. It has also been referred to as Limanowska. The camp is listed neither in Dubyk, *Dovidnyk pro tabory*, nor in USHMM, *Encyclopedia of Camps and Ghettos*. Its existence is confirmed, however, in Kysla, "Vyzhyvannia za ekstremal'nykh umov," 15, 22, 24, 31.

dig bunkers. Some later hid in these bunkers in the woods, including Burgman. The Banderites, however, came looking for them and killed many. Burgman said he had heard rumors that the Banderites were killing Jews, but he did not want to believe it. But he and his brother had to flee their bunker when the Banderites did come. When they returned to the bunker later, they saw that the food that they had left there was doused with gasoline. This was to spoil the food so that they would have nothing to eat.[1350]

Meir Chameides was hiding with his father in the attic of a building in Boryslav. "The news arriving from the outside world were [sic] depressing. A new term was added to the lexicon of murderers of Jews, 'Banderowcy.' Those were bands of Ukrainian nationalists who were gathering in the forests and preparing for a confrontation with the Red Army. In the meanwhile, they were spending their time hunting for bunkers of Jews, seizing their possessions and murdering them."[1351]

Leon Knebel was hiding in the woods near the village of Opaka, near Boryslav in Lviv oblast, from mid-April until the Soviets came in early August. Of the group of twelve Jews he was hiding with, three were killed by the Banderites. "The Banderites were cruel," he wrote. "They also lived in the woods and simply hunted the Jews." They did not merely kill those they caught but tortured them. One day twenty-four victims were murdered. "Later we found the corpse of a young Jewish woman, Mala Ehrenfeld; both of her hands were cut off and strips of skin had been cut out of her body."[1352] Ignacy Goldwasser was hiding in the same forest. In the two months preceding the return of the Soviets, he had to hide from the Banderites, who were destroying Jewish bunkers and killing Jews.[1353] Also in the same forest was Edzia Szpeicher. She said that Banderites posed as pro-Soviet partisans and invited the Jews in her bunkers to join them. Suspicious, she and some others managed to escape, but the Banderites caught over twenty others, forced them

---

1350 Shoah Foundation, 15542 Murray Bergman, 105-12.
1351 Chameides, *That War and Me*, 100.
1352 AŻIH, 301/679, 6-7.
1353 AŻIH, 301/2193, 10-11.

to undress, and murdered them.[1354] An eleven-year-old girl described the murderers in the Opaka woods as Germans and Ukrainian policemen.[1355]

Near Peremyshliany (P Przemyślany), in the Ostałowiecki forest,[1356] there was a group of a hundred Jews hiding. Unfortunately, their footprints in the snow revealed the location of the bunkers. The woods were searched a number of times before several hundred Ukrainians launched a major attack on the morning of 2 March 1944. Of the hundred Jews mentioned in the testimony of Lipa Stricker, only ten survived. He himself managed to hide in the bushes. The slaughter lasted an hour. All the Jews were killed with knives. Stricker's son had ten knife wounds, six in his chest, four in his back. Stricker's wife lay murdered and naked. Her sister and her two adult daughters were also murdered there.[1357]

The Friedman family was hiding in the countryside near Brody, Lviv oblast, in the fall of 1943. They feared the Banderites because, they believed, "they did not simply kill—they would cut off the penis or breasts of a Jew, torture their victim endlessly, then torch and bury the corpse."[1358] "One evening Father heard the Banderas marching toward our hiding place and he assumed we had been discovered. He took out his razor blade and prepared to slit our throats. 'We will not be tortured,' he whispered to Isaac and me. 'Otherwise, we will give away your mother and Sarah.'" Referring to December 1943, he recalled hiding from German patrols and Bandera bandits. "Both groups wanted to kill us." Referring to early 1944, he wrote: "The retreat of the Germans had left a clear field for the Banderas. They went about their business of murdering Poles....The Banderas seemed to have gone berserk, killing every

---

1354 AŻIH, 301/3359, 5.

1355 AŻIH, 301/1205, 8-9.

1356 The Ostałowiecki family had been large landowners in the Peremyshliany region. There is a village called Ostalovychi (P Ostałowice) about ten kilometers south of Peremyshliany.

1357 AŻIH, 301/1136, Lipa Stricker, 4. Perhaps the incident described here is connected with the series of incidents described below with regard to Svirzh; see 397-98. A Polish researcher listed by name eight Jews killed by UPA in 1944 in Peremyshliany county. Wyspiański, *Osoby zamordowane*, 35, 41, 48, 50, 55.

1358 Friedman, *I'm no Hero*, 23

Pole they got their hands on. I had never heard or seen such wailing, and I hope to God I never do again....The Banderas were now desperate to find Jacob Friedman [the author's father]. Nearly every prominent Jewish man in the area around Brody had been accounted for, except Father."[1359]

In March 1944 a thirteen-year old boy was given shelter by a Ukrainian family in the village of Berlyn (P̲ Berlin) near Brody. He tried to convince the family he was Christian by reciting prayers. The woman of the household insisted he take a bath, and when he took off his clothes, she saw he was Jewish. She said she was afraid because there were so many Banderites in the area and asked him to move to a village closer to the front.[1360] Also near Brody a friend of Szyja Rajzer perished at the hands of the Banderites.[1361]

Berl Lieblein was being hidden by a Ukrainian in the village of Korostiv (P̲ Korostów), just southwest of Skole in Lviv oblast. The Ukrainian who hid them was very afraid of being discovered by the Banderites. "The Banderites in particular maltreated Jews in a cruel way. The bandit Suslynets,[1362] who had a mass of murders on his conscience, was famous for his cruelties throughout the region. He lured twelve Jews to his bunker, promising them he would hide them, and then with the help of his band he murdered all of them. Another time he got in his clutches two Jewish girls, whom he hanged on a branch upside down. Under them he placed a pile of branches which he set on fire and thus burned both victims."[1363]

A survivor who hid in the woods between Horodenka and Borshchiv (P̲ Borszczów) wrote: "These bloody outfits ["Banderowtzes" who turned against the Germans in 1943] always killed Jews who had managed to survive by hiding in the woods, whenever they found them."[1364] Basically the same was said by another survivor from the Horodenka area.[1365]

1359 Ibid, 33-37.
1360 AŻIH, 301/198, Leon Knebel, 5.
1361 AŻIH, 301/2986, 14.
1362 This is likely a reference to Dmytro Suslynets, who commanded a company (*sotnia*) in the Hoverla military district.
1363 Hochberg-Mariańska and Grüss, *Dzieci oskarżają*, 139.
1364 Bernard, *In the Eye of the Storm*, 141-42.
1365 AŻIH, 301/3647, 3.

A teenage girl hiding in Skala-Podilska, Ternopil oblast, also remembered the Banderites, whom she defined as "the roaming 'partisan' gangs that had arrived in the region from the forest." "I was convinced," she wrote, "[that] I would be just as vulnerable in the house as on the road. *Banderowtzi* swooped down on village or town and took what they wanted. No sport short of obliterating a German division would give them more pleasure than to roister through this place and kill Jews."[1366] Mendel Rosenkranz was working on a *folwark*, an agricultural labor camp in Korolivka (P Korolówka), southeast of Borschiv. In early 1944 "the Banderites, who were Ukrainian nationalists, became active. They murdered Jews in all the camps. Then we went our separate ways and into hiding."[1367]

The Soviets liberated the Jewish labor camp in Tovste at the end of March 1944. They learned that in a neighboring village, Banderites had come and lured Jews as if to the pro-Soviet partisans, but in reality they took them into the woods and killed them all.[1368] The intense persecution of Jews in this area by the Banderites finds corroboration in the testimony of Hilary Kenigsberg. He was working in the same labor camp system in Tovste. He said that beginning in early 1944 the Banderites began to comb the nearby woods for Jewish bunkers, and when they found Jews they killed them in a horrible way. Their terror in the woods was so great that Jews were actually fleeing from the woods to the Germans for protection.[1369] There exists another account of murders of dozens of Jews by Banderites in these woods in the first three months of 1944, with particular intensity in March. The narrator witnessed many of the fresh corpses himself and helped gather up the survivors. He lost many relatives, including his own father, in these killings.[1370]

1366 Heller, *Strange and Unexpected Love*, 211, 213.
1367 Hochberg-Mariańska and Grüss, *Dzieci oskarżają*, 38.
1368 Shoah Foundation, 18287 Benno Noskovich, 100-02. The testimony refers to the camp in Rozhanivka, which is very close to Tovste. That the camp was in Tovste and liberated by the Soviets in late March 1944 is confirmed in USHMM, *Encyclopedia of Camps and Ghettos*, s.v. "Tłuste," by Alexander Kruglov and Martin Dean.
1369 AŻIH, 301/3337, 14.
1370 AŻIH, 301/6012, Leon Hejnysz, 2-4.

Many Jews were hiding in forests north of Rohatyn. According to one of them, Jack Glotzer, numerous Banderites appeared in the vicinity in 1944, and they were particularly dangerous because they knew every inch of the woods. They stayed for about five or six months. As the Red Army approached, the Bandera movement searched for the Jews in order to kill them. They said that when the Russians came the Jews would inform on them.[1371] In Glotzer's opinion, if it were not for the Ukrainians, many more Jews would have survived. The Soviets stopped about sixty kilometers from where Glotzer was hiding. If they had gone further, many more Jews would also have survived.[1372] This is corroborated by the fate of Natan Arsen. Local Ukrainians told his older brother Borys that Natan managed to survive in a bunker in the environs of Rohatyn until April 1944. At that time a unit of SB OUN was ethnically cleansing the territory of Jews and Poles. They found Natan's hideout, tied him to the tail of a horse, and drove the horse across the frozen fields. The Ukrainians did not know where the remains were, nor could they name the individuals responsible for the murder.[1373]

A Jewish partisan witnessed Banderites torturing a Jewish family of four that had been hiding in a bunker near Oleshiv (P Oleszów) just east of Stanyslaviv. The Banderites subsequently put them on a cart and took them to the woods to kill them.[1374]

Mozes Ehrlich escaped to the forest from the Janowska camp on the outskirts of Lviv some time after mid-April 1943. He ended up in a family camp of thirty-four Jews. "We were most vexed by the Banderites, Ukrainian German nationalists. I will describe the following fact. In one forest there were about eighty Jews, so they surrounded the forest and killed every single one of them. They

---

1371 An UPA report from "Bilhorod" (apparently a cryptonym) in Galicia from December 1943 noted that two Jews were executed for knowing everything that was happening in the *stanytsia* and also for spying on a training course. Rusnachenko, *Narod zburenyi*, 136, citing TsDAVO, fond 3836, op. 1, spr. 64, f. 97. Motyka, *Ukraińska partyzantka*, 294.

1372 Shoah Foundation, 20586 Jack Glotzer, 12-15.

1373 Arsen, *Moia hirka pravda*, 316.

1374 AŻIH, 301/4680, 14.

quartered their victims and hung the quarters on trees with a notice that said 'This is Jewish meat.'"[1375]

Survivor Joseph Adler wrote: "The Ukrainian nationalist bands policy [sic] was the murdering of Jews. So, for example, when Bandera's people got information about Rozia Adler hiding in the village of Hoszow [Hoshiv, P̱ Hoszów, south of Stryi], they requested that she be handed over. After robbing her, she was was murdered. This happened in early summer of 1944."[1376]

Frank Golczewski has found German documentation that supports what the Jewish eyewitness accounts say was happening in Galicia. In May 1944, the Germans and UPA were negotiating a tactical alliance. The German 1st Armored High Command noted that "in the event of an agreement," UPA would be expected, among other things, to provide "active help against Soviet paratroopers, Red Army stragglers, Bolshevik, Polish and Jewish gangs." In April 1944 Wehrmacht intelligence reported: "By our own reconnaissance, a gang of Jews was observed east of Bibrka, the planned destruction of which could not ensue due to use of the intended troops in another operation. The UPA has successfully taken up pursuit of the Jewish gangsters and up to now shot almost 100."[1377] Dieter Pohl also quotes a German document: In March or April 1944 UPA leaders told German officials that they were going to cleanse the Chełm-Rava Ruska (P̱ Rawa Ruska) region of "Poles, bandits, and Jews."[1378]

In summary, all evidence points to the routine murder of Jews by OUN-B during the course of its national insurgency. Except for moments of Banderite-German rapprochement in the spring of 1944, the murders occurred while OUN-B had broken with the Germans and was even conducting a desultory resistance against them.

1375 AŻIH, 301/1247, 2.
1376 Adler, "Chapters," 222.
1377 Golczewski, "Shades of Grey," 143.
1378 Pohl, *Nationalsozialistische Judenverfolgung in Ostgalizien*, 376.

Poles

The primary target of ethnic cleansing in both Volhynia and Galicia was the Polish population. UPA's murder of Poles resulted in tens of thousands of deaths.[1379] UPA also massacred other national minorities.[1380] These murders were in line with the slogan "Ukraine for Ukrainians" that OUN had been pursuing since the outbreak of the war. The campaign against the Poles was particularly important, however. This was UPA's baptism of fire. The murders of Polish civilians in Volhynia set off a vast conflagration of violence, as Poles retaliated and collaborated with their other enemies, the Germans and the Soviets, in order to acquire weapons and military backing.

In the fierce war between Poles and Ukrainians, many Jews chose the Polish side, or had that side chosen for them.[1381] As the Jewish survivor Seweryn Dobroszklanka said, the emergence of UPA improved relations between Jews and Poles in Volhynia, since they were both in danger from the same source.[1382] The same held true in Galicia.[1383] Polish testimonies note that Jews joined Polish self-defence units. A self-defence unit in the military colony

---

1379 There is a huge literature on this subject, but in my opinion it requires renewed study using updated methodology, new sources, and a more objective approach. Valuable contributions to the literature include: Il'iushyn, *Volyns'ka trahediia*; Motyka, *Ukraińska partyzantka*; Rossoliński-Liebe, "Der polnisch-ukrainische Historikerdiskurs"; Snyder, *Reconstruction of Nations*, 154-78; Snyder, "To Resolve the Ukrainian Question Once and for All"; Siemaszko and Siemaszko, *Ludobójstwo*.

1380 The destruction of ethnic German villages is recorded in Serhiichuk, *OUN-UPA v roky viiny*, 312. The Siemazkos tallied the number of murders by Ukrainian nationalists in Volhynia in 1941-45 as mentioned in the many, mainly Polish testimonies they examined. By their calculations and estimates, the testimonies attest also to the murder of 342 Czechs, at least 135 Russians, and dozens of Roma. Siemaszko and Siemaszko, *Ludobójstwo*, 2:19. There are also reports that UPA killed a family of Roma in Smerek, Lesko county, in the Lemko region on 21 October 1945. Dalecki, *Zbrodnie nacjonalistów ukraińskich*, 164. On OUN hostility to "Gypsies" as a people that "does not even have the right to life," see Diukov, *Vtorostepennyi vrag*, 78.

1381 For example, after attacks by Ukrainian police and local inhabitants, Jews in Mlyniv (P Młynów), northwest of Dubno, fled for protection to the Poles and Czechs who lived in the village. Siemaszko and Siemaszko, *Ludobójstwo*, 1:90.

1382 AŻIH, 301/1222, 6.

1383 Shoah Foundation, 6347 Samuel Drix, 22.

Bortnytsia (P Bortnica), less than ten kilometers south of Dubno, consisted of fifteen Poles and eight Jews. When Ukrainians attacked the colony on Roman Catholic Christmas day 1943, eight Poles and three Jews fell in battle. The colony was burned down.[1384] The Polish colony of Ziniówka, Dubno county, which no longer exists, had a self-defence unit which included Jews who were being hid. Attacked by UPA on 14 July 1943, the self-defence unit evacuated to the Polish-Czech colony of Kurdybań Warkowicki, which was also in Dubno county and also no longer exists.[1385] Twenty-five Jews served in Kurdybań Warkowicki's self-defence unit (of sixty Jews who had found refuge in that colony).[1386] There is first-hand testimony of a Jewish partisan who sided with the Poles against Ukrainian bands around Tovste and Buchach in Ternopil oblast.[1387] Many OUN and UPA documents from 1943 and 1944 show that the Ukrainian nationalists considered the Jews and Poles to be allies against the Ukrainians.[1388] Working with a different source base, the Fortunoff Video Archive of Holocaust Testimonies at Yale, Timothy Snyder came to the same conclusion as I did: "As the UPA brought much of the countryside under its control, Jews who were staying with Poles were killed along with their rescuers, sometimes as Poles and sometimes as Jews."[1389]

Thus the logic of the situation was that the Jews were identified with the Poles during the ethnic cleansing of Volhynia, which lasted from the spring through the fall of 1943, by which time most of the Poles had left, and during the ethnic cleansing of Galicia, which began in earnest in January 1944. Just as UPA killed Poles in this period, it also killed Jews in Polish self-defence units, Jews whom Poles sheltered, and, in fact, as we have seen, Jews in general. As a Banderite insurgent told a Ukrainian Baptist in Volhynia in January 1944, the future Ukraine was to have neither Poles nor Jews.[1390]

1384 Siemaszko and Siemaszko, *Ludobójstwo*, 1:60.
1385 Ibid., 1:109.
1386 Ibid., 1:107.
1387 Wermuth, "The Jewish Partisans of Horodenka."
1388 They are cited in Bruder, *"Den ukrainischen Staat erkämpfen,"* 168.
1389 Snyder, *Sketches from a Secret War*, 190.
1390 Podvorniak, *Viter z Volyni*, 206.

There was a widespread view among Ukrainian nationalists in Volhynia that once the Jews had been killed, it was time to proceed to the Poles. Polish testimonies noted that UPA units in Volhynia were heard to be singing: *Vyrizaly my zhydiv, vyrizhemo i liakhiv, i staroho, i maloho do iednoho; Poliakiv vyrizhem, Ukrainu zbuduiem.*[1391]

Jewish testimonies also state that UPA killed Jews at the same time it was killing Poles. The Poles who had been hiding Vera Shchetinkova and her brother in 1943 were killed by the Banderites, and the Banderites also killed Jews.[1392] Polish testimonies corroborate that UPA killed Jews together with Poles. On 23 July 1943 UPA soldiers tried to kill a Jew in the largely Ukrainian village of Okhnivka (P Ochnówka), about ten kilometers north of Volodymyr-Volynskyi, but the man managed to escape. They killed his son and severely beat and wounded his wife, who was Polish.[1393] An UPA attack in July or August 1943 on the village of Medwedówka,[1394] near Liudvypil, left fifty-seven dead, mainly Poles, but also four Jews who were hiding among them.[1395] In late August 1943 an UPA unit killed Jews who were hiding with Poles in the colony of Głęboczyca, Volodymyr-Volynskyi county.[1396] On 30 August 1943 Ukrainian detachments headed by Fedir Halushko and recruited from local nationalists and communists burned the Polish village of Myslyna (P Myślina), just over ten kilometers north of Kovel, and murdered the inhabitants, mainly Poles, but also four Jewish families, including three children.[1397] When UPA attacked the Polish

---

1391 Translation: We slaughtered the Jews, we'll slaughter the Poles, old and young, every one; we'll slaughter the Poles, we'll build Ukraine. Siemaszko and Siemaszko, *Ludobójstwo*, 1:872, 2:1269. The message that the Poles would be next after the Jews was spread throughout Volhynia. Ibid., 1:285, 1:309, 1:571, 1:737, 1:747, 1:7842:1269.

1392 Shoah Foundation, 45238 Vera Shchetinkova, 140-43.

1393 Siemaszko and Siemaszko, *Ludobójstwo*, 1:929.

1394 I have been unable to locate this village on present-day maps; it probably did not survive the war.

1395 Siemaszko and Siemaszko, *Ludobójstwo*, 1:270.

1396 Ibid., 1:872, 874. Głęboczyca no longer exists. According to Polish testimonies, in August 1943 UPA killed a Jew in Głęboczyca by the name of Aron who had owned an oil press. The Pole who hid him was also murdered. Ibid., 1:872.

1397 Ibid., 1:367.

village of Rudnia Potasznia, about fifty kilometers east of Kostopil, in October 1943, they also killed a Jewish couple.[1398]

Then about twelve years old, Seweryn Dobrszklanka, remembered the emergence of the Banderite UPA in Volhynia. He was Jewish and staying with a Polish family in a forested area near Berezne in Rivne oblast. His situation there was good, and the family would have let him stay beyond the spring of 1943 if UPA had not started killing Poles and Jews in the area. He fled to the forest, but one day the Banderites surrounded the forest and searched it. They found three Jewish bunkers and killed over two hundred Jews with grenades and rifles. They also killed dozens of other Jews at different times. Later the boy went to work for a Ukrainian farmer. The Banderites saw him, but did not touch him. They said that they were no longer going to kill Jews, but it turned out, according to Dobroszlanka, that this was a trap. Many Jews were deceived and came out of the forest, settling in the homes of Poles who had fled or been killed. His mother was in a house with both Jews and Poles. Ukrainians came to the door, and most of the house's inhabitants did not expect that they were in danger, since the killing seemed to have stopped. His mother, however, and some others managed to escape. The Banderites told those who remained in the house to lie on the floor. They proceeded to kill a dozen Jews and ten Poles using a machine gun. His mother went to another house in the predawn hours to check on her other son, Seweryn's brother, and found his corpse and that of a little girl. The mother then took Seweryn away from the Ukrainian farmer, whom they no longer trusted. This could have been in mid-October 1943. His mother and he went deep into the forest where about a hundred Jews were living in bunkers. Some Polish partisans were also nearby. In late December UPA attacked the forest. They caught about twenty Jews and let them go, saying that this was now Ukrainian territory. But Seweryn and his mother did not trust them, sure that this was another trap.[1399]

1398 Ibid., 1:277. It seems that a cemetery is all that is left of Rudnia Potasznia.
1399 AŻIH, 301/1222, 5-9.

Polish testimonies also speak of UPA denouncing Polish set-tlements to the Germans for harboring Jews. On 16 June 1943 a Ger-man battalion surrounded the Polish village of Huta (P Huta Ste-pańska), about forty kilometers north of Kostopil, as a result of UPA denunciations that the villagers had organized a well armed parti-san unit that received drops from aircraft, had a short-wave radio and artillery, printed and distributed anti-German leaflets, cooper-ated with Soviet partisans, and hid Jews. After investigating and finding the claims exaggerated, the Germans left the village.[1400] In fact, though, young Jewish refugees, the brothers Waks, had come to Huta precisely because it was a well armed camp. At first the Poles did not trust them, suspecting them of being Ukrainians or spies from the Ukrainians, and threatened to kill them.[1401] But a man on horseback told the Polish police to let them go. In late spring 1943, according to Mordechai Waks, but more likely in July, "the Ukrainian bandit army" attacked the village to kill the Poles, and the Waks brothers fled together with the Poles to Rafalivka.[1402]

Another survivor's account also discussed the situation in and around Huta:

> My uncle escaped to the forest, but was caught by the Ukrainian na-tionalists and killed....
> The situation in the village [Velyke Verbche, P Werbcze Duże, near Sarny] got worse. The Germans along with their partners, the Ukrain-ians, increased the searching from house to house, from threshing floor to threshing floor, and we were forced to wander and hide all the time in inhumane conditions. My brother Sheptel was caught by the Ukrainians and the Germans, and was tortured in order that he would reveal our hiding place. But he withstood the inhumane tor-turing for four days, and didn't reveal to them anything, and in the end he died.

1400 Siemaszko and Siemaszko, *Ludobójstwo*, 1:287.
1401 Battles with the Banderites and the Poles' distrust of Jewish partisans also fig-ure in the account of survivor Gitla Szwarcblatt. AŻIH, 301/1237, 2v-3v.
1402 Shoah Foundation, 13213 Mike Walsh (Mordechai Waks), 55-60. Another memoirist from the Rafalivka region noted: "Ukrainian nationalists attacked the small Polish villages and, of course, the Jews were the first victims." Reu-ven and Lea Portnoy, "Wanderings, Separation and Reunion," https://www.jewishgen.org/yizkor/rafalovka/raf098.html (accessed 31 March 2020).

I got sick of life, and at midnight I turned to the head of the Ukrainian nationalist gang in the village by the name of Helkon Zinka, who had studied with me in school in the past, and I said to him: "I have come so you can kill me." He responded: "No, I don't want to kill you. But I command you and your brothers hiding in the village to leave today, because in the end you will be caught by my friends and they will kill you." At this period of time, the nationalist Ukrainians began to attack Polish towns, and thus most of the Poles were centralized in the area of the village, Hota-Stepanseka [Huta], and they organized themselves for defense. We fled from Vervecha [Velyke Verbche] to Hota-Stepanseka. Here we were taken in willingly by the Poles as an additional work force and for defending ourselves together.[1403]

The Polish colony of Ludwikówka, Dubno county, had been attacked unsuccessfully several times by UPA. UPA denounced the colony to the SS for harboring Jews and Soviet partisans. On the night of 13 July 1943, a large unit of SS, Vlasovites, and Ukrainian police attacked the village and burned most of the colony's inhabitants in a barn.[1404]

For Jews hiding in the woods near Svirzh (P Swirz), about ten kilometers west of Peremyshliany, it became "very dangerous," because the Banderites were attacking.[1405] A young girl who was living in these same woods said that her group was protected by both Polish and Soviet partisans and that they fought against the Banderites.[1406] There is another testimony from this same area with more details. It says that the Banderites conducted a search of the woods in March 1944. One of the Banderites warned the Jews hiding in the bunkers of the upcoming attack, and five hundred Jews then fled to the nearby Polish village of Hanaczów.[1407] The next morning at 7:00 the Banderites attacked the rest of the Jews, burning

---

1403 Yitzhak Wachs, "Between Life and Death," https://www.jewishgen.org/yizkor/stepan/stee274.html (accessed 3 April 2020).

1404 Siemaszko and Siemaszko, *Ludobójstwo*, 1:88. Ludwikówka no longer exists.

1405 AŻIH, 301/790, 3.

1406 AŻIH, 301/843, 11.

1407 Called Hanaki in the testimony. I am grateful to Krzysztof Janiga for identifying the correct locality and for pointing me to sources on what transpired there. There is a good map of Hanaczów and environs on line: http://www.hanaczow.pl/images/maps/mapa.jpg (accessed 17 October 2012). Hanaczów no longer exists.

any structures they had above ground and throwing grenades into their bunkers. Later the Banderites attacked Hanaczów, which was defended by a self-defence unit composed of Poles and Jews. Two Jewish families perished in that attack. The Banderites attacked the village again on Roman Catholic Easter Sunday 1944 and killed both Poles and Jews, but again met combined Polish and Jewish resistance.[1408]

In Reklynets (P Rekliniec), about thirty kilometers south of Sokal, in the winter of 1943-44 "the Ukrainians-Banderites began to organize. They began to attack the Poles. They murdered some Polish families in the village. They burned Jewish houses." Jews who were hiding in the village feared for their lives. The Ukrainian who was sheltering the narrator, Szyja Rajzer, and other Jews also began to fear for his life and told the Jews to leave. This had become very dangerous now, because the peasants had set up a guard around the village "organized especially against Jews and Poles."[1409] A Polish testimony said that in September 1943 UPA murdered two Jewish boys, Abram and Berko, hiding in the Polish colony of Piłsudszczyzna, near Svyniukhy (P Świniuchy, now called Pryvitne), about fifty kilometers southwest of Lutsk.[1410]

In fall 1943 dozens of Jews were hiding in bunkers in forests near Naraiv (P Narajów), about fifteen kilometers northwest of Berezhany. When five went out to obtain some potatoes, they were attacked by Banderites, and one was badly wounded. In March 1944 the Banderites terrorized a Pole who they knew was helping to feed these Jews and made him lead them to the Jews' hideout. The Banderites tried to lure the Jews out, speaking in Russian and telling them that they were looking to employ chauffeurs and mechanics. When the Jews refused to come above ground, they

---

1408   AŻIH, 301/808, Edmund Adler, 2-3. The attack on Hanaczów is described in Węgierski, *W lwowskiej Armii Krajowej*, 105-08, and in Yones, *Evrei L'vova*, 309-11. Various armed forces roamed the Hanaczów region in addition to UPA: German units, the Polish Home Army (AK), Ukrainian auxiliary police, and Soviet partisans.

1409   AŻIH, 301/2986, 22-23. Elderly nationalists interviewed in Lviv in 2009 recounted how their fathers joined the village guard, armed with axes, scythes, and pitchforks. Himka and Himka, "Absence and Presence."

1410   Siemaszko and Siemaszko, *Ludobójstwo*, 1:191. Piłsudszczyzna no longer exists.

threatened to suffocate them in the bunkers. Then all went out except the narrator and his two cousins. The Banderites shot all the Jews who came out, a total of fifty-one people, including the narrator's father and both of his brothers. After UPA left, the survivors went out. Accompanied by one of their Polish protectors, they found the corpses stacked in a huge pile. The Pole who was with them told them that the Banderites first shot the children, then the adults. Not long afterwards, the Pole who protected them had to flee, because the Banderites were burning down all the Poles' houses. In the intervening months before the Red Army arrived, the Jews in this group were still endangered by Banderites patrolling the area, but managed to keep out of their sight.[1411]

A similar story concerned the vicinity of Bytkiv (P Bitków), west of Nadvirna in Ivano-Frankivsk oblast. Nuchim Werner was, with other Jews, hiding in a bunker in the forest. One day Banderites surrounded the bunker and, pretending they were Soviets, spoke Russian to the Jews. When the Jews left the bunker and saw Banderites they began to flee. The Banderites shot at the Jews, killing about twenty. Fourteen remained alive, however, including a wounded boy. While these survivors were hiding in the woods, a Jewish boy joined them. He told them he had been captured by the Banderites and tied up in a barn. The next day they were planning to torture him to make him reveal the location of bunkers where Jews were hiding, but at night the boy cut through his bonds and fled to the group in the woods.[1412]

There is second-hand testimony about the murder of Jews and Poles together from a Ukrainian memoirist from the Rohatyn area in Galicia. Petro Maslii, a veteran of the Waffen-SS Division Galizien who ended up in Britain, wrote in an unpublished memoir about two young Jewish women who were hiding near his village, Luchyntsi (P Łuczyńce). As to their ultimate fate, he first wrote that he would not say, since he left the village in June 1944. Then a little later in his memoir he wrote: "I heard that at the time Polish colonists were being murdered, those who ignored the request to leave

---

1411 AŻIH, 301/879, Mojżesz Kin, 2-4.
1412 Hochberg-Mariańska and Grüss, *Dzieci oskarżają*, 150.

Ukrainian lands and return to indigenous Poland, these [two Jewish women] were also murdered and buried in the fields where there was once a wonderful meadow. I cannot guarantee this, because I only heard about it."[1413]

Partisans

UPA veteran and Canadian political scientist Peter J. Potichnyj, responding to accusations that UPA killed Jews, told a *Washington Post* correspondent that most Ukrainian Jews were dead in 1943, when the insurgent army gained strength. "'But there were some remnants, and the remnants were either working with the Ukrainian underground or they were working with the Soviets.' Those allied with the Red partisans were obviously enemies of the underground, he said."[1414] Indeed, in addition to killing Jews because they were Jews and because they were allies with the Poles, UPA killed Jews who were associated with or protected by the Soviet partisan movement.

Postwar Western Ukrainian testimonies always refer to the Soviets as the "liberators" in quotation marks, that is, ironically. Jewish testimonies, however, use the word liberators with genuine appreciation for their deliverance. The crux of the matter was that for Ukrainian nationalists, the Soviet Union was the ultimate evil, the Germans a lesser evil; for the Jews, the Germans were the ultimate evil, and the Soviets either a lesser evil or, for some, a positive good. The Soviets brought life to surviving Jews, but death to Ukrainian nationalists.

Thousands of Jews joined the pro-Soviet partisans, mortal enemies of UPA. For example, Szlojme Katz showed his interviewers from the Jewish Historical Commission a certificate from his commander that he had killed twelve Germans and six Banderites. He had joined pro-Soviet partisans in the Zhytomyr region in late May 1943, one of about twenty-five Jews in a unit comprised of about a

---

1413 Letter of P. Maslij to the Ukrainian Canadian Documentation Centre (Toronto), 29 January 1991, UCRDC, "Spomyny," no. 51.
1414 Pancake, "In Ukraine."

thousand partisans. (The rest, he said, were Russians and Poles.) In his testimony he listed a number of battles in the environs of Rivne in which his unit, though outnumbered, killed many Banderites and took their horses.[1415] Other Jewish testimonies also confirm that Jews in pro-Soviet partisan units were at war with Ukrainian nationalist partisans.[1416]

Paula Last joined Dmitrii Medvedev's partisan unit. She felt lucky to have encountered Russian partisans; Ukrainian partisans (she mentions "Banderovtses") would often kill Jews, and actively looked for them.[1417]

At the age of twelve, Mordekhai Kleinman fled from the Liudvypil ghetto to the woods. He was in a small group of armed Jews, about twenty in all, who were associated with the Soviet partisans. The Germans did not attempt to round up the Jews in these woods because all kinds of partisans ruled the forest including Ukrainian partisans. "The Ukrainian nationalist partisan group shot at the Jews."[1418]

An armed Jewish group from Horodenka attacked Banderites and both joined the Soviet partisan movement and cooperated with Poles.[1419] A Jewish partisan band from Stanyslaviv, connected with the Soviets, engaged in a tough battle with the Banderites and were defeated. Fifteen Jewish partisans died in the encounter, and thirty-three were taken prisoner. The Banderites forced the prisoners to dig their own graves with their hands and then hanged them from trees.[1420]

Jewish survivor Zelda Baller-Lior survived in a family camp protected by Soviet partisans in the vicinity of Manevychi (P Maniewicze), about forty kilometers east of Rafalivka. She remembered that in the summer of 1943 bands of armed Ukrainians, the Banderites and Bulbaites, appeared in the region. "Members of these gangs were local people and knew the forests and all the

---

1415 AŻIH, 301/589, 1-2.
1416 For example, AŻIH, 301/926, 4; AŻIH, 301/1488, 2; AŻIH, 301/4680, 12-14.
1417 Shoah Foundation, 44158 Paula Last.
1418 YIVO, RG 104, folder 145, Mordekhai Kleinman. AŻIH, 301/75, 1.
1419 Yones, *Evrei L'vova*, 302.
1420 Ibid., 304.

roads and tracks. Our situation grew worse daily. Any Jew found in the forest or hiding in the farms was killed by them."[1421]

In 1943 UPA destroyed a Jewish civilian camp located in the woods south of Sernyky (P Serniki), in Rivne oblast near the Belarusian border; the camp was associated with Soviet partisans under the command of Maksim Misiura. One of the partisans, himself Jewish, came to the camp to recruit one of his two cousins living there. But the next morning UPA attacked the camp and killed just under fifty Jews, including both of the partisan's cousins.[1422] Other Jewish survivor accounts confirm UPA's destruction of the civilian camp. Lazar Bromberg joined the Misiura partisans in early 1943. Of the original group of eight with which he left Sernyky, only two survived; the rest died in battles with the "Bulbaites." At one point he quarrelled with the partisan leadership and left his unit together with some other Jewish partisans. They went to the Jewish civilian camp, which was about ten kilometers distant. They stayed there four days, but the Bulbaites attacked and slaughtered all the civilians, including the children. He and his Jewish partisans managed to fight their way out, but were unable to save any of the civilians.[1423]

In the same area in mid-1943, in the villages and forests between Stepanhorod (P Stepangród) and the Udrytsk-Sarny railway line, there was a Banderite gang led by a priest's son, Sashko, reputed to be a cruel killer. Sashko had first started working for the Germans as a translator and then as a judicial investigator (*sudebnyi sledovatel'*). In the hamlet of Verba (P Werba), which helped the partisans, Jews would come for shelter and food. There were some

1421 Zelda (Zoya) Baller-Lior, "A Child without a Childhood," https://www.jew-ishgen.org/yizkor/Melnitsa/mele047.html (accessed 28 March 2020).

1422 Shoah Foundation, 1979 Milton Turk, 64-68. Another interview concerning the Misiura group in the same woods mentions reports that Ukrainian partisans were killing Poles, Jews, and "Gypsies." Shoah Foundation, 46178 Nathan Dinerman.

1423 AŻIH, 301/1046, 1-2. Milton Turkienicz, also a Misiura partisan, recalled that Ukrainian nationalist partisans killed forty Jews in the forest. "Ukrainians knew the forest as well as we did." Shoah Foundation, 1979 Milton Turkienicz, 66. The massacre of the family camp by UPA was also remembered by another Misiura partisan: Shoah Foundation, 35697 Benjamin Dubowski.

partisans in Verba when Sashko's band attacked. They had no chance, since Sashko had two hundred men under his command. The Jews fled to the forest. The Banderites cut off two villagers' heads until a third one agreed to lead them to the Jews in the woods. The Banderites slaughtered the Jews.[1424]

Also in the north, in Rivne oblast near the Belarusian border, "Banderite and Bulbaite gangs fell on the villages and fields. Near the village of Vychivka [P Wiczówka] not far from the Jewish partisan base stood the Jewish family camp. Murderous gangs attacked this camp at night and killed seventy five Jews. The battle that ensued between the Jewish partisans and the Ukrainian murderers after this slaughter lasted all that night and only in the morning did the partisans force the Banderites to retreat."[1425] Further north, across the Belarusian border, near Pinsk "a large gang of Bulbaites who were searching for Jews in the woods attacked the [partisan] camp and set up ambushes for partisans when they left. Under the pressure of the gangs, the partisans were forced to retreat and temporarily abandon the forest. The refugee [i.e. family] camp fell victim to the Ukrainians' murderous lust. Sixty Jews were massacred by the Bulbaites, while the rest went barefoot and worn out into the wetlands toward the Polish village of Stara Huta [P Huta Stara, northwest of Kovel], which the Germans had set on fire. The forest refugees tried to flee toward Rafalivka, but the Jews were also persecuted there by Bulbaite and Banderite thugs."[1426]

Attempts to join the partisans were dangerous in areas where UPA was active. About three hundred Jews from Ustyluh (P Uściług), near Volodymyr-Volynskyi, escaped during the liquidation action. "Only a few found hiding places with Poles or joined the partisans. Five youths of the Sepasow family armed themselves with weapons and attempted to join the partisans through the intermediation of a Ukrainian acquaintance. The acquaintance

---

1424 Bakal'chuk-Felyn, *Vospominaniia*, 133-35.
1425 *Sefer ha-partizanim ha-Yehudim*, 1:629. Translation by Alan Rutkowski.
1426 Ibid., 1:680. Translation by Alan Rutkowski.

brought them to the units of the U.P.A. who murdered them all."[1427]
Two Jewish girls and five Poles in the Sarny-Kostopil area went towards the forest to join Soviet partisans. "On the way, they ran into
shooting by the Ukrainian nationalists and most of the group was
killed."[1428]

Labor Camps

The Holocaust had a devastating effect on branches of the economy
involving craftsmen. Over two-thirds of the craftsmen in Volhynia
before World War II were Jewish. Even the Germans recognized
that the mass murder of Jews would have serious consequences for
their armed forces because of the lack of leather workers of all sorts,
tailors, metal workers, and the like.[1429] This is the context that led
OUN-UPA to institute labor camps in which Jewish craftsmen and
professionals could work for the Ukrainian cause. Unfortunately,
the vast majority of Jews who worked in the Banderite camps were
executed as the Soviets closed in in the winter of 1943-44.

Vera Shchetinkova recalled how she was hiding with about
eighty-five other Jews in the general vicinity of the county capital
Sarny in mid-January 1944. The Banderites discovered their bunkers and decided to destroy all the Jews who lived in them. In her
view, this was so that there would be no witnesses left when the
Soviets came. Their goal was to round up all the Jews, take them to
the village of Stepan (P Stepań), about thirty or so kilometers north
of Kostopil, and there shoot them. They had surrounded the bunkers and were setting up a machine gun, but the Jews rushed out of
the bunkers and ran in all directions before they finished setting up
the gun. The young fled, and the Banderites ended up only with the
elderly and invalids. They told the Jews they did catch that they
should go to Stepan, where they would not be shot but given work.

1427 "Translation of 'Uscilug' Chapter from Pinkas Hakehillot Polin," https://
www.jewishgen.org/yizkor/pinkas_poland/pol5_00032.html (accessed 24
March 2020).
1428 Batya Scheinboim, "Escape from the Murderers," https://www.jewishgen.org
/yizkor/stepan/stee274.html (accessed 3 April 2020).
1429 Spector, *Holocaust of Volhynian Jews*, 92, 109-10. Armstrong, *Ukrainian Nationalism*, 170.

A few of the Jews who escaped decided to go to that village. However, they met a woodcutter, a Stundist[1430] from (P) Kazimierka (now Kuzmivka), who told them not to go there. He said that graves had already been dug for them and advised them to wait a few days until the Soviets arrived.[1431] Several other Jewish survivor memoirs also recount that Banderites encouraged Jews hiding in the forest to come to Stepan to work but killed them all as the Soviets approached.[1432] A memoir of an UPA veteran confirms that Jews worked in a labor camp near Stepan, set up by Ivan Lytvynchuk, commander of the Zahrava military district. In a footnote the veteran wrote: "Unfortunately, in the postwar memories of Jews perhaps there are no mentions [of the camp]. And certainly someone must have survived. But it is possible that with the arrival of the Soviets in 1944 they could have been repressed for collaboration with UPA."[1433]

Pola Jasphy related her experience to the Shoah Foundation. She was hiding with some other Jews in the forests near Antonivka (P Antonówka), about half way between Rafalivka and Sarny, where armed Ukrainians had murdered and driven out the Polish population. Many Jews found refuge in the houses abandoned by the Poles, while others hid nearby in the forest. She estimated that there were several hundred Jewish refugees in the area in the fall of 1943. They made contact with the Banderites, who said that they were not going to kill Jews, and the surviving Jews of the area went

---

1430 A type of Evangelical Protestant.
1431 Shoah Foundation, 45238 Vera Shchetinkova, 152-59.
1432 J. Peri, "Death and Sorrow," https://www.jewishgen.org/yizkor/stepan/stee 214.html (accessed 2 April 2020); also J. Peri, "Stories of Escapes," https://www.jewishgen.org/yizkor/stepan/stee274.html (accessed 3 April 2020). Aaron Grossman, "Among the Gentiles," https://www.jewishgen.org/yizkor/stepan/stee274.html (accessed 3 April 2020). Fredel Maggid, "The Struggle for Life," https://www.jewishgen.org/yizkor/stepan/stee274.html (accessed 3 April 2020). "...Three dressmakers from Ostrozhets and Olyka, as well as several artisans from Stepan, were murdered; all of them were employed by the UPA." Spector, *Holocaust of Volhynian Jews*, 271.
1433 Petrenko, *Za Ukrainu*, 173. Lev Shankovsky has denied that OUN killed the Jews in labor camps, ascribing the death of these Jews to a major offensive of the Germans against UPA in July-August 1943. In this monograph, however, the labor camps discussed existed in a later period, the winter of 1943-44. Shankovs'kyi, "Initsiiatyvnyi komitet," 59-60 n. 26.

to work for them. This lasted until early January 1944. On the 4th of the month she learned that all the Jews who were living near the formerly Polish houses (she in the meantime had moved to another part of the forest) had been killed by the Ukrainians. She and a few others managed to hide in the hay in a barn. The next day some Ukrainians came searching for them with pitchforks, but missed them by a meter. She stayed in that barn for eight days. In her opinion, the Banderites had deliberately gathered the Jews together in order to kill them.[1434]

Doba Melamed, a Jew who fled to the forest with her family from the Tuchyn ghetto, told much the same story in relation to the labor camp near Antonivka: "In the summer of 1943 the Banderites began to kill the Poles....We found out that near the town of Antonivka in the village of Rezyca,[1435] Jews were living in liberty, that the Banderites had announced that they will not kill the Jews because they are fighting against a common enemy. We went to Rezyca. In fact there were two hundred Jews living at liberty, working for the peasants as tanners, tailors, cobblers, and the like." The Melameds were suspicious and fled further. "The houses of the Poles stood empty. Then the Banderites announced that England and America, as countries with which they were allied, had forbidden them to kill Jews, that they will allow Jews to take over the homes abandoned by the Poles....In December 1943 the Banderites again began to register the Jews. After registration they announced that if one Jew escaped, the rest would be killed....In December 1943 a certain Jew knocked on our window pane and shouted: 'Run for it, the Banderites have killed the Antonivka Jews.' We fled to the forest. We sent the forester to investigate. He came back with the news that the Banderites had killed all the Jews, with axes and knives."[1436]

The memoirs of Jacob Biber resonate with the previous two testimonies. Biber's cousin had been invited by the "Bulbas" to set up a tannery in the Stubicki forest, southeast of Lutsk, near

---

1434 Shoah Foundation, 37150 Pola Jasphy, 230-39; also 150-63.
1435 I have been unable to identify this locality.
1436 AŻIH, 301/397, 12-14.

Siomaky. Siomaky is very close to Antonivka, only ten kilometers distant, so it is likely that Biber is also referring to the same labor camp or labor camp complex as Jasphy and Mełamed. Biber's Ukrainian employer and protector told him: "See...they are not touching any Jews."[1437] Biber went to visit his cousin, who said: "The Bulbas are treating me well,...but...I don't trust the Bulbas, because there are too many killers among them who do not need witnesses around with the times changing the way they are. The Soviets are winning the war and getting nearer." His cousin also told him about a Jewish girl who went to work for the Bulbas in Stubicki forest and was later found shot to death in the forest.[1438] In mid-December 1943 Biber visited his cousin again. He "told us he was working with a whole crew at the Bulbas' tannery and had acquired an assistant. He advised us again to be extremely careful, as some of the Bulbas were still killing any Jews they could find."[1439]

Yet another such tale, probably describing events in the vicinity of Radyvyliv, Rivne oblast, at the beginning of 1944, was told by Mina Grinzajd. She was in a group of 376 Jews who reached an agreement with the Banderites to work for them as tailors, cobblers, and leather workers. From time to time the Banderites "resettled" some of the workers in groups of twenty to thirty, in reality shooting them. At the end of three months, the original group was reduced to thirty-four.[1440]

From another locality, forests near Kupychiv (P Kupiczów), about twenty-five kilometers south of Kovel, comes yet another such description. The Banderites set up a labor camp in which

---

1437 Biber, *Survivors*, 137.
1438 Ibid., 139.
1439 Ibid., 145.
1440 AŻIH, 301/2888. I have relied on S. Arm's Polish translation and Franziska Bruder's German translation of this Yiddish-language testimony. Bruder, *"Den ukrainischen Staat erkämpfen,"* 218-19. The place name mentioned in the testimony is "Kritniv," rendered by both Arm and Bruder as Krytyniw. I suspect this is Korytne, about twenty-five kilometers north of Radyvyliv. Mina Grinzajd wrote that the agreement with the Banderites was reached in January 1943. This would have been too early for the establishment of a work camp associated with the Ukrainian nationalists; all the other examples we know of come much later in the year, after the emergence of UPA. I suspect she meant January 1944. That timing fits perfectly with the many other cases.

seventy Jews were working. They gave Jews in nearby bunkers an equivalent of the Germans' *Kennkarte*, which would allow the Jews to leave their bunkers for work without being harmed. In fact, though, the Banderites attacked the bunkers three times, killing seventeen of the inhabitants. All seventy Jews who worked in the labor camp were murdered.[1441]

Sonyah Sherer was hiding with a Ukrainian farmer in Khorokhoryn. Nearby was a small wooded area where about half a dozen Jews were hiding. According to her testimony, Banderites were in the vicinity and "pasted announcements up on the trees — let all the Jews come to them, and they will do them no harm. It was winter, it was cold — they went to those Ukrainians, to the Banderites, and they shot them all."[1442]

There was another camp near Mizoch. In 1943 survivor Volf Oks was taken to "the leader of the Bandera Gangs" by the latter's son. The Banderites were "then fighting only for an independent Ukraine, not against the Jews, and he led me and a group of Jews to a camp, a pit on an island." Oks fled the camp after eight days, so we do not know the fate of the Jews who worked there.[1443]

From the region of Ratne and Kamin-Kashirskyi (P Kamień Koszyrski) in Volhynia oblast comes this survivor narrative:

> A change took place with the Ukrainians who had collaborated with the Germans. They decided to sever their covenant with the Germans and begin to struggle to establish an independent Ukrainian state. These people were headed by a Ukrainian general named Bulba, and they were called "Bulbovchi" after his name. They fought against the retreating Germans as well as the advancing Russians....One day two representatives of the Ukrainian organization suddenly appeared accompanied by the farmer who had saved us. They had a unanimous announcement: since my father had a trade and knew how to fix weapons, our entire family had to move to their camp near Khoteshov [Khoteshiv, P Chocieszów], where they would protect us.

1441 AŻIH, 301/1510, Fefer Bajla, 2-3.

1442 Shoah Foundation, 17221 Sonyah Sherer. This testimony was in Hebrew; I am grateful to Mykhailo Tiahlyi for providing me with a Ukrainian translation.

1443 Volf Oks, "The Destruction of the Jewish Village of Mizoch," https://www.jewishgen.org/yizkor/kremenets3/kre339.html#Page366 (accessed 27 March 2020).

My father would work at fixing weapons, I would help him, and my mother and sister would weave scarves and socks for their fighters. We could not refuse, and we moved to their base, where a small house was put at our disposal. They treated us well in accordance with the explicit directive of their commander....

Everything had now changed with our way of life. We slept on a bench rather than a pile of straw and fodder. We ate at a table rather than in a barn or sheep pen. We felt that the "Bulbovchi" Camp was like a royal palace...[1444] We lived with them and enjoyed our freedom for seven months. Indeed, this was a very forced freedom, for we knew very well what these Ukrainians had perpetrated against the Jews in the past. We also knew that they did not maintain us out of love, and if they reached the conclusion that we were no longer of benefit to them, they would not spare our lives....My father became friendly with one of the captains, a member of the staff that was responsible for us. He greatly valued our work at repairing the weapons and weaving the scarves. His nickname was "Stochka" and he had been a policeman in his time. He revealed a secret to my father: they had decided in their group that in the event that the partisans were to advance to us and attempt to conquer the area, they would kill us. He swore that he would save us if such a time came.

One evening, I visited the house of one of the farmers along with the friendly captain. The host brought refreshments and liquor. Our friend became drunk, and "when wine enters, secrets come out." He said that the situation had become serious, the partisans were pressing from all sides, there would be a need to retreat, and they would be forced to carry out the plan that he had told my father secretly. Before we returned home, the captain tapped my shoulders and said, "Do not worry, as long as I am alive, no harm will befall you."....

Toward the next evening, the Ukrainians retreated from the area due to the pressure of the partisans who had begun to clear the area to prepare for the advancing Russian Army.... Our friend Stochka returned to us toward morning. He was tired and unshaven. He told us that they wanted to come at night to kill us, but he convinced his friends to refrain from carrying out their plan, and promised them to turn us over to them. He advised us to flee in the direction of the partisans, and asked that we remember him positively. Tears flowed from his eyes, and, from the appearance of his face, we sensed that he was speaking the truth. We felt sorry for him, and we advised him

---

1444 Ellipsis in the original.

to escape together with us, but he did not want to betray his friends. We parted from him in great agony.[1445]

By the winter of 1943-44 there were few Poles left in Volhynia, and none in unprotected settlements, so they have left no accounts of UPA's labor camps in the forests.

It is, in my opinion, difficult to doubt that the Jewish survivor testimonies, collected over a span of fifty years in different countries and converging in so many details, reflect a genuine OUN-UPA policy, one that the nationalists learned while they cooperated with the Germans: they assembled Jews in forced labor camps, occasionally issued registration papers that would protect them temporarily, and then executed them when no longer required. With the imminent arrival of the Soviets, the Jewish laborers were not simply no longer required but posed, in OUN-B's opinion, a security concern.

However, there is one survivor memoir, that of Zelig Broiderman, that credits UPA with saving a Jewish family camp. This memoir appeared not in any of the collections of Jewish survivor testimonies, but in an article compiled by the Israeli journalist Leo Heiman for the *Ukrainian Quarterly*. I do not doubt that this is a genuine memoir, since other materials included in Heiman's compilations[1446] are surely genuine.[1447] Broiderman wrote that the family camp he was in, near Kovel in Volhynia, had appealed for protection to the Polish Home Army, the Polish People's Army (*Armia Ludowa*), and Soviet partisans. None of these partisan formations were willing to help and, in fact, threatened the camp. UPA, however, and notably a certain Roman Polishchuk,[1448] set up a special labor

---

1445 Ben-Zion Kamintzky, "Sorrowful Memories," *Translation of* Ratne; sipura shel kehila yehudit she-hushmeda, ed. Nachman Tamir (Tel Aviv: Ratno Society in Israel, 1983), https://www.jewishgen.org/yizkor/Ratno/rat159.html#f170-1r (accessed 23 March 2020).

1446 He also produced a related compilation for the *Ukrainian Quarterly*: Heiman, "They Saved Jews."

1447 The veracity of Broiderman's memoir is also accepted by Spector, *Holocaust of Volhynian Jews*, 272.

1448 A Roman Polishchuk was a notorious killer of Jews in the Tuchyn region. He killed Jews as an OUN militiaman, as a policeman, and as a nationalist insurgent. Testimony of Bella Shpilman, 25 November 1944: USHMM RG-22.002M, reel 25; TsGAOR, fond 7021, op. 71, spr. 68, ff. 71-72. But Polishchuk is a very

camp not far from the local UPA headquarters. "One of our people was a precision-tool mechanic, and we soon opened small work-shops to manufacture bomb-fuses and explosive mechanisms for the UPA saboteurs. Two tailors and a shoemaker helped take care of UPA uniforms." The Soviet approach endangered the Jewish family/labor camp: "If we came out into the open, the Soviets would consider us as enemies, because of our association with the UPA. This meant death, or at least deportation to Siberia." The Jews were saved by Polishchuk and his family, who placed them in hiding with local Ukrainian families. At least twenty survivors of this group ended up in Israel. However, Broiderman included a number of qualifiers in his memoir: "Smaller unarmed Jewish groups were murdered by pro-Nazi 'pseudo-partisans' who posed as UPA guerrillas....The Polish AK units shot us on sight, as did the bands of 'independent' Ukrainian renegades headed by various 'ataman' chieftans, who posed as UPA formations to kill and loot for personal gain....the real UPA, as distinct from the bandits who misused the UPA's name and reputation, never harmed us....To be quite objective, I cannot say today whether the kind treatment we received was the general policy in all UPA units, or only in the unit commanded by Roman Polishchuk."[1449] My own interpretation of this memoir is that Broiderman was at pains to express his gratitude to an UPA commander and unit that saved him and his companions, but he knew that this was not UPA's normal policy. He therefore made a distinction between a genuine UPA that saved Jews and an imposter UPA that killed Jews.

To prepare for the arrival of the Soviets, the OUN-B leadership called for a reduction of the front against the Poles. In January 1944 it issued these instructions: "The following should be destroyed:....Active sympathizers of the Bolsheviks....In places where military strongholds are planned [*plianovanykh osidok*] to undertake a complete purge of elements that could be threatening in the

---

common Ukrainian last name, and Tuchyn is quite some distance from Kovel. Moreover, Broiderman's Roman Polishchuk was killed in combat by Soviet forces, while the other Roman Polishchuk was working at the mill in Tuchyn at least until late November 1944.

1449 Heiman, "We Fought for Ukraine," 35-36.

reality under the Soviets....To create on the circle and county levels execution units—militant units. Their task will be:....Conducting mass liquidation actions...." The document also prohibited the local population from entering the forests on pain of death. It continued:

> To use the chaos at the front for the mass liquidation of hostile elements, who are, in the first place:
> a) organized members of the Bolshevik underground
> b) partisan units,
> c) active sympathizers of the Bolsheviks,
> d) Russian POWs who are politically activated,
> e) the Polish element capable of leadership and military action, who will become the servant of the new Soviet occupation.
> To execute all the liquidation actions as discreetly as possible.[1450]

Although this document makes no specific mention of Jews, it does imply the kind of operations against the Jews that we have examined above.

Other sources state unequivocally that the military wing of OUN-B included Jews in these mass liquidation actions. Jewish survivor Borys Arsen linked his brother's murder with an order issued by Roman Shukhevych, supreme commander of UPA "to annihilate all potential adversaries of Ukraine."[1451] Mykola Todorovych Slobodiuk,[1452] a subraion commander of SB OUN, was interrogated by the Soviets on 13 April 1944. He related that in early August 1943 he was summoned to a meeting of the local SB OUN leadership. The commander of the Rivne raion SB OUN, whose pseudonym was "Makar," instructed the subraion officers as follows: "To destroy all 'the enemies of UPA,' understood to be all Poles, Czechs, Jews, Komsomol members, officers of the Red Army, militia personnel, and any Ukrainians who even in the least measure sympathized with Soviet authority."[1453] Oleksii Kyryliuk, who was the personal adjutant of "Makar," told his interrogators on 27 June

---

1450 Polishchuk, *Integralny nacjonalizm ukraiński*, 5:19-21, citing DARO, fond R-30, opys 2, spr. 16, ff. 112-14.

1451 Melamed, "Organized and Unsolicited Collaboration," 222.

1452 There was another Mykola Slobodiuk with a different patronymic in the same subraion SB OUN unit.

1453 Polishchuk, *Integralny nacjonalizm ukraiński*, 5:100, citing DARO, acts of case no. 10012, vol. 2, ff. 406-13.

1944: "Generally the leadership of OUN placed the following obligations on its security service: 1. Destroy all 'enemies' of UPA and OUN, who are the Poles, Czechs, Jews, komsomol members, communists, officers and soldiers of the Red Army, militia personnel, and persons from the local population expressing their sympathies for Soviet authority."[1454]

After Liberation

In this section I will look at how the relationship between OUN-UPA and the surviving Jewish population developed in the immediate aftermath of the Soviet reconquest of Western Ukraine. Soviet authority took years to take firm hold there, since the Red Army was still marching to Berlin many months after Lutsk, Rivne, and Lviv were liberated (2 February, 5 February, 27 July 1944, respectively). The Soviets found themselves overextended for a considerable period after World War II came to an end. I am not aiming here at a comprehensive survey, just a sketch of the trends that can be easily observed in this chaotic period.

The tentative attempts to revise OUN's position on the Jews that we noticed earlier[1455] continued after the Germans were gone. An indication of this was a response to an antisemitic article written by the nationalist ideologue Dmytro Dontsov in 1944. A young member of OUN's supreme council, Osyp Pozychaniuk, called for a complete renunciation of antisemitism and of any other form of xenophobia. His response still, however, bore the marks of its origin in the antisemitic environment of the nationalists. He wrote that the Ukrainian people were not going to be attracted to the movement by an antisemitic line, but "not because the people sympathizes with the Jews." Rather, "the people has endured at the hands of the universal carriers of this antisemitism—the Hitlerite hordes—an even greater tragedy than the Jews."[1456] A change in

---

1454 Polishchuk, *Integralny nacjonalizm ukraiński*, 5:153, citing DARO, acts of case no. 10012, vol. 2, ff. 327-36.

1455 See above, 351.

1456 V"iatrovych, *Stavlennia OUN do ievreiv*, 84-85. See also Radchenko, "From Staryi Uhryniv to Munich," 442-45.

official policy is indicated by a secret order from the Buh military region of UPA in Galicia, dated 5 September 1944, which called for restoring relations with the Poles and for treating the Jews as a national minority.[1457] An OUN-UPA instruction issued two days later said, under the heading "Jewish Question": "Take no actions against the Jews. The Jewish issue is no longer a problem, there are so few of them left."[1458]

There was at least one case in which UPA spared Jewish lives in the aftermath of the war. The story only came out in 2001, when a representative of a Jewish relief agency met two Jewish women in Starunia, south of Bohorodchany in Ivano-Frankivsk oblast. Fellow villagers, Ukrainians, had written to the agency to request help for the two old Jewish women, who were sisters. When the representative met the women, they were still afraid to be recognized as Jews. They had managed to survive the war by successfully posing as poor Ukrainian women; a wealthy individual in Ternopil had given them jobs. After liberation they had difficulties legalizing themselves, since they had no documents. They returned therefore to Starunia, where their house, robbed entirely of its belongings, was occupied by another family. A local farmer gave them shelter, but people began to demand they leave the village. This was in 1945-46, when "the boys from the forest" called the tune. Eventually the sisters had to hide in their host's attic whenever anyone came over. Then one day two men from the forest came to the farmer who was sheltering them and demanded he bring out the two Jewish women. The sisters thought they had met their end. But the senior of the two men told them: "Girls, don't be afraid, and remember that as long as we are in charge of your region no one will dare to lay a finger on you." From then on they were greeted on the street, even with smiles.[1459]

1457 TsDAVO 3833-2-3, http://io.ua.1532331p (accessed 28 May 2009). Motyka, *Ukraińska partyzantka*, 296.

1458 USHMM RG-31.026, reel 9; TsDAHO, fond 1, op. 23, spr. 931, f. 169. Also cited in Bruder, *"Den ukrainischen Staat erkämpfen,"* 223, and Motyka, *Ukraińska partyzantka*, 296.

1459 This story is told in Arsen, *Moia hirka pravda*, 351-53.

However, antisemitism was so deeply rooted in OUN attitudes, experience, and practices that it did not disappear. Interrogated by his Soviet captors, Volodymyr Porendovsky told them
that in 1941-42 OUN openly preached a racist ideology, called for
the annihilation of the Jews, and took part in their murder. Later
OUN began to be ashamed of this and repudiated participation in
such actions, "but in reality until the very end the 'leadership' of
OUN stood on antisemitic positions." He related that in 1945 the
director of the political section (*referentura*) of the central OUN leadership, Dmytro Maievsky, told him: "It was a good thing that the
Germans annihilated the Jews, because in this way OUN got rid of
some of its enemies." Another important figure in the OUN leadership, Yaroslav Starukh, had told him much the same thing in fall
1946.[1460] Starukh at that time was leading UPA troops on the territory of Poland (Zakerzonnia).[1461] Antisemitic formulations — "Jewish commissars,"[1462] "Jewish-Bolshevik dictatorship"[1463] — remained embedded in texts issued by the OUN-UPA underground.[1464] A memorial monument to Holocaust victims at Sosenky
forest near Rivne, erected in 1945 by a dozen Jewish survivors from
the area, was destroyed several times by Banderites.[1465]

The murder of Jews wound down but did not cease. In every
region where OUN-B and UPA remained active, there are reports
that they killed Jews. Neta Kiperman was in a hospital in Sverd-
lovsk when he received news he could return home to Kozyn (P
Kozin) in Volhynia. This was after the Soviets had recaptured
Rivne. But "along the roads were bands of 'Banderas' (Ukrainian

---

1460 HDA SBU, fond 13, spr. 372, vol. 2, f. 198 (15 February 1948).

1461 *Encyclopedia of Ukraine*, s.v. "Starukh, Yaroslav."

1462 Peter Potichnyj Collection on Insurgency and Counter-Insurgency in Ukraine,
University of Toronto, box 81, file "1947," lystivka "Chervonoarmiitsi," December 1944. I am grateful to Yuri Radchenko for transcripts of materials from
the Potichnyj Collection.

1463 Armstrong, *Ukrainian Nationalism*, 118.

1464 See also Peter Potichnyj Collection on Insurgency and Counter-Insurgency in
Ukraine, University of Toronto, box 75, file "1944," letter of I.P. Ivaniuk, 6 December 1944; TsDAHO, fond 1, op. 23, spr. 929.

1465 Burds, *Holocaust in Rovno*, 103.

fascists) who killed Russians and, above all, Jews."[1466] Similarly, after Sarny was liberated, recalled another survivor, "life was tense. We heard shooting at frequent intervals. With the onset of darkness, everyone closeted themselves in their houses for fear of the *Banderovtsy* that roamed through the streets at that time."[1467] Yet another survivor returned to Lanivtsi after 1945. He recalled:

> There was no transportation. The Ukrainians walked everywhere but I was afraid to join them because the roads were full of Bandarovtze who murdered Jews. Their fellow Ukrainians would inform the Bandarovtze of every Jew or person suspected of being Jewish....
> There [the Christian cemetery in Shumsk] I was shown two graves and was told that these were of Jews from Shumsk who had returned here to their pitiful homes after the war. One of them was Bryk and the name of the other was not known. Banderovtze stabbed them to death on the road. On their tombstones Russian stars were carved but no names were inscribed.
> Near these graves were also the graves of Banderovtze leaders whom the Soviets had caught and buried like dogs, in their clothing.[1468]

Murders were also reported in Galicia. Le'ah Rozentsvayg, a survivor from Rava Ruska, was asked by her interviewer from the USC Shoah Foundation if she returned to the town after the war. She answered: "In Vienna I met my girlfriends who also fled from Rava Ruska and returned. They told me: 'There is nothing there for you to look for, no one is alive. Moreover, there is mortal danger there, there are Banderites there, i.e., Ukrainians....'" The interviewer asked: "This was after the war?" She answered in the affirmative: "After the war. There were Ukrainian nationalists who killed those who returned."[1469] After the liberation of Skole in November 1944, Berl Lieblein and his uncle returned there. A few days later Banderites attacked the city, and a Jewish boy was killed in battle.

1466 Neta Kiperman, "My Wanderings," https://www.jewishgen.org/yizkor/kremenets3/kre339.html#Page366 (accessed 27 March 2020).

1467 Meir Walkin, "After the Victory," https://www.jewishgen.org/yizkor/sarny/sar370.html (accessed 2 April 2020).

1468 Munya (Nathan) Fuks, "Wanderings of a Boy from Shumsk," https://www.jewishgen.org/yizkor/szumsk/szu110.html (accessed 2 April 2020).

1469 Shoah Foundation, 34376 Le'ah Rozentsvayg. This testimony was in Hebrew; I am grateful to Mykhailo Tiahlyi for providing me with a Ukrainian translation.

Banderites searched Lieblein's uncle's home. Lieblein and his uncle were hiding in some nearby ruins, and they could hear the Banderites asking each other if they'd seen the uncle. Clearly, Lieblein thought, someone had hired them to kill the uncle. The uncle suspected it was a Ukrainian teacher with whom he and other Jews had left many things for safekeeping.[1470] A ten-year-old boy, Munio Inslicht, told the Central Jewish Historical Commission with tears in his eyes that his father, along with another Jewish man, had been murdered by Banderites just two months previously while he was travelling on business between Tlumach (P Tłumacz) and Stanyslaviv. This was in 1945, already after Soviet rule had returned.[1471] A Jewish survivor and his wife made their way to Stanyslaviv shortly after the Soviets reoccupied it (27 July 1944). They had left their baby girl with a family in the village of Puzhnyky (P Puźniki). After a few weeks in Stanyslaviv, they wanted to go after their daughter, but felt it was unsafe: "At that time...the area was infested with *banderowcy* (Ukrainian nationalist guerillas) who were killing Jews."[1472] In May 1945 the Jews of Zhuravno moved to the larger nearby town of Stryi. According to a Jewish survivor from Zhuravno, "they were afraid of the gangs of Ukrainian Nationalists."[1473] Banderites killed a Jewish woman as well as about twenty Poles in the village of Piątkowa, Przemyśl county, in 1944-45, according to a Polish testimony.[1474]

Murder and terror continued also in Bukovina. After the Germans were driven out by the Soviets, the Wiesenfeld family wanted to return to Nyzhni Stanivtsi, which had been the scene of a bloody pogrom in 1941.[1475] It was now 1945. But there were Banderites in the woods, whom Chana Wiesenfeld characterized as left-over Germans in combination with Ukrainian fascists. When the nationalists discovered that Jews were coming back to Nyzhni Stanivtsi, they started to shoot at the house they were in. They killed several

1470 Hochberg-Mariańska and Grüss, *Dzieci oskarżają*, 141.
1471 AŻIH, 301/803.
1472 Tannenzapf, *Memories from the Abyss*, 47.
1473 Tal, *The Fields of Ukraine*, 155.
1474 Dalecki, *Zbrodnie nacjonalistów ukraińskich*, 184.
1475 See above, 292-97.

people, including a doctor. The rest, who were lying on the floor, survived. They also left a letter saying, "We don't need you dirty Jews; if you do not leave this town, you will be killed in the morning." So the Wiesenfelds asked a Russian officer to put them on a tank, which took them to Vashkivtsi, not far from Galicia. The Banderites were there too, and they were also shooting Jews. But in this bigger town the Soviets had the upper hand and were able to keep the Banderites under control.[1476] Leizer Roll was from Berehomet (Ro Berehomet pe Siret), east of Storozhynets. In the spring of 1944, after most of Bukovina was reoccupied by the Soviets, he and some other Jews arrived in Storozhynets (Ro Storojineţ) but could not go back to the village of Berehomet. The Banderites were in charge there and killed Jews who dared to return. A friend of his who returned was killed the first night with axes, cut in half, together with his wife and small child. The dismembered corpses were piled on a table. They also took a Jewish doctor to the woods and tied him between two bent trees. When they let go of the trees, the doctor was ripped in half.[1477]

UPA also killed Jews in other Ukrainian- or Rusyn-inhabited territories. There is a report that UPA killed a Jewish woman in the Lemko region (Faja Dym in Kalnica, Lesko county) on 13 February 1945.[1478] In December 1945 an UPA unit killed and robbed eleven Jews in Kolbasov in Eastern Slovakia.[1479]

With the arrival of the Red Army and Soviet partisans, surviving Jews could take revenge on the Ukrainian police, OUN militias, and UPA. Revenge, in fact, had played a major role in motivating Jewish partisans.[1480] Around the time of the Soviet reconquest, a Soviet partisan unit captured Velyki Mezhyrichi (P Międzyrzec), east

---

1476 Shoah Foundation, 15665 Chana Wiesenfeld, 11.
1477 Shoah Foundation, 11289 Leizer Roll, 39-41. The murder of the doctor is modeled on the fate of the Rus' Prince Igor, a story the nationalists would have been familiar with. Igor's legs were tied to two bent birch trees, and when the trees were released, the prince's body was torn in two.
1478 Dalecki, *Zbrodnie nacjonalistów ukraińskich*, 113.
1479 This has been carefully documented in Tokarczuk, *Medzi troma hranicami*, esp. 18-24.
1480 On the importance of revenge for Jewish partisans, see Ejack, "The Jewish Soviet Partisan," 46-50.

of Korets in Rivne oblast. One of the Jewish partisans identified twenty-eight Ukrainian policemen to the commander, who had them summarily executed. Another Jewish partisan helped with the execution, killing the policemen with his knife. "I want to see them bleeding like they bled my parents," he told his friend; "I feel good when I see their blood."[1481]

Some Jews volunteered for the Soviet militia, NKVD, and destruction battalions in order to eradicate Ukrainian nationalist insurgents and former policemen.[1482] A Jewish commander within a Soviet partisan subunit, Yitzhak Zakuska joined an "NKVD battalion fighting the UPA remnants."[1483] Jewish survivors Chaim and Yakov Waks joined the NKVD after the Soviets returned in order to "take care of the Ukrainian Nazis." Chaim was killed by UPA in 1944 in the village of Malynsk (P Małyńsk), north of Kostopil. His brother Yakov afterwards went on a drunken shooting spree in the village, which resulted in fatalities.[1484] A Jewish doctor who survived the war in Galicia wrote in his memoirs: "We were also co-opted onto the Russian army draft board for participation in operations against the Ukrainian nationalists. I took part in this activity willingly and showed them no mercy: I drafted them into the army or sent them to the Donbass coal mines for hard labor....I sat on medical committees with Soviet army personnel and Communist Party officials who regularly got falling-down drunk. Sometimes I joined in, to forget or to harden my heart toward the Ukrainian population which, here too, had collaborated with the Germans."[1485] Yosef Laufer of Zhuravno in Galicia also volunteered for Soviet police auxiliaries to fight the Banderites.[1486] Survivor Lew Akiwa, from near Sambir reported two Banderites to the NKVD, one of whom killed his father as well as hundreds of other Jews.[1487] When

---

1481 Shoah Foundation, 1222, Samuel Honigman, 27.
1482 Bruder, "Den ukrainischen Staat erkämpfen," 239, cites many examples of OUN-UPA documents referring to Jews collaborating with the organs of repression in the aftermath of the return of Soviet power.
1483 Spector, Holocaust of Volhynian Jews, 311.
1484 Ejack, ""The Jewish Soviet Partisan," 51.
1485 Milch, Can Heaven Be Void? 245-46.
1486 Tal, The Fields of Ukraine, 150.
1487 AŻIH, 301/2238, 7.

the Red Army took over Khorokhoryn in Volhynia oblast, Sonyah Sherer had been hiding with a half-Ukrainian, half-Polish villager. "Suddenly in the morning a Russian came, a Jew it seems....and he said: 'We will pay back all the Ukrainians and all the Poles for killing Jews.'....Then more Russians came to us. Well, I immediately went around the villages to find out when some gentile exposed Jews, and when some gentile in some manner helped the Jews."[1488]

Jews in UPA

Just as the mass murder of Jews caused a shortage of craftsmen and professionals, it also devastated personnel in the health professions. Surviving Jewish physicians, paramedics, and dentists were in great demand in various partisan formations, including Soviet partisans,[1489] the Polish Home Army,[1490] and UPA.

Numerous sources document the presence of Jewish medical personnel serving with UPA, including Soviet interrogations. Prominent UPA officer Yevhen Basiuk told his interrogator the names of two Jewish paramedics who worked with UPA.[1491] A Ukrainian policeman, Osyp Velychuk, was asked by his NKVD interrogators in Hrymailiv, if he knew anyone who joined UPA. He replied: "I know that Gudz Nikolai took Markevich Miacheslav [sic], a Jew, into an 'UPA' band in the fall of 1943. In the winter of 1944 my mother Velichuk Ekaterina received a letter from him with a cancellation from the city of Ternopil; he wrote that he was living well, but where he was living he did not write."[1492] Shaia Varm had survived on false papers and maintained a medical practice in Sviichiv (P Swojczów) near Volodymyr-Volynskyi until May 1943. At that time he was drafted as a physician for UPA and served the

1488 Shoah Foundation, 17221 Sonyah Sherer. This testimony was in Hebrew; I am grateful to Mykhailo Tiahlyi for providing me with a Ukrainian translation.
1489 Spector, *Holocaust of Volhynian Jews*, 326. Shoah Foundation, 35697 Benjamin Dubowski. Shoah Foundation, 9245 Manya Feldman. Shoah Foundation, 24104 Nina Merrick. Shoah Foundation, 46178 Nathan Dinerman.
1490 Spector, *Holocaust of Volhynian Jews*, 263-64.
1491 "Vytiah z protokolu dopytu Ie. Basiuka," 128.
1492 USHMM RG-31.018M, reel 83; GDA SBU Ternopil', spr. 31025, vol. 1, Herman H.M., Velychuk, O.Z., f. 57.

insurgents until he was arrested by the Soviet authorities in September 1944. During his interrogation, he described his recruitment to UPA:

> One night in May 1943 two armed Banderites came to my home. One of them, who had the pseudonym "Sokil," was the commandant of the police. He stated: "We need a physician, come with us." They put my modest belongings on a cart and took me and my wife Bronislava. They took us to the village of Vovchok [Urochyshche Vovchak, P Wowczak] in Turiisk raion and gave us an apartment. From that time on I worked as a doctor in UPA. About a week later fighting started and wounded appeared. At that time I worked in the hospital in Vovchok, but in July we transferred our base to the forest.[1493]

Jewish survivors also mentioned fellow Jews who worked in health care for UPA. Borys Arsen, whose brother was killed by UPA near Rohatyn, had a cousin, Moisei Zilber, who served for a long time as a dentist for UPA. Arsen did not know what happened to him in the end.[1494] According to Shmuel Spector, "Dr. Elbirt of Lutsk, who carried papers attesting to his being a Karaite, joined the UPA by mistake and was murdered by his comrades-in-arms on the eve of liberation. A similar fate befell two physicians and their wives from Lvov who were brought to the Ludvipol [Liudvypil] area."[1495] Basing himself on two Hebrew-language testimonies, Eliyahu Yones recounted that in the summer of 1943, in the Kurovychi [P Kurowice] labor camp about thirty kilometers southeast of Lviv, Ukrainian partisans convinced two physicians, Drs. Staropolsky and Kalfus, as well as a dentist to join them in the forest

1493 *Litopys neskorenoi Ukrainy*, 413. Varm's fate has not been established with certainty. A woman who knew Varm (her mother supervised UPA hospitals) said that he was sentenced to twenty years in a labor camp, but that supposedly the Jewish community intervened on his behalf. Ibid., 415. Eliyahu Yakira, a doctor serving with the Polish Home Army, said that after the Soviets arrested Varm, he was sentenced to death with the entire captured UPA unit. Dr. Yakira intervened on his behalf and an appeal was made to Stalin himself. As a result, his sentence was first commuted to life imprisonment and then reduced to fifteen years; in the end, he was pardoned. Spector, *Holocaust of Volhynian Jews*, 263-66, 271. *Medychna opika v UPA*, 363-64, reprints the decision of a military tribunal sentencing Varm to twenty years hard labor on 16 September 1944.
1494 Arsen, *Moia hirka pravda*, 12.
1495 Spector, *Holocaust of Volhynian Jews*, 271.

and treat their sick and wounded. The partisans promised the Jews that they would be spared and not liquidated. "The Jews agreed and joined their units, but as the front got closer, the Ukrainians killed them all."[1496] Yones also wrote that before the liquidation of the Ternopil ghetto (thus before June 1943), Ukrainian partisans convinced some Jewish physicians to join them, but killed them later as the Red Army approached.[1497]

Ukrainian sources say that many Jews served in UPA as physicians.[1498] Mykola Omeliusik wrote about UPA's lack of doctors and how Jews filled that gap:

> In the situation, the OUN organization proposed to Jewish doctors that they join UPA. Many of them joined and were secretly transported to their assigned place. Many of them were stolen out of the ghettos with their families, where they were under police guard. I did not hear of a case in which the Jewish doctors tried to go over to the side of the Red partisans. There were instances when a unit had to disperse when confronted with a more powerful enemy, and without exception the doctors would reappear in their unit. In one case a Jewish doctor had to hide from the Red partisans up to his neck in mud for a whole day before he could get back to his unit.[1499]

One of the elderly nationalists whom Eva Himka interviewed in Lviv in 2009 also stated that Jewish doctors who served in UPA never betrayed it and that most of these Jews died in battle.[1500] UPA veteran Roman Petrenko recalled:

> In the Zahrava military district, two Jewish doctors worked for "Dubovyi" [Ivan Lytvynchuk]. In the UPA hospital in the city of Kolky [P Kołki] the Jewish doctor "Bilyi" worked together with his wife. When it was necessary to transfer this hospital to the medical center in the Kovel region, I personally transported Dr. "Bilyi" and his wife there. We met accidentally after the war in 1946 in Germany, in the city of Ingolstadt. This was at the railroad station. In our brief

---

1496 Yones, *Evrei L'vova*, 298. Three to four hundred Jews worked in the Kurovychi camp. Among the main tasks of the forced laborers were roadwork and breaking rocks for gravel. On the camp, see ibid., 227-28.

1497 Ibid., 302 (based on testimonies).

1498 For example, Potichnyj, *My Journey*, 55.

1499 Omeliusik, "UPA na Volyni v 1943 rotsi," no. 2: 20-21. This article is a very one-sided account of UPA's treatment of the Polish population of Volhynia in 1943.

1500 Himka and Himka, "Absence and Presence."

conversation he spoke about the past and said that he was off to Israel. Unfortunately, we parted without thinking about further contact. I met another two Jewish doctors, husband and wife, in the "Sich" in the region of Volodymyr-Volynskyi.[1501]

Other physicians who worked for UPA include: Dr. Margosh ("Havrysh"), chief of medical services of the Western Division of UPA; Samuel Neuman ("Maksymovych"), who was taken from the ghetto together with his mother and then served at a training school for UPA officers in Verkhnia Rozhanka (P Rożanka Wyżna) in the Carpathians; Dr. "Kum," chief of an underground UPA hospital in Trukhaniv (P Truchanów), near Skole in the Carpathians (he was killed in a battle against Soviet forces); and Roman Vynnytsky ("Sam").[1502]

Philip Friedman asked: "Ukrainian sources speak of a considerable number of Jewish physicians, dentists, and hospital attendants who served in the ranks of the UPA. The question is: Why did only a small number of them remain alive?"[1503] I do not know whether this is a question that can be answered by citing evidence. We do not know how many health workers of Jewish nationality served with UPA, and we only have anecdotal information about their fates. All that can be said with certainty is that UPA killed some, some escaped to liberated areas, some survived because of UPA, and some were victims of the Soviet reconquista. Without more information — and I do not see how we will get it — we cannot determine the proportion between the various outcomes.

Before leaving the topic of Jewish medical personnel in UPA, we should look at three very different accounts by Jewish survivors of their service in UPA.

1501 Petrenko, *Za Ukrainu*, 173. It is most likely that the last-mentioned husband and wife team were Shaia and Bronislava Varm. In his interrogation, Varm mentioned "the Sich in the Svynaryn forest. This was near the village of Vovchok, Turiisk raion, where the Sich officer staff was located." *Litopys neskorenoi Ukrainy*, 414. Danylo Shumuk remembered three Jewish doctors working in the Sich. Shumuk, *Life Sentence*, 77.

1502 Motyka, *Ukraińska partyzantka*, 291. Friedman, "Ukrainian Jewish Relations," 204 n. 59. *Medychna opika v UPA*, 349-58.

1503 Friedman, "Ukrainian Jewish Relations," 188-89.

Collecting oral history on the town of Berezhany, the Israeli scholar Shimon Redlich interviewed a Jew who had been a physician with UPA. He granted the interview on the condition that his real name not be revealed, which, he felt, might endanger him. Poldek, as he called himself for the interview, had become friends with a man who was the chief of police in a village and a member of UPA. This man suggested he serve with the nationalist partisans, and Poldek agreed. "I was asked to translate books of basic medicine from Polish and German into Ukrainian and to teach young Ukrainian women to be nurses for the underground." He refused some tasks that UPA assigned him. One was to perform surgical experiments on a Soviet partisan they had captured in battle; another was to save the life of a wounded SS man. He escaped from the unit in summer 1944 and returned to Berezhany, then in Soviet hands.[1504]

A memoir that was much more favorable to UPA was published by Leo Heiman in the *Ukrainian Quarterly*.[1505] It was so favorable that I was initially concerned that it might have been a fake, like the Stella Krenzbach memoir.[1506] However, thanks to the investigation of Israeli journalist Fredi Gruber, I was able to confirm that the author of the memoir, Dr. Abraham Sterzer, had indeed existed and that various personal details included in his account were true.[1507] Moreover, Sterzer was also mentioned, though not by name, in Philip Friedman's study of Ukrainian-Jewish relations during the Second World War.[1508] Although very interesting, Sterzer's memoir is, unfortunately, too long to quote in full. It opens with a lengthy exposition of Ukrainian-Jewish relations, contextualizing the outbreaks of antisemitism among Ukrainians. "Now, nothing I have said so far justifies the excesses and brutalities

---

1504 Redlich, *Together and Apart in Brzezany*, 23, 127.
1505 Heiman, "We Fought for Ukraine," 37-41. Reprinted as Abraham Sterzer, "We Fought for Ukraine!" in *Medychna opika v UPA*, 341-45.
1506 See above, 112-15.
1507 Email from Fredi Gruber to the author, 8 October 2017. Dr. Sterzer was born in 1902 and died in 2004.
1508 "Another Jewish physician who served in the Bandera group and was thus saved, together with his brother, lives now in a village near Tel Aviv." This was clearly Sterzer. Friedman, "Ukrainian Jewish Relations," 204 n. 59.

committed during the war. Nothing justifies the murder of women and children, the physical annihilation of entire communities. And this brings us to the UPA. To me, my brother Arieh, and some other Jews, the UPA freedom fighters were saviour-angels sent by Heaven. The UPA was a legitimate national-liberation resistance movement, which had to operate under complicated and very difficult conditions of a three-cornered fight." Sterzer then outlined UPA's activities, differentiating UPA from the "dregs, scum, and criminal elements from the slums and villages, [who] joined the Nazi auxiliary militia to kill Jews." Given the fierce repression of the Germans towards those who harbored fugitive Jews, the protection of UPA commanders was "a miracle of good will." Sterzer described how before the war he had close contacts in Ukrainian circles:

> I flirted with Ukrainian girls, danced with them, nearly married one of them....I made sincere efforts to learn their language, make lasting friendships and integrate myself in their cultural and social lives as much as possible. Both of our national groups—the Jews and the Ukrainians—were oppressed minorities in reactionary Poland. We were natural allies. I understood that. I wish I could say as much about other Jews. They were blind and they were stupid.

He was recruited into the nationalist insurgency even before the formation of UPA:

> I escaped from the [Lviv] ghetto in 1942, and made my way on foot in the southeastern direction, towards my village where I had friends and acquaintances. About 40 kilometers east of Lviv, I was intercepted on a field track by a group of armed men. At first I thought they were one of the pro-Nazi outfits set up by the Gestapo to catch fugitive Jews, partisans and freedom fighters....In fact, they were Ukrainian Nationalist guerrillas. The UPA was not born yet at that time, but various Nationalist resistance units were organized in the rural districts, to protect the populace against German slave-labor round-ups, abduction of Ukrainian girls for Nazi military brothels and the depredations of Polish and Russian guerrillas.

Sterzer admitted to being a Jew (at first the nationalists suspected he was connected with the communist underground). When he told them that he was a doctor, they asked if he would tend to their wounded. He agreed and "served as a doctor with the UPA for the next 12 months." One day he learned that his brother and other Jews were hiding in a family camp in a forest near Stanyslaviv. His UPA commander released him from duty and arranged for an underground agent to accompany him to the UPA command in the Stanyslaviv region.

> Now I have heard and read evidence that some Ukrainian "independent" bands led by anarchistic "atamans" massacred Jews whom they found hiding in the forest. But the UPA was a disciplined force. In my case, the people in charge of UPA operations in our district were friends of mine, or friends of friends. They authorized the establishment of an independent Jewish guerrilla unit under my command, and the UPA's protection, in the famous Black Forest near Stanislaviv. The local peasants were encouraged by the UPA to bring us food and clothes. We also received some arms and ammunition. If the situation demanded it, I visited the underground UPA hospital to help the Ukrainian medical personnel treat the casualties. I also gave free medical treatment to the local populace, insofar as I could leave my forest hideout without getting caught by Gestapo agents or Nazi police. But my brother and I, our wives and relatives, and other Jews I know, survived the bestial Nazi holocaust only thanks to the friendly attitude of Ukrainian freedom-fighters.[1509]

In evaluating Sterzer's memoir, two things should be pointed out. First, his story concerns Galicia and not Volhynia, which was the scene of the greatest carnage and where UPA was most active. In fact, I wonder how he could have been serving with UPA for twelve months in 1942-43, since UPA during that entire period was based in Volhynia and moved operations to Galicia only in 1944. This said, I do not doubt his story. Second, Sterzer blamed all the violence against Jews on socially marginal elements. We know, however, that the "dregs, scum and criminal elements" who entered the auxiliary militias were often OUN militants. Elsewhere in the memoir he blames "dregs from the slums and underworld elements, Polish elements" for "the notorious Lviv pogroms and bloody massacres." We know that this was not the whole story either.

1509 Heiman, "We Fought for Ukraine," 37-41. *Medychna opika v UPA*, 341-45.

A completely different narrative, reflecting a completely different experience, comes from a Jewish woman who served as a
nurse with UPA in Volhynia. Lea Goldberg was hiding with some
Stundists in the village of Polytsi (P̱ Police) outside her native Rafalivka. She was about fourteen when UPA attacked the Stundist
community.[1510] The UPA men had little ammunition[1511] and apparently did not want to waste it, so they started beating her to death
with clubs. She protested that she was a Ukrainian girl who believed in independent Ukraine, and one of the UPA partisans ordered the others to stop. He said that they could always kill her
later, but in the meantime she could be of some use. She was taken
to their camp to serve as a nurse. One of the first things she heard
in the camp was someone declaring that the hated Jews had to be
killed for the sake of Ukraine. She witnessed many atrocities committed by these partisans, including knife murders of Jewish babies.
After she had served for about six months, one of the Banderites,
drunk, forced his way into her room and tried to kill her. She managed to wound him with his own gun, and that night she escaped
from the camp. Her closest friend among the Stundists led her to
some Soviet partisans, and thus she survived the war.[1512] (On the
shooting of nurses, Jacob Biber heard the following from a fellow
Jew in hiding who worked in an UPA tannery: "Just recently one of
them killed the nurse, Elka Berelson, who survived for a long time
on one of the farms. They had been happy at headquarters to get
Elka to come and work for them, because she had been the head

---

1510 The Banderites' deep antipathy to Ukrainian evangelical Christians comes out
    clearly in the memoirs of a Ukrainian Baptist in Volhynia: Podvorniak, *Viter z
    Volyni*, 137, 156-59, 181, 184, 187-88, 191, 206. The same memoirs also attest to
    Baptist rescue of Jews. Ibid., 156-59. Kost Pankivsky mentioned an incident of
    a Banderite speaking against Baptists in a village, calling them "of the German
    faith." Pan'kivs'kyi, *Roky nimets'koi okupatsii*, 332.
1511 A Ukrainian Baptist was forcibly recruited into UPA in 1944. He was given an
    old rifle, which he suspected to be of tsarist Russian provenance. All the re-
    cruits in his group were given several bullets each and told to hold on to them
    because there were no more. Podvorniak, *Viter z Volyni*, 206-07.
1512 AŻIH, 301/1011. This testimony is in Yiddish. I read it in an English translation
    in a manuscript in preparation at Florida Atlantic University entitled "First
    Reports: An Anthology of Early Holocaust Testimonies Taken from Record
    Group 301 of the Jewish Historical Institute of Poland," ed. Felix Tych et al.

nurse of the hospital and they needed someone like her very badly. Yet, she too, was shot secretly by one of them."[1513])

Other Jews could be found in UPA outside the medical service. Joseph Grossman told his interesting story to the USC Shoah Foundation. He was ten years old in the spring and summer of 1943 and hiding in the forest with some Poles near Huta. He explained to his interviewer that the Ukrainian nationalists in the Bandera movement were fighting for an independent Ukraine but a Ukraine without other nationalities — no Jews, no Poles, just Ukrainians. But at one point he and a friend left the woods and went to a peasant acquaintance to ask if rumors he had heard were true, whether the Banderites had stopped killing the Jews and were now fighting the Germans. The Ukrainian acquaintance told him that this was a trap and not to believe the propaganda. Later, he and other Jews in his group were attacked by a band whom he believed were probably Banderites. His attackers did not want to waste a bullet and therefore beat him until he showed no signs of life. But he did not die, and a Ukrainian peasant took the boy to his home, nursed him back to health, and put him to work helping with farm chores. The peasant lived alone with his wife, because his three sons were gone: one had been murdered, another had been taken for forced labor to Germany, and the third had joined UPA. The local peasants were illiterate, and the local UPA unit needed a person who could read and write. The young Grossman was recruited to help them. He wrote their confidential missives and sometimes even delivered them himself. It reached a point that UPA taught him how to disable land mines and work with explosives. They knew he was a Jew but never caused him trouble on that account. After the Soviets took over, he continued to work for UPA for a while, then managed to legalize himself in Stepan. Over fifty years after these events, he expressed amazement to his interviewers that he remained alive and that UPA did not kill him, since UPA normally killed all the Jews it encountered.[1514]

1513 Biber, *Survivors*, 145.
1514 Radchenko, "Stavlennia UPA do ievreiv," part 2, citing Shoah Foundation, 40428 Joseph Grossman.

The memoir of an UPA veteran mentioned that it used a Jewish woman to translate for them in the Matsiiv area because so few Ukrainians in Volhynia knew German. But the local *Gebietskommissar* ordered them to replace her.[1515]

In Leo Heiman's compilation on UPA for the *Ukrainian Quarterly* there is the memoir of a Jewish soldier who fought in the ranks of UPA. The memoir was signed simply Lt. Col. Gershon K.; as Heiman explained, "his full name may not be disclosed as he is on active service with the Israeli Army." He was fourteen when the Germans took his native Ternopil. The rest of his family was killed by, in Heiman's words, "German storm troops and local pro-Nazi auxiliaries." Gershon managed to escape from a truck and was taken in by a Ukrainian farmer, Ivan Hordiichuk. When young Gershon went swimming with some other boys, without their clothes, it was discovered he was Jewish. Hordiichuk took him to a friend in UPA for protection. Hordiichuk himself was killed for harboring a Jew: "he was tortured by Ukrainian renegades who worked for the Gestapo." As to Gershon: "Two UPA agents took me to the forest....In the UPA unit, the commanding officer, his deputy, and all platoon and squad leaders knew I was a Jew. Some of the men who learned about it teased me good-naturedly, but I never had to suffer because of it. I was a scout with the reconnaisance platoon till the summer of 1944." Gershon K. went on to detail the anti-German actions of his unit. As the front closed in, his commander advised him to find other Jewish survivors and use the skills he had acquired to fight for the establishment of a Jewish state in Palestine. He went through Lviv, Kraków, Prague, and Vienna, to Austria, where he met up with the Palestine Jewish Brigade. He was smuggled to Palestine in British Army vehicles.[1516]

Largely due to the efforts of pro-OUN circles in Ukraine, a few other Jews who served in UPA have been discovered in recent years. Mandyk Khasman, a native of Drohobych, was twelve years old in the summer of 1942 when the Germans killed his parents. Taken in by a Ukrainian family, he received a new identity as

---

1515 Lebid', "Chasy nimets'koi okupatsii," 201.
1516 Heiman, "We Fought for Ukraine," 41-44.

Volodymyr Dmytrenko. When his guardian signed him up for forced labor in Germany, he fled to the woods. There he met up with Ukrainian nationalist partisans and became part of their unit. In battle with NKVD forces in 1945, he lost both his legs. He was repressed but survived at least until 2012, when he was interviewed by an OUN youth group. He did not reveal his true identity, as Mandyk Khasman and not Volodymyr Dmytrenko, until 1949 when he was drafted into the Red Army. But in 2013 Khasman claimed that the Banderites in whose unit he served knew that he was Jewish.[1517]

The Security Service of Ukraine published documents on its website about Leiba-Itsyk Dobrovsky, a Jew who served as a political consultant and propagandist for UPA Army-North.[1518] A brief biography posted on the internet informs us that Dobrovsky served in the Red Army and was captured by the Germans. He was able to obtain false papers that changed his nationality from "Jew" to "Ukrainian" and Ukrainianized his name and patronymic. He escaped from the camp and went to the town of Korets in Rivne oblast. There he found work in the local gymnasium and took his meals at the cafeteria of the Ukrainian police. He made friends with some members of OUN, who directed him to UPA in July 1943. He was a well-educated individual — he had finished the law faculty at Kyiv University and was well versed in history — so UPA entrusted him with propaganda work. Dobrovsky concealed his Jewish identity from his comrades in UPA. SMERSH apprehended him on 1 February 1944 and learned his real identity and nationality.[1519]

1517 V"iatrovych, "Povstans'kyi Havrosh Mandyk Khasman." "Mandyk Khasman — ievrei v UPA," https://www.youtube.com/watch?v=qKm_aySS80Y&list=PLQ ul8lc-DWlz_zJCr1njx64Ftx-4zcXMP (accessed 10 December 2020). Nataliia Zubryts'ka, "Na Volyni zhyve ievrei-voin UPA," *zaxid.net*, 12 February 2013, https://zaxid.net/na_volini_zhive_yevreyvoyin_upa_n1277630 (accessed 22 April 2021).

1518 "U Sluzhbi bezpeky Ukrainy vidbulys' Hromads'ki istorychni slukhannia 'Ievrei v Ukrains'komu vyzvol'nomu rusi,'" press release of the Security Service of Ukraine, 14 April 2008. This used to be found on the Service's website at http://www.sbu.gov.ua/sbu/control/uk/index (accessed 24 October 2009).

1519 McBride, "Ukraine's Invented a 'Jewish-Ukrainian Nationalist.'" Oleksandr Namozov, "Ukrains'kyi povstanets' Leiba Dobrovs'kyi?" Viche Kostopil'shchyny, 20 June 2009, http://www.kostopilpost.com/index.php?op

It remains to correct one error that has crept into the literature. Yakiv Suslensky was a former Soviet political prisoner who devoted great effort to fostering good relations between Ukrainians and Jews. He wrote a book about Ukrainians who helped Jews during the Holocaust. In it he cited the testimony of Shave (Isiah) Litwak who had joined Hryn Babii's partisan group in the Dolyna forest; he made no mention of the politics of the Babii group.[1520] Both Aharon Weiss and Dieter Pohl mistakenly understood the Babii group to be an UPA unit.[1521] In fact it was communist.[1522] This pro-Soviet unit was led by Stakh (Hryn) Babii.[1523] But there was also an Oleksii Babii, who led a partisan group affiliated with OUN-M. This Babii had killed Jews before he led a partisan unit, which was mainly engaged on the anti-Polish front.[1524]

Mercy and Rescue

We have already encountered a number of examples of nationalist partisans sparing or rescuing Jews.[1525] Here I will look at other cases that I am aware of.

When the Security Service of Ukraine was promoting a positive image of UPA supreme commander Roman Shukhevych, it stated that Shukhevych helped his wife rescue a Jewish girl named Iryna Raikhenberh in 1942-43.[1526] The Security Service did not release information on the circumstances and motivation of the rescue. In the Ukrainian village of Hodovychi (P̲ Godowicze), west of

---

tion=com_content&task=view&id=109&Itemid=26 (accessed 26 October 2009). Oleksandr Nechytailo, "Neimovirna odisseia kyivs'koho ievreia, iakyi borovsia za nezalezhnist' Ukrainy v lavakh UPA," Vector News, 6 June 2018, https://www.vectornews.net/exclusive/63399-neymovrna-odsseya-kiyivsk ogo-yevreya-yakiy-borovsya-za-nezalezhnst-ukrayini-v-lavah-upa.html (accessed 12 December 2020).

1520 Suslensky, *They Were True Heroes*, 142-43.
1521 Weiss, "Jewish-Ukrainian Relations," 417. Pohl, *Nationalsozialistische Judenverfolgung*, 375.
1522 Friedman, "Ukrainian-Jewish Relations," 189.
1523 AŻIH, 301/510, Widman Baruch.
1524 Radchenko, "The Biography of the OUN(m) Activist Oleksa Babii."
1525 See above, 397, 409-10.
1526 "U Sluzhbi bezpeky Ukrainy."

Kovel, the Omelianiuk family rescued a Jew and has been recognized for this by Yad Vashem. They had two relatives in UPA who passed on information to them that helped them keep their refugee from harm.[1527]

Genya Finkelstein told the story of a compassionate man who saved her as a child, but who at the same time was an antisemite, a Banderite nationalist who later fought with UPA. She lived with a Ukrainian family in Babyn from summer 1942 through summer 1944. At first she claimed to be a Ukrainian orphan from Kyiv, but they discovered she was Jewish when she talked Yiddish in her sleep. The woman maltreated her, but the husband was relatively kind. He felt compassion for her and kept his wife from reporting her to the Gestapo. Also, he promised to marry her to his younger brother when she got older. "Her husband, Petro, was a good-hearted man but a Jew-hater since the days when he had worked as chief butcher in a restaurant owned by a Jewish family in the city of Lvov....Petro belonged to a group of Ukrainians who were fighting for Ukrainian independence."[1528]

One of the more unusual tales to come out of the Holocaust in Volhynia is that of Oleksii Melnychuk of the village of Tumyn (P Tumin), east of Volodymyr-Volynskyi in Volhynia oblast. From mid-1943 he had been helping a group of Jews living in the forest near his village. According to materials housed at Yad Vashem, one of the Jews convinced Melnychuk to join the Banderites in order to find out in advance about pogroms or forest searches. When the Red Army came, Melnychuk was arrested for his association with OUN, but the testimony of the Jews he saved resulted in his release.[1529]

1527 Shoah Foundation, 36160 Dmitrii Omelianiuk, 203-04. Stepan Omelianiuk and Mariya Omelianiuk, Dmitrii's parents, were recognized as Righteous among the Nations on 27 January 1982. *The Righteous among the Nations Database*, https://righteous.yadvashem.org/?search=Omelyanyuk&searchType=righteous_only&language=en&itemId=4035711&ind=0 (accessed 17 December 2020).

1528 Finkelstein, *Genya*, 77-97; quote 77-78.

1529 Yad Vashem recognized Aleksey Melnichuk as Righteous among the Nations on 22 December 1993. *The Righteous among the Nations Database*, https://righte

Most often, OUN-UPA militants spared Jews because of a personal connection. In the course of the January 1944 UPA murders described by Vera Shchetinkova, a Banderite recognized one of the Jewish women as a former classmate and friend; he shot in the air, let her and her sister and her daughter go, and told them that Rivne was already in Soviet hands.[1530] Jacob Biber reported on his meeting with Ivan Ryzhy, who had been a notorious killer as a policeman, who later became a leader of the "Bulbas," and who in the end was hanged by the Bulbas for extorting pigs from Ukrainian villagers. He told Biber and his wife that he was their friend, that he and his men would do them no harm, that he had grown up with Jews and played soccer with them, that he had even saved some Jews from the Germans.[1531] Another "Bulba," Volodia Masliuk, was leading a large unit on horseback. But he broke away from his unit, and told the Biber family, who were genuinely personal friends: "I'm glad you have survived until now. Watch yourself. We have many bad boys among us."[1532] Fedir Vovk, a native of the Poltava region, was the principal of a school in Nikopol in Dnipropetrovsk oblast when the Germans invaded. He joined OUN-B in 1941 after the arrival of an expeditionary group and proceeded to organize the OUN underground in the Nikopol region. As the Soviets pushed westward in 1943, he moved to Galicia, where he was appointed vice-president of the UHVR. In 1998 Yad Vashem recognized him and his wife as Righteous among the Nations because they had saved a Jewish friend, the school teacher Sara Bakst, and her family.[1533]

ous.yadvashem.org/?search=aleksey%20melnichuk&searchType=righteous_only&language=en&itemId=4016382&ind=0 (accessed 18 December 2020).
1530 Shoah Foundation, 45238 Vera Shchetinkova, 153-55. And see above, 404.
1531 Biber, *Survivors*, 138, 151.
1532 Ibid., 144.
1533 *The Righteous among the Nations Database*, https://righteous.yadvashem.org/?searchType=righteous_only&language=en&itemId=4045141&ind=0 (accessed 16 December 2020). Although vice-president of the UHVR, Vovk did not join the *dviikari* in emigration. After the war he changed his name to Ivan Vovchuk and remained loyal to the Bandera movement until his death in 1979. "Pravednyk narodiv svitu rodom z Poltavshchyny: urodzhenets' Semenivshchyny Fedir Vovk," *Novyny Poltavshchyny*, 7 May 2020, https://np.pl.ua/2020/05/pravednyk-narodiv-svitu-rodom-z-poltavshchyny-urodzhen

Faina Liakher, who accepted Christianity and eventually became a nun, was protected by a member of the OUN underground—her former boyfriend, Volodymyr Zaplatynsky.[1534]

A moving tale originates from the vicinity of Shumsk in Volhynia:

> Snow was already everywhere. We made ourselves a hut from wooden shingles. Both of us, my daughter Freida, who was 22 years old, and I, worked energetically. We sat in the hut for a few nights, and when we went out it was as if we were hunted animals. When we went out we met a robber, a leader of a gang of Banderovtze. I recognized him immediately. He was the son of Olsko, a longtime acquaintance and customer. I had once given Olsko 80 zloty and he was supposed to bring me wood, which he didn't deliver. His son had a pistol on him, and my daughter was shaking with fear. For some reason I felt he would not harm us. He asked me in Ukrainian, "What are you doing here?" I said to him, "Olsko, I'm very hungry. Give me something to eat." He answered, "I would invite you to our home, but they are searching us every evening for weapons, and so I can't invite you." From him I learned that there were Russian partisans in the area. I said to him, "You know me." He didn't ask any more questions, just said, "Stay here. I'll bring you some straw and you will stay here." My daughter didn't believe him and wanted to run away, but I said, "If he comes accompanied by someone else, I'll grapple with him and take his pistol and we'll escape. But if he comes alone it's a sign that he doesn't intend to harm us."
> After a quarter of an hour we saw him skipping and running in our direction with baskets of food in hand, and I knew that his intentions were good. The basket had hot soup and bread. He said, "During the day you can come to my house, but don't come at night."
> And then he added, "You know, I have an account to settle with you." I was so frightened my stomach turned. In spite of this, I summoned up my courage and said, "I haven't come to settle accounts." But he said, decisively, "This can't be," and he told me that his father had passed away, and before his death he had commanded his children to pay me 80 zloty. "It isn't fitting to die owing money," he had said. I said that I would forgo the money, of course. But he ordered us to remain there. "Tomorrow I'll come and bring you previk

---

ets-semenivshchyny-fedir-vovk/ (accessed 16 December 2020). I am grateful to Raisa Ostapenko for bringing Vovk/Vovchuk to my attention.
1534 Nina Polishchuk, "Faina Liakher." Shoah Foundation, 45446 Faina Liakher.

[*pervak*]," which was a kind of whiskey that he made himself. We agreed that he would knock twice on a tree as a signal that it was he who had come to us.[1535]

Kalman Shmirgold, a Jewish survivor from the small Volhynian town of Berestechko (P Beresteczko), had to leave his hiding place near a small village. With no place to go, he simply started walking down the road. A sled with Banderites passed him by. They stopped to check his papers. Kalman's fake identification as Mykola Konopka did not convince them: they recognized him personally.

> Banderites: Hey, we know you, we used to go to school together.
> Kalman: Yes, you know me, we went to school together. You can kill me. I was kicked out of my hiding place. There is nowhere I can go to.

Kalman broke into tears and asked for his life to be spared: "Help me, maybe tomorrow I will be of some use to you." The Ukrainians discussed this between themselves, then ordered Kalman on the sled. He thought they were taking him to a nearby police precinct, and that would mean eventual death. When the sled passed by the hill, the Ukrainians ordered him out. He started climbing up the hill, not daring to turn back, expecting a shot at every minute. No shots were fired. They had set him free.[1536]

These personal acts of rescue and mercy do not exonerate OUN and UPA. Nazis and Wehrmacht personnel performed similar acts. Examples well known from popular films include Nazi-party member Oskar Schindler's rescue of twelve hundred Jews in his employ and Captain Wilm Hosenfeld's protection of the Polish-Jewish pianist and composer Władysław Szpilman. But there are numerous more obscure examples, including the Wehrmacht officers who protected surviving Jews of the Buchach area from Ukrainian mobs as the Germans retreated.[1537] These acts of mercy and rescue do not change the fact that the Nazi party and the Wehrmacht

---

1535 Wolf Berensztejn, "This Is How It Began," https://www.jewishgen.org/yizkor/szumsk/szu021.html (accessed 2 April 2020).
1536 Melamed, "Organized and Unsolicited Collaboration," 224.
1537 Bartov, *Anatomy of a Genocide*, 261-62.

were chiefly responsible for the murder of the great majority of Europe's Jews.

* *
*

Numerous testimonies of Jewish survivors indicate that for UPA, killing Jews was standard procedure. This conclusion is also borne out by field reports of UPA units, confessions of UPA and SB OUN officers to the NKVD, the testimonies of Polish witnesses, and the existence of orders — particularly to units of the SB OUN — to kill Jews and those hiding them. This evidence is hardly startling given the nature of UPA. Many of its officers were former Ukrainian policemen who already had the blood of many Jews on their hands. UPA was also the armed force of OUN-B, which, like both factions of OUN, strove not just for an independent Ukrainian state, but one that was cleansed of other nationalities, a "Ukraine for Ukrainians." The latter goal found expression not only in the murder of Jews, but also in the murder of Poles, primarily civilians, and other minorities, almost all of whom were civilians. Jews who fled to the Poles were also killed as allies of the Poles. Jews hiding in the forest who found protection in nearby Soviet partisan formations were also considered condemned to death by UPA. They were the embodiment of Judeocommunism. In the winter of 1943-44, UPA assembled surviving Jews in labor camps in Volhynia; when the Soviets came too close, UPA or SB OUN liquidated the camps and their Jewish workers. In that whole episode of the camps and their liquidation, patterns introduced by the Germans and internalized by the Ukrainian policemen are clearly evident.

There is also a mythology, spread by the OUN itself and perpetuated by the movement's defenders for decades afterwards, that UPA represented a departure from the "integral nationalism" of OUN. A key moment in the mythos are the resolutions of the Third Extraordinary Assembly of August 1943. The declaration of equal rights for minorities did not prevent UPA from engaging in an intense slaughter of Poles at the same time. From the diary of Oleksandr Povshuk we can understand that the fine declarations of

August 1943 were not promulgated to rank-and-file UPA soldiers until quite late, if at all. We also see from Povshuk's diary that the embrace of minority rights did not prevent a young man who had been in UPA for a year from developing an image of Poles as the arrogant enemies of Ukrainians and of Jews as the backbone of the Soviet regime. We have also seen that the propaganda turn of 1943 vis-à-vis Jews was often conceptualized in antisemitic ways: Jews control the Western Allies, so we need to be careful with them; the Germans have killed most of the Jews, so they are not such a problem now; and Muscovites are the priority, Jewish survivors are for later. Clearly, UPA wanted to dissociate itself from the murder of the Jews, even trying to alter the historical record,[1538] but it did not actually decide to stop murdering Jews.

OUN-UPA apologists have often pointed to the service of Jews as medical personnel in UPA as though it were a proof that UPA was not anti-Jewish. But the fate and stories of some of these Jewish physicians and nurses confirm that some were murdered by UPA and others deliberately escaped. I can imagine that doctors and nurses, by saving soldiers' lives, could win the personal loyalty of the units they served and thus be spared liquidation. Occasionally, other Jews could be saved by UPA, generally also for personal reasons. Jews who served in other capacities in UPA had to hide their origins. Pro-OUN figures in the government of Ukraine managed to find two Jews who served in UPA outside the medical sphere, namely Leiba Dobrovsky and Mandyk Khasman, but we know that UPA had no idea that Dobrovsky was Jewish. The memoir of Gershon K., who was fourteen or fifteen when he was taken into UPA, makes it clear that only platoon and squad leaders were informed that he was Jewish. In short, the kind of evidence marshalled by apologists of OUN-UPA is both meager and feeble.

How many Jews did UPA and SB OUN kill in the period 1943-44? Numerical estimates provided by testimonies usually reflect perceptions rather than offer reliable data. A Jewish survivor and resistance fighter estimated that three thousand Jews had fled to the woods and the neighboring steppe from the Tuchyn ghetto, but

---

1538 See above, 85.

only several dozen survived the war. The rest died "in partisan battles and during the attacks of fascist-bandit murderers."[1539]

The testimonies consulted by the Siemaszkos attest to 1210 plus an additional unknown quantity of Jews killed by Ukrainian nationalists in Volhynia in 1941-45; seventy-nine of these Jews have been identified by name. However, the Siemaszkos argue that many more were killed. They cite estimates by Shmuel Spector that there were 200,000 Jews in Volhynia; that 150,000 of these were killed during the liquidation of the ghettos; and that 3500 Volhynian Jews survived the war. Thus there is a remainder of 46,000 Jews who were murdered by Ukrainians or else died of hunger, exposure, disease, or exhaustion during the time they were hiding.[1540] I am uncomfortable with calculations based on such global estimates. Spector himself spoke of "thousands of survivors...slaughtered by the Ukrainian nationalist partisans."[1541] A Polish historian of UPA, Grzegorz Motyka, has also estimated that UPA killed one or two thousand Jews, mainly in Volhynia.[1542]

Furthermore, there is a consensus developing among scholars that Ukrainians killed about sixty thousand Poles in 1943-45. UPA bears the most responsibility for this crime. UPA was able to surround whole villages and herd the inhabitants into churches which they burned to the ground. If they only succeeded in killing tens of thousands of a population concentrated in entire settlements, it is difficult to imagine that they could have killed anywhere near as many Jews, who had already been greatly reduced in number and who were dispersed, hiding underground, and seeking out remote places.

An estimate in the lower thousands is far from certain, however. Consider the case of the Jews in the forests near Svirzh, described above, in which five hundred Jews were able to escape certain death at the hands of the Banderites by what amounted to a fluke.[1543] Jews in the woods tended to cluster together for safety. If

---

1539 AŻIH, 301/652, Bakalczuk Melech, 5.
1540 Siemaszko and Siemaszko, *Ludobójstwo*, 2:1079-80.
1541 Spector, *The Holocaust of Volhynian Jews*, 256.
1542 Motyka, *Ukraińska partyzantka*, 295-97.
1543 See above, 397.

the survivor populations were concentrated enough, it may prove necessary to ascribe a larger death toll to UPA and to the OUN SB. In any case, UPA made the survivor experience in Western Ukraine even more hellish.

8. Conclusions

Defenders of the reputation of OUN and UPA have dealt with the nationalists' perpetration during the Holocaust in several ways. One has been to point to the declarations of equality for national minorities issued by the Third Extraordinary Great Assembly in August 1943 and by the Ukrainian Supreme Liberation Council (UHVR) in July 1944. I think this monograph has shown clearly that these declarations reflected OUN's realization that Germany had lost the war on the Eastern front and that the organization had to present itself as more democratic if it wished to gain support from the Western Allies. The timing of these programmatic "turns" are one indication of this. Before the Third Extraordinary Great Assembly concluded, the Soviets had already taken Kharkiv. UHVR was founded on the eve of the Soviet reconquest of Galicia. In this same period and in the same situation, Hitler's allies in Hungary and Romania were sending out feelers to the West. Hitler felt he had to invade his Hungarian ally in March 1944 to prevent defection from the Axis cause, and Romania completely switched sides in August 1944. Moreover, at the same time as OUN proclaimed the equality of nationalities, its internal reports and orders demonstrate that it was killing Poles, Jews, and other national minorities in great numbers. The evidence of OUN's internal documents is also confirmed by what OUN-UPA militants confessed to their Soviet interrogators. I remind the reader that the arrested nationalists never challenged accounts that their units engaged in the murder of communists, Jews, and others; what they denied was their own personal participation in the killings. Evidence from Jewish and Polish survivors, Soviet partisans, and the Germans also confirms that the declarations were more than meaningless: they were a subterfuge. This study also demolishes the myth that it was OUN's experience in the eastern and southern Ukrainian lands that led to an ideological revolution, jettisoning fascism in favor of democracy.

Another way OUN's defenders have responded to the movement's Holocaust history has been to simply leave Jews and their destruction out of memoirs and histories published in the post-

World-War-II diaspora. This also entailed doctoring documents they published and even creating the fiction of the Stella Krenzbach memoir. The working group in independent Ukraine that rehabilitated OUN-UPA also avoided writing about OUN's antisemitism and mass murder of Jews, because for them this was not an issue of importance. Later, other historians, notably those gathered around Volodymyr Viatrovych and his institutions (the Center for the Study of the Liberation Movement, the Ukrainian Institute of National Memory), did engage not so much with the Holocaust itself as with accusations that OUN and UPA participated actively in it. They produced one-sided polemics, sometimes backed with better scholarship (e.g., Serhii Riabenko), sometimes with extremely poor scholarship (e.g., Viatrovych). They also disseminated a deceptive document, the Book of Facts, which was the precise opposite of what its title indicated.

The OUN defenders have also tried to hide the organization's wartime crimes by blaming these on criminal and lumpen elements. It was the latter, they say, who carried out pogroms, who as policemen took part in anti-Jewish actions, and who killed Jews during the national insurgency. Andriy Zayarnyuk put it well in reference to the Lviv pogrom of 1941: "Soon after the pogrom, educated Ukrainians in conversations with their Jewish colleagues blamed the pogrom on the proverbial 'city scum.' Later, it became a standard explanation Ukrainian patriots used to exonerate the Ukrainian community....Lviv's underclass was blamed for the crimes instigated by more 'respectable' patriots."[1544]

Defenders also point to some cases of Jews who served in UPA. The presence of Jewish medical staff in UPA is held up as evidence that UPA could not have been antisemitic. But the urgent need for doctors in the conditions of warfare diminishes the force of this argument, as does the murder of some of the physicians and nurses who served. It was rare, but it happened that some Jews ended up in UPA as soldiers or scouts. I have been able to learn of only four such cases. In two of them, these were young teens, boys, whom UPA units adopted; and in one of these two cases, only the

---

1544 Zayarnuk, *Lviv's Uncertain Destination*, 167.

officers were supposed to know that their young recruit was Jewish. In another case, which has been trumpeted by the Viatrovych group, that of the propagandist Dobrovsky, he hid his Jewish identity altogether.

Finally, these defenders of OUN-UPA argue that various acts of mercy and rescue prove that the nationalists were not involved in the Holocaust. But this argument conflates individuals and an organization. Neither OUN nor UPA as organizations attempted to rescue Jews; as organizations they killed Jews. But individuals within these organizations were sometimes moved to spare people they knew or who awakened their sympathy. Nationalist historians prefer to operate as if there were no middle ground between individual Ukrainians and the Ukrainian nation. In order to save the good name of the Ukrainian nation, they often insist that war crimes and genocide were the work of criminal individuals and cannot reflect on the nation as a whole. But the framing of the argument is all wrong. Nations exist, especially as concepts, but nations are not homogeneous; they consist of all kinds of people, good and bad. Particular organizations can claim to speak on behalf of the entire nation, but this remains merely a claim, since nations are too amorphous to appoint spokespersons. States and their institutions can do so, but not nations conceived as ethnicities, as separate from states. This is especially true of the stateless Ukrainian nation. In this study, I have not been interested in the reputation of the nation nor in the guilt or innocence of particular individuals, but rather in the evaluation of OUN and its armed forces, the Ukrainian National Militia and UPA. In the Holocaust, individuals' actions were less important than those of organizational actors: the Wehrmacht, the SS and SD, the local civil administrations, the occupation press, and OUN and UPA. Nationalists who argue that Holocaust perpetration was entirely the work of individuals should also be ready to accept that acts of mercy and rescue were the work of individuals too.

Once we dismiss these deliberate mystifications, we can examine OUN's record during the Holocaust in its proper light. What we see is that in the second half of the 1930s, before the war broke out, OUN expressed its solidarity with Nazi Germany, fascist Italy, and antisemitic Romania; it propagated antisemitism and particularly the concept of Judeocommunism; and its ideologues began to envision a Ukrainian state that was both imperialist and cleansed of non-Ukrainian minorities. Then, as Germany was preparing to attack the Soviet Union in the spring of 1941, the very top leadership of the Bandera faction of OUN collectively authored the text "The Struggle and Activities of OUN in Wartime." The document was permeated with antisemitism, and it devoted many pages to instructions for the formation of a militia, one of whose primary tasks was to deal with the Jewish population. The document instructed the militias to register Jews and put them in internment camps; this proved impossible to achieve when the German-Soviet war, and the accompanying "Ukrainian national revolution," actually broke out. "The Struggle and Activities of OUN in Wartime" had already specified certain categories of Jews to be killed, but the absence of internment camps meant that many more Jews were killed instead of being imprisoned. From late June and at least into early August 1941, OUN militias killed Jews throughout Galicia, Bukovina, and Volhynia, sometimes helping the Germans or Romanians, and sometimes just on their own leadership's initiative. When the Germans dissolved the militias, OUN militants entered the police forces the Germans set up, the Ukrainian Auxiliary Police in Galicia and the Schutzmannschaften in Volhynia. The police were involved in the persecution of Jews in ghettos and labor camps, the robbery of the Jewish population, the roundup of Jews for the Germans to kill by poison gas or bullets, the murder of Jews in the course of and sometimes immediately after the roundups, and the murder of Jews who were hiding with local families or in the forests after the liquidation of the ghettos. Then in spring 1943 thousands of these policemen deserted to UPA. They continued to kill Jews all during the nationalist insurgency. They routinely killed Jews they discovered in hiding, they killed Jews who were associated with the Poles or the Red partisans, they killed Ukrainians who rescued Jews, and they lured Jews from their forest bunkers, placed them in labor camps, and then liquidated them as the Soviets closed in. They also killed Jews who tried to return to their villages after the Soviets reconquered Western Ukraine. I think all this has been solidly established in this monograph.

I have tried to give voice to the members of OUN through their own documents, memoirs, and confessions. But their reticence about the Holocaust and denial of participation in it have been a hindrance to gaining a fuller understanding of what made young patriots think that killing their neighbors was the right thing to do. Perpetrators of a crime are less willing to be forthcoming about it than the victims are.

I have adduced the voices of many Jewish survivors of the Holocaust in Western Ukraine. I think it is important to convey what Jewish men, women, and children experienced at the hands of OUN and UPA. Although many details of these testimonies must be incorrect, given the fragility of human memory, the overall chorus of voices sings the same sad and frightening song. The survivors' stories fit together almost seamlessly, even though they have been collected over a period of over half a century, in different historical and political environments, and from several continents. I have often been able to corroborate their accounts with other evidence, from German and OUN documentation, from Soviet sources, and from Polish testimonies.

I need to say a few words about the creation of a murderous mental environment. I do not think OUN and UPA would have been so willing to kill Jews and others if it were not for the influence of Hitler and the Nazi leadership. It was their propaganda and example that radicalized the thinking of OUN in the 1930s. Just as many anticolonial struggles in the 1960s and 1970s drew inspiration, support, and ideological direction from the Soviet Union, Cuba, and the People's Republic of China, so too did OUN look for guidance and funding to Nazi Germany. Then, with the invasion of the USSR, the Germans embarked on the mass slaughter of Jews throughout Eastern Europe. And OUN joined in. The Germans created a poisonous atmosphere and taught genocide by example. But it also needs to be understood that OUN itself did much to spread anti-Jewish sentiment and to encourage anti-Jewish violence in the general population of Galicia, Volhynia, and Bukovina. OUN was instrumental in the establishment of the local civil administration, which aided both the Germans and OUN in the murder of Jews. OUN identified the struggle for Ukrainian statehood with the policy of liquidating national minorities in the name of "Ukraine for Ukrainians." OUN militias and UPA openly killed Jews, demonstrating how patriots should act. After the ghettos and most camps were liquidated by the Germans and the police, OUN and UPA spread the word in Ukrainian villages that anyone who protected Jews would be killed. In these circumstances, rescue on the part of the Ukrainian civilian population was difficult.

Yet when we read survivor accounts, time and again we come across aid Jews received — food, shelter, information — from ordinary Ukrainian households and individuals. These individual acts, courageous and honorable, have yet to find their historian.[1545]

Finally, I want to state that I do not believe in definitive monographs. All I hope for is that I have cleared some ground for future historians to work. The history of the destruction of the Jews in Ukraine, the country which accounted for a quarter of all Holocaust deaths, has many uninvestigated and underinvestigated questions that need to be addressed.

1545 But research on this topic is underway. Raisa Ostapenko at the Sorbonne is writing her doctoral dissertation on rescue in Ukraine.

Bibliography

Abramson, Henry. *A Prayer for the Government: Ukrainians and Jews in Revolutionary Times, 1917-1920* (Cambridge, Mass.: Distributed by Harvard University Press for the Ukrainian Research Institute and Center for Jewish Studies, Harvard University, 1999).

Adamczyk, Mieczysław, Janusz Gmitruk, and Adam Koseski, eds. *Ziemie Wschodnie. Raporty Biura Wschodniego Delegatury Rządu na Kraj 1943-1944*. Warsaw and Pułtusk: Muzeum Historii Polskiego Ruchu Ludowego, Wyższa Szkoła Humanistyczna im. Aleksandra Gieysztora, 2005.

Adler, Joseph. "Chapters of Annihilation." In *Memorial Book of Bolekhov (Bolechów), Ukraine*, edited by Y. Eshel, 196-224. New York: JewishGen, [2015].

Ainsztein, Reuben. *Jewish Resistance in Nazi-Occupied Eastern Europe with a Historical Survey of the Jew as Fighter and Soldier in the Diaspora*. London: Paul Elek, 1974.

Aleksiun, Natalia. "The Central Jewish Historical Commission in Poland 1944-1947." *Polin* 20 (2008): 74-97.

Aleksiun, Natalia. "An Invisible Web: Philip Friedman and the Network of Holocaust Research." In *Als der Holocaust noch keinen Namen hatte: Zur frühen Aufarbeitung des NS-Massenmordes an den Juden / Before the Holocaust Had Its Name: Early Confrontations of the Nazi Mass Murder of the Jews*, edited by Regina Fritz, Éva Kovács, and Béla Rásky, Beitrage zur Holocaustforschung des Wiener Wiesenthal Instituts für Holocaust-Studien, 149-65. 2. Vienna: new academic press, 2016.

Aleksiun, Natalia. "Philip Friedman and the Emergence of Holocaust Scholarship: A Reappraisal." *Jahrbuch des Simon-Dubnow-Instituts* 11 (2012): 333-46.

Al'tman, I.A., ed. *Kholokost na territorii SSSR: entsyklopediia*. 2nd ed. Moscow: Rosspen, 2011.

Amar, Tarik Cyril. "A Disturbed Silence: Discourse on the Holocaust in the Soviet West as an Anti-Site of Memory." In *The Holocaust in the East: Local Perpetrators and Soviet Responses*, edited by Michael David-Fox et al., 158-84. Pittsburgh: University of Pittsburgh Press, 2014.

Amar, Tarik Cyril. *The Paradox of Ukrainian Lviv: A Borderland City between Stalinists, Nazis, and Nationalists*. Ithaca, NY, Cornell University Press, 2015.

Amar, Tarik Cyril [Syril], Ihor Balyns'kyi, and Iaroslav Hrytsak, eds. *Strasti za Banderoiu*. Kyiv: Hrani-T, 2010.

Andrzej. "Tadeusz Zaderecki, postać nieznana." *modlitwa.pl*, 28 July 2018, http://modlitwa.pl/nowy-testament/tadeusz-zaderecki/ (accessed 26 November 2018).

Angrick, Andrej. "Power Games: The German Nationality Policy (*Volkstumpolitik*) in Czernowitz before and during the Barbarrosa Campaign." *Dapim: Studies on the Holocaust* 24, no. 1 (2010): 89-135.

Angrick, Andrej [Andriei Anhrik]. "U vzaiemodii syl. Do pytannia pro nimets'kyi vplyv na natsional'nu polityku v Chernivtsiakh do pochatku ta pid chas realizatsii planu 'Barbarossa.'" *Holokost i suchasnist'*, no. 1 (7) (2010): 9-61.

Anotovanyi dovidnyk antyradians'koho rukhu oporu: struktura, kerivnyi ta dopomizhnyi sklad pidpillia OUN i UPA (1940-1954 rr.). Chastyna 1. Chernivets'ka oblast'. Chastyna 2. Zakarpats'ka oblast'. Kyiv: Haluzevyi derzhavnyi arkhiv Sluzhby bezpeky Ukrainy, Ukrains'kyi instytut natsional'nyi pam"iati, 2019.

Antoniuk, Iaroslav. *Diial'nist SB OUN na Volyni.* Lutsk: Volyns'ka knyha, 2007.

Antoniuk, Iaroslav. *Ukrains'kyi vyzvol'nyi rukh u postatiakh kerivnykiv. Volyns'ka ta brests'ka oblasti (1935-1955).* Litopys UPA Biblioteka, 13. Toronto and Lviv: Litopys UPA, 2014.

Arel, Dominique, comp. *The Ukraine List*, no. 441, 16 February 2010.

Arel, Dominique, comp. *The Ukraine List*, no. 442, 15 March 2010.

Arendt, Hannah. *Eichmann in Jerusalem: A Report on the Banality of Evil.* Rev. and enlarged ed. Harmondsworth: Penguin, 1994.

Armstrong, John A. "Heroes and Human: Reminiscences concerning Ukrainian National Leaders during 1941-1944." *Ukrainian Quarterly* 51, no. 2-3 (summer-fall 1995): 213-27.

Armstrong, John A. *Ukrainian Nationalism.* 2nd ed. Littleton, CO.: Ukrainian Academic Press, 1980.

Arsen, B.S. *Moia hirka pravda. Ia i Kholokost na Prykarpatti.* Nadvirna: Nadvirnians'ka drukarnia, 2004.

Artizov, A.N., et al., eds. *Ukrainskie natsionalisticheskie organizatsii v gody Vtoroi mirovoi voiny. Dokumenty.* 2 vols. Moscow: Rosspen, 2012.

Atlas, Zygfryd. *Just One Life.* Caulfield North, UK: Rocham Pty Ltd, 1999.

Bahrianyi, Ivan. *Publitsystyka. Dopovidi, statti, pamflety, refleksii, ese.* Edited by Oleksii Konoval. Kyiv: Vydavnytstvo "Smoloskyp," Fundatsiia im. Ivana Bahrianoho, 1996.

Bakal'chuk-Felyn, Meilakh. *Vospominaniia evreia-partizana.* Moscow: Vozvrashchenie, 2003.

Bakanov, Aleksei. *"Ni katsapa, ni zhida, ni liakha." Natsional'nyi vopros v ideologii Organizatsii ukrainskikh natsionalistov, 1929-1945 gg.* Vostochnaia Evropa. XX vek, 5. Moscow: Fond "Istoricheskaia pam"iat'," 2014.

Baran, Volodymyr, and Vasyl' Tokars'kyi. *"Zachystka": politychni represii v zakhidnykh oblastiakh Ukrainy, 1939-1941.* Lviv: Instytut ukrainoznavstva im. I. Kryp"iakevycha NAN Ukrainy, 2014.

Barber, John. "Popular Reactions in Moscow to the German Invasion of June 22, 1941." *Soviet Union/Union Sovietique* 18, no. 1-3 (1991): 5-18.

Bartov, Omer. *Anatomy of a Genocide: The Life and Death of a Town Called Buczacz.* New York: Simon & Schuster, 2018.

Bartov, Omer. "Eastern Europe as the Site of Genocide." *Journal of Modern History* 80 (September 2008): 557-93.

Bartov, Omer. "Wartime Lies and Other Testimonies: Jewish-Christian Relations in Buczacz, 1939-1944." *East European Politics and Societies* 25, no. 3 (August 2011): 486-511.

Bauer, Yehuda. *A History of the Holocaust.* New York, London, Toronto, Sydney: Franklin Watts, 1982.

Bauman, Zygmunt. *Modernity and the Holocaust.* Ithaca, N.Y.: Cornell University Press, 2000.

Bechtel, Delphine. "De Jedwabne à Zolotchiv: Pogromes locaux en Galicie, juin-juillet 1941." In *Cultures d'Europe Centrale, 5: La destruction des confins,* 69-92. Paris: CIRCE, 2005.

Berkhoff, Karel. "Babi Yar: A Summary of the Current State of Knowledge." Paper presented at the Experts Roundtable of the Ukrainian Jewish Encounter Initiative, Potsdam and Berlin, 27-30 June 2011.

Berkhoff, Karel C. *Harvest of Despair: Life and Death in Ukraine under Nazi Rule.* Cambridge, MA, and London: The Belknap Press of Harvard University Press, 2003.

Berkhoff, Karel C., and Marco Carynnyk. "The Organization of Ukrainian Nationalists and Its Attitude toward Germans and Jews: Iaroslav Stets'ko's 1941 *Zhyttiepys.*" *Harvard Ukrainian Studies* 23, no. 3-4 (1999): 149-84.

Berkhoff, Karel. C. "A Power Terrible for Its Opponents." *Yad Vashem Studies* 43, no. 2 (2015): 191-207.

Berkhoff, Karel. C. "'Total Annihilation of the Jewish Population': The Holocaust in the Soviet Media, 1941-45." In *The Holocaust in the East: Local Perpetrators and Soviet Responses,* edited by Michael David-Fox et al., 84-117. Pittsburgh: University of Pittsburgh Press, 2014.

Berkhoff, Karel C. "Ukraine under Nazi Rule (1941-1944): Sources and Finding Aids." *Jahrbücher für Geschichte Osteuropas* 45, no. 1 (1997): 85-103; no. 2 (1997): 273-309.

Bernard, Frederic L. *In the Eye of the Storm: Surviving in Nazi-Occupied Poland*. Sarasota, FL, 1995.

Bertelsen, Olga, and Myroslav Shkandrij. "The Secret Police and the Campaign against Galicians in Soviet Ukraine, 1929-1934." *Nationalities Papers* (2013): 1-26.

Biber, Jacob. *Survivors: A Personal Story of the Holocaust*. Studies in Judaica and the Holocaust, 2. San Bernardino: R. Reginald, The Borgo Press, 1989.

Bilas, Ivan. *Represyvno-karal'na systema v Ukraini 1917-1953. Suspil'no-politychnyi ta istoryko-pravovyi analiz*. 2 vols. Kyiv: Lybid', Viis'ko Ukrainy, 1994.

Blitt, Laizer. *No Strength to Forget: Survival in the Ukraine, 1941-44*. London and Portland, OR: Vallentine Mitchell, 2007.

Bohachevsky-Chomiak, Martha. *Ukrainian Bishop, American Church: Constantine Bohachevsky and the Ukrainian Catholic Church*. Washington, DC: The Catholic University of America Press, 2018.

Bohunov, Serhii, et al., eds. *Mytropolyt Andrei Sheptyts'kyi u dokumentakh radians'kykh orhaniv derzhavnoi bezpeky (1939-1944 rr.)*. Kyiv: Kyivs'kyi natsional'nyi universytet imeni Tarasa Shevchenka, Tsentr ukrainoznavstva; Derzhavnyi arkhiv Sluzhby bezpeky Ukrainy, 2005.

Bolianovs'kyi, Andrii. *Dyviziia "Halychyna". Istoriia*. Lviv: Instytut ukrainoznavstva im I. Kryp"iakevycha NANU, 2000.

Bolianovs'kyi, Andrii. "Natsional'na polityka natsysts'koi Nimechchyny v Halychyni u 1941-1944 rr." *Visnyk L'vivs'koho universytetu. Seriia istorychna* 32 (1997): 226-35.

Bolianovs'kyi, Andrii. "Polityko-pravovyi status Halychyny v systemi okupovanykh nimechchynoiu terytorii: Poshuk al'ternatyv natsysts'koi skhidnoi polityky u 1941-1944 rr." In *Materialy zasidan' Istorychnoi ta Arkheohrafichnoi komisii NTSh v Ukraini*, vyp. 2: *(1995-1997 rr.)*, edited by Iaroslav Hrytsak, 3-14. Lviv, 2000.

Bolianovs'kyi, Andrii. "Sotsial'nyi aspekt hitlerivs'koho 'novoho poriadku' v Halychyni u 1941-1944 rokakh." *Visnyk L'vivs'koho universytetu. Seriia istorychna* 33 (1998): 186-94.

Bolianovs'kyi, Andrii. *Ukrains'ki viis'kovi formuvannia v zbroinykh sylakh Nimechchyny (1939-1945)*. Lviv: L'vivs'kyi Natsional'nyi Universytet im. I.Franka, Kanads'kyi instytut ukrains'kykh studii Al'berts'koho universytetu. 2003.

Boll, Bernd. "Złoczów. July 1941: The Wehrmacht and the Beginning of the Holocaust in Galicia: From a Criticism of Photographs to a Revision of the Past." In *Crimes of War: Guilt and Denial in the Twentieth Century*, edited by Omer Bartov, Atina Grossmann, and Mary Nolan, 61-99, 275-83. New York: The New Press, 2002.

Brandon, Ray, and Wendy Lower, eds. *The Shoah in Ukraine: History, Testimony, Memorialization*. Bloomington and Indianapolis: Indiana University Press, 2008.

Breitman, Richard. "Himmler's Police Auxiliaries in the Occupied Soviet Territories." *Simon Wiesenthal Center Annual* 7 (1990): 23-39.

Browning, Christopher R. *Collected Memories: Holocaust History and Postwar Testimony*. Madison: University of Wisconsin Press, 2003.

Browning, Christopher R. *Ordinary Men: Reserve Police Battalion 101 and the Final Solution in Poland*. New York: HarperCollins, 1992.

Bruder, Franziska. "'Der Gerechtigkeit zu dienen': Die ukrainischen Nationalisten als Zeugen im Auschwitz-Prozess." In *Im Labyrinth der Schuld: Täter – Opfer – Ankläger*, ed. Irmtrud Wojak and Susanne Meinl, 133-62. Frankfurt and New York: Campus Verlag, 2003.

Bruder, Franziska. *"Den ukrainischen Staat erkämpfen oder sterben!" Die Organisation Ukrainischer Nationalisten (OUN) 1929-1948*. Berlin: Metropol, 2007.

Büchler, Yehoshua R. "Local Police Force Participation in the Extermination of Jews in Occupied Soviet Territory 1941-1942." *Shevut* 20 (1996): 79-98.

Bul'ba-Borovets', Taras. *Armiia bez derzhavy. Slava i trahediia ukrains'koho povstans'koho rukhu: spohady*. Winnipeg: Volyn', 1981.

Burds, Jeffrey. "AGENTURA: Soviet Informants' Networks and the Ukrainian Rebel Underground in Galicia, 1944-1948." *East European Politics and Societies* 11, no. 1 (winter 1997): 89-130.

Burds, Jeffrey. *The Early Cold War in Soviet West Ukraine, 1944-1948*. The Carl Beck Papers in Russian and East European Studies, 1505. Pittsburgh: The Center for Russian and East European Studies, University of Pittsburgh, 2001.

Burds, Jeffrey. "Gender and Policing in Soviet West Ukraine, 1944-1948." *Cahiers du Monde russe* 42/2, no. 3-4 (April-December 2001): 279-319.

Burds, Jeffrey. *Holocaust in Rovno: The Massacre at Sosenki Forest, November 1941*. New York: Palgrave Macmillan, 2013.

Carynnyk, Marco. "Foes of Our Rebirth: Ukrainian Nationalist Discussions about Jews, 1929-1947." *Nationalities Papers* 39, no. 3 (May 2011): 315-52.

Carynnyk, Marco. "'Jews, Poles, and Other Scum': Ruda Różaniecka, Monday, 30 June 1941." Paper presented at the Fourth Annual Danyliw Research Seminar on Contemporary Ukrainian Studies, Chair of Ukrainian Studies, University of Ottawa, 23-25 October 2008.

Carynnyk, Marco. "'A Knife in the Back of Our Revolution': A Reply to Alexander J. Motyl's 'The Ukrainian Nationalist Movement and the Jews: Theoretical Reflections on Nationalism, Fascism, Rationality, Primordialism, and History.'" http://www.aapjstudies.org/mana ger/external/ckfinder/userfiles/files/Carynnyk Reply to Motyl.pdf (accessed 17 June 2014).

Carynnyk, Marco. "The Palace on the Ikva — Dubne, September 18th, 1939 and June 24th, 1941." In *Shared History — Divided Memory: Jews and Others in Soviet-Occupied Poland, 1939-1941*, edited by Elazar Barkan, Elizabeth A. Cole, and Kai Struve, 263-301. Leipzig: Leipziger Universitätsverlag, 2007.

Carynnyk, Marco [Marko Tsarynnyk]. "Zolochiv movchyt'." *Krytyka* 9, no.10 (2005): 14-17.

Chameides, Meir. *That War and Me: Growing up in the Shadow of the Holocaust*. N.p., 2001.

Chodakiewicz, Marek Jan. "The Dialectics of Pain: The Interrogation Methods of the Communist Secret Police in Poland, 1944-1955." *Glaukopis* 2/3 (2004-05): 1-54.

"Christopher Browning Talks about the Changing Attitudes of Witness Testimony in Genocide Studies." *USC Shoah Foundation*, https://sfi. usc.edu/news/2018/03/21626-christopher-browning-talks-about-c hanging-attitudes-witness-testimony-genocide (accessed 26 September 2018).

Coleman, Heather J., et al. "A Roundtable on Lynne Viola's *Stalinist Perpetrators on Trial: Scenes from the Great Terror in Soviet Ukraine*." *Canadian Slavonic Papers* 61, no. 2 (2019): 225-43.

Conason, Joe. "To Catch a Nazi." *The Village Voice*, 11 February 1986.

Dalecki, Maciej, et al. *Zbrodnie nacjonalistów ukraińskich na ludności cywilnej w południowo-wschodniej Polsce (1942-1947)*. Przemyśl: Polski Związek Wschodni w Przemyślu, 2001

Danylenko, Vasyl', and Serhii Kokin, eds. *Radians'ki orhany derzhavnoi bezpeky u 1939-chervni 1941 r. Dokumenty HDA SB Ukrainy*. 2nd rev. ed. 2 parts. [Kyiv:] Vydavnychyi dim "Kyievo-Mohylians'ka akademiia," 2013.

Dean, Martin. *Collaboration during the Holocaust: Crimes of the Local Police in Belorussia and Ukraine, 1941-44*. New York: St. Martin's Press, published in association with the United States Holocaust Memorial Museum, 2000.

Dean, Martin. "German Ghettoization in Occupied Ukraine: Regional Patterns and Sources." Paper prepared for the Experts Roundtable of the Ukrainian Jewish Encounter Initiative, Potsdam, 27-30 June 2011.

Desbois, Patrick. *The Holocaust by Bullets: A Priest's Journey to Uncover the Truth behind the Murder of 1.5 Million Jews*. New York: Palgrave Macmillan, 2008.

Diukov, A.R. *Vtorostepennyi vrag. OUN, UPA i reshenie "evreiskogo voprosa."* Moscow: Fond "Istoricheskaia pamiat'," 2008.

Diukov, A.R. *Vtorostepennyi vrag. OUN, UPA i reshenie "evreiskogo voprosa."* 2nd rev. ed. Moscow: Fond "Istoricheskaia pamiat'," 2009.

Dobrovol's'kyi, O.B. *OUN na Donechchyni (zbirnyk dokumentiv ta materialiv)*. Vol. 1. Donetsk: Skhidnoukrains'kyi doslidnyts'kyi tsentr "Spadshchyna," 2013.

"Dokumenty SBU sprostovuiut' zvynuvachennia proty batal'ionu 'Nakhtihal'," press release of the Embassy of Ukraine in Canada, 22 March 2008.

Dubyk, M., ed. *Dovidnyk pro tabory, tiurmy ta hetto na okupovanii terytorii Ukrainy (1941-1944). Handbuch der Lager, Gefängnisse und Ghettos auf dem besetzten Territorium der Ukraine (1941-1944)*. Kyiv: Derzhavnyi komitet arkhiviv Ukrainy, Ukrains'kyi natsional'nyi fond "Vzaiemorozuminnia i prymyrennia" pry kabineti ministriv Ukrainy, 2000.

Dumitru, Diana. "An Analysis of Soviet Postwar Investigation and Trial Documents and Their Relevance for Holocaust Studies." In *The Holocaust in the East: Local Perpetrators and Soviet Responses*, edited by Michael David-Fox et al., 142-57. Pittsburgh: University of Pittsburgh Press, 2014.

Dumitru, Diana, and Carter Johnson. "Constructing Interethnic Conflict and Cooperation: Why Some People Harmed Jews and Others Helped Them during the Holocaust in Romania." *World Politics* 63, no. 1 (January 2011): 1-42.

Dziuban, Orest, ed. *Ukrains'ke derzhavotvorennia. Akt 30 chervnia 1941. Zbirnyk dokumentiv i materialiv*. L'viv-Kyiv: Piramida, 2001.

Eikel, Marcus, and Valentina Sivaieva. "City Mayors, Raion Chiefs and Village Elders in Ukraine, 1941-4: How Local Administrators Co-operated with the German Occupation Authorities." *Contemporary European History* 23, no. 3 (2014): 405-28.

The Einsatzgruppen Reports: Selections from the Dispatches of the Nazi Death Squads' Campaign against the Jews July 1941-January 1943. Edited by Yitzak Arad, Shmuel Krakowski and Shmuel Spector. New York: Holocaust Library, 1989.

Ejack, Stephen. "The Jewish Soviet Partisan as an Identity Construct." Honors thesis, Department of History and Classics, University of Alberta, 2011.

Encyclopedia of Ukraine. 5 vols. Edited by Volodymyr Kubijovyč and Danylo Husar Struk. Toronto: University of Toronto Press, 1984-93.

Erlacher, Trevor. "The Furies of Nationalism: Dmytro Dontsov, the Ukrainian Idea, and Europe's Twentieth Century." PhD dissertation: University of North Carolina at Chapel Hill, 2017.

Finder, Gabriel N., and Prusin, Alexander V. "Collaboration in Eastern Galicia: The Ukrainian Police and the Holocaust," *East European Jewish Affairs* 34, no. 2 (Winter 2004): 95-118.

Finder, Gabriel N. "The Trial of Szepsl Rotholc and the Politics of Retribution in the Aftermath of the Holocaust." *Gal-Ed: On the History & Culture of Polish Jewry* 20 (2006): 63-89.

Finkelstein, Genya. *Genya*. N.p., 1998.

Forum on Jan Gross's *Neighbors* in *Slavic Review* 61, no. 3 (Fall 2002): 453-89.

Fostii, Ivan. "Diial'nist' OUN na Bukovyni u 1940-1941 rr." http://www.sb u.gov.ua/sbu/doccatalog%5Cdocument?id=42164 (accessed 24 May 2011).

Fostii, Ivan. *Pivnichna Bukovyna i Khotynshchyna u Druhii svitovii viini 1939-1945 rr.* Chernivtsi: Oblasne viddilennia Poshukovo-vydavnychoho ahenstva "Knyha pam"iati Ukrainy," 2005.

Friedman, Henry. *I'm no Hero: Journeys of a Holocaust Survivor.* Seattle and London: University of Washington Press, 1999.

Friedman, Philip. "The Destruction of the Jews of Lwów." In Philip Friedman, *Roads to Extinction: Essays on the Holocaust,* edited by Ada June Friedman, 244-321. New York: Conference on Jewish Social Studies, Jewish Publication Society of America, 1980.

Friedman, Philip [Filip Friedmann]. *Die galizischen Juden im Kampfe um ihre Gleichberechtigung (1848-1868).* Veröffentlichungen der Dr. S.A. Bettelheim Memorial Foundation, 3. Frankfurt a.M.: J. Kauffmann Verlag, 1929.

Friedman, Philip. "Ukrainian-Jewish Relations during the Nazi Occupation." In Philip Friedman, *Roads to Extinction: Essays on the Holocaust,* edited by Ada June Friedman, 176-208. New York: Conference on Jewish Social Studies, Jewish Publication Society of America, 1980.

Friedman, Philip [Filip]. *Zagłada Żydów lwowskich w okresie okupacji niemieckiej.* 2nd, expanded ed. Munich, 1947.

Geissbühler, Simon. *Blutiger Juli: Rumäniens Vernichtungskrieg und der vergessene Massenmord an den Juden 1941.* Paderborn: Ferdinand Schöningh, 2013.

Geissbühler, Simon. "'He Spoke Yiddish Like a Jew': Neighbors' Contribution to the Mass Killing of Jews in Northern Bukovina and Bessarabia, July 1941." *Holocaust and Genocide Studies* 28, no. 3 (Winter 2014): 430-49.

Geissbühler, Simon. "What We Now Know about Romania and the Holocaust—and Why It Matters." In *Romania and the Holocaust: Events—Contexts—Aftermath*, edited by Simon Geissbühler, 241-66. Stuttgart: ibidem-Verlag, 2016.

Gerstenfeld-Maltiel, Jacob. *My Private War: One Man's Struggle to Survive the Soviets and the Nazis.* London: Vallentine Mitchell & Co. Ltd., 1993.

Gilbert, Martin. *Atlas of the Holocaust.* London: Michael Joseph, 1982.

Gilley, Christopher. "Reconciling the Irreconcilable? Left-Wing Ukrainian Nationalism and the Soviet Regime." *Nationalities Papers* 47, no. 3 (May 2019): 341-54.

Gitelman, Zvi. "Politics and the Historiography of the Holocaust in the Soviet Union." In *Bitter Legacy: Confronting the Holocaust in the USSR*, edited by Zvi Gitelman, 14-42. Bloomington and Indianapolis: Indiana University Press, 1997.

Golczewski, Frank. *Deutsche und Ukrainer 1914-1939.* Paderborn: Ferdinand Schöningh, 2010.

Golczewski, Frank. "Die Kollaboration in der Ukraine." In *Beiträge zur Geschichte des Nationalsozialismus*, vol. 19: *Kooperation und Verbrechen: Formen der "Kollaboration" im östlichen Europa 1939-1945*, ed. Christoph Dieckmann, Babette Quinkert, and Tatjana Tönsmeyer, 151-82. Göttingen: Wallstein Verlag, 2003.

Golczewski, Frank. "Local Government in German Occupied Ukraine." In *Local Government in Occupied Europe (1939-1945)*, ed. Bruno De Wever, Herman Van Goethem, and Nico Wouters, 241-57. Gent: Academia Press, 2006.

Golczewski, Frank. "Shades of Grey: Reflections on Jewish-Ukrainian and German-Ukrainian Relations in Galicia." In *The Shoah in Ukraine: History, Testimony, Memorialization*, edited by Ray Brandon and Wendy Lower, 114-55. Bloomington and Indianapolis: Indiana University Press, 2008.

Gomza, Ivan. "Elusive Proteus: A Study in the Ideological Morphology of the Organization of Ukrainian Nationalists." *Communist and Post-Communist Studies* 48 (2015): 195-207.

Grabowski, Jan. *Hunt for the Jews: Betrayal and Murder in German-Occupied Poland.* Bloomington and Indianapolis: Indiana University Press, 2013.

Grimsted, Patricia Kennedy. "'Trophy' Archives and Non-Restitution: Russia's Cultural 'Cold War' with the European Community." *Problems of Post-Communism* 45, no. 3 (May-June 1998): 3-16.

Gross, Jan T. *Fear: Anti-Semitism in Poland after Auschwitz: An Essay in Historical Interpretation.* New York: Random House, 2006.

Gross, Jan Tomasz, with Irena Grudzińska Gross. *Golden Harvest: Events at the Periphery of the Holocaust.* Oxford: Oxford University Press, 2012.

Gross, Jan T. *Neighbors: The Destruction of the Jewish Community in Jedwabne, Poland.* Princeton: Princeton University Press, 2001.

Gross, Jan T. *Revolution from Abroad: The Soviet Conquest of Poland's Western Ukraine and Western Belorussia.* Princeton: Princeton University Press, 1988.

Gyidel, Ernest. "The Ukrainian Legal Press of the General Government: The Case of *Krakivs'ki visti*, 1940-1944." PhD dissertation: University of Alberta, 2019.

Hanusiak, Michael. *Lest We Forget.* Greatly enlarged ed. New York, 1975.

Havryshko, M.I. "Choloviky, zhinky i nasyl'stvo v OUN ta UPA v 1940-1950-kh rr." *Ukrains'kyi istorychnyi zhurnal*, no. 4 (2016): 89-107.

Havryshko, Marta. "Illegitimate Sexual Practices in the OUN Underground and UPA in Western Ukraine in the 1940s and 1950s." *The Journal of Power Institutions in Post Soviet Societies* 17 (2016). https://journals.openedition.org/pipss/4214 (accessed 12 October 2018).

Headland, Ronald. *Messages of Murder: A Study of the Reports of the Einsatzgruppen of the Security Police and the Security Service, 1941-1943.* Rutherford, Madison, Teaneck: Fairleigh Dickinson University Press; London and Toronto: Associated University Presses, 1992.

Heer, Hannes. "Lemberg 1941: Die Instrumentalisierung der NKVD-Verbrechen für Judenmord." In *Kriegsverbrechen im 20. Jahrhundert*, ed. Wolfram Wette and Gerd R. Ueberschär), 165-77. Darmstadt: Primus Verlag, 2001.

Heiman, Leo. "They Saved Jews: Ukrainian Patriots Defied Nazis." *Ukrainian Quarterly* 17, no. 4 (Winter 1961): 320-32.

Heiman, Leo. "We Fought for Ukraine! The Story of Jews with the UPA." *Ukrainian Quaterly* 20, no. 1 (Spring 1964): 33-44.

Hellbeck, Jochen. "Fashioning the Stalinist Soul: The Diary of Stepan Podlubnyi, 1931-9." In Sheila Fitzpatrick, ed., *Stalinism: New Directions*, 77-116. Rewriting Histories. London and New York: Routledge, 2000.

Heller, Fanya Gottesfeld. *Strange and Unexpected Love: A Teenage Girl's Holocaust Memoirs.* Hoboken: KTAV Publishing House, 1993.

Hempel, Adam. *Pogrobowcy klęski: Rzecz o policji "granatowej" w Generalnym Gubernatorstwie 1939-1945.* Warsaw: Państwowe Wydawnictwo Naukowe, 1990.

Herasymenko, P. [H. Polikarpenko]. *Orhanizatsiia Ukrains'kykh Natsionalistiv pidchas Druhoi svitovoi viiny*. 4th ed., ed. B. Mykhailiuk. Canada, 1951.

[Hescheles, Janina.] *Oczyma dwunastoletniej dziewczyny*. Kraków: Centralny Komitet Żydów Polskich, 1946.

Heyer, Friedrich. *Kirchengeschichte der Ukraine im 20. Jahrhundert: Von der Epochenwende des ersten Weltkrieges bis zu den Anfängen in einem unabhängigen ukrainischen Staat*. Göttingen: Vandenhoeck & Ruprecht, 2003.

Hilberg, Raul. *The Destruction of the European Jews*. 3rd ed. 3 vols (with continuous pagination). New Haven and London: Yale University Press, 2003.

Hilberg, Raul. *The Politics of Memory: The Journey of a Holocaust Historian*. Chicago: Ivan R. Dee, 1996.

Himka, Eva, and John-Paul Himka. "Absence and Presence of Genocide and Memory: The Holocaust and the Holodomor in Interviews with Elderly Ukrainian Nationalists in Lviv." Paper presented at the Fifth Annual Danyliw Research Seminar in Contemporary Ukrainian Studies, sponsored by the Chair of Ukrainian Studies, University of Ottawa, 29-31 October 2009.

Himka, John-Paul. "Be Wary of Faulty Nachtigall Lessons." *Kyiv Post*, 27 March 2008.

Himka, John-Paul. "Christianity and Radical Nationalism: Metropolitan Andrei Sheptytsky and the Bandera Movement." In *State Secularism and Lived Religion in Soviet Russia and Ukraine*, edited by Catherine Wanner, 93-116. Washington and New York: Woodrow Wilson Center Press and Oxford University Press, 2012.

Himka, John-Paul. "Debates in Ukraine over Nationalist Involvement in the Holocaust, 2004-2008." *Nationalities Papers* 39, no. 3 (May 2011): 353-70.

Himka, John-Paul [Ivan Khymka]. "Dostovirnist' svidchennia: reliatsiia Ruzi Vagner pro l'vivs'kyi pohrom vlitku 1941 r." *Holokost i suchasnist'* no. 2 (4) (2008): 43-79.

Himka, John-Paul. "Ethnicity and the Reporting of Mass Murder: *Krakivs'ki visti*, the NKVD Murders of 1941, and the Vinnytsia Exhumation." In *Shatterzone of Empires: Coexistence and Violence in the German, Habsburg, Russian, and Ottoman Borderlands*, edited by Omer Bartov and Eric D. Weitz, 378-98. Bloomington: Indiana University Press, 2013.

Himka, John-Paul. "How to Think about Difficult Things: Daniel Mendelsohn's *The Lost*." *Harvard Ukrainian Studies* 32-33 (2011-14): 315-24.

Himka, John-Paul. "The Importance of the Situational Element in East Central European Fascism." *East Central Europe* 37 (2010): 353-58.

Himka, John-Paul. "*Krakivski visti* and the Jews, 1943: A Contribution to the History of Ukrainian-Jewish Relations during the Second World War." *Journal of Ukrainian Studies* 21, no. 1-2 (Summer-Winter 1996): 81-95.

Himka, John-Paul. "Legislating Historical Truth: Ukraine's Laws of 9 April 2015." *Ab imperio*, 21 April 2015, http://net.abimperio.net/node/3442.

Himka, John-Paul. "The Lontsky Street Prison Memorial Museum: An Example of Post-Communist Holocaust Negationism." In *Perspectives on the Entangled History of Communism and Nationalism: A Comnaz Analysis*, ed. Klas-Göran Karlsson, Johan Stenfeldt, and Ulf Zander, 137-66. Lanham, MD: Lexington Books, 2015.

Himka, John-Paul. "The Lviv Pogrom of 1941: The Germans, Ukrainian Nationalists, and the Carnival Crowd." *Canadian Slavonic Papers* 53, no. 2-3-4 (June-September-December 2011): 209-43.

Himka, John-Paul. "Metropolitan Andrei Sheptytsky and the Holocaust." *Polin* 26 (2013): 337-59.

Himka, John-Paul. "The Organization of Ukrainian Nationalists and the Ukrainian Insurgent Army: Unwelcome Elements of an Identity Project." *Ab Imperio* 4 (2010): 83-101.

Himka, John-Paul. "Problems with the Category of Genocide and with Classifying the Ukrainian Famine of 1932-33 as a Genocide." In *Holodomor 1932-1933 rokiv v Ukraini: prychyny, demohrafichni naslidky, pravova otsinka* (Kyiv: Vydavnychyi dim "Kyievo-Mohylians'ka Akademiia," 2009), 413-20.

Himka, John-Paul. "Refleksje żołnierza Ukraińskiej Powstańczej Armii. Pamiętnik Ołeksandra Powszuka (1943–1944)." In *Prawda historyczna a prawda polityczna w badaniach naukowych. Przykład ludobójstwa na Kresach południowo-wschodniej Polski w latach 1939-1946*, ed. Bogusław Paź, 179-90. Wrocław: Wydawnictwo Uniwersytetu Wrocławskiego, 2011.

Himka, John-Paul. Review of Dieter Pohl, *Nationalsozialistische Judenverfolgung in Ostgalizien 1941-1944: Organisation und Durchführung eines staatlichen Massenverbrechens. Journal of Ukrainian Studies* 24, no. 1 (summer 1999): 97-99.

Himka, John-Paul [Ivan-Pavlo Khymka]. "'Skazhite, mnogo liudei vy rasstreliali?' 'Net, ne mnogo—chelovek 25-30.'" *Ukraina moderna*, 4 July 2012, http://www.uamoderna.com/md/173 (accessed 19 June 2020).

Himka, John-Paul. "Ukrainian Collaboration in the Extermination of the Jews during the Second World War: Sorting Out the Long-Term and Conjunctural Factors." In *The Fate of the European Jews, 1939-1945: Continuity or Contingency*, ed. Jonathan Frankel (New York, Oxford: Oxford University Press, 1997), *Studies in Contemporary Jewry* 13 (1997): 170-89.

Himka, John-Paul. "Ukrainian-Jewish Antagonism in the Galician Country-side during the Late Nineteenth Century." In *Ukrainian-Jewish Relations in Historical Perspective*, ed. Peter J. Potichnyj and Howard Aster (Edmonton: Canadian Institute of Ukrainian Studies, 1988), 111-58.

Himka, John-Paul. "Ukrainian Memories of the Holocaust: The Destruction of Jews as Reflected in Memoirs Collected in 1947." *Canadian Slavonic Papers* 54, no. 3-4 (September-December 2012): 427-42.

Himka, John-Paul. *Ukrainians, Jews and the Holocaust: Divergent Memories.* Saskatoon: Heritage Press, 2009.

Himka, John-Paul. "Western Ukraine between the Wars." *Canadian Slavonic Papers* 34, no. 4 (December 1992): 391-412.

Himka, John-Paul. "What Were They Thinking? The Organization of Ukrainian Nationalists: Its Attitudes toward Jews on the Eve of the Holocaust." In *Jews and Non-Jews during the Holocaust in the USSR: The Perspective of Interethnic Relations*, edited by Arkadi Zeltser. Jerusalem: Yad Vashem, forthcoming.

Hirsch, Marianne. "Surviving Images: Holocaust Photographs and the Work of Postmemory." *Yale Journal of Criticism* 14, no. 1 (Spring 2001): 5-33.

Hochberg-Mariańska, Maria, and Noe Grüss, eds. *Dzieci oskarżają*. Kraków: Centralna Żydowska Komisja Historyczna, 1947.

Homin voli: Spivanyk natsionalistychnykh pisen'. Part 1. N.p., 1940.

Hon, Maksym. "Ievreis'ke pytannia v Zakhidnii Ukraini naperedodni Druhoi svitovoi viiny (za materialamy hromads'ko-politychnoi periodyky kraiu)." *Holokost i suchasnist'* 1 (2005): 9-27.

Hon, Maksym. *Iz kryvdoiu na samoti. Ukrains'ko-ievreis'ki vzaiemyny na zakhidnoukrains'kykh zemliakh u skladi Pol'shchi (1935-1939). Monohrafiia.* Rivne: Volyns'ki oberehy, 2005.

Hrushevs'kyi, Mykhailo. *Vybrani pratsi. Vydano z nahody 25-richchia z dnia ioho smerty (1934-1959)*, edited by Mykola Halii. New York, 1960.

Hryciuk, Grzegorz. "Victims 1939-1941: The Soviet Repressions in Eastern Poland." In *Shared History – Divided Memory: Jews and Others in Soviet-Occupied Poland, 1939-1941*, edited by Elazar Barkan, Elizabeth A. Cole, and Kai Struve, 173-200. Leipzig: Leipziger Universitätsverlag, 2007.

Hrynevch, Vladyslav. *Nepryborkane riznoholossia: Druha svitova viina i suspi'lno-politychni nastroi v Ukraini, 1939 – cherven' 1941 rr.* Kyiv-Dnipropetrovsk: Vydavnytstvo "Lira," 2012.

Hrytsak, Iaroslav. *Strasti za natsionalizmom: istorychni esei.* Kyiv: Krytyka, 2004.

Hryvul, Taras. "Chysel'nist' pidpil'noi merezhi OUN na terytoriï URSR v 1940-1941 rokakh." *Ukraina: kul'turna spadshchyna, natsional'na svidomist', derzhavnist'* 52 (2012): 260-68.

Hunczak, Taras. "Problems of Historiography: History and Its Sources." *Harvard Ukrainian Studies* 25, no. 1-2 (2001): 129-42.

Hunczak, Taras. "A Reappraisal of Symon Petliura and Ukrainian-Jewish Relations, 1917-1921." *Jewish Social Studies* 31 (1969): 163-83.

Hunczak, Taras. "Ukrainian-Jewish Relations during the Soviet and Nazi Occupations." In *Ukraine during World War II: History and Its Aftermath: A Symposium,* edited by Yury Boshyk, 39-57. Edmonton: Canadian Institute of Ukrainian Studies, 1986.

Hunczak [Hunchak], Taras, and Roman Solchanyk [Sol'chanyk], eds. *Ukrains'ka suspil'no-politychna dumka v 20 stolitti. Dokumenty i materialy.* 3 vols. N.p.: Suchasnist', 1983.

"Iak tvorylasia lehenda pro Nachtigall", *Dzerkalo tyzhnia,* 16 February 2008, website of the Security Service of Ukraine: http://www.ssu.gov.ua/sbu/control/uk/publish/article?art_id=74855&cat_id=74589 (accessed 6 April 2013).

Ianiv, Volodymyr. "Za dobre im"ia ukrains'koho narodu (Do zlobnoi kharakterystyky Kogona v ioho knyzhtsi pro nimets'ki kontstabory)." *Chas* (Fürth), 18 May 1947.

Iashan, Vasyl. *Pid brunatnym chobotom. Nimets'ka okupatsiia Stanyslavivshchyny v Druhii svitovii viini, 1941-1944.* Toronto: New Pathway Publishers, 1989.

"Ievhen Smuk...." *Iavorivs'ka raionna derzhavna admynistratsiia. Istorychni podii,* 6 January 2019, http://javoriv-rda.gov.ua/istorychni-podiji/6-sichnya-1915-roku-narodyvsya-providnyk-oun-upa-yavorivschyny-evhena-smuka/ (accessed 20 September 2019).

Il'iushyn, I.I. "Boiovi dii OUN i UPA na antypol's'komu fronti." In *Orhanizatsiia ukrains'kykh natsionalistiv i Ukrains'ka povstans'ka armiia. Istorychni narysy,* edited by Stanislav Kul'chyts'kyi, 222-302. Kyiv: Naukova dumka, 2005.

Il'iushyn, Ihor. *Ukrainsk'a povstans'ka armiia i Armiia kraiova. Protystoiannia v Zakhidnii Ukraini (1939-1945 rr.).* Kyiv: Vydavnychyi dim "Kyievo-Mohylians'ka Akademiia," 2009.

Il'iushyn, I.I. *Volyns'ka trahediia 1943-1944 rr.* Kyiv: Natsional'na akademiia nauk Ukrainy, Instytut istorii Ukrainy; Kyivs'kyi slavistychnyi universytet, 2003.

Ilnytzkyj, Roman. *Deutschland und die Ukraine 1934-1945: Tatsachen europäischer Ostpolitik: Ein Vorbericht.* 2 vols. 2nd ed. Munich: Osteuropa-Institut, 1958.

Isaievych, Iaroslav. "1943 rik u pam"iati poliakiv i ukraintsiv." *Den'*, 15 March 2003. http://www.ji-magazine.lviv.ua/dyskusija/volyn/day 15-03.htm (accessed 3 September 2018).

Ishchuk, Oleksandr, and Valerii Ohorodnik. *Heneral Mykola Arsenych: zhyttia ta dial'nist' shefa SB OUN.* Kolomyia: Vik, 2010.

Ivanushchenko, Hennadii, ed. *OUN-UPA na Sumshchyni.* Vol. 1. Vinnytsia: Vydavnytstvo DP DKF, 2007.

Justiz und NS-Verbrechen: Sammlung deutscher Strafurteile wegen nationalsozialistischer Tötungsverbrechen, edited by D.W. de Mildt and C.F. Rüter. Amsterdam: University Press Amsterdam, 1968- . Online edition, https://www.junsv.nl/ (accessed 30 October 2018).

Kasianov, Georgiy. "History, Politics and Memory (Ukraine 1990s-2000s)." In *Memory and Change in Europe: Eastern Perspectives*, edited by Małgorzata Pakier and Joanna Wawrzyniak, 193-211. New York and Oxford: Berghahn Books, 2015.

Katchanovski [Kachanovs'kyi], Ivan. "OUN(b) ta natsysts'ki masovi vbyvstva vlitku 1941 roku na istorychnii Volyni." *Ukraina Moderna* 20 (2014): 215-45.

Katchanovski, Ivan. "Terrorists or National Heroes? Politics of the OUN and the UPA in Ukraine." Paper presented at the Fifteenth Annual World Convention of the Association for the Study of Nationalities, New York, 15-17 April 2010.

Katzmann, Friedrich. *Rozwiązanie kwestii żydowskiej w Dystrykcie Galicja. Lösung der Judenfrage im Distrikt Galizien.* Edited by Andrzej Żbikowski. Dokumenty, 5. Warsaw: Instytut Pamięci Narodowej, 2001.

Kazanivs'kyi, Bohdan. *Shliakhom Legendy. Spomyny.* London: Ukrains'ka vydavnycha spilka, 1975.

Kedryn Rudnyts'kyi, Ivan. *Zhytiia – podii – liudy. Spomyny i komentari.* New York: Chervona Kalyna, 1976.

Kentii, A., et al. *Borot'ba proty UPA i natsionalistychnoho pidpillia: informatsiini dokumenty TsK KP(b)U, obkomiv partii, NKVS-MVS, MDB-KDB 1943-1959*, book 1: *1943-1945 Litopys UPA*, new series, 4. Kyiv and Toronto: Natsional'na Akademiia nauk Ukrainy, 2002.

Kentii, A.V. "'Dvofrontova' borot'ba UPA (1943–persha polovyna 1944 rr." In *Orhanizatsiia ukrains'kykh natsionalistiv i Ukrains'ka povstans'ka armiia. Istorychni narysy*, edited by Stanislav Kul'chyts'kyi, 160-221. Kyiv: Naukova dumka, 2005.

Kentii, A.V. *Narysy istorii Orhanizatsii ukrains'kykh natsionalistiv v 1941-1942 rr.* Kyiv, 1999.

Kentii, A.V. "Perekhid OUN(B) na antynimets'ki pozytsii (1941-1942)." In *Orhanizatsiia ukrains'kykh natsionalistiv i Ukrains'ka povstans'ka armiia. Istorychni narysy*, edited by Stanislav Kul'chyts'kyi, 88-113. Kyiv: Naukova dumka, 2005.

Kentii, A.V. *Ukrains'ka povstans'ka armiia v 1942-1943 rr.* Kyiv, 1999.

Kentii, A.V. *Ukrains'ka povstans'ka armiia v 1944-1945 rr.* Kyiv, 1999.

Khonigsman, Ia.S. *Katastrofa evreistva Zapadnoi Ukrainy. Evrei Vostochnoi Galitsii, Zapadnoi Volyni, Bukoviny i Zakarpat'ia v 1933-1945 gg.* Lviv, 1998.

Khonigsman, Iakov. *Katastrofa l'vovskogo evreistva.* Lviv: L'vovskoe obshchestvo evreiskoi kul'tury im. Sholom Aleikhema, 1993.

Kiebuzinski, Ksenya, and Alexander Motyl, eds. *The Great West Ukrainian Prison Massacre of 1941: A Sourcebook.* Amsterdam: Amsterdam University Press, 2017.

Klee, Ernst; Willi Dressen; and Volker Riess, eds. *"The Good Old Days": The Holocaust as Seen by Its Perpetrators and Bystanders.* New York: The Free Press, 1991.

Klid, Bohdan. "Stanislav Kulchytsky: A Historian and His Writings in Changing Times." In Stanislav Kulchytsky, *The Famine of 1932-1933 in Ukraine: An Anatomy of the Holodomor*, xi-xvii. Edmonton and Toronto: Canadian Institute of Ukrainian Studies Press, 2018.

Klymenko, Oleh, and Serhii Tkachov. *Ukraintsi v politsii v dystrykti "Halychyna" (Ternopil's'kyi okruh). Nimets'kyi okupatsiinyi rezhym v Ternopoli ta okolytsiakh u 1941-1944 rr.* Kharkiv: Ranok-NT, 2013.

Klymenko, Oleh, and Serhii Tkachov. *Ukraintsi v politsii v reikhskomisariati "Ukraina" (Pivdenna Volyn'). Nimets'kyi okupatsiinyi rezhym na Kremenechchyni u 1941-1944 rr.* Kharkiv: Ranok-NT, 2012.

Klymyshyn, Mykola. *V pokhodi do voli. Spomyny.* 2nd ed. Vol.1. Detroit: Peredruk Ukrains'koi knyharni, 1987.

Knyha faktiv teroru nimets'kykh i bol'shevyts'kykh okupantiv ta borot'by proty nykh Orhanizatsii ukrains'kykh natsionalistiv i Ukrains'koi povstans'koi armii, iak tezh inshykh, zviazanykh z tsym podii. Part 1: *1941-1943 r.r.* N.p.: Vydannia Ukrains'koi povstans'koi armii, 1947.

Kohn, Nahum, and Howard Roiter. *A Voice from the Forest: Memoirs of a Jewish Partisan.* New York: Holocaust Library, 1980.

Kolesnichenko, Vadym. "Reabilitatsiia ta heroizatsiia usikh, khto borovsia proty antyhitlerivs'koi koalitsii bude zaboronena v Ukraini (zakonoproekt)." *Ukrains'ka pravda, Blohy*, 8 May 2013, https://blogs.pra vda.com.ua/authors/kolesnichenko/518a35535beb4/ (accessed 24 October 2018).

"Kolesnichenko vydav zbirnyk pro UPA ta OUN." *Istorychna pravda*, 23 May 2012, http://www.istpravda.com.ua/short/2012/05/23/86770/ (accessed 24 October 2018).

"Kolesnichenko znovu potsupyv chuzhu pratsiu." *Istorychna pravda*, 9 April 2013, http://www.istpravda.com.ua/short/2013/04/9/120043/?fbcli d=IwAR0EnbG3GMoJ8IMlge7fMn9K8Ns5L7oTcw_tcqwTbSdimydS W4kjEQp2KLU (accessed 24 October 2018).

Kolodzins'kyi, Mykhailo. "Natsionalistychne povstannia. Rozdil iz pratsi 'Voienna doktryna ukrains'kykh natsionalistiv.'" *Ukraina Moderna* 20 (2013): 257-95.

Konovalets', Evhen. *Prychynky do istorii ukrains'koi revoliutsii*. Prague: Nakladom Provodu Ukrains'kykh Natsionalistiv, 1928.

Kopstein, Jeffrey S., and Jason Wittenberg. "Deadly Communities: Local Political Milieus and the Persecution of Jews in Occupied Poland." *Comparative Political Studies* 20 (10) (2010): 1-25.

Kopstein, Jeffrey S., and Jason Wittenberg. *Intimate Violence: Anti-Jewish Pogroms on the Eve of the Holocaust*. Ithaca and London: Cornell University Press, 2018.

Kordiuk, B. "Pro liudei, spovnenykh samoposviaty." *Suchasna Ukraina*, 20 July 1958.

Korzen, Meir. "The Extermination of Two Ukrainian Jewish Communities: Testimony of a German Army Officer." *Yad Vashem Studies* (1959): 303-20.

Kostiuk, Ivan R. "Pam"iati Andriia Tershakivtsia." *Svoboda* (Jersey City), 27 July 1979.

Kosyk, Volodymyr [Wolodymyr], ed. *Das Dritte Reich und die ukrainische Frage: Dokumente 1934-1944*. Munich: Ukrainisches Institut, [1985].

Kosyk, Volodymyr, ed. *Ukraina v Druhii svitovii viini u dokumentakh. Zbirnyk nimets'kykh arkhivnykh materialiv*. Vol. 1. Lviv, 1997.

Kosyk, Volodymyr, ed. *Ukraina v Druhii svitovii viini u dokumentakh*. Vol. 2: *Zbirnyk nimets'kykh arkhivnykh materialiv (1941-1942)*. Lviv: L'vivs'kyi derzhavnyi universytet im. I. Franka, Instytut ukrains'koi arkheohrafii ta dzhereloznavstva im. M. Hrushevs'koho NAN Ukrainy, Instytut ukrainoznavstva im. I. Kryp"iakevycha NAN Ukrainy, 1998.

Koval', V.S. "Za shcho i z kym borolysia OUN-UPA." in *Ukraina XX st. Problemy natsional'noho vidrodzhennia. Zbirnyk naukovykh prats'*, ed. I.S. Khmil' et al., 91-116. Kyiv: Naukova dumka, 1993.

Kovaliuk, V.R. "Kul'turolohichni ta dukhovni aspekty 'radianyzatsii' Zakhidnoi Ukrainy (veresen' 1939 r.–cherven' 1941 r.)." *Ukrains'kyi Istorychnyi Zhurnal*, no. 2-3 (1993): 3-17.

Kovaliv, Yuriy B. "Herasymenko (Herasymenko-Volkovinsky), Polykarp." *Ukrainians in the United Kingdom: Online Encyclopaedia*, http://www.ukrainiansintheuk.info/eng/02/herasymenko-e.htm (accessed 31 March 2018).

Kovba, Zhanna. *Liudianist' u bezodni pekla. Povedinka mistsevoho naselennia Skhidnoi Halychyny v roky "ostatochnoho rozv"iazannia ievreis'koho pytannia."* Biblioteka Instytutu iudaiky. Kyiv: Instytut iudaiky, 1998.

Kraft, Robert N. "Archival Memory: Representations of the Holocaust in Oral Testimony." *Poetics Today* 27, no. 2 (Summer 2006): 311-30.

Krakowski, Shmuel. *The War of the Doomed: Jewish Armed Resistance in Poland, 1942-44*. Translated by Orah Blaustein. New York, London: Holmes & Meier Publishers, Inc., 1984.

Krentsbakh, Stella. "Zhyvu shche zavdiaky UPA." In *V riadakh UPA. Zbirka spomyniv buv. voiakiv Ukrains'koi povstans'koi armii*, edited by Petro Mirchuk and V. Davydenko, 342-49. New York: T[ovarystvo] b. Voiakiv UPA v ZDA i Kanadi, 1957.

Kruglov, Aleksandr. "Pogromy v Vostochnoi Galitsii letom 1941 g.: organizatory, uchastniki, masshtaby i posledstviia." In *Voina na unichtozhenie. Natsistskaia politika genotsida na territorii Vostochnoi Evropy. Materialy mezhdunarodnoi nauchnoi konferentsii (Moskva, 26-28 aprelia 2010 goda)*, edited by A.R. Diukov and O.E. Orlenko, 324-41. Moscow: Fond "Istoricheskaia pamiat'," 2010.

Kruglov, A. *Sbornik dokumentov i materialov ob unichtozhenii natsistami evreev Ukrainy v 1941-1944 godakh*. Kyiv: Institut iudaiki, 2002.

Kudelia, Mykola P. *Kriz' buri lykholit'*. Minneapolis: "STYR" Publishing Co., 1999.

Kul'chyts'kyi, Stanislav. *Orhanizatsiia ukrains'kykh natsionalistiv i Ukrains'ka povstans'ka armiia. Fakhovyi vysnovok robochoi hrupy istorykiv pry Uriadovii komisii z vyvchennia diial'nosti OUN i UPA*. Kyiv, 2005.

Kul'chyts'kyi, Stanislav, ed. *Orhanizatsiia ukrains'kykh natsionalistiv i Ukrains'ka povstans'ka armiia. Istorychni narysy*. Kyiv: Naukova dumka, 2005.

Kul'chyts'kyi, Stanislav, ed. *Problema OUN-UPA. Poperednia istorychna dovidka*. Kyiv: Natsional'na Akademiia Nauk Ukrainy, Instytut istorii Ukrainy, 2000.

Kulińska, Lucyna. "Dowody zbrodni popełnionych przez nacjonalistów ukraińskich z formacji OUN-UPA na ludności żydowskiej w świetle ukraińskich dokumentów archiwalnych zgromadzonych przez Wiktora Poliszczuka." In *OUN, UPA i zagłada Żydów*, edited by Andrzej A. Zięba, 67-103. Kraków: Księgarnia Akademicka, [2017].

Kuromiya, Hiroaki. *Freedom and Terror in the Donbas: A Ukrainian-Russian Borderland, 1870s-1990s*. Cambridge Russian, Soviet and Post-Soviet Studies, 104. Cambridge and New York: Cambridge University Press, 1998.

Kuropas, Myron B. *The Ukrainian Americans: Roots and Aspirations 1884-1954*. Toronto: University of Toronto Press, 1991.

Kurylo, Taras, and John-Paul Himka [Ivan Khymka]. "Iak OUN stavylasia do ievreiv? Rozdumy nad knyzhkoiu Volodymyra V"iatrovycha." *Ukraina Moderna* 13 (2008): 252-65.

Kurylo, Taras. "The 'Jewish Question' in the Ukrainian Nationalist Discourse of the Inter-War Period." *Polin* 26 (2014): 233-73.

Kurylo, Taras. "Shche raz pro OUN ta faszyzm." *zaxid.net*, 15 March 2012, https://zaxid.net/shhe_raz_pro_oun_ta_fashizm_n1250264 (accessed 19 March 2019).

Kurylo, Taras. "Syla ta slabkist' ukrains'koho natsionalizmu v Kyievi pid chas nimets'koi okupatsii (1941-1943)." *Ukraina moderna* 13 (2) (2008): 115-30.

Kysla, Iuliia. "Vyzhyvannia za ekstremal'nykh umov: Holokost u Boryslavi (1941-1944)." *Holokost i suchasnist'* 1 (11) (2012): 9-33.

Lahola, Ivan, and Stepan Andrusiak. *Spohady politychnoho v"iaznia no. 154820 fashysts'kykh taboriv smerti*. Lviv: NVF "Ukrains'ki tekhnolohii," 2002.

Lebed', Mykola. *UPA*. Part 1: *Nimets'ka okupatsiia Ukrainy*. N.p.: Vydannia Presovoho B"iura UHVR, 1946.

Lebid', Mykhailo. "Chasy nimets'koi okupatsii v Matiivs'kim raioni na Volyni. (Spohady kol. holovy raionovoi upravy." In *Volyn' i Polissia. Nimets'ka okupatsiia. Book 3: Spomyny uchasnykiv z anhliis'kymy reziume*, edited by Ievhen Shtendera, 197-222. Litopys UPA, 5. Toronto: Vydavnytstvo "Litopys UPA," 1984.

Lehmann, Rosa. *Symbiosis and Ambivalence: Poles and Jews in a Small Galician Town*. New York and Oxford: Berghahn Books, 2001.

Levin, Alex. *Under the Yellow and Red Stars*. Azrieli Series of Holocaust Survivor Memoirs, Series 2. Toronto: The Azrieli Foundation, 2009.

Lewin, Kurt I. *Przeżyłem. Saga Świętego Jura spisana w roku 1946 przez syna rabina Lwowa*. Warsaw: Fundacja Zeszytów Literackich, 2006.

Lewytzkyj [Levyts'kyi], Borys. "Natsional'nyi rukh pid chas Druhoi svitovoi viiny: Interv"iu z B. Levyts'kym." *Diialoh* 2 (1979): 4-31.

Litopys neskorenoi Ukrainy. Dokumenty, materialy, spohady. Edited by Petro Maksymuk et al. Book 1. Lviv: Prosvita, 1993.

Liubchenko, Arkadii. *Shchodennyk Arkadiia Liubchenka.* Edited by George Luckyj [Iurii Luts'kyi]. Lviv-New York, Vydavnytstvo M.P. Kots', 1999.

Livneh, Nathan, ed. *Pinkas hak'hilah Trisk: sefer isskor.* Israel: Trisk-Committe [sic] in Israel, 1975.

Longereich, Peter, with Dieter Pohl, eds. *Die Ermordung der europäischen Juden: Eine umfassende Dokumentation des Holokaust 1941-1945.* Munich and Zürich: Piper, 1989.

Lower, Wendy. *The Diary of Samuel Golfard and the Holocaust in Galicia.* Documenting Life and Destruction, Holocaust Sources in Context. Lanham, MD: AltaMira Press in association with the United States Holocaust Memorial Museum, 2011.

Lower, Wendy. *Hitler's Furies: German Women in the Nazi Killing Fields.* Boston: Houghton Mifflin Harcourt, 2013.

Lower, Wendy. *Nazi Empire-Building and the Holocaust in Ukraine.* Chapel Hill: The University of North Carolina Press in association with the United States Holocaust Memorial Museum, 2005.

Lower, Wendy. "Pogroms, Mob Violence and Genocide in Western Ukraine, Summer 1941: Varied Histories, Explanations and Comparisons." *Journal of Genocide Research* 13, no. 3 (September 2011): 217-46.

Magocsi, Paul Robert. *With Their Backs to the Mountains: A History of Carpathian Rus' and Carpatho-Rusyns.* Budapest and New York: Central European University Press, 2015.

Marchuk, Ihor, and Iaroslav Perekhod'ko. *Kurinnyi UPA Stepan Trofymchuk-"Nedolia."* Litopys UPA, Seriia "Podii i Liudy," 31. Toronto-Lviv: Vydavnytstvo "Litopys UPA," 2015.

Marples, David R. *Heroes and Villains: Creating National History in Contemporary Ukraine.* Budapest and New York: Central European University Press, 2007.

Martynenko, Taras. "Ukrains'ka Dopomizhna Politsiia v okruzi L'viv-misto: shtrykhy do sotsial'noho portreta." *Visnyk L'vivs'koho universytetu. Seriia istorychna* 48 (2013): 152-67.

Martynets', V. *Zhydivs'ka probliema v Ukraini.* London: Williams, Lea & Co., 1938.

Martynowych, Orest T. "Sympathy for the Devil: The Attitude of Ukrainian War Veterans in Canada to Nazi Germany and the Jews, 1933-1939." In *Re-imagining Ukrainian Canadians: History, Politics, and Identity,* edited by Rhonda L. Hinther and Jim Mochoruk, 173-220. Toronto: University of Toronto Press, 2011.

Matthäus, Jürgen. "Operation Barbarossa and the Onset of the Holocaust, June-December 1941." In Christopher R. Browning, with contributions by Jürgen Matthäus, *The Origins of the Final Solution: The Evolution of Nazi Jewish Policy, September 1939-March 1942*, 244-308. Lincoln, NE, and Jerusalem: University of Nebraska Press and Yad Vashem, 2004.

McBride, Jared. *Contesting the Malyn Massacre: The Legacy of Inter-Ethnic Violence and the Second World War in Eastern Europe*. Carl Beck Papers, 2405. Pittsburgh: University Library System, University of Pittsburgh, 2016.

McBride, Jared. "How Ukraine's New Memory Commissar Is Controlling the Nation's Past." *The Nation*, 13 August 2015. https://www.thenation.com/article/how-ukraines-new-memory-commissar-is-controlling-the-nations-past/ (accessed 12 October 2018).

McBride, Jared Graham. "'A Sea of Blood and Tears': Ethnic Diversity and Mass Violence in Nazi-Occupied Volhynia, Ukraine, 1941-44." PhD dissertation: University of California, Los Angeles, 2014.

McBride, Jared. "'To Be Stored Forever." *Ab Imperio*, no. 1 (2012): 434-45.

McBride, Jared. "Ukraine's Invented a 'Jewish-Ukrainian Nationalist' to Whitewash Its Nazi-era Past." *Haaretz*, 9 November 2017. https://www.haaretz.com/opinion/ukraine-nationalists-are-using-a-jew-to-whitewash-their-nazi-era-past-1.5464194?v=1603208641337 (accessed 12 December 2020).

McBride, Jared. "Ukrainian Holocaust Perpetrators Are Being Honored in Place of Their Victims." *Tablet*, 20 July 2016. http://www.tabletmag.com/jewish-news-and-politics/208439/holocaust-perpetrators-honored?utm_source=tabletmagazinelist&utm_campaign=2f2e517c76-July_21_20167_21_2016&utm_medium=email&utm_term=0_c308bf8edb-2f2e517c76-207199705 (accessed 11 August 2016).

McBride, Jared. "Who's Afraid of Ukrainian Nationalism?" *Kritika: Explorations in Russian and Eurasian History* 17, no. 3 (2016): 647-63.

Mechnyk, S.M. *Neskoreni. Dokumental'na povist' pro herois'ku borot'bu chleniv revoliutsiinoi OUN*. London: Ukrains'ka vydavnycha spilka, 1965.

Mechnyk, S. *Pid trioma okupantamy. Spohady revoliutsionera-pidpil'nyka*. London: Ukrains'ka vydavnycha spilka, 1958.

Medychna opika v UPA. Edited by Modest Ripets'kyi. Litopys UPA, 23. Toronto-Lviv: Litopys UPA, 1992-93.

Mędykowski, Witold. *W cieniu gigantów. Pogromy 1941 r. w byłej sowieckiej strefie okupacyjnej. Kontekst historyczny, społeczny i kulturowy*. Warsaw: Instytut Studiów Politycznych Polskiej Akademii Nauk, 2012.

Melamed, Vladimir. "Organized and Unsolicited Collaboration in the Holocaust: The Multifaceted Ukrainian Context." *East European Jewish Affairs* 37, no. 2 (August 2007): 217-48.

Mel'nyk, Oleksandr. "Stalins'ka iustytsiia iak mistse pam"iati: anty-ievreis'ke nasyllia v Kyievi u veresni 1941 roku kriz' pryzmu radians'kykh slidchykh materialiv." 2 parts. *Historians.in.UA*, 14-15 February 2013, http://www.historians.in.ua/index.php/en/doslidzhe nnya/582-oleksandr-melnyk-stalinska-iustytsiia-iak-mistse-pamiati-anty-ievreiske-nasyllia-v-kyievi-u-veresni-1941-roku-kriz-pryzmu-r adianskykh-slidchykh-materialiv-chastyna-1 and http://www.histo rians.in.ua/index.php/en/doslidzhennya/584-oleksandr-melnyk-st alinska-iustytsiia-iak-mistse-pamiati-anty-ievreiske-nasyllia-v-kyiev i-u-veresni-1941-roku-kriz-pryzmu-radianskykh-slidchykh-material iv-chastyna-2 (accessed 27 August 2019).

"Michael Hanusiak, Activist and Journalist, 93." *People's World*, 21 September 2007. http://www.peoplesworld.org/article/michael-hanusiak-activist-and-journalist-93/ (accessed 17 May 2018).

Michlic, Joanna. "Coming to Terms with the 'Dark Past': The Polish Debate about the Jedwabne Massacre." *Analysis of Current Trends in Antisemitism*, no. 21. The Vidal Sassoon International Center for the Study of Antisemitism. 2002.

Mick, Christoph. *Kriegserfahrungen in einer multiethnischen Stadt: Lemberg 1914-1947*. Wiesbaden: Harrassowitz Verlag, 2010.

Milch, Baruch. *Can Heaven Be Void?* Jerusalem: Yad Vashem, 2003.

Minenko, Tymofii. *Pravoslavna tserkva v Ukraini pid chas Druhoi svitovoi viiny 1939-1945 (Volyns'kyi period)*. Vol. 1. Winnipeg-Lviv: Vydavnytstvo L'vivs'koho muzeiu istorii relihii "Lohos," 2000.

Mirchuk, Petro. *In the German Mills of Death 1941-1945*. 2nd ed. Rochester, NY: The Survivors of the Holocaust and the Ukrainian American Freedom Foundation, Inc., 1985.

Mirchuk, Petro. *Mykola Mikhnovs'kyi. Apostol ukrain'koi derzhavnosty*. Philadelphia: T-vo Ukrains'koi Studiiuiuchoi Molodi im. M. Mikhnovs'koho, 1960.

Mirchuk, Petro. *Narys istorii Orhanizatsii Ukrains'kykh Natsionalistiv*. Vol. 1: *1920-1939*. Edited by Stepan Lenkavs'kyi. Munich: Ukrains'ke vydavnytstvo, 1968.

Mirchuk, Petro. *Ukrains'ka Povstans'ka Armiia 1942-1952*. Munich: Cicero, 1953.

Mitrynga, Ivan [Serhii Oreliuk]. *Nash shliakh borot'by*. 2 parts. ([Kraków, 1940-41]).

Mondzelevs'kyi, Eduard. "Pochatok viiny na Fastivshchyni." *Borovaia*, http://borova.org/?page_id=149 (accessed 30 September 2011).

Moroz, Volodymyr. *Zynovii Tershakovets'-"Fedir."* Litopys Ukrains'koi povstans'koi armii, Seriia "Podii I liudy," 12. Toronto and Lviv: Vydavnytstvo "Litopys UPA," 2011.

Motyka, Grzegorz. *Ukraińska partyzantka 1942-1960: działalność Organizacji Ukraińskich Nacjonalistów i Ukraińskiej Powstańczej Armii.* Warsaw: Instytut Studiów Politycznych PAN; RYTM, 2006.

Motyl, Alexander J. *The Turn to the Right: The Ideological Origins and Development of Ukrainian Nationalism, 1919-1929.* Boulder: East European Monographs, 1980.

Motyl, Alexander J. "The Ukrainian Nationalist Movement and the Jews: Theoretical Reflections on Nationalism, Fascism, Rationality, Primordialism, and History." *Polin: Studies in Polish Jewry*, 26 (2014): *Jews and Ukrainians*, ed. Yohanan Petrovsky-Shtern and Antony Polonsky, 275-95.

Musial, Bogdan. *"Konterrevolutionäre Elemente sind zu erschießen": Die Brutalisierung des deutsch-sowjetischen Krieges im Sommer 1941.* Berlin: Propyläen, 2000.

Myshlovska, Oksana. "Establishing the 'Irrefutable Facts' about OUN and UPA: The Role of the Working Group of Historians on OUN-UPA Activities in Mediating Memory-based Conflict in Ukraine." *Ab Imperio*, no. 1 (2018): 223-54.

Nakhmanovych, V.R. "Bukovyns'kyi kurin' i masovi rozstrily ievreiv Kyieva voseny 1941 r." *Ukrains'kyi istorychnyi zhurnal*, 2007, no. 3 (474): 76-97.

Nakonechnyi, Ievhen. *"Shoa" u L'vovi.* 2nd ed. Lviv: Piramida, 2006.

Nazarko, Ir[ynei]. "Piznaimo zhydiv!" *Kaliendar Misionaria* 27 (1930): 54-60.

Nimchuk, Ivan. *595 dniv soviets'kym viaznem.* Toronto: Drukarnia OO. Vasyliian, 1950.

Novick, Peter. *The Holocaust in American Life.* Boston and New York: Houghton Mifflin, 1999.

Nowak, Szymon. "'Droga do nikąd. Wojna polska z UPA' A.B. Szcześniak, W.Z. Szota–recenzja." *Historia. org.pl*, 28 August 2013. https://historia.org.pl/2013/08/28/droga-do-nikad-wojna-polska-z-upa-a-b-szcz esniak-w-z-szota-recenzja/ (accessed 16 May 2018).

Omeliusik, Mykola. "UPA na Volyni v 1943 rotsi." *Visti kombatanta*, no. 1 (22) (1966): 10-17; no. 2 (23) (1966): 16-25.

OUN v svitli postanov Velykykh zboriv, konferentsii ta inshykh dokumentiv z borot'by 1929-1955 r. Zbirka dokumentiv. [Munich:] Vyd. Zakordonnykh chastyn Orhanizatsii ukrains'kykh natsionalistiv, 1955.

Pan'kivs'kyi, Kost'. *Roky nimets'koi okupatsii*. New York and Toronto: Zhyttia i mysli, 1965.

Pan'kivs'kyi, Kost'. *Vid derzhavy do komitetu*. New York and Toronto: Zhyttia i mysli, 1957.

Paperno, Irina. "Exhuming the Bodies of Soviet Terror." *Representations* 75 (Summer 2001): 89-118.

Patryliak, I.K. *Viis'kova diial'nist OUN (B) u 1940-1942 rokakh*. Kyiv: Kyivs'kyi natsional'nyi universytet imeni Tarasa Shevchenka Instytut istorii Ukrainy NAN Ukrainy, 2004.

Patryliak, Ivan. "Zbroini vystupy OUN proty pol's'koi derzhavy na pochatku Druhoi svitovoi viiny." *Voienna istoriia*, no. 5 (47) (2009). http://warhistory.ukrlife.org/5_09_6.html (accessed 19 January 2021).

Paulovicova, Nina. "Rescue of Jews in the Slovak State (1939-1943)." PhD dissertation: University of Alberta, 2012.

Penter, Tanja. "Collaboration on Trial: New Source Material on Soviet Postwar Trials against Collaborators." *Slavic Review* 64, no. 4 (Winter 2005): 782-90.

Penter, Tanja. "Local Collaborators on Trial: Soviet War Crimes Trials under Stalin (1943-1953)." *Cahiers du Monde russe* 49, no. 2-3 (April-September 2008): 1-24.

Perechodnik, Calel. *Czy ja jestem mordercą?* Edited by Paweł Szapiro. Warsaw: Karta, 1995.

Petelycky, Stefan. *Into Auschwitz, for Ukraine*. Kingston and Kyiv: The Kashtan Press, 1999. http://www.uccla.ca/InAuschwitz-Petelycky. pdf (accessed 9 April 2015).

Petrenko, Roman. *Za Ukrainu, za ii voliu (Spohady)*. Litopys UPA, 27. Toronto: Vydavnytstvo Litopys UPA, 1997.

Plum, Günter. [Report on OUN involvement in 1941 pogroms.] Munich: Institut für Zeitgeschichte, 1965. Institut für Zeitgeschichte, Gutachten 3547 (ID 50, 191). Typescript also in Mykola Lebed archives, consulted at Harvard Ukrainian Research Institute, box 1, file 3.

Podvorniak, Mykhailo. *Viter z Volyni. Spohady*. Winnipeg: Tovarystvo "Volyn'," 1981.

Pohl, Dieter. "Anti-Jewish Pogroms in Western Ukraine—A Research Agenda." In *Shared History—Divided Memory: Jews and Others in Soviet-Occupied Poland, 1939-1941*, edited by Elazar Barkan, Elizabeth A. Cole, and Kai Struve, 305-13. Leipzig: Leipziger Universitätsverlag, 2007.

Pohl, Dieter. *Nationalsozialistische Judenverfolgung in Ostgalizien 1941-1944: Organisation und Durchführung eines staatlichen Massenverbrechens*. Munich: R. Oldenbourg Verlag, 1997.

Pohl, Dieter. Review of "*Konterrevolutionäre Elemente sind zu erschießen*": *Die Brutalisierung des deutsch-sowjetischen Krieges im Sommer 1941* in *H-Soz-Kult*, 30 April 2001, https://www.hsozkult.de/publicationrevie w/id/rezbuecher-546 (accessed 24 September 2018).

Polishchuk, Nina. "Faina Liakher—khrystyianka Anna i monakhynia Mariia. Istoriia z pidpillia i hlybyn dushi." *Khrystyianyn i svit*, http://xic. com.ua/z-istoriji-duhu/14-molytva/364-fajina-ljaher-hrystyjanka-a nna-j-monahynja-marija-istorija-z-pidpillja-i-glybyn-dushi (accessed 17 December 2020).

Polishchuk [Poliszczuk], Viktor [Wiktor]. *Bitter Truth: The Criminality of the Organization of Ukrainian Nationalists (OUN) and the Ukrainian Insurgent Army (UPA) (The Testimony of a Ukrainian)*. Toronto, 1999.

Polishchuk, Viktor. *Hirka pravda. Zlochynnist' OUN-UPA (spovid' ukraintsia)*. Toronto, 1995.

Polishchuk [Poliszczuk], Viktor [Wiktor]. *Integralny nacjonalizm ukraiński jako odmiana faszyzmu*. 5 vols. Toronto, 1998-2003.

Polishchuk, Viktor. *Rik 1943: OUN Bandery na Volyni. Diial'nist' OUN Bandery u svitli 'Vidkrytykh lystiv do Orhanizatsii Ukrains'kykh Natsionalistiv Stepana Bandery' avtorstva Tarasa Bul'by-Borovtsia. Prychynok do politychnoi i iurydychnoi otsinky OUN Bandery*. Toronto, 1943.

Polonsky, Antony, and Joanna B. Michlic, eds. *The Neighbors Respond: The Controversy over the Jedwabne Massacre in Poland*. Princeton and Oxford: Princeton University Press, 2004.

Pol'shcha ta Ukraina u trydsiatykh-sorokovykh rokakh XX stolittlia: Nevidomi dokumenty z arkhiviv spetsial'nykh sluzhb, vol. 4: *Poliaky i Ukraintsi mizh dvoma totalitarnymy systemamy 1942-44*. Vol. 4, part 1. Warsaw-Kyiv: Derzhavnyi arkhiv Sluzhby bezpeky Ukrainy et al., 2005.

Posivnych, Mykola. "Vydannia K[r]aiovoi Ekzekutyvy OUN 1931 r." *Ukrains'kyi vyzvol'nyi rukh*, no. 2 (2003): 7-14.

Postanovy II. Velykoho zboru Orhanizatsii ukrains'kykh natsionalistiv. N.p., 1941. http://avr.org.ua/index.php/viewDoc/11977/ (accessed 12 March 2019).

Potichnyj, Peter J. *My Journey*. Litopys UPA, Series "Events and People," 4. Toronto-Lviv: Vydavnytstvo "Litopys UPA," 2008.

Potichnyj, Peter J., and Yevhen Shtendera, eds. *Political Thought of the Ukrainian Underground 1943-1951*. Edmonton: Canadian Institute of Ukrainian Studies, 1986.

Potichnyj, Peter J., and Howard Aster, eds. *Ukrainian-Jewish Relations in Historical Perspective*. Edmonton: Canadian Institute of Ukrainian Studies, 1988.

Potichnyj, Peter J., and Howard Aster, eds. *Ukrainian-Jewish Relations in Historical Perspective*. 2nd ed. Edmonton: Canadian Institute of Ukrainian Studies, 1990.

Preston, David Lee. "A Bird in the Wind." *The Philadelphia Inquirer Magazine* (8 May 1983): 12-16, 28-30.

Provid ukrains'kykh natsionalistiv. *Politychna prohrama i ustrii Orhanizatsii ukrains'kykh natsionalistiv*. Argentina (?), 1940.

Prus, Edward. *Holocaust po banderowsku: czy Żydzi byli w UPA?* Wrocław: Wydawnictwo "Nortom," 1995.

Prusin, Alexander Victor. "'Fascist Criminals to the Gallows!': The Holocaust and Soviet War Crimes Trials, December 1945-February 1946." *Holocaust and Genocide Studies* 17, no. 1 (Spring 2003): 1-30.

Prusin, Alexander [Aleksandr]. "Ukrainskaia politsiia i Kholokost v general'nom okruge Kiev, 1941-1943: deistviia i motivatsii." *Holokost i suchasnist'* 1 (2007): 31-59.

Prusin, Alexander V. "A 'Zone of Violence': The Anti-Jewish Pogroms in Eastern Galicia in 1914-1915 and 1941." In *Shatterzone of Empires: Coexistence and Violence in the German, Habsburg, Russian, and Ottoman Borderlands*, edited by Omer Bartov and Eric D. Weitz, 362-77. Bloomington: Indiana University Press, 2013.

Prystans'ka, Nataliia. "U lisakh Ivano-Frankivshchyny znaishly dva dosi nevidomi arkhivy OUN ta UPA." *Zaxid.net*, 8 October 2019, https://zaxid.net/u_lisah_ivano_frankivshhini_znayshli_dva_dosi_nevido mi_arhivi_oun_ta_upa_n1490624 (accessed 8 October 2019).

Radchenko, Iurii [Yuri]. "The Biography of the OUN(m) Activist Oleksa Babii in the Light of His 'Memoirs on Escaping Execution' (1942)." *Journal of Soviet and Post-Soviet Politics and Society* 6, no. 1 (2020): 237-67.

Radchenko, Iurii [Yuri]. "From Staryi Uhryniv to Munich: The First Scholarly Biography of Stepan Bandera." *Journal of Soviet and Post-Soviet Politics and Society* 1, no. 2 (2015): 429-58.

Radchenko, Iurii. "'Ioho choboty ta esesivs'ka forma buly zabryzkani krov"iu...': Taiemna pol'ova politsiia, politsiia bezpeky ta SD, dopomizhna politsiia u terorii shchodo ievreiv Kharkova (1941-1943 rr.)." *Holokost i suchasnist'* 2 (10) (2011): 46-86.

Radchenko, Iurii. "'I todi braty z Moskvy i braty-zhydy prykhodyly i obbyraly brativ ukraintsiv do nytky': Olena Teliha, Babyn Yar ta ievrei." *uamoderna*, 27 March 2017, http://uamoderna.com/blogy/yurij-radc henko/teliha (accessed 3 December 2018).

Radchenko, Iurii. "Nashi 'sukyni deti'. Zashchishchat' ili...." *Khadashot,* http://hadashot.kiev.ua/content/istorik-yuriy-radchenko-boycy-b ukovinskogo-kurenya-sotrudnichali-s-nacistami (accessed 12 July 2020).

Radchenko [Radczenko], Iurii [Jurij]. "'Niemcy znaleźli u nich zrabowane żydowskie rzeczy i dlatego ich rozstrzelali': Kureń Bukowiński, Holokaust w Kijowie i świadectwo Marty Zybaczynskiej." *Zagłada Żydów. Studia i Materiały* 14 (2018): 580-617.

Radchenko, Iurii. "Stavlennia OUN do ievreiv: dyskusiia bez 'spil'nykh deklaratsii'. Chastyna 1." *Historians.in.ua,* 3 July 2016, http://historia ns.in.ua/index.php/en/dyskusiya/1932-yurii-radchenko-stavlenni a-oun-do-ievreiv-dyskusiia-bez-spilnykh-deklaratsii-chastyna-1 (accessed 5 August 2016).

Radchenko, Iurii. "Stavlennia OUN do ievreiv: dyskusiia bez 'spil'nykh deklaratsii'. Chastyna 2." *Historians.in.ua,* 5 July 2016, http://histori ans.in.ua/index.php/en/dyskusiya/1935-yurii-radchenko-stavlenn ia-oun-do-ievreiv-dyskusiia-bez-spilnykh-deklaratsii-chastyna-2 (accessed 20 August 2016).

Radchenko, Iurii [Yuri]. "'Two Policemen Came...': The Auxiliary Police, the Local Administration, and the Holocaust in the Recollections of Non-Jewish Residents of the Donbas." *Yad Vashem Studies* 45, no. 1: 61-100.

Radchenko, Iurii [Yuri]. "Ukrainian Historiography of the Holocaust through the Prism of Modern Discourse on Collaboration on the Territory of Ukraine." *Dapim: Studies on the Holocaust* 31, no. 3 (2017): 313-21.

Radziejowski, Janusz. *The Communist Party of Western Ukraine 1919-1929.* Edmonton: Canadian Institute of Ukrainian Studies, 1983.

Rasevych, Vasyl'. "L'vivs'kyi pohrom." *zaxid.net,* 14 August 2008, https://zaxid.net/lvivskiy_pogrom_n1058971 (accessed 12 October 2018).

Rasevych, Vasyl'. "Vyverty propahandy." *zaxid.net,* 30 September 2015, https://zaxid.net/viverti_propagandi_n1367592 (accessed 12 October 2018).

Redlich, Shimon. "Jewish-Ukrainian Relations in Inter-War Poland as Reflected in Some Ukrainian Publications," *Polin* 11 (1998): 232-46.

Redlich, Shimon. *Together and Apart in Brzezany: Poles, Jews, and Ukrainians, 1919-1945.* Bloomington and Indianapolis: Indiana University Press, 2002.

Redner, Ben Z. *A Jewish Policeman in Lwów: An Early Account, 1941-1943.* Jerusalem: Yad Vashem, 2015.

Relacje z czasów Zagłady. Inwentarz. Archiwum ZIH-INB, zespół 301. 7 vols. Warsaw: Żydowski Instytut Historyczny, Instytut Naukowo-Badawczy, 1998-2005.

Riabenko, Serhii. "Do pytannia stvorennia militsii u L'vovi ulitku 1941 r." https://www.academia.edu/1500597/%D0%94%D0%BE_%D0%BF%D0%B8%D1%82%D0%B0%D0%BD%D0%BD%D1%8F_%D1%81%D1%82%D0%B2%D0%BE%D1%80%D0%B5%D0%BD%D0%BD%D1%8F_%D1%83%D0%BA%D1%80%D0%B0%D1%97%D0%BD%D1%81%D1%8C%D0%BA%D0%BE%D1%97_%D0%BC%D1%96%D0%BB%D1%96%D1%86%D1%96%D1%97_%D1%83_%D0%9B%D1%8C%D0%B2%D0%BE%D0%B2%D1%96_%D1%83%D0%BB%D1%96%D1%82%D0%BA%D1%83_1941_%D1%80 (accessed 12 July 2019).

Riabenko, Serhii. "'Knyha faktiv.' Istoriia dzherela." *Ukrains'kyi vyzvol'nyi rukh* 19 (2014): 89-120.

Riabenko, Serhii. "Slidamy 'L'vivs'koho pohromu' Dzhona-Pola Khymky." *Istorychna pravda*, 20 February 2013, http://www.istprav da.com.ua/articles/2013/02/20/112766/ (accessed 17 December 2019).

Riabenko, Serhii. "Ukrains'ka militsiia L'vova: 'banderivs'ka' chy robitny-cha-selians'ka'?" *Istorychna pravda*, 30 June 2018, http://www.istpra vda.com.ua/articles/2018/06/30/152654/ (accessed 16 November 2019).

Rich, David Alan. "Armed Ukrainians in L'viv: Ukrainian Militia, Ukrainian Police, 1941-1942." *Canadian-American Slavic Studies* 48 (2014): 271-87.

Rodal, Alti. "A Village Massacre: The Particular and the Context." In *Romania and the Holocaust: Events — Contexts — Aftermath*, edited by Simon Geissbühler, 59-88. Stuttgart: ibidem-Verlag, 2016.

Romaniv, Oleh, and Inna Fedushchak. *Zakhidnoukrains'ka trahediia 1941.* Lviv and New York: Naukove tovarystvo im. Shevchenka, 2002.

Rosenfeld, Klara. *From Lwów to Parma: A Young Woman's Escape from Nazi-Occupied Poland.* Vallentine Mitchell: London and Portland, OR, 2005.

Rosov, Oleg. "Chem zanimalas' SB OUN. Sovetnik predsedatelia SBU vnov' otzhigaet." *Live Journal*, 15 February 2008, https://novoross-73.livejournal.com/23549.html (accessed 12 November 2020).

Rossoliński-Liebe, Grzegorz. "Die antijüdische Massengewalt ukrainischer Nationalisten in der antikommunistischen, deutschen, jüdischen, polnischen, ukrainischen und sowjetischen Historiographie." In *Gewalt — Gedächtnis — Erkenntnis. Nationale und transnationale Erinnerungsräume im östlichen Europa*, edited by Kerstin Schoor, Stefanie Schüler-Springorum, 206-226. Göttingen: Wallstein, 2016.

Rossoliński-Liebe, Grzegorz. "Debating, Obfuscating and Disciplining the Holocaust: Post-Soviet Historical Discourses on the OUN-UPA and Other Nationalist Movements." *East European Jewish Affairs* 42, no. 3 (December 2012): 199-241.

Rossoliński-Liebe, Grzegorz. "Erinnerungslücke Holocaust: Die ukrainische Diaspora und der Genozid an den Juden." *Vierteljahrshefte für Zeitgeschichte* 62, no. 3 (July 2014): 397-430.

Rossoliński-Liebe, Grzegorz. *The Fascist Kernel of Ukrainian Genocidal Nationalism*. Carl Beck Papers, 2042. Pittsburgh: University Library System, University of Pittsburgh, 2015.

Rossoliński-Liebe, Grzegorz. "Der polnisch-ukrainische Historikerdiskurs über den polnisch-ukrainischen Konflikt 1943-1947." *Jahrbücher für Geschichte Osteuropas* 57 (2009): 54-84.

Rossoliński-Liebe, Grzegorz. *Stepan Bandera: The Life and Afterlife of a Ukrainian Nationalist: Fascism, Genocide, and Cult*. Stuttgart: ibidem-Verlag, 2014.

Rossoliński-Liebe, Grzegorz. "Survivor Testimonies and the Coming to Terms with the Holocaust in Volhynia and Eastern Galicia: The Case of the Ukrainian Nationalists." *East European Politics and Societies and Cultures* 34, no. 1 (February 2020): 221-40.

Rossoliński-Liebe, Grzegorz. "The 'Ukrainian National Revolution' of 1941: Discourse and Practice of a Fascist Movement." *Kritika: Explorations in Russian and Eurasian History* 12, no. 1 (Winter 2011): 83-114.

Rossoliński-Liebe, Grzegorz. "Ukraińska policja, nacjonalizm i zagłada Żydów w Galicji Wschodniej i na Wołyniu," *Zagłada Żydów. Studia i Materiały* 13 (2017): 57-79.

Rossoliński-Liebe, Grzegorz. "Der Verlauf und die Täter des Lemberger Pogroms vom Sommer 1941: Zum aktuellen Stand der Forschung." *Jahrbuch für Antisemitismusforschung* 22 (2013): 207-43.

Roth, Karl Heinz. "Heydrichs Professor: Historiographie des 'Volkstums' und der Massenvernichtungen: Der Fall Hans Joachim Beyer." In *Geschichtsschreibung als Legitimationswissenschaft 1918-1945*, edited by Peter Schöttler, 262-342. Frankfurt am Main: Suhrkamp, 1997.

Rothenberg, Samuel. *List o zagładzie Żydów w Drohobyczu*. Edited by Edmund Silberner. London: Poets and Painters Press, 1984.

"Round-Table Discussion." In *Ukrainian-Jewish Relations in Historical Perspective*, edited by Peter J. Potichnyj and Howard Aster, 479-12. Edmonton: Canadian Institute of Ukrainian Studies, 1988.

Rud'ko, Vasyl' [R. Lisovyi]. *Rozlam v OUN. Krytychni narysy z nahody dvadtsiatylittia zasnuvannia OUN*. N.p.: Vyd-vo Ukraina, 1949.

Rudling, Per Anders. "Bogdan Musial and the Question of Jewish Responsibility for the Pogroms in Lviv in the Summer of 1941." *East European Jewish Affairs* 35, no. 1 (June 2005): 69-89.

Rudling, Per Anders. "The Khatyn Massacre in Belorussia: A Historical Controversy Revisited." *Holocaust and Genocide Studies* 26, no. 1 (spring 2012): 29-58.

Rudling, Per Anders. "'Not Quite Klaus Barbie, but in That Category': Mykola Lebed, the CIA, and the Airbrushing of the Past." In *Rethinking Holocaust Justice: Essays across Disciplines*, edited by Norman J. W. Goda, 158-187. New York: Berghahn Books, 2018.

Rudling, Per Anders. *The OUN, the UPA and the Holocaust: A Study in the Manufacturing of Historical Myths.* Carl Beck Papers in Russian & East European Studies, 2107. Pittsburgh: Center for Russian & East European Studies, University Center for International Studies, University of Pittsburgh, 2011.

Rudling, Per Anders. "Rehearsal for Volhynia: Schutzmannschaft Battalion 201 and Hauptmann Roman Shukhevych in Occupied Belorussia, 1942." *East European Politics and Societies and Cultures* 34, no. 1 (February 2020): 158-93.

Rudling, Per Anders. "Terror and Local Collaboration in Occupied Belarus: The Case of the Schutzmannschaft Battalion 118." *Historical Yearbook*, Romanian Academy "Nicolae Iorga" History Institute, 8 (2011): 195-214; 9 (2012): 99-121.

Rudling, Per Anders. "Yushchenko's Fascist: The Bandera Cult in Ukraine and Canada." *Journal of Soviet and Post-Soviet Politics and Society* 3, no. 2 (2017): 129-78.

Rudnytsky [Rudnyts'kyi], Ivan Lysiak-. "Natsionalizm i totalitaryzm (Vidpovid' M. Prokopovi)." *Journal of Ukrainian Studies* 7, no. 2 (13) (fall 1982): 80-86.

Rukkas, Andrii. "Zbroini zahony Orhanizatsii ukrains'kykh natsionalistiv na Berezhanshchyni (veresen' 1939 r.)." *Ukrains'kyi vyzvol'nyi rukh* 3:145-59.

Rusnachenko, Anatolii. *Narod zburenyi: natsional'no-vyzvol'nyi rukh v Ukraini i natsional'ni rukhy oporu v Bilorusii, Lytvi, Latvii, Estonii u 1940-50-kh rokakh.* Kyiv: Pul'sary, 2002.

Rybakov, Dmitrii. "Marko Tsarynnyk: Istorychna napivpravda hirsha za odvertu brekhniu." *LB.ua*, 5 November 2009, http://lb.ua/news/200 9/11/05/13147_marko_tsarinnik_istorichna.html (accessed 17 June 2014).

Sandkühler, Thomas. *"Endlösung" in Galizien: Der Judenmord in Ostpolen und die Rettungsinitiativen von Berthold Beitz, 1941-1944.* Bonn: Dietz, 1996.

"SBU: Zvynuvachennia proty 'Nakhtihaliu' — istorychna pravda chy politychni tekhnolohii." *Memorial*, 8 February 2008, http://www.memor ial.kiev.ua/novyny/612-sbu-zvynuvachennja-proty-nahtigalju-istor ychna-pravda-chy-politychni-tehnologiji.html (accessed 16 December 2019).

Sefer ha-partizanim ha-Yehudim. 2 vols. Merhavia: Sifriyat Po'alim, 1958.

Segal, Raz. "Beyond Holocaust Studies: Rethinking the Holocaust in Hungary." *Journal of Genocide Research* 16, no. 1 (2014): 1-23.

Semelin, Jacques. *Purify and Destroy: The Political Uses of Massacre and Genocide*. New York: Columbia University Press, 2007.

Serhiichuk, Volodymyr. *Nasha krov — na svoii zemli*. Kyiv: Ukrains'ka Vydavnycha Spilka, 2000.

Serhiichuk, Volodymyr. *OUN-UPA v roky viiny. Novi dokumenty i materialy*. Kyiv: Dnipro, 1996.

Shankovs'kyi, Lev. "Initsiiatyvnyi komitet dlia stvorennia Ukrains'koi Holovnoi Vyzvol'noi Rady. Postannia i diia v 1943-1944 rr. Spohad i komentar." In *Ukrains'ka Holovna Vyzvol'na Rada. Dokumenty, ofitsiini publikatsii, materialy*. Book 4: *Dokumenty i spohady*, compiled by Yevhen Shtendera and edited by Peter J. Potichnyj, 28-71. Litopys UPA, 26. Toronto: Vydavnytstvo Litopys UPA, 2000.

Shankovs'kyi, Lev. *Pokhidni hrupy OUN (Prychynky do istorii pokhidnykh hrup OUN na tsentral'nykh i skhidnikh zemliakh Ukrainy v 1941-1943 rr.)*. Munich: Ukrains'kyi samostiinyk, 1958.

Shapoval, Iurii. "Chy podolano 'volyns'kyi syndrom'?" *Den'*, 15 March 2003. http://www.ji-magazine.lviv.ua/dyskusija/volyn/day15-03.htm (accessed 3 September 2018).

Shapoval, Iurii. "Pro vyznannia i znannia." *Krytyka* 15, no. 1-2 (2011): 17-20.

Shepelev, Georgii. "Fotografii, sdelannye nemetskimi soldatami na territorii SSSR (1941-1944 gg.), kak istochnik po natsitskoi istrebitel'noi politike." In *Voina na unichtozhenie. Natsistskaia politika genotsida na territorii Vostochnoi Evropy. Materialy mezhdunarodnoi nauchnoi konferentsii (Moskva, 26-28 aprelia 2010 goda)*, edited by A.R. Diukov and O.E. Orlenko, 429-47. Moscow: Fond "Istoricheskaia pamiat'," 2010.

[Sheptyts'kyi, Andrei.] *Pys'ma-poslannia Mytropolyta Andreia Sheptyts'koho ChSVV. z chasiv nimets'koi okupatsii*. Biblioteka Lohosu, 30. Yorkton, SK.: 1969.

Shevchuk F.N., et al., eds. *Reabilitovani istoriieiu u dvadtsiaty semy tomakh*. Book 1: Ternopil's'ka oblast'. Ternopil: Zbruch, 2008.

Shkandrij, Myroslav [Miroslav Shkandrii]. "*Radio Vena*: radioperedachi Organizatsii Ukrainskikh Natsionalistov (1938-1939 gg.)." *Forum noveishei vostochnoevropeiskoi istorii i kul'tury* 2 (2014), 195-213.

Shkandrij, Myroslav. *Ukrainian Nationalism: Politics, Ideology, and Literature, 1929-1956*. New Haven and London: Yale University Press, 2015.

Shliakhtych, Roman. "Arkhivno-slidchi spravy politsaiv iak dzherelo shchodo vyvchennia Holokostu na terytorii Kryvoho Rohu v roky nimets'koi okupatsii." Paper presented at the conference on "Genocides, Mass Murders and Deportations on Ukrainian Lands during World War II: How to Work with Sources." Center for Interethnic Relations Research in Eastern Europe, Kharkiv, Ukraine, 17-19 April 2018.

Shliakhtych, Roman. "Stvorennia ta funktsionuvannia mistsevoi dopomizhnoi politsii na Kryvorizhzhi v roky nimets'koi okupatsii." *Problemy istorii Holokostu: ukrains'kyi vymir*, no. 9 (2017): 10-26.

Shliakhtych, Roman. "Uchast' mistsevoi dopomizhnoi politsii u Holokosti na Kryvorizhzhi." *Holokost i suchasnist'* 1 (14) (2016): 75-88.

Shtul', Oleh [O. Shuliak]. *V im"ia pravdy (do istorii povstanchoho rukhu v Ukraini)*. Rotterdam, 1947.

Shumuk, Danylo. *Life Sentence: Memoirs of a Ukrainian Political Prisoner*. Edited by Ivan Jaworsky. Edmonton: Canadian Institute of Ukrainian Studies, 1984.

Siemaszko, Ewa. "Bilans zbrodni." *Biuletyń Instytut Pamięci Narodowej*, no. 7-8 (116-17) (July-August 2010): 77-94.

Siemaszko, Władysław, and Ewa Siemaszko. *Ludobójstwo dokonane przez nacjonalistów ukraińskich na ludności polskiej Wołynia, 1939-1945*. 2 vols. Warsaw: Wydawnictwo von borowiecky, 2000.

Skakun, Roman. *"Patsyfikatsiia": Pol's'ki represii 1930 roku v Halychyni*. Lviv: Vydavnytstvo Ukrains'koho katolyts'koho universytetu, 2012.

Skorobohatov, A.V. "OUN u Kharkovi za chasiv okupatsii (1941-1943 rr.)." *Ukrains'kyi istorychnyi zhurnal*, no. 6 (1999): 81-89.

Slyvka, Iurii, ed. *Deportatsii. Zakhidni zemli Ukrainy kintsia 30-kh–pochatku 50-kh rr. Dokumenty, materialy, spohady u tr'okh tomakh*. Vol. 1: 1939-1945 rr. Lviv: Natsional'na akademiia nauk Ukrainy, Instytut ukrainoznavstva im. I. Kryp"iakevycha, 1996. Vol. 2: 1946-1947 rr. 1998.

Snyder, Timothy. *Black Earth: The Holocaust as History and Warning*. New York: Tim Duggan Books, 2015.

Snyder, Timothy. *The Reconstruction of Nations: Poland, Ukraine, Lithuania, Belarus, 1569-1999*. New Haven & London: Yale University Press, 2003.

Snyder, Timothy. *Sketches from a Secret War: A Polish Artist's Mission to Liberate Soviet Ukraine*. New Haven and London: Yale University Press, 2005.

Snyder, Timothy. "To Resolve the Ukrainian Question Once and for All: The Ethnic Cleansing of Ukrainians in Poland, 1943-1947." *Journal of Cold War Studies* 1, no. 2 (Spring 1999): 86-120.

Solchanyk, Roman. "The Communist Party of Western Ukraine, 1919-1938." PhD dissertation: University of Michigan, 1973.

Solod'ko, Pavlo. "Iak Kolesnichenko oskandalyvsia pered zakhidnymy istorykamy." *Istorychna pravda*, 5 June 2012, http://www.istpravda. com.ua/columns/2012/06/5/87087/ (accessed 24 October 2018).

Solonari, Vladimir. "Patterns of Violence: The Local Population and the Mass Murder of Jews in Bessarabia and Northern Bukovina, July-August 1941." In *The Holocaust in the East: Local Perpetrators and Soviet Responses*, edited by Michael David-Fox et al., 51-82. Pittsburgh: University of Pittsburgh Press, 2014.

Solonari, Vladimir. *Purifying the Nation: Population Exchange and Ethnic Cleansing in Nazi-Allied Romania.* Washington, DC, and Baltimore: Woodrow Wilson Center Press and The Johns Hopkins University Press, 2010.

Solonari [Solonar'], Vladimir. "Stavlennia do ievreiv Bukovyny z boku radians'koi ta rumuns'koi administratsii u 1940-1944 r." *Holokost i suchasnist'* no. 2 (8) (2010): 117-48.

Sorokina, Marina. "People and Procedures: Toward a History of the Investigation of Nazi Crimes in the USSR." In *The Holocaust in the East: Local Perpetrators and Soviet Responses*, edited by Michael David-Fox et al., 118-41. Pittsburgh: University of Pittsburgh Press, 2014.

Spector, Shmuel. *The Holocaust of Volhynian Jews 1941-1944.* Jerusalem: Yad Vashem, The Federation of Volhynian Jews, 1990.

Stakhiv, Ievhen. *Kriz' tiurmy, pidpillia i kordony. Povist' moho zhyttia.* Kyiv: Rada, 1995.

Statiev, Alexander. "The Nature of Anti-Soviet Armed Resistance, 1942-44: The North Caucasus, the Kalmyk Autonomous Republic, and Crimea." *Kritika: Explorations in Russian and Eurasian History* 6, no. 2 (spring 2005): 285-318.

Statiev, Alexander. "The Organization of Ukrainian Nationalists as the Leader of a Unique Fascist Armed Resistance." In *Violent Resistance: From the Baltics to Central, Eastern and Southeastern Europe 1944-1956*, edited by Michael Gehler and David Schriffl, 143-71. Leiden: Ferdinand Schöningh, 2020.

Statiev, Alexander. *The Soviet Counterinsurgency in the Western Borderlands.* Cambridge: Cambridge University Press, 2010.

Stebel's'kyi, Ivan. *Shliakhamy molodosti i borot'by. Spohady, statti, lystuvannia.* Kyiv: Smoloskyp, 1999.

Steinhart, Eric C. *The Holocaust and the Germanization of Ukraine*. New York: United States Holocaust Memorial Museum, German Historical Institute, and Cambridge University Press, 2015.

Stets'ko, Iaroslav S. *30 chervnia 1941. Proholoshennia vidnovlennia derzhavnosty Ukrainy*. Toronto: Liga vyzvolennia Ukrainy, 1967.

Stets'ko, Iaroslav [Zynovii Karbovych]. "Zhydivstvo i my." *Novyi shliakh* (Winnipeg), 8 May 1939.

Stobniak-Smogorzewska, Janina. *Kresowe osadnictwo wojskowe 1920-1945*. Warsaw: Instytut Studiów Politycznych PAN, Oficyna wydawnicza RYTM, 2003.

Strutyns'ka, Mariia [V. Mars'ka]. *Buria nad L'vovom. Povist' u dvokh chastynakh*. Philadelphia: Kyiv, 1952.

Strutyns'ka, Mariia. *Daleke zblyz'ka*. Winnipeg: Tryzub, 1975.

Struve, Kai. *Bauern und Nation in Galizien: Über Zugehörigkeit und soziale Emanzipation im 19. Jahrhundert*. Göttingen: Vandenhoek & Ruprecht, 2005.

Struve, Kai. *Deutsche Herrschaft, ukrainischer Nationalismus, antijüdische Gewalt: Der Sommer 1941 in der Westukraine*. Berlin and Boston: De Gruyter Oldenbourg, 2015.

Struve, Kai. "Masovi vbyvstva v"iazniv l'vivs'kykh tiurem: shcho vidomo pro mistsia ta kil'kist' zhertv?" *Ukraina moderna*, 9 September 2018, http://uamoderna.com/md/struve-lonckoho (accessed 24 September 2018).

Struve, Kai. "Rites of Violence? The Pogroms of Summer 1941." *Polin* 24 (2012): 257-74.

Struve, Kai. "Ritual und Gewalt—Die Pogrome des Sommers 1941." In *Synchrone Welten: Zeitenräume jüdischer Geschichte*, ed. Dan Diner, 225-50. Göttingen: Vandenhoeck & Ruprecht, 2005.

Struve, Kai. "Tremors in the Shatter-Zone of Empires: Eastern Galicia in Summer 1941." In *Shatterzone of Empires: Coexistence and Violence in the German, Habsburg, Russian, and Ottoman Borderlands*, ed. Omer Bartov and Eric D. Weitz, 463-84. Bloomington and Indianapolis: Indiana University Press, 2013.

Stsibors'kyi, Mykola. *Natsiokratiia*. Vinnytsia: Derzhavna kartohrafichna fabryka, 2007.

Styrkul, Valery. *We Accuse: Documentary Sketch*. Kyiv: Dnipro, 1984.

Surmach, Oksana. *Dni kryvavykh svastyk. Hreko-katolyts'ka tserkva v period nimets'koho okupatsiinoho rezhymu v Ukraini (1941-1944 rr.)*. Lviv: Spolom, 2005.

Suslensky, Yakov. *They Were True Heroes: Citizens of Ukraine, Righteous among the Nations*. Kyiv: Society "Ukraine," 1995.

Svarnyk, Halyna. *Arkhivni ta rukopysni zbirky Naukovoho tovarystva im. Shevchenka v Natsional'nii bibliotetsi u Varshavi: kataloh-informator.* Warsaw: Ukrains'kyi arkhiv, 2005.

Szajkowski, Zosa. "'A Reappraisal of Symon Petliura and Ukrainian-Jewish Relations, 1917-1921': A Rebuttal." *Jewish Social Studies* 31 (1969): 184-213.

Szarota, Tomasz. *U progu Zagłady: zajście antyżydowskie i pogromy w okupowanej Europie: Warszawa, Paryż, Amsterdam, Antwerpia, Kowno.* Warsaw: Wydawnictwo Sic!, 2000.

Szcześniak, Antoni B., and Wiesław Z. Szota. *Droga do nikąd. Działalność Organizacji Ukraińskich Nacjonalistów i jej likwidacja w Polsce.* Warsaw: Wydawnictwo Ministerstwa Obrony Narodowej, 1973.

Tal, Haim. *The Fields of Ukraine: A 17-Year-Old's Survival of Nazi Occupation: The Story of Yosef Laufer written by Haim Tal.* Denver: Dallci Press, 2009.

Tannenzapf, William. *Memories from the Abyss.* Toronto: Azrieli Foundation, 2009.

Tokarczuk, Wiesław. *Medzi troma hranicami: Vampír z Bieščad v Uličskej doline.* Snina, Slovakia: Edícia Retrospektíva, 2019.

Tokarski, Sławomir. *Ethnic Conflict and Economic Development: Jews in Galician Agriculture 1868-1914.* Warsaw: Wydawnictwo "Trio", 2003.

Törnquist-Plewa, Barbara. "The Jedwabne Killings—A Challenge for Polish Collective Memory: The Polish Debate on *Neighbours*." In Klas-Göran Karlsson and Ulf Zander, eds., *Echoes of the Holocaust: Historical Cultures in Contemporary Europe* (Lund: Nordic Academic Press, 2003), 141-76.

Torzecki, Ryszard. *Kwestia ukraińska w polityce III Rzeszy.* Warsaw: Książka i Wiedza, 1972.

Torzecki, Ryszard. "Mav ia do dila z endets'kym murom." *Svoboda*, 23 March 2001.

Trunk, Isaiah. *Judenrat: The Jewish Councils in Eastern Europe under Nazi Occupation.* New York: Macmillan / London: Collier-Macmillan, 1972.

"Ukraintsi i zhydy." *Ukrains'ka trybuna* (Munich), 1 May 1947.

Usach, Andrii. "Chy mozhemo pochuty holos mistsevoho vynuvattisa natsysts'koho nasyl'stva v Ukraini?" Paper presented at the conference on "Genocides, Mass Murders and Deportations on Ukrainian Lands during World War II: How to Work with Sources." Center for Interethnic Relations Research in Eastern Europe, Kharkiv, Ukraine, 17-19 April 2018.

"U Sluzhbi bezpeky Ukrainy vidbulys' Hromads'ki istorychni slukhannia 'Zvynuvachennia proty "Nakhtihaliu" — istorychna pravda chy politychni tekhnolohii,'" press release of the Security Service of Ukraine, 6 February 2008, http://www.ssu.gov.ua/sbu/control/uk/publish /article?art_id=74369&cat_id=74549 (accessed 6 April 2013; now a dead link).

Veryha, Wasyl, comp. *The Correspondence of the Ukrainian Central Committee in Cracow and L'viv with the German Authorities 1939-1944.* 2 pts. Research Report No. 61. Edmonton: Canadian Institute of Ukrainian Studies Press, 2000.

Veselova, O., et al., eds. *OUN i UPA v 1943 rotsi. Dokumenty.* Kyiv: Instytut istorii Ukrainy NAN Ukrainy, 2008.

Veselova, O., et al., eds. *OUN v 1941 rotsi. Dokumenty.* 2 parts. Kyiv: Instytut istorii Ukrainy NAN Ukrainy, 2006.

Veselova, O., et al., eds. *OUN v 1942 rotsi. Dokumenty.* Kyiv: Instytut istorii Ukrainy NAN Ukrainy, 2006.

V"iatrovych, Volodymyr. "Povstans'kyi Havrosh Mandyk Khasman." *Istorychna pravda,* 8 June 2011, http://www.istpravda.com.ua/articles/ 2011/06/8/41955/ (accessed 12 December 2020).

V"iatrovych, Volodymyr. *Stavlennia OUN do ievreiv: formuvannia pozytsii na tli katastrofy.* Lviv: Vydavnytstvo Ms, 2006.

"Vidkopaly arkhiv UPA zi spyskamy represovanykh radians'koiu vladoiu ukraintsiv." *Gazeta.ua,* 5 September 2017, https://gazeta.ua/articles /history/_vidkopali-arhiv-upa-zi-spiskami-represovanih-radyansk oyu-vladoyu-ukrayinciv/791416 (accessed 30 October 2018).

Viola, Lynne. *Stalinist Perpetrators on Trial: Scenes from the Great Terror in Soviet Ukraine.* New York: Oxford University Press, 2017.

Virna, Nadiia. "Do rokovyn nyshchennia bukovyntsiv sovietamy." *Chas,* 14 June 2013, https://chas.cv.ua/history/11272-do-rokovin-nischen nya-bukovincv-sovyetami.html (accessed 29 June 2020).

"Vytiah z protokolu dopytu F. Vorobtsia." In *Borot'ba proty povstans'koho rukhu i natsionalistychnoho pidpillia: Protokoly dopytiv zaareshtovanykh radians'kymy orhanamy derzhavnoi bezpeky kerivnykiv OUN i UPA: 1944-1945,* edited by O. Ishchuk and S. Kokin, 651-700. Litopys UPA, new series, 9. Kyiv-Toronto: Litopys UPA, 2007.

"Vytiah z protokolu dopytu Ie. Basiuka." In *Borot'ba proty povstans'koho rukhu i natsionalistychnoho pidpillia: Protokoly dopytiv zaareshtovanykh radians'kymy orhanamy derzhavnoi bezpeky kerivnykiv OUN i UPA: 1944-1945,* edited by O. Ishchuk and S. Kokin, 111-36. Litopys UPA, new series, 9. Kyiv-Toronto: Litopys UPA, 2007.

Ward, James Mace. *Priest, Politician, Collaborator: Jozef Tiso and the Making of Fascist Slovakia.* Ithaca and London: Cornell University Press, 2013.

Węgierski, Jerzy. *W lwowskiej Armii Krajowej.* Warsaw: Instytut Wydawniczy PAX, 1989.

Weiner, Amir. *Making Sense of War: The Second World War and the Fate of the Bolshevik Revolution.* Princeton and Oxford: Princeton University Press, 2001.

Weiss, Aharon. "Jewish-Ukrainian Relations in Western Ukraine during the Holocaust." In *Ukrainian-Jewish Relations in Historical Perspective,* edited by Peter J. Potichnyj and Howard Aster, 409-20. Edmonton: Canadian Institute of Ukrainian Studies, 1988.

Weiss, Aharon. "The Relations between the Judenrat and the Jewish Police." *Yad Vashem Shoah Research Center,* https://www.yadvashem.org/odot _pdf/Microsoft%20Word%20-%203224.pdf (accessed 30 July 2020). Originally published in *Patterns of Jewish Leadership in Nazi Europe 1933-1945: Proceedings of the Third Yad Vashem International Historical Conference, April 4-7 1977* (Jerusalem: Yad Vashem, 1979), 201-18.

Weissbrod, Abraham. *Death of a Shtetl.* N.p., 1995.

Wells, Leon Weliczker. *The Janowska Road.* New York: Macmillan, 1963.

Welzer, Harald, Sabine Moller, and Karoline Tschuggnall. *"Opa war kein Nazi": Nationalsozialismus und Holocaust im Familiengedächtnis.* Frankfurt am Main: Fischer Taschenbuch Verlag, 2002.

Wermuth, Joshua. "The Jewish Partisans of Horodenka." In *They Fought Back: The Story of the Jewish Resistance in Nazi Europe,* edited by Yuri Shul, 2nd ed., 226-30. New York: Schocken Books, 1975.

Wieviorka, Annette. "The Witness in History." *Poetics Today* 27, no. 2 (Summer 2006): 385-97.

Wildt, Michael. *An Uncompromising Generation: The Nazi Leadership of the Reich Security Main Office.* Translated by Tom Lampert. Madison: The University of Wisconsin Press, 2009.

Wnuk, Rafał. "Recent Polish Historiography on Polish-Ukrainian Relations during World War II and Its Aftermath." *InterMarium* 7, no. 1 (2004), https://web.archive.org/web/20100604234037/http://ece.columbi a.edu/research/intermarium/vol7no1/wnuk.pdf (accessed 3 September 2018).

Wroński, Stanisław, and Maria Zwolakowa, eds. *Polacy Żydzi 1939-1945.* Warsaw: Książka i Wiedza, 1971.

Wysocki, Roman. *Organizacja Ukraińskickh Nacjonalistów w Polsce w latach 1929-1939. Geneza, struktura, program, ideologia.* Lublin: Wydawnictwo Uniwersytetu Marii Curie-Skłodowskiej, 2003.

Wyspiański, Józef. *Osoby zamordowane przez nacjonalistów ukraińskich w pow. Przemyślany w latach 1939-1945.* Lublin, 2012.

Yones, Eliyahu [Eliiakhu Iones]. *Evrei L'vova v gody Vtoroi Mirovoi Voiny i Katastrofy evropeiskogo evreistva, 1939-1944.* Moscow and Jerusalem: Rossiiskaia biblioteka Kholokosta, 1999.

Yones, Eliyahu. *Die Juden in Lemberg während des Zweiten Weltkriegs und im Holocaust 1939-1944.* Edited by Susanne Heim and Grzegorz Rossoliński Liebe. Stuttgart: ibidem-Verlag, 2018.

Yones, Eliyahu. *Smoke in the Sand: The Jews of Lvov in the War Years 1939-1944.* Jerusalem and New York: Gefen, 2004.

Yones, Eliyahu. *Die Strasse nach Lemberg: Zwangsarbeit und Widerstand in Ostgalizien 1941-1944.* Frankfurt am Main: Fischer Taschenbuch Verlag, 1999.

Yurkevich, Myroslav. "Ukrainian Nationalists and DP Politics, 1945-50." In *The Refugee Experience: Ukrainian Displaced Persons after World War II,* edited by Wsevolod W. Isajiw, Yury Boshyk, and Roman Senkus, 125-43. Edmonton: Canadian Institute of Ukrainian Studies Press, 1992.

Zaderecki, Tadeusz. "Gdy swastyka Lwowem władała...(Wycinek z dziejów okupacji hitlerowskiej)." YVA, 06/28.

Zaitsev, Oleksandr. "Chy isnuvav ukrains'kyi natsional'no-vyzvol'nyi faszhyzm?" *zaxid.net,* 12 March 2012, https://zaxid.net/chi_isnuvav _ukrayinskiy_natsionalnovizvolniy_fashizm_n1249957 (accessed 19 March 2019).

Zaitsev, Oleksandr. "Defiliada v Moskvi ta Varshavi: 'Voienna doktryna ukrains'kykh natsionalistiv' Mykhaila Kolodzins'koho." *uamoderna,* 27 November 2013, http://www.uamoderna.com/event/186 (accessed 12 October 2018).

Zaitsev, Oleksandr. "Fascism or Ustashism? Ukrainian Integral Nationalism in Comparative Perspective, 1920s-1930s." *Communist and Post-Communist Studies* 30 (2015): 1-11.

Zaitsev, Oleksandr, et al. *Natsionalizm i relihiia: Hreko-Katolyts'ka Tserkva ta ukrains'kyi natsionalistychnyi rukh u Halychyni (1920–1930-ti roky).* Lviv: Vydavnytstvo Ukrains'koho Katolyts'koho Universytetu, 2011.

Zaitsev, O.Iu. "OUN i avtorytarno-natsionalistychni rukhy mizhvoiennoi Ievropy." *Ukrains'kyi istorychnyi zhurnal,* no. 1 (2012): 89-101.

Zaitsev, Oleksandr. "OUN i fashyzm. Sim tez do dyskusii." *zaxid.net,* 30 March 2012, https://zaxid.net/oun_i_fashizm_sim_tez_do_diskusiy i_n1251429 (accessed 20 March 2019).

Zaitsev, Oleksandr. *Ukrains'kyi integral'nyi natsionalizm (1920–1930-ti) roky. Narysy intelektual'noi istorii.* Kyiv: Krytyka, 2013.

Zaitsev, Oleksandr. "Voienna doktryna Mykhaila Kolodzins'koho." *Ukraina Moderna* 20 (2013): 245-56.

Zaplitnyi, Ievhen. *Za tebe, kraiu mii. Natsional'no-vyzvol'nyi rukh na Hrymail-ivshchyni v 30-50 rokakh XX stolittia.* Ternopil: Dzhura, 2002.

Zayarnyuk, Andriy. *Lviv's Uncertain Destination: A City and Its Train Terminal from Franz Joseph I to Brezhnev.* Toronto: University of Toronto Press, 2020.

Zhulyns'kyi, Hryhorii, and Mykola Zhulyns'kyi. *"To tvii, synu, bat'ko." Ukrains'ka dusha – na Holhofi XX stolittia. Montazh svidchen', dokumentiv ta komentari Volodymyra Drozda.* Kyiv: Iaroslaviv Val, 2005.

Zięba Andrzej A., ed. *OUN, UPA i zagłada Żydów.* Kraków: Księgarnia Akademicka, [2017].

Zięba Andrzej A. "Ukraińcy, Polacy i niemiecka zagłada Żydów." In *OUN, UPA i zagłada Żydów,* edited by Andrzej A. Zięba, xix-lii. Kraków: Księgarnia Akademicka, [2017].

Zlochyny komunistychnoi Moskvy v Ukraini v liti 1941 roku. New York: Proloh, 1960.

Place and Name Index

UKRAINIAN VOICES

Collected by Andreas Umland